MATTHEW

This book is a verse-by-verse analysis of the New Testament Gospel of Matthew. It provides a comprehensive introduction to the gospel, which describes the world of Jesus and his first followers. This commentary explores the historical, social, and religious contexts of Matthew and examines the customs, beliefs, and ideas that inform the text. Unfamiliar to many readers of the New Testament, this background will help readers fully understand the text of Matthew, which focuses on what Jesus taught and why the religious authorities in Jerusalem rejected his message and gave him up to the Roman governor for execution. This book will be an important tool for clergy, scholars, and other interested readers of Matthew.

Craig A. Evans is Payzant Distinguished Professor of New Testament at Acadia Divinity College in Nova Scotia. He is the author of several books about Jesus and the New Testament, including *Ancient Texts for New Testament Studies* (2005) and *Jesus, the Final Days* (2009).

NEW CAMBRIDGE BIBLE COMMENTARY

GENERAL EDITOR: Ben Witherington III

HEBREW BIBLE/OLD TESTAMENT EDITOR: Bill T. Arnold

The *New Cambridge Bible Commentary* (NCBC) aims to elucidate the Hebrew and Christian Scriptures for a wide range of intellectually curious individuals. While building on the work and reputation of the *Cambridge Bible Commentary* popular in the 1960s and 1970s, the NCBC takes advantage of many of the rewards provided by scholarly research over the last four decades. Volumes utilize recent gains in rhetorical criticism, social scientific study of the Scriptures, narrative criticism, and other developing disciplines to exploit the growing advances in biblical studies. Accessible jargon-free commentary, an annotated "Suggested Readings" list, and the entire New Revised Standard Version (NRSV) text under discussion are the hallmarks of all volumes in the series.

PUBLISHED VOLUMES IN THE SERIES
Genesis, Bill T. Arnold
Exodus, Carol Meyers
Judges and Ruth, Victor H. Matthews
1–2 Corinthians, Craig S. Keener
The Gospel of John, Jerome H. Neyrey
James and Jude, William F. Brosend II
Revelation, Ben Witherington III

FORTHCOMING VOLUMES
Deuteronomy, Brent Strawn
Joshua, Douglas A. Knight
1–2 Chronicles, William M. Schniedewind
Psalms 1–72, Walter Brueggemann and William H. Bellinger, Jr.
Psalms 73–150, Walter Brueggemann and William H. Bellinger, Jr.
Isaiah 1–39, David Baer
Jeremiah, Baruch Halpern
Hosea, Joel, and Amos, J. J. M. Roberts
The Gospel of Luke, Amy-Jill Levine and Ben Witherington III
The Letters of John, Duane F. Watson

Matthew

Craig A. Evans
Acadia Divinity College, Acadia University

CAMBRIDGE
UNIVERSITY PRESS

32 Avenue of the Americas, New York NY 10013-2473, USA

Cambridge University Press is part of the University of Cambridge.

It furthers the University's mission by disseminating knowledge in the pursuit of education, learning and research at the highest international levels of excellence.

www.cambridge.org
Information on this title: www.cambridge.org/9780521011068

First published 2012

A catalogue record for this publication is available from the British Library

Library of Congress Cataloguing in Publication data
Evans, Craig A.
  Matthew / Craig A. Evans.
    p.   cm. – (New Cambridge Bible commentary)
  Includes bibliographical references and index.
  ISBN 978-0-521-81214-6 (hardback) – ISBN 978-0-521-01106-8 (paperback)
  1. Bible. N.T. Matthew – Commentaries.   I. Title.
  BS2575.53.E93   2011
  226.2'077–dc2   2011018888

ISBN 978-0-521-81214-6 Hardback
ISBN 978-0-521-01106-8 Paperback

Contents

Supplementary Sections

Preface

In keeping with the stated purpose of the *New Cambridge Bible Commentary*, I have written the present commentary on Matthew for a "wide range of intellectually curious individuals." It is not written primarily for the scholar, though I hope scholars will find it useful. My commentary is not an example of what is sometimes called a "commentary on commentaries," which given the modest size of the commentaries in this series would not have been possible had I wished to do so. I have therefore kept the engagement with scholarly literature to a minimum.

Although I benefited greatly from many learned commentaries on Matthew, I refer to them only occasionally in the notes. Other studies, usually specialized studies in certain passages or themes in Matthew, appear in the footnotes, though again only sparingly. Because it is anticipated that not too many readers of this commentary read languages other than English, references to literature in foreign languages have been kept to a minimum. My constant companions were the weighty commentaries by John Nolland (2005) and Dick France (2007). I benefited also from the detailed redactional analysis of the text offered in Robert Gundry's commentary (1982, revised 1994) and from the rich selection of primary materials related to the Mediterranean world found in Craig Keener's commentary (1999).

Readers will notice that I have written a rather brief Introduction. The purpose of the Introduction is to orient readers toward the basic issues and the positions taken in the commentary, not to offer an exhaustive review of the almost endless discussion of critical issues with which scholars today grapple. Readers are invited to consult the commentaries and other books in the Suggested Readings list for further discussion of introductory matters.

I offer my thanks to the New Cambridge Bible Commentary editorial board for inviting me to write this commentary and for patiently awaiting its completion. I also thank Brian LePort and Jesse Richards for their assistance in preparing the indexes. I dedicate the commentary to the memory of two great New Testament scholars, Graham Stanton and Martin Hengel, both of whom died in the summer of 2009. I learned much from these Christian gentlemen and was blessed by their friendship and professional encouragement.

A Word about Citations

All volumes in the *New Cambridge Bible Commentary* (NCBC) include foot-notes, with full bibliographical citations included in the note when a source is first mentioned. Subsequent citations include the author's initial or initials, full last name, abbreviated title for the work, and date of publication. Most readers prefer this citation system to endnotes that require searching through pages at the back of the book.

The Suggested Reading lists, also included in all NCBC volumes after the Introduction, are not a part of this citation apparatus. Annotated and organized by publication type, the self-contained Suggested Reading list is intended to intro-duce and briefly review some of the most well-known and helpful literature on the biblical text under discussion.

Abbreviations

ABD	*The Anchor Bible Dictionary*, edited by D. N. Freedman (6 vols., New York: Doubleday, 1992)
ABG	Arbeiten zur Bibel und ihre Geschichte
ABR	*Australian Biblical Review*
ABRL	Anchor Bible Reference Library
AGJU	Arbeiten zur Geschichte des antiken Judentums und des Urchristentums
ANF	The Ante-Nicene Fathers
ANTJ	Arbeiten zum Neuen Testament und Judentum
ArBib	The Aramaic Bible
AUSS	*Andrews University Seminary Studies*
BA	*Biblical Archaeologist*
BAG	W. Bauer, W. F. Arndt, and F. W. Gingrich, *A Greek-English Lexicon of the New Testament* (1957)
BAGD	W. Bauer, W. F. Arndt, F. W. Gingrich, and F. W. Danker, *A Greek-English Lexicon of the New Testament* (1979)
BAR	*Biblical Archaeology Review*
BBR	*Bulletin for Biblical Research*
BETL	Bibliotheca ephemeridum theologicarum lovaniensium
Bib	*Biblica*
BibOr	Biblica et orientalia
BibSem	The Biblical Seminar
BJRL	*Bulletin of the John Rylands University Library of Manchester*
BJS	Brown Judaic Studies
BK	*Bibel und Kirche*
BR	*Biblical Research*
BRev	*Bible Review*
BT	*The Bible Translator*
BTB	*Biblical Theology Bulletin*

BToday	*Bible Today*
BZ	*Biblische Zeitschrift*
BZNW	Beihefte zur *Zeitschrift für die neutestamentliche Wissenschaft*
CBQ	*Catholic Biblical Quarterly*
CIL	*Corpus inscriptionum latinarum*
ConBNT	Coniectanea biblica, New Testament Series
CTM	*Concordia Theological Monthly*
DDD	*Dictionary of Deities and Demons in the Bible*, rev. ed., edited by K. van der Toorn, B. Becking, and P. W. van der Horst (Leiden: Brill, 1999)
DJG	*Dictionary of Jesus and the Gospels*, edited by J. B. Green, S. McKnight, and I. H. Marshall (Downers Grove, IL: InterVarsity, 1992)
DSD	*Dead Sea Discoveries*
EBR	*Encyclopedia of the Bible and Its Reception*, edited by H.-J. Klauck et al. (Berlin: de Gruyter, 2009–)
EpReview	*Epworth Review*
ETL	*Ephemerides theologicae lovanienses*
ETR	*Études théologiques et religieuses*
EvQ	*Evangelical Quarterly*
EvT	*Evangelische Theologie*
ExpT	*Expository Times*
FAT	Forschungen zum Alten Testament
FBBS	Facet Books, Biblical Series
FRLANT	Forschungen zur Religion und Literatur des Alten und Neuen Testaments
GNS	Good News Studies
HBT	*Horizons in Biblical Theology*
HeyJ	*Heythrop Journal*
HTR	*Harvard Theological Review*
HUCA	*Hebrew Union College Annual*
IBS	*Irish Biblical Studies*
ICC	International Critical Commentary
IDB	*The Interpreter's Dictionary of the Bible*, edited by G. A Buttrick (Nashville, TN: Abingdon, 1962)
IEJ	*Israel Exploration Journal*
Int	*Interpretation*
IRT	Issues in Religion and Theology
ITQ	*Irish Theological Quarterly*
JBL	*Journal of Biblical Literature*
JCP	Jewish and Christian Perspectives
JETS	*Journal of the Evangelical Theological Society*
JGRChJ	*Journal of Greco-Roman Christianity and Judaism*
JJS	*Journal of Jewish Studies*

JSHJ	*Journal for the Study of the Historical Jesus*
JSJ	*Journal for the Study of Judaism in the Persian, Hellenistic and Roman Period*
JSNT	*Journal for the Study of the New Testament*
JSNTSup	Journal for the Study of the New Testament, Supplement Series
JSOTSup	Journal for the Study of the Old Testament, Supplement Series
JSP	*Journal for the Study of the Pseudepigrapha*
JSS	*Journal of Semitic Studies*
JTS	*Journal of Theological Studies*
LNTS	Library of New Testament Studies
LSJ	Liddell, Scott, Jones, *Greek-English Lexicon*
Neot	*Neotestamentica*
NewDocs	*New Documents Illustrating Early Christianity*, edited by G. H. R. Horsley et al. (9 vols., Sydney: Macquarie University, 1976–2002)
NGS	New Gospel Studies
NICNT	New International Commentary on the New Testament
NIDB	*The New Interpreter's Dictionary of the Bible*, edited by K. D. Sakenfeld et al. (5 vols., Nashville, TN: Abingdon, 2006–2009)
NIGTC	New International Greek Testament Commentaries
NovT	*Novum Testamentum*
NovTSup	Novum Testamentum, Supplements
NTS	*New Testament Studies*
NTTS	New Testament Tools and Studies
PEQ	*Palestine Exploration Quarterly*
PG	*Patrologia graeca*, edited by J. Migne
PGM	*Papyri graecae magicae*, edited by K. Preisendanz
PIBA	*Proceedings of the Irish Biblical Association*
RB	*Revue biblique*
RestQ	*Restoration Quarterly*
RevQ	*Revue de Qumran*
RHPR	*Revue d'histoire et de philosophie religieuses*
SBL	Society of Biblical Literature
SBLDS	Society of Biblical Literature Dissertation Series
SBLSP	*Society of Biblical Literature Seminar Papers*
SBT	Studies in Biblical Theology
ScEs	*Science et esprit*
SEG	*Supplementum Epigraphicum Graecum*
SIG	*Sylloge Inscriptionum Graecarum*
SJT	*Scottish Journal of Theology*
SNTSMS	Society for New Testament Studies Monograph Series
SNTU	*Studien zum Neuen Testament und seiner Umwelt* (journal)
SNTU	Studien zum Neuen Testament und seiner Umwelt (monograph series)

SPB	Studia postbiblica
SSEJC	Studies in Scripture in Early Judaism and Christianity
ST	*Studia theologica*
STDJ	Studies on the Texts of the Desert of Judah
TBei	*Theologische Beiträge*
TDNT	*Theological Dictionary of the New Testament*, edited by G. Kittel and G. Friedrich (1964–74)
TSK	*Theologische Studien und Kritiken*
TynBul	*Tyndale Bulletin*
TZ	*Theologische Zeitschrift*
VC	*Vigiliae christianae*
WBC	Word Biblical Commentary
WD	*Wort und Dienst*
WMANT	Wissenschaftliche Monographien zum Alten und Neuen Testament
WTJ	*Westminster Theological Journal*
WUNT	Wissenschaftliche Untersuchungen zum Neuen Testament
ZAW	*Zeitschrift für die alttestamentliche Wissenschaft*
ZDPV	*Zeitschrift des deutschen Palästina-Vereins*
ZNW	*Zeitschrift für die neutestamentliche Wissenschaft*
ZTK	*Zeitschrift für Theologie und Kirche*

I. Introduction

Study of a document, whether ancient or modern, is aided by data outside the document that may tell us important things about the circumstances and context in which the document was originally composed, circulated, and read. This is especially so in the case of the New Testament Gospels. Yet, as is almost always the case when we study a document from the distant past, we possess little external data and so find ourselves making educated guesses. The Gospel of Matthew is no exception. Nevertheless, the limited external data we have, when interpreted in the light of the text of Matthew itself, at least give us a general sense of the world in which this Gospel was written and why it was written.

ORIGINS OF THE GOSPEL OF MATTHEW

Who Wrote the Gospel of Matthew?

Sometime in the early second century A.D. (some say between 130 and 140; others think before 110), Papias apparently linked the apostle Matthew with the Gospel of Matthew, or at least that is how some interpret his comment. Papias also seems to contrast the Gospel of Matthew with the Gospel of Mark, although just how is also disputed. Here is the passage in question (frags. 3.14–16 from Eusebius, *Hist. Eccl.* 3.39.14–16):

For our present purpose we must add to his statements already quoted above a tradition concerning Mark, who wrote the Gospel, that has been set forth in these words: "And the elder used to say this: 'Mark, having become Peter's interpreter, wrote down accurately everything he remembered, though not in order, of the things either said or done by Christ. For he neither heard the Lord nor followed him, but afterward, as I said, followed Peter, who adapted his teachings as needed but had no intention of giving an ordered account of the Lord's sayings. Consequently Mark did nothing wrong in writing down some things as he remembered them, for he made it his one concern not to omit anything that he heard or to make any false statement in them.'"

Such, then, is the account given by Papias with respect to Mark. But with respect to Matthew the following is said: "So Matthew composed the oracles in the Hebrew language and each person interpreted them as best he could."[1]

What have just been quoted are extracts from a five-volume work entitled *Expositions of the Sayings of the Lord*, authored by Papias, who for a number of years served as bishop of Hierapolis in Asia Minor (what is now Turkey). Eusebius, apologist and church historian of the early fourth century, says these volumes still circulated in his time (*Hist. Eccl.* 3.39.1). Today we only have some two dozen quotations from this work.

The quoted passage is quite suggestive at a number of points. The "elder" who is mentioned is a Christian who was either acquainted with an apostle or was an apostle (the apostle John?). Either way, we have an early and very important link to apostolic tradition. This elder, according to Papias, tells us that Mark (presumably John Mark, a relative of Barnabas; see Acts 12:25) was Peter's interpreter (Greek: *hermeneutes*), who wrote down what he learned from Peter. Papias is surely talking about the Gospel of Mark, as implied by the larger context, in which Papias states his preference for the "living voice" over written books; that is, the Gospels (frag. 3.3). Papias says Mark did not write an "ordered account [Greek: *suntaxis*] of the Lord's sayings." This lack of order contrasts with what is said of Matthew, "who composed the oracles." What is translated as "composed" could also be translated as "ordered" (Greek: *sunetaxato*). The verb "ordered" is cognate to the noun "order." Perusal of the Gospel of Matthew shows how it is indeed a well-ordered account.

Furthermore, Papias says that Matthew ordered the oracles (or sayings) of Jesus "in the Hebrew language," or, in Greek, *Hebraidi dialekto*. The Greek word *dialektos* can and often does mean "language" or "dialect," as Eusebius, who quotes this passage, probably understood (see *Hist. Eccl.* 5.8.2, where he quotes late second-century church father Irenaeus: "Now Matthew published among the Hebrews a written Gospel also in their own language [*dialekto*]"). But the word also means "discussion," "debate," "arguing," or "way of speaking" (see LSJ, as well as the cognate Greek verb *dialegomai*, meaning "converse with" or "argue with"). In other words, Papias may be saying that Matthew ordered the sayings of Jesus in a Hebrew (or Jewish) way of presenting material or making an argument. This understanding matches well what we see in the Gospel of Matthew. Of course, the possibility that the evangelist wrote a Hebrew or Aramaic version of his Gospel cannot be ruled out (after all, Josephus wrote an Aramaic version of *The Jewish Wars* as well as the Greek

---

[1] The translation is from M. W. Holmes, *The Apostolic Fathers: Greek Texts and English Translations*, 3rd edition (Grand Rapids, MI: Baker Academic, 2007), 739, 741, with Greek text on facing pages (i.e., 738, 740). For an informative discussion of this Papian fragment, see R. H. Gundry, *Matthew: A Commentary on His Literary and Theological Art* (Grand Rapids, MI: Eerdmans, 1982), 609–22.

one that is extant today),[2] but the Gospel of Matthew that we have today is in Greek (and not a Greek translation of a Hebrew or Aramaic text).[3]

Finally, the Papian tradition may imply that Mark was written first and that Matthew was written later, a conclusion that has been reached by almost all Gospel scholars. (More will be said on this topic.) It may also imply, with the words "each person interpreted them [i.e., the sayings of Jesus, as Matthew ordered them] as best he could," that it was Matthew's Gospel (not Mark's) that Christian teachers tended to study. As it so happens, this seems to be the case, for in the first century of the history of the church Matthew's Gospel was clearly the favorite,[4] and it remained so until the nineteenth century.

To be sure, what survives of the Papian tradition leaves unanswered many questions, but taken at face value it appears to lend important, early support to the apostle Matthew as the author of the Gospel of Matthew. Not all Gospel scholars accept what Papias has to say and suggest instead that the tradition of Matthew's authorship arose no earlier than the second century. This may be so, but it is far from evident that the Gospels circulated anonymously for years, even decades, before some imagined ecclesiastical authority assigned authors to them.[5] There is no evidence that such a body existed or that, if it did, it could exert the influence necessary to produce unanimity. After all, there is no evidence that anyone disputed Matthean attribution (or the attributions with respect to the other Gospels, for that matter). Surely, a late, arbitrary, and (from a scholarly point of view) pseudonymous attribution of authorship could not have gone unchallenged. Yet there is not a hint that anyone claimed someone else as the author of Matthew.

Another point should be made. If attributions were made on bases other than historical ones, then why select the apostle Matthew as the author of this Gospel? All we know of Matthew was that he was a tax collector (Matt 9:9) who invited

---

[2] At the opening of his Greek version of *The Jewish Wars*, Josephus explains: "I have proposed … to translate those books into the Greek tongue, which I formerly composed in my native [language]" (*J.W.* 1.3).

[3] On the possibility of a Hebrew version of Matthew, see G. Howard, *The Gospel of Matthew According to a Primitive Hebrew Text* (Macon, GA: Mercer University Press, 1987); J. R. Edwards, *The Hebrew Gospel and the Development of the Synoptic Tradition* (Grand Rapids, MI: Eerdmans, 2009). There are still a few scholars who argue that our Greek Matthew is but a translation of a Hebrew (or Aramaic) version. I do not agree. The Semitic flavor of the New Testament Gospels is due to the influence of the Greek Old Testament and the way Greek was spoken by Jews who also spoke Aramaic or Hebrew.

[4] This observation has been ably documented in É. Massaux, *The Influence of the Gospel of Saint Matthew on Christian Literature before Saint Irenaeus* (NGS 5.1–3, ed. A. J. Bellinzoni; 3 vols., Macon, GA: Mercer University Press, 1990–1993).

[5] This point has been well argued in M. Hengel, *Four Gospels and the One Gospel of Jesus Christ: An Investigation of the Collection and Origin of the Canonical Gospels* (Harrisburg, PA: Trinity Press International, 2000), 48–56. Hengel argues that the four New Testament Gospels never circulated anonymously. See also R. T. France, *Matthew: Evangelist & Teacher* (New Testament Profiles; Downers Grove, IL: InterVarsity, 1998), 50–60.

friends to hear Jesus (Luke 5:29–32). Nothing is said of him in the Book of Acts apart from his name appearing in a list. Surely, better candidates would have come to mind. Why not Peter or his brother Andrew, or one of the Zebedee brothers? If names were simply picked out of a hat, as it were, then why not select names of apostles who figured more prominently in the ministry of Jesus and in the leadership of the church?[6] There is nothing in the Gospel of Matthew that rules out the apostle Matthew as its author, and there is nothing in the life of the early church that compelled it to select the apostle Matthew.

When Was the Gospel of Matthew Written?

Related to the question of authorship is the question of date. Many scholars date Matthew a few years after the end of the Jewish revolt in 70 A.D. A few even date the Gospel to sometime in the 80s. The principal argument for a post-70 date is the possible allusion to the burning of Jerusalem in the parable of the wedding banquet (Matt 22:1–14). In the parable, the enraged king "sent his troops, destroyed those murderers, and burned their city" (v. 7). This is taken by many as an allusion to the Roman destruction of Jerusalem and its temple, which eyewitness Josephus describes in very fiery terms (e.g., *The Jewish Wars* [hereafter *J.W.* in citations] 6.165–68, 177–85, 190–92, 228–35, 250–84, 316, 346, 353–55, 407, 434). But the Gospel of Matthew appears to presuppose the continuing function of the temple (Matt 5:23–24; 17:24–27; 23:16–22). Moreover, the detail of fiery destruction in Matthew's parable may be nothing more than biblical language. Both the narrative books and the prophets repeatedly refer to the fiery destruction of the city of Jerusalem and its magnificent temple (e.g., 2 Kings 25:9; 2 Chron 36:19; Neh 1:3; 2:3, 13, 17; 4:2; Isa 64:11, "Our holy and beautiful house … has been burned by fire"; Jer 21:10, "this city … shall be given into the hands of the king of Babylon, and he shall burn it with fire"; 32:29, "The Chaldeans who are fighting against this city shall come, set it on fire, and burn it"; 34:2, "am going to give this city into the hand of the king of Babylon, and he shall burn it with fire"). Of course, it is possible that after 70 A.D. the parable was glossed to reflect the destruction of Jerusalem. Scribes did gloss Scripture here and there, as the discovery of early New Testament manuscripts has shown.

Closely related to the question of the date of Matthew is the date of the Gospel of Mark. Most Markan scholars think Mark was composed and circulated either during the Jewish revolt (perhaps in 68 or 69 A.D.) or shortly after the capture of the city (perhaps in 70 or 71 A.D.). A few scholars have argued that Mark (and Matthew) should be dated much earlier. One scholar recently concluded on the basis of the attitude toward the Jewish law and in comparison to what is said in the Book of Acts about the first decade or so of the early church that Mark was probably not

---

6   On this point, see R. T. France, *Matthew* (1998), 66–74.

written later than the mid-40s A.D.[7] If so, then Mark's Gospel could have circulated and been read and studied for years before Matthew composed his more Jewish and orderly account well before the 60s A.D. and the agitation that led to the Jewish revolt. It has also been pointed out that the Book of Acts, the second volume in the Luke-Acts work, brings its narrative to an end no later than 62 A.D., before the death of James, the brother of the Lord.[8] This, too, could suggest that Luke, which also makes use of Mark, could have been written before the outbreak of the Jewish revolt. Thus we see reasonable arguments for the writing and circulation of all three Synoptic Gospels sometime prior to the war of 66–70 A.D. Recent major commentaries on Matthew have reached this conclusion.[9]

Where and in What Setting Was the Gospel of Matthew Written?

A number of scholars have suggested that the Gospel of Matthew was composed in the city of Antioch, a prominent city in Syria,[10] or perhaps in Damascus, much farther to the south. Odessa, also in Syria, is sometimes mentioned. Others have suggested Palestine, perhaps Galilee.[11] Admittedly, Antioch was a major center of Christian activity in the early decades of the church (see, e.g., Acts 11:19–27; 13:1; 14:26; 15:22), but the suggestion that Matthew was written there is nothing more than an educated guess. In one place in Matthew, we may have an important clue. The evangelist rewrites Mark's reference to people seeking Jesus (Mark 1:36–37) to say that Jesus' "fame spread throughout all Syria" (Matt 4:24). The reference to "Syria" sticks out like a sore thumb. Matthew did not get this reference from Mark or from any other source we know of. Why not say "throughout all Israel" or "throughout all Galilee"? Matthew may have mentioned Syria because it was in this region that he lived and traveled and by the time he was writing his Gospel Jesus had become well known, even "throughout all Syria."[12] Admittedly, this is not much to go on either.

---

[7]   See J. G. Crossley, *The Date of Mark's Gospel: Insight from the Law in Earliest Christianity* (JSNTSup 266; London: T. & T. Clark International, 2004).

[8]   See also J. A. T. Robinson, *Redating the New Testament* (Philadelphia: Westminster, 1976), 97–107, who dates Matthew to a time before 62 A.D.

[9]   See J. Nolland, *The Gospel of Matthew* (NIGTC; Grand Rapids, MI: Eerdmans; Bletchley: Paternoster, 2005), 12; R. T. France, *The Gospel of Matthew* (NICNT; Grand Rapids, MI: Eerdmans, 2007), 19.

[10] Antioch as the place of writing has recently been defended by D. C. Sim, *The Gospel of Matthew and Christian Judaism: The History and Social Setting of the Matthean Community* (Edinburgh: T. & T. Clark, 1998).

[11] B. Witherington III, *Matthew* (Smyth & Helwys Bible Commentary; Macon, GA: Smyth & Helwys, 2006), 22–28. Witherington plausibly suggests Capernaum.

[12] It is possible, of course, that "Syria" may have been understood from a Roman perspective, as referring to a much larger region, including southern territories such as Galilee and perhaps even Judea (see Macrobius, *Saturnalia* 2.4.11, who calls the kingdom of Herod the Great "Syria," rather than Israel or Judea). If so, Matthew's reference in 4:24 to

Perhaps we should say no more than "Matthew may have been written in Syria" and leave it at that.

Of more pressing importance is why Matthew wrote his Gospel. It has been argued, primarily on the basis of the Great Commission, in which the risen Jesus commands his apostles to convert and teach "all Gentiles" (Matt 28:19), that the Jewish mission had concluded and that Matthew's interest was oriented exclusively toward Gentiles.[13] However, this interpretation runs against the strong emphasis on the validity of the Law (cf. Matt 5:17–20), not to mention the critical comments directed against Gentiles (cf. Matt 5:46–47; 6:7–8, 31–32; 18:17). In view of such data, a number of scholars have reached the opposite conclusion, namely that Matthew is still in the Jewish community, struggling to convince a skeptical synagogue that Jesus really is Israel's Messiah, that his teaching really does measure up to the righteous requirements of the Law of Moses, and that his death and resurrection really have fulfilled prophecy.[14]

In my opinion, the latter view is closer to the truth, though it may underestimate the degree to which Jesus in Matthew distances himself from and condemns scribal Judaism, the forerunner in some sense to rabbinic Judaism, as well as the Jerusalem temple establishment, which would still have existed and exerted influence if Matthew wrote before 66–70 A.D. The Jesus of Matthew is sharply critical of the scribes and Pharisees (see especially Matthew 23). The evangelist Matthew seems to have written his Gospel in a time of transition, when he and his primary readers, most of whom were ethnically Jewish but were evangelizing Gentiles,[15] had been driven out of the synagogue and had begun to form a

Syria would not necessarily rule out the Gospel's origin in Galilee. On Galilee as the place of composition, see B. Witherington III, *Matthew* (2006), 21–28. Nevertheless, I find it unlikely that the evangelist himself would refer to any part of Israel as "Syria," however Rome may have understood this regional or political reference.

13   D. R. A. Hare, *The Theme of Jewish Persecution of Christians in the Gospel According to St. Matthew* (SNTSMS 6; Cambridge: Cambridge University Press, 1967); D. R. A. Hare and D. J. Harrington, "'Make Disciples of All Gentiles' (Mt 28:19)," *CBQ* 37 (1975): 359–69.

14   Among the most recent and better argued, J. A. Overman, *Matthew's Gospel and Formative Judaism: A Study of the Social World of the Matthean Community* (Minneapolis: Fortress Press, 1990); J. A. Overman, *Church and Community in Crisis: The Gospel According to Matthew* (Valley Forge, PA: Trinity Press International, 1996); A. J. Saldarini, *Matthew's Christian-Jewish Community* (Chicago: University of Chicago Press, 1994); D. C. Sim, *The Gospel of Matthew and Christian Judaism* (1998).

15   And here is where I disagree with D. C. Sim (see note 14); Matthew remains committed to the evangelization of Gentiles. See W. Carter, "Matthew and the Gentiles: Individual Conversion and/or Systemic Transformation?" *JSNT* 26 (2004): 259–82. See also D. A. Hagner, "Matthew: Apostate, Reformer, Revolutionary," *NTS* 49 (2003): 193–209. Hagner contends, against Overman, Saldarini, and Sim, that Matthew's community should not be described as a form of Christianized Judaism. It is fully Christian but still understands itself in relation to Israel.

community of faith distinct from it.[16] Although estranged from the synagogue, Matthew firmly believed that the followers of Jesus constituted the true "sons of the kingdom" (Matt 13:38), comprising a congregation or assembly (Matt 16:18; 18:17), and that when gathered in the name of Jesus, even if only two or three, the Shekinah, the dwelling presence of God – now experienced in his Son Messiah Jesus – was "in their midst" (Matt 18:19–20; cf. *m. 'Abot* 3:2, "if two sit together … the Shekinah rests between them"). Graham Stanton has dubbed those who belonged to the congregation of Jesus a "new people," a people who have left the synagogue and are aggressively evangelizing the Gentiles, in fulfillment of the risen Lord's command.[17]

MATTHEW AND THE OTHER GOSPELS

Matthew is one of the three New Testament Gospels called the "Synoptic Gospels." They are called "Synoptic" (from the Greek compound word *sunopsis*) because they can be "seen together" (*opsis* = "seen" + *sun* = "with" or "together") when presented in parallel columns. The other Synoptic Gospels are Mark and Luke. The Gospel of John is not a Synoptic Gospel. Its contents and writing style are quite distinctive.

Almost from the beginning, Christians have wondered how the Gospels of Matthew, Mark, and Luke relate to one another. From the great theologian Augustine until the scholars of the early nineteenth century, it was believed that Matthew was the first Gospel written, with Mark seen as an abbreviation of Matthew, or perhaps as a combination and abbreviation of both Matthew and Luke. But, in the nineteenth century, a number of scholars began to suspect that Mark was the first Gospel to circulate and that Matthew and Luke made use of Mark and another body of material, comprising mostly the teachings of Jesus, known today by the siglum Q. Today, most New Testament scholars hold this view because, in the words of one commentator on Matthew, "it provides the framework for what seem to be the most cogent explanations of the similarities and differences of detail among the synoptics."[18] For most scholars today, the relationship of the three

[16] W. Carter, "Matthew's Gospel: Jewish Christianity, Christian Judaism, or Neither?" in M. Jackson-McCabe (ed.), *Jewish Christianity Reconsidered: Rethinking Ancient Groups and Texts* (Minneapolis: Fortress Press, 2007), 155–79. Carter reminds us that the synagogue was not Matthew's only point of reference; the difficulties of life in the Roman Empire must be factored in also.

[17] G. N. Stanton, *A Gospel for a New People: Studies in Matthew* (Edinburgh: T. & T. Clark, 1992; Louisville, KY: Westminster/John Knox, 1993), 280–81.

[18] R. H. Gundry, *Matthew* (1982), 3. There are, of course, a few dissenters (such as the late W. R. Farmer). For a discussion of Markan priority and Matthew's use of Mark, see R. H. Stein, *Studying the Synoptic Gospels: Origin and Interpretation* (Grand Rapids, MI: Baker, 2001), 29–169.

Synoptic Gospels is seen as giving Mark "priority" (i.e., that Mark was written and circulated first) and that Matthew and Luke utilized Mark and Q as their primary sources. This solution does not rule out the possibility of some contact between Matthew and Luke. Indeed, some scholars think that at some point in composing his Gospel the evangelist Matthew may have had access to the Gospel of Luke.[19] Some think Matthew made use of all or some of the *Didache*, an early epitome of Jesus' teaching (the Greek word *didache* means "teaching") that today is classified with the mostly second-century writings of those known as the "Apostolic Fathers."[20]

THE STRUCTURE OF MATTHEW

Paul Wernle long ago described the Gospel of Matthew as a "retelling" of the Gospel of Mark,[21] a description with which most Matthean scholars today concur.[22] Although Luke also made use of Mark, calling Luke a "retelling" of Mark does not sound quite right. Luke made use of only 60 percent of Mark and freely rearranged the sequence of the narrative. In contrast, Matthew made use of almost 90 percent of Mark's content and very rarely departed from Mark's sequence.

I mention this at the outset because it has a bearing on how we understand the structure of Matthew. How did the evangelist arrange and structure his Gospel? Long ago, attention focused on the five major discourses in Matthew (Chapters 5–7, 10, 13, 18, and 24–25), believed to be a deliberate parallel to the five books of Moses.[23] But these discourses do not account for the whole of Matthew's structure. It has been suggested that Matthew divides into three major parts, 1:1–4:16, 4:17–16:20, and 16:21–28:20, on the basis of the statements "From that time Jesus

[19]   For example, see R. V. Huggins, "Matthean Posteriority: A Preliminary Proposal," *NovT* 34 (1992): 1–21. Huggins thinks Matthew regarded Mark as his primary source and Luke as a supplemental source in that Matthew was informed by but not determined by material in Luke (such as the infancy narrative). Others wonder if it goes the other way, that Luke edited his Gospel in the light of Matthew. See R. H. Gundry, *Matthew* (1982), 5.

[20]   For arguments on Matthew's use of the *Didache*, see A. J. P. Garrow, *The Gospel of Matthew's Dependence on the Didache* (JSNTSup 254; London: T. & T. Clark International, 2004).

[21]   P. Wernle, *Die synoptische Frage* (Freiburg: Mohr Siebeck, 1899), 161.

[22]   As, for example, in the classic collection of studies by G. Bornkamm, G. Barth, and H. J. Held, *Tradition and Interpretation in Matthew* (Philadelphia: Westminster, 1963). See Held's comment on p. 165.

[23]   B. W. Bacon, "The Five Books of Matthew against the Jews," *The Expositor* 15 (1918): 56–66. Bacon was correct in recognizing the presence of the five discourses and surmising that their number paralleled the number of books of Moses (i.e., Genesis – Deuteronomy). Less convincing was his view that the five discourses of Jesus were somehow "against the Jews" or explained the Gospel of Matthew as a whole.

began to proclaim" in 4:17 and "From that time on, Jesus began to show" in 16:21.[24] These three major divisions are labeled the "Preparation for Jesus Messiah, Son of God," the "Proclamation of Jesus to Israel," and the "Passion and Resurrection of Jesus Messiah, Son of God," respectively.[25] This division may work for the first two sections, but the third section includes too much material, for some of the material has nothing to do with the Passion. Other structural proposals have been suggested, in which key events or "kernels" are identified.[26] But again, nothing approaching consensus has been achieved.

Perhaps it is better to view Matthew's arrangement and structure as an expansion and adaptation of Mark's relatively simple outline of a ministry in Galilee, then a journey south to Judea and Jerusalem, and finally the Passion in Jerusalem. Matthew has worked within this framework, prefacing Mark's Gospel with an infancy narrative, concluding it with an evangelistic commission, and enriching the interior with additional materials, not least five impressive discourses.[27]

Before concluding this section, a word needs to be said about Matthew's writing style. The Jewish orientation of the evangelist is revealed at several points. He is acquainted with Scripture (i.e., the Old Testament) in three languages: the Hebrew, the Greek translation, and even the Aramaic paraphrase (the Targum, indicated

---

[24] J. D. Kingsbury, *Matthew: Structure, Christology, Kingdom* (Philadelphia: Fortress, 1975), 7–17. Kingsbury's interpretation has been followed and elaborated by two of his students: D. R. Bauer, *The Structure of Matthew's Gospel: A Study in Literary Design* (JSNTSup 31; Sheffield: Almond Press, 1988); and J. A. Gibbs, *Matthew 1:1–11:1* (Concordia Commentary; St. Louis, MO: Concordia Academic Press, 2006).

[25] See D. R. Bauer, *The Structure of Matthew's Gospel* (1988), 73–108.

[26] For example, F. Matera, "The Plot of Matthew's Gospel," *CBQ* 49 (1987): 233–53, who identifies a number of "kernels" around which a series of narrative "blocks" (Matt 1:1–4:11; 4:12–11:1; 11:2–16:12; 16:13–20:34; 21:1–28:15; and 28:16–20) are identified, all of which trace Jesus' movement away from Israel, which has rejected him, to the Gentiles. See the response by W. Carter, "Kernels and Narrative Blocks: The Structure of Matthew's Gospel," *CBQ* 54 (1992): 463–83. Carter identifies the kernels and major events (Matt 1:18–25; 4:17–25; 11:2–6; 16:21–28; 21:1–27; 28:1–10) and the corresponding narrative blocks (Matt 1:1–4:16; 4:17–11:1; 11:2–16:20; 16:21–20:34; 21:1–27:66; 28:1–20) somewhat differently.

[27] See the succinct summary of views, including a prudent conclusion with which I agree, in D. C. Allison, Jr. and W. D. Davies, *A Critical and Exegetical Commentary on the Gospel According to Saint Matthew* (ICC; 3 vols., Edinburgh: T. & T. Clark, 1988–1997), 1:58–72. Matthew's structure is "mixed." It is sometimes suggested that Matthew produced six discourses, not five (the extra discourse is Matthew 23, the denunciation of the scribes and Pharisees). This position is taken in G. S. Sloyan, *Preaching from the Lectionary: An Exegetical Commentary* (Minneapolis: Fortress Press, 2004), 176; B. Witherington III, *Matthew* (2006), 15: "definitely six, not five." It is not wrong to identify Matthew 23 as a discourse or diatribe, but it is quite different from the five discourses that have been mentioned and does not conclude with the Mosaic phrase, "When Jesus finished ...," as do the five discourses.

herein by *Tg.* when citing specific texts), which in the first century was only in its beginning stages.[28] Matthew makes extensive use of Scripture, many times citing it as "fulfilled." Matthew is very concerned with the Law of Moses and how it is to be fulfilled. Related to this is the question of what constitutes righteousness. We find words and phrases that remind us of the way the Rabbis discussed Scripture and debated among themselves. There is little doubt that Matthew was familiar with some aspects of midrash (what in time became standard practice among the Rabbis).[29] We see this sometimes in his interpretation of Scripture and perhaps also in ways that revised or supplemented what he inherited from Mark and Q. But I do not think Matthew engaged in wholesale invention or transformation of stories. This matter will be addressed in the infancy narrative and elsewhere.

OUTLINE OF MATTHEW

    I. Birth and Preparation of the Messiah (1:1–4:11)
      A. Infancy Narrative (1:2–2:23)
      B. Baptism and Temptation (3:1–4:11)
   II. The Messiah's Proclamation and Ministry (4:12–11:1)
      A. Narrative: Beginnings of Ministry (4:12–25)
      B. Discourse 1: The Sermon on the Mount: The Messiah's Call to Righteousness (5:1–7:29)
      C. Narrative: The Messiah's Ministry (8:1–9:35)
      D. Discourse 2: The Messiah's Summons to All Israel (9:36–11:1)
  III. Reactions and Responses to the Messiah (11:2–20:34)
      A. Narrative: A Mixed Response to the Messiah (11:2–12:50)
      B. Discourse 3: The Messiah's Teaching about the Kingdom (13:1–53)
      C. Narrative: Intensification of the Mixed Response (13:54–17:27)
      D. Discourse 4: The Messiah's Teaching on Community Life (18:1–19:1)
      E. Narrative: The Messiah's Teaching on the Way to Jerusalem (19:2–20:34)
  IV. The Rejection and Vindication of the Messiah (21:1–28:20)
      A. Narrative: The Messiah Confronts Jerusalem (21:1–23:39)
      B. Discourse 5: The Messiah Prophesies Coming Judgment (24:1–26:2)
      C. Narrative: The Messiah Is Judged but Vindicated (26:3–28:20)

[28] The later, fully preserved Targums are not in view here. What we find are verbal, thematic, and exegetical points of coherence between Jesus and other first-century teachers and distinctive readings in the Targums. This coherence suggests that the later Targums in some instances preserve readings and interpretations that reach back to the first century and probably earlier. It was with some of these readings and interpretations that Jesus was familiar. For a discussion of the relevance of the Targums for understanding Matthew as a writer, see C. A. Evans, "Targumizing Tendencies in Matthean Redaction," in D. J. Harrington et al. (eds.), *When Judaism and Christianity Began: Essays in Memory of Anthony J. Saldarini* (JSJSup 85; 2 vols., Leiden: Brill, 2004), 1:93–116.

[29] Midrash (from *darash*, to "search") means searching, or interpreting Scripture.

Some Significant Dates in New Testament Background and the Origins of Christianity

587 B.C.	The capture of Jerusalem, the destruction of the temple, and the deportation of many Jews to Babylonia.
333–32 B.C.	Alexander the Great sweeps through Israel and conquers the Middle East.
270 B.C.	The death of Epicurus (founder of Epicureanism).
ca. 265 B.C.	The death of Zeno (founder of Cynicism).
ca. 250 B.C.	The beginning of the work of translation of the Hebrew Scriptures into Greek, leading to the Septuagint (LXX).
167 B.C.	The desecration of the temple by the Seleucid ruler Antiochus IV "Epiphanes" (i.e., "[Divine] Manifestation").
164 B.C.	Judas Maccabeus (the "hammer") defeats General Lysias; Antiochus IV dies; Judas rules Judea and begins to enlarge its borders; the Hasmonean dynasty is founded.
63 B.C.	Pompey enters Jerusalem, thus beginning the era of Roman dominance.
40 B.C.	The Roman senate, at the prompting of Mark Antony, declares Herod (son of Antipater II) "King of the Jews"; the Parthians support Antigonus (son of Aristobulus II), the last Hasmonean ruler.
37 B.C.	Herod defeats Antigonus, last of the Hasmonean rulers, and becomes king of Israel in fact and marries Mariamne (granddaughter of Hyrcanus II). During his reign, he rebuilds Jerusalem and the temple, founds several cities and fortresses, and marries, divorces, and/or murders ten wives.
31 B.C.	Octavian defeats Mark Antony and Cleopatra at Actium, becomes Roman emperor, changes his name to Augustus, and forgives Herod for siding with Mark Antony.
6 or 5 B.C.	The birth of Jesus
4 B.C.	The death of Herod the Great.
6 A.D.	Archelaus (son of Herod the Great) is deposed.
6 A.D.	Annas (or Ananus) is appointed high priest.
18 A.D.	Joseph bar Caiaphas (son-in-law of Annas) is appointed high priest.
19 or 25 A.D.	Pontius Pilate succeeds Gratus as prefect of Samaria and Judea.
30 or 33 A.D.	Jesus is crucified.
34 A.D.	The death of Herod Philip (son of Herod the Great).
37 A.D.	Pontius Pilate and Joseph bar Caiaphas are removed from office.

37 A.D.	The death of Tiberius, succeeded by Gaius Caligula; the birth of Josephus, Jewish historian and apologist.
39 A.D.	Caligula banishes Herod Antipas (son of Herod the Great) to Gaul.
44 A.D.	The death of Herod Agrippa I (son of Aristobulus and Bernice, grandson of Herod the Great), after brief rule over Israel (41–44); see Acts 12:1–23.
ca. 50 A.D.	The death of Philo of Alexandria, Jewish allegorist, philosopher, and apologist.
54 A.D.	The death of Claudius, succeeded by Nero.
ca. 50–60 A.D.	The Gospel of Mark is published.
60–62 A.D.	Tenure of the Roman governor Festus in Caesarea.
62 A.D.	Ananus (son of Annas) becomes high priest and without Roman approval puts to death James, the brother of Jesus; Albinus removes Ananus from office.
62–64 A.D.	Tenure of the Roman governor Albinus in Caesarea; the Gospel of Luke and Acts are published; the Gospel of Matthew is published.
64–66 A.D.	Tenure of the Roman governor Gessius Florus in Caesarea.
65 A.D.	The death of Seneca.
66 A.D.	The Jewish revolt begins; governor Florus is murdered (or escapes).
ca. 67 A.D.	The death of Paul.
68 A.D.	The death of Nero; he is succeeded by Galba.
68–69 A.D.	Brief reigns of Galba, Otho, and Vitellius.
69 A.D.	General Vespasian, commander of the Roman forces against the Jews, is proclaimed emperor.
70 A.D.	Jerusalem is captured by Titus (son of Vespasian). The temple is badly damaged by fire; it is later demolished.
71 A.D.	Emperor Vespasian and sons Titus and Domitian celebrate victory over Judea in a triumph held in Rome.
73 A.D.	General Silva captures Masada.
ca. 78 A.D.	Josephus publishes *The Jewish Wars*.
79 A.D.	The death of Vespasian; he is succeeded by Titus.
81 A.D.	The death of Titus; he is succeeded by Domitian (brother of Titus).
ca. 85 A.D.	Christians are excluded from some synagogues.
90 A.D.	The Gospel of John is published.

ca. 93 A.D.	The death of Agrippa II (son of Agrippa I), after ruling portions of Israel beginning in 49 (see Acts 25:13–26:32); Bernice was his sister.
96 A.D.	The death of Domitian; he is succeeded by Nerva.
98 A.D.	The death of Nerva; he is succeeded by Trajan. The death of Josephus (?).
ca. 110 A.D.	Papias publishes *Expositions of the Sayings of the Lord.*
ca. 112 A.D.	The death of Ignatius.
115 A.D.	Jewish revolt in North Africa.
117 A.D.	The death of Trajan; he is succeeded by Hadrian.
ca. 120 A.D.	Tacitus publishes *The Annals.*
132–135 A.D.	The great Jewish revolt led by Simon ben Kosiba, dubbed "bar Kokhba" (i.e., "son of the star").
138 A.D.	The death of Hadrian; he is succeeded by Antoninus Pius.

THE GREEK TEXT OF MATTHEW

The New Cambridge Bible Commentary is based on the New Revised Standard Version (NRSV). This English version of the Bible is based on the third (corrected) edition of the United Bible Societies Greek New Testament, though the New Testament translators had access to the apparatus of the fourth edition.[30] (The apparatus lists the important variant readings in the various ancient Greek manuscripts.) The editors-in-chief of the NRSV are the late Professor Bruce M. Metzger (whose principal responsibility was the New Testament and books of the Old Testament Apocrypha) and Father Roland E. Murphy (whose principal responsibility was the Old Testament). A number of other great scholars labored with them in bringing to fruition this remarkable achievement. Readers are encouraged to peruse both the Editors' Preface and the "To the Reader" statement that usually accompany a published edition of the NRSV.[31]

---

[30]   See K. Aland, M. Black, C. M. Martini, B. M. Metzger, and A. Wikgren (eds.), *The Greek New Testament*, corrected 3rd edition (Stuttgart: Deutsche Bibelgesellschaft and United Bible Societies, 1983); B. Aland, K. Aland, J. Karavidopoulos, C. M. Martini, and B. M. Metzger (eds.), *The Greek New Testament*, 4th edition (Stuttgart: Deutsche Bibelgesellschaft and United Bible Societies, 1993).

[31]   As in B. M. Metzger and R. E. Murphy (eds.), *The New Oxford Annotated Bible with Apocryphal/Deuterocanonical Books: New Revised Standard Version* (New York: Oxford University Press, 1991), v–vi (Editors' Preface), ix–xiv (To the Reader). See also B. M. Metzger, R. C. Dentan, and W. Harrelson, *The Making of the New Revised Standard Version of the Bible* (Grand Rapids, MI: Eerdmans, 1991).

Oldest Papyrus Fragments of the Gospel of Matthew

P¹ (1:1–9, 12, 14–20; 2:14; third century)
P³⁵ (25:12–15, 20–23; third or fourth century)
P³⁷ (26:19–52; third or fourth century)
P⁴⁵ (20:24–32; 21:13–19; 25:41–46; 26:1–39; third century)
P⁵³ (26:29–40; third century)
P⁶⁴ (26:7–8, 10, 14–15, 22–23, 31–33; late second or early third century)
P⁶⁷ (3:9, 15; 5:20–22, 25–28; late second or early third century)
P⁷⁰ (2:13–16, 22–23; 3:1; 11:26–27; 12:4–5; 24:3–6, 12–15; third century)
P⁷⁷ (23:30–39; late second or early third century)
P⁸⁶ (5:13–16, 22–25; fourth century)
P¹⁰¹ (3:10–12, 16–17; 4:1–3; third century)
P¹⁰² (4:11–12, 22–23; third or fourth century)
P¹⁰³ (13:55–57; 14:3–5; late second or early third century)
P¹⁰⁴ (21:34–37, 43, 45; late second century)
P¹⁰⁵ (27:62–64; 28:2–5; fifth or sixth century)
P¹¹⁰ (10:13–14, 25–27; fourth century)

See K. S. Min, *Die früheste Überlieferung des Matthäusevangeliums (bis zum 3./4. Jh.): Edition und Untersuchung* (Arbeiten zur neutestamentlichen Textforschung 34; Berlin: de Gruyter, 2005).

Oldest Uncials of the Gospel of Matthew

א (Codex Sinaiticus, fourth century)
A (Codex Alexandrinus, fifth century)
B (Codex Vaticanus, fourth century)
C (Codex Ephraemi Rescriptus, fifth century)
D (Codex Beza, fifth century)
W (Codex Washington, fifth century)

See T. J. Kraus and T. Nicklas (eds.), *New Testament Manuscripts: Their Texts and Their World* (Texts and Editions for New Testament Study 2; Leiden: Brill, 2006).

II. Suggested Readings on the Gospel of Matthew

In the bibliography that follows, I list the commentaries on Matthew that I consulted. These are occasionally referenced in the footnotes as well. Following the commentaries, I list a number of books that I consulted. Most of these are monographs or collections of studies devoted to the Gospel of Matthew. Finally, I list a selected number of shorter studies concerned with Matthew. Other books and studies, not included here, appear in the footnotes. I have placed asterisks beside commentaries and other works that I think students and clergy will find especially helpful.

COMMENTARIES

W. F. Albright and C. S. Mann, *Matthew* (AB 26; Garden City, NY: Doubleday, 1971).

W. Allen, *A Critical and Exegetical Commentary on the Gospel According to St. Matthew* (ICC; Edinburgh: T. & T. Clark, 1907).

*D. C. Allison, Jr. and W. D. Davies, *A Critical and Exegetical Commentary on the Gospel According to Saint Matthew* (ICC; 3 vols., Edinburgh: T. & T. Clark, 1988–1997).

A. W. Argyle, *The Gospel According to Matthew* (Cambridge Bible Commentary; Cambridge: Cambridge University Press, 1963).

F. W. Beare, *The Gospel According to Matthew: A Commentary* (Oxford: Blackwell; New York: Harper & Row, 1981).

*C. L. Blomberg, *Matthew* (NAC 22; Nashville, TN: Broadman, 1992).

P. Bonnard, *L'évangile selon Saint Matthieu* (Commentaire du Nouveau Testament 1; Paris: Éditions Delachaux et Niestlé, 1963).

J. A. Broadus, *Commentary on the Gospel of Matthew* (An American Commentary on the New Testament; Philadelphia: American Baptist Publication Society, 1886).

A. Carr, *The Gospel According to St Matthew* (The Cambridge Bible for Schools and Colleges; Cambridge: Cambridge University Press, 1905).

*D. A. Carson, "Matthew," in F. E. Gaebelien (ed.), *The Expositor's Bible Commentary*, vol. 8 (Grand Rapids, MI: Zondervan, 1984), 1–599.

*W. Carter, *Matthew: Storyteller, Interpreter, Evangelist*, revised edition (Peabody, MA: Hendrickson, 2004).

H. Clarke, *The Gospel of Matthew and Its Readers: A Historical Introduction to the First Gospel* (Bloomington: Indiana University Press, 2003).

G. E. P. Cox, *Saint Matthew: Introduction and Commentary* (Torch Bible Commentaries; London: SCM Press, 1952).

P. Dausch, "Das Matthäusevangelium," in *Die drei älteren Evangelien*, 4th edition (Die heilige Schrift des Neuen Testamentes 2; Bonn: Hanstein, 1932), 41–369.

J. C. Fenton, *Saint Matthew* (Pelican Gospel Commentaries; Harmondsworth: Penguin, 1963).

F. Filson, *Commentary on St. Matthew* (HNTC; New York: Harper, 1960).

R. T. France, *The Gospel According to Matthew: An Introduction and Commentary* (TNTC; Grand Rapids, MI: Eerdmans, 1985).

The Gospel of Matthew (NICNT; Grand Rapids, MI: Eerdmans, 2007).

H. Frankemölle, *Matthäus: Kommentar 1* (Düsseldorf: Patmos Verlag, 1994).

P. Gaechter, *Das Matthäus Evangelium: Ein Kommentar* (Innsbruck: Tyrolia-Verlag, 1963).

*D. Garland, *Reading Matthew: A Literary and Theological Commentary on the First Gospel* (New York: Crossroad, 1995).

*J. A. Gibbs, *Matthew 1:1–11:1* (Concordia Commentary; St. Louis, MO: Concordia Academic Press, 2006).

Matthew 11:2–20:34 (Concordia Commentary; St. Louis, MO: Concordia Academic Press, 2010).

J. Gnilka, *Das Matthäusevangelium* (HTKNT 1.1–2; 2 vols., Freiburg: Herder, 1986–1988).

F. W. Green, *The Gospel According to Saint Matthew* (The Clarendon Bible; Oxford: Clarendon Press, 1936).

H. B. Green, *The Gospel According to Matthew* (The New Clarendon Bible; Oxford: Clarendon Press, 1975).

W. Grundmann, *Das Evangelium nach Matthäus*, 5th edition (THNT 3; Berlin: Evangelische Verlagsanstalt, 1981).

*R. H. Gundry, *Matthew: A Commentary on His Handbook for a Mixed Church under Persecution*, revised edition (Grand Rapids, MI: Eerdmans, 1994). Original edition published as *Matthew: A Commentary on His Literary and Theological Art* (Grand Rapids, MI: Eerdmans, 1982).

*D. A. Hagner, *Matthew* (WBC 33; 2 vols., Dallas: Word, 1993–1995).

D. R. A. Hare, *Matthew* (Interpretation: A Bible Commentary for Teaching and Preaching; Louisville, KY: John Knox Press, 1993).

*D. J. Harrington, *The Gospel of Matthew* (Sacra Pagina 1; Collegeville, MN: Liturgical Press, 1991).

D. Hill, *Matthew* (NCB; Grand Rapids, MI: Eerdmans, 1972).

H. J. Holtzmann, *Die Synoptiker*, 3rd edition (Hand-Commentar zum Neuen Testament I/1; Tübingen: Mohr [Siebeck], 1901).

*C. S. Keener, *A Commentary on the Gospel of Matthew* (Grand Rapids, MI: Eerdmans, 1999).

E. Klostermann, *Das Matthäusevangelium*, 4th edition (HNT 4; Tübingen: Mohr [Siebeck], 1971).

S. T. Lachs, *A Rabbinic Commentary on the New Testament: The Gospels of Matthew, Mark and Luke* (Hoboken, NJ: Ktav, 1987).

M.-J. Lagrange, *Évangile selon Saint Matthieu*, 2nd edition (ÉBib; Paris: Gabalda, 1923).

A.-J. Levine, "Matthew," in C. A. Newsom and S. H. Ringe (eds.), *The Women's Bible Commentary* (Louisville, KY: Westminster John Knox Press, 1992), 252–62.

E. Lohmeyer, *Das Evangelium des Matthäus*, 2nd edition, W. Schmauch (ed.) (MeyerK 1; Göttingen: Vandenhoeck & Ruprecht, 1958).

U. Luck, *Das Evangelium nach Matthäus* (Züricher Bibelkommentare; Zurich: Theologischer Verlag, 1993).

*U. Luz, *Matthew* (Hermeneia; 3 vols., Minneapolis: Fortress, 2001–2007).

S. Mason and T. Robinson, "Matthew: The Book of the Genesis of Jesus the Messiah," in *Early Christian Reader* (Peabody, MA: Hendrickson, 2004), 327–96.

A. H. McNeile, *The Gospel According to St. Matthew* (London: Macmillan, 1915).

J. P. Meier, *Matthew* (Wilmington, DE: Glazier, 1980).

C. G. Montefiore, *The Synoptic Gospels: Edited with an Introduction and a Commentary*, 2nd edition (2 vols., London: Macmillan, 1927), 2:1–359.

*L. Morris, *The Gospel According to Matthew* (PNTC; Grand Rapids, MI: Eerdmans; Leicester: Apollos, 1992).

*R. H. Mounce, *Matthew* (NIBC 1; Peabody, MA: Hendrickson, 1991).

*J. Nolland, *The Gospel of Matthew* (NIGTC; Grand Rapids, MI: Eerdmans; Bletchley: Paternoster, 2005).

D. Patte, *The Gospel According to Matthew: A Structural Commentary of Matthew's Faith* (Philadelphia: Fortress Press, 1987).

A. Plummer, *An Exegetical Commentary on the Gospel of Matthew* (London: James Clarke, 1909).

E. H. Plumptre, "The Gospel According to St. Matthew," in C. J. Ellicott (ed.), *A New Testament Commentary for English Readers*, vol. 1: *The Four Gospels* (London: Cassell, 1897).

T. H. Robinson, *The Gospel of Matthew* (MNTC; London: Hodder & Stoughton, 1928).

A. Sand, *Das Evangelium nach Matthäus*, 5th edition (RNT; Regensburg: Pustet, 1965).

A. Schlatter, *Der Evangelist Matthäus: Seine Sprache, sein Ziel, seine Selbständigkeit*, 5th edition (Stuttgart: Calwer, 1959).

J. Schmid, *Das Evangelium nach Matthäus* (RNT 1; Regensburg: Pustet, 1959).

R. Schnackenburg, *The Gospel of Matthew* (Grand Rapids, MI: Eerdmans, 2002).

J. Schniewind, *Das Evangelium nach Matthäus*, 11th edition (NTD 2; Göttingen: Vandenhoeck & Ruprecht, 1964).

E. Schweizer, *The Good News According to Matthew* (Atlanta: John Knox, 1977).

*D. Senior, *Matthew* (Abingdon New Testament Commentaries; Nashville, TN: Abingdon, 1998).

W. F. Slater, *St. Matthew*, revised edition by G. H. Box (The New Century Bible; Edinburgh: T. C. & E. C. Jack; New York: Henry Frowde, 1925).

B. T. D. Smith, *The Gospel According to St. Matthew* (Cambridge Greek Testament; Cambridge: Cambridge University Press, 1927).

D. Smith, *The Gospel According to St. Matthew* (Westminster New Testament; London: Andrew Melrose, 1908).

H. L. Strack and P. Billerbeck, *Kommentar zum Neuen Testament aus Talmud und Midrasch* (6 vols., Munich: C. H. Beck, 1922–1928), 1:1–1055.

R. V. G. Tasker, *The Gospel According to St. Matthew: An Introduction and Commentary* (TNTC; London: Tyndale, 1961).

W. Trilling, *The Gospel According to St. Matthew* (2 vols., New York: Herder & Herder; London: Burns & Oates, 1969).

M. J. Wilkins, *Matthew* (NIV Application Commentary; Grand Rapids, MI: Zondervan, 2004).

*B. Witherington III, *Matthew* (Smyth & Helwys Bible Commentary; Macon, GA: Smyth & Helwys, 2006).

T. Zahn, *Das Evangelium des Matthäus*, 3rd edition (Leipzig: Deichert, 1910).

MONOGRAPHS AND COLLECTED STUDIES

D. C. Allison, Jr., *The New Moses: A Matthean Typology* (Minneapolis: Fortress Press, 1993).

  Studies in Matthew: Interpretation Past and Present (Grand Rapids, MI: Baker Academic, 2005).

J. C. Anderson, *Matthew's Narrative Web: Over, and Over, and Over Again* (JSNTSup 91; Sheffield: Sheffield Academic Press, 1994).

W. E. Arnal, *Jesus and the Village Scribes: Galilean Conflicts and the Setting of Q* (Minneapolis: Fortress, 2001).

*D. E. Aune (ed.), *The Gospel of Matthew in Current Study* (Grand Rapids, MI: Eerdmans, 2001).

B. W. Bacon, *Studies in Matthew* (New York: Henry Holt, 1930).

D. Balch (ed.), *Social History of the Matthean Community* (Minneapolis: Fortress Press, 1991).

D. R. Bauer, *The Structure of Matthew's Gospel: A Study in Literary Design* (JSNTSup 31; Sheffield: Almond Press, 1988).

D. R. Bauer and M. A. Powell (eds.), *Treasures Old and New: Contributions to Matthean Studies* (SBL Symposium Series 1; Atlanta: Scholars Press, 1996).

G. R. Beasley-Murray, *Jesus and the Kingdom of God* (Grand Rapids, MI: Eerdmans, 1986).

Jesus and the Last Days: The Interpretation of the Olivet Discourse (Peabody, MA: Hendrickson, 1993).

R. Beaton, *Isaiah's Christ in Matthew's Gospel* (SNTSMS 123; Cambridge: Cambridge University Press, 2002).

H. D. Betz, *Essays on the Sermon on the Mount* (Philadelphia: Fortress, 1985).

The Sermon on the Mount (Hermeneia; Philadelphia: Fortress, 1995).

S. L. Black, *Sentence Conjunctions in the Gospel of Matthew: καί, δέ, τότε, γάρ, οὖν and Asyndeton in Narrative Discourse* (JSNTSup 216; SNTG 9; London: Sheffield Academic Press, 2002).

G. Bornkamm, G. Barth, and H. J. Held, *Tradition and Interpretation in Matthew* (Philadelphia: Westminster, 1963).

R. G. Bratcher, *A Translator's Guide to the Gospel of Matthew* (Helps for Translators; London: United Bible Societies, 1981).

S. H. Brooks, *Matthew's Community: The Evidence of his Special Sayings Material* (JSNTSup 16; Sheffield: JSOT Press, 1987).

J. K. Brown, *The Disciples in Narrative Perspective: The Portrayal and Function of the Matthean Disciples* (Academia Biblica 9; Leiden: Brill, 2002).

R. E. Brown, *The Birth of the Messiah: A Commentary on the Infancy Narratives in the Gospels of Matthew and Luke* (Garden City, NY: Doubleday, 1977; revised edition, ABRL; New York: Doubleday, 1993).

The Death of the Messiah: From Gethsemane to the Grave. A Commentary on the Passion Narratives in the Four Gospels (ABRL; 2 vols., New York: Doubleday, 1994).

R. E. Brown, K. P. Donfried, and J. E. Reumann (eds.), *Peter in the New Testament: A Collaborative Assessment by Protestant and Roman Catholic Scholars* (Minneapolis: Augsburg; New York: Paulist, 1973).

T. Buckley, *Seventy Times Seven: Sin, Judgment, and Forgiveness in Matthew* (Zacchaeus Studies: New Testament; Collegeville, MN: The Liturgical Press, 1991).

S. Byrskog, *Jesus the Only Teacher: Didactic Authority and Transmission in Ancient Israel, Ancient Judaism and the Matthean Community* (ConBNT 24; Stockholm: Almqvist & Wiksells International, 1994).

P. S. Cameron, *Violence and Kingdom: The Interpretation of Matthew 11:12* (ANTJ 5; Frankfurt am Main: Peter Lang, 1984).

C. E. Carlston, *The Parables of the Triple Tradition* (Philadelphia: Fortress, 1975).

W. C. Carter, *Households and Discipleship: A Study of Matthew 19–20* (JSNTSup 103; Sheffield: Sheffield Academic Press, 1994).

    Matthew and the Margins: A Socio-Political and Religious Reading (JSNTSup 204; Sheffield: Sheffield Academic Press, 2000).

    *What Are They Saying about Matthew's Sermon on the Mount? (New York: Paulist, 1994).

W. C. Carter and J. P. Heil (eds.), *Matthew's Parables: Audience-Oriented Perspectives* (CBQMS 30; Washington, DC: Catholic Biblical Association, 1998).

L. Cerfaux, *Apostle and Apostolate: According to the Gospel of St. Matthew* (Paris: Desclée, 1960).

B. Charette, *Restoring Presence: The Spirit in Matthew's Gospel* (JPTSup 18; Sheffield: Sheffield Academic Press, 2000).

    The Theme of Recompense in Matthew's Gospel (JSNTSup 79; Sheffield: JSOT Press, 1992).

*J. H. Charlesworth, with M. Harding and M. Kiley, *The Lord's Prayer and Other Prayer Texts from the Greco-Roman Era* (Valley Forge, PA: Trinity Press International, 1994).

J. H. Charlesworth and W. P. Weaver (eds.), *What Has Archaeology To Do with Faith?* (Faith and Scholarship Colloquies; Philadelphia: Trinity Press International, 1992).

F. H. Chase, *The Lord's Prayer in the Early Church* (Texts and Studies 1, no. 3; Cambridge: Cambridge University Press, 1891).

O. L. Cope, *Matthew: A Scribe Trained for the Kingdom of Heaven* (CBQMS 5; Washington, DC: Catholic Biblical Association, 1976).

J. R. Cousland, *The Crowds in the Gospel of Matthew* (NovTSup 102; Leiden: Brill, 2002).

W. D. Davies, *The Setting of the Sermon on the Mount* (Cambridge: Cambridge University Press, 1964; repr. BJS 186; Atlanta: Scholars Press, 1989).

R. Deines, *Die Gerechtigkeit der Tora im Reich des Messias: Mt 5,13–20 als Schlüsseltext der matthäischen Theologie* (WUNT 177; Tübingen: Mohr Siebeck, 2004).

C. Deutsch, *Hidden Wisdom and the Easy Yoke: Wisdom, Torah and Discipleship in Matthew 11.25–30* (JSNTSup 18; Sheffield: JSOT Press, 1987).

Lady Wisdom, Jesus, and the Sages: Metaphor and Social Context in Matthew's Gospel (Valley Forge, PA: Trinity Press International, 1996).

C. H. Dodd, *The Parables of the Kingdom* (London: Nisbet, 1935).

T. L. Donaldson, *Jesus on the Mountain: A Study of Matthean Theology* (JSNTSup 8; Sheffield: JSOT Press, 1985).

*J. D. G. Dunn, *Jesus Remembered* (Christianity in the Making 1; Grand Rapids, MI: Eerdmans, 2003).

R. A. Edwards, *The Sign of Jonah: In the Theology of the Evangelists and Q* (SBT 18; London: SCM Press, 1971).

E. Eve, *The Jewish Context of Jesus' Miracles* (JSNTSup 231; London: Sheffield Academic Press, 2002).

L. Finkelstein, *The Pharisees: The Sociological Background of Their Faith* (2 vols., Philadelphia: JPSA, 1938; 3rd edition, 1962).

P. Foster, *Community, Law and Mission in Matthew's Gospel* (WUNT 2, no. 117; Tübingen: Mohr Siebeck, 2004).

*R. T. France, *Matthew: Evangelist & Teacher* (New Testament Profiles; Downers Grove, IL: InterVarsity, 1998).

G. Friedlander, *The Jewish Sources of the Sermon on the Mount* (London: Bloch, 1911; repr. New York: Ktav, 1969).

D. E. Garland, *The Intention of Matthew 23* (NTTS 52; Leiden: Brill, 1979).

B. Gerhardsson, *The Mighty Acts of Jesus According to Matthew* (Scripta Minora Regiae Societatis Humaniorum Litterarum Lundensis 5; Lund: Gleerup, 1979).

J. B. Gibson, *The Temptations of Jesus in Early Christianity* (JSNTSup 112; Sheffield: Sheffield Academic Press, 1995).

S. W. Gray, *The Least of My Brothers: Matthew 25:31–46: A History of Interpretation* (SBLDS 114; Atlanta: Scholars Press, 1989).

H. B. Green, *Matthew, Poet of the Beatitudes* (JSNTSup 203; Sheffield: Sheffield Academic Press, 2000).

*R. A. Guelich, *The Sermon on the Mount: A Foundation for Understanding* (Waco, TX: Word, 1982).

R. H. Gundry, *The Use of the Old Testament in St. Matthew's Gospel with Special Reference to the Messianic Hope* (NovTSup 18; Leiden: Brill, 1967).

D. M Gurtner, *The Torn Veil: Matthew's Exposition of the Death of Jesus* (SNTSMS 139; Cambridge: Cambridge University Press, 2007).

C. Ham, *The Coming King and the Rejected Shepherd: Matthew's Reading of Zechariah's Messianic Hope* (New Testament Monographs 4; Sheffield: Sheffield Phoenix, 2005).

D. R. A. Hare, *The Theme of Jewish Persecution of Christians in the Gospel According to St. Matthew* (SNTSMS 6; Cambridge: Cambridge University Press, 1967).

J. P. Heil, *The Death and Resurrection of Jesus: A Narrative-Critical Reading of Matthew 26–28* (Minneapolis: Fortress Press, 1991).

*M. Hengel, *The Four Gospels and the One Gospel of Jesus Christ: An Investigation of the Collection and Origin of the Canonical Gospels* (Harrisburg, PA: Trinity Press International, 2000).

G. Howard, *The Gospel of Matthew According to a Primitive Hebrew Text* (Macon, GA: Mercer University Press, 1987).

B. J. Hubbard, *The Matthean Redaction of a Primitive Apostolic Commissioning* (SBLDS 19; Missoula, MT: Scholars Press, 1974).

*A. J. Hultgren, *Jesus and His Adversaries: The Form and Function of the Conflict Stories in the Synoptic Tradition* (Minneapolis: Augsburg, 1979).

R. Hummel, *Die Auseinandersetzung zwischen Kirche und Judentum im Matthäusevangelium*, 2nd edition (BEvT 33; Munich: Kaiser Verlag, 1966).

G. Jackson, *'Have Mercy on Me': The Story of the Canaanite Woman in Matthew 15.21–28* (JSNTSup 228; CIS 10; London: Sheffield Academic Press, 2002).

M. D. Johnson, *The Purpose of the Biblical Genealogies with Special Reference to the Settings of the Genealogies of Jesus* (SNTSMS 8; Cambridge: Cambridge University Press, 1969).

I. H. Jones, *The Matthean Parables: A Literary and Historical Commentary* (NovTSup 80; Leiden: Brill, 1995).

G. D. Kilpatrick, *The Origins of the Gospel According to St. Matthew* (Oxford: Clarendon Press, 1946).

J. D. Kingsbury, *Matthew: Structure, Christology, Kingdom* (Philadelphia: Fortress, 1975).
    The Parables of Jesus in Matthew 13: A Study in Redaction-Criticism (Richmond, VA: John Knox Press, 1969).

W. S. Kissinger, *The Sermon on the Mount: A History of Interpretation and Bibliography* (American Theological Library Association Monograph 3; Lanham, MD: Scarecrow Press, 1975).

M. Knowles, *Jeremiah in Matthew's Gospel: The Rejected Prophet Motif in Matthaean Redaction* (JSNTSup 68; Sheffield: JSOT Press, 1993).

D. D. Kupp, *Matthew's Emmanuel: Divine Presence and God's People in the First Gospel* (SNTSMS 90; Cambridge: Cambridge University Press, 1996).

J. Lambrecht, *The Sermon on the Mount: Proclamation and Exhortation* (GNS 14; Wilmington, DE: Glazier, 1985).

X. Léon-Dufour, *The Gospels and the Jesus of History* (London: Collins, 1968).

R. H. Lightfoot, *History and Interpretation in the Gospels* (The Bampton Lectures; London: Harper & Brothers, 1934).

E. Lohmeyer, *The Lord's Prayer* (London: Collins, 1965).

U. Luz, *Matthew in History: Interpretation, Influence, and Effects* (Minneapolis: Fortress Press, 1994).
    Studies in Matthew (Grand Rapids, MI: Eerdmans, 2005).
    The Theology of Matthew (New Testament Theology; Cambridge: Cambridge University Press, 1995).

*B. J. Malina and J. H. Neyrey, *Calling Jesus Names: The Social Value of Labels in Matthew* (Foundations & Facets; Sonoma, CA: Polebridge, 1988).

J. P. Meier, *Law and History in Matthew's Gospel: A Redactional Study of Matt. 5.17–48* (AnBib 71; Rome: Biblical Institute, 1976).

A Marginal Jew: Rethinking the Historical Jesus (4 vols., New York: Doubleday, 1991–2001; New Haven, CT: Yale University Press, 2009).

The Vision of Matthew: Christ, Church, and Morality in the First Gospel (Mahwah, NJ: Paulist, 1979).

P. S. Minear, *Commands of Christ: Authority and Implications* (Nashville, TN: Abingdon, 1972).

A. D. A. Moses, *Matthew's Transfiguration Story in Jewish-Christian Controversy* (JSNTSup 122; Sheffield: Sheffield Academic Press, 1996).

P. Nepper-Christensen, *Das Matthäusevangelium: Ein judenchristliches Evangelium?* (Acta Theologica Danica 1; Aarhus: Universitetforlaget, 1958).

B. M. Newman and P. C. Stine, *A Handbook on the Gospel of Matthew* (UBS Helps for Translators; New York: United Bible Societies, 1988).

K. G. C. Newport, *The Sources and Sitz im Leben of Matthew 23* (JSNTSup 117; Sheffield: Sheffield Academic Press, 1995).

*J. H. Neyrey, *Honor and Shame in the Gospel of Matthew* (Louisville, KY: Westminster John Knox Press, 1998).

L. Novakovic, *Messiah, the Healer of the Sick: A Study of Jesus as the Son of David in the Gospel of Matthew* (WUNT 2, no. 170; Tübingen: Mohr Siebeck, 2003).

D. E. Orton, *The Understanding Scribe: Matthew and the Apocalyptic Ideal* (JSNTSup 25; Sheffield: JSOT Press, 1989).

*J. A. Overman, *Church and Community in Crisis: The Gospel According to Matthew* (Valley Forge, PA: Trinity Press International, 1996).

Matthew's Gospel and Formative Judaism: A Study of the Social World of the Matthean Community (Minneapolis: Fortress Press, 1990).

E. C. Park, *The Mission Discourse in Matthew's Interpretation* (WUNT 2, no. 81; Tübingen: Mohr Siebeck, 1995).

B. Przybylski, *Righteousness in Matthew and His World of Thought* (SNTSMS 41; Cambridge: Cambridge University Press, 1980).

C. L. Quarles, *Midrash Criticism: Introduction and Appraisal* (Lanham, MD: University Press of America, 1997).

B. Repschinski, *The Controversy Stories in the Gospel of Matthew: Their Redaction, Form and Relevance for the Relationship between the Matthean Community and Judaism* (FRLANT 189; Göttingen: Vandenhoeck & Ruprecht, 2000).

*P. Richardson, *Herod: King of the Jews and Friend of the Romans* (Columbia, SC: University of South Carolina Press, 1996).

W. Rothfuchs, *Die Erfüllungszitate des Matthäus-Evangeliums: Eine biblisch-theologische Untersuchung* (BWANT 88; Stuttgart: Kohlhammer, 1969).

*A. J. Saldarini, *Matthew's Christian-Jewish Community* (Chicago: University of Chicago Press, 1994).

Pharisees, Scribes, and Sadducees in Palestinian Society: A Sociological Approach (Wilmington, DE: Glazier, 1988).

A. Sand, *Das Gesetz und die Propheten: Untersuchungen zur Theologie des Evangeliums nach Matthäus* (Biblische Untersuchungen 11; Regensburg: Pustet, 1974).

J. Schaberg, *The Father, the Son, and the Holy Spirit: The Triadic Phrase in Matthew 28:19b* (SBLDS 61; Chico, CA: Scholars Press, 1982).

The Illegitimacy of Jesus: A Feminist Theological Interpretation of the Infancy Narratives (San Francisco: Harper & Row, 1987; repr. BibSem 28; Sheffield: Sheffield Academic Press, 1995).

The Resurrection of Mary Magdalene: Legends, Apocrypha, and the Christian Testament (New York: Continuum, 2002).

W. Schenk, *Die Sprache des Matthäus* (Göttingen: Vandenhoeck & Ruprecht, 1987).

H.-M. Schenke, *Das Matthäus-Evangelium im mittelägyptischen Dialekt des Koptischen (Codex Schøyen)* (Manuscripts in the Schøyen Collection 2: Coptic Papyri 1; Oslo: Hermes, 2001). [see review by T. Baarda, *NovT* 46 (2004): 302–6]

*R. Schnackenburg, *All Things Are Possible to Believers: Reflections on the Lord's Prayer and the Sermon on the Mount* (Louisville, KY: Westminster John Knox Press, 1995).

E. Schweizer, *Matthäus und seine Gemeinde* (SBS 71: Stuttgart: Katholisches Bibelwerk, 1974).

B. B. Scott, *Hear Then the Parable: A Commentary on the Parables of Jesus* (Minneapolis: Fortress, 1989).

*D. Senior, *The Passion of Jesus in the Gospel of Matthew* (Collegeville, MN: Liturgical Press, 1985).

P. Sigal, *The Halakah of Jesus of Nazareth According to the Gospel of Matthew* (Lanham, MD: University Press of America, 1986).

D. C. Sim, *Apocalyptic Eschatology in the Gospel of Matthew* (SNTSMS 88; Cambridge: Cambridge University Press, 1996).

The Gospel of Matthew and Christian Judaism: The History and Social Setting of the Matthean Community (Edinburgh: T. & T. Clark, 1998).

M. Slee, *The Church in Antioch in the First Century CE: Communion and Conflict* (JSNTSup 244; London: Sheffield Academic Press, 2003).

*K. R. Snodgrass, *Stories with Intent: A Comprehensive Guide to the Parables of Jesus* (Grand Rapids, MI: Eerdmans, 2007).

G. M. Soares Prabhu, *The Formula Quotations in the Infancy Narrative of Matthew* (AnBib 63; Rome: Pontifical Biblical Institute Press, 1976).

*G. N. Stanton, *A Gospel for a New People: Studies in Matthew* (Edinburgh: T. & T. Clark, 1992; Louisville, KY: Westminster/John Knox, 1993).

*The Gospels and Jesus, 2nd edition (Oxford: Oxford University Press, 2002).

(ed.), *The Interpretation of Matthew* (IRT 3; London: SPCK; Philadelphia: Fortress, 1983).

Jesus of Nazareth in New Testament Preaching (SNTSMS 27; Cambridge: Cambridge University Press, 1974).

K. Stendahl, *The School of St. Matthew and Its Use of the Old Testament* (ASNU 20; Lund: Gleerup; Copenhagen: Munksgaard; revised edition, Philadelphia: Fortress, 1968).

A. Stock, *The Method and Message of Matthew* (Collegeville, MN: Liturgical Press, 1994).

G. Strecker, *The Sermon on the Mount: An Exegetical Commentary* (Nashville, TN: Abingdon, 1988).

M. J. Suggs, *Wisdom, Christology, and Law in Matthew's Gospel* (Cambridge, MA: Harvard University Press, 1970).

**C. H. Talbert, *Reading the Sermon on the Mount: Character Formation and Decision Making in Matthew 5–7* (Columbia: University of South Carolina Press, 2004; repr. Grand Rapids, MI: Baker Academic, 2006).

W. G. Thompson, *Matthew's Advice to a Divided Community: Matt 17:22–18:35* (AnBib 44; Rome: Biblical Institute Press, 1970).

S. van Tilborg, *The Jewish Leaders in Matthew* (Leiden: Brill, 1972).

D. J. Verseput, *The Rejection of the Humble Messianic King: A Study of the Composition of Matthew 11–12* (Frankfurt am Main: Peter Lang, 1986).

E.-J. Vledder, *Conflict in the Miracle Stories: A Socio-Exegetical Study of Matthew 8 and 9* (JSNTSup 152; Sheffield: Sheffield Academic Press, 1997).

F. Vouga, *Jésus et la loi selon la tradition synoptique* (Le monde de la Bible 563; Paris: Labor et Fides, 1988).

E. M. Wainwright, *Shall We Look for Another? A Feminist Reading of the Matthean Jesus* (Maryknoll, NY: Orbis Books, 1998).

D. Weaver, *Matthew's Missionary Discourse: A Literary Critical Analysis* (JSNTSup 38; Sheffield: JSOT Press, 1990).

D. Wenham, *The Rediscovery of Jesus' Eschatological Discourse* (Gospel Perspectives 4; Sheffield: JSOT Press, 1984).

J. W. Wenham, *Redating Matthew, Mark and Luke: A Fresh Assault on the Synoptic Problem* (London: Hodder & Stoughton, 1991).

M. J. Wilkins, *The Concept of Disciple in Matthew's Gospel as Reflected in the Use of the Term μαθητής* (NovTSup 59; Leiden: Brill, 1988).

M. O. Wise, M. G. Abegg, Jr., and E. M. Cook, *The Dead Sea Scrolls: A New Translation* (San Francisco: HarperCollins, 1996).

G. Yamasaki, *John the Baptist in Life and Death: Audience-Oriented Criticism of Matthew's Narrative* (JSNTSup 167; Sheffield: Sheffield Academic Press, 1998).

Y.-E. Yang, *Jesus and the Sabbath in Matthew's Gospel: The Background, Significance and Implication* (JSNTSup 139; Sheffield: Sheffield Academic Press, 1997).

J. Zumstein, *La condition du croyant dans l'Évangile selon Matthieu* (OBO 16; Göttingen: Vandenhoeck & Ruprecht, 1977).

SELECTED SHORTER STUDIES

E. L. Abel, "Who Wrote Matthew?" *NTS* 17 (1971): 138–52.

*D. C. Allison, Jr., "The Embodiment of God's Will: Jesus in Matthew," in B. R. Gaventa and R. B. Hays (eds.), *Seeking the Identity of Jesus: A Pilgrimage* (Grand Rapids, MI: Eerdmans, 2008), 117–32.

D. L. Barr, "The Drama of Matthew's Gospel: A Reconsideration of Its Structure and Purpose," *Theology Digest* 24 (1976): 349–59.

S. Brown, "The Matthean Community and the Gentile Mission," *NovT* 22 (1980): 193–221.

C. E. Carlston, "Interpreting the Gospel of Matthew," in J. L. Mays (ed.), *Interpreting the Gospels* (Philadelphia: Fortress Press, 1981), 55–65.

*W. Carter, "Matthew and the Gentiles: Individual Conversion and/or Systemic Transformation?" *JSNT* 26 (2004): 259–82.

  *"Matthew's Gospel: Jewish Christianity, Christian Judaism, or Neither?" in M. Jackson-McCabe (ed.), *Jewish Christianity Reconsidered: Rethinking Ancient Groups and Texts* (Minneapolis: Fortress Press, 2007), 155–79.

A. Cohen, "The Christology of Matthew's Gospel," *Mishkan* 39 (2003): 59–64.

H. J. B. Combrink, "The Structure of the Gospel of Matthew as Narrative," *TynBul* 34 (1983): 61–90.

O. L. Cope, "'To the Close of the Age': The Role of Apocalyptic Thought in the Gospel of Matthew," in J. Marcus and M. Soards (eds.), *Apocalyptic in the New Testament: Essays in Honor of J. Louis Martyn* (JSNTSup 24; Sheffield: JSOT Press, 1989), 113–24.

P. A. Cunningham, "Actualizing Matthean Christology in a Post-Supersessionist Church," in D. J. Harrington, A. J. Avery-Peck, and J. Neusner (eds.), *When Judaism and Christianity Began: Essays in Memory of Anthony J. Saldarini* (JSJSup 85; 2 vols., Leiden: Brill, 2004), 2:563–75.

F. W. Danker, "Matthew: A Patriot's Gospel," in C. A. Evans and W. R. Stegner (eds.), *The Gospels and the Scriptures of Israel* (JSNTSup 104; SSEJC 3; Sheffield: Sheffield Academic Press, 1994), 94–115.

D. C. Duling, "'Egalitarian' Ideology, Leadership, and Factional Conflict within the Matthean Group," *BTB* 27 (1997): 124–37.

  *"The Matthean Brotherhood and Marginal Scribal Leadership," in P. Esler (ed.), *Modelling Early Christianity: Social-Scientific Studies of the New Testament in Its Context* (London: Routledge, 1995), 159–82.

"The Therapeutic Son of David: An Element in Matthew's Christological Apologetic," *NTS* 24 (1977–1978): 392–410.

M. S. Enslin, "The Gospel According to Matthew," in M. S. Enslin, *Christian Beginnings*, Part III: *The Literature of the Christian Movement* (New York: Harper & Row, 1938), 389–402.

C. A. Evans, "The Jewish Gospel Tradition," in O. Skarsaune and R. Hvalvik (eds.), *Jewish Believers in Jesus: The Early Centuries* (Peabody, MA: Hendrickson, 2007), 241–77.

"Targumizing Tendencies in Matthean Redaction," in D. J. Harrington, A. J. Avery-Peck, and J. Neusner (eds.), *When Judaism and Christianity Began: Essays in Memory of Anthony J. Saldarini* (JSJSup 85; 2 vols., Leiden: Brill, 2004), 1:93–116.

P. Foster, "The Use of Zechariah in Matthew's Gospel," in C. M. Tuckett (ed.), *The Book of Zechariah and Its Influence: Papers of the Oxford-Leiden Conference* (Aldershot: Ashgate, 2003), 65–85.

R. T. France, "Jewish Historiography, Midrash, and the Gospels," in R. T. France and D. Wenham (eds.), *Studies in Midrash and Historiography* (Gospel Perspectives 3; Sheffield: JSOT Press, 1983), 99–127.

S. Freyne, "Vilifying the Other and Defining the Self: Matthew's and John's Anti-Jewish Polemic in Focus," in J. Neusner and E. S. Frerichs (eds.), *"To See Ourselves as Others See Us": Christians, Jews, "Others" in Late Antiquity* (Chico, CA: Scholars Press, 1985), 117–43.

L. Gaston, "The Messiah of Israel as Teacher of the Gentiles: The Setting of Matthew's Christology," in J. L. Mays (ed.), *Interpreting the Gospels* (Philadelphia: Fortress Press, 1981), 78–96.

F. C. Grant, "The Ecclesiastical Gospel: Matthew," in *The Gospels: Their Origin and Their Growth* (London: Faber & Faber, 1957), 134–53.

*D. A. Hagner, "Matthew: Christian Judaism or Jewish Christianity?" in S. McKnight and G. R. Osborne (eds.), *The Face of New Testament Studies: A Survey of Recent Research* (Grand Rapids, MI: Baker Academic, 2004), 263–82.

*"Matthew's Eschatology," in T. E. Schmidt and M. Silva (eds.), *To Tell the Mystery: Essays on New Testament Eschatology in Honor of Robert H. Gundry* (JSNTSup 100; Sheffield: Sheffield Academic Press, 1994), 49–71.

*"Righteousness in Matthew's Theology," in M. J. Wilkins and T. Paige (eds.), *Worship, Theology and Ministry in the Early Church: Essays in Honour of Ralph P. Martin* (JSNTSup 87; Sheffield: JSOT Press, 1992), 101–20.

D. R. Hare, "Current Trends in Matthean Scholarship," *Word and World* 18 (1998): 405–10.

D. J. Harrington, "Matthean Studies since Joachim Rohde," in *The Light of All Nations: Essays on the Church in New Testament Research* (GNS 3; Wilmington, DE: Glazier, 1982), 93–109.

J. P. Heil, "Significant Aspects of the Healing Miracles in Matthew," *CBQ* 41 (1979): 274–87.

P. Hertig, "Geographical Marginality in the Matthean Journeys of Jesus," *SBL 1999 Seminar Papers* (1999): 472–89.

*D. Hill, "The Figure of Jesus in Matthew's Story: A Response to Professor Kingsbury's Literary-Critical Probe," in C. A. Evans and S. E. Porter (eds.), *The Synoptic Gospels: A Sheffield Reader* (BibSem 31; Sheffield: Sheffield Academic Press, 1995), 81–96.

"Son and Servant: An Essay on Matthean Christology," in C. A. Evans and S. E. Porter (eds.), *The Synoptic Gospels: A Sheffield Reader* (BibSem 31; Sheffield: Sheffield Academic Press, 1995), 13–27.

L. A. Huizenga, "The Incarnation of the Servant: The 'Suffering Servant' and Matthean Christology," *HBT* 27 (2005): 25–58.

A. Ito, "Matthew and the Community of the Dead Sea Scrolls," in C. A. Evans and S. E. Porter (eds.), *The Synoptic Gospels: A Sheffield Reader* (BibSem 31; Sheffield: Sheffield Academic Press, 1995), 28–46.

M. D. Johnson, "Reflections on a Wisdom Approach to Matthew's Christology," *CBQ* 36 (1974): 44–64.

S. E. Johnson, "The Gospel According to St. Matthew," in *The Theology of the Gospels* (Studies in Theology 56; London: Duckworth, 1966), 50–64.

*J. Kampen, "Communal Discipline in the Social World of the Matthean Community," in J. V. Hills (ed.), *Common Life in the Early Church: Essays Honoring Graydon F. Snyder* (Harrisburg, PA: Trinity Press International, 1998), 158–74.

"The Sectarian Form of the Antitheses within the Social World of the Maatthean Community," *DSD* 1 (1994): 338–63.

T. J. Keegan, "Introductory Formulae for Matthean Discourses," *CBQ* 44 (1982): 415–30.

G. D. Kilpatrick, "Matthew on Matthew," in C. M. Tuckett (ed.), *Synoptic Studies: The Ampleforth Conferences of 1982 and 1983* (JSNTSup 7; Sheffield: JSOT Press, 1984), 177–85.

J. D. Kingsbury, "The Figure of Jesus in Matthew's Story: A Literary-Critical Probe," in C. A. Evans and S. E. Porter (eds.), *The Synoptic Gospels: A Sheffield Reader* (BibSem 31; Sheffield: Sheffield Academic Press, 1995), 47–80.

"The Figure of Jesus in Matthew's Story: A Rejoinder to David Hill," in C. A. Evans and S. E. Porter (eds.), *The Synoptic Gospels: A Sheffield Reader* (BibSem 31; Sheffield: Sheffield Academic Press, 1995), 97–117.

"The Form and Message of Matthew," in J. L. Mays (ed.), *Interpreting the Gospels* (Philadelphia: Fortress Press, 1981), 66–77.

"The Title 'Son of David' in Matthew's Gospel," *JBL* 95 (1976): 591–602.

J. R. D. Kirk, "Conceptualising Fulfilment in Matthew," *TynBul* 59 (2008): 77–98.

E. Krentz, "The Extent of Matthew's Prologue: Toward the Structure of the First Gospel," *JBL* 83 (1964): 409–15.

A. M. Leske, "Isaiah and Matthew," in W. H. Bellinger and W. R. Farmer (eds.), *Jesus and the Suffering Servant: Isaiah 53 and Christian Origins* (Harrisburg, PA: Trinity Press International, 1998), 152–69.

W. R. G. Loader, "Son of David, Blindness, and Duality in Matthew," *CBQ* 44 (1982): 570–85.

U. Luz, "The Son of Man in Matthew: Heavenly Judge or Human Christ?" *JSNT* 48 (1992): 3–21.

R. K. MacIver, "Twentieth Century Approaches to the Matthean Community," *AUSS* 37 (1999): 23–38.

T. W. Manson, "The Gospel According to St. Matthew," in M. Black (ed.), *Studies in the Gospels and Epistles* (Philadelphia: Westminster, 1962), 68–104.

J. P. Martin, "The Church in Matthew," in J. L. Mays (ed.), *Interpreting the Gospels* (Philadelphia: Fortress Press, 1981), 97–114.

*L. M. McDonald, "The Gospel of Matthew," in L. M. McDonald and S. E. Porter, *Early Christianity and Its Sacred Literature* (Peabody, MA: Hendrickson, 2000), 297–302.

*S. McKnight, "A Loyal Critic: Matthew's Polemic with Judaism in Theological Perspective," in C. A. Evans and D. A. Hagner (eds.), *Anti-Semitism and Early Christianity: Issues of Polemic and Faith* (Minneapolis: Fortress, 1993), 55–79.

*"Matthew, Gospel of," in J. B. Green, S. McKnight, and I. H. Marshall (eds.), *Dictionary of Jesus and the Gospels* (Downers Grove, IL: InterVarsity, 1992), 526–41.

C. F. D. Moule, "St. Matthew's Gospel: Some Neglected Features," in *Essays in New Testament Interpretation* (Cambridge: Cambridge University Press, 1982), 67–74.

R. L. Mowery, "Subtle Differences: The Matthean 'Son of God' References," *NovT* 32 (1990): 193–200.

M. Müller, "The Theological Interpretation of the Figure of Jesus in the Gospel of Matthew: Some Principal Features in Matthean Christology," *NTS* 45 (1999): 157–73.

D. J. Neville, "Toward a Teleology of Peace: Contesting Matthew's Violent Eschatology," *JSNT* 30 (2007): 131–61.

M. Pamment, "The Kingdom of Heaven According to the First Gospel," *NTS* 27 (1981): 211–32.

P. B. Payne, "Midrash and History in the Gospels with Special Reference to R. H. Gundry's *Matthew*," in R. T. France and D. Wenham (eds.), *Studies in Midrash and Historiography* (Gospel Perspectives 3; Sheffield: JSOT Press, 1983), 177–215.

*M. A. Powell, "The Plot and Subplots of Matthew's Gospel," *NTS* 38 (1992): 187–204.

C. J. Reedy, "Rhetorical Concerns and Argumentative Techniques in Matthean Pronouncement Stories," *SBL 1983 Seminar Papers* (1983): 219–22.

B. Repschinski, "Re-imaging the Presence of God: The Temple and the Messiah in the Gospel of Matthew," *ABR* 54 (2006): 37–49.

P. Rolland, "From the Genesis to the End of the World: The Plan of Matthew's Gospel," *BTB* 2 (1972): 155–76.

*A. Runesson, "Rethinking Early Jewish-Christian Relations: Matthean Community History as Pharisaic Intragroup Conflict," *JBL* 127 (2008): 95–132.

*A. J. Saldarini, "Boundaries and Polemics in the Gospel of Matthew," *BibInt* 3 (1995): 239–65.

T. E. Schmidt, "Hostility to Wealth in the Gospel of Matthew," in *Hostility to Wealth in the Synoptic Gospels* (JSNTSup15; Sheffield: JSOT Press, 1987), 121–34.

*D. Senior, "Between Two Worlds: Gentile and Jewish Christians in Matthew's Gospel," *CBQ* 61 (1991): 1–23.

*"Directions in Matthean Studies," in *The Gospel of Matthew in Current Studies: Studies in Memory of William G. Thompson, S.J.*, edited by David E. Aune (Grand Rapids, MI: Eerdmans, 2001), 5–21.

G. N. Stanton, "The Origin and Purpose of Matthew's Gospel: Matthean Scholarship from 1945 to 1980," *ANRW* II.25.3 (1985): 1889–951.

*W. R. Stegner, "Leadership and Governance in the Matthean Community," in J. V. Hills (ed.), *Common Life in the Early Church: Essays Honoring Graydon F. Snyder* (Harrisburg, PA: Trinity Press International, 1998), 147–57.

C. H. Talbert, "Indicative and Imperative in Matthean Soteriology," *Biblica* 82 (2001): 515–38.

V. Taylor, "The Gospel of Matthew," in *The Gospels: A Short Introduction*, 10th edition (London: Epworth, 1962 [orig. 1930]).

W. G. Thompson, "An Historical Perspective in the Gospel of Matthew," *JBL* 93 (1974): 243–62.

C. C. Torrey, "The Biblical Quotations in Matthew," in *Documents of the Primitive Church* (New York: Harper & Bros., 1941).

D. Verseput, "The Role and Meaning of the 'Son of God' Title in Matthew's Gospel," *NTS* 33 (1987): 532–56.

F. P. Viljoen, "The Matthean Community According to the Beginning of His Gospel," *Acta Theologica* 26 (2006): 242–62.

E. J. Vledder, "The Social Stratification of the Matthean Community," *Neot* 28 (1994): 511–22.

*E. M. Wainwright, "Tradition Makers / Tradition Shapers: Women of the Matthean Tradition," *Word and World* 18 (1998): 380–88.

III. Commentary

MATTHEW 1:1–17 – THE GENEALOGY OF THE MESSIAH

1:1: An account of the genealogy of Jesus the Messiah, the son of David, the son of Abraham.

1:2: Abraham was the father of Isaac, and Isaac the father of Jacob, and Jacob the father of Judah and his brothers,

1:3: and Judah the father of Perez and Zerah by Tamar, and Perez the father of Hezron, and Hezron the father of Aram,

1:4: and Aram the father of Aminadab, and Aminadab the father of Nahshon, and Nahshon the father of Salmon,

1:5: and Salmon the father of Boaz by Rahab, and Boaz the father of Obed by Ruth, and Obed the father of Jesse,

1:6: and Jesse the father of King David. And David was the father of Solomon by the wife of Uriah,

1:7: and Solomon the father of Rehoboam, and Rehoboam the father of Abijah, and Abijah the father of Asaph,

1:8: and Asaph the father of Jehoshaphat, and Jehoshaphat the father of Joram, and Joram the father of Uzziah,

1:9: and Uzziah the father of Jotham, and Jotham the father of Ahaz, and Ahaz the father of Hezekiah,

1:10: and Hezekiah the father of Manasseh, and Manasseh the father of Amos, and Amos the father of Josiah,

1:11: and Josiah the father of Jechoniah and his brothers, at the time of the deportation to Babylon.

1:12: And after the deportation to Babylon: Jechoniah was the father of Salathiel, and Salathiel the father of Zerubbabel,

1:13: and Zerubbabel the father of Abiud, and Abiud the father of Eliakim, and Eliakim the father of Azor,

1:14: and Azor the father of Zadok, and Zadok the father of Achim, and Achim the father of Eliud,

1:15: and Eliud the father of Eleazar, and Eleazar the father of Matthan, and Matthan the father of Jacob,

1:16: and Jacob the father of Joseph the husband of Mary, of whom Jesus was born, who is called the Messiah.

1:17: So all the generations from Abraham to David are fourteen generations; and from David to the deportation to Babylon, fourteen generations; and from the deportation to Babylon to the Messiah, fourteen generations.

*M*atthew's opening verse has a decidedly Jewish ring to it: "An account of the genealogy of Jesus the Messiah, the son of David, the son of Abraham" (v. 1). As "son of David," Jesus stands in the royal, messianic line; as "son of Abraham," Jesus stands in the line of Israel's patriarchs. To begin the narrative as (literally) "the book of the genealogy" is to suggest that the story of Jesus is part of Israel's scriptural story. What is translated as "genealogy" is in the Greek *genesis*, and could be translated in this context as "generations." This is exactly how it is understood in Gen 5:1 in reference to the first man: "This is the book of the generations of Adam." The Hebrew for "generations" is *toledoth*, but in the Greek version of the Old Testament it is *genesis*, the same word used by Matthew. Thus, Matthew's "book of the genesis," or "generations," deliberately recalls the first biblical book's "book of the generations."[1] Matthew implies that the story of Jesus parallels in importance the story of the very first human being. His interesting genealogy that follows will clarify this.[2]

Matthew's opening verse, or incipit, stands in noticeable contrast to the incipit of Mark, Matthew's narrative source. Mark 1:1 reads: "The beginning of the good news of Jesus Christ [or Messiah], Son of God." Mark's words allude unmistakably to the Roman imperial cult of the divine emperor. One immediately thinks of the calendar inscriptions in honor of Caesar Augustus, one of which reads: "the birthday of the god Augustus was the beginning of the good news for the world" (see *OGIS* 458; ca. 9 B.C.). Or, closer to the time of the publication of Mark and Matthew is the reference to the megalomaniac Nero, who in a papyrus is described

---

[1]   In Matthew's time, the first book of Moses was sometimes called "the book of Genesis," as in Philo (*Abr.* 1; *Poster C.* 127; *Aet. Mund.* 19). It seems most probable that in beginning his Gospel narrative with the words *biblos geneseos* Matthew intends his readers to think of the book of Genesis – a book of beginnings and a book of genealogies.

[2]   W. B. Tatum, "'The Origin of Jesus Messiah' (Matt 1:1, 18a): Matthew's Use of the Infancy Traditions," *JBL* 96 (1977): 523–35.

as the "good god of the inhabited world, the beginning of all good things" (P.Oxy. 1021; ca. 65 A.D.).[3]

Mark's incipit should be seen as a direct challenge to the Roman imperial cult. In essence, he is asserting that the true Son of God, the beginning of the good news (or gospel) for the world is not the Roman emperor but Jesus Messiah. Matthew would have understood the import of these words and would have agreed with them.[4] The decision to rewrite Mark's incipit, thus dropping the implied criticism of the Roman cult, underscores Matthew's desire to redirect the thrust of the entire gospel story. For Matthew, the real challenge lies not in the context of the Roman Empire and its sycophantic support of the Julian-Claudian dynasty, now in ruins with the death of Nero, but that of the Jewish synagogue that has rejected Jesus as a failed Messiah and false teacher.

Matthew's preference for "son of David" instead of Mark's "Son of God" is all the more remarkable when one remembers that the scribal habit of referring to the Messiah as "son of David" was called into question by Jesus in Mark 12:35–37, a passage with which Matthew was familiar and that he edited (see Matt 22:41–46).[5] Accordingly, we must conclude that Matthew was strongly committed to a Jewish perspective, where epithets such as "son of Abraham" and "son of David" were highly valued. However, this does not mean that Matthew's understanding of Davidic messianism is essentially that of many of his Jewish contemporaries. On the contrary, Matthew will redefine the messianic "son of David" on his own terms.[6]

A Closer Look: Incipits in Late Antiquity

The opening sentence (or paragraph) of books in late antiquity usually functioned as an incipit, or "beginning," of the writing. These incipits served more or less as titles and/or abstracts of the work. Mark's incipit, "the beginning of the good news of Jesus Christ, Son of God" (Mark 1:1), announces to the reader (or hearer) that the story to follow concerns the good news Jesus proclaimed and performed. The evangelist's choice of language deliberately

---

[3] On this point, see C. A. Evans, "Mark's Incipit and the Priene Calendar Inscription: From Jewish Gospel to Greco-Roman Gospel," *JRGRChJ* 1 (2000): 67–81.

[4] W. Carter, "Matthaean Christology in Roman Imperial Key: Matthew 1.1," in J. K. Riches and D. Sim (eds.), *The Gospel of Matthew in Its Roman Imperial Context* (JSNTSup 276; Early Christianity in Context; London: T. & T. Clark International, 2005), 143–65. See the commentary on Matt 14:33.

[5] J. M. Jones, "Subverting the Textuality of Davidic Messianism: Matthew's Presentation of the Genealogy and the Davidic Title," *CBQ* 56 (1994): 256–72.

[6] Rightly J. M. Jones, "Subverting the Textuality of Davidic Messianism: Matthew's Presentation of the Genealogy and the Davidic Title," *CBQ* 56 (1994): 256–72.

alludes to the Roman imperial cult, in which Caesar was understood as the son of God and as the beginning of the good news for the world. Matthew's incipit, "An account of the genealogy of Jesus the Messiah, the son of David, the son of Abraham" (Matt 1:1), orients readers to the Jewish world, while Luke's incipits for volume 1 (i.e., the Gospel of Luke) and volume 2 (i.e., the Book of Acts) of his work orient readers to aspects of the Roman juridical process: "… I too decided, after investigating everything carefully from the very first, to write an orderly account for you, most excellent Theophilus, so that you may know the truth concerning the things about which you have been instructed" (Luke 1:1–4); "In the first book, Theophilus, I wrote about all that Jesus did and taught from the beginning …" (Acts 1:1–2). The juridical or quasi-legal flavor of Luke's language is seen in a comparison with the incipits Josephus employs to introduce the two volumes of his work against the anti-Semite Apion: "In my history of our Antiquities, most excellent Epaphroditus, I have, I think, made sufficiently clear to any who may peruse that work the extreme antiquity of our Jewish race.… I consider it my duty to devote a brief treatise to all these points; in order at once to convict our detractors of malignity and deliberate falsehood, to correct the ignorance of others, and to instruct all who desire to know the truth …" (*Against Apion* 1.1–3); and "In the first volume of this work, my most esteemed Epaphroditus, I demonstrated the antiquity of our race …" (*Against Apion* 2.1). One might also compare Philo's incipit that introduces *On the Life of Moses* (see 1.1–4). The fourth Gospel begins with a poetic prologue (see John 1:1–18) that orients the narrative away from biography and history to wisdom, drama, and metaphor: "In the beginning was the Word, and the Word was with God, and the Word was God.…"

Matthew's form of Jesus' genealogy is thoroughly Jewish and biblical in style and arrangement. Literally it reads: "Abraham begat Isaac, Isaac begat Jacob, Jacob begat Judah and his brothers," and so on. Once again, Matthew reminds us of Gen 5:1: "Adam begat … Seth, and Seth begat … Enosh, and Enosh begat … Kenan," and so on (see also Ruth 4:18–22; 1 Chron 2:10–13, 17–22, 36–49).

Not only is Jesus the "son of David," he is also the "son of Abraham." The claim of being a "son of Abraham" or of having Abraham as one's "father" carried with it implications of election and right-standing before God. See Matt 3:9 (= Luke 3:8), where John the Baptist articulates the views of some Jews that "We have Abraham as our father"; or Luke 13:16, where Jesus says of the woman with the curved spine, "this woman, a daughter of Abraham"; or Luke 16:24, where the rich man in the parable cries out, "Father Abraham, have mercy on me!"; or Luke 19:9, where Jesus says of Zacchaeus the tax collector, "Today salvation has come to this house, since he also is a son of Abraham"; or the polemical passages in the fourth Gospel, where Jesus' critics claim to be the seed of Abraham (cf. John 8:33, 37, 39, 53, 56).

There are three important features in the Matthean genealogy that require comment. First, Matthew breaks his biblical pattern in vv. 3 ("by Tamar"), 5 ("by Rahab ... by Ruth"), and 6 ("by the wife of Uriah"). Why does he do this? Matthew breaks the pattern in order to remind his readers of four women who in various ways are rather surprising members of the messianic genealogy. Tamar bore children by her father-in-law Judah (see Gen 38). Rahab was the harlot who hid the spies (see Josh 2, 6) and became the mother of Boaz. Ruth was the Moabite widow who married Boaz and became the mother of Obed (see Ruth 4:17). Finally, Bathsheba, who is not named in the Matthean genealogy, was the wife of Uriah, whom King David had murdered (see 2 Sam 11) in a desperate bid to cover up his adultery. What is common to these four women is the unusual, exceptional element, not their sinfulness (for Ruth was not sinful, and in the case of Bathsheba, David is to blame). In all four cases, God acted in an extraordinary and unexpected way – just as he did in the case of Mary.

Nevertheless, these irregularities – and outright sinfulness in the cases of Tamar and Rahab – leave these four women open to accusations of improper sexual conduct. The situations of all four are set aright "by the actions of men who acknowledge guilt and/or accept responsibility for them, drawing them under patriarchal protection, legitimating them and their children-to-be."[7] Judah admits his guilt in the case of Tamar. Rahab, who almost certainly is the harlot of Jericho,[8] is vindicated by Joshua and later praised by James (James 2:25). Ruth the Moabitess accepts the God of Israel and his people and in return is redeemed by the honorable Boaz, who offers her protection. And finally, in the case of Bathsheba, it is David who is blamed (2 Sam 11:27), but it is Bathsheba who plays an important role in securing the throne for her son Solomon (1 Kings 1:11–31).

Alluding to these four women, Matthew places Mary the mother of Jesus into a carefully nuanced context, with special reference to the major male figures in the

---

[7] J. Schaberg, "Before Mary: The Ancestresses of Jesus," *Bible Review* 20, no. 6 (2004): 12–23, at 23. For further discussion, see E. D. Freed, "The Women in Matthew's Genealogy," *JSNT* 29 (1987): 3–19; J. Schaberg, "The Foremothers and the Mother of Jesus," in A. Brenner (ed.), *A Feminist Companion to the Hebrew Bible* (The Feminist Companion to the Bible 10; Sheffield: Sheffield Academic Press, 1996), 149–58. See also J. Nolland, "Genealogical Annotation in Genesis as Background for the Matthean Genealogy of Jesus," *TynBul* 47 (1996): 115–22; J. Nolland, "The Four (Five) Women and Other Annotations in Matthew's Genealogy," *NTS* 43 (1997): 527–39; F. S. Spencer, "Those Riotous – yet Righteous – Foremothers of Jesus: Exploring Matthew's Comic Genealogy," in A. Brenner (ed.), *Are We Amused? Humour about Women in the Biblical Worlds* (JSOTSup 383; London: T. & T. Clark, 2003), 7–30.

[8] Y. Zakowitch, "Rahab als Mutter des Boas in der Jesus-Genealogie (Matth. I 5)," *NovT* 17 (1975): 1–5; R. E. Brown, "*Rachab* in Mt 1,5 Probably is Rahab of Jericho," *Bib* 63 (1982): 79–80.

genealogy: Judah, David, and Jesus.[9] He is suggesting that Mary is the fifth woman in the messianic line that for one reason or another was vulnerable to accusation but was vindicated by the actions of others. Just as Tamar was protected by Judah the patriarch, or Ruth was protected by righteous Boaz, so now Mary will be protected by her husband, Joseph, described as a righteous man (Matt 1:19), who in turn will be guided by an angel of the Lord (Matt 1:20). Seen in this context, the unusual experience of Mary places her in a special category, suggesting that God indeed had worked in her.

A Closer Look: Other Special Women

Matthew classifies Mary with four other women who through various circumstances find themselves a part of and contributing to the messianic genealogy. However, this class of women is but a subclass of a larger class of women who through trial and prayer are not only vindicated but become heroes and defenders of the people of God.

Sarah. Probably the best-known woman in this larger category is the great matriarch Sarah, wife of Abraham. Sarah, known for her beauty (Gen 12:10–20), gave birth to Isaac, as promised, in her old age (Gen 21:1–7).

Rebekah. Though barren, Rebekah conceived and gave birth to Esau and Jacob after her husband, Isaac, prayed for her (Gen 25:21).

Rachel. God heard Rachel's prayers and enabled her to conceive and give birth to Joseph (Gen 30:22–24).

Wife of Manoah. The unnamed wife of Manoah was unable to conceive but received a vision and gave birth to Samson (Judg 13:2–25). Manoah's wife is given the name Eluma in Ps.–Philo, *Bib. Ant.* 42:1.

Hannah. Elkanah's wife, Hannah, was unable to conceive until after sacrifice and prayer (1 Sam 1:1–20). She gave birth to Samuel the priest and prophet,

---

[9]   The purpose of this context is much debated. For important discussion, see M. D. Johnson, *The Purpose of the Biblical Genealogies: With Special Reference to the Setting of the Genealogies of Jesus* (SNTSMS 8; Cambridge: Cambridge University Press, 1969), 146–79; R. E. Brown, *The Birth of the Messiah: A Commentary on the Infancy Narratives in the Gospels of Matthew and Luke* (Garden City, NY: Doubleday, 1977; updated edition, 1993), 69–74; J. Schaberg, *The Illegitimacy of Jesus: A Feminist Theological Interpretation of the New Testament Infancy Narratives* (New York: Crossroad, 1990; repr. BibSem 28; Sheffield: Sheffield Academic Press, 1995), 20–34; R. Bauckham, *Gospel Women: Studies of the Named Women in the Gospels* (Grand Rapids, MI: Eerdmans, 2002), 17–46; P.-B. Smit, "Something about Mary? Remarks about the Five Women in the Matthean Genealogy," *NTS* 56 (2010): 191–207.

the last of Israel's judges, who anointed Saul, Israel's first king, and then later David.[10]

Esther. The courage and wisdom of Esther and Mordecai, her cousin and father by adoption, saved the Jewish people in the Persian Empire.

Susanna. Falsely accused by corrupt and lustful judges, Susanna is vindicated by the young Daniel (see Susanna, one of the additions to Daniel).

Judith. The chaste and beautiful Judith saves her people from Holofernes and his threatening army through faith and cunning (see Judith, one of the deutero-canonical books).

Second, Matthew divides the genealogy into three sections, "from Abraham to David ... from David to the deportation to Babylon ... and from the deportation to Babylon to the Messiah" (**v. 17**). The threefold division suggests that "from Abraham to David" (about 1,000 years), the divine promises were fulfilled: Israel had gained land, seed, and blessing (see Gen 12, 15, 17). Then, "from David to the deportation to Babylon" (about 400 years), Israel squandered its blessings by violating the covenant. The Davidic dynasty had come to an end, the temple had been destroyed, the city of Jerusalem had been sacked, and most of the population had been deported. But "from the deportation to Babylon to the Messiah" (about 600 years), the promises were once again fulfilled. The exile has ended, the Messiah has come.[11]

Third, Matthew very artificially provides us with three sets of *fourteen* generations (**v. 17**). Not all interpreters agree, but the evangelist probably meant the number to refer to the numerical value of the name *David*, which in Hebrew (*dvd*) has the numerical value of 14 (i.e., $d = 4$, $v = 6$, $d = 4$; therefore, $4 + 6 + 4 = 14$). Interpreting the numerical value of the letters that make up a name (called *gematria* in Hebrew) may strike us today as very strange, but it held significance for the ancients and was practiced by Jewish interpreters of Scripture (e.g., *b. Shab.* 70a, in reference to Ex 35:1) and Greek interpreters of oracles and various traditions.

Matthew concludes the genealogy with the words "Joseph the husband of Mary, of whom Jesus was born, who is called the Messiah" (**v. 16**). The relative pronoun "of whom" is feminine and refers to Mary (Greek: *Marias, ex hes*). In other words, Jesus is indeed the offspring of Mary, but he is not the physical descendent of Joseph.[12]

---

[10] For an interesting study of seven special, barren women in rabbinic tradition, see M. Callaway, *Sing, O Barren One: A Study in Comparative Midrash* (SBLDS 91; Atlanta: Scholars Press, 1986), 117–23.

[11] For a discussion of the various spans of time, see G. F. Moore, "Fourteen Generations – 490 years," *HTR* 14 (1921): 97–103.

[12] On the genealogy tracing legal lineage to Joseph yet spiritual lineage to God, see C. H. Gordon, "Paternity at Two Levels," *JBL* 96 (1977): 101; B. M. Metzger, *New Testament*

In v. 1, Jesus was introduced as the Messiah, and in v. 17 he will again be identified as the Messiah in the context of the climax of Israel's history. Here in v. 16 Jesus is he "who is called the Messiah" (Greek: *ho legomenos Christos*),[13] which closely parallels the language of Josephus, the first-century Jewish historian and apologist, who in *The Antiquities of the Jews* (hereafter *Ant.* in citations) recounts the murder of James, "the brother of Jesus, who is called the Messiah [Greek: *tou legomenou Christou*]" (*Ant.* 20.200).[14] Josephus wrote his *Antiquities* a decade or more after the time of Matthew. By then, not only in Jewish circles but also in non-Jewish ones, Jesus of Nazareth had become known as he "who is called Messiah."[15]

Interpreters have rightly recognized that Matthew's genealogy reveals much about the narrative that follows.[16] No one familiar with the synagogue   whether still a member in good standing or not – could possibly read Matthew's incipit and then all that follows and fail to hear claims and counterclaims that were of the greatest significance to the Jewish people who longed for the appearance of God's Messiah.

Despite the irregularity of Jesus' conception and birth, whereby he may well have been regarded as a *mamzer*,[17] Matthew affirms that Jesus is indeed a "son of Abraham" (that is, a true descendant of the first great patriarch of the Jewish people) and a "son of David," and therefore the legitimate messianic heir. Having made this bold confession, the evangelist then marshals the witness of Scripture, underscoring correspondences with biblical patterns and fulfillments of biblical prophecies.

Studies: Philological, Versional, and Patristic (NTTS 10; Leiden: Brill, 1980), 105–13; L. Cantwell, "The Parentage of Jesus," *NovT* 24 (1982): 304–15.

[13] For more on this topic, see E. L. Abel, "The Genealogies of Jesus *ho christos*," *NTS* 20 (1974): 203–10.

[14] In *Ant.* 18.63–64, Josephus refers to Jesus, his arrest, and his execution by Pilate. In later Christian hands, this passage is expanded with at least three glosses, one of which reads: "He was the Messiah." There is no question that this gloss is inauthentic, for nowhere in his extant writings does Josephus discuss Jewish messianism or how it is that Jesus is the Messiah. His reference in *Ant.* 20.200 to Jesus as the one "called the Messiah" simply informs his readers that the brother of James was none other than the Jesus who founded the Christian movement. Josephus has identified James and Jesus; he has not defined messianism or explained what it is that the followers of Jesus believe about their master.

[15] An early Roman attestation is seen in Cornelius Tacitus (c. 110): "… whom the crowd called 'Christians.' Christus, the author of their name, had suffered the death penalty during the reign of Tiberius, by sentence of the procurator Pontius Pilate" (*Annals* 15.44); "… instigated by Chrestus …" (Suetonius, *Claudius* 25.4); "… to Christus as to a god …" (Pliny the Younger, *Epistles* 10.96).

[16] D. E. Nineham, "The Genealogy in St. Matthew's Gospel and Its Significance for the Study of the Gospels," *BJRL* 58 (1975–1976): 421–44; H. C. Waetjan, "The Genealogy as the Key to the Gospel According to Matthew," *JBL* 95 (1976): 205–30; D. R. Bauer, "The Literary Function of the Genealogy in Matthew's Gospel," *SBL 1990 Seminar Papers* (1990): 451–68.

[17] That is, one whose birth is suspect. See the commentary on Matt 1:18–25.

The purpose of this apologetic is to bolster the faith of those who believe in Jesus (both Jews and Gentiles) and to reply to the objections and criticisms emanating from the synagogue. It is in this direction that the incipit of Matthew points.

MATTHEW 1:18–25 – THE BIRTH OF JESUS MESSIAH

1:18: Now the birth of Jesus the Messiah took place in this way. When his mother Mary had been engaged to Joseph, but before they lived together, she was found to be with child from the Holy Spirit.

1:19: Her husband Joseph, being a righteous man and unwilling to expose her to public disgrace, planned to dismiss her quietly.

1:20: But just when he had resolved to do this, an angel of the Lord appeared to him in a dream and said, "Joseph, son of David, do not be afraid to take Mary as your wife, for the child conceived in her is from the Holy Spirit.

1:21: She will bear a son, and you are to name him Jesus, for he will save his people from their sins."

1:22: All this took place to fulfill what had been spoken by the Lord through the prophet:

1:23: "Look, the virgin shall conceive and bear a son, and they shall name him Emmanuel," which means, "God is with us."

1:24: When Joseph awoke from sleep, he did as the angel of the Lord commanded him; he took her as his wife,

1:25: but had no marital relations with her until she had borne a son; and he named him Jesus.

*M*atthew's birth narrative broadly fits the genre of the birth announcement, attested in the Old Testament and other literature.[18] Although it is usually referred to as a "birth narrative," what the evangelist actually narrates is the conception of Jesus, not his birth.

When Joseph discovered that Mary his betrothed was "with child" (**v. 18**), he decided to "dismiss her," that is divorce her, though "quietly," in order not "to expose her to public disgrace" (**v. 19**). Joseph is understood to be following the Law of Moses: "Suppose a man enters into marriage with a woman, but she does not please him because he finds something objectionable about her, and so he writes her a certificate of divorce, puts it in her hand, and sends her out of his house ..." (Deut 24:1).

---

[18]   E. W. Conrad, "The Annunciation of Birth and the Birth of the Messiah," *CBQ* 47 (1985): 656–63; T. D. Finlay, *The Birth Report Genre in the Hebrew Bible* (FAT 2, no. 12; Tübingen: Mohr Siebeck, 2005); J. A. Sanders, "The Function of Annunciations in Scripture," in W. H. Brackney and C. A. Evans (eds.), *From Biblical Criticism to Biblical Faith* (Macon, GA: Mercer University Press, 2007), 24–40.

The Law of Moses required a certificate of divorce, but it did not require public exposure and humiliation. One thinks of Tamar, daughter-in-law of the patriarch Judah. When her pregnancy was discovered, she was brought out in public, accused of harlotry, and threatened with death (Gen 38:24–26; cf. Deut 22:23–24). There is evidence that as early as the first century B.C. divorce was believed to be required if one's wife had committed adultery or some other form of sexual sin (or an engagement would have to be broken off in cases of fornication or sexual sin).[19] As a "righteous man," Joseph must comply with the Law of Moses and put away the unfaithful Mary.[20]

Matthew states as a matter of fact that the pregnancy was "from the Holy Spirit," but Joseph does not yet know this. No doubt many ancient readers snickered at such a claim, but others would have been open to this possibility, at least in principle. The mighty works of Jesus, not least the Resurrection, would have convinced many that an unusual birth would be expected of such an amazing figure. Moreover, the ancients – Jews as well as pagans – appreciated the workings of God in everyday life. Accordingly, Philo remarks in reference to Sarah's conception in her advanced age: "For when a barren woman gives birth, it is not by way of generation but the work of divine power" (*Quaest. et Solut. in Gen.* 18). If this is true in the case of a barren but married woman, how much more so in the case of an unwed virgin? In another place, Philo likens the soul to a woman who has given birth and then is "transformed into a pure virgin" (*Praem. et Poen.* 158–59).[21] Statements such as these do not explain Mary's miraculous conception, but they are illustrative of the mindset of the Jewish people in late antiquity.

A Closer Look: The Holy Spirit

By the time of Jesus and the early church, the "Holy Spirit" appears to have been well established as part of the Godhead. The full expression "Holy Spirit" only occurs three times in the Old Testament (Ps 51:11; Isa 63:10–11) and three times in the deutero-canonical books (Wisd of Sol 9:17; Sus 45; 2 Esd 14:22), though many references to "Spirit" (*ruach*), "Spirit of God" (*ruach elohim*), or "Spirit of the Lord" (*ruach Yahweh*) should be understood as references to the Holy Spirit (e.g., Gen 41:38; Exod 31:3; Judg 3:10; 6:34; Isa 61:1).

---

[19]   On this, see M. N. A. Bockmuehl, "Matthew 5.32; 19.9 in the Light of Pre-rabbinic Halakhah," *NTS* 35 (1989): 291–95. For evidence from the first century B.C., Bockmuehl appeals to 1QapGen 20:15, where Abram will lose Sarah if she has sexual intercourse with Pharaoh, even if against her will.

[20]   According to Num 5:11–31, a woman suspected of adultery is put to a test by a priest. But in cases where sexual activity is known to occur (as in evidence of pregnancy), Deut 22:23–27 is applied. On these questions, see A. Tosato, "Joseph, Being a Just Man (Matt 1:19)," *CBQ* 41 (1979): 547–51.

[21]   M. Callaway, *Sing, O Barren One* (1986), 99.

The full form "Holy Spirit" occurs more than forty times in the Dead Sea Scrolls, though often meaning no more than "spirit of holiness" (as opposed to a spirit of wickedness) or the holy spirit of a righteous individual. Some references in the scrolls clearly refer to the Holy Spirit in a sense probably the same as in the writings of the New Testament. According to the *Community Rule* Scroll, only the repentant person is able to "gaze upon the light of life and so be joined to His truth by His (God's) Holy Spirit" (1QS 3:7). Several times, the author of the Hymn Scroll addresses God, saying "Your Holy Spirit" (e.g., 1QH[a] 4:26; 6:13; 8:11–12, 16, 21; 15:6; 17:32; 20:12). The pronominal suffix implies that the noun spirit (*ruach*) is definite (i.e., "the Holy Spirit of you"). Whether "Holy Spirit" at Qumran was understood in terms of personification, or hypostasis, is another matter. "Holy Spirit" appears in a few pseudepigraphical texts (e.g., ms P of *T. Job* 51:2, though "holy angel" is probably the better reading; *T. Abr.* [A] 4:7, "I shall send my Holy Spirit upon his son Isaac"; *T. Mos.* frag. 2 [Gélase de Cyzique, *Hist. Eccl.* 2.21.7], "for from his Holy Spirit we all were created"; *Odes Sol.* 11:2, "the Most High circumcised me by his Holy Spirit"; *Pr. Levi* 8 [= *T. Levi* 2:3 *apud* ms Mount Athos], "Show me, Master, your Holy Spirit"). Most of these passages are late, and some of them probably are Christian interpolations. Josephus sometimes speaks of a "divine spirit" (*theion pneuma*; see, e.g., *Ant.* 4.108; 6.56; 6.166) or "Spirit of God" (e.g., *Ant.* 4.119).

It is sometimes asserted that Mary's miraculous conception is little more than a reflection of popular ideas and myths about gods impregnating mortal women. One of the best-known examples is Dionysius, the god of wine, whose father was the supreme god, Zeus, and whose mother was the mortal Semele. Another was the mighty Hercules, whose father was Zeus and mother the mortal Alcmene. Even in the case of Julius Caesar, certainly known to have a mortal father (Gaius) and a mortal mother (Aurelia), we nonetheless find an inscription (*SIG* 760) declaring that his father was Ares (or Mars), the god of war, and his mother was the goddess Aphrodite (or Venus). Of course, many Greek despots and Roman emperors were routinely hailed as "god" or "son of god" (for more examples, see A Closer Look: Omens).[22]

It is not likely, however, that early Jewish Christians, including the evangelist Matthew, would present Jesus in pagan garb. Jewish teachers were highly critical of pagan morals and myths. The idea of gods and goddesses having sexual relations with mortals was repugnant. To compare, even if only implicitly, the God of

[22] For surveys of parallels, see E. Nellesen, *Das Kind und seine Mutter* (SBS 39; Stuttgart: Katholisches Bibelwerk, 1969), 97–109; R. J. Miller, *Born Divine: The Births of Jesus and Other Sons of God* (Santa Rosa, CA: Polebridge, 2003).

Abraham to a pagan deity like Zeus and to imagine him as somehow impregnating Mary would have been viewed as idolatrous and quite scandalous.[23] Moreover, there was no expectation of a virgin birth in Jewish messianism.[24] No, it is much more likely that Mary's miraculous conception would have been understood very much in terms of the powerful working of God's Spirit, as seen in every conception (as in Philo), and especially seen in the examples in the Old Testament in which elderly or otherwise barren women conceive. Mary's virginal conception tops them all, for her child is none other than Israel's awaited Messiah and God's Son.[25]

Joseph's problem is solved when an "angel of the Lord appeared to him in a dream" and explained everything (vv. 20–21). The association of the name Joseph with dreams would instantly call to mind the well-known patriarch who had dreams and interpreted them (Gen 37:5; 40:8–9, 16; 41:15, 17), dreams of saving import. The dreams of Joseph the patriarch also concerned the salvation of his family, in Egypt, just as the dreams of Joseph, husband of Mary, concerned the salvation of his family, which also had to flee to Egypt. We again see typology at work in the Matthean narrative.

A Closer Look: The Angel of the Lord

The "angel of the Lord" (*mal'ak Yahweh / angelos kuriou*) appears to Hagar in the wilderness (Gen 16:7, 9–11) and again to Abraham (Gen 22:11, 15). This mysterious being appears to Moses (Exod 3:2), to the donkey of Balaam the hired prophet (Num 22:23–27), and eventually to Balaam himself (Num 22:31–35). The angel of the Lord appears to various people in the Book of Judges, including Gideon (Judg 6:11–22) and the parents of Samson (Judg 13:3–20), and several more times elsewhere in other narrative books, the Psalms, and the Prophets. Perhaps the most interesting passages are in Zechariah (e.g., Zech 1:11–12; 3:1, 5–6; 12:8). The Hebrew *mal'ak* and the Greek *angelos* mean "messenger." (The name Malachi means "my messenger.")

A Closer Look: Dreams

Dreams were taken very seriously in antiquity among Gentiles (Homer, *Iliad* 1.63; 5.150; Virgil, *Aeneid* 4.556–557; Ovid, *Metamorphoses* 9.685–701; Arrian,

---

[23]   G. H. Box, "The Gospel Narratives of the Nativity and the Alleged Influences of Heathen Ideas," *ZNW* 6 (1905): 80–101.

[24]   Many commentators regard the infancy narratives of Matthew and Luke as comprising little more than Jewish midrash. For a critique of this perspective, see C. L. Quarles, *Midrash Criticism: Introduction and Appraisal* (Lanham, MD: University Press of America, 1997).

[25]   A. Milavec, "Matthew's Integration of Sexual and Divine Begetting," *BTB* 8 (1978): 108–16.

Alexander 2.18.1) and the Jewish people (1QapGen 19:14–23, where Abraham is warned in a dream; *Jub.* 27:21–24; 32:1; 41:24; Ps.-Philo, *Bib. Ant.* 9:10; 42:3; 4 Ezra 10:59; *b. B. Bat.* 10a; *b. Ber.* 55a–58a) alike. Philo devotes his treatise *On Dreams* to the meaning of dreams. A Roman historian tells us that a leading citizen named Quintus Catulus once had a dream in which he saw a boy sitting in the lap of the god Jupiter. When he tried to remove the boy, "the god warned him to desist, declaring that the boy was being reared to be the savior of his country. When Catulus the next day met Augustus, whom he had never seen before, he looked at him in great surprise and said that he was very like the boy of whom he had dreamed" (Suetonius, *Augustus* 94).

It is significant that Joseph is addressed as "son of David" (**v. 20**). It recalls the incipit, where Jesus is introduced as the "son of David" (Matt 1:1), as well as the tripartite division of Israel's history, centered on the name and numerical value of David (Matt 1:17), and underscores the royal, Davidic descent of Jesus.[26]

Joseph is commanded "to name him Jesus, for he will save his people from their sins" (**v. 21**). The full form of the Hebrew name Yeshua (or Yehoshua, which in English is usually rendered Joshua) meant in Matthew's time "Yahweh saves." This meaning is also reflected in the works of first-century writer and apologist Philo: "Jesus is interpreted to mean 'salvation of the Lord'" (*On the Change of Names* 121, commenting on Num 13:16 and the meaning of the name of Moses' successor Joshua, son of Nun). Given his saving mission, the name Yeshua, or, in its Greek form, "Jesus," is suitable.

However, Messiah Jesus will save his people "from their sins." Had the angel of the Lord only said "he will save his people," many Jews likely would have understood this promised salvation in very militant terms. The anticipated Messiah described in some literature of the time was expected to lead armies against Gentiles and especially the hated Romans. Indeed, according to one scroll from Qumran, the Messiah, "Branch of David," would in fact kill the Roman emperor (see 4Q285 frag. 5, where the Roman emperor is dubbed the "king of the Kittim").[27] No, Jesus the Messiah will save his people "from their sins." The greatest danger that humans face is not oppressive humans but enslaving sin, sin that estranges humans from God. The hope that the Messiah will forgive his people of their sins probably reflects the Song of the Suffering Servant (Isa 52:13–53:12). The Servant will bear "the sin of many" and make "intercession for the transgressors" (53:12).

---

[26] For a further discussion, see D. R. Bauer, "The Kingship of Jesus in the Matthean Infancy Narrative: A Literary Analysis," *CBQ* 57 (1995): 306–23.

[27] Matthew, at the time of writing his Gospel, knows perfectly well that the Jewish people remain under the Roman thumb; grievously so, if he wrote after the destruction of Jerusalem in 70 A.D.

In the Aramaic paraphrase (or Targum) of this famous passage, the Servant is identified as the Messiah (see 52:13; 53:10).[28] Scholars dispute this, of course, but in my view it is the best explanation for understanding the Messiah's mission in terms of forgiving sins. That the evangelist Matthew identifies Jesus with the Servant is seen in Matt 8:16–17 ("to fulfill what had been spoken through the prophet Isaiah, 'He took our infirmities and bore our diseases'"), where Isa 53:4 is formally cited.[29] The unique and special nature of Jesus' task explains his unique and special conception.

Joseph is therefore to proceed with the marriage, for Mary has not been unfaithful; rather, her pregnancy "is from the Holy Spirit." The child is not called Son of God in this passage, but that clearly is the implication of the quotation of Isaiah in **v. 23** ("God with us"). Jesus will be addressed as "Son of God" in Matt 4:3, 6; 8:29; and 27:54, and the prophecy of Hos 11:1 ("My Son") will be applied to him in Matt 2:15. At the Baptism (3:17) and at the Transfiguration (17:5), God will address Jesus as "My beloved Son."

A Closer Look: Omens that Accompany Birth of Saviors

Mysterious circumstances surrounding the conception and/or birth of someone were viewed with special interest in late antiquity. In reference to the birth of the great Roman emperor Augustus (ruled 30 B.C. – 14 A.D.), the Roman historian Suetonius relates the story that, while she was in the temple of Apollo, the mother of Augustus was visited by a serpent: "In the tenth month after that, Augustus was born and was therefore regarded as the son of Apollo" (Suetonius, *Augustus* 94). The mother of Augustus also had a dream in which the significance of her conception was invested with great importance. To be raised as a son of a human father yet understood to be the offspring of deity was not viewed as contradictory. For example, some thought Plato's father was Apollo, while his mother was mortal (see Diogenes

---

[28]   The intercessory role of the Servant Messiah is also emphasized in the Aramaic version, where it is said that he will "purify [the people's] soul from sins" (Isa 53:10) and through his intercession even those who rebel against the law "will be forgiven" (Isa 53:12). The Isaiah Targum that is extant dates from well after the first century, but some of its distinctive terminology and interpretation dates back to the time of Jesus and earlier.

[29]   R. Beaton, *Isaiah's Christ in Matthew's Gospel* (SNTSMS 123; Cambridge: Cambridge University Press, 2002), 110–19; see also A. M. Leske, "The Influence of Isaiah on Christology in Matthew and Luke," in W. R. Farmer (ed.), *Crisis in Christology: Essays in Quest of Resolution* (Livonia: Dove, 1995), 241–69; O. Betz, "Jesus and Isaiah 53," in W. H. Bellinger and W. R. Farmer (eds.), *Jesus and the Suffering Servant: Isaiah 53 and Christian Origins* (Harrisburg, PA: Trinity Press International, 1998), 70–87, especially 81.

Laertius, *Lives of Eminent Philosophers*, "Plato" 3.1–2, 45). This was also the case with Pythagoras (see Iamblichus, *Life of Pythagoras* 2.3–5: "a Samian poet says that Pythagoras was son of Apollo"). In the case of an ancestor of Pythagoras (ibid. 2.3), "the story goes that Ancaeus ... was sired by Zeus." In the case of Alexander the Great, there was a rumor that on his father's side he was a descendant of Hercules (see Plutarch, *Parallel Lives*, "Life of Alexander" 2.1–3.2).

The strange circumstances surrounding the birth of Jesus, the meaning of his name, and the purpose of his mission "took place to fulfill what had been spoken by the Lord through the prophet" (**v. 22**). This is Matthew's first formula introduction of a fulfilled prophecy of Scripture. Four more times in the infancy narrative, the evangelist will appeal to this Scripture or that as "fulfilled" (cf. Mic 5:2 in Matt 2:6; Hos 11:1 in Matt 2:15; Jer 31:15 in Matt 2:18; and Judg 13:5 / Isa 11:1 in Matt 2:23).

A Closer Look: Jewish Son of God Texts

2 Sam 7:14 – "I will be a father to him, and he shall be a son to me."

Ps 2:7 – "You are my son; today I have begotten you."

Ps 89:26 – "He shall cry to me, 'You are my Father, my God, and the Rock of my salvation!'"

1QSa 2:11–12 "When God has begotten the Messiah."

4Q246 2:1 – "He will be called the Son of God, they will call him the Son of the Most High."

The birth of Jesus, Matthew says, fulfilled the prophecy of Isa 7:14: "Look, the virgin shall conceive and bear a son, and they shall name him Emmanuel" (**v. 23**). This prophecy was originally spoken in a time of national danger (Isa 7:1–2; ca. 734–733 B.C.). Judah's King Ahaz was considering a new treaty with mighty Assyria. Isaiah the prophet warned him to have faith in God instead (Isa 7:9, "If you will not believe, you surely shall not endure," an allusion to the Davidic Covenant of 2 Sam 7:16, "your house and your kingdom shall endure before Me forever"). The prophet offered Ahaz a sign to assure him that God indeed was speaking through him. The king did not want a sign, but a sign was promised in any event. The prophecy and its interpretation in full are as follows:

Therefore the Lord Himself will give you a sign: Behold, a virgin will be with child and bear a son, and she will call His name Immanuel. He will eat curds and honey at the time He knows enough to refuse evil and choose good. For before the boy will know enough to refuse evil and choose good, the land whose two kings you dread will be forsaken. (Isa 7:14–16)

The sign is simple: a young woman will give birth to a child, whom she will name Immanuel ("God is with us"), and by the time he is old enough to know the difference between right and wrong the land of the two neighboring kings who frighten Ahaz so much will be desolate. And this is exactly what took place; within a few years Syria and Ephraim, the two kingdoms that plotted against Ahaz (hoping either to coerce him into a foolish rebellion against Assyria or to replace him with a more compliant monarch) had been annihilated.

A Closer Look: 1QpHab and Pesher Interpretation

The distinctive style of biblical interpretation found in the Dead Sea Scrolls is called *pesher* (meaning interpretation or solution). The word also appears in several places in Daniel, usually in reference to interpreting the meaning of a dream or vision. Among the scrolls are found several commentaries, or *pesharim*, on the Prophets and Psalms. The principles of *pesher* exegesis are nowhere more clearly spelled out than in the following passages, taken from the *pesher* on the Book of Habakkuk.

[... "For the wicked man hems in] the righteous man" (Hab 1:4b). The "wicked man" refers to the Wicked Priest, and "the righteous man" is the Teacher of Righteousness ... [... "Look, traitors, and see, and be shocked, for the Lord is doing something in your time that you would not believe it if] told" (Hab 1:5). [This passage refers to] the traitors with the Man of the Lie, because they did not [listen to the words of] the Teacher of Righteousness from the mouth of God. It also refers to the trai[tors to the] New [Covenant], because they did not believe in God's covenant [and desecrated] his holy name; and finally, it refers [to the trai]tors in the Last Days. They are the cru[el Israel]ites who will not believe when they hear everything that [is to come upon] the latter generation that will be spoken by the Priest in whose [heart] God has put [the ability] to explain all the words of his servants the prophets, through [whom] God has foretold everything that is to come upon his people and [...]. (1QpHab 1:10–2:10)

Then God told Habakkuk to write down what is going to happen to the generation to come; but when that period would be complete He did not make known to him. When it says, "so that with ease someone can read it," this refers to the Teacher of Righteousness to whom God made known all the mysterious revelations of his servants the prophets. "For a prophecy testifies of a specific period; it speaks of that time and does not deceive" (Hab 2:3a). This means that the Last Days will be long, much longer than the prophets

> had said; for God's revelations are truly mysterious. "If it tarries, be patient,
> it will surely come true and not be delayed" (Hab 2:3b). This refers to those
> loyal ones, obedient to the Law, whose hands will not cease from loyal service
> even when the Last Days seems long to them, for all the times fixed by God
> will come about in due course as He ordained that they should by his inscru-
> table insight. (1QpHab 7:1–14)[30]

Isaiah's prophecy was not intended to be fulfilled seven centuries later; it was
to be, and was, fulfilled in the lifetime of the feckless King Ahaz. The birth of the
child who was named Immanuel took place long ago and had nothing to do with
an awaited Messiah (and we in fact do not know who the young woman was – a
new bride for Isaiah, or for Ahaz? – and we do not know who the young son was).
But the event, which was indeed prophetic and is recorded in Scripture, took on
typological significance for later generations. In the birth of Jesus, Matthew sees
biblical history repeating itself, which is what typology is all about – the conviction
that God will act in the future the way he acted in the past.[31] If the birth of an infant,
foretold with respect to a young woman, a virgin not yet wed,[32] was a sign that God
was with his people, to save and deliver, then how else was the surprising pregnancy
of Mary to be understood?

This is well and good when seen in the light of Jesus' astounding public activities
and his even more astounding resurrection. But as he grew up, there can be no doubt
that family, friends, and neighbors would have viewed Mary's pregnancy as out of
wedlock, whether involving Joseph or someone else. Even years later, as an adult,
there are allusions to and hints of the doubt surrounding Jesus' conception and

---

[30]   Translation based on M. O. Wise, M. G. Abegg, Jr., and E. M. Cook, *The Dead Sea Scrolls:
A New Translation* (San Francisco: HarperCollins, 1996), 116, 119.

[31]   J. T. Willis, "The Meaning of Isaiah 7:14 and Its Application in Matthew," *RestQ* 21 (1978):
1–18; R. E. Watts, "Immanuel: Virgin Birth Proof Text or Programmatic Warning of
Things to Come (Isa 7:14 in Matt 1:23)?" in C. A. Evans (ed.), *From Prophecy to Testament:
The Function of the Old Testament in the New* (Peabody, MA: Hendrickson, 2004), 92–113.
On the possibility of an allusion to Deut 32:18 ("the Rock that bore you … the God who
gave you birth"), see B. D. Crowe, "The Song of Moses and Divine Begetting in Matt 1,20,"
Bib 90 (2009): 47–58.

[32]   In the Hebrew Isa 7:14, we hear of a "young woman" or "maiden" (*'almah*) who will conceive, but in Matthew's Greek quotation the word *parthenos* ("virgin") is used. Although
some think it is problematic, it is not. Given the cultures of both Old Testament times
and the time of Jesus, it was assumed that a not yet married maiden (*'almah* in the
Hebrew; *kore*, *pais*, or *paidiske* in the Greek) was in fact a virgin. Moreover, Greek literature often refers to a girl or maiden as a *parthenos*. Accordingly, the Greek translation,
which Matthew has followed, is not wrong. The use of *parthenos*, of course, suits his purpose in making the point that the conception of Jesus was through the Holy Spirit and
not through Joseph or another man.

birth. We see this when teachers reply to Jesus, "We are not illegitimate children!" (John 8:41), and probably in the reference to Jesus as "son of Mary" (Mark 6:3).[33] A person of suspect birth was called a *mamzer*, a status no one wanted: "Those born of an illicit union [*mamzer*] shall not be admitted to the assembly of the Lord. Even to the tenth generation, none of their descendants shall be admitted to the assembly of the Lord" (Deut 23:2; cf. Zech 9:6, where *mamzer* means "mongrel," whereas in the targumic tradition it is understood as "foreigner").[34]

Joseph did as he was instructed (**vv. 24–25**). Mary remained a virgin until she gave birth, and the child was named Jesus. For the holy family, however, the adventure was only beginning. The question of the history behind the infancy narrative will be taken up at the end of the commentary on Matt 2:13–23.

MATTHEW 2:1–12 – THE WISE MEN

2:1: In the time of King Herod, after Jesus was born in Bethlehem of Judea, wise men from the East came to Jerusalem,

2:2: asking, "Where is the child who has been born king of the Jews? For we observed his star at its rising, and have come to pay him homage."

2:3: When King Herod heard this, he was frightened, and all Jerusalem with him;

2:4: and calling together all the chief priests and scribes of the people, he inquired of them where the Messiah was to be born.

2:5: They told him, "In Bethlehem of Judea; for so it has been written by the prophet:

2:6: 'And you, Bethlehem, in the land of Judah, are by no means least among the rulers of Judah; for from you shall come a ruler who is to shepherd my people Israel.'"

---

[33] H. K. McArthur, "Son of Mary," *NovT* 15 (1973): 38–58. One also thinks of the accusation that Jesus was a "Samaritan" (John 8:42), implying doubt about his birth, as well as the accusation that he was a "sinner" (John 9:16), which in the context of the healing of the man *born* blind could well have implied that Jesus, too, had been born in sin.

[34] For a discussion of Jesus as *mamzer*, see B. D. Chilton, *Rabbi Jesus: An Intimate Biography. The Jewish Life and Teaching that Inspired Christianity* (New York: Doubleday, 2000), 3–22. For early rabbinic discussion of this topic, see *m. Hag.* 1:7; *Yebam.* 2:4–5; 4:12–13; 6:2; 7:5; 9:1–3; 10:1, 3–4; *Ketub.* 1:9; 3:1; 11:6; *Sota* 4:1; 8:3, 5; *Git.* 8:5; 9:2; *Qidd.* 2:3; 3:12–13; 4:8. See some of the cautious clarifications in S. McKnight, "Jesus as *Mamzer* ('Illegitimate Son')," in S. McKnight and J. B. Modica (eds.), *Who Do My Opponents Say that I Am? An Investigation of the Accusations against the Historical Jesus* (LNTS 327; London: T. & T. Clark, 2008), 133–63. For a less sympathetic assessment of Chilton's interpretation, see C. L. Quarles, "Jesus as *Mamzer*: A Response to Bruce Chilton's Reconstruction of the Circumstances Surrounding Jesus' Birth in *Rabbi Jesus*," *BBR* 14 (2004): 243–55.

2:7: Then Herod secretly called for the wise men and learned from them the exact time when the star had appeared.

2:8: Then he sent them to Bethlehem, saying, "Go and search diligently for the child; and when you have found him, bring me word so that I may also go and pay him homage."

2:9: When they had heard the king, they set out; and there, ahead of them, went the star that they had seen at its rising, until it stopped over the place where the child was.

2:10: When they saw that the star had stopped, they were overwhelmed with joy.

2:11: On entering the house, they saw the child with Mary his mother; and they knelt down and paid him homage. Then, opening their treasure chests, they offered him gifts of gold, frankincense, and myrrh.

2:12: And having been warned in a dream not to return to Herod, they left for their own country by another road.

*M*atthew's infancy narrative invites comparison of the kingship of Jesus with that of the Idumean puppet Herod the Great. The kingship of Jesus is rooted in prophecy and will result in the salvation of his people. This stands in sharp contrast to the self-serving kingship of Herod, whose rule results in terror and death. The infancy narrative, especially here in Chapter 2, prepares readers for the passion and resurrection narratives, where the kingship of Jesus will once again come to the fore.[35]

After going to the trouble to narrate the unusual circumstances surrounding the conception of Jesus, it is surprising that Matthew says nothing about the actual birth of Jesus apart from the rather perfunctory notice that "Jesus was born in Bethlehem of Judea" (v. 1). In contrast to Luke (cf. Lk 2:4), Matthew does not prepare his readers for Jesus' birth in Bethlehem; he simply states that it happened. Later, in Matt 2:4–6, an explanation (a prophetic one) will be given. However, the evangelist does provide a temporal reference, saying that Jesus' birth took place "in the time of King Herod." Although "King Herod" could refer to the king's son Archelaus, who succeeded his father as ethnarch of Judea and Samaria (governed 4 B.C.–6 A.D. and mentioned in Lk 1:5),[36] it is probable that the reference is to Herod the Great, who

[35] D. R. Bauer, "The Kingship of Jesus in the Matthean Infancy Narrative: A Literary Analysis," *CBQ* 57 (1995): 306–23.

[36] As is argued by M. D. Smith, "Of Jesus and Quirinius," *CBQ* 62 (2000): 278–93. Smith argues that the only firm date of the administration of Quirinius is after 6 A.D., when Archelaus was removed from office. Matthew wishes "Herod" to be understood as Herod the Great (who notoriously executed three of his sons in his later life and ordered popular Jews executed at his death) in order to facilitate a typological comparison with the story of Pharaoh, whose slaughter of the Hebrew infants constituted a grave threat to Moses.

ruled from 37 B.C. until his death in 4 B.C. Herod is called "the great" (*ho megas*) only once by Josephus (*Ant.* 18.130). Although his sons were sometimes called "king" (e.g., in Mark 6:14, where Antipas the tetrarch is called "King Herod"), only Herod the Great officially possessed this title, conferred upon him by the Roman Senate.[37]

A Closer Look: Herodian Kings and Princes of Israel

Antipater (procurator of Judea), father of Herod the Great
Herod the Great (king of the Jews) 37–4 B.C.
Archelaus (ethnarch of Judea, Idumea, and Samaria) 4 B.C.–6 A.D.
Philip (tetrarch of Gaulanitis, Batanea, and Trachonitis) 4 B.C.–34 A.D.
Antipas (tetrarch of Galilee and Perea) 4 B.C.–39 A.D.
Herod Agrippa I 41–44 A.D. (some territory received in 37 and 39 A.D.)
Herod Agrippa II 49–93 A.D.

Reference to King Herod sets the stage for the story of the "wise men from the east" (**v. 1**). The NRSV translates the verse as "wise men," but this may not be the proper sense (as will be discussed further). It is probably better to use the term magi (Greek: *magoi*). These men are probably magicians (not in the modern sense of illusionists) or astronomers from the region of Chaldea, perhaps of priestly vocation. As stargazers and scholars, often in the employ of kings (cf. Strabo, *Geography* 15.1.68; Xenophon, *Cyropaedia* 8.1.23–24), they would be expected to observe and understand strange phenomena in the heavens. The Chaldeans were famous in antiquity for magic and astrology (Arrian, *Alexander* 7.18.2, 4; Juvenal, *Satires* 6.553–564; Philo, *Dreams* 1.53; *Sibylline Oracles* 3.227). Because the gifts that the magi brought parallel Isa 60:3 and Ps 72:10–11, in which kings bring gifts to Israel (see the commentary on Matt 2:11), it is not surprising that the tradition arose that the magi were themselves "kings" (as seen, for example, in Caesarius of Arles, *Sermo* 139 [*PL* 39.2018], but qualified in Tertullian, *Against Marcion* 3.13.8; see also the reference to Pliny in the commentary on v. 2). And, of course, the magi were spoken of as "wise men" (as seen, for example, in Chrysostom, *Matt. Hom.* 7.3 [*PG* 57.75–76]: "wise men from on high"). In one inscription, from Cappadocia and perhaps from the third century B.C., reference is made to "becoming a magus," meaning to assume the office of a magus.[38]

---

[37]   The title would later be conferred on his grandson Julius Agrippa I in 41 A.D.

[38]   É. Lipinski, *Studies in Aramaic Inscriptions and Onomastics* (2 vols., Orientalia Lovaniensia Analecta 1, 57; Leuven: Peeters and Leuven University Press, 1975–1994), 1:173–84. The Greek inscription reads: "Sagarios, [son] of Maipharnes, commander of Ariaramneia, became magus [*emageuse*] of Mithra." For a learned review of ancient documentation, see J. Bidez and F. Cumont, *Les mages hellénisés: Zoroastre, Ostanès, et Hystaspe d'après la tradition grecque* (2 vols., Paris: Société d'Éditions "Les belles lettres," 1938). For a recent

Modern interpreters have also puzzled over the identity and vocation of the three magi.[39] The Chaldean and Persian background has been investigated.[40] The assumption that the magi were Gentiles has recently been challenged; perhaps they should be understood as Jewish.[41] Indeed, the habit of calling these men "wise men" has been challenged recently. It has been argued that this is a more or less modern view, in which the magi are portrayed as scholars of a sort, whose learning rightly leads them to search for the Messiah. Matthew's readers, however, especially those who were Jewish, would have viewed the magi with suspicion and would have had little regard for their magian knowledge. Indeed, the hated Balaam, in time viewed as the archenemy of the Jewish people, was regarded as a magus (cf. Philo, *Moses* 1.276). The visit of the magi should be understood as the travel of ignorant men in search of the wisdom that can come only from Israel's Messiah and God's Son (cf. Matt 11:28–30). Likewise, the magi should not be viewed as kings.[42]

The magi inquire where they might find the recently born "king of the Jews" (**v. 2**). The title "king of the Jews" is the Roman designation of Israel's monarch and was applied to Herod the Great, appointed as such by the Roman Senate in 40 B.C., upon the recommendation of Herod's friend Mark Antony (see Josephus, *J.W.* 1.282).[43] Throughout the writings of Josephus, Herod is regularly called "king of the Jews." It would only be natural for the visiting magi to refer to Herod's successor by this title. There is no reason to think that the magi saw this as controversial or as

study that focuses on the magi story in Matthew, see R. D. Kotansky, "The Star of the Magi: Lore and Science in Ancient Zoroastrianism, the Greek Magical Papyri, and 'St. Matthew's Gospel," *Annali di storia dell'esegesi* 24 (2007): 379–421.

[39] H. J. Richards, "The Three Kings (Mt. II.1–12)," *Scripture* 8 (1956): 23–28; J. E. Bruns, "The Magi Episode in Matthew 2," *CBQ* 23 (1961): 51–54; E. M. Yamauchi, "The Episode of the Magi," in J. Vardaman and E. M. Yamauchi (eds.), *Chronos, Kairos, Christos: Nativity and Chronological Studies Presented to Jack Finegan* (Winona Lake, IN: Eisenbrauns, 1989), 15–39.

[40] A. Hultgård, "The Magi and the Star: The Persian Background in Texts and Iconography," in P. Schalk and M. Stausberg (eds.), *"Being Religious and Living through the Eyes": Studies in Religious Iconography and Iconology* (Uppsala: Uppsala University Library, 1998), 215–25. See also the interesting comparative approach in R. D. Aus, *Barabbas and Esther and Other Studies in the Judaic Illumination of Earliest Christianity* (South Florida Studies in the History of Judaism 54; Atlanta: Scholars Press, 1992), 95–111.

[41] D. C. Sim, "The Magi: Gentiles or Jews?" *Hervormde Teologiese Studies* 55 (1999): 980–1000.

[42] For more on this line of interpretation, see M. A. Powell, "The Magi as Wise Men: Re-examining a Basic Supposition," *NTS* 46 (2000): 1–20; M. A. Powell, "The Magi as Kings: An Adventure in Reader-Response Criticism," *CBQ* 62 (2000): 459–80. Powell suggests that the magi in the Matthean infancy narrative are not kings but representatives of kings, who recognize in the newborn Messiah the true king. Similarly, see J. A. Gibbs, *Matthew 1:1–11:1* (2006), 125.

[43] Rome and only Rome bestowed the title and office of "king of the Jews" on Israel's rule in the Roman period. Other would-be kings of the Jews, be they the last Hasmonean prince, Antigonus (Dio Cassius, *Roman History* 49.22.6), or the Galilean Jesus of Nazareth (Matt 27:26), were flogged and crucified.

a threat to Herod himself. That Herod had to summon the magi (v. 7) would have made it clear to the visitors that this newborn king of the Jews was not himself a son of the aged and unwell king. The chaotic and uncertain state of Herod's succession surely played a role in the development and transmission of the story of the birth of Jesus and attendant dangers.

The magi explain that they have seen "his star at its rising" (v. 2). The births (and deaths) of great men were often augured by the appearance of a star (as in Alexander the Great, Julius Caesar, and others).[44] The star to which the magi refer is surely related in some way to the prophecy of Num 24:17: "I see him, but not now; I behold him, but not near – a star shall come out of Jacob, and a scepter shall rise out of Israel; it shall crush the borderlands of Moab, and the territory of all the Shethites." In the Aramaic paraphrase, this passage is understood in an explicitly messianic sense: "I see him, but not now; I behold him, but not near. When the strong king from those of the house of Jacob shall rule, and the Messiah and the strong rod from Israel shall be anointed ..." (Ps.-Jonathan; cf. Onqelos and Neofiti). The antiquity of this tradition is attested by the Dead Sea Scrolls (cf. CD 7:18–8:1 [= 4Q266 frag. 3, col. iii, lines 20–23; 4Q269 frag. 5, lines 3–4]; 1QSb 5:27; 1QM 11:6–7; 4Q175 1:9–13). In all probability, it is to Num 24:17 that Josephus also refers when he says that it was an "ambiguous oracle" that more than anything else incited his countrymen to revolt against Roman authority (Josephus, *J.W.* 6.312–13), an oracle thought to have been fulfilled by a star or comet, "resembling a sword," seen in the sky above Jerusalem (*J.W.* 6.289).[45]

Modern astronomers tell us that there were celestial phenomena that could have had some significance for Jews and others in the Middle East of late antiquity: an alignment of Jupiter and Saturn in 7 B.C. would have created a star of unusual brightness, and an alignment of Venus and Saturn in 3 B.C. would have done the same; other alignments and configurations in 3 and 2 B.C. have also been suggested.[46]

There may well have been a celestial phenomenon of one sort or another, but astronomical interpretations ultimately cannot explain Matthew's text. In the evangelist's time, stars were viewed as living beings.[47] This is what Tatian meant in the second century when he spoke of a "spirit in the stars, spirit in angels ... spirit in humans, spirit in animals" (*Oratio ad Graecos* 12.4).[48] This understanding is also

---

[44] For a discussion and more examples, see R. A. Rosenberg, "The 'Star' of the Messiah Reconsidered," *Bib* 53 (1972): 105–9.

[45] T. Nicklas, "Balaam and the Star of the Magi," in G. H. van Kooten and J. van Ruiten (eds.), *The Prestige of the Pagan Prophet Balaam in Judaism, Early Christianity and Islam* (Themes in Biblical Narrative 11; Leiden: Brill, 2008), 233–46.

[46] See K. Ferrari-D'Occhieppo, "The Star of the Magi and Babylonian Astronomy," in J. Vardaman and E. M. Yamauchi (eds.), *Chronos, Kairos, Christos* (1989), 41–53.

[47] D. C. Allison, Jr., *Studies in Matthew: Interpretation Past and Present* (Grand Rapids, MI: Baker Academic, 2005), 17–41.

[48] For Greek text and English translation, see M. Whittaker, *Tatian: Oratio ad Graecos and Fragments* (Oxford: Clarendon Press, 1982), 24–25.

seen in Philo, the Jewish philosopher and interpreter, who lived a century earlier: "the stars ... are living creatures" (*Plant.* 12); "the stars are souls divine" (*Gig.* 8); and "the heavenly bodies ... living creatures endowed with mind" (*Opif.* 73). The same idea is found in the Magical Papyri: "[A star] will descend and come to a stop in the middle of the housetop, and when the star [has dissolved] before your eyes, you will behold an angel whom you have summoned and who has been sent" (*PGM* I.74–77). Many texts describe angels as bright light (e.g., 2 Cor 11:14; *T. Job* 3:1; 4:1; 1QS 3:20; 1QM 13:9–10; *Joseph and Aseneth* 14:1–7). Accordingly, we should not be surprised that the apocryphal *Arabic Gospel of the Savior* says that "there appeared to them [i.e., the magi] an angel in the form of a star which had guided them on their journey; and they went away, following the guidance of its light."[49] Theophylact likewise says: "When you hear 'star,' do not think that it was a star such as we see, but a divine and angelic power that appeared in the form of a star ... the star was an angelic power."[50] The decision at the Second Council of Constantinople in 553 that belief that the sun, moon, and stars are living beings is heresy discouraged interpreting the magi's star as an angel.[51]

Some think Jesus may have been born in the spring; yet others have suggested the fall. Inferences based on when shepherds tended their sheep out in the fields are flimsy, and, in any case, this is borrowing a detail from Luke. There is no compelling argument against a midwinter date.[52] All things considered, it is probably still best to think Jesus was born in or around 5 B.C., not too long before the death of Herod the Great.[53]

The magi assert that they "have come to pay him homage" (**v. 2**). The underlying Greek word is sometimes translated as "worship" (as in the RSV), but *proskunesai* also means to "pay homage," which is what it means here. The magi do not seek to worship Jesus as God but to show him the respect due a great king. Of course, Matthew's original readers may have surmised that the magi knew more than ordinary persons and so may have rightly recognized in the Christ child the presence of God himself (cf. Matt 1:23; 2:15). One also thinks of the words of Tiridates, king of Armenia, who traveled from the east to pay respects to Caesar (i.e., Nero, ca. 60 A.D.): "I have come to you, my god, to pay homage" (Pliny, *Natural History* 30.6.16–17).[54]

When Herod heard of the purpose of the visit of the magi, "he was frightened" (**v. 3**). And when Herod was frightened, so was everyone else. Herod was very

[49]   *Arabic Gospel of the Savior* §7; cf. *ANF* 8:406; Allison, *Studies in Matthew* (2005), 29.
[50]   *Comm. Matt.* on Matt 2:1–12; *PG* 123:161.
[51]   Allison, *Studies in Matthew* (2005), 31.
[52]   According to *m. Sheqalim* 7:4, livestock were out in pasture (from Jerusalem to Bethlehem) throughout the year, including the winter months.
[53]   For a detailed discussion, see H. W. Hoehner, *Chronological Aspects of the Life of Christ* (Grand Rapids, MI: Zondervan, 1977), 11–27.
[54]   Pliny also refers to Tiridates and his company as magi.

possessive about his throne, and in his declining years had become paranoid, which sometimes led to terrible acts of violence (such as his plan to have a number of prominent citizens slaughtered the moment he died, thus guaranteeing that the day of his death would not be celebrated; see Josephus, *Ant.* 17.180–81).

Hoping to learn more, Herod summoned "all the chief priests and scribes of the people" (**v. 4**). That is, Herod has assembled all of the religious authorities, those who would know the contents of Scripture and related literature and how they were to be interpreted. It is probable that the Jewish high priest, along with ruling priests, advised the secular authorities, including Roman governors. One thinks of Theudas, who summoned the poor to join him at the Jordan, the waters of which would part at his command (Josephus, *Ant.* 20.97–98), or the Jew from Egypt who persuaded many to join him atop the Mount of Olives, where he promised they would see the walls of Jerusalem collapse (Josephus, *Ant.* 20.169–70), or the Samaritan prophet of renewal who claimed to know where the vessels of the long-destroyed Samaritan temple could be found (Josephus, *Ant.* 18.85–87). In every case, Roman authorities seem to understand the import of these would-be prophets. They knew what was happening because "chief priests and scribes of the people" informed them.

Herod "inquired of them where the Messiah was to be born" (**v. 4**). The prophecy that the Messiah would be born in a particular city is paralleled in a prophecy said to have portended the birth of Augustus: "In ancient days, when a part of the wall of Velitrae had been struck by lightning, the prediction was made that a citizen of that town would one day rule the world … at last long afterward the event proved that the omen had foretold the rule of Augustus" (Suetonius, *Augustus* 94). Of course, Herod's inquiry provides Matthew with the opportunity to underscore the Bethlehem prophecy and its fulfillment.

The ruling priests and scribes answer Herod's question, explaining that the Messiah is to be born "in Bethlehem of Judea; for so it has been written by the prophet" (**v. 5**). Bethlehem "of Judea" is identified, so as not to be confused with Bethlehem of Galilee, about six miles west of Nazareth. Because Jesus grew up in Galilee, some may have thought of the wrong Bethlehem. The scribes explain to Herod that the birthplace of Israel's king is Bethlehem because this is what "has been written in the prophet." To speak of something written by a prophet or in a book of a particular prophet is commonplace at Qumran (e.g., 4Q174 3:15, "as it is written in the book of Isaiah the prophet"; 3:16, "it is written in the book of Ezekiel the prophet"; 4:3, "it is written in the book of Daniel the prophet"; 4Q177 1:2, 5, 6, 9; 2:13; 4Q265 frag. 1 line 3; 4Q285 frag. 4 line 3; frag. 7 line 1).

Unlike the prophecies "fulfilled" in Matt 1:22–23 (Isa 7:14) or 2:15 (Hos 11:1), the prophecy of Mic 5:2 has been fulfilled in a more conventional sense. Nevertheless, an element of typology remains in that a pattern of salvation is present: God saved Israel long ago by raising up David from Bethlehem of Judea; he has done it again by raising up his Messiah, the son of David, from "Bethlehem of Judea."

The quotation that the ruling priests and scribes recite to Herod (**v. 6**) does not agree exactly with either the Hebrew or the Greek. Moreover, the quotation is a conflation of Mic 5:2 ("But you, O Bethlehem of Ephrathah, who are one of the little clans of Judah, from you shall come forth for me one who is to rule in Israel") and 2 Sam 5:2b ("It is you who shall be shepherd of my people Israel, you who shall be ruler over Israel").[55] The Targum understands the royal ruler in messianic terms. The Hebrew's "from you shall come forth for me one who is to rule in Israel" is rendered in Aramaic as "from you shall come forth before Me the Messiah, to exercise dominion over Israel." One of the tasks of the awaited Messiah was to shepherd his people, which sometimes are likened to "sheep that have no shepherd" (cf. Num 27:17; 1 Kings 22:17; 2 Chron 18:16; Zech 10:2; Mark 6:34; John 10).

It is not implausible that Herod would consult with visiting magi. We hear of Roman officials receiving magi (e.g., Dio Cassius, *Roman History* 63.1.7; Suetonius, *Nero* 13). Herod calls for the magi "secretly" (**v. 7a**) because he does not want to alert the ruling priests and scribes. The last thing the unpopular monarch wants is for his subjects, who hate him, to learn of the existence of a rival. Herod wishes to learn from the magi "the exact time when the star had appeared" (**v. 7b**). By knowing when the "star had appeared," Herod can calculate the approximate date of the birth of the child "born king of the Jews." To play it safe, Herod decides to slay males two years and under (Matt 2:16).

Herod "sent them to Bethlehem" (**v. 8a**) because of what he had learned from the ruling priests and scribes in Matt 2:4–6. Herod, of course, has no intention of seeking out the child to "pay him homage" (**v. 8b**); he has other plans.

The magi do as Herod requests. The star went ahead of them "until it stopped over the place where the child was" (**v. 9**). The idea that the star "stopped [literally stood] over" the place where Jesus was is formally paralleled in Josephus' description of the star that "stood over the city" of Jerusalem (*J.W.* 6.289). Josephus and Matthew use the same or similar words for "star" (*astron/aster*) and "stood" (*histemi*).[56]

When the magi found Jesus and his parents, they "offered him gifts of gold, frankincense, and myrrh" (**v. 11**). Interpreters have proposed symbolic significance for these gifts. The parallel is to gifts Israel's monarchs in the past have received; for

---

[55] For a detailed discussion of the text of the quotation, see R. H. Gundry, *The Use of the Old Testament in St. Matthew's Gospel with Special Reference to the Messianic Hope* (NovTSup 18; Leiden: Brill, 1967), 91–93; A. J. Petrotta, "A Closer Look at Matt 2:6 and Its Old Testament Sources," *JETS* 28 (1985): 47–52; D. A. Hagner, *Matthew* (WBC 33; 2 vols., Dallas: Word, 1993–1995), 1:28–29.

[56] "And the magi went out. And behold, the star which they saw in the east went before them until they entered the cave, and it stood over the head of the cave. And the magi saw the child with Mary his mother" (*Protevangelium of James* 21:3). Some manuscripts read "... stood over the head of the child ...," very similar to the variant in Codex D: "[the star] stood above the child," instead of "[the star] stood above the place where the child was."

example, "May the kings of Tarshish and of the islands render him tribute [*dora*]; may the kings of Sheba and Seba bring gifts [*dora*]. May all kings fall down before him, all nations give him service" (Ps 72:10–11 [LXX: 71:10–11]), or "Nations shall come to your light, and kings to the brightness of your dawn.... The wealth of the nations shall come to you.... A multitude of camels shall cover you, the young camels of Midian and Ephah; all those from Sheba will come. They shall bring gold and frankincense, and shall proclaim the praise of the Lord" (Isa 60:3, 5, 6). In the Aramaic paraphrase, this passage from Isaiah envisions the return of Israel's exiles in the last days. These allusions imply that all kings will recognize the supreme authority of Israel's Messiah, Jesus born in Bethlehem.

The magi escape the guile and wrath of Herod, "having been warned in a dream not to return to Herod" (**v. 12**). Human beings are from time to time either warned or instructed in dreams. For example, in an apocryphal story, Abraham is warned by God in a dream (see 1QapGen 19:14–23). In Matthew's narrative, Joseph, engaged to Mary but vexed by her unexpected pregnancy, has already been instructed in a dream (Matt 1:20). Later in the infancy narrative, Joseph will again be instructed in dreams (Matt 2:13, 19, 22). One wonders if Matthew saw a comparison between the patriarch Joseph, who dreamed and interpreted dreams (cf. Gen 37:5–10; 40:9–13, 16–19; 41:1–36). Of course, during the Passion it will be the wife of Pilate who will receive a warning of sorts in a dream (Matt 27:19).

The magi escape Herod, but their quest for the king of the Jews will have tragic consequences, for Herod, the dying vengeful monarch, has also been warned.

MATTHEW 2:13–23 – TO EGYPT AND BACK

2:13: Now after they had left, an angel of the Lord appeared to Joseph in a dream and said, "Get up, take the child and his mother, and flee to Egypt, and remain there until I tell you; for Herod is about to search for the child, to destroy him."

2:14: Then Joseph got up, took the child and his mother by night, and went to Egypt,

2:15: and remained there until the death of Herod. This was to fulfill what had been spoken by the Lord through the prophet, "Out of Egypt I have called my son."

2:16: When Herod saw that he had been tricked by the wise men, he was infuriated, and he sent and killed all the children in and around Bethlehem who were two years old or under, according to the time that he had learned from the wise men.

2:17: Then was fulfilled what had been spoken through the prophet Jeremiah:

2:18: "A voice was heard in Ramah, wailing and loud lamentation, Rachel weeping for her children; she refused to be consoled, because they are no more."

2:19: When Herod died, an angel of the Lord suddenly appeared in a dream to Joseph in Egypt and said,

2:20: "Get up, take the child and his mother, and go to the land of Israel, for those who were seeking the child's life are dead."

2:21: Then Joseph got up, took the child and his mother, and went to the land of Israel.

2:22: But when he heard that Archelaus was ruling over Judea in place of his father Herod, he was afraid to go there. And after being warned in a dream, he went away to the district of Galilee.

2:23: There he made his home in a town called Nazareth, so that what had been spoken through the prophets might be fulfilled, "He will be called a Nazorean."

$\mathcal{T}$he report of the holy family's flight to Egypt (Matt 2:13–15) anticipates Herod's evil intentions (Matt 2:16–18). Of course, it also forms the expected sequel to the previous pericope, in which the fearful and agitated Herod seeks to learn where he may find the infant. The brief paragraphs that make up this part of the infancy narrative also provide Matthew with the opportunity to cite three more instances of the fulfillment of Scripture (vv. 15, 17–18, and 23). The theme of danger, plots, dramatic deliverance, and the fulfillment of Scripture replays in important ways the story of Israel, from the calling of Abraham to the return to Israel after the exile.

We have yet another warning "in a dream" (**v. 13a**; see the commentary on Matt 1:20 and 2:12), this time for the holy family to flee to Egypt. Thus we have, because of Herod's murderous wrath, the magi fleeing to the east and Jesus and his parents fleeing to the south. On "angel of the Lord," see the commentary on Matt 1:20.

The angel instructs Joseph to "flee to Egypt, and remain there until I tell you; for Herod is about to search for the child, to destroy him" (**v. 13b**). What Matthew has given us is a Moses typology: just as Pharaoh tried to destroy the Hebrew males (Exod 1:15–2:10), so now Herod tries to destroy the Messiah by killing Hebrew males born in and around Bethlehem. Just as Moses fled from Egypt to escape the wrath of Pharaoh (Exod 2:11–15), Jesus and his parents flee to Egypt to escape the wrath of Herod. Just as Moses departed from Egypt to deliver Israel from the Egyptians, Jesus will depart from Egypt (Matt 2:15) to begin his ministry of deliverance. The Moses typology continues in Matthew when Jesus ascends the mount (i.e., the Sermon on the Mount in Matthew 5–7), even as Moses did to receive the Law; when Jesus utters ten beatitudes (i.e., Matt 5:3–12), as Moses received the Ten Commandments; and when Jesus delivers his teaching in five major blocks of material (i.e., his five discourses in Matthew 5–7, 10, 13, 18, 24–25), even as Moses delivered his in five books (i.e., the five books of the Law, or the Pentateuch).

The holy family remains in Egypt "until the death of Herod" (**v. 15a**). For background details related to the "death of Herod," see the commentary on Matt 2:16–18.

The sojourn in and return from Egypt fulfill the prophecy of Hos 11:1: "Out of Egypt I have called my son" (**v. 15b**).[57] The "fulfillment" of this passage is similar to the earlier fulfillment of Isa 7:14 in Matt 1:22–23 (see the commentary there). Perusal of the context of Hosea 11 makes it clear that the prophet is referring to God's past deliverance of the nation of Israel, collectively referred to as "my son." The passage is not predictive, nor is it messianic. So in what sense may Matthew cite it as having been fulfilled in Jesus' return from Egypt? We again have an example of typology: Just as God saved his people by calling them out of Egypt (i.e., the exodus), so will he save his people once again by calling his "son" (this time understood singularly, not collectively) "out of Egypt." Accordingly, the exodus of God's son, Israel, foreshadowed the deliverance of God's son Jesus, whose ministry will save God's people in an even greater way than they were saved long ago.

> **A Closer Look: Herod's Harsh Acts, According to Josephus**
>
> And now Herod accused the captains and Tero in an assembly of the people, and brought the people together in a body against them; and accordingly there were they put to death, together with [Trypho] the barber; they were killed by the pieces of wood and the stones that were thrown at them. (*J.W.* 1.550)
>
> He also sent his sons to Sebaste, a city not far from Caesarea, and ordered them to be there strangled; and as what he had ordered was executed immediately, so he commanded that their dead bodies should be brought to the fortress Alexandrium, to be buried with Alexander their grandfather by the mother's side. And this was the end of Alexander and Aristobulus. (*J.W.* 1.551)
>
> As soon as ever Antipater heard that, he took courage, and with joy in his looks, besought his keepers, for a sum of money, to loose him and let him go; but the principal keeper of the prison did not only obstruct him in that his intention, but ran and told the king what his designs were; hereupon the king cried out louder than his distemper would well bear, and immediately sent some of his guards and slew Antipater; he also gave order to have him buried at Hyrcanium, and altered his testament again – and therein made Archelaus, his eldest son, and the brother of Antipas, his successor; and made Antipas tetrarch. (*J.W.* 1.663–64)[173] ... though he were near his death, he contrived the following wicked designs. [174] He commanded that all the principal men of the entire Jewish nation wheresoever they lived, should be called to

---

[57]   Matthew's quotation of Hos 11:1 follows the Hebrew more closely than it does the Greek translation (the LXX). For a detailed study, see R. H. Gundry, *The Use of the Old Testament in St. Matthew's Gospel* (1967), 93–94.

him. Accordingly, there were a great number that came, because the whole nation was called.... And now the king was in a wild rage against them all, the innocent as well as those that had afforded him ground for accusations;[175] and when they were come, he ordered them all to be shut up in the hippo-drome, and sent for his sister Salome, and her husband Alexas, and spoke thus to them: "I shall die in a little time, so great are my pains; which death ought to be cheerfully borne, and to be welcomed by all men; but what prin-cipally troubles me is this, that I shall die without being lamented, and with-out such mourning as men usually expect at a king's death." [176] For that he was not unacquainted with the temper of the Jews, that his death would be a thing very desirable, and exceedingly acceptable to them; because during his lifetime they were ready to revolt from him ...[177] he shall have a great mourn-ing at his funeral, and such as never any king had before him; for then the whole nation would mourn from their very soul, which otherwise would be done in sport and mockery only. [178] He desired therefore that as soon as they see he has died, they shall place soldiers round the hippodrome, while they do not know that he is dead; and that they shall not declare his death to the multitude till this is done, but that they shall give orders to have those that are in custody shot with their arrows; and that this slaughter of them all will cause that he shall not miss to rejoice on a double account; that as he is dying, they will make him secure that his will shall be executed in what he charges them to do; and that he shall have the honor of a memorable mourning at his funeral. (*Ant.* 17.173–78)

Eventually Herod learns that the magi have departed his realm without provid-ing the requested intelligence. Not surprisingly, "he was infuriated, and he sent and killed all the children in and around Bethlehem who were two years old or under" (**v. 16**). Herod's action strikes most people today as hardly credible, but it is in fact very much in keeping with what we know of him (see the examples in the preced-ing box).

Herod, growing weaker and suffering from dementia in his declining years, and entangled with various palace intrigues involving his children, his current wife, and ex-wives and various other friends and relatives, executed his sons Alexander and Aristobulus, whose mother was the Hasmonean princess Mariamme I. Sometime later, Herod's oldest son, Antipater, who also had contributed to the plot that had led to the execution of his brothers, became involved in yet another plot, this time to poison the ailing king. Herod imprisoned him and then had him exe-cuted just four days before his own death. Although a full account is provided by Josephus, we find an interesting reference in a work by a fifth-century Latin writer: "When he [i.e., Augustus] heard that among the boys under the age of two years, whom in Syria [i.e., Israel] Herod the king of the Jews had ordered to be put to death, was the king's own son, he exclaimed: 'I'd rather be Herod's pig than Herod's son'" (Macrobius, *Saturnalia* 2.4.11). Because this text, influenced by Matthew's story of the slaughter of the infants (and somewhat confused, for Antipater was not "among the boys under the age of two"), is written in Latin, the play on words does not work (i.e., *porcum* ["pig"] in contrast to *filium* ["son"]). The original language must have been Greek: "I would rather be Herod's pig [*hus*] than his son [*huios*]." Augustus implies that the life of a pig, which Jews do not slaughter and eat, would be longer than that of a royal prince, whom Herod was very apt to have put to death. Macrobius or the tradition before him has linked the remarkable pun of Augustus, originally in reference to Herod's brutality near the end of his life, to Herod's murder of the infants.

As a final act of madness, Herod even arranged to have several prominent citizens executed the day he died, lest the day of his death occasion celebration (cf. Josephus, *Ant.* 17.180–81, and the preceding box). Fortunately, the order was rescinded by Herod's son Archelaus, who succeeded him as ethnarch over Judea.

The strange story of Herod's murder of the infants finds a parallel in Roman literature. In reference to the circumstances leading to the birth of Augustus, Rome's greatest emperor, Suetonius relates: "According to Julius Marathus, a few months before Augustus was born, a portent was generally observed at Rome, which gave warning that nature was pregnant with a king for the Roman people; thereupon the senate in consternation decreed that no male child born that year should be reared" (*Augustus* 94). That is, the Senate, fearing that its supremacy over Rome would be eclipsed, desired that no male child born the year of the portent be allowed to live. Jews, of course, would see Herod's murder of the infants in and around the village of Bethlehem as in some way parallel to Pharaoh's killing of the Hebrew male infants (as noted earlier).

Herod's murderous action and the grief that it provoked are said to have "fulfilled what had been spoken through the prophet Jeremiah" (**v. 17**). Matthew then quotes most of Jer 31:15 (**v. 18**). Once again, we have an example of typology in the quotation of prophecy and the claim that it has been fulfilled. Jeremiah's poetry originally referred to the destruction of the northern tribes, particularly the descendants of Joseph and Benjamin (Gen 30:22; 35:16–20; for Ramah, see 1 Sam 10:2). Matthew understands the slaughter of the children in Bethlehem, resulting from the violence of a murderous monarch, as parallel to what happened to the northern tribes, caused by the violence of a foreign king, in this case the king of Assyria.

"When Herod died" (probably in March or April 4 B.C.), "an angel of the Lord suddenly appeared in a dream" (**v. 19**) instructing Joseph to take his family and return to Israel (on dreams, see the commentary on Matt 1:20). Most of the danger has passed. Nevertheless, because the violent Archaelaus has been granted rule over Judea (and Samaria), Joseph settles in the north, in Galilee, in a small village called Nazareth (**vv. 22–23**). Because Archelaus hoped to gain all of his father's kingdom and therefore would tolerate no rivals, Joseph may have believed that living in

Judea, in the jurisdiction of the new ethnarch, would be too dangerous. In contrast, the younger Antipas, appointed tetrarch of Galilee, was more tolerant.

A Closer Look: Josephus on Archelaus

This Archelaus, son of such a tyrant … anxious apparently not to be taken for a bastard son of Herod, ushered in his reign with the massacre of three thousand citizens; that was the grand total of the victims which he offered to God on behalf of his throne, that was the number of corpses with which he had filled the Temple at a festival! (*J. W.* 2.87–98, quoting the delegation opposed to Archaelaus, who refer to the Passover violence described in *J. W.* 2.11–13; cf. *Ant.* 17.218)

In Galilee, Joseph "made his home in a town called Nazareth" (**v. 23**). This is the first mention of Nazareth in Matthew's Gospel. Because Jesus was known as "Jesus of Nazareth," the evangelist may well have assumed that everyone knew that Nazareth was in fact the home village of Joseph and Mary (cf. Luke 1:26; 2:4).[58] Nevertheless, it is a bit odd that Matthew does not explain how it was that Mary gave birth in Bethlehem rather than in Nazareth. According to Luke 2:1–7, Joseph, who was of the house of David, went to Bethlehem (the "City of David") to register as part of a census. There is tradition that descendants of David relocated from Bethlehem of Judea to Nazareth of Galilee.[59] Indeed, the name Nazareth itself may allude to the Davidic legacy (as will be discussed later).

Nazareth is located in the Nazareth Mountains in lower Galilee, about 1600 feet above sea level. The name "Nazareth" appears inscribed on a stone tablet that lists the priestly courses. The tablet was found in the ruins of a third- or fourth-century synagogue in Caesarea Maritima.[60] Estimations of the population of Nazareth at the turn of the era vary. Most think no more than a few hundred people lived in this small village. Recent excavations in and around Nazareth (which today is a city of about 63,000) suggest that the village in the time of Jesus was economically active. There is evidence of viticulture, quarrying, and terrace farming. We should also assume the presence of livestock and perhaps also tanning hides. The sentimental view of Nazareth as a sleepy village, whose inhabitants needed to seek

---

[58] And not Capernaum, though this fishing village on the northwest shore of the Sea of Galilee would become Jesus' headquarters. See J. S. Kennard, "Was Capernaum the Home of Jesus?" *JBL* 65 (1946): 131–41.

[59] C. R. Page II, *Jesus and the Land* (Nashville, TN: Abingdon Press, 1995), 33–38.

[60] M. Avi-Yonah, "A List of Priestly Courses from Caesarea," *IEJ* 12 (1962): 137–39; M. Avi-Yonah, "The Caesarea Inscription of the Twenty-Four Priestly Courses," in E. J. Vardaman and J. L. Garrett (eds.), *The Teacher's Yoke: Studies in Memory of Henry Trantham* (Waco, TX: Baylor University Press, 1964), 46–57.

employment elsewhere, has been put to rest. Nevertheless, the network of roads and evidence of travel and commerce throughout Galilee do leave open the possibility of employment opportunities in a city like Sepphoris, some four miles northwest of Nazareth, which during the first two decades of the first century underwent significant expansion.[61]

Matthew tells us that Joseph made his home in Nazareth, "so that what had been spoken through the prophets might be fulfilled, 'He will be called a Nazorean'" (**v. 23**). This is the fifth fulfillment in Matthew's Gospel related to Jesus' birth and infancy (for the four others, see Isa 7:14 in Matt 1:22–23; Mic 5:2 in Matt 2:5–6; Hos 11:1 in Matt 2:15; and Jer 31:15 in Matt 2:17–18). This time the evangelist says "prophets," probably because he has at least two prophecies in mind, not one. Nowhere in the Old Testament do we find the words "He will be called a Nazorean." What we have here is a summary, not a quotation. It is a summary of Judg 13:5 ("For behold, you shall conceive and give birth to a son, and no razor shall come upon his head, for the boy shall be a Nazirite to God from the womb; and he shall begin to save Israel") and Isa 11:1 ("a shoot will spring from the stem of Jesse, and a branch from his roots will bear fruit"), both involving key words whose consonants approximate those in the name Nazareth; that is, **N**, **Z**, and **R**. In Judges, the parents of Samson, who have been unable to have a child, are promised a boy who will be a NAZIrITE, while the prophet Isaiah foretells the coming of a "branch" (NEZEr) from the roots of Jesse, the father of David. Thus the "prophets" have indeed foretold that the coming Messiah "will be called a Nazarene."[62]

Of the two prophecies, Isa 11:1 is the most important. What Matthew and perhaps other early Christians found attractive about Judg 13:5 was the prophecy that Samson would "save Israel," which relates to the meaning of Jesus' name and alludes to his mission: Mary "will bear a son, and you are to name him Jesus, for he will save his people from their sins" (Matt 1:21). Isaiah 11, however, was cited and interpreted

[61] For a discussion of Nazareth, including archaeological excavations, see S. E. Johnson, *Jesus and His Towns* (GNS 29; Wilmington, DE: Glazier, 1989), 26–37; J. F. Strange, "Nazareth," in D. N. Freedman et al. (eds.), *The Anchor Bible Dictionary* (6 vols., New York: Doubleday, 1992), 1050–51; B. Bagatti and V. Tzaferis, "Nazareth," in E. Stern et al. (eds.), *The New Encyclopedia of Archaeological Excavations in the Holy Land* (4 vols., Jerusalem: The Israel Exploration Society, 1993), 1103–6. On Sepphoris, see R. M. Nagy, C. L. Meyers, E. M. Meyers, and Z. Weiss (eds.), *Sepphoris in Galilee: Crosscurrents of Culture* (Winona Lake, IN: Eisenbrauns, 1996).

[62] For discussion of the meaning of these terms, see W. F. Albright, "The Names 'Nazareth' and 'Nazorean'," *JBL* 65 (1946): 397–401; J. S. Kennard, "Nazorean and Nazareth," *JBL* 66 (1947): 79–81; G. Allan, "He Shall Be Called – a Nazirite?" *ExpT* 95 (1983): 81–82; R. Pesch, "'He will be Called a Nazorean': Messianic Exegesis in Matthew 1–2," in C. A. Evans and W. R. Stegner (eds.), *The Gospels and the Scriptures of Israel* (JSNTSup 104; SSEJC 3; Sheffield: Sheffield Academic Press, 1994), 129–78; J. A. Sanders, "Ναζωραῖος in Matt. 2.23," in C. A. Evans and W. R. Stegner (eds.), *The Gospels and the Scriptures of Israel* (1994), 116–28.

widely in late antiquity in reference to the awaited royal Messiah, who will save Israel and subdue the nation's enemies (cf. 1QSb 5:20–29; 4QpIsa[a] frags. 8–10 lines 15–29; 4Q285 frag. 5 lines 1–6; *Pss. Sol.* 17:29, 36, 37; *Tg.* Isa 11:1–6).

At this point, we may inquire more closely into the question of history. Some commentators have suggested that the various components of the infancy narrative were produced through theological and typological interpretation of the scriptures of Israel. According to this line of thought, early Christian interpreters and apologists combed through the scriptures looking for clarification of the significance of the life, ministry, and death of Jesus. Various texts, or "prophecies," were identified, which in turn created narratives. Understood this way, the infancy stories of the miraculous conception (Matt 1:18–25), the birth in Bethlehem and the inquiry of the magi (Matt 2:1–12), the flight to Egypt (Matt 2:13–15), and the murder of the infants (Matt 2:16–18) are not actual events of history but theological and midrashic creations.

All of this is possible, of course, but the evidence for it and the logic behind it are not as compelling as some think. It is not at all clear that the prophecy of Isa 7:14 would have given rise to a story about a virginal conception. There is no history of interpretation that anticipates either a miraculous conception or a messianic identity of the child in Isaiah 7. Neither was there an expectation that the Messiah was to be born of a virgin. Indeed, had the conception and birth of Jesus been conventional, one wonders why anyone would have introduced a story involving a divine conception. Such a story would have created difficulties, for in Jewish circles it could have been viewed in terms of pagan mythology, in which a god produces a child through intercourse with a mortal woman. It is more likely that Mary's conception was indeed unexpected and unusual, and given the outcome – the amazing power of Jesus demonstrated in his public ministry and his astounding resurrection following his passion – the claim of his conception by an act of the Holy Spirit of God becomes plausible.

It is probably better to see the tradition of Mary's unusual conception and the belief that it was of God's Spirit as generating an appeal to Scripture, not the Scripture generating the story of Mary's immaculate conception. In other words, Isa 7:14 was understood to explain the irregularities surrounding the conception and birth of Jesus. The prophecy of Isaiah not only foreshadows the unusual conception of Jesus but places it into the context of Israel's history, in which God's saving work is revealed.

Jesus is said to have been born in Bethlehem of Judea, the famous "City of David" (Luke 2:4). Was he really a descendant of David? The Gospels of Matthew and Luke explicitly state that he was, and they provide genealogies that trace the lineage of Jesus back to Israel's famous king (cf. Matt 1:6; Luke 3:31–32). In Mark, blind Bartimaeus hails Jesus as "son of David" (Mark 10:47, 48). In the triumphal entry, the crowd praises God in anticipation of the arrival of the "kingdom of our ancestor David" (Mark 11:10; cf. Matt 21:9, "Hosanna to the Son of David!"). But perhaps most importantly, Paul, almost in passing, refers to Jesus as being "descended from David according to the flesh" (Rom 1:3; cf. 15:12, "the root of Jesse"; 2 Tim 2:8, "a descendant of David"). In Paul's Christology, the Davidic descent of Jesus plays hardly any role but seems at best simply taken for granted. Could Paul have been mistaken? Contrary to those who think all we have here is a theological idea that lacks any basis in fact,[63] it seems most unlikely. After all, Paul was personally acquainted with some of Jesus' disciples, such as Peter and John, and was acquainted with James the brother of Jesus (Gal 1:18–19; 2:9; Acts 21:18).

Thus, it is hard to see how a fiction such as the claim that Jesus descended from David could have circulated in the early community with the knowledge, even acquiescence, of close friends and family members who would have known there was no truth to it. Moreover, there were other would-be royal deliverers of Israel who did not claim Davidic descent, or even claimed descent from the tribe of Judah. And, if Jesus were God's Son, raised up in power and glory, would claims of Davidic descent even be necessary? Recall, too, that Jesus himself called into question the validity of the scribal habit of referring to the Messiah as "son of David" (Mark 12:35–37; cf. Matt 22:41–46). Jesus did not deny the Davidic descent of the Messiah, but he apparently regarded the epithet "son of David" as inadequate. A fair reading of the evidence leads to the conclusion that it is highly probable that Jesus was indeed a descendant of the family of David.[64]

If it is acknowledged that Jesus was of the family of David, this lends strength to the story of the visit to Bethlehem and Jesus' birth there.[65] It is also consistent with Nazareth as the home village of Joseph and Mary, for there is a tradition that the name Nazareth is linked to the *nezer*, or "branch," of the Davidic prophecy of Isaiah 11 (Epiphanius, *Pan.* 29.6.2–4). There is also a tradition that descendants of David lived in Nazareth (Africanus, *apud* Eusebius, *Hist. Eccl.* 1.7.13–14). A link between the name of the village and the Isaianic prophecy would have encouraged calling Jesus the "Nazarene" and his followers the "Nazarenes" (e.g., Acts 24:5; Epiphanius, *Pan.* 29.1.3; Tertullian, *Adv. Marc.* 4.8; *b. Sanh.* 43a, "Shall Nezer be executed? Is it not written, 'A Nezer shall grow out of his roots' [Isa 11:1]? Yes, they said, Nezer shall be executed, since it is [also] written, 'But you are cast forth away from your grave like Nezer, an abhorrent offshoot' [Isa 14:19]").[66] If the name Nazareth had no

---

[63] For example, see C. Burger, *Jesus als Davidssohn* (FRLANT 98; Göttingen: Vandehoeck & Ruprecht, 1979), 178. Burger believes that the tradition of Jesus' Davidic descent resulted from Easter faith, not credible knowledge that he really was of the family of David.

[64] On this important question, see J. P. Meier, *A Marginal Jew: Rethinking the Historical Jesus.* Volume One: *The Roots of the Problem and the Person* (ABRL; New York: Doubleday, 1991), 216–19, 237–41 (notes).

[65] J. Murphy-O'Connor, "Where Was Jesus Born? Bethlehem ... of course," *Bible Review* 16 (2000): 40–45, 50.

[66] For a discussion of the early evidence, see R. A. Pritz, *Nazarene Jewish Christianity: From the End of the New Testament Period until Its Disappearance in the Fourth Century* (SPB 37; Leiden: Brill, 1988; repr. Jerusalem: Magnes, 1992), 11–18; W. Kinzig, "The Nazoraeans,"

special meaning, it is hard to see why it was used to give Jesus and his movement its name, at least early on. In time, of course, the followers of Jesus became known as Christians. But if the sobriquet "Nazarene" alluded to the *nezer*, the Davidic shoot, of Isaiah 11, then the shift from Nazarene to Christian becomes all the more intelligible.

We might also ask about the story of the flight to and brief sojourn in Egypt. It is not surprising that some think the story was spun from Hos 11:1 ("out of Egypt I called my son").[67] This is possible, but there are factors that weigh against it. First, the Greek translation of the verse from Hosea actually reads: "I have called back his [Israel's] children." Although he was not unacquainted with the Hebrew version of Scripture, the evangelist Matthew normally makes use of the Greek. Not even the Greek and the Hebrew compel the invention of a story about a flight to Egypt in order to be called out of Egypt later. However, if the holy family spent time in Egypt, fearing Herod's wrath at a time of growing political instability surrounding the question of his succession, and then returned to Israel following Herod's death, it is not surprising that Matthew would appeal to the passage in Hosea. Second, there was a large Jewish population in Egypt and, as both the papyri and Josephus make clear, Jews in fact did travel back and forth between Israel and Egypt, sometimes to escape danger in Israel (e.g., Josephus, *Ant.* 12.387–88, Onias the high priest flees to Ptolemy, king of Egypt; 14.21, during civil war many of the Jewish upper class flee to Egypt; 15.45–46, Cleopatra advises Alexandra "to escape secretly with her son and come to her in Egypt"). Third, Roman Egypt extended north, almost to Gaza. Accordingly, it is not necessary to think that the holy family traveled as far as Alexandria or some other city in Egypt proper. They simply removed themselves from Herod's territory. It is likely, then, that we have here yet another example in which Matthew seeks out a passage from the prophets that he can apply, in a typological sense, to an event in the life of Jesus.

The same should be said of the shocking story of the murder of the young children. Matthew appeals to Jer 31:15 ("a voice is heard in Ramah … Rachel is weeping for her children") not only because of the reference to weeping for lost children but perhaps also because the passage is in the context of the hope for redemption, seen especially in the promise of a new covenant (Jer 31:31). But would Jer 31:15 in itself inspire a fictional story, whatever its typological value, of the murder of children in and around Bethlehem? Like Hos 11:1, Jer 31:15 is neither messianic nor eschatological. Rather, the prophet is looking back on the death and exile of the people of Israel or, in poetic terms, the matriarch Rachel's children.[68] And why appeal to Jer 31:15 if

---

in O. Skarsaune and R. Hvalvik (eds.), *Jewish Believers in Jesus: The Early Centuries* (Peabody, MA: Hendrickson, 2007), 463–87, especially 468–71.

[67] R. H. Gundry, *Matthew* (1982), 32–34.

[68] The prophet speaks of Ramah, which is about five miles north of Jerusalem, in the territory of the tribe of Benjamin (see Jer 40:1), where the Jewish captives were gathered before the march to Babylon. If Matthew knew that this was the Ramah of which the prophet

it is an allusion to Pharaoh's murder of the Hebrew male infants that is intended? Perhaps the better explanation is that Matthew has made use of tradition that can be exploited as part of his Jesus as New Moses typology and has found a passage from the prophets that, as in the case of his use of Hos 11:1, he can present as additional evidence that the advent of Jesus Messiah means redemption for the people of Israel. Exploiting the story as part of a Moses typology and then appealing to Jer 31:15 as supplying a prophetic witness makes more sense than the reverse – that Jer 31:15 inspired a fictional story.[69]

MATTHEW 3:1–12 – THE MINISTRY OF JOHN THE BAPTIST

3:1: In those days John the Baptist appeared in the wilderness of Judea, proclaiming,

3:2: "Repent, for the kingdom of heaven has come near."

3:3: This is the one of whom the prophet Isaiah spoke when he said, "The voice of one crying out in the wilderness: 'Prepare the way of the Lord, make his paths straight.'"

3:4: Now John wore clothing of camel's hair with a leather belt around his waist, and his food was locusts and wild honey.

3:5: Then the people of Jerusalem and all Judea were going out to him, and all the region along the Jordan,

3:6: and they were baptized by him in the river Jordan, confessing their sins.

3:7: But when he saw many Pharisees and Sadducees coming for baptism, he said to them, "You brood of vipers! Who warned you to flee from the wrath to come?

3:8: Bear fruit worthy of repentance.

---

spoke, then there would be even less reason to think Jer 31:15 inspired a story about the death of children in Bethlehem. Of course, it is possible that Matthew was thinking of the Ramah (or Ramah Rahel), which is about three miles northeast of Bethlehem.

[69] For arguments in favor of pre-Matthean tradition and perhaps even the historicity of the story of Herod's murder of the children, see R. T. France, "Herod and the Children of Bethlehem," *NovT* 21 (1979): 98–120; R. T. France, "The 'Massacre of the Innocents' – Fact or Fiction?" in E. A. Livingstone (ed.), *Studia Biblica 1978*: II. *Papers on the Gospels* (JSNTSup 2; Sheffield: JSOT Press, 1980), 83–94. On the general question of the birth stories and history, see R. T. France, "Scripture, Tradition and History in the Infancy Narratives of Matthew," in R. T. France and D. Wenham (eds.), *Studies of History and Tradition in the Four Gospels* (Gospel Perspectives 2; Sheffield: JSOT Press, 1981), 239–66. The evidence is summed up well in J. P. Meier, *Matthew* (1980), 17: "[W]e can be fairly sure that Jesus was born in Bethlehem towards the end of the reign of King Herod, that his mother was Mary and his putative father Joseph, and that he was brought up in Nazareth."

3:9: Do not presume to say to yourselves, 'We have Abraham as our ancestor'; for I tell you, God is able from these stones to raise up children to Abraham.

3:10: Even now the ax is lying at the root of the trees; every tree therefore that does not bear good fruit is cut down and thrown into the fire.

3:11: "I baptize you with water for repentance, but one who is more powerful than I is coming after me; I am not worthy to carry his sandals. He will baptize you with the Holy Spirit and fire.

3:12: His winnowing fork is in his hand, and he will clear his threshing floor and will gather his wheat into the granary; but the chaff he will burn with unquenchable fire."

$\mathcal{T}$he ministry of Jesus begins, as it were, with the ministry of John the Baptist (or "the one who baptizes"). John's appearance "in the wilderness" (**v. 1**), where in the Jordan River he baptizes people, would have evoked powerful thoughts and images of restoration and redemption. Every Jew in the time of Jesus knew that the people of Israel entered the Promised Land by crossing the Jordan River (Joshua 4). John's ministry at this important place set the stage for Jesus, whose ministry would soon get under way. But John's call for repentance and his location at the Jordan River would have caught the attention of political authorities. John's was no mere religious revival; it was a movement with significant social and political implications.[70]

The proclamation of Matthew's John, "Repent, for the kingdom of heaven has come near" (**v. 2**), draws upon Jesus' proclamation in Mark 1:15 ("The time is fulfilled, and the kingdom of God has come near; repent, and believe in the good news"). By presenting it as the first thing spoken by John (and the historical John in all probability uttered such words), Matthew strengthens the continuity between John the forerunner and Jesus the Messiah. The forerunner anticipates the message of his mightier successor.

Because the quotation formula specifically refers to "the prophet Isaiah" (**v. 3a**), Matthew deletes the words from Mal 3:1 ("See, I am sending my messenger ..."), which appear in Mark (Mark 1:2), Matthew's principal narrative source. Throughout his Gospel, we observe that Matthew is more of a stickler for such details, preferring verbatim quotations (as opposed to Mark's allusions and loose paraphrases), formal introductions to many of these quotations, and often displaying acquaintance with traditions that were circulating in the synagogue and among the sages. The deleted passage from Malachi will appear later in Matthew's narrative (Matt 11:3, 10).

---

[70] For a selection of recent studies of John the Baptist, see E. Bammel, "The Baptist in Early Christian Tradition," *NTS* 18 (1971): 95–128; J. P. Meier, "John the Baptist in Matthew's Gospel," *JBL* 99 (1980): 383–405; R. L. Webb, *John the Baptizer and Prophet: A Socio-Historical Study* (JSNTSup 62; Sheffield: JSOT Press, 1991); J. E. Taylor, *The Immerser: John the Baptist within Second Temple Judaism* (Studying the Historical Jesus; Grand Rapids, MI: Eerdmans, 1997).

Isaiah's reference to the "voice of one crying out in the wilderness" (**v. 3b**) provides the rationale for John's presence and preaching in the wilderness. The Baptist's association with the Jordan River, his call for repentance, his promise of the coming of "one who is more powerful" (v. 11), and the appeal to Isa 40:3 place John in the context of the various renewal movements active in the first century. The verse plays an important part in Qumran's Community Rule (1QS 8:12–14; 9:19–20), a work that anticipates Israel's renewal and restoration. One is also reminded of Theudas, who during the administration of Fadus (44–46 A.D.) persuaded many to take up their possessions and follow him to the Jordan River. He claimed to be a prophet and that at his command the river would be parted, providing easy passage (Josephus, *Ant.* 20.97–98). Evidently, Theudas saw himself as a Joshua figure, probably the promised prophet like Moses (Deut 18:15–19). Crossing the Jordan River was but a prelude to a new conquest of the promised land and a restoration of a theocracy based on the Law of Moses. John's presence at this river, his appeal to Isa 40:3, and the promise of the coming of a mighty one seem related to the hopes expressed by Qumran, Theudas, and others. The mighty one of John's expectations will baptize people "with the Holy Spirit and fire."

Matthew tells us that "John wore clothing of camel's hair with a leather belt around his waist, and his food was locusts and wild honey" (**v. 4**). The dress is an unmistakable allusion to Elijah and the prophetic tradition modeled after him (cf. 2 Kings 1:8; Zech 13:4). Moreover, Elijah was prophesied to return "before the great and terrible day of the Lord comes" (Mal 4:5–6; cf. Sir 48:10, "At the appointed time, it is written, you are destined to calm the wrath of God before it breaks out in fury, to turn the hearts of parents to their children, and to restore the tribes of Jacob"). John's food, "locusts and wild honey," likely represented a very strict *kashrut*, perhaps in keeping with a Nazirite vow (cf. Luke 1:15–16, "He must never drink wine or strong drink.... He will turn many of the people of Israel to the Lord their God"), or even an Essene vow.[71] Elijah the prophet was also found in the wilderness, sometimes at the Jordan River (2 Kings 2:6–13).

Matthew says that John's popularity was such that "the people of Jerusalem and all Judea were going out to him, and all the region along the Jordan" (**v. 5**). This is not hyperbole, for Josephus says much the same. In fact, John's great popularity worried Antipas, tetrarch of Galilee, fearing that it could lead to a revolt (*Ant.* 18.118, "the great influence John had over the people might put it into his power and inclination to raise a rebellion"; see the A Closer Look box that follows).[72]

The people who went to John were baptized and were "confessing their sins" (**v. 6**). This confession of sin was in response to the Baptist's call to repent (v. 2).

[71]   S. L. Davies, "John the Baptist and Essene Kashruth," *NTS* 29 (1983): 569–71; A. S. Geyser, "The Youth of John the Baptist," *NovT* 1 (1956): 70–75.

[72]   E. Rivkin, "Locating John the Baptizer in Palestinian Judaism: The Political Dimension," *SBL 1983 Seminar Papers* (1983): 79–85; R. L. Webb, "John's Baptizing Activity in the Context of First-Century Judaism," *Forum* n.s. 2, no. 1 (1999): 99–123.

Whereas the Greek concept of repentance largely meant "to change one's thinking," the Hebrew meaning of repentance was "to return" (*teshuvah*, "returning" or "repentance," from the verb *shuv*, "to return"). The call for repentance or the lament that Israel has in fact not repented is common in the Prophets (Isa 31:6; 45:22; 55:7; Jer 3:7, 10, 14, 22; 4:1; 8:5; and many more). The Jewish custom of ritual immersion for purity was probably part of the background to John's baptism. The theme of repentance is found in the most important sectarian scrolls at Qumran (e.g., CD and 1QS). Ritual immersion was also very important at Qumran, as the many immersion pools attest.[73]

Matthew finds John's angry "Brood of Vipers" speech (**vv. 7–10**) in Q, the source that he has in common with Luke, a source that mostly consists of the teaching of Jesus. However, the evangelists introduce the words of John differently. Whereas Luke has the Baptist address the "crowds" (Luke 3:7), Matthew has him address the "Pharisees and Sadducees" (**v. 7**). Consistent with his criticism of the Jewish religious leaders, Matthew refers to the Sadducees seven times (Matt 3:7; 16:1, 6, 11, 12; 22:23, 24), more than any of the other Gospel writers. In contrast, Luke mentions the Sadducees only once (Luke 20:27; six times if Acts is counted).

Josephus provides us with a great deal of information about the Pharisees and the Sadducees. The "Pharisees," we are told, "are supposed to excel others in the accurate knowledge of the laws of their country" (*Life* 191) and "are esteemed most skillful in the exact explication of their laws" (*J.W.* 2.162). They believe that "some actions, but not all, are the work of fate, and some of them are in our own power" (*Ant.* 13.172; cf. *J.W.* 2.162). The Pharisees have great "power over the multitude, that when they say anything against the king or against the high priest, they are presently believed" (*Ant.* 13.288). They are more lenient in matters of punishment (*Ant.* 13.294). The "Pharisees have delivered to the people a great many observances by succession from their fathers, which are not written in the law of Moses," holding to things that "are derived from the tradition of our forefathers" (*Ant.* 13.297; cf. 13.408). Whereas "the Sadducees are able to persuade none but the rich, and have not the populace obsequious to them, the Pharisees have the multitude on their side" (*Ant.* 13.298; cf. 13.408–9). The "Pharisees are friendly to one another" (*J.W.* 2.166). They "live simply, and despise delicacies in diet"; they "believe that souls have an immortal vigor in them, and that under the earth there will be rewards or punishments, according as they have lived virtuously or viciously in this life; and the latter are to be detained in an everlasting prison, but that the former shall have power to revive and live again" (*Ant.* 18.12, 14; cf. *J.W.* 2.163).

---

[73] It has been customary to think of John as a prophet and his baptism as eschatological. Other possibilities have been explored. See D. Smith, "Jewish Proselyte Baptism and the Baptism of John," *RestQ* 25 (1982): 13–32; B. D. Chilton, "John the Purifier," in B. D. Chilton and C. A. Evans, *Jesus in Context: Temple, Purity, and Restoration*, with Bruce Chilton (AGJU 39; Leiden: Brill, 1997), 203–20.

The portrait of the "Sadducees" is not so charitable. They

suppose that God is not concerned in our doing or not doing what is evil; and they say, that to act what is good, or what is evil, is at men's own choice, and that the one or the other belongs so to every one, that they may act as they please. They also take away the belief of the immortal duration of the soul, and the punishments and rewards in Hades. (*J. W.* 2.164–65; cf. *Ant.* 13.173)

In other words, Sadducees believe that "souls die with the bodies" (*Ant.* 18.16). Unlike the Pharisees, they do not "regard the observation of anything besides what the law enjoins them" and "think it an instance of virtue to dispute with those teachers of philosophy whom they frequent" (*Ant.* 18.16). Sadducees "are very rigid in judging offenders" (*Ant.* 20.199). Few accept their doctrine, so for this reason they grudgingly adopt some of the "notions of the Pharisees" (*Ant.* 18.17).

It is not strange to imagine Pharisees "coming for baptism," but one may wonder why Sadducees would show any interest. The explanation may, if Josephus is to be believed, lie in the delight some take in disputations. After all, we are told of an instance where Sadducees ask Jesus about the resurrection, a doctrine they do not accept (cf. Mark 12:18–27; Matt 22:23–33; Luke 20:27–40). Of course, Saducean interest in John could have had as much to do with curiosity, perhaps even concern. Who is this fellow? Why is he so popular? Is trouble brewing?

John's nasty epithet for the religious leaders, "You brood of vipers" (**v. 7**), is part of the speech that Matthew has found in Q, also used by Luke (Luke 3:7). Matthew will make use of it in a later polemic directed against the Pharisees (cf. Matt 12:34, "You brood of vipers! How can you speak good things, when you are evil?," and 23:33, "You snakes, you brood of vipers! How can you escape being sentenced to hell?"). Scripture makes figurative use of poisonous snakes and vipers (e.g., Deut 32:33; Isa 11:8; 59:5; Ps 140:3, with reference to the wicked, "They make their tongue sharp as a snake's, and under their lips is the venom of vipers"; Prov 23:32, "At the last it bites like a serpent, and stings like an adder"). In the second century A.D., Rabbi Eliezer is remembered to have warned that the sting of the sages is "the sting of a scorpion and their hiss the hiss of a serpent" (*m. 'Abot* 2:10). Various politicians and other groups are called "vipers" or "brood of vipers" in Greco-Roman sources (e.g., Aeschylus, *Choephori* 994; Euripides, *Ion* 1262; Euripides, *Orestes* 479, "mother-killing dragon"!).

Perhaps the best contemporary parallels are found in the Dead Sea Scrolls: "They did not separate from the people, but arrogantly threw off all restraint, living by wicked customs, of which God had said, 'their wine is the poison of serpents, the cruel venom of asp' [Deut 32:33]. 'The snakes' are the kings of the Gentiles, and 'their wine' is their customs and 'the poison of vipers' is the chief of the kings of Greece, who comes to wreak vengeance on them" (CD 8:8–12); "You shut the mouth of the young lions whose teeth are like a sword, and whose fangs are as a sharp spear. All their evil plans for abduction are like the poison of serpents; they lie in wait, but have not opened their mouths wide against me" (1QHa 13:8–13); "they devise the ruination of their heart; [and with the words of] Belial they have exhibited a lying tongue; as the poison of serpents it bursts forth continuously. As those who crawl in the dust, they cast forth to sei[ze …] serpents which cannot be charmed" (1QHa 13:28–30).

John warns of the "wrath to come" (**v. 7**), a warning that echoes prophetic language: "See, the day of the Lord comes, cruel, with wrath and fierce anger, to make the earth a desolation, and to destroy its sinners from it" (Isa 13:9); "See, the name of the Lord comes from far away, burning with his anger, and in thick rising smoke; his lips are full of indignation, and his tongue is like a devouring fire" (Isa 30:27); "that day will be a day of wrath" (Zeph 1:15). This language is common in the Dead Sea Scrolls; for example, "the outpouring of wrath upon the pretenders and the time of anger for all which belongs to Belial" (1QHa 11:29).

John demands that the people "Bear fruit worthy of repentance" (**v. 8**). John expects the lives and deeds of those who repent to change; their deeds will prove the sincerity of their repentance. The idea is similar to Jesus' statement, itself proverbial, that "the tree is known by its fruit" (Matt 12:33 = Luke 6:44; cf. Prov 11:30, "The fruit of the righteous is a tree of life"; Hos 10:12; Amos 6:12). One also thinks of James, who exhorts his readers to act and not simply mouth pious words, such as "Go in peace; keep warm and eat your fill" (James 2:16).

John warns the people that they must not speak presumptuously by saying, "We have Abraham as our ancestor" (**v. 9**). The reassuring "Abraham our ancestor" occurs frequently in the Jewish literature of late antiquity (e.g., *Jub.* 25:5; *T. Levi* 6:9; 8:15, "the seed of Abraham our father"; *4 Macc* 16:20; *m. ʾAbot* 3:16; 5:3, 4, 9, 22, "of the disciples of Abraham our father"; *m. Taʿanit* 2:5). The epithet "Abraham … our ancestor" may well allude to Isa 51:1–2, "Look to the rock from which you were hewn, and to the quarry from which you were dug. Look to Abraham your father." John the Baptist will go on to say that God will be able to raise up children to Abraham from these stones (i.e., from a new rock quarry, and the Aramaic version of Isa 51:1 adds the words "hewn stone").

What John the Baptist objects to is the assumption that by being a descendant of Abraham one need not fear judgment. The religious leaders he criticized may very well have voiced something like the following, preserved in a later text: "the disciples of Abraham our father inherit the Garden of Eden and inherit the world to come" (*m. ʾAbot* 5:22).

John asserts that "God is able from these stones to raise up children to Abraham" (**v. 9**). It is probable that John is referring to "these stones" of Joshua 4, where twelve stones were placed by the Jordan River as a symbol of God's deliverance of the twelve tribes of Israel: "'Take twelve stones from here out of the midst of the Jordan …' And these twelve stones, which they took out of the Jordan River, Joshua set up in Gilgal, and he said to the people of Israel, 'When your children ask their fathers in time to come, "What do these stones mean?" then you shall let your children know,

"Israel passed over this Jordan on dry ground"'" (Josh 4:2, 20–22, RSV). This stone symbolism reappears in the Elijah narrative: "Elijah took twelve stones, according to the number of the tribes of the sons of Jacob, to whom the word of the Lord came, saying, 'Israel shall be your name'; with the stones he built an altar in the name of the Lord" (1 Kings 18:31–32). Like Elijah of old, so now John, the promised Elijah of the last days (Mark 9:13, "I tell you that Elijah has come"), has placed a monument of twelve stones at the Jordan River and has summoned the tribes of Israel to repent and prepare themselves for the coming of the Lord's anointed. In continuity with this aspect of John's ministry, Jesus appoints twelve disciples (cf. Mark 3:14, 16).[74]

Behind John's "children to Abraham," in either Aramaic or Hebrew, may be a wordplay between the similar sounding words "stones" and "children," for stone in Hebrew is *eben* and son (or child) is *ben*. This wordplay is found in various Jewish sources (e.g., Josephus, *J.W.* 5.272; *Tg. Onq.* Gen 49:24; *Tg. Zech* 10:4; *Tg. Ps* 118:22; *Exod. Rab.* 37.1 [on Exod 27:20]). In effect, the Baptist has said that God can "raise up" from "these" twelve "stones" (that represent the twelve tribes of Israel) "children to Abraham"; fulfillment of the Almighty's promises is not contingent upon faithless stewards. They may presume nothing.

John then explains that "every tree therefore that does not bear good fruit is cut down and thrown into the fire" (**v. 10**). What is thrown into the fire is worthless. John's warning is echoed in Jesus' teaching as well: "Every tree that does not bear good fruit is cut down and thrown into the fire" (Matt 7:19); "See here! For three years I have come looking for fruit on this fig tree, and still I find none. Cut it down! Why should it be wasting the soil?'" (Luke 13:7). John's language may very well reflect the warnings of Malachi: "But who can endure the day of his coming, and who can stand when he appears? For he is like a refiner's fire and like fullers' soap.... See, the day is coming, burning like an oven, when all the arrogant and all evildoers will be stubble; the day that comes shall burn them up, says the Lord of hosts, so that it will leave them neither root nor branch" (Mal 3:2; 4:1). The words "day," "fire," and "root nor branch" cohere with John's proclamation. We shall see that John's condemnation of Herod's divorce and affair with his sister-in-law Herodias is also consistent with Malachi's message (cf. 2:16 "I hate divorce").[75] Cutting down a tree and throwing it into the fire also recalls language in Jeremiah: "... they will cut down your choicest cedars and throw them on the fire" (Jer 22:7).[76]

---

[74]   O. J. F. Seitz, "'What Do These Stones Mean?'" *JBL* 79 (1960): 247–54; C. A. Evans, "The Baptism of John in a Typological Context," in A. R. Cross and S. E. Porter (eds.), *Dimensions of Baptism: Biblical and Theological Studies* (JSNTSup 234; Sheffield: Sheffield Academic Press, 2002), 45–71; C. S. Keener, "Human Stones in a Greek Setting: Luke 3.8; Matthew 3.9; Luke 19.40," *JGRChJ* 6 (2009): 28–36.

[75]   J. A. Trumbower, "The Role of Malachi in the Career of John the Baptist," in C. A. Evans and W. R. Stegner, *The Gospels and the Scriptures of Israel* (1994), 28–41.

[76]   J. D. G. Dunn, "John the Baptist's Use of Scripture," in C. A. Evans and W. R. Stegner, *The Gospels and the Scriptures of Israel* (1994), 42–54.

John declares, "I baptize you with water for repentance" (**v. 11a**). In Mark's version, John said, "I have baptized you with water" (Mark 1:8a). Matthew's version, which includes "for repentance," clarifies the nature of John's baptism and underscores the difference between it and the ministry of his anticipated successor. By repenting, the people of Israel have prepared themselves for Jesus and his message of the saving, redeeming rule of God.

In contrast to his baptism of water, John says that one who follows him, who is "more powerful than I," will "baptize you with the Holy Spirit and fire" (**v. 11b**). In Mark's version, John only says, "He will baptize you with the Holy Spirit" (Mark 1:8b). But Matthew and Luke, probably drawing on parallel material from Q, both read "Holy Spirit and fire" (cf. Luke 3:16). The linkage of Spirit and fire is interesting. In the Prophets, fire is often associated with judgment (e.g., Isa 31:9; Amos 7:4; Mal 3:2). Spirit (*pneuma*, which can also mean "wind") and fire (*pur*) occur together in a few passages: "You conceive chaff, you bring forth stubble; your breath [*pneuma*] is a fire [*pur*] that will consume you" (Isa 33:11); "On the wicked He will rain coals of fire [*pur*] and sulfur; a scorching wind [*pneuma*] shall be the portion of their cup" (Ps 11:6 [LXX 10:6]); "Fire [*pur*] and hail, snow and frost, stormy wind [*pneuma*] fulfilling his command!" (Ps 148:8). Spirit/wind (*ruah*) and fire (*esh*) are found together in some Qumran texts as well (e.g., 1QM 11:10; 1QHa 16:12–13, "the mystery of powerful warriors, holy spirits, and the whirling flame of fire so that none may [come to the] fountain of life"; 4Q287 frag. 2, line 4, "angels of fire and spirits of cloud"; 4Q403 frag. 52, line 9, "divine spirits, fiery shapes"; 4Q405 frags. 20–22, col. ii, line 10, "His chariot-throne's glorious [w]heels appear something like a fire of spirits. All around are what appear to be streams of fire, resembling electrum, and [sh]ining handiwork"). The combination of spirit/wind and fire in other Jewish texts of late antiquity is also attested (e.g., *1 Enoch* 67:13; *T. Isaac* 5:21; *Life of Adam and Eve* 25:3). Moreover, "water" and "fire" can be linked as well, as seen in the Rabbis, who anticipate a river of fiery judgment to overtake the wicked and purify the righteous (e.g., *Mek.* on Exod 18:1; *b. Zebah.* 116a; cf. *T. Abraham* 12–13).

John says that he is "not worthy to carry his sandals"; that is, the sandals of his mighty successor. By this he means that in relation to his successor he is not even worthy of the role of servant (for servants removed the sandals and washed the feet of their masters). Of course, reference to sandals makes it clear that the successor to whom John refers is a human and not God himself.[77]

The Baptist has drawn on this well-known apocalyptic imagery to give vividness to his warning. Right now he immerses people in the water of the Jordan River, but his successor will immerse all Israel, indeed all of humanity, in Spirit/wind and fire, which will consume some and purify others.[78] The category in which one will be found is determined by whether one repents and obeys the summons.

---

[77] P. G. Bretscher, "'Whose Sandals'? (Matt 3:11)," *JBL* 86 (1967): 81–87.
[78] J. D. G. Dunn, "Spirit-and-Fire Baptism," *NovT* 14 (1972): 81–92.

In reference to his mighty successor, John declares, "His winnowing fork is in his hand, and he will clear his threshing floor" (**v. 12**). His colorful agrarian imagery is vivid and builds upon the wind and fire theme in the previous verse. The "winnowing fork" flings the harvested chaff and wheat up into the air, where the wind separates it by blowing the chaff away and allowing the heavier wheat to fall to the "threshing floor."[79] The result of the winnowing is what one should expect: the eschatological judge "will gather His wheat into the granary," where it will be protected from the elements and from predators; not so the chaff. The "chaff he will burn with unquenchable fire." John's "unquenchable fire" alludes to Isa 66:24 ("their worm shall not die, their fire shall not be quenched"), which in the Aramaic paraphrase also mentions Gehenna (cf. Mark 9:42–48). See also Jer 7:30–34.

Thus the Spirit/wind and fire of John's imagery clarify his warning of coming judgment. One will either be saved by the wind and fire, or one will be judged.

A Closer Look: Josephus on John the Baptist

[116] But to some of the Jews the destruction of Herod's army seemed to be divine vengeance, for his treatment of John, surnamed the Baptist. [117] For Herod had put him to death, though he was a good man and had exhorted the Jews to lead righteous lives, to practice justice toward their fellows and piety towards God, and so doing to join in baptism. In his view this was a necessary preliminary if baptism was to be acceptable to God. They must not employ it to gain pardon for whatever sins they committed, but as a consecration of the body implying that the soul was already thoroughly cleansed by right behavior. [118] When others too joined the crowds about him, because they were aroused to the highest degree by his sermons, Herod became alarmed. Eloquence that had so great an effect on people might lead to some form of sedition, for it looked as if they would be guided by John in everything that he did. Herod decided therefore that it would be much better to strike first and be rid of him before his work led to an uprising, than to wait for an upheaval, get involved in a difficult situation and see his mistake. [119] Though John, because of Herod's suspicions, was brought in chains to Machaerus, the stronghold that we have previously mentioned, and there put to death, yet the verdict of the Jews was that the destruction of Herod's army was a vindication of John, since God saw fit to inflict such a blow on Herod. (*Ant.* 18.116–19)

---

79   R. L. Webb, "The Activity of John the Baptist's Expected Figure at the Threshing Floor (Matthew 3.12 = Luke 3.17)," *JSNT* 43 (1991): 103–11.

Translation is based on L. H. Feldman, *Josephus IX* (LCL 433; London: Heinemann, 1969), 81, 83, 85. See C. A. Evans, "Josephus on John the Baptist and Other Jewish Prophets of Deliverance," in D. C. Allison, Jr., J. D. Crossan, and A. J. Levine (eds.), *The Historical Jesus in Context* (Princeton Readings in Religions; Princeton, NJ: Princeton University Press, 2006), 55–63.

MATTHEW 3:13–17 – THE BAPTISM OF JESUS

3:13: Then Jesus came from Galilee to John at the Jordan, to be baptized by him.

3:14: John would have prevented him, saying, "I need to be baptized by you, and do you come to me?"

3:15: But Jesus answered him, "Let it be so now; for it is proper for us in this way to fulfill all righteousness." Then he consented.

3:16: And when Jesus had been baptized, just as he came up from the water, suddenly the heavens were opened to him and he saw the Spirit of God descending like a dove and alighting on him.

3:17: And a voice from heaven said, "This is my Son, the Beloved, with whom I am well pleased."

On a historical level, John's baptism of Jesus is hardly surprising. Jesus identified with John (Matt 17:11–13), spoke of him (Matt 11:7–15, 16–19; 21:25–26, 32), and was queried by him (Matt 9:14; 11:2–5). Accordingly, we should not find it strange that Jesus joined John in the latter's ministry of baptism.[80] However, in the aftermath of Easter and the early community's proclamation of Jesus as the risen Lord and as Israel's Messiah and Son of God, "who knew no sin" (2 Cor 5:21), the baptism of Jesus became a theological embarrassment. After all, John's baptism was "a baptism of repentance for the forgiveness of sins," at least as defined by the evangelist Mark (Mark 1:4). If Jesus was sinless, why was it necessary for him to go to John for baptism?

With this important question in mind, the evangelist Matthew edits the tradition. First, John's baptism is no longer defined as a baptism of repentance for the forgiveness of sins. Rather, he is baptizing and calling on people to repent (Matt 3:1–2), and people do just that: they go to John, are baptized, and confess their sins (Matt 3:5–6).

[80] M. S. Enslin, "John and Jesus," *ZNW* 66 (1975): 1–18; J. Murphy-O'Connor, "John the Baptist and Jesus: History and Hypotheses," *NTS* 36 (1990): 359–74; R. L. Webb, "John the Baptist and His Relationship to Jesus," in B. D. Chilton and C. A. Evans (eds.), *Studying the Historical Jesus: Evaluations of the State of Current Research* (NTTS 19; Leiden: Brill, 1994), 179–229.

Therefore, according to Matthew's narrative, when Jesus goes to John for baptism, it is not necessarily "for the forgiveness of sins." And, of course, when Jesus is baptized, there is no mention of confession of sin. Second, when Jesus approaches John, John initially refuses, stating that Jesus should baptize him. In saying this, John has acknowledged an important element in his preaching, namely that his successor will be greater (Matt 3:11). If his successor is greater, then the successor should baptize the predecessor and not the other way around.

When Jesus, along with others "from Galilee" (**v. 13**), approaches John for baptism, "John would have prevented him, saying, 'I need to be baptized by you, and do you come to me?'" (**v. 14**). Mark says nothing of this. It is important for Matthew, who tries to resolve some tension in the story. Two verses earlier, John had said that the one coming after him was mightier than himself and that he (John) was not worthy to release the strap of his sandal (Matt 3:11). Because it is assumed that he who baptizes is greater than he who is baptized, Matthew cannot simply repeat Mark's brief version of the story. Yes, Jesus was baptized by John, but only after the latter acknowledged his unworthiness and the former insisted on being baptized. Moreover, John called Israel to repent and to be baptized for the forgiveness of sins. By going to John for baptism, was Jesus admitting to sin, to a need for repentance? Matthew's version of the story mitigates these difficult questions.

The embellished version of the story that we find in the Jewish *Gospel of the Hebrews* (excerpt §2, from Jerome, *Commentary on Isaiah* 4 [on Isa 11:2]) grapples with this same difficulty, but with much greater imagination. This version says:

And it came to pass when the Lord came up out of the water that the whole fount of the Holy Spirit descended upon him and rested on him and said to him: "My Son, in all the prophets was I waiting for you that you should come and I might rest in you. For you are my rest; you are my first-born Son that reigns forever."

An even more fanciful version is found in the Jewish *Gospel of the Ebionites* (i.e., the "Poor Ones") §3 (from Epiphanius, *Against Heresies* 30.13.7–8):

When the people were baptized, Jesus came and was baptized by John. And as he came up from the water, the heavens opened and he saw the Holy Spirit in the form of the dove, descending and entering into him. And a voice from heaven [was] saying: "You are my beloved son, in whom I have taken pleasure"; and again, "Today I have begotten you." And immediately a great light shone round about the place. Seeing this, it says, John says to him, "Who are you, Lord?" And again a voice from heaven [sounded forth] to him: "This is my beloved son, in whom I have taken pleasure." And then it says: John, falling on his face, was saying, "I beg you, Lord, baptize me!" But he forbade him, saying, "Permit, for thus it is proper that all things be fulfilled."

The dependence on Matthew's version of the story is obvious.

Notwithstanding John's objections, Jesus insists on being baptized, telling the baptizer, "Let it be so now; for it is proper for us in this way to fulfill all righteousness" (v. 15). Jesus' reply satisfies John (and evidently Matthew and his readers also). Moreover, it gives Matthew the opportunity to introduce an important theme in his Gospel – that of righteousness. "Righteous" (*dikaios*), "righteousness" (*dikaiosune*), and "to be righteous" (*dikaioun*) occur more than two dozen times in Matthew, far more than in Mark (twice) or Luke (seventeen times). Although earlier Matthew had referred to Joseph as a "righteous" (or "just") man (Matt 1:19), it is here in Matt 3:15 that the theme of righteousness begins to unfold (e.g., in Matt 5:6, 10, 20, 45; 6:1; etc. See especially the comment on Matt 5:20 in the commentary on Matt 5:17–20).[81] Indeed, the words of Jesus "to fulfill all righteousness," in reference to baptism, may anticipate the command in the Great Commision (Matt 28:18–20) to baptize converts and thus begin instruction in the way of righteousness as Jesus taught his disciples.[82]

John baptizes Jesus and "as he came up from the water, suddenly the heavens were opened to him and he saw the Spirit of God descending like a dove and alighting on him" (v. 16). Mark 1:10 simply says "Spirit"; Matthew adds "of God." Matthew replaces Mark's "into him" (NASB: "upon Him") with "and alighting on him," possibly because Mark's description may leave the impression that until his baptism Jesus did not possess the Spirit (compare the *Gospel of Ebionites* §3, quoted earlier, which reads in part: "And as he came up from the water, the heavens opened and he saw the Holy Spirit in the form of the dove, descending and *entering into* him" [emphasis added]). The descent of the Spirit "like a dove" implies that the Spirit was visible to Jesus. But it is not clear why the Spirit is said to have appeared as a dove. The suggestion that it is meant to recall the dove sent out by Noah, after the floodwaters had begun to abate (Gen 8:8–12), is not persuasive.[83]

---

[81] On "righteousness" in Matthew, see D. A. Hagner, "Righteousness in Matthew's Theology," in M. J. Wilkins and T. Paige (eds.), *Worship, Theology and Ministry in the Early Church: Essays in Honour of Ralph P. Martin* (JSNTSup 87; Sheffield: JSOT Press, 1992), 101–20; R. Deines, *Die Gerechtigkeit der Tora im Reich des Messias: Mt 5,13–20 als Schlüsseltext der matthäischen Theologie* (WUNT 177; Tübingen: Mohr Siebeck, 2004), 121–36. See also the commentary on Matt 5:17–20.

[82] On this interesting suggestion, see J. Nolland, "'In Such a Manner It Is Fitting for Us to Fulfil All Righteousness': Reflections on the Place of Baptism in the Gospel of Matthew," in S. E. Porter and A. R. Cross (eds.), *Baptism, the New Testament and the Church: Historical and Contemporary Studies in Honour of R. E. O. White* (JSNTSup 171; Sheffield: Sheffield Academic Press, 1999), 63–80; J. A. Gibbs, *Matthew 1:1–11:1* (2006), 181: John and Jesus "perform the saving deeds of God."

[83] L. E. Keck, "The Spirit and the Dove," *NTS* 17 (1970): 41–67; S. Gero, "The Spirit as Dove at the Baptism of Jesus," *NovT* 18 (1976): 17–35; P. Garnet, "The Baptism of Jesus and the Son of Man Idea," *JSNT* 9 (1980): 49–65.

The opening of heaven and the descent of the Spirit may have been understood as a fulfillment of the prophet's prayer that God "tear open the heavens and come down" (Isa 63:19 [Eng. 64:1]; cf. 1 Cor 2:9, where Paul applies Isa 64:4 to the revelatory work of the Holy Spirit). There is also an important parallel in the *Testaments of the Twelve Patriarchs*: "The heavens will be opened ... and the spirit of understanding and sanctification shall rest upon him" (*T. Levi* 18:6–7). The significance of this parallel is seen in its eschatological perspective. One thinks also of Ezek 1:1, which in the Greek version says: "the heavens were opened, and I saw visions of God." The opening of heaven and God's Spirit coming upon Jesus offer important early evidence that in Jesus "God is with" his people (cf. Matt 1:23).[84]

Matthew's "alighting on him" is reminiscent of Old Testament language where the Spirit of God "came upon" Israel's mighty deliverers, such as Othniel the son of Kenaz, Caleb's younger brother (Judg 3:10), Gideon (Judg 6:34), Jephthah (Judg 11:29), Samson (Judg 14:6, 19; 15:14), Saul (1 Sam 10:6; 11:6), and various minor figures such as Amasai (1 Chron 12:18) and Jahaziel the son of Zechariah (2 Chron 20:14). Indeed, the Spirit of God even came upon the notorious Balaam (Num 24:2), whose intended curse was altered to a blessing.

As Jesus came up from the water, "a voice from heaven said, 'This is my Son, the Beloved, with whom I am well pleased'" (**v. 17**). The reference to Jesus as the "beloved son" probably echoes Ps 2:7 ("You are my son"). The adjective "beloved" may reflect the Aramaic tradition, as preserved in *Tg.* Ps 2:7 ("You are as beloved to me as a son is to a father"), but this Targum is quite late. Perhaps God's address to Jesus is also meant to recall God's command to Abraham to sacrifice his "beloved son" Isaac (LXX Gen 22:2).[85] In any case, the heavenly voice confirms Jesus as the "mighty one" of whom John the Baptist had preached. No greater attestation could be expected. God himself had spoken. The mighty one, upon whom the Spirit of God has descended, is now ready to be tested by God's adversary (i.e., in the wilderness temptations, narrated in Matt 4:1–11).

The opening of heaven and the divine declaration that Jesus is God's beloved Son may have something to do with Jesus' habit of referring to himself as the "Son of Man." On the occasion of healing the paralytic and declaring his sins forgiven, Jesus says that the "Son of Man has authority on earth to forgive sins" (Matt 9:6). In Dan 7:13–14, the being described as (literally) "one like a son of man" (NRSV: "like a human being") approaches the throne of God and receives "dominion and glory and kingship." In the Greek translation of this passage, "dominion" is rendered *exousia*, which in English is usually translated as "authority" or "power." This power

---

[84]   For more on this idea, see D. B. Capes, "Intertextual Echoes in the Matthean Baptismal Narrative," *BBR* 9 (1999): 37–49.

[85]   For another suggestion, see P. G. Bretscher, "Exodus 4:22–23 and the Voice from Heaven," *JBL* 87 (1968): 301–11.

received in heaven clarifies Jesus' declaration in Matt 9:6 that he as "Son of Man has authority [*exousia*] on earth to forgive sins." The qualifying phrase, "on earth," seems unnecessary, until it is recognized that what is meant is that the authority granted the Son of Man in heaven is now exercised on earth.

When did Jesus, as the Son of Man, receive this heavenly authority? Although admittedly beyond our ability to confirm, it may well be that the prophetic vision of Dan 7:9–13, in which the heavenly court convenes in preparation for passing judgment on evil, was fulfilled when Jesus was baptized and heaven was opened.[86] The very Spirit of God descended from heaven and rested upon Jesus, empowering him with the authority of the Son of Man, as portrayed in Daniel 7. Jesus, the fulfillment of the Son of Man vision, now exercises his authority "on earth." As the empowered Son of Man, he represents a serious threat to the authority of Satan, whose demise is adumbrated in the Book of Daniel. It is not surprising that shortly after the baptism Satan challenges Jesus.

MATTHEW 4:1–11 – THE TEMPTATION OF JESUS IN THE WILDERNESS

4:1: Then Jesus was led up by the Spirit into the wilderness to be tempted by the devil.

4:2: He fasted forty days and forty nights, and afterwards he was famished.

4:3: The tempter came and said to him, "If you are the Son of God, command these stones to become loaves of bread."

4:4: But he answered, "It is written, 'One does not live by bread alone, but by every word that comes from the mouth of God.'"

4:5: Then the devil took him to the holy city and placed him on the pinnacle of the temple,

4:6: saying to him, "If you are the Son of God, throw yourself down; for it is written, 'He will command his angels concerning you,' and 'On their hands they will bear you up, so that you will not dash your foot against a stone.'"

4:7: Jesus said to him, "Again it is written, 'Do not put the Lord your God to the test.'"

4:8: Again, the devil took him to a very high mountain and showed him all the kingdoms of the world and their splendor;

---

[86] Long ago, S. E. Johnson ("Son of Man," *IDB* 4:416) suggested a connection between the epithet Son of Man and the Johannine understanding of the baptism of Jesus. For a more recent consideration of this possibility, and in reference to Mark 2:10 (= Matt 9:6), see J. Marcus, "Authority to Forgive Sins upon the Earth: The *Shema* in the Gospel of Mark," in C. A. Evans and W. R. Stegner (eds.), *The Gospels and the Scriptures of Israel* (1994), 196–211, especially 205–8.

4:9: and he said to him, "All these I will give you, if you will fall down and worship me."

4:10: Jesus said to him, "Away with you, Satan! for it is written, 'Worship the Lord your God, and serve only him.'"

4:11: Then the devil left him, and suddenly angels came and waited on him.

*T*he identification of Jesus as the beloved "Son" of God (Matt 3:17) sets the stage for the Satanic wilderness temptation. The temptations do not directly challenge the divine sonship of Jesus; rather, they attempt to misdirect it and, if successful, render it powerless and ineffective. The mission of Jesus is to "save his people from their sins" (Matt 1:21). If he cannot save himself from the temptations of Satan, he cannot save his people and therefore does not qualify for his messianic role.[87]

Matthew has taken over and expanded Mark's brief temptation narrative, though some details have been omitted (such as the reference to the "wild beasts" in Mark 1:13) and others modified. Most of the expansion comes from the source shared with Luke that is known as Q.[88] The Q material here comprises three specific temptations. In each case, Jesus replies with a quotation from Deuteronomy. The noticeable difference between Matthew and Luke is the difference in the order of the second and third temptations. Which order was original is not easy to determine, for the third temptation in Matthew (offer of the kingdoms of the world) and the third temptation in Luke (leaping from the temple in Jerusalem) fit the theological perspectives of the two respective evangelists very well.[89]

The temptation narrative begins with the notice that "Jesus was led up by the Spirit into the wilderness to be tempted by the devil" (**v. 1**). Matthew understandably replaces Mark's "drove" (*ekballein*) (cf. Mark 1:12, literally "cast out") with "led up" (*anagein*). This change not only paints a more dignified picture but also avoids using the verb that is normally used in reference to casting out (*ekballein*) demons. This detail argues in favor of Mark's priority and Matthew's prior reading of Mark before making use of it as a source. In reading Mark (probably many times), Matthew would have observed the regular use of *ekballein* in reference to

---

[87] J. A. Kirk, "The Messianic Role of Jesus and the Temptation Narrative: A Contemporary Perspective," *EvQ* 44 (1972): 11–29, 91–102.

[88] P. Hoffmann, "Die Versuchungsgeschichte in der Logienquelle," *BZ* 13 (1969): 207–23; C. M. Tuckett, "The Temptation Narrative in Q," in F. Van Segbroeck et al. (eds.), *The Four Gospels 1992: Festschrift Frans Neirynck* (BETL 100; 3 vols., Leuven: Peeters and Leuven University Press, 1992), 1:479–507.

[89] P. Doble, "The Temptations," *ExpT* 72 (1960): 91–93; J. T. Fitzgerald, "The Temptation of Jesus: The Testing of the Messiah in Matthew," *RestQ* 15 (1972): 152–60; P. Pokorny, "The Temptation Stories and Their Intention," *NTS* 20 (1974): 115–27; W. Stegemann, "Die Versuchung Jesu im Matthäusevangelium: Mt 4,1–11," *EvT* 45 (1985): 29–44; F. Neugebauer, *Jesu Versuchung: Wegentscheidung am Anfang* (Tübingen: Mohr-Siebeck, 1986).

the casting out of evil spirits (cf. Mark 1:34, 39; 3:15, 22, 23; 6:13; 7:26; 9:18, 28, 38). It is not surprising therefore that both Matthew (4:1) and Luke (4:1) replace "drive out" with forms of "lead (up)." Had Matthew written first and Mark later, it would be difficult to explain Mark's replacement of *anagein* with *ekballein*. Matthew's use of *anagein*, moreover, may also have been intended to recall Israel's being led up from Egypt, through the wilderness, and on to the promised land (cf. Num 20:5; LXX 1 Sam 12:6; LXX Ps 80:1).

A Closer Look: Demons in the Desert

First-century readers and hearers of this account would immediately have thought of the dangers of evil spirits in the "wilderness."[90] It was widely believed in late antiquity that wilderness areas were haunted by evil spirits, who often took the form of or inhabited various animals, such as jackals and poisonous snakes. (It is to this popular belief that Mark 1:13 refers when "wild beasts" are mentioned.) The angel Raphael binds the demon Azael and casts him into the desert (*1 Enoch* 10:4). In answer to Abraham's prayer, "wild beasts came out of the desert, and devoured" men who had committed murder (*T. Abr.* B 12:10–11). In the face of martyrdom, the righteous Israelite woman declares: "No destroyer of the desert injured me; nor did the destructive, deceitful snake make spoil of my chaste virginity …" (*4 Macc* 18:8). The linkage of evil spirits and wilderness is illustrated in one of the fragmentary texts from Qumran:

⁴ And I, the Instructor, proclaim His glorious splendor so as to frighten and to te[rrify] ⁵ all the spirits of the destroying angels, spirits of the bastards, demons, Lilith, howlers, and [desert dwellers …] ⁶ and those which fall upon men without warning to lead them astray from a spirit of understanding and to make their heart and their […] desolate during the present dominion of ⁷ wickedness … (4Q510 frag. 1, lines 4–7 = 4Q511 frag. 10, lines 1–3)

The devil's temptation of Jesus may also recall the temptation Abraham faced when God commanded him to sacrifice his son Isaac (LXX Gen 22:1, "God tested [*peirazein*] Abraham and said to him …"), especially if the heavenly confirmation, "This is my Son, the Beloved" (Matt 3:17), does indeed allude to Gen 22:2 (LXX Gen 22:1). The Genesis story, at least as it is preserved in the Hebrew and the Greek (LXX), says nothing about Satan (or the devil). However, in later Jewish interpretations, Satan is understood as the motivating force behind the temptation. According

---

⁹⁰ For a review of the linguistic, thematic, and geographical dimensions of the idea of "wilderness" in Jewish thought in late antiquity, see R. W. Funk, "The Wilderness," *JBL* 77 (1959): 205–14.

to *Jubilees* (second century B.C.), "Prince Mastema" (i.e., Satan) urges God to put Abraham to the test to see if he is truly faithful (*Jub.* 17:16; 18:12; the same interpretive tradition reappears in the late rabbinical writing *Pirqe de-Rabbi Eliezer*). This interpretive tradition was probably inspired by the story of Satan's testing of Job.

The word "devil" is not really a personal name (any more than Satan is). Devil (Greek: *diabolos*) means "one who slanders," "accuses," or "speaks against." We see this in the Book of Job, where Satan (literally "the satan," the one who opposes) accuses Job of not having a deep commitment to God (Job 1:9–11). In the time of Jesus, several epithets were applied to the devil, including Satan (1 Chron 21:1; Job 1:6; Zech 3:1; *T. Dan* 3:6; *T. Gad* 4:7), Beelzebul (*T. Sol.* 3:1; Matt 10:25; 12:24), Beliar (*T. Reub.* 2:2; *T. Sim.* 5:3; 2 Cor 6:15); Belial (in the Dead Sea Scrolls: CD 4:13; 1QM 1:1; 1QHa 10:18, 24), and Mastemah (4Q225 frag. 2, col. i, line 9; 4Q390 frag. 1, line 11, "angels of Mastemah").[91]

Mark says nothing about fasting, so we should assume that this detail was part of the longer Q version of the story. Matthew tells us that Jesus "fasted forty days and forty nights" (**v. 2**). The lengthy fast sets the stage for the temptations that follow, in which the first one tempts Jesus to turn stones into bread. Mark says nothing about fasting, but he does say that Jesus was in the wilderness "forty days" (Mark 1:13). Matthew also adds "and forty nights," recalling the duration of the rain at the time of the flood (cf. Gen 7:4, 12), the length of Moses' stay on Mount Sinai (cf. Exod 24:18; 34:28), and the length of time that Elijah, on the run and hiding in the wilderness, was sustained by the food that an angel had provided (cf. 1 Kings 19:5–8). The last example is what Matthew's language is intended to evoke, for it offers a close parallel to Jesus' experience in the wilderness (cf. Matt 4:11, where after the temptation ends, angels minister to Jesus, presumably to feed him). It may be noted that fasting sometimes precedes visionary experiences (e.g., 1 Sam 28:20; Dan 10:3; 4 Ezra 5:20; 2 *Bar* 20:5–6). Another interesting parallel is found in the *Apocalypse of Abraham*, a work that dates to the late first century A.D.: "And we went, the two of us alone together, forty days and nights; and I ate no bread and drank no water, because [my] food was to see the angel who was with me, and his discourse with me was my drink" (12:1–2). See also *Hist. Rechab.* 19:6 ("he led me through the wilderness for forty days").

After forty days of fasting, Jesus "was famished" (**v. 2**). His great hunger sets the stage for the first temptation. It also anticipates Jesus' beatitude "Blessed are those who hunger and thirst for righteousness, for they will be filled" (Matt 5:6).

After mentioning Jesus' hunger, Matthew tells us that the "tempter came" (**v. 3**), who is, of course, the devil (vv. 1, 5). The description of the devil as "tempter" (*ho peirazon*) recalls the word used in v. 1 (*peirasthenai*, "to be tempted"). In Matt 16:1,

---

[91]   For a further discussion, see H. A. Kelly, "The Devil in the Desert," *CBQ* 26 (1964): 190–220.

the evangelist will apply this word to the designs of the Pharisees and Sadducees (cf. Matt 19:3; 22:18, 35). Paul refers to the devil as the tempter in 1 Thess 3:5, and in Rev 2:10 the devil and temptation are linked.

The devil begins with the words, "If You are the Son of God" (**v. 3**). Greek has four distinct types of "if-then" sentences. The type here (called a first-class conditional sentence) understands the word "if" (*ei*) as being equivalent to "because" (i.e., "Because you are the Son of God ...."). The tempter is not questioning the reality of Jesus' sonship (and after God himself acknowledged it, what would be the point?); he is suggesting that Jesus do something *in light of his divine sonship*. In a sense, the devil is saying to Jesus, "If you are the Son of God, prove it."

In the Greco-Roman world, the epithet "son of God" evokes ideas of the semi-divine man (often the Roman Caesar) who mediates between heaven and humanity. A text from Qumran speaks of an expected "son of God" and "son of the Most High" (see 4Q246 2:1). However, there are also ideas of "son of God" and "sons of God" in the Hebrew Bible and other early Jewish texts. We think of the mysterious Nephilim and "sons of God" in Gen 6:2, 4, and even more pertinent are the "sons of God" in Job, among whom also was Satan himself (see Job 1:6; also 2:1; 38:7). Also of interest is Ps 82:6–7, "You are gods, children of the Most High, all of you; nevertheless you shall die like mortals, and fall like any prince," a passage that Jesus applies to himself in the Gospel of John (John 10:34).

The devil's proposition, "If (or since) you are the son of God," probably pre-supposes these Old Testament traditions, thus conceding Jesus' place among the heavenly "sons." But if "gods" and "sons of the Most High" can "die like men" (Ps 82:6–7), then there is still a chance that Jesus, too, just like the Israelites of old (to whom Psalm 82 is making reference; cf. *Mek.* on Exod 20:18–19; *Sipre Deut.* §320 [on Deut 32:20]), can be ensnared in sin and destroyed. Or at least the devil hopes.

To demonstrate his divine sonship, Jesus should "command that these stones become loaves of bread" (**v. 3**). The tempter is not asking Jesus to prove anything (and there is no crowd of onlookers on hand to witness what happens); he is tempting Jesus to (mis)use his power to feed himself in the wilderness. Given the Scripture Jesus recites, the parallel is with the Israelites in the wilderness, who grumbled about their lack of bread (cf. Exod 16:1–8). It is interesting to note that in the *Testament of Job* Satan tempts Job, through his wife, by posing as a seller of bread (cf. *T. Job* 22–25).

Jesus replies, "It is written" (**v. 4**), responding to the satanic temptation with an appeal to Scripture. "It is written" is a standard introductory formula found in the Old Testament itself, though with some variations: Josh 8:31, "as it is written in the book of the law of Moses"; 2 Sam 1:18, "it is written in the Book of Jashar"; 2 Kings 23:21, "as it is written in this book of the covenant"; 2 Chron 23:18, "as it is written in the law of Moses"; 2 Chron 25:4, "as it is written in the law in the book of Moses"; 2

Chron 31:3, "as it is written in the law of the Lord"; 2 Chron 35:12 / 1 Esd 1:11, "as it is written in the book of Moses"; Neh 8:15, "as it is written"; Sir 48:10, "it is written."

This introductory formula is commonplace in the Dead Sea Scrolls: CD 7:19, "as it is written"; 1QS 5:15, "for thus it is written"; 4Q174 3:2–3, "as it is written in the book of [Moses]"; 4Q174 3:15, "as it is written in the book of Isaiah the prophet"; 4Q174 3:16, "it is written in the book of Ezekiel the prophet"; 4Q174 4:3, "it is written in the book of Daniel the prophet." In later times, it was routine simply to say "it is written" without specifying where.

There are some interesting variations in some of the Pseudepigrapha. *Jubilees* and the *Testament of Levi* speak of what "is written on heavenly tables" or "tablets" (*Jub.* 4:5; 33:10; 50:12; *T. Levi* 5:4) or "written and ordained" (*Jub.* 5:18; 33:10). Rabbi Yose ben Kisma refers to what "is written in the book of Psalms, by the hands of David, king of Israel" (*m. 'Abot* 6:10).

Jesus quotes part of Deut 8:3: "One does not live by bread alone...." It is the first of three quotations from the Book of Deuteronomy, in the time of Jesus the most often cited book in the Law of Moses.[92] The point is that there is more to sustenance than food for the physical body. This was a lesson that the wilderness generation had difficulty learning, demanding that God provide them with bread (cf. Exodus 16). The bread that the devil suggests Jesus command into existence, as amazing as it may be, will not provide life. Humans live "by every word that comes from the mouth of God." Luke's quotation only includes the first part of the quotation from Deut 8:3 (Luke 4:3, "Man shall not live on bread alone"). It is probable that Matthew added the second clause, and not that Luke omitted it. Matthew's addition is in keeping with his high regard for the Law (cf. Matt 5:17). One is reminded of an old rabbinic saying, "Great is Torah, for it gives to them that practice it life in this world and [life] in the world to come" (*m. 'Abot* 6:7).

For the second temptation of Jesus, "the devil took him to the holy city" (**v. 5**). The "holy city" is Jerusalem (which is how it reads in Luke 4:9); the phrase comes from Matthew and is found in Scripture in reference to Jerusalem (e.g., Isa 52:1, "Put on your beautiful garments, O Jerusalem, the holy city" [also quoted in 4Q176 frags. 8–11, line 2]; Neh. 11:1, "to live in Jerusalem, the holy city"; Tob 13:9, "O Jerusalem, the holy city"; *Pss. Sol.* 8:4, "towards Jerusalem, the holy city").

---

[92]   For studies that have examined the role of Deuteronomy and other scriptural traditions in Matthew's temptation narrative, see J. Dupont, "L'arrière-fond biblique du récit des tentations de Jésus," *NTS* 3 (1957): 287–304; A. B. Taylor, "Decision in the Desert: The Temptation of Jesus in the Light of Deuteronomy," *Int* 14 (1960): 300–9; B. Gerhardsson, *The Testing of God's Son (Matt 4:1–11 & Par.): An Analysis of Early Christian Midrash* (ConBNT 2/1; Lund: Gleerup, 1966); W. R. Stegner, "The Use of Scripture in Two Narratives of Early Jewish Christianity (Matthew 4.1–11; Mark 9.2–8)," in C. A. Evans and J. A. Sanders, *Early Christian Interpretation of the Scriptures of Israel: Investigations and Proposals* (JSNTSup 148; SSEJC 5; Sheffield: Sheffield Academic Press, 1997), 98–120, especially 99–110.

How the devil took Jesus to the city is not clear; it is probably visionary.[93] There are traditions of miraculous transport. Probably the most pertinent is found in Ezekiel, where the prophet says an angel

stretched out the form of a hand and caught me by a lock of my head; and the Spirit lifted me up between earth and heaven and brought me in the visions of God to Jerusalem, to the entrance of the north gate of the inner court, where the seat of the idol of jealousy, which provokes to jealousy, was located. (Ezek 8:3)

Similarly, in Bel and the Dragon, one of the later additions to the Book of Daniel, an angel of the Lord lifts the prophet Habakkuk "by the crown of his head" and conveys him to the den of lions in Babylon to feed Daniel (Bel and the Dragon 36 = Dan 14:36 in the Vulgate).

The devil places Jesus "on the pinnacle of the temple." We are not certain of the precise location of the temple's pinnacle. An old description may give us a rough idea: "But in order that we might gain complete information, we ascended to the summit of the neighboring citadel and looked around us. It is situated in a very lofty spot, and is fortified with many towers, which have been built up to the very top of immense stones, with the object, as we were informed, of guarding the temple precincts" (*Letter of Aristeas* 100). In describing the great height of the Royal Portico, which was part of the temple complex, Josephus says that looking down into the valley below made one "dizzy" (*Ant.* 15.411–12).

The devil once again tempts Jesus, reminding him that he is the "Son of God," urging him to throw himself down from the pinnacle of the temple. And why not? After all, "it is written, 'He will command his angels concerning you'" (**v. 6**). Satan counters Jesus with a Scripture quotation of his own. After all, in the first temptation, Jesus said that one lives "by every word that comes from the mouth of God" (v. 4). So the devil has taken Jesus at his word. One of the words "from the mouth of God" is his assurance that his angels will protect his people. Because Jesus is the Son of God, he may throw himself from the pinnacle of the temple without fear, knowing that God will protect him with his angels.

Satan has quoted from Ps 91:11–12. It was an appropriate passage to select, given the context, for in late antiquity Psalm 91 was understood as providing assurance and aid against demons. "You will not fear the terror of the night, or the arrow that flies by day" in v. 5 becomes in the Aramaic paraphrase "Be not afraid of the terror of demons who walk at night, of the arrow of the angel of death that he looses during the day." "Or the pestilence that stalks in darkness, or the destruction that wastes at noonday" in v. 6 becomes in the Aramaic paraphrase "Of the death that walks in darkness, of the band of demons that attacks at noon." And finally, "No evil shall

93 D. A. Hagner, *Matthew* (1993–1995), 1:66: "In his trance-like vision Jesus sees himself perched upon one of the highest points of the temple." See also R. T. France, *The Gospel of Matthew* (2007), 131–32.

befall you, no scourge come near your tent" in v. 10 becomes in the Aramaic "No harm shall happen to you; and no plague or demon shall come near to your tents."

It is quite interesting to observe that in one of the Psalms scrolls from Qumran's cave 11 (11Q11), Psalm 91 is preceded by three apocryphal psalms devoted to exorcism. This contextualization suggests that Psalm 91 was understood very much the way it is paraphrased in the later Aramaic version. Thus, it would seem that the devil quoted from Psalm 91 as part of his ploy to assure Jesus that he has nothing to fear, that he may throw himself down and be assured that God's angels will protect him. That Jesus understood Psalm 91 as offering protection against evil spirits is seen in his own allusion to it when the seventy disciples return rejoicing because of their power over evil spirits. Jesus is remembered to have replied: "I watched Satan fall from heaven.... I have given you authority to tread on snakes and scorpions, and over all the power of the enemy" (Luke 10:18–19). The words "authority to trample [*patein*] on snakes and scorpions" probably allude to Ps 91:13 (LXX: "on asp and cobra you will tread [*katapateseis*]"), which are also alluded to in *T. Levi* 18:12 ("Beliar will be bound by him, and he will give authority to his children to trample [*patein*] upon the evil spirits") in a context that is clearly in reference to Satan.

Notwithstanding the devil's quotation of an appropriate and reassuring passage of Scripture, Jesus counters, "Again it is written" (**v. 7**). Jesus rebuts the devil's offer with another Scripture. Playing one Scripture against another was part of Jewish interpretation in late antiquity. In a sense, Jesus and the devil are disputing with one another in a rabbinic fashion.

Once again, Jesus appeals to a passage from Deuteronomy: "Do not put the Lord your God to the test." Jesus counters with a quotation of part of Deut 6:16, which referred to Israel's failure at Massah, where the people demanded water as proof of God's fidelity (cf. Exod 17:2–7; Ps 95:7–9). Jesus will not place himself in danger in order to put God to the test. We hear similar expressions in the works of the Rabbis. For example, Rabbi Yannai is remembered to have said: "A man should never stand in place of danger [purposely] saying that God will perform a miracle for him, for perchance no miracle will be performed for him" (*b. Shab.* 32a).

For the third temptation, the devil took Jesus "to a very high mountain" (**v. 8**). Again, this is visionary, so we should not expect to be able to identify a specific mountain in or near Israel. Nevertheless, "high" mountains do figure significantly in Jewish traditions (see Isa 40:9; Ezek 17:23; 20:40; 40:2; Bar 5:7). Two passages from intertestamental writings could be especially pertinent. The patriarch Levi describes a dream: "And I beheld a high mountain, and I was upon it" (*T. Levi* 2:5). A vision is explained to Enoch: "This high mountain which you have seen, whose summit is like the throne of God, is his throne, where the Holy Great One, the Lord of Glory, the Eternal King, will sit, when he shall come down to visit the earth with goodness" (*1 Enoch* 25:3).

The devil showed Jesus "all the kingdoms of the world and their splendor" (**v. 8**). Taking Jesus up to a high mountain, that he may see "all the kingdoms of the world," may allude to Deut 34:1–4, where God showed Moses the length and breadth of the Promised Land. But the parallel is inexact, for the devil shows Jesus the kingdoms of the world, not the land of Israel, and offers to give them to him, not withhold them. We should understand these kingdoms as Gentile kingdoms, some of which have oppressed Israel and some, like the Roman Empire, that still do. The devil promises to give "all these" to Jesus. This is a dream offer for a would-be messianic leader of Israel itching to throw off the Gentile yoke. The language of the devil's offer, "all these I will give you," parallels the *Testament of Job*, in which the devil gains authority over all that Job owns (*T. Job* 8:1–3; 16:2).

There is only one catch: to gain mastery of all of the kingdoms of the world, Jesus must "fall down and worship" the devil. Falling down and worshiping (or paying homage) occurs two other times in Matthew (i.e., Matt 2:11; 18:26) and occurs ten other times elsewhere in the New Testament (e.g., Acts 10:25; 1 Cor 14:25). These words in combination occur in the Greek Old Testament (i.e., the Septuagint, abbreviated LXX) several times as well (e.g., Ruth 2:10; 1 Sam 20:41; 25:23). In 2 Chron 7:3; 20:18; 29:30; Jth 6:18; 1 Macc 4:55; and Sir 50:17, Israelites fall down and worship God (see also *1 Enoch* 48:5; 57:3; 62:9; 63:1). But in Dan 3:5–7, 10–11, 15, Nebuchadnezzar insists that all in his kingdom, including the Jewish exiles, fall down and worship his golden image. This Daniel will not do. We probably have here our closest parallel to Satan's offer to Jesus. Ironically, if Jesus worships the devil, then he is no longer God's Son; he becomes Satan's servant.

In response to the third temptation, by far the most blasphemous and spiritually dangerous, Jesus commands, "Away with you, Satan!" (**v. 10**). Jesus' command "Away!" parallels his exorcisms, where he orders unclean spirits to depart: "Go!" (Matt 8:32); "I command you, come out of him, and never enter him again!" (Mark 9:25). One again thinks of the *Testament of Moses*, in which the hope is expressed that when the kingdom of God appears, "then Satan will be no more, and sorrow shall depart with him" (*T. Moses* 10:1).

Jesus cites Deuteronomy yet again, instructing Satan: "Worship the Lord your God, and serve him only." In his third reply to the devil, Jesus quotes from Deut 6:13. Thus we see Jesus quoting from Deuteronomy three times, and in descending order: 8:3; 6:16; and 6:13. (There are four texts if we count Deut 9:9, which tells of Moses being with the Lord "forty days and forty nights," eating no bread and drinking no water, perhaps alluded to in Matt 4:2.)

The contest for now is over. The NRSV translates, "Then the devil left him" (**v. 11**). However, the Greek text reads literally "the devil leaves him." The present tense may suggest that the struggle is not over (cf. Luke 4:13). The devil departs and "suddenly angels came and waited on him." Just as Elijah was sustained for forty days thanks to the food brought to him by an angel of the Lord (1 Kings 19:4–8), now angels minister to Jesus after his forty-day fast. At this moment of trial, Jesus accepts angelic ministrations, but during his Passion, the very evening of his arrest, he refuses to request angelic aid (cf. Matt 26:53).

MATTHEW 4:12–17 – PROCLAMATION IN GALILEE

4:12: Now when Jesus heard that John had been arrested, he withdrew to Galilee.

4:13: He left Nazareth and made his home in Capernaum by the sea, in the territory of Zebulun and Naphtali,

4:14: so that what had been spoken through the prophet Isaiah might be fulfilled:

4:15: "Land of Zebulun, land of Naphtali, on the road by the sea, across the Jordan, Galilee of the Gentiles –

4:16: the people who sat in darkness have seen a great light, and for those who sat in the region and shadow of death light has dawned."

4:17: From that time Jesus began to proclaim, "Repent, for the kingdom of heaven has come near."

*W*ith the arrest of John the Baptist, the ministry of Jesus of Nazareth begins. Matthew's narrative is an expansion of Mark 1:14–15. Its distinctive feature is the citation of Isa 9:1–2, which is to show that Jesus' ministry in Galilee fulfills prophetic Scripture.

After his baptism in the Jordan and temptation in the wilderness, Jesus returns to Galilee (**v. 12**). But he does not take up residence in Nazareth, his hometown, but rather in Capernaum (**v. 13**). Capernaum is located on the northwest shore of Lake Gennesaret (a.k.a. the Sea of Galilee). The name literally means "village of Nahum." It was a bustling fishing village in Jesus' day, with a population of about 1,000.[94] In the 1980s, a first-century fishing boat was recovered not far from Capernaum.[95] Archaeological excavations have uncovered the black basalt foundation of an ancient synagogue (on top of which the white limestone ruins of a fourth-century A.D. synagogue rest). In all probability, this is the very synagogue in which Jesus preached, healed, and debated (cf. Matt 8:5; 17:24). The building was made up primarily of two large rooms, one for worship and one for social activity. In the former, Jesus preached (Matt 13:53–58); in the latter, he healed (Matt 12:9–14).[96] Byzantine

---

[94]   S. E. Johnson, *Jesus and His Towns* (1989), 67–71; J. E. Sanderson, "Capernaum," in R. K. Harrison (ed.), *Major Cities of the Biblical World* (Nashville, TN: Thomas Nelson, 1985), 72–82.

[95]   For a discussion of this find, along with photographs, see S. Wachsmann et al., *The Excavations of an Ancient Boat in the Sea of Galilee (Lake Kinneret)* ('Atiqot English Series 19; Jerusalem: Israel Antiquities Authority, 1990).

[96]   See A. Runesson, D. D. Binder, and B. Olsson, *The Ancient Synagogue from Its Origins to 200 CE: A Source Book* (Leiden: Brill, 2010), 25–32; A. Runesson, "Architecture, Conflict, and Identity Formation: Jews and Christians in Capernaum from the First to the Sixth Century," in J. Zangenberg et al. (eds.), *Religion, Ethnicity, and Identity in Ancient Galilee: A Region in Transition* (WUNT 210; Tübingen: Mohr Siebeck, 2007), 231–57.

Christians built a small octagonal church over and around the remains of a house
that evidently belonged to a fisherman, in the belief that it was the very house of
Simon Peter (Matt 8:14). Millstones have been uncovered in and around Capernaum.
These stones, if tied around the neck of a person who was then thrown into the lake,
would prove fatal (Matt 18:6). Finally, recent excavations may have uncovered the
remains of Roman buildings (see the commentary on Matt 8:5–13).[97]

Matthew explains that Capernaum is "by the sea, in the territory of Zebulun
and Naphtali" (**v. 14**). This geographical information is preparation for the quotation that follows: "so that what had been spoken through the prophet Isaiah might
be fulfilled: 'Land of Zebulun, land of Naphtali, on the road by the sea, across the
Jordan, Galilee of the Gentiles ...'" (**vv. 14–15**). Matthew is fond of formal quotations
of Scripture to show how Jesus has fulfilled this or that passage. Here he appeals to
Isa 9:1–2 to show that the coming of the Messiah to Galilee, in which Gentiles reside
(especially in the eastern part of the province and to the east of the Jordan, in the
area called the Decapolis), fulfills Scripture.

The coming of Jesus to Galilee will give "the people who sat in darkness" and
"in the region and shadow of death" the opportunity to see the dawning of "light"
(**v. 15**). The passage is well chosen, for in the Targum Isa 9:1–7 is rendered in a
messianic sense. The Hebrew's "For a child has been born for us, a son given to us;
authority rests upon his shoulders; and he is named Wonderful Counselor, Mighty
God, Everlasting Father, Prince of Peace" (Isa 9:6) reads in the Aramaic version "*The
prophet said to the house of David,* 'For to us a child is born, to us a son is given; and
he will accept the Law upon himself to keep it, and his name will be called *before the*
Wonderful Counselor, *the* Mighty God, existing forever, *The Messiah in whose days
peace will increase upon us*'" (*Tg.* Isa 9:6, with italics indicating departures from the
Hebrew). The Aramaic reader understands the passage as pertaining to a prophetic
oracle that applies to the "house of David." However, the exalted titles "Wonderful
Counselor" and "Mighty God" ("Father" drops out, leaving behind "everlasting" or
"existing forever") are understood to refer to God, not to the Messiah. That is the
significance of the insertion of "before." In other words, the Messiah will not be
called "Mighty God" but "The Messiah in whose days peace will increase upon us"
before or *in the presence of* God Almighty, the Wonderful Counselor, who exists forever. The Aramaic version respects Jewish monotheistic sensitivities in that it will
not allow divine attributes to be applied to David's descendent, but it does recognize
this descendant as the Messiah, who accepts the Law and keeps it. This latter feature

[97] J. F. Strange, "Has the House Where Jesus Stayed in Capernaum Been Found?" *BAR* 8, no.
6 (1982): 26–37; J. F. Strange and H. Shanks, "Synagogue Where Jesus Preached Found at
Capernaum," *BAR* 9, no. 6 (1983): 24–31; V. Tzaferis, "New Archaeological Evidence on
Ancient Capernaum," *BA* 46 (1983): 198–204; J. C. H. Laughlin, "Capernaum from Jesus'
Time and After," *BAR* 19, no. 5 (1993): 54–61, 90; J. J. Rousseau and R. Arav, *Jesus and His
World: An Archaeological and Cultural Dictionary* (Minneapolis: Fortress, 1995), 39–47;
H. I. MacAdam, "Domus Domini: Where Jesus Lived (Capernaum and Bethany in the
Gospels)," *Theological Review* 25 (2004): 46–76.

is entirely consistent with Matthew's portrait of Jesus the Messiah, for he, too, keeps the Law (cf. Matt 5:17–20).

The "land of Zebulun" refers to the territory that was allotted to the tribe of Zebulun when the people of Israel settled in the Promised Land (Josh 19:10; 19:16, 27; 21:34; Judg 1:30). Zebulun was the sixth son of Jacob and Leah; the name means "dwelling" (cf. Gen 30:20). The "land of Naphtali" likewise refers to the territory allotted to the tribe of Naphtali. Naphtali was the second son of Bilhah, Rachel's maid; the name means "wrestling" (cf. Gen 30:8; 35:25). The tribe of Naphtali also settled in the north (cf. Deut 33:23; 34:2; Josh 19:32; 20:7, "So they set apart Kedesh in Galilee in the hill country of Naphtali, and Shechem in the hill country of Ephraim, and Kiriath-arba (that is, Hebron) in the hill country of Judah").

Matthew tells us that "from that time" (that is, from the time of John's arrest) "Jesus began to proclaim, 'Repent, for the kingdom of heaven has come near'" (**v. 17**). The very words of Jesus' message are identical to the words of John the Baptist (cf. Matt 3:2), thus drawing the two preachers closer together and underscoring how in fact John prepared the way for Jesus' proclamation of God's rule.[98] The introduction of Jesus' preaching with the quotation of Isa 9:1–2 shows that this preaching is the fulfillment of the prophetic promise that someday light will dawn on the people of Galilee.[99]

With his arrest, John's public ministry has come to an end. With his (implied) successful completion of the period of testing, Jesus' public ministry may commence. We were told in Matt 3:1 that John was preaching in the wilderness near the Jordan. Now we are told in Matt 4:12–17 that Jesus was preaching the "kingdom of heaven" in Galilee. Whereas John called for repentance and baptized those who came to him (Matt 3:1, 6), promising the coming of a mightier one who would baptize with fire (Matt 3:11–12), Jesus now proclaims that the "kingdom of heaven has come near" (Matt 4:17). The call for repentance continues an important aspect of John's message and mission.

> **A Closer Look: Kingdom of "God" and Kingdom of "Heaven"**
>
> Readers of the Synoptic Gospels will readily perceive Matthew's preference for the expression "kingdom of heaven." This expression occurs twenty-two times in Matthew and not once in Mark and Luke. In Mark, we find "kingdom of God" fourteen times; in Luke, we find the expression thirteen times. However, "kingdom of God" also occurs in Matthew, some four times. Two

---

[98] H. Merklein, "Die Umkehrpredigt bei Johannes dem Täufer und Jesus von Nazaret," *BZ* 25 (1981): 29–46.

[99] G. M. Soares-Prabhu, "Matthew 4:14–16: A Key to the Origin of the Formula Quotations of Matthew," *Indian Journal of Theology* 20 (1971): 70–91.

of the occurrences of "kingdom of God" in Matthew have been carried over from the evangelist's sources: that in Matt 12:28 from Q (cf. Luke 11:20) and that in Matt 19:24 from Mark (Mark 10:25). The two other occurrences appear in what seems to be special Matthean material: Matt 21:31, 43. No distinction should be made between "kingdom of God" and "kingdom of heaven." Both expressions refer to God's rule. Matthew's preference for "kingdom of heaven" was probably out of respect for the sanctity of God's name. By saying "heaven," he avoided saying "God," though his hearers all knew that "heaven" in fact referred to God. In pious Jewish circles, the name of God was often avoided. Instead of pronouncing the holy name Yahweh, Jews would (and still do) pronounce Adonai ("Lord"). Other substitutions were used, such as "Blessed," "Power," or "heaven." Sometimes the grammar was altered so that "God" would not have to be mentioned (e.g., saying "he was delivered," instead of "God delivered him," or what is called the "divine passive").[100]

What did Jesus mean by speaking of the "kingdom of heaven (God)"? As we shall see in Matt 4:23, the kingdom is the central datum of his proclamation of the good news, or gospel. This question will be treated in the commentary on Matt 4:23–25.

MATTHEW 4:18–22 – THE CALL OF THE FIRST DISCIPLES

4:18: **As he walked by the Sea of Galilee, he saw two brothers, Simon, who is called Peter, and Andrew his brother, casting a net into the sea – for they were fishermen.**

4:19: **And he said to them, "Follow me, and I will make you fish for people."**

4:20: **Immediately they left their nets and followed him.**

4:21: **As he went from there, he saw two other brothers, James son of Zebedee and his brother John, in the boat with their father Zebedee, mending their nets, and he called them.**

4:22: **Immediately they left the boat and their father, and followed him.**

*M*atthew 4:18–22 represents a slight reworking of Mark 1:16–20. Jesus calls his first disciples, though they will not be referred to as "disciples" until Matt 5:1 (or perhaps not until 10:1, where we find reference to the "twelve disciples"). The story raises several questions: (1) Why does Jesus call these men? The call is abrupt;

---

[100] For the suggestion that "kingdom of heaven" in Matthew may have involved more than a mere circumlocution out of respect for the name of God, see R. Foster, "Why on Earth use 'Kingdom of Heaven'? Matthew's Terminology Revisited," *NTS* 48 (2002): 487–99.

there is no preparation for it. (2) What does the odd saying "I shall make you fish for people" mean? (3) Why do these fishermen drop everything and follow Jesus? These features evidently troubled Luke, who narrates Jesus' teaching and the miraculous catch of fish (Luke 5:1–11) before the call of the first disciples. Moreover, Luke omits the odd saying about fishing for people. The second question is not too difficult, but the first and third questions cannot be answered with more than speculation.

Matthew may have appreciated, in the story of the abruptness of the summons to discipleship, the authority of Jesus. When he calls, people jump. Little or no preamble is required. Most impressive is the comment that James and John "left the boat and their father, and followed him" (**v. 22**).[101]

The toponym "Sea of Galilee" (**v. 18**) also appears in Matt 4:18 and 15:29 (cf. Mark 1:16; 3:7; 7:31; John 6:1). The lake is also called the Sea of Tiberias or Lake of Tiberias (John 21:1; Josephus, *J.W.* 3.57), a name reflecting the prominent lakeside city Tiberias (John 6:6; Josephus, *J.W.* 2.68; Josephus, *Ant.* 18.36; Pausanias, *Descr.* 5.7.4; *t. Sukkah* 3.9). The distinctive *Sea* of Galilee (instead of Lake of Galilee, Kinneret Lake, Lake of Gennesar, or Lake of Tiberias) may have suggested itself to early Christian narrators of the story of Jesus who were under the influence of Isa 8:23 (Eng. 9:1), where Galilee is linked with the "way of the sea, the land beyond the Jordan." Thus, the toponym "Sea of Galilee" may have had a Christian origin.[102]

The Sea of Galilee is some 630 feet below sea level (second-lowest lake in the world; only the Dead Sea is lower, at 1,300 feet). The Golan Heights lie to the northwest. Approximately 33 miles in circumference, the lake is about 13 miles long (north to south) and about 8 miles wide at its widest point. It is fed by springs, the Jordan River (from the north), and a few other small streams. The Jordan River continues its flow out of the south end of the lake and continues south to the Dead Sea. The Sea of Galilee supported (and still supports) a thriving fishing industry.

The Synoptic accounts of Jesus' calling of his disciples are modeled after Elijah's call of Elisha (1 Kings 19:19–21; cf. Luke 5:1–11; and especially 9:59–60).[103] Matthew's narrative follows Mark's closely, though Matthew adds to the mention of Simon's name the phrase "who is called Peter" (**v. 18**; see also Matt 10:2; 16:18) and omits

---

[101]   Jesus' distinctive summons of disciples has generated considerable scholarly interest. See M. Hengel, *The Charismatic Leader and His Followers* (New York: Crossroad, 1981); J. D. G. Dunn, *Jesus' Call to Discipleship* (Cambridge: Cambridge University Press, 1992). For studies on discipleship in Matthew, see M. J. Wilkins, *The Concept of Disciple in Matthew's Gospel as Reflected in the Use of the Term* μαθητής (NovTSup 59; Leiden: Brill, 1988); J. A. Cabrido, "A Typology for Discipleship: The Narrative Function of PAIDION in Matthew's Story of Jesus," *ABR* 57 (2009): 47–60.

[102]   For more on this question, see R. S. Notley, "The Sea of Galilee: Development of an Early Christian Toponym," *JBL* 128 (2009): 183–88.

[103]   A. J. Droge, "Call Stories in Greek Biography and the Gospels," *SBL 1983 Seminar Papers* (1983): 245–57; J. R. Butts, "The Voyage of Discipleship: Narrative, Chreia, and Call Story," in C. A. Evans and W. F. Stinespring (eds.), *Early Jewish and Christian Exegesis: Studies in Memory of William Hugh Brownlee* (Homage 10; Atlanta: Scholars Press, 1987), 199–219.

Mark's "with the hired men" (Mark 1:20). On "boat" (**v. 21**), see the discussion of the Galilee boat in Matt 8:23.

Jesus summons Simon and Andrew (and presumably the two sons of Zebedee as well) with the words, "Follow me, and I will make you fish for people" (**v. 19**). The comparison between catching fish and catching people cannot be pressed. After all, catching fish is not for the benefit of the fish! The point of the comparison is that in following Jesus these Galilean fishermen will no longer be pursuing fish; they will be pursuing human beings.[104]

MATTHEW 4:23–25 – THE BEGINNINGS OF MINISTRY

4:23: Jesus went throughout Galilee, teaching in their synagogues and proclaiming the good news of the kingdom and curing every disease and every sickness among the people.
4:24: So his fame spread throughout all Syria, and they brought to him all the sick, those who were afflicted with various diseases and pains, demoniacs, epileptics, and paralytics, and he cured them.
4:25: And great crowds followed him from Galilee, the Decapolis, Jerusalem, Judea, and from beyond the Jordan.

*M*atthew 4:23–25 represents a thorough revision of Mark 1:35–39. In the Markan passage, Jesus seeks solitude, and when told that people are searching for him, he tells his disciples it is time to go elsewhere. It almost sounds as if Jesus' goal is to avoid people. Matthew (and Luke, too) understandably rewrites the passage, transforming it into a summary of Jesus' ministry, a ministry of preaching the good news of the kingdom and healing the sick and demonized.

Matthew says that Jesus traveled throughout Galilee, "teaching in their synagogues and proclaiming the good news of the kingdom and curing" (**v. 23**). With three participles – teaching, proclaiming (or preaching), and curing (or healing) – Matthew summarizes Jesus' Galilean ministry. For Jesus, works of power always accompany his powerful words.

Twentieth-century archaeology has uncovered a number of ancient synagogues, some clearly dating to the time before the destruction of the second temple in 70 A.D. These synagogues include those at Capernaum, Gamala, Jericho, Masada, Herodium, Qumran, and Migdal.[105] The Theodotos inscription, found in the 70 A.D.

---

[104] For more discussion, see J. Mánek, "Fishers of Men," *NovT* 2 (1958): 138–41; W. Wuellner, *The Meaning of "Fishers of Men"* (Philadelphia: Westminster, 1967); J. Murphy-O'Connor, "Fishers of Fish, Fishers of Men: What We Know of the First Disciples from Their Profession," *Bible Review* 15, no. 3 (1999): 22–27, 48–49.
[105] The discovery of the synagogue from the second-temple era was reported by the Israel Antiquities Authority in September 2009. Among other things are a mosaic and a stone

rubble of Jerusalem, and the North African inscription, dating from 55 A.D., indicate two more synagogues from before 70 A.D. The synagogues at Delos (one of the small islands of the Aegean Sea) and Ostia in Italy (near the mouth of the Tiber River) may also be older than 70 A.D. The Capernaum synagogue, which has been partially restored, dates to the third or fourth century. However, the underlying black basalt foundation dates to the first century, if not earlier.[106]

In the synagogues and out in the open air, Jesus proclaimed the good news of God's rule. The Greek word "good news" or "gospel" (*euaggelion*) in earliest Christianity in all probability derives from Isaiah (Hebrew: *besora*) and not from Greco-Roman usage (though later the parallel would be exploited, as in Mark 1:1, which alludes to the cult of the divine emperor). Isaiah 40, 52, and 61 contributed to the substance and manner of Jesus' preaching and teaching (Matt 11:2–6 = Luke 7:18–23; Luke 4:16–30). Isaiah had promised the good news of God's reign (Isa 52:7, "Your God reigns!"; *Tg.* Isa 52:7, "the kingdom of your God is revealed"; cf. *Tg.* Isa 40:9), which Jesus now proclaims (Matt 4:17, "the kingdom of God has come near"). The "gospel," or good news, is that the promised and awaited kingdom of God is now here.

If we follow the lead of the Targum (the Aramaic paraphrase of the Old Testament), then we should understand the kingdom of God as a way of speaking of the presence and reign of God,[107] a concept that includes realm or sphere.[108] The clearest indication of this is seen in synoptic traditions outside of Mark, where Jesus says, "If by the finger of God I cast out demons, the kingdom of God has come upon you" (Luke 11:20). Mark, however, displays only modest interest in the kingdom.

---

relief depicting the menorah. There are now seven synagogues found in the land of Israel that are known to date to a time before the destruction of Jerusalem. The Theodotos inscription refers to an eighth. One should consult A. Runesson, D. D. Binder, and B. Olsson, *The Ancient Synagogue from Its Origins to 200 CE* (2010).

[106] J. F. Strange and H. Shanks, "Synagogue Where Jesus Preached Found at Capernaum," *BAR* 9, no. 6 (1983): 24–31; Y. Tsafrir, "The Synagogues at Capernaum and Meroth and the Dating of the Galilean Synagogue," in J. H. Humphrey (ed.), *The Roman and Byzantine Near East: Some Recent Archaeological Research* (Journal of Roman Archaeology, Supplementary Series 14; Ann Arbor: University of Michigan, 1995), 151–61. Not long ago, a first-century synagogue was discovered at Magdala, presumably Mary Magdalene's hometown. See J. K. Zangenberg, "Archaeological News from the Galilee: Tiberias, Magdala and Rural Galilee," *Early Christianity* 1 (2010): 471–84, especially 476–77.

[107] On the relevance of the Targum for understanding the meaning of "kingdom of God" in Jesus' preaching, see B. D. Chilton, "Regnum Dei Deus Est," *SJT* 31 (1978): 261–70; B. D. Chilton, *God in Strength: Jesus' Announcement of the Kingdom* (SNTU B1; Freistadt: Plöchl, 1979; repr. BibSem 8; Sheffield: JSOT Press, 1987), 97–121. On Matthew's specific expression "kingdom of heaven," see R. Deines, *Die Gerechtigkeit der Tora im Reich des Messias* (2004), 103–20.

[108] Most modern lexica dismiss the meaning of *realm* when referring to the *basileia* of God. This needs to be rethought. The point has been well argued recently by H. Kvalbein (in a paper read at the annual SNTS meeting in Berlin in 2010, to be published in due course).

More often than not, references to the kingdom have more to do with membership and who may enter the kingdom and who may not and why. For Mark, Christology is paramount. Recognizing Jesus' messianic identity and divine sonship is more important than emphasizing the kingdom.

Matthew says that Jesus was "curing every disease and every sickness among the people" (**v. 23**). The evangelist's combined reference to disease (*nosos*) and sickness (*malakia*) reappears in Matt 9:35 and 10:1 and may allude to Deut 7:15, "the Lord will remove from you all sickness [LXX: *malakia*]; and he will not inflict on you any of the harmful diseases [LXX: *nosos*] of Egypt which you have known, but he will lay them on all who hate you" (cf. 2 Chron 21:15, 19; *T. Joseph* 17:7). If so, it may suggest that Matthew sees Jesus' ministry of healing as being in fulfillment of promises linked to the Promised Land and hopes of national renewal. This interpretation is consistent with the wilderness theme and quotations of and allusions to Deuteronomy that were observed in the temptation narrative (Matt 4:1–11). Good health, plenty, and relief from disease and oppression were part of the messianic hope of late antiquity (cf. Isa 26:19; 29:18; 35:5–6; 61:1; *Jub.* 23:28–30; 2 *Bar* 73:2–3; 4 Ezra 8:53; 4Q521).

Because of Jesus' proclamation of the good news of God's rule and his remarkable ability to heal, "his fame spread throughout all Syria" (**v. 24a**). Matthew has reworked Mark 1:28 ("his fame began to spread throughout the surrounding region of Galilee"). It has been suggested that Matthew adds "Syria" (and apart from the mention of Quirinius, governor of Syria, no other Gospel mentions Syria) because he came from this part of the world, perhaps Antioch (e.g., Acts 15:23, "the believers of Gentile origin in Antioch and Syria"). Perhaps, but it is more likely that Syria, the smaller region north of Galilee extending from Damascus to Antioch and favored by a significant Jewish population (cf. Josephus, *J. W.* 7.43, "the Jewish race … particularly numerous in Syria"), was understood by Matthew to be part of greater Israel, which in the messianic era would be included in a restored and renewed Israel (cf. Gen 15:18, "from the river of Egypt to the great river, the river Euphrates"; Exod 23:31; Num 13:21; 34:7–9; Deut 1:7–8, "and the Lebanon, as far as the great river, the river Euphrates"; Ezek 47:15–17, "the boundary shall run from the sea to Hazarenon, which is north of the border of Damascus, with the border of Hamath to the north"). In the Targums and rabbinic literature, the northern border of restored Israel will include Syria.[109]

---

[109] See the Introduction to the commentary (pp. 5–6). For a discussion of the greatly enlarged boundaries of Israel envisioned in the messianic era, see S. Freyne, "The Geography of Restoration: Galilee-Jerusalem in Early Jewish and Christian Experience," *NTS* 47 (2001): 289–311, especially 292–97; J. Zangenberg, "Pharisees, Villages and Synagogues: Observations on the Theological Significance of Matthew's Geography of Galilee," in V. A. Lehnert and U. Rüsen-Weinhold (eds.), *Logos – Logik – Lyrik: Engagierte exegetische Studien zum biblischen Reden Gottes* (FS K. Haacker; ABG 27; Leipzig: Evangelische Verlagsanstalt, 2007), 151–69.

Jesus' fame was such that people "brought to him all the sick, those who were afflicted with various diseases and pains, demoniacs, epileptics, and paralytics, and he cured them" (**v. 24b**). Matthew piles up an impressive string of maladies. The point is simple: whatever illness or condition afflicted someone, Jesus could heal it. It has been noted that the principal reason Jesus drew large crowds was because of his ability to heal. Historians, archaeologists, and anthropologists have suggested that a large percentage of the population in the time of Jesus was ill, injured, or incapacitated. Jesus' healing power (and refusal to accept payment; see Matt 10:8) would have attracted a very large following.[110]

Not surprisingly, "great crowds followed him from Galilee, the Decapolis, Jerusalem, Judea, and from beyond the Jordan" (**v. 25**). Matthew expands Mark's "he went throughout Galilee, proclaiming the message in their synagogues" (Mark 1:39) to include a much wider area. He does not necessarily mean that Jesus himself went to all of these places but that people from all of these places "followed him," so great was Jesus' fame.

The "Decapolis" (literally "ten cities") included an area within and to the east of the Jordan Valley. Jerash (or Gerasa) and Scythopolis (site of ancient Beth She'an) were two of the larger cities (whose impressive ruins have been partly restored). Significant Gentile populations were present in these cities.

It has been fashionable in recent scholarship to speak of "peasants" in Galilee and Judea. These imagined peasants are often assumed to live at subsistence level. Seen in this light, questions have been raised about literacy (i.e., Who would have time to study? Who could afford books?) and the leisure and means to travel, to name a few. Much of this thinking is the result of projecting modern concepts of powerless, impoverished peasants (in stark contrast to populations that enjoy power and affluence) onto the populations of late antiquity. Fortunately, ongoing research is bringing a much-needed corrective to this important field of study.[111]

MATTHEW 5:1–2 – THE SETTING OF THE SERMON ON THE MOUNT

5:1: When Jesus saw the crowds, he went up the mountain; and after he sat down, his disciples came to him.

5:2: Then he began to speak, and taught them, saying:

---

[110]   On health and healing in first-century Jewish Palestine, see J. J. Pilch, "The Health Care System in Matthew," *BTB* 16 (1986): 102–6; J. Zias, "Death and Disease in Ancient Israel," *BA* 54 (1991): 146–59; J. T. Carroll, "Sickness and Healing in the New Testament Gospels," *Int* 49 (1995): 130–42; C. M. Dauphin, "Illness and Healing: Review Article," *PEQ* 130 (1998): 63–67; P. Elbert, "The Devil, Disease and Deliverance: Origins of Illness in New Testament Thought – an Appreciation and Critique," *Asian Journal of Pentecostal Studies* 3 (2000): 139–54.

[111]   On this issue, see S. L. Mattila, "Jesus and the 'Middle Peasants'? Problematizing a Social-Scientific Concept," *CBQ* 72 (2010): 291–313.

*M*atthew presents Jesus' major teaching in five blocks of material, presented as discourses. The first of these discourses is the well-known Sermon on the Mount (Chapters 5–7; the four other discourses are found in Chapters 10, 13, 18, and 24–25).[112] Matthew has drawn much of this material from Q, the source also used by Luke (see Luke 6:20–49), only Matthew assembles more of Jesus' ethical teaching, creating a discourse of three chapters, compared with Luke's half chapter. Because both Matthew and Luke place their respective discourses (or sermons) on or in the vicinity of a mountain, a mountain setting was probably part of the source itself. Matthew, perhaps assuming his readers would think of the smaller hills of Galilee (and his word *oros* can mean "mount," "mountain," or "hill"), does not think it necessary to explain how Jesus and a large crowd could sit on a mountain. Luke, who was perhaps from Asia Minor, where mountains are larger, and whose readers may not be familiar with Galilean topography, explains why Jesus descended from the mountain and "stood on a level place" (Luke 6:17).[113] In any case, the mountain setting lends the sermon an added degree of authority, recalling Moses ascending Mount Sinai, where he received the Law from God.[114] Jesus, cast in Matthew as the new lawgiver, has also ascended the mountain, where he will deliver to God's people what he has received from his Father.[115]

The chapter division at this point is somewhat arbitrary. Matthew 5:1–2 belongs as much to Matt 4:23–25 as it does to the Sermon on the Mount, which follows. Taken together, Matt 4:23–5:2 provides a transition from the report of settling in Capernaum and the calling of the first disciples in Matt 4:12–22 to the giving of the first major block of teaching, the Sermon on the Mount. Jesus has established his

---

[112] B. W. Bacon, "The 'Five Books' of Moses against the Jews," *Expositor* 15 (1918): 56–66. There are formal traits that mark these five discourses. Each discourse concludes with the verb *telein* ("to finish") (e.g., Matt 7:28, "When Jesus finished these words …"; cf. 11:1; 13:53; 19:1; 26:1). These concluding sentences draw on language from the five books of Moses (e.g., Deut 31:1, "When Moses finished [*suntelein*] speaking all these words"; (cf. Num 16:31; Deut 31:24; 32:45). For an additional discussion, see T. J. Keegan, "Introductory Formulae for Matthean Discourses," *CBQ* 44 (1982): 415–30.

[113] J. Mánek, "On the Mount – On the Plain (Mt. v 1–Lk. vi 17)," *NovT* 9 (1967): 124–31.

[114] T. L. Donaldson, *Jesus on the Mountain: A Study of Matthean Theology* (JSNTSup 8; Sheffield: JSOT Press, 1985), 105–21.

[115] For important studies on the Sermon on the Mount, see G. Friedlander, *The Jewish Sources of the Sermon on the Mount* (London: Bloch, 1911; repr. 1969); W. D. Davies, *The Setting of the Sermon on the Mount* (Cambridge: Cambridge University Press, 1964; repr. BJS 186; Atlanta: Scholars Press, 1989); W. S. Kissinger, *The Sermon on the Mount: A History of Interpretation and Bibliography* (American Theological Library Association Monograph 3; Lanham, MD: Scarecrow Press, 1975); R. A. Guelich, *The Sermon on the Mount: A Foundation for Understanding* (Waco, TX: Word, 1982); G. Strecker, *The Sermon on the Mount: An Exegetical Commentary* (Nashville, TN: Abingdon, 1988); H. D. Betz, *The Sermon on the Mount* (Hermeneia; Philadelphia: Fortress, 1995); C. H. Talbert, *Reading the Sermon on the Mount: Character Formation and Decision Making in Matthew 5–7* (Columbia: University of South Carolina Press, 2004; repr. Grand Rapids, MI: Baker Academic, 2006).

base of operations, in fulfillment of Scripture (Isa 9:1–2), has begun proclaiming the kingdom of God, has chosen disciples, and now sets forth his teaching.

Some years ago, Hans Dieter Betz presented an interesting hypothesis in which he argued that the Sermon on the Mount was composed and circulated as an independent epitome of Jesus' teaching. This epitome was subsequently incorporated, in its entirety and with no editing, into Matthew's Gospel (as Matt 5:3–7:27) as the first of five major discourses. Scholarly reaction to this theory, however, has been quite skeptical.[116] It is a brilliant tour de force, but in the end it fails to convince. The Sermon on the Mount parallels too closely the composition of the other discourses, and the genre analysis of the Sermon as a Greek epitome strikes most as strained.

Eleven times in Matthew's Gospel, Jesus goes up and comes down a mountain. The Sermon on the Mount begins the same way. These mountain references, especially the one here in Matt 5:1, are part of the evangelist's Moses typology. Readers are meant to recall the revelation given at Mount Sinai long ago.[117]

A Closer Look: Jesus on the Mountain in Matthew

Again, the devil took him to a very high mountain and showed him all the kingdoms of the world and their splendor (4:8).

When Jesus saw the crowds, he went up the mountain … (5:1).

When Jesus had come down from the mountain, great crowds followed him (8:1)

And after he had dismissed the crowds, he went up the mountain by himself to pray (14:23).

After Jesus had left that place, he passed along the Sea of Galilee, and he went up the mountain, where he sat down (15:29).

Six days later, Jesus took with him Peter and James and his brother John and led them up a high mountain … (17:1).

---

[116]   See, for example, C. E. Carlston, "Betz on the Sermon on the Mount: A Critique," *CBQ* 50 (1988): 47–57. Carlston is evaluating the thesis as presented in H. D. Betz, *Essays on the Sermon on the Mount* (Philadelphia: Fortress, 1985), though he notes that Betz had presented the hypothesis in a series of essays published between 1978 and 1984 (of which some are reprinted in the *Essays* volume). Betz continues to argue his hypothesis in *The Sermon on the Mount*, 42–44 (see the preceding footnote). For additional criticism of his hypothesis, see G. N. Stanton, *A Gospel for a New People* (1992/1993), 310–25; R. H. Gundry, "H. D. Betz's Commentary on the Sermon on the Mount," in Charles Prebish et al. (eds.), *Critical Review of Books in Religion 1997* (Atlanta: Scholars Press, 1998), 39–57. For criticism of Betz's claim that the Sermon lacks even implicit Christology, see the review of his 1995 commentary by J. Topel in *CBQ* 59 (1997): 370–72; and R. H. Gundry, "H. D. Betz's Commentary on the Sermon on the Mount," 47–52.

[117]   D. A. Allison, Jr., "Jesus and Moses (Mt 5.1–2)," *ExpT* 98 (1987): 203–5.

> As they were coming down the mountain, Jesus ordered them, "Tell no one about the vision ..." (17:9).
>
> When they had come near Jerusalem and had reached Bethphage, at the Mount of Olives ... (21:1).
>
> When he was sitting on the Mount of Olives, the disciples came to him privately ... (24:3).
>
> When they had sung the hymn, they went out to the Mount of Olives (26:30).
>
> Now the eleven disciples went to Galilee, to the mountain to which Jesus had directed them (28:16).

As a Jewish teacher (or rabbi), Jesus "sat down" (**v. 1**). As a Jewish teacher, Jesus has disciples; accordingly, they "came to him." Here "disciples" refers to an undefined group, presumably larger in number than the twelve, who will not be named and numbered until Matt 10:1–5. With his disciples (literally "learners") at his feet, Jesus "taught them" (**v. 2**). We should imagine two groups of people, the disciples and crowds. The phrase in the NRSV translates as "he began to speak," but the Greek literally reads "having opened his mouth he was teaching them" (or "began teaching them"). The Greek sounds strange to our ears, but it is actually translating a Semitic idiom often found at the beginning of a public address (e.g., Job 3:1–2 LXX; Ps 35:21; 78:2; 109:2; Judg 11:35–36; Ezek 33:22; Dan 10:16; *Jub.* 25:11; *1 Enoch* 106:3; Luke 1:64; Acts 8:35; 10:34; 18:14; Eph 6:19).[118] The verb "was teaching" is an imperfect (Greek: *edidasken*) and probably has an inceptive sense: "he began to teach" (see also Matt 13:54; Mark 1:21; 10:1; 11:17; Luke 4:15; 5:3).

MATTHEW 5:3–12 – THE BEATITUDES

5:3: "Blessed are the poor in spirit, for theirs is the kingdom of heaven.

5:4: Blessed are those who mourn, for they will be comforted.

5:5: Blessed are the meek, for they will inherit the earth.

5:6: Blessed are those who hunger and thirst for righteousness, for they will be filled.

5:7: Blessed are the merciful, for they will receive mercy.

5:8: Blessed are the pure in heart, for they will see God.

5:9: Blessed are the peacemakers, for they will be called children of God.

---

[118] D. A. Black, "The Translation of Matthew 5.2," *BT* 38 (1987): 241–43.

5:10: Blessed are those who are persecuted for righteousness' sake, for theirs is the kingdom of heaven.

5:11: Blessed are you when people revile you and persecute you and utter all kinds of evil against you falsely on my account.

5:12: Rejoice and be glad, for your reward is great in heaven, for in the same way they persecuted the prophets who were before you.

*T*he Sermon on the Mount begins with a series of beatitudes (from the Latin *beatus*, meaning "blessed" or "happy"). The underlying Greek is *makarios* (which is a man's name in modern Greek); the underlying Hebrew is *esher* (or *ashre* in the plural construct form). The latter is also a Hebrew name (and, indeed, is the name of the patriarch and tribe Asher). Beatitudes (a.k.a. makarisms) are found in Greco-Roman literature, as well as in Jewish and early Christian writings. For Greeks, of course, it was the gods who were truly blessed (e.g., Homer, *Odyssey* 5.7).[119]

There are dozens of isolated beatitudes in all parts of the Old Testament, including Law, Prophets, and the Writings. There are no strings of beatitudes as we find in Matthew 5 and Luke 6, though we do find several couplets. Here is one example:

"Happy are those whose transgression is forgiven, whose sin is covered" (Ps 32:1).

"Happy are those to whom the Lord imputes no iniquity, and in whose spirit there is no deceit" (Ps 32:2).

Other couplets include Ps 84:4–5; 119:1–2; 128:1–2; 137:8–9; Sir 14:1–2; 25:8–9; Tob 13:13–14. Other isolated beatitudes in the Old Testament Apocrypha and Pseudepigrapha include Bar 4:4; *Pss. Sol.* 4:23; 5:16; 6:1; 10:1; 17:44; *1 Enoch* 58:2; *Life of Adam and Eve* 21:2; 29:10. Some beatitudes have an eschatological orientation that comes closer in spirit to Jesus' beatitudes:

Happy are those who persevere and attain the thousand three hundred thirty-five days. (Dan 12:12)

Blessed are those born in those days, to see the good things of Israel, which God will do in the assembly of the tribes. (*Pss. Sol.* 17:44)

---

[119]   For a selection of studies of the beatitudes, see M. Black, "The Beatitudes," *ExpT* 64 (1953): 125–26; C. H. Dodd, "The Beatitudes: A Form-Critical Study," in C. H. Dodd, *More New Testament Studies* (Manchester: Manchester University Press; Grand Rapids, MI: Eerdmans, 1968), 1–10; G. Strecker, "Die Makarismen der Bergpredigt," *NTS* 17 (1971): 255–75; E. Schweizer, "Formgeschichtliches zu den Seligpreisungen," *NTS* 19 (1973): 121–26; R. A. Guelich, "The Matthean Beatitudes: 'Entrance Requirements' or Eschatological Blessings?" *JBL* 95 (1976): 415–34; H. D. Betz, "Die Makarismen der Bergpredigt (Matthäus 5,3–12): Beobachtungen zur literarischen Form und theologischen Bedeutung," *ZTK* 75 (1978): 1–19; N. J. McEleney, "The Beatitudes of the Sermon on the Mount/Plain," *CBQ* 43 (1981): 1–13.

> **A Closer Look: Isolated Beatitudes in the Old Testament**
>
> "Happy are you, O Israel!" (Deut 33:29).
>
> "Blessed are all those who wait for Him" (Isa 30:18; cf. 56:2).
>
> "Happy are your people! Happy are these your servants, who continually attend to you and hear your wisdom!" (2 Chron 9:7).
>
> Most of the Old Testament beatitudes are found in the Psalms and wisdom writings, such as Proverbs, Job, and Ecclesiastes. Some of these include:
>
> "Happy are those who do not follow the advice of the wicked, nor take the path that sinners tread, or sit in the seat of scoffers" (Ps 1:1).
>
> "Happy are those who take refuge in him" (Ps 34:8).
>
> "Happy are those who find wisdom, and those who get understanding" (Prov 3:13).
>
> "How happy is the one whom God reproves; therefore do not despise the discipline of the Almighty" (Job 5:17).[120]

Not all of Jesus' beatitudes are found in the Sermon on the Mount; we find a few in different contexts:

"And blessed is anyone who takes no offense at me" (Matt 11:6).

"But blessed are your eyes, for they see, and your ears, for they hear" (Matt 13:16).

"Blessed are you, Simon son of Jonah! For flesh and blood has not revealed this to you, but my Father in heaven" (Matt 16:17).

Other Gospel characters utter beatitudes, such as the woman who says to Jesus: "Blessed is the womb that bore you and the breasts that nursed you!" (Luke 11:27), or the man who says to Jesus and the other banquet guests: "Blessed is anyone who will eat bread in the kingdom of God!" (Luke 14:15). The risen Jesus says to his disciples: "Blessed are those who have not seen and yet have come to believe" (John 20:29). The apostle Paul declares: "Blessed are those who have no reason to condemn themselves because of what they approve" (Rom 14:22). James, the Lord's brother, says: "Blessed is anyone who endures temptation" (James 1:12). John the seer pronounces many beatitudes (e.g., Rev 1:3; 14:13; 16:15; 19:9; 20:6; 22:7, 14).

[120] For a study of beatitudes in the Old Testament, see W. Janzen, "*asre* in the Old Testament," *HTR* 58 (1965): 215–26. For a comparison of Old Testament beatitudes with those of the Sermon on the Mount, see W. Zimmerli, "Die Seligspreisungen der Bergpredigt und das Alte Testament," in E. Bammel, C. K. Barrett, and W. D. Davies (eds.), *Donum Gentilicium: New Testament Studies in Honour of David Daube* (Oxford: Clarendon Press, 1978), 8–26.

Not until the discovery of 4Q525, one of the Dead Sea Scrolls, which probably dates to the first century B.C., do we find a string of beatitudes beyond the few examples just noted that contain couplets. In this fragmentary scroll, we have five beatitudes at least (with the first one partially restored), though the first two or three (or more) may be missing. The final beatitude that blesses "the man who attains wisdom" is followed by a development of this theme. In this, we have a parallel with Jesus' last beatitude in Matt 5:11–12. The obvious difference between Jesus' beatitudes and the several beatitudes of 4Q525 is that the former contain eschatological promises (e.g., "for theirs is the kingdom of heaven"; "for they shall inherit the earth"), whereas the latter do not. However, there may be an eschatological element in the fragmentary ending of 4Q525, "[wisdom/Law] places a crown [of something] upon his head, and with kings [wisdom/Law] shall seat him."

A Closer Look: 4Q525 Fragments 2 and 3, Column ii, Lines 1–9

["Blessed is the one who …] with a clean heart and does not slander with his tongue.

"Blessed are those who hold fast to its statutes and do not hold fast to the ways of injustice.

"Ble[ssed] are those who rejoice in it, and do not burst forth on paths of folly.

"Blessed are those who seek it with pure hands, and do not search for it with a deceitful [hea]rt.

"Blessed is the man who attains wisdom, and walks in the law of the Most High: establishes his heart in its ways, restrains himself by its corrections, is continually satisfied with its punishments, does not forsake it in the face of [his] trials, at the time of distress he does not abandon it, does not forget it [in the day of] terror, and in the humility of his soul he does not abhor it. But he meditates on it continually, and in his trial he reflects [on the law, and with al]l his being [he gains understanding] in it, [and he establishes it] before his eyes so as not to walk in the ways [of injustice, and …] together, and perfects his heart by it, [and … and places a crown of … upon] his [hea]d, and with kings it shall se[at him, and …] "

Translation based on M. O. Wise, M. G. Abegg, Jr., and E. M. Cook, *The Dead Sea Scrolls: A New Translation* (San Francisco: HarperCollins, 1996), 423–24.

4Q525 provides startling pre-Christian documentation outside of the Sermon on the Mount itself of the stringing together of beatitudes, combining wisdom and eschatological elements. As such, it provides at this time our most important parallel.[121]

One of the striking features of Jesus' beatitudes are the many parallels with Isa 61:1–11. The "poor in spirit" of v. 3 echoes Isa 61:1, "mourn" and "comforted" in v. 4 echo Isa 61:2, "inherit the earth" of v. 5 echoes Isa 61:5, "righteousness" in vv. 6 and 10 echoes Isa 61:3, 8, 11, the promise to be "filled" in v. 6 echoes Isa 61:6, the "pure in heart" in v. 8 may allude to Isa 61:1 (the "brokenhearted"), and "be glad" in v. 12 alludes to Isa 61:10. Not only does Jesus exposit Isaiah 61 in the Nazareth sermon (Luke 4:16–30, with Isa 61:1–2 quoted in Luke 4:18–19), he attaches a beatitude to his allusion to the prophecy when he replies to the imprisoned John: "… the poor have good news brought to them. And blessed is anyone who takes no offense at me" (Matt 11:5–6 = Luke 7:22–23). These beatitudes, which are also salted with allusions to words and phrases from the Book of Psalms, especially the lament psalms, go to the heart of Jesus' message of the kingdom and the rule of God.

The appearance of allusions to Isaiah *and the Psalms* in these beatitudes should occasion no surprise when it is remembered that in late antiquity the Psalter was regarded as prophetic. We see this in the Dead Sea Scrolls, particularly the *pesharim* (or commentaries), which are devoted to the Prophets and Psalms, understanding both as containing prophecies, and in the New Testament, where psalms are cited as "fulfilled" or as "spoken beforehand" (e.g., Acts 1:15–20; 2:25–31, 34–35; 4:24–28; 13:32–37) and where they are closely linked to the Prophets (e.g., in Luke 24:44, where the risen Jesus speaks of everything written about him in "the Prophets and Psalms").

The first beatitude, "Blessed are the poor in spirit" (**v. 3**; cf. Luke 6:20), alludes to Isa 61:1 ("the Spirit of the Lord God is upon me … to bring good news to the oppressed [or poor] …"), which appears elsewhere in Jesus' teaching (e.g., in his response to the imprisoned and discouraged John the Baptist: Matt 11:5, "the poor have good news brought to them"; cf. Luke 4:16–30). Matthew's "in spirit" directs

---

[121] G. J. Brooke, "The Wisdom of Matthew's Beatitudes (4QBeat and Mt. 5:3–12)," *Scripture Bulletin* 19, no. 2 (1989): 35–41. Brooke rightly notes that although the beatitudes of Jesus stand in the tradition of Jewish wisdom, they do contain new elements, such as eschatology and judgment. See also H.-J. Fabry, "Der Makarismus – mehr als nur eine weisheitliche Lehrform: Gedanken zu dem neu-edierten Text Q 525," in J.-Z. Hausmann (ed.), *Alttestamentlicher Glaube und biblische Theologie* (FS H. Dietrich; Stuttgart: Kohlhammer, 1992), 362–71; J. H. Charlesworth, "The Qumran Beatitudes (4Q525) and the New Testament (Mt 5:3–11, Lk 6:20–26)," *RHPR* 80 (2000): 13–35. É. Puech believes that 4Q525 originally contained eight beatitudes. On this basis, he speculates that Matthew originally contained only eight beatitudes instead of nine (or ten). See É. Puech, "4Q525 et la péricope des Béatitudes en Ben Sira et Matthieu," *RB* 98 (1991): 80–106; É. Puech, "The Collection of Beatitudes in Hebrew and in Greek (4Q525 1–4 and Mt 5,3–12)," in F. Manns and E. Alliata (eds.), *Early Christianity in Context: Monuments and Documents* (SBF 38; Jerusalem: Franciscan Printing Press, 1993), 353–68.

the emphasis away from a socioeconomic perspective (as seen in Luke's beatitudes and woes; cf. Luke 6:20–26) to one's attitude – toward God ("hunger and thirst for righteousness"; "pure in heart") and toward fellow humans ("the meek"; "the merciful"; "the peacemakers"). As such, this beatitude is appropriate as the first in the string that follows, for it denotes the true attitude and spirit of the righteous.[122] In the Prophets, the poor are associated with the meek (Isa 11:4), will receive good news (Isa 61:1–2), are contrite (Isa 66:2), are linked with the righteous (Amos 2:6–7), and are devout (*Pss. Sol.* 10:6).

A group's self-understanding as "the poor" is documented in the Dead Sea Scrolls (e.g., 1QSb 5:21, where the Messiah will "with righteousness judge the poor"; 1QpHab 12:3, which complains of villainous treatment of the poor; 1QpHab 12:10, where the Wicked Priest [i.e., the high priest of Jerusalem] robbed the wealth of the poor; and 1QM 14:7, where we find the actual phrase "poor in spirit"). The "poor" in 1QM 14:7 (= 4Q491 frags. 8–10, col. i, line 5) stand opposite those who have a "hard heart" and those who are "haughty" in 4Q427 (frag. 7, col. ii, line 8) and 4Q431 (frag. 2, line 7). The "poor" is not a technical term or an official self-designation, but it is a way of referring to the righteous, to those who rely upon God and not upon power, wealth, or reputation.

Jesus says that the poor in spirit are blessed because "theirs is the kingdom of heaven" (**v. 3**).[123] Why is this so? According to Matthew, it is necessary to repent in order to enter the kingdom (cf. Matt 3:2; 4:17). Matthew's readers would therefore assume that the poor in spirit have repented. But the Matthean Jesus also says that "unless your righteousness exceeds that of the scribes and Pharisees, you will never enter the kingdom of heaven" (Matt 5:20). Presumably, the righteousness of the poor in spirit does exceed that of the scribes and Pharisees. The Matthean Jesus also warns that not everyone who says to him, "'Lord, Lord,' will enter the kingdom of heaven," but only the one who does the will of his "Father in heaven" (Matt 7:21; cf. the warning in Matt 8:11–12 that some of the "heirs of the kingdom will be thrown into the outer darkness," meaning ethnic Israelites who are not "poor in spirit").

The opposite of the poor in spirit are "violent men" who try to take the kingdom of heaven by force (Matt 11:12), men who will not humble themselves and become like children (Matt 18:3; 19:14). They may also be persons who cannot part with their

---

[122]   See D. Flusser, "Blessed are the Poor in Spirit," *IEJ* 10 (1960): 1–13; E. Best, "Matthew 5,3," *NTS* 6 (1961): 255–58.

[123]   *Gospel of Thomas* §54 reads "Blessed are the poor, for yours is the kingdom of heaven." Contrary to the opinion of some scholars, *Thomas'* mixed form of the saying represents a conflation of Matt 5:3, whose protasis, "Blessed are the poor," is third person, and Luke 6:20, whose apodosis, "for yours is the kingdom of God," is second person. *Thomas'* mixed form does not represent independent tradition but late second-century Syrian tradition, as seen in the Syriac version of Matt 5:3, which reads "Blessed are the poor in spirit, for yours is the kingdom of heaven." The Syrian tradition at this point probably reflects Tatian's *Diatessaron*, which also omits the phrase "in spirit." Syrian Christians emphasized the blessedness of literal poverty.

wealth (Matt 19:23, "it is hard for a rich person to enter the kingdom of heaven"). They may also be scribes and Pharisees, whose righteousness is inadequate (Matt 5:20) and who in fact "lock people out of the kingdom of heaven" but do not enter it themselves (Matt 23:13).

Similar sentiment is expressed in rabbinic literature: "Concerning them … who are humble of spirit, Scripture declares: 'Thus says the Lord … to him who is despised of men … kings shall see and arise, princes shall also bow down' [Isa 49:7]" (*Derek 'Erets Rabba* 2.14).

The second beatitude in Matthew's list, "Blessed are those who mourn" (**v. 4**), alludes to Isa 61:2, "… to comfort all who mourn," and to Isa 61:3, "to provide for those who mourn in Zion – to give them a garland instead of ashes, the oil of gladness instead of mourning, the mantle of praise instead of a faint spirit. They will be called oaks of righteousness, the planting of the Lord, to display his glory" (cf. also Isa 66:10, "Rejoice with Jerusalem, and be glad for her, all you who love her; rejoice with her in joy, all you who mourn over her").

The second beatitude promises comfort to those who mourn. Mourning and comfort are combined a few times in Scripture (e.g., Gen 37:35; Isa 40:1–2; Jer 16:7; 31:13; 1 Chron 7:22; Job 29:25; 4 Ezra 10:41; *Jub.* 36:22). The most important passage is Isa 61:2 ("to comfort all who mourn"), though Jer 31:13 may also be relevant: "Then shall the young women rejoice in the dance, and the young men and the old shall be merry. I will turn their mourning into joy, I will comfort them, and give them gladness for sorrow." This verse is part of a larger complex of oracles in Jeremiah 31 that speak of Israel's redemption, restoration, and covenant renewal.

The association of comfort with the eschatological period may account for the rabbinic tradition in which the Messiah is sometimes called *Menahem*, or "Comforter" (from the Hebrew verb *naham*, which is found in Isa 61:2 and Jer 31:13): "What is the name of the Messiah? … His name is 'Comforter'" (*Lam. Rab.* 1:16 §51); "What is the name of the Messiah? 'Comforter'" (*y. Ber.* 2.4). See also "Concerning them who sigh, grieve, and look forward to [national] salvation and mourn for Jerusalem, Scripture declares: 'To provide for those who mourn in Zion – to give them a garland instead of ashes' [Isa 61:3]" (*Derek 'Erets Rabba* 2.20).

Thus, the promise of comfort evokes the prophetic assurance that in the last days the righteous and those that mourn "will be comforted" by God. It is part of the task of Messiah Jesus to bring that comfort.

The third beatitude, "Blessed are the meek, for they will inherit the earth" (**v. 5**), alludes to Ps 37:11, "But the meek [LXX: *praus*] shall inherit the land, and delight themselves in abundant prosperity" (but see also Ps 37:22, "For those blessed by the Lord shall inherit the land"; and 37:29, "The righteous shall inherit the land"). It is significant that this passage from the Psalms is interpreted in an eschatological sense in one of the *pesharim* (i.e., commentaries) of the Dead Sea Scrolls: "'But the meek shall inherit the land, and delight themselves in abundant prosperity' [Ps 37:11]. Its interpretation concerns the company of the poor who endure the time of error but are delivered from all the snares of Belial. Afterwards they will enjoy all the [...] of the earth and grow fat on every ..." (4Q171 frags. 1–10, col. ii, lines 8–10). This Qumran interpretation not only understands Ps 37:11 in an eschatological sense, as does Jesus in Matt 5:5, but also applies the promise of inheriting the earth to the "poor," thus offering yet another important overlap (cf. Matt 5:3).

The promise that the meek will "inherit the earth" (Greek: *kleronomein* and *ge*) recalls God's promise to Abraham: "I am the Lord who brought you out of Ur of the Chaldeans, to give you this land [*ge*] to inherit [*kleronomein*] it" (Gen 15:7 RSV; cf. 28:4). The promise is again recalled at the time of the exodus (cf. Exod 23:30) and in preparation for entry into the promised land (cf. Deut 4:1; passim). The theme is found in prophetic literature, as part of Israel's hope of restoration: "Your people shall all be righteous; they shall possess the land forever. They are the shoot that I planted, the work of my hands, so that I might be glorified" (Isa 60:21). It is noteworthy that the theme of inheriting the land is found in Isaiah 61, the passage that contributes to themes in the first two beatitudes: "Instead of your shame you will have a double portion, and instead of humiliation they will shout for joy over their portion. Therefore they will possess a double portion in their land, everlasting joy will be theirs" (Isa 61:7).

Jesus' third beatitude, then, speaks to Israel's hope for national renewal, which includes, in some instances, regaining the land itself. It must be remembered that many in Israel in Jesus' day were poor and had been disinherited, possibly because the law of the jubilee (cf. Leviticus 25), whereby debts are forgiven and land seized in foreclosure is returned, had not been observed. Jesus' beatitude and its allusion to the promised re-inheriting of the land would strike a hopeful chord in the hearts of his hearers.

The fourth beatitude, "Blessed are those who hunger and thirst for righteousness" (v. 6), may allude to Ps 107:5–6, in which the words for hunger (*peinan*) and thirst (*dipsan*) appear in the Greek version (LXX Ps 106:5–6): "hungry and thirsty, their soul fainted within them. Then they cried out to the Lord in their trouble, and he delivered them from their distress." But the prophetic tradition may once again have made a contribution. One thinks of Isa 49:10, "they shall not hunger or thirst, neither scorching wind nor sun shall strike them down, for he who has pity on them will lead them, and by springs of water will guide them," or Jer 31:15, which in the Greek version (LXX Jer 38:25) reads, "I have saturated every thirsting soul and I have filled every hungering soul."

Jesus' promise that those who hunger and thirst for righteousness "will be filled" speaks to the prophetic hope found in Isa 25:6, "the Lord of hosts will make for all peoples a feast of rich food, a feast of well-aged wines, of rich food filled with marrow, of well-aged wines strained clear" (cf. Isa 41:17–18; 43:20; 44:3; 49:9–10; 55:1–3), a passage that contributes to the theme of the messianic banquet in the age to come and in the light of which Jesus' parable of the Great Banquet should be understood (cf. Luke 14:15, "Blessed is anyone who will eat bread in the kingdom of God!";

14:15–24, "Someone gave a great dinner and invited many"; 15:23, "get the fatted calf and kill it, and let us eat and celebrate"). Qumran likewise expected a banquet over which the priest and Messiah would preside. This is seen in 1QSa 2:11–21, part of which reads: "The procedure for the [mee]ting of the men of reputation [when they are called] to the banquet held by the Council of the Yahad, when [God] has begotten the Messiah among them: [the Priest,] as head of the entire congregation of Israel, shall enter first.... Then the [Mess]iah of Israel may en[ter] ... [When] they gather [at the] communal [tab]le, [having set out bread and w]ine so the communal table is set [for eating] and [the] wine (poured) for drinking ..." The Rabbis linked those who pursue righteousness with the promise of divine protection (*Derek 'Erets Rabbah* 2.24).

Although a beatitude and not an exhortation, the fifth beatitude, "Blessed are the merciful" (**v. 7**), presupposes the warning to "be merciful as your Father is merciful" (Luke 6:36) and the assurance that a merciful God will indeed have mercy on his people: "imploring the Lord of heaven that mercy and safety may be granted to you" (Tob 6:18; cf. *1 Enoch* 60:5 on God's patience and mercy toward humans), for it is in God's character to be merciful (e.g., LXX Exod 22:27, "I am merciful"; cf. Exod 34:6). Those who are merciful may then expect to "receive mercy."

We have parallels in rabbinic literature: "So long as you are merciful, he will have mercy on you" (*t. B. Qam.* 9.30 [Gamaliel], "So long as you are merciful, he will have mercy on you"; *Sipre Deut.* §96 [on Deut 13:18]; *b. Sanh.* 51b; *b. Shab.* 151b; cf. *Derek 'Erets Rabba* 2.21); "My people, children of Israel, as our Father is merciful in heaven, so shall you be merciful on earth" (*Tg. Ps.-J.* Lev 22:28).

The sixth beatitude, "Blessed are the pure in heart" (**v. 8**), probably alludes to Ps 24:3–4: "Who shall ascend the hill of the Lord? And who shall stand in his holy place? Those who have clean hands and pure hearts" (cf. Ps 73:1; *T. Joseph* 4:6). Those who are "pure in heart," Jesus promises, "will see God." Here again we probably have an allusion to Psalm 24: "Such is the company of those who seek him, who seek the face of the God of Jacob" (Ps 24:6), perhaps under the influence of Isaiah ("I saw the Lord," Isa 6:1) or Job ("after my skin has been thus destroyed, then in my flesh I shall see God," Job 19:26; cf. 33:26; Ps 17:15, "I shall behold your face in righteousness"; Ps 63:2, "I have looked upon you in the sanctuary"; 4 Ezra 7:98; *Jub.* 1:28). The promise to see God stands in tension, of course, with the story in which Moses is denied his request to see God's face (Exod 33:20). But in the eschatological day, the righteous may "see God."

In rabbinic literature, we find: "Concerning them ... who are pure of heart, Scripture declares: 'Surely God is good to Israel, to those who are pure in heart' [Ps 73:1]" (*Derek 'Erets Rabba* 2.19; cf. *Gen. Rab.* 41.1 [on Gen 12:17]; *Midr. Ps.* 24.8 [on Ps 24:4]).

The seventh beatitude, "Blessed are the peacemakers" (**v. 9**), is distinctive. The noun peacemaker only occurs here in the New Testament, and not once in the Septuagint (LXX). The verb, however, does occur once in the Septuagint: "He who winks with his eyes deceitfully brings grief to men, but he who reproves honestly makes peace" (LXX Prov 10:10). The promised Messiah is called "Prince of Peace" (Isa 9:6) and will win peace from the nations (Zech 9:9–10). One of the scrolls from Qumran anticipates the coming of an anointed messenger, who will proclaim the peace foretold in Isa 52:7 (cf. 11QMelchizedek 2:16–19).

The peacemakers, Jesus promises, "will be called sons of God." The righteous are called "sons of God" in a few places in the Old Testament and related literature: "You are children of the Lord your God" (Deut 14:1); "Children of the living God" (Hos 1:10; 2:1); "Blessed be my son Jacob and all the children of God Most High, to all the ages" (*Jub.* 22:11; see also Exod 4:22; Jer 31:9). In rabbinic literature, we see "loving peace and pursuing peace" (*m. 'Abot* 1:12) and "making peace between" people (*m. Peah* 1:1).

In several New Testament passages, believers are called "son of God" (e.g., Luke 20:36, "they are like angels and are children of God"; Rom 8:14, "all who are led by the Spirit of God are children of God"; Rom 8:19; Gal 3:26). The epithet is found in Hellenistic Jewish literature (Wisd of Sol 12:19; Philo, *Spec. Leg.* 1.318) and in rabbinic literature as well (e.g., *m. 'Abot* 3:19, "Beloved are Israel, that they are called children of God"). Reference to righteous persons as children of God is also found in Greco-Roman literature; for example, "A chaste and sinless person has power in God's sight as a child of God" (Sextus, *Sentences* 60).

The eighth beatitude, "Blessed are those who are persecuted for righteousness' sake" (**v. 10**), alludes to an interesting eschatological element. Apocalyptic literature of late antiquity foretells the coming persecution of the righteous: "Woe to you, sinners, for you persecute the righteous; for you shall be delivered up and persecuted because of injustice, and heavy shall its yoke be upon you" (*1 Enoch* 96:7); "you will make void the law, and despise the words of the prophets by evil perverseness. And you will persecute righteous persons, and hate the godly; the words of the faithful you will abhor" (*T. Levi* 16:2); "there shall be false prophets like tempests, and they shall persecute all righteous persons" (*T. Judah* 21:9).

Jesus' beatitude accords well with the perspective expressed in Wisd of Sol 1:16–5:23. Part of this passage reads as follows (beginning with the designs of the wicked): "Let us oppress the righteous poor man.... Let us lie in wait for the righteous man, because he is inconvenient to us and opposes our actions.... He professes to have knowledge of God, and calls himself a child of the Lord ... he calls the last end of the righteous happy [*makarizei*], and boasts that God is his father ... if the righteous man is God's child, he will help him, and will deliver him from the hand of his adversaries.... In the eyes of the foolish they seemed to have died, and their departure was thought to be a disaster, and their going from us to be their destruction; but they are at peace. For though in the sight of men they were punished, their hope is full of immortality" (Wisd of Sol 2:10, 12, 13, 16, 18; 3:2–4).

Those who experience such persecution, Jesus says, will receive the kingdom (*basileia*) of heaven. We again have agreement with Wisdom of Solomon, which promises that, despite severe persecution, even death, the righteous "will govern nations and rule [*basileusei*] over peoples, and the Lord will reign over them forever" (Wisd of Sol 3:8). Jesus' beatitude may be alluded to in 1 Pet 3:14 ("But even if you do suffer for doing what is right, you are blessed").

The ninth beatitude, "Blessed are you when people revile you and persecute you" (v. 11), alludes to some of the lament psalms, such as LXX Ps 34:7 (= 35:7 in Hebrew and English): "For without cause they hid their net for me; without cause they cast reproach on my soul" (see also Ps 42:10; 44:16; 52:12; 69:9; 74:10).

The wicked hate the righteous "and utter all kinds of evil against" the followers of Jesus. Speaking "evil against" (*poneron kata*) the righteous alludes to yet another lament psalm: "Let this be the reward of my accusers from the Lord, and of those who speak evil against [*poneron kata*] my soul" (LXX Ps 108:20 = Ps 109:20 in Hebrew and English). In all of the beatitudes, Jesus draws heavily on the language of the Prophets and Psalms. The words "when people revile you and persecute you … on my account" find a parallel in Isa 66:5, "our own people who hate you and reject you for my name's sake…."

Jesus concludes with what could be regarded as a tenth beatitude. However, it does not begin with a descriptive makarism, "Blessed," but rather with two imperatives: "Rejoice and be glad" (v. 12). If v. 12 may be regarded as a beatitude, then we have ten in all, which corresponds to the Mosaic pattern of Ten Commandments received on Mount Sinai (Exodus 20) and, as such, furthers Matthew's typology.

Jesus' imperatives are found together in Tobit's prayer, "Rejoice and be glad for the children of the righteous; for they will be gathered together, and will praise the Lord of the righteous" (Tob 13:13). Tobit's exhortation coheres with the prophetic hope expressed in Habakkuk: "Yet I will rejoice in the Lord; I will exult in the God of my salvation" (Hab 3:18). See also *4 Bar* 6:20: "Rejoice and be glad, for God has not permitted us to depart from this body grieving for the city [Jerusalem] that has been laid waste and outraged." We may also have another allusion to Isa 61:10, which in the Greek version (the LXX) reads: "My soul will rejoice in the Lord."

The righteous are to rejoice and be glad, for their "reward in heaven is great." We find no exact parallel in the Old Testament, but one is reminded of God's promise to Abraham, "Your reward shall be very great" (Gen 15:1), and of the promise found in Wisdom of Solomon that "the righteous live for ever, and their reward is with the Lord; the Most High takes care of them" (Wisd of Sol 5:15; see also *2 Enoch* 63:1, "When man clothes the naked and fills the hungry, he will find reward from God").

Jesus underscores the reassurance that he has given by appealing to precedence. The righteous should rejoice in the face of persecution and slander at the hands of the wicked, "for in the same way they persecuted the prophets who were before you." There are a few examples in the Old Testament of prophets who were reviled and persecuted. We think of Elijah, who was pursued by Ahab and Jezebel (1 Kings 19:2–18). The discouraged prophet complains: "the Israelites have forsaken your covenant, thrown down your altars, and killed your prophets with the sword. I alone am left, and they are seeking my life, to take it away" (1 Kings 19:10; cf. v. 14). In 2 Chron 24:20–21, the priest Zechariah son of Jehoida the priest is stoned to death for speaking the word of the Lord. Jeremiah is placed in stocks (Jer 20:1–2) and cast into a pit (Jer 38:6). There was a tradition that the prophet Isaiah, found hiding in a hollow log, was sawed in two by order of Manasseh (*Mart. Isa.* 5:1), a tradition possibly alluded to in Heb 11:37. We are also told that Elijah reproved Ahaziah, king of Samaria, for slaying the prophets of God (*Mart. Isa.* 2:14). The Chronicler summarizes Israel's long history of rejecting God's prophets and messengers (2 Chron 36:15–16, "mocking the messengers of God, despising his words, and scoffing at his prophets"). The first-century anthology known as the *Lives of the Prophets* recounts the ministries and deaths of some two dozen prophets, though only a few of them suffered martyrdom. It seems that there were enough examples of persecution and martyrdom that Jesus could generalize by saying: "Jerusalem, Jerusalem, the city that kills the prophets and stones those who are sent to it!" (Luke 13:34 = Matt 23:37).

Jesus wants the "poor in spirit," the "pure in heart," and the "peacemakers" to know that to be "persecuted for righteousness' sake" and "on account of" Jesus is to share company with God's prophets. They may suffer, they may be insulted, but they are blessed nonetheless. It is in this context that the balance of the Sermon on the Mount that follows (Matt 5:13–7:27) should be understood.

MATTHEW 5:13–16 – SALT AND LIGHT

5:13: "You are the salt of the earth; but if salt has lost its taste, how can its saltiness be restored? It is no longer good for anything, but is thrown out and trampled under foot.

5:14: "You are the light of the world. A city built on a hill cannot be hid.

5:15: No one after lighting a lamp puts it under the bushel basket, but on the lampstand, and it gives light to all in the house.

5:16: In the same way, let your light shine before others, so that they may see your good works and give glory to your Father in heaven.

*M*atthew adds to his nine (or ten) beatitudes (see the commentary on Matt 5:3–12) a series of admonitions. His people are the "salt of the earth"; they are the "light of the world," and therefore they should let their "light shine before others" that they might "give glory to God." Most of Matthew's material is drawn from Q, the source that he has in common with Luke (cf. Luke 14:34–35 [= Matt 5:13]; Luke 8:16 + 11:33 [= Matt 5:15]), though there is some overlap with Mark (cf. Mark 9:50 [= Matt 5:13]; Mark 4:21 [= Matt 5:15]). The closest verbal agreements are with Luke.[124]

---

[124]   For a recent and comprehensive treatment of Matt 5:13–16, see R. Deines, *Die Gerechtigkeit der Tora im Reich des Messias* (2004), 183–256.

What does it mean to be "salt of the earth" (**v. 13**)? A great number of suggestions have been made. The context suggests that, like salt, Jesus' disciples are of benefit to the world, whether in reference to purity and preservation (Exod 30:35; 2 Kings 19–23) or in reference to wisdom (Col 4:5; *m. Sota* 9:15) and peacemaking (Matt 5:9; Mark 9:50). Of course, when salt "has lost its taste," it has lost its value and is no longer good for anything. It is "thrown out" into the street, like so much dust swept from a house.

There are some interesting parallels in rabbinic literature: "The Torah has been compared to salt ... the world cannot exist without salt ... it is impossible for the world to exist without Scripture" (*Soperim* 15.8); "When salt becomes unsavory, with what is it to be salted?" (*b. Bekorot* 8b); "The wisdom of the scribes will become insipid" (*m. Sota* 9:15).[125]

Likewise, Jesus' followers are to be the "light of the world" (**v. 14**), a designation with scriptural and traditional antecedents (e.g., Isa 49:6; *Apoc. Abr.* 9:3; *b. Babba Batra* 4a). God's people are supposed to be the light of the world (*T. Levi* 14:3). In John's Gospel, Jesus says, "I am the light of the world" (John 8:12; 9:5). The Roman politician and author Cicero (106–43 B.C.) describes Rome as a "light to the whole world" (*In Catalinam* 4.6). The light of the world, of course, originates with God himself, who created the earth and brought light into being (Gen 1:3–4, 15–18; Jer 4:23), who provides light and illumination for this people (Ps 18:28; 56:13; 118:27), who sends his Messiah to bring light to a darkened Israel (Isa 9:1–2), and who someday will himself be the source of light (Isa 60:19; Rev 22:5).

"A city built on a hill cannot be hidden" links the "light of the world" saying with the "lamp" and "lampstand" saying in **v. 15**.[126] The meaning of the saying in v. 15 no doubt explains the meaning of the "city built on a hill" saying. Two cities have sometimes been mentioned as cities Jesus and the public would have had in mind. Sepphoris, just four miles north of Nazareth, is located on a hill. The lights of this large, sophisticated city, with Roman-style buildings, would have been plainly visible to the inhabitants of nearby Nazareth. The adult Jesus may have been thinking of Sepphoris as "a city built on a hill," whose light "cannot be hid." Another candidate is Gamla, situated high in the Golan Heights, east of the north end of the Sea of Galilee. The lights of this lofty city were plainly visible to anyone on or near the great lake and would therefore have been seen by Jesus and his followers as they wandered about in the region. It is more likely, however, that behind the statement that "a city built on a hill cannot be hid" lies a prophetic exhortation with Jerusalem very much in mind. The city is named in Matthew thirteen times. It is referred to several more times as "the holy city" (Matt 4:5; 27:53) or "city of the Great King"

[125] For a learned review of the primary literature and the various scholarly options that have been proposed, see R. Deines, *Die Gerechtigkeit der Tora im Reich des Messias* (2004), 185–217.

[126] The parallel saying in *Gospel of Thomas* §33b is not independent but a version of the Lukan form of the saying (cf. Luke 8:16).

(Matt 5:35), or simply "the city" (Matt 21:17, 18; 23:37; 26:18; 28:11). Implicit in the saying is the point that if God's people let their light shine (see the next verse) in their good works and pursuit of righteousness, then the city of Jerusalem will indeed shine throughout the world like a lamp placed on a lampstand.[127]

Jesus enjoins his listeners to "let your light shine before others, so that they may see your good works" (**v. 16**). There are no antecedents to this summarizing statement, though there are a few parallels to its components. The Psalmist bids people to "Come and see what God has done" (Ps 66:5), while the dying patriarch Benjamin, in the pseudepigraphical work *Testaments of the Twelve Patriarchs*, explains to his sons that "where there is reverence for good works and light in the mind, even darkness flees away from him" (*T. Benjamin* 5:3). Naphtali similarly instructs his children: "God will be glorified among the Gentiles through you" (*T. Naphtali* 8:4). In John's Gospel, Jesus defends himself by saying, "I have shown you many good works from the Father" (John 10:32), and Paul declares that believers are "what he has made us, created in Christ Jesus for good works" (Eph 2:10). The "good works" clarify what is meant by "let your light shine." The good works become a testimonial to humans everywhere.

When people see the good works of true believers, people who are "poor in spirit," who "hunger and thirst for righteousness," and who are "peacemakers" (Matt 5:3–9), then they will "give glory to your Father in heaven" (v. 16). Matthew's "Father in heaven" is typical of Jewish piety (cf. *m. 'Abot* 5:23, "do the will of your Father who is in heaven"; *m. Yoma* 8:9, "Blessed are you, O Israel. Before whom are you made clean, and who makes you clean? It is your Father who is in heaven"; *m. Sota* 9:15, "On whom may we rely? On our Father who is in heaven"). It is acknowledged in some literature that all humanity will glorify God, though not until judgment day (*T. Gad* 7:2, "all flesh shall die; and offer praise to God"). Jesus wants his disciples to let their light shine, as seen in their good works, so that all humanity will glorify God in the present age.

A characteristic mark of Jesus in his prayers is his habit of addressing God as "Father." Many examples appear in Matthew; for example, Matt 6:6, 8, 9, 15; 7:1; 11:25, "I thank you, Father, Lord of heaven and earth"; 11:26, "Yes, Father, for such was your gracious will"; 26:39, "My Father, if it is possible, let this cup pass from me"; 26:42, "My Father, if this cannot pass unless I drink it. . . ."

MATTHEW 5:17–20 – FULFILLMENT AND RIGHTEOUSNESS

5:17: "Do not think that I have come to abolish the law or the prophets; I have come not to abolish but to fulfill.

---

[127]   See K. M. Campbell, "The New Jerusalem in Matt. 5:14," *SJT* 31 (1978): 335–63; H. D. Betz, *The Sermon on the Mount* (1995), 161–62.

5:18: For truly I tell you, until heaven and earth pass away, not one letter, not one stroke of a letter, will pass from the law until all is accomplished.

5:19: Therefore, whoever breaks one of the least of these commandments, and teaches others to do the same, will be called least in the kingdom of heaven; but whoever does them and teaches them will be called great in the kingdom of heaven.

5:20: For I tell you, unless your righteousness exceeds that of the scribes and Pharisees, you will never enter the kingdom of heaven.

In Matt 5:17–20, we have the most important part of the Sermon on the Mount. In this section, particularly in v. 17, Matthew sets the record straight: Jesus did not come to abolish the Law of Moses. On the contrary, he came to fulfill it. Some of this material is traditional, to be sure (cf. Luke 16:17), but the passage is for the most part Matthew's summary of the importance of Jesus' teaching. If Matthew's apologetic is to make any headway in the setting of the synagogue, he will have to show that Jesus was not a lawbreaker and did not encourage his followers to break the law. The discontinuity between Jesus and the teachers of the synagogue is because of the law's fulfillment, not its abandonment. There is no question that Jesus transgressed the oral law, but the written law, understood in the light of the whole of Scripture, he fulfilled.[128]

Each verse in this passage conveys an important truth. The passage begins with a correction of an allegation: "Do not think" (**v. 17**) or "do not suppose" (Greek: *nomizein*). The language here is reminiscent of the determined words of the heroes

---

[128] For a selection of important studies of this passage, see K. Berger, *Die Gesetzesauslegung Jesu: Ihr historischer Hintergrund im Judentum und im Alten Testament.* Teil I: *Markus und Parallelen* (WMANT 40; Neukirchen-Vluyn: Neukirchener Verlag, 1972), 209–27; R. Banks, "Matthew's Understanding of the Law: Authenticity and Interpretation in Matthew 5:17–20," *JBL* 93 (1974): 226–42; J. P. Meier, *Law and History in Matthew's Gospel: A Redactional Study of Matt. 5.17–48* (AnBib 71; Rome: Biblical Institute, 1976), especially 65–89, 120–24; U. Luz, "Die Erfüllung des Gesetzes bei Matthäus (5,17–20)," *ZTK* (1978): 398–435; D. Wenham, "Jesus and the Law: An Exegesis on Matthew 5:17–20," *Themelios* 4 (1979): 92–96; H. D. Betz, "Die hermeneutischen Prinzipien in der Bergpredigt (Mt. 5:17–20)," in E. Jüngel et al. (eds.), *Verifikationen: Festschrift für Gerhard Ebeling zum 70. Geburtstag* (Tübingen: Mohr-Siebeck, 1982), 27–41; D. Moo, "Jesus and the Authority of the Mosaic Law," *JSNT* 20 (1984): 3–49, especially 23–28; F. Vouga, *Jésus et la loi selon la tradition synoptique* (Le monde de la Bible 563; Paris: Labor et Fides, 1988), 189–99; K. R. Snodgrass, "Matthew and the Law," in D. R. Bauer and M. A. Powell (eds.), *Treasures Old and New: Contributions to Matthean Studies* (SBL Symposium Series 1; Atlanta: Scholars Press, 1996), 99–127; W. R. G. Loader, *Jesus' Attitude towards the Law: A Study of the Gospels* (WUNT 2, no. 97; Tübingen: Mohr [Siebeck], 1997), 165–73; É. Cuvillier, "Torah Observance and Radicalization in the First Gospel: Matthew and First-Century Judaism: A Contribution to the Debate," *NTS* 55 (2009): 144–59, especially 148–54; J. P. Meier, *A Marginal Jew* (1991–2009), 4:40–47, 67–73.

of the books of the Maccabees, who were concerned with preserving the temple and keeping the Law. A martyr says to a tyrant (i.e., Antiochus IV Epiphanes), "But do not think that you will go unpunished for having tried to fight against God!" (2 Macc 7:19); or again in a later version, "Therefore do not suppose that it would be a petty sin if we were to eat defiling food" (4 *Macc* 5:19); or yet again, "Therefore, tyrant, put us to the test; and if you take our lives because of our religion, do not suppose that you can injure us by torturing us" (4 *Macc* 9:7). Jesus' opening words, "Do not think …," followed by a discussion of the value and permanence of the Law, may well have evoked these venerated expressions of fidelity.

Jesus' declaration "I have come" is the first of several such declarations in the Gospel of Matthew (Matt 5:17a, 17b; 9:13; 10:34a, 34b, 35; 20:28). These declarations reinforce the theme, with which the Gospel begins, that Jesus has indeed come to save his people (Matt 1:21). His words, deeds, suffering, death, and resurrection demonstrate the presence of God in his ministry (Matt 1:23), things that Jesus has come to fulfill.[129]

What Jesus' critics should not think is that he came "to abolish the Law." Again, this was the very concern of the Maccabean struggle – to prevent the abolition of the Law. In the preface to his work, the author of 2 Maccabees summarizes the history of Jason that he is about to recount, namely how Judas Maccabeus and his brothers "regained possession of the temple famous throughout the world, and liberated the city, and re-established the laws that were about to be abolished" (2 Macc 2:22). Again, the words of one of the martyrs parallel the words of Jesus: "I do not so pity my old age as to break the ancestral law by my own act" (4 *Macc* 5:33). In the pseudepigraphical *Testaments of the Twelve Patriarchs*, the dying Levi warns his sons that they will have priestly descendents who will "make void the law, and despise the words of the prophets by evil perverseness" (*T. Levi* 16:2).

Jesus refers to "the Law and the Prophets," the first two divisions of the three-part canon of the Old Testament, or what the Jewish people call the Tanak, an acronym for the *Torah* (the Law), *Nebi'im* (the Prophets), and *Ketuvim* (the Writings).[130] Although by the time of Jesus there was agreement that there were sacred writings outside of the Law and the Prophets, there was no consensus as to their precise number. Three other times in Matthew, Jesus refers to the Law and the Prophets (Matt 7:12; 11:13, where the order is intentionally reversed; and 22:40, "the whole Law and the Prophets"). The phrase "Law and the Prophets" is found in the preface to the Book of the Wisdom of ben Sira, where ben Sira's grandson says that his grandfather devoted himself "especially to the reading of the Law and the Prophets." The phrase also occurs in 2 Macc 15:9 and 4 *Macc* 18:10, and several times in rabbinic

---

[129]   On this important topic, see W. Carter, "Jesus' 'I have come' Statements in Matthew's Gospel," *CBQ* 60 (1998): 44–62.

[130]   In this context, "the law and the prophets" refers to the entirety of Jewish Scripture. See G. Strecker, *The Sermon on the Mount* (1988), 57; D. Moo, "Jesus and the Authority of the Mosaic Law," *JSNT* 20 (1984): 27–28.

literature (e.g., *b. Ta'anit* 20a, where we have the standard tripartite reference to the canon of Scripture: "the Law, the Prophets, and the Writings"; cf. *b. Ta'anit* 17b, where we have "Moses and the Prophets").

No, Jesus did not come to abolish Scripture but "to fulfill" it; that is, obey it.[131] Matthew's readers will have already sensed the truth of this claim, for five times in the infancy narrative actions or circumstances surrounding Jesus' birth were said to "fulfill" this or that Scripture. At his baptism, Jesus urged John "to fulfill all righteousness" (Matt 3:15), and the inception of his ministry in Galilee fulfilled prophecy (Matt 4:14). Now Jesus has the opportunity to show that he has indeed come to fulfill the Law, not just messianic prophecies. Only Jesus as Israel's Messiah and God's Son can fulfill the Law and the Prophets.[132] How he fulfills the Law will be illustrated in the antitheses of Matt 5:21-48.[133] (For examples of the words "Law" and "fulfill" together, see 2 *Bar* 57:2; *T. Naphtali* 8:7.)

There is an interesting rabbinic tradition in which the words of Jesus are presented somewhat differently: "I did not come to destroy the Law of Moses nor did I come to add to the Law of Moses" (*b. Shabbath* 116a–b). This version may have been influenced by a saying of Agesilaus, as collected by Plutarch (ca. 45–125 A.D.): "I would not become a lawgiver to enact another set of laws, for in the present laws I would make no addition, subtraction, or revision" (*Moralia* 214 BC: "Sayings of the Spartans," 73).

A Closer Look: The Law (*nomos*) Passages in Matthew

"Do not think that I have come to abolish the law or the prophets; I have come not to abolish but to fulfill." (5:17)

"For truly I tell you, until heaven and earth pass away, not one letter, not one stroke of a letter, will pass from the law until all is accomplished." (5:18)

"In everything do to others as you would have them do to you; for this is the law and the prophets." (7:12)

"For all the prophets and the law prophesied until John came." (11:13)

---

[131] K. R. Snodgrass, "Matthew and the Law," in D. R. Bauer and M. A. Powell (eds.), *Treasures Old and New* (1996), 115: "Matthew's point is that Jesus came so that people would live according to the scriptures." Yes, but live according to the Scriptures *as Jesus understood and taught them*. This is why Matthew says Jesus came to "fulfill" the Law and the Prophets. Others may "do," "keep," or "observe" the Law, but only Jesus fulfills it. See J. P. Meier, *A Marginal Jew* (1991–2009), 4:41–42. Only Jesus can fulfill it by virtue of his unique relationship to God. See D. Moo, "Jesus and the Authority of the Mosaic Law," *JSNT* 20 (1984): 29–30.

[132] See R. Deines, *Die Gerechtigkeit der Tora im Reich des Messias* (2004), 257–87.

[133] É. Cuvillier, "Torah Observance and Radicalization in the First Gospel," *NTS* 55 (2009): 148–49.

> "Or have you not read in the law that on the sabbath the priests in the temple break the sabbath and yet are guiltless?" (12:5)
>
> "Teacher, which commandment in the law is the greatest?" (22:36)
>
> "On these two commandments hang all the law and the prophets." (22:40)
>
> "Woe to you, scribes and Pharisees, hypocrites! For you tithe mint, dill, and cummin, and have neglected the weightier matters of the law: justice and mercy and faith. It is these you ought to have practiced without neglecting the others." (23:23)

Verses 18–20 reinforce the solemn declaration of v. 17. Jesus begins with the words "truly I say to you" (**v. 18a**). What is translated as "truly" is literally "amen." Jesus' use of amen is somewhat distinctive of his manner of speaking and teaching. In our oldest sources, "amen" was used as an emphatic agreement with something just spoken, often a law or decree (as in Num 5:22; Deut 27:15–26; 1 Kings 1:36) or a blessing (1 Chron 16:36; Neh 8:6; Ps 41:13). It later became customary as a concluding affirmation of a prayer (Tob 8:8; Pr of Man 15; *4 Macc* 18:24; *m. Ber.* 5:4). Amen is common enough as a conclusion to a prayer (especially in the ancient Jewish prayers of the synagogue, such as the Amidah and the Qaddish; for examples in other Jewish writings, see 1 Chron 16:36; Neh 8:6; *1 Enoch* 105:2; *2 Enoch* 68:7; *3 Bar* 17:4; *4 Macc* 18:24), but using it to begin a statement is not common (especially the "amen, amen" sayings in John and in Num 5:22; Neh 8:6; Pss 41:13; 72:19; 89:52; but note the triple amen at the end of the story of Ahiqar and his treacherous nephew Nadin in *Ahiqar* 8:38: "This chronicle is finished with the help of God, may he be exalted: amen, amen, amen").

Jesus' purpose was to fulfill the Law and Prophets.[134] This fulfillment means, metaphorically speaking, that the Law remains in effect "until heaven and earth pass away." In Jewish thinking, the heaven and earth would endure until God himself recreated them (as in Isa 65:17, "I am about to create new heavens and a new earth"; cf. 66:22; *1 Enoch* 91:16; 2 Pet 3:13; Rev 21:1). But until that eschatological moment, creation should be thought of as permanent. One thinks of the Psalmist, who extols God for creating the heavens, the sun, the moon, and the stars, adding, "He has established them forever; he has made an ordinance, and it shall not pass away" (LXX Ps 148:6), or, "For he knew that his time was but short, but that heaven and earth endure always" (*2 Bar* 19:2). Thus, Jesus' language is implicitly eschatological: the Law will endure "until" the End. His disciples will obey the Law for as long as they live.[135]

---

[134] R. G. Hamerton-Kelly, "Attitudes to the Law in Matthew's Gospel: A Discussion of Matthew 5,18," *BR* 17 (1972): 19–32; R. Deines, *Die Gerechtigkeit der Tora im Reich des Messias* (2004), 289–370.

[135] This point is disputed. It is taken in an eschatological sense in J. P. Meier, *Law and History in Matthew's Gospel* (1976), 164; and as "until everything takes place" in U. Luz, *Matthew* (Hermeneia; 3 vols., Minneapolis: Fortress, 2001–2007), 1:218–19.

The Law is so important that "not one letter, not one stroke of a letter, will pass from the law until all is accomplished" (**v. 18b**). God's Law is just as permanent as creation itself (see, e.g., 4 Ezra 9:37, "the Law, however, does not perish but remains in its glory"; Bar 4:1, "the Law that endures for ever"; *1 Enoch* 99:2, "the eternal Law"; *2 Bar* 77:15, "though we depart, yet the Law abides"; Philo, *Life of Moses* 2.14, "But Moses is alone in this, in that his laws, firm, unshaken, immovable, stamped, as it were, with the seals of nature herself, remain secure from the day they were first enacted to now, and we may hope that they will remain for all future ages as though immortal, so long as the sun and the moon and the whole heaven and universe exist"; *Gen. Rab.* 10.1 [on Gen 2:1], "everything has an end, even heaven and earth have an end; only one thing has no end: and what is that? The Law").

The "one letter" and "one stroke of a letter" (literally "one yota or one serif") refer to the Hebrew letter *yod*, which as a consonant makes either a *y* sound or a *j* sound (often it is *j* in English but *y* in Hebrew, German, and other European languages), and the small strokes that distinguish similar letters from one another (such as distinguishing *h* from *t* or *d* from *r*). The logic is that if the smallest letter and the tiniest mark will not pass away, then one may be sure that the major teaching of the Law will not either.[136]

But the "Law," too, comes to an end, just as does creation (with all due respect to the rabbinic exegesis cited earlier). It comes to an end when "all is accomplished." Matthew's "accomplished" clarifies what is meant by "fulfill" in v. 17. Jesus has come to accomplish all that the Law contains, and all of it will be accomplished, or fulfilled, before it passes away.

The language of "until heaven and earth pass away" and "not one letter, not one stroke of a letter" is hyperbolic. It is the use of exaggeration to make a point.[137] Jesus is saying that there is nothing in God's Law that is unimportant. All must be respected; all must be obeyed. Of course, we must ask what is in the Law and how it must be obeyed. That is where Jesus differed sharply with many of the religious teachers of his day, as the examples in Matt 5:21–48 will make clear.

In light of the validity of the Law, anyone who "breaks one of the least of these commandments, and teaches others to do the same, will be called least [*elachistos*] in the kingdom of heaven" (**v. 19**).[138] It has been suggested that we have here an allusion to the apostle Paul, who refers to himself as the "least [*elachistos*] of the apostles" (cf. 1 Cor 15:9).[139] Because of his emphasis on liberty (see, e.g., 1 Cor 6:12; 10:23, "All things are lawful"), he did not teach Gentiles to keep the Law; in fact, he vigorously criticized those (i.e., the "Judaizers") who did (cf. the argument in Galatians and in the later *Letter of Barnabas*). In Matthew's Gospel, Jesus may therefore be

---

[136] For a detailed discussion of this manner of speaking, see R. Deines, *Die Gerechtigkeit der Tora im Reich des Messias* (2004), 294–335.

[137] K. R. Snodgrass, "Matthew and the Law," in D. R. Bauer and M. A. Powell (eds.), *Treasures Old and New* (1996), 117.

[138] R. Deines, *Die Gerechtigkeit der Tora im Reich des Messias* (2004), 371–412.

[139] H. D. Betz, *The Sermon on the Mount* (1995), 188–89.

trying to put Paul in his place: Paul may be in the "kingdom of heaven," but he shall be held in low esteem.[140]

In the *Testament of Moses*, a pseudepigraphical work dating from about 30 A.D., we find strong criticism of those "who sin and nullify the commandments" of God; they shall be "without the blessing" mentioned previously, and they shall be "punished with many torments," but they will not be destroyed (*T. Moses* 12:10–12). We find a similar idea expressed in Dio Chrysostom (ca. 40–120 A.D.): "If anyone chisels out only one word from any official tablet, you will put him to death … and if anyone should … erase one jot of the law, or one single syllable … you will treat this man as you would any person who should [commit a very serious crime]" (*Thirty-First Discourse* 86). A rabbinic tradition says that the letter *yod*, in reaction to Solomon's understanding of the Law, reacted in fear, saying: "Master of the Universe, have you not said that no letter shall ever be abolished from the Law? Behold, Solomon has now arisen and abolished one. Who knows? Today he has abolished one letter, tomorrow he will abolish another until the whole Law will be nullified!" (*Exod. Rab.* 6.1 [on Exod 6:2]).[141]

The reference to Paul (whose name in Latin means "small") is possible, but it is far from certain. The adjective *elachistos* ("least") occurs five times in Matthew (and four times in Luke, but not once in Mark or John) and seems to be part of his vocabulary. We have references to other "least" people in Matthew (cf. Matt 25:40, 45). In the Micah prophecy cited in Matt 2:6, Bethlehem is called "least." Seeing a reference to Paul in Matt 5:19 may be reading into the passage a nuance that is not present. The "least" of v. 19 probably refers to the "least" (or, as the NASB puts it, "smallest") of v. 18 and not necessarily to Paul's self-deprecating assessment. Moreover, Paul was by no means the only Christian teacher in the first century who proclaimed freedom from the Law of the Moses in view of the Messiah's completed work.[142]

In the minds of many Jews in the first century, the benchmark of fidelity to the Law had been established by the Pharisees. But Jesus is not impressed by their interpretations or their claims of obedience. He tells his disciples that their "righteousness" must exceed "that of the scribes and Pharisees" (**v. 20**).[143] Matthew

[140]   To be "least" in the kingdom is not to be excluded from it. See J. P. Meier, *Law and History in Matthew's Gospel* (1976), 92–95.

[141]   The translation is based on H. Freedman and M. Simon (eds.), *Midrash Rabbah*, 3rd edition (10 vols., London: Soncino, 1983), 3:103. For a discussion of this passage and related passages, see E. Bammel, "Any Deyathiqi Cancelled Is Completely Cancelled," *JSS* 5 (1960): 355–58.

[142]   See also D. C. Sim, "Are the Least Included in the Kingdom of Heaven? The Meaning of Matthew 5:19," *Hervormde Teologiese Studies* 54 (1998): 573–87.

[143]   R. Deines, *Die Gerechtigkeit der Tora im Reich des Messias* (2004), 413–34; É. Cuvillier, "Torah Observance and Radicalization in the First Gospel," *NTS* 55 (2009): 153–54; J. D. Charles, "Garnishing with the 'Greater Righteousness': The Disciple's Relationship to the Law (Matthew 5:17–20)," *BBR* 12 (2002): 1–15.

returns to his all-important theme of righteousness (see the commentary on Matt 3:15). To satisfy Jesus, one's righteousness must surpass "that of the scribes and Pharisees," the very persons who criticize Jesus and his followers for not following the Law, or at least their understanding of it. The premise that runs throughout the Synoptic Gospels is that the scribes and Pharisees represent the pinnacle of fidelity to the Law, including their oral traditions, which were intended to build a protective fence around the written Law. If anyone had attained the degree of righteousness that pleases God, surely they have (cf. *1 Enoch* 15:1, "Fear not, Enoch, righteous man and scribe of righteousness"). In the balance of the Sermon on the Mount, Jesus will explain how righteousness can and must exceed the righteousness of the scribes and Pharisees.

If the Law is ignored, if one's righteousness is no better than that of the self-serving Pharisees, then one "will never enter the kingdom of heaven." Entering the kingdom of heaven, of course, is the hope of every Torah-observant Jew. This is its first mention in Matthew (cf. Matt 7:21; 18:3; 19:23–24; 23:13). This language appears in the other Synoptic Gospels also (cf. Mark 9:47; 10:15, 24–25; Luke 18:17, 25; Acts 14:22) and in the fourth Gospel (cf. John 3:5). The last occurrence in Matthew is especially poignant: "But woe to you, scribes and Pharisees, hypocrites! For you lock people out of the kingdom of heaven. For you do not go in yourselves, and when others are going in, you stop them" (Matt 23:13). Not only are the scribes and Pharisees in danger of not entering the kingdom of heaven, but their teachings and activities hinder others from entering also. No wonder Jesus insists that his disciples' righteousness must surpass that of the scribes and Pharisees.[144]

Jesus' command that his disciples exceed the righteousness of the scribes and Pharisees, and the examples that he offers them in what we call the "antitheses" (in Matt 5:21–48), reflect his Messianic authority, an authority that not only explains how the Law is to be understood and obeyed but is greater than the Law itself. In v. 18, Jesus said, "until heaven and earth pass away, not one letter, not one stroke of a letter, will pass from the law until all is accomplished." In Matt 24:35, Jesus tells his disciples, "Heaven and earth will pass away, but my words will not pass away." A comparison of Matt 5:18 with Matt 24:35 suggests that the Law remains valid until all is accomplished (through Jesus' teaching, ministry, death, and resurrection), but Jesus' words never expire. His teaching – what the Law really means and how it is truly fulfilled – remains valid for all time.[145]

---

[144] For a major study of the Old Testament and Jewish materials related to the meaning of "righteous" and "righteousness," see R. Deines, *Die Gerechtigkeit der Tora im Reich des Messias* (2004), 501–638.

[145] In light of this language, É. Cuvillier, "Torah Observance and Radicalization in the First Gospel," *NTS* 55 (2009): 152, finds that "Jesus does have authority over the law."

MATTHEW 5:21–26 – EXAMPLE ONE: MURDER

5:21: "You have heard that it was said to those of ancient times, 'You shall not murder'; and 'whoever murders shall be liable to judgment.'

5:22: But I say to you that if you are angry with a brother or sister, you will be liable to judgment; and if you insult a brother or sister, you will be liable to the council; and if you say, 'You fool,' you will be liable to the hell of fire.

5:23: So when you are offering your gift at the altar, if you remember that your brother or sister has something against you,

5:24: leave your gift there before the altar and go; first be reconciled to your brother or sister, and then come and offer your gift.

5:25: Come to terms quickly with your accuser while you are on the way to court with him, or your accuser may hand you over to the judge, and the judge to the guard, and you will be thrown into prison.

5:26: Truly I tell you, you will never get out until you have paid the last penny.

*M*atthew has assembled five examples of how Jesus understands the Law, five ways the righteousness of his disciples may surpass the righteousness of the scribes and Pharisees (as in Matt 5:20). These examples are usually called antitheses, in that Jesus counters ("but I say to you") a scribal or Pharisaic interpretation of a given passage of legal scripture. The five examples appear in Matt 5:21–48. They are Matt 5:21–26 (on murder), 5:27–32 (on adultery and divorce), 5:33–37 (on swearing oaths), 5:38–42 (on retaliation), and 5:43–48 (on love of enemies).[146] The antitheses do not appear in Luke, though elements of the material they contain do. There are some parallels with material in the Gospel of Mark also.

It must be emphasized that Jesus does not correct Scripture;[147] he only challenges certain interpretations and applications that some of his critics think are warranted by Scripture.[148] Jesus can hardly claim to fulfill the Law (Matt 5:17) if he then

---

[146] Some commentators count six antitheses instead of five. To do this, they count 5:31–32 as a separate antithesis. However, one should notice the change in form in v. 31 ("It was also said"). The shortened introduction ("It was said") links vv. 31–32 to vv. 27–30. It does not introduce a new antithesis that is unrelated to the others. Unlike the other antitheses, this is a compound antithesis that is made up of two parts: the first deals with adultery (vv. 27–30) and the second deals with divorce (vv. 31–32). Exactly how the two components are linked will be explained in the commentary on Matt 5:27–32.

[147] J. R. Levison, "A Better Righteousness: The Character and Purpose of Matthew 5:21–48," *Studia Biblica et Theologica* 12 (1982): 171–94. Levison rightly argues that the antitheses are not antithetical to the Law itself.

[148] The antitheses reflect intramural debates of first-century Judaism. See J. Kampen, "The Sectarian Form of the Antitheses within the Social World of the Matthean Community," *DSD* 1 (1994): 338–63.

contradicts it. Jesus fulfills the Law in the light of his conviction that it is summed up in two commands: to love God with all that one is and has (Deut 6:4–5) and to love one's neighbor as oneself (Lev 19:18; cf. Matt 22:34–40).[149]

Each antithesis begins with "you have heard that it was said" (although vv. 21 and 33 read a bit longer: "You have heard that it was said to those of ancient times"), implying that most people have *heard* Scripture read in the synagogue or recited in various settings and assuming that not too many people have actually *read* the commandments for themselves. By and large, that is probably true. But it should not be inferred from this (if the assumption is correct) that few Jews were literate in Jesus' time. (On the question of Jesus and literacy, see the commentary on Matt 13:53–58.)[150]

The first antithesis, like the third, refers to "those of ancient times," literally "the ancient ones" (**v. 21**; cf. v. 33). Who were they? The adjective "ancient" (Greek: *archaios*) may refer to "ancient generations" of people (as in Sir 2:10), including the "ancients" who committed "lawless deeds" and saw the temple destroyed (as in LXX Ps 78:8 [Hebrew and English 79:8]), or "ancient days" or "days of old" (as in Isa 37:26; Lam 1:7). But the ancients who were told the Law were the people of the wilderness generation who heard God speak from Sinai and heard the Law read to them by Moses (as in Exodus 20; cf. vv. 18–19, "all the people witnessed the thunder and lightning, the sound of the trumpet … and said to Moses, 'You speak to us, and we will listen'"). But there are passages that refer to the ancient wise men, who studied the Law and taught it to their students. We find pertinent examples in LXX 1 Sam 24:13 ("As the proverb of the ancients says …"), LXX 1 Kings 4:30 ("Solomon's wisdom surpassed the wisdom of all the ancients"), and especially Sir 39:1 ("He seeks out the wisdom of all the ancients, and is concerned with prophecies").

In view of these passages, it may be that "those of ancient times" that Jesus has in mind should not be limited to the people of the wilderness generation who first heard the Law at Sinai but may include subsequent ancients who studied the Law and generated the oral traditions, some of which Jesus will now oppose in Matt 5:21–48.

The first antithesis (vv. 21–26) concerns murder and begins by citing the sixth commandment (cf. Exod 20:13 = Deut 5:17): "You shall not murder." The second quotation, "whoever murders shall be liable to judgment," summarizes the juridical

---

[149] K. R. Snodgrass, "Matthew and the Law," in D. R. Bauer and M. A. Powell (eds.), *Treasures Old and New* (1996), 99–127.

[150] For more on the antitheses, see C. Dietzfelbinger, *Der Antithesen der Bergpredigt* (Munich: Kaiser, 1975); R. A. Guelich, "The Antitheses of Matthew v. 21–48: Traditional and/or Redactional?" *NTS* 22 (1976): 444–57; G. Strecker, "Die Antithesen der Bergpredigt (Mt 5.21–48 par.)," *ZNW* 69 (1978): 36–72; M. J. Suggs, "The Antitheses as Redactional Products," in R. H. Ruller (ed.), *Essays on the Love Commandment* (Philadelphia: Fortress, 1978), 93–107; C. Dietzfelbinger, "Die Antithesen der Bergpredigt im Verständnis des Matthäus," *ZNW* 70 (1979): 1–15.

process outlined in Exod 21:12; Lev 24:17; Num 35:12; and Deut 17:8–13. No Torah-observant Jew would disagree with the sixth commandment or with the laws that go with it.[151]

The rub comes in **v. 22**: "But I say to you that if you are angry with a brother or sister, you will be liable to judgment." It is not enough to refrain from committing actual murder; one must refrain from hating one's brother or sister. Jewish and Gentile ethicists in antiquity would have agreed with Jesus' position here, at least in principle. Jesus is demanding that his followers put the principle into practice to an extreme; if not, one could end up in court (literally "judgment"). Whoever says "if you insult a brother or sister, you will be liable to the council" (literally "If you say to your brother, 'Raca'"). "Raca" (or *reqa'*) is an Aramaic word brought into Matthew's Greek text (probably because his readers, whether or not they speak Aramaic, know what it means); it means "empty head" (or, in today's parlance, "airhead"). Such an insult could lead to an appearance before the "council" (literally "Sanhedrin"). But whoever says "You fool" (literally "moron") "will be liable to the hell of fire" (literally "gehenna of fire"). The progression in the hyperbole is plain enough: anger leads to the court, an insult leads to the highest court in Israel, and a grievous, degrading insult leads to hell itself (for more on hell, or Gehenna, see the commentary on Matt 18:9).[152] This logic is seen elsewhere in Jewish literature (Sir 22:24, "insults precede bloodshed"; *T. Gad* 2:1, "I confess now my sin.... I often wished to kill him, because I hated him"; 4:6, "as love would make alive even the dead ... so hatred would kill the living"; *b. Baba Mesia* 58b).

What is one to do? **Verses 23–25** explain how to avoid judgment. One mends the situation not by offering "a gift at the altar" (as if making things right with God makes it unnecessary to make things right with one's brother or sister) but by being "reconciled." Only then is it useful to offer a gift. The same teaching is found in rabbinic literature: "For transgressions between human and human, the Day of Atonement atones, only if the man will regain the good will of his friend" (*m. Yoma* 8:9). Similarly, one is well advised to "come to terms quickly" with one's "accuser," lest the situation escalate and one ends up in prison. One will not get out of there until the penalty is fully paid, literally "the last quadrans" (**v. 26**). An approximate parallel is found in Sextus, *Sentences* 39: "After he is released from his body, the evil person will be called to account by an evil demon until the last penny [*quadrans*] is paid up."[153]

[151] M. Weise, "Mt 5.21f. – ein Zeugnis sakraler Rechtsprechung in der Urgemeinde," *ZNW* 49 (1958): 16–23; C. F. D. Moule, "The 'Angry Word': Mt 5,21f.," *ExpT* 81 (1969): 10–13.

[152] P. Wernberg-Møller, "A Semitic Idiom in Matt. v. 22," *NTS* 3 (1956): 71–73; R. A. Guelich, "Matthew 5, 22: Its Meaning and Integrity," *ZNW* 64 (1973): 39–52; D. Garlington, "'You Fool!' Matthew 5:22," *BBR* 20 (2010): 61–84. Garlington suggests that the point is that in calling a believer a "fool" is in effect to call that believer an apostate or unbeliever. Such a harsh (and unfair) word could result in judgment upon the one who utters it. Rabbi Yohanan is said to have called an insolent student a "fool" (*reqa'*) and then "set his eyes on him" and the student died (*b. B. Bat.* 75a = *b. Sanh.* 100a).

[153] See *NewDocs* 9 (2002): 59–61: "I ask, if it seems right, to order his arrest, until he makes repayment to me."

It has been suggested that "gift," "brother," and the subject of hatred and murder may recall the tragic story of Cain, whose offering (LXX: "gift") was rejected, and his brother Abel, whose offering was accepted and who was killed by the resentful Cain (cf. Genesis 4). In the Greco-Roman world, we have the warning of Plutarch, who says that wickedness, once it takes hold, can very quickly convert anger into murder: "Wickedness, when by reason of power it possesses rapid speed, forces every passion to emerge, making of anger murder, of love adultery, of covetousness confiscation" (cf. *Moralia* 782C: "To an Uneducated Reader" 6).[154]

MATTHEW 5:27–32 – EXAMPLE TWO: ADULTERY AND DIVORCE

5:27: "You have heard that it was said, 'You shall not commit adultery.'

5:28: But I say to you that everyone who looks at a woman with lust has already committed adultery with her in his heart.

5:29: If your right eye causes you to sin, tear it out and throw it away; it is better for you to lose one of your members than for your whole body to be thrown into hell.

5:30: And if your right hand causes you to sin, cut it off and throw it away; it is better for you to lose one of your members than for your whole body to go into hell.

5:31: "It was also said, 'Whoever divorces his wife, let him give her a certificate of divorce.'

5:32: But I say to you that anyone who divorces his wife, except on the ground of unchastity, causes her to commit adultery; and whoever marries a divorced woman commits adultery.

The first antithesis concerned murder, hatred, and reconciliation (Matt 5:21–26). The second antithesis concerns adultery, lust, divorce, and remarriage (vv. 27–32). It is in fact one antithesis, even though it is made up of two parts, the first treating the commandment not to commit adultery (vv. 27–30) and the second treating divorce law (vv. 31–32). They are tied together, as will become clear in the commentary. The second part of the antithesis has drawn upon material in Mark (cf. Mark 10:2–12).[155]

The second antithesis (v. 27) begins with a quotation of the seventh commandment, "You shall not commit adultery" (Exod 20:14 = Deut 5:18). Jesus' selection of the topic of adultery is very interesting when we remember that adultery,

[154] G. B. Caird, "Expounding the Parables: I. The Defendant (Matthew 5.25f.; Luke 12.58f.)," *ExpT* 77 (1965): 36–39.
[155] P. J. du Plessis, "The Ethics of Marriage According to Matt 5:27–32," *Neot* 1 (1967): 16–27.

divorce, and remarriage constituted the gist of John the Baptist's criticism of Herod Antipas, the tetrarch of Galilee (cf. Matt 14:1–12). On the face of it, there is nothing controversial about the prohibition of adultery. No one would disagree with Moses. But what constitutes divorce? That is the question, and Jesus' answer will unsettle some.

It is not enough, Jesus says, to refrain from physical contact: "But I say to you that everyone who looks at a woman with lust has already committed adultery with her in his heart" (**v. 28**). To look "at a woman with lust" (literally "looking at a woman to lust for her") is in itself adultery and, in fact, is what often leads to divorce (which is the point of the second part of the antithesis, in vv. 31–32). Sinning with one's thoughts, whether or not these thoughts lead to sinful deeds, is discussed in late antiquity (Plato, *Crat.* 420a; Aristotle, *Eth. Nic.* 1167a–b, "love begins with the eye"). Most think thoughts and deeds are tied together (see, e.g., *Letter of Aristeas* 133; *T. Gad* 5:5; *T. Joseph* 17:3; Ps.-Phocylides 52, "It is each person's intention that is examined"), though there is disagreement in some rabbinic traditions (e.g., *b. Qiddushin* 39b, "evil intention is not combined with deeds"). To "lust for her" (as the Greek literally reads) probably alludes to Exod 20:17, "you shall not covet [or lust for] your neighbor's wife." According to Sextus, *Sentences* 233, "Know that you are an adulterer, even if you merely think of committing adultery. And let your attitude about every sin be the same." Jesus' focus is entirely on the man, not on the woman.[156]

In saying "If your right eye causes you to sin, tear it out and throw it away" (**v. 29**), Jesus employs graphic hyperbole to make his point: better maimed in heaven than whole in hell. The danger is that if people cannot or will not control their urges, they risk falling into sin and judgment. What is rendered "thrown into hell" in the NRSV is literally "thrown into Gehenna." Gehenna is an Aramaic word, from "Valley of Hinnom," with sinister connotations. Unlike the word "Hades," which was not necessarily negative, Gehenna referred to a place of fire, death, and destruction. The word is ubiquitous in rabbinic and targumic literature (for further comments, see the commentary on Matt 18:7–9).

Lust usually begins with what the eye sees. This in turn often leads to something that the hand does; that is, it reaches out to touch or take. This is why Jesus next says, "And if your right hand causes you to sin, cut it off and throw it away" (**v. 30**). Loss of the right hand constituted a terrible disability. Nevertheless, "it is better for you to lose one of your members than for your whole body to go into hell."[157]

---

[156]   *Pace* K. Haacker, "Der Rechtssatz Jesu zum Thema Ehebruch (Mt 5, 28)," *BZ* 21 (1977): 113–16. Rightly, see K. E. Brower, "Jesus and the Lustful Eye: Glancing at Matthew 5:28," *EvQ* 76 (2004): 291–309.

[157]   For a discussion of rabbinic ideas about members of the body that cause offense, see H. W. Basser, "The Meaning of 'Shtuth': Gen. R. 11 in Reference to Matthew 5.29–30 and 18.8–9," *NTS* 31 (1985): 148–51.

The relationship between the first part of the antithesis and the second part now becomes clear. Lust for a woman to whom one is not married sometimes leads to divorce. But lust for another woman is hardly grounds for divorce. Jesus knew that this was precisely what some men did and yet they claimed to have committed no sin. It is true that no physical adultery has occurred, but lust for the other woman led to the divorce of one's wife so that a "lawful" remarriage could take place. Jesus saw through this practice and criticized it.

The second part of the antithesis begins, "It was also said, 'Whoever divorces his wife, let him give her a certificate of divorce'" (**v. 31**). The law of divorce is treated in Deut 24:1–4. Moses required a man to write out a certificate of divorce ("... she does not please him because he finds something objectionable about her, and so he writes her a certificate of divorce, puts it in her hand, and sends her out of his house ..."). The divorce proceedings were intended to place limits on the man, who in ancient near eastern culture had great power over his wife. The "certificate of divorce" forced the man to declare his grounds for divorce, thus making him accountable to his neighbors and, more importantly, to his wife's family. His reasons for divorce had better be good ones. In some rabbinic discussions, grounds for divorce, based on interpretation of Deut 24:1–4, were quite flimsy and were very much in the man's favor.[158] The certificate also made it possible for the woman socially and legally to remarry. It also prevented the man from taking the woman back or, as the case may well have been, taking advantage of her sexually in the future. Under no circumstances, however, was the Mosaic Law intended to encourage divorce or accommodate lustful desires.[159]

Divorcing one's wife to marry another woman is adultery, Jesus says, "except on the ground of unchastity" (**v. 32**). If the woman has been unchaste, then her husband is not liable to the charge of causing her to commit adultery, either through remarriage (which is forbidden, on the same grounds that apply to the man) or, worse, through fornication or prostitution. What the NRSV translates as "unchastity" (Greek: *porneia*) may refer either to adultery or to incest (cf. 1 Cor 5:1), but it is probable that the primary reference is to adultery (as implied in Deut 24:1 and in

---

[158] D. Moo, "Jesus and the Authority of the Mosaic Law," *JSNT* 20 (1984): 20, where Moo rightly remarks that "the root problem which Jesus attacks is a liberal divorce procedure based on the Deuteronomy passage." Although not all rabbis adhered to such liberal interpretations, the views of Hillel and Aqiba, two very influential sages of the first and second centuries, were likely held by many of their contemporaries. According to the Mishna (*Git.* 9:10), "And the School of Hillel say: '[He may divorce her] even if she spoiled a dish for him, for it is written, "Because he has found in her indecency in" anything.' Rabbi Aqiba says: 'Even if he found another fairer than she, for it is written, "And it shall be if she find no favor in his eyes ..."'" (trans. based on H. Danby, *The Mishnah* [Oxford: Oxford University Press, 1933], 321).

[159] G. J. Wenham, "Gospel Definitions of Adultery and Women's Rights," *ExpT* 95 (1984): 330–32. Wenham rightly recognizes that Jesus' teaching on divorce was to protect women.

subsequent rabbinic interpretation; cf. *m. Gittin* 9:10; *Sipre Deut.* §269 [on Deut 24:1]; *b. Gittin* 90a–b).[160]

Jesus completes his teaching on this sensitive topic by adding "and whoever marries a divorced woman commits adultery" (**v. 32**). Why is this so? If the divorced woman was divorced because of unchastity on her part, then it would be wrong for a man to marry her (because she is an adulteress). But if she has been unlawfully divorced by her husband, then she really is not free to remarry. Therefore, to marry her is in effect to marry another man's wife. However, if the woman herself has committed adultery or some other sexual sin, the man has not committed adultery in divorcing her and marrying another.[161] (For more on the theme of divorce, see the commentary on Matt 19:3–9.)

MATTHEW 5:33–37 – EXAMPLE THREE: HONEST SPEECH

5:33: "Again, you have heard that it was said to those of ancient times, 'You shall not swear falsely, but carry out the vows you have made to the Lord.'

5:34: But I say to you, Do not swear at all, either by heaven, for it is the throne of God,

5:35: or by the earth, for it is his footstool, or by Jerusalem, for it is the city of the great King.

5:36: And do not swear by your head, for you cannot make one hair white or black.

5:37: Let your word be 'Yes, Yes' or 'No, No'; anything more than this comes from the evil one.

*T*he third antithesis is concerned with vows and oaths. Oaths in antiquity, probably dating back to preliterary times, were a common part of contracts, agreements, and treaties. Because humans often cannot be trusted (either to comply with or remember the terms), agreements often invoked the gods as witnesses and

---

[160] D. Daube, "Origen and the Punishment of Adultery in Jewish Law," in C. M. Carmichael (ed.), *Collected Works of David Daube*, Volume One: *Talmudic Law* (Studies in Comparative Legal History; Berkeley: University of California Press, 1992), 167–71.

[161] For more on the "exception clause," see B. Vawter, "The Divorce Clauses in Matt. 5,32 and 19,9," *CBQ* 16 (1954): 155–67; A. Mahoney, "A New Look at the Divorce Clauses in Mt 5,32 and 19,9," *CBQ* 30 (1968): 29–38; L. Sabourin, "The Divorce Clauses (Mt 5:32, 19:9)," *BTB* 2 (1972): 80–86; J. J. Kilgallen, "To What Are the Matthean Exception-Texts (5,32 and 19,9) an Exception?" *Bib* 61 (1980): 102–5; G. J. Wenham, "Matthew and Divorce: An Old Crux Revisited," *JSNT* 22 (1984): 95–107; B. Witherington III, "Matthew 5.32 and 19.19 – Exception or Exceptional Situation?" *NTS* 31 (1985): 571–75; M. N. A. Bockmuehl, "Matthew 5.32; 19.9 in the Light of Pre-Rabbinic Halakhah," *NTS* 35 (1989): 291–95. Bockmuehl finds that divorce was not only permitted in cases of adultery but required.

guarantors of the agreement,[162] complete with threats against the violator of the agreement.[163] The antithesis regarding oaths begins, like the four other antitheses, with a quotation from the Law: "You shall not swear falsely, but carry out the vows you have made to the Lord" (v. 33).[164] (On "those of ancient times," see the commentary on Matt 5:21.)

The quotation summarizes several laws, but the closest parallel is perhaps Lev 19:12, "you shall not swear falsely by My name, so as to profane the name of your God; I am the Lord" (see also Exod 20:7; Num 30:3–15; Deut 23:21–23), and the latter part of the quoted commandment, "carry out" [literally pay] "the vows you have made to the Lord," may allude to Ps 50:14, "pay your vows to the Most High" (cf. LXX Ps 49:14).

The Greek verb that underlies "You shall not swear falsely," *epiorkein*, can refer either to the commission of perjury (false testimony under oath)[165] or making a vow that is not kept.[166] Given the second part of the quoted commandment, "carry out the vows you have made to the Lord," it is clear that the second meaning is intended.[167] The ways in which people felt they could leave their vows unfulfilled will be considered shortly.

---

[162] Agamemnon assures Odysseus: "This I am willing to swear, and my heart bids me, nor will I swear falsely [*epiorkeso*] before god" (Homer, *Iliad* 19.188). The reference is from J. A. L. Lee, "Led Astray by Punctuation: The Meaning of ἐπιορκέω in Matt 5:33," *NovT* 52 (2010): 24–36 at 29. Lee draws our attention to an error in the presentation of Bauer's lexical data in the English edition of BAG and BAGD.

[163] The Athenians pray "for the one who observes this oath [to honor democracy], that there may be many blessings, but for the one who breaks his oath [*epiorkounti*], that he and his family may be wiped out" (Andocides, *Myst.* 98). Again, the citation is from Lee. See J. A. L. Lee, "Led Astray by Punctuation," *NovT* 52 (2010): 30. Observe also the juxtaposition of treaties and oaths in the accusation "… what they both did in violating oaths [*epiorkesan*] and breaking treaties …" (Plutarch, *Comp. Demetrius et Antonius* 5.3); J. A. L. Lee, "Led Astray by Punctuation," *NovT* 52 (2010): 31.

[164] G. Dautzenberg, "Ist das Schwurverbot Mt 5,33–7; Jak 5,12 ein Beispiel für die Torakritik Jesu?" *BZ* 25 (1981): 47–66, thinks the antithesis does not go back to Jesus. To be sure, the material has been edited and glossed, but the radical nature of the teaching bears the characteristics of authentic Jesus tradition. For a rebuttal of Dautzenberg, see A. Ito, "The Question of the Authenticity of the Ban on Swearing (Matthew 5.33–37)," *JSNT* 43 (1991): 5–13. James alludes to the tradition, and Paul apparently was aware of it.

[165] As in Philo, "For an oath is nothing else than to call God to bear witness in a disputed matter" (*Spec. Leg.* 2.10), cited by C. H. Talbert, *Reading the Sermon on the Mount* (2004), 84. To call upon God as witness, in the giving of false testimony, is "the most impious of all things" (ibid.).

[166] As in Cicero, writing in the first century B.C., "an oath is an assurance backed by religious sanctity; and a solemn promise given, as before God as one's witness, is to be sacredly kept" (*De off.* 3.104), cited by C. H. Talbert, *Reading the Sermon on the Mount* (2004), 84.

[167] J. A. L. Lee, "Led Astray by Punctuation," *NovT* 52 (2010): 35, recommends as the translation: "You shall not break a sworn promise, but you shall fulfill to the Lord your sworn promises."

But it is not enough to refrain from making false vows. Jesus commands his disciples, "Do not swear at all" (**v. 34**). Jesus himself refused to take the oath the high priest would have imposed on him (in Matt 26:63). Jesus will make no exception; oaths are to be avoided, whether "by heaven," "by the earth," or "by Jerusalem." What do these qualifications mean?[168]

Jesus forbids vows and oaths because of the risk of profaning God; that is, of making light of His person and character. Ultimately what lies behind Jesus' prohibition is the commandment "You shall not make wrongful use of the name of the Lord your God" (Exod 20:7). So what if one swears an oath "by heaven"? That is inappropriate, says Jesus, because it is "the throne of God." In other words, even the mention of heaven comes too close because it is the dwelling of God (cf. Ps 11:4, "The Lord is in his holy temple; the Lord's throne is in heaven").

Jesus forbids swearing "by the earth, for it is his footstool" (**v. 35**). The same rationale applies to swearing by the earth. This, too, comes too close, for the earth is God's "footstool" (cf. Isa 66:1, "Thus says the Lord: 'Heaven is my throne and the earth is my footstool'"). Jesus' teaching finds expression in the letter of James: "Above all, my beloved, do not swear, either by heaven or by earth or by any other oath, but let your 'Yes' be yes and your 'No' be no, so that you may not fall under condemnation" (James 5:12).

And finally, Jesus forbids swearing "by Jerusalem, for it is the city of the great King" (v. 35). Again, the same logic applies to swearing by Jerusalem. Such a qualification still comes too close to profaning God's name, for Jerusalem is the "city of the great King" (cf. Ps 48:2, "Beautiful in elevation, is the joy of all the earth, Mount Zion, in the far north, the city of the great King").[169] As D. C. Duling has shown, the title "great king" was a commonplace in the eastern Mediterranean of late antiquity, and even Agrippa I struck coins whose legend referred to him as the "great king."[170]

Jesus concludes his teaching on oaths by exhorting his disciples, "And do not swear by your head, for you cannot make one hair white or black" (**v. 36**). Well, if one must not swear or make an oath by heaven, earth, or Jerusalem, may one qualify an oath by reference to himself? No, Jesus says, because a human being has no power, not even over himself, even to do something trivial. Oaths, along with their various qualifications, run the risk of being unfulfilled, dishonest, and even blasphemous.

---

[168] Jesus of Nazareth was not the only sage to express misgivings about oaths. Ben Sira has this to say: "Do not accustom your mouth to oaths, nor habitually utter the name of the Holy One.... The one who swears many oaths is full of iniquity, and the scourge will not leave his house. If he swears in error, his sin remains on him, and if he disregards it, he sins doubly; if he swears a false oath, he will not be justified, for his house will be filled with calamities" (Sir 23:9–11).

[169] Qumran opposed swearing by the name of God and even forbade swearing by the Law of Moses "because the name of God is written out fully in it" (CD 15:1–3).

[170] D. C. Duling, "Against Oaths: Crossan *Sayings Parallels* 59," *Forum* 6, no. 2 (1990): 99–138.

Jesus and his contemporaries were well aware of the kinds of shenanigans and deceit that often played a part in vows and oaths. Here is an example of a rabbinic discussion of oaths: "If he said to him, 'If one litigant said to the other, "I accept my father as reliable"; "I accept your father as reliable"; "I accept as reliable three herdsmen [to serve as judges]"' – R. Meir says, 'He has the power to retract.' And sages say, 'He has not the power to retract.' If one owed an oath to this fellow, and this fellow said, '[Instead of an oath], take a vow to me *by the life of your head*,' R. Meir says, 'He has the power to retract.' And sages say, 'He has not the power to retract'" (*m. Sanh.* 3:2, emphasis added). The "power to retract" means that one can make his vow void. In effect, it means that his vow was false and so, by Jesus' understanding, one has violated the commandment not to swear falsely (Lev 19:12). The whole debate presupposes ways of backing out of one's vow.[171] Jesus will not allow his disciples to do this.

Instead, Jesus says, "Let your word be 'Yes, Yes' or 'No, No'" (**v. 37**). Accordingly, Jesus' disciples are not to swear by this or that, but they are to be truthful. "Yes," they will pay such and such, or "No," they will not do such and such. Whether one answers Yes or one answers No, it is the truth and it will be done as affirmed.[172] Jesus' disciples are to be men and women of their word, not prevaricators and dissemblers, whose complicated and heavily qualified vows and oaths may in fact serve as camouflage for deceit. (Some readers will remember a recent holder of high office who tried to justify his perjury by saying that it depended on "what the meaning of 'is' is.") Gentile ethicists agreed, asserting that it is better to demonstrate the integrity of his word rather than relying on appeals to the gods (Diogenes Laertius, *Lives of Eminent Philosophers* 8.22). Jesus' teaching may be echoed in Paul's comment to the Corinthian Christians: "Therefore, I was not vacillating when I intended to do this, was I? Or that which I purpose, do I purpose according to the flesh, that with me there should be yes, yes and no, no at the same time? But as God is faithful, our word to you is not yes and no" (2 Cor 1:17–18).[173]

Jesus concludes by saying that "anything more than this comes from the evil one." This final comment probably derives from Matthew himself and is not intended to be a word of Jesus. (Where to begin and end quotations in the Gospels is not always clear, as seen, for example, in John 3.) The point of this concluding comment is that

---

[171]   Rabbinic literature also has a saying about making the wing of a black raven white: "If all the nations of the world should gather together to make white one wing of a raven they would not be able to accomplish it" (*Lev. Rab.* 19.2 [on Lev 15:25]; cf. *Song Rab.* 5:11 §3).

[172]   E. Kutsch, "Eure Rede aber sei ja ja, nein nein," *EvT* 20 (1960): 206–18; P. Minear, "Yes or No: The Demand for Honesty in the Early Church," *NovT* 13 (1971): 1–13, reprinted in P. S. Minear, *Commands of Christ: Authority and Implications* (Nashville, TN: Abingdon, 1972), 30–46.

[173]   *2 Enoch* 49:1–2 offers a very close parallel to Matt 5:33–37. However, *2 Enoch* is heavily influenced by Christian tradition and so 49:1–2 is probably no more than a gloss. Indeed, *2 Enoch* may actually be a Christian composition.

what goes beyond an honest Yes or No "comes from the evil one." The Greek's *ek tou ponerou* is ambiguous. It could mean "from evil" or "of evil." But the adjective could be substantival and mean "from the evil one," the devil. The NRSV evidently understands it in this latter sense. An allusion to the devil is entirely appropriate, for in Judeo-Christian circles he had the well-earned reputation for trickery and deceit.

\

MATTHEW 5:38–42 – EXAMPLE FOUR: ON RETALIATION

5:38: "You have heard that it was said, 'An eye for an eye and a tooth for a tooth.'

5:39: But I say to you, Do not resist an evildoer. But if anyone strikes you on the right cheek, turn the other also;**

5:40: and if anyone wants to sue you and take your coat, give your cloak as well;**

5:41: and if anyone forces you to go one mile, go also the second mile.**

5:42: Give to everyone who begs from you, and do not refuse anyone who wants to borrow from you.**

*T*he fourth antithesis concerns retaliation, forgiveness, and generosity. The commandment that Jesus quotes, "An eye for an eye and a tooth for a tooth" (**v. 38**), comes from Exod 21:23–25 ("If any harm follows, then you shall give life for life, eye for eye, tooth for tooth, hand for hand, foot for foot, burn for burn, wound for wound, stripe for stripe"), Lev 24:19 ("Anyone who maims another shall suffer the same injury in return: fracture for fracture, eye for eye, tooth for tooth; the injury inflicted is the injury to be suffered"), and Deut 19:21 ("Show no pity: life for life, eye for eye, tooth for tooth, hand for hand, foot for foot").[174] Although there are variations in these lists of injuries and penalties (such as "burn," "wound," and "stripe" in Exodus, "fracture" in Leviticus), common to all three passages is "eye for an eye and a tooth for a tooth."

The principle underlying this law is *jus talionis* ("justice of kind") or *lex talionis* ("law of kind"), or justice of equal measure. The idea is that one compensates another for damages, but one is not required to pay over the amount of the actual damages; nor is it satisfactory to pay under the amount.[175] The law is an ancient one, attested not only in the Law of Moses but also in the Babylonian Code of Hammurabi (eighteenth century B.C.). It was still in practice in the time of Jesus and the early church (e.g., *Jub.* 4:31–32; Josephus, *Ant.* 4.280; 11Q19 61:9–12, "If it turns out that the witness has falsely accused his comrade, then you shall do to him what he had schemed

[174]   And in a nonlegal context: "skin for skin" (Job 2:4).

[175]   One may have the injury done to him that he did to another, or a payment can be made, usually at the discretion of the injured party. See Philo, *Spec. Leg.* 3.181–204, and Josephus, *Ant.* 4.280, for discussions of how the law was applied in their time, the approximate time of Jesus and the early church.

to do to his comrade. Thus you will purge the evil one from your midst."). The point of *jus talionis* was not to condone personal revenge or petty payback (as in slapping back, or returning insult for insult) but to compensate fairly.[176]

That revenge and retaliation are in mind is seen in the commands: "Do not resist an evildoer. But if anyone strikes you on the right cheek, turn the other also" (**v. 39**). This has nothing to do with just compensation for loss or damage. Jesus commands his disciples not only to forego revenge but even to forego just compensation (a wish that reappears in Paul's letters as well; cf. 1 Cor 6:7, "In fact, to have lawsuits at all with one another is already a defeat for you. Why not rather be wronged? Why not rather be defrauded?"). Therefore, if anyone wants to sue you and take your coat, give your cloak as well (**v. 40**), or, "if anyone forces you to go one mile" (as Roman law permitted),[177] "go also the second mile" (**v. 41**).[178] Instead of exacting revenge or repayment, "Give to everyone who begs from you, and do not refuse anyone who wants to borrow from you" (**v. 42**).

Similar sentiments are found in some of the Greco-Roman philosophers. Musonius said that "he would never indict anyone who had injured him, nor would he advise anyone else to do so" (Musonius 10). Seneca remarked: "If someone gets angry with you, challenge him with kindness in return. Enmity immediately tumbles away when one side lets it fall" (*De Ira* 2.34.5); "It is a pitifully small-minded person who gives bite for bite" (*De Ira* 2.34.1). Or even closer to the examples in Jesus' teaching, one thinks of the forgiving Spartan, as related by Epictetus: "Who is there among us who does not admire Lycourgos of Sparta, in his response to being blinded in one eye by a fellow citizen. The people handed the young man over to

---

[176] J. F. Davis, *Lex Talionis in Early Judaism and the Exhortation of Jesus in Matthew 5.38–42* (JSNTSup 281; London: T. & T. Clark International, 2005); H. D. Betz, *The Sermon on the Mount* (1995), 275–77.

[177] On compulsory public service in the Roman Empire related to transportation, see *NewDocs* 7:58–92, especially 85–87. We may actually have an example of compulsory service in Simon of Cyrene, who was compelled to assist Jesus in carrying the cross to the place of crucifixion. See Matt 27:32; Mark 15:21; Luke 23:26. Advice in Epictetus shows the currency of the practice: "If a soldier commandeers your donkey, let it go" (*Discourses* 4.1.79).

[178] H. Clavier, "Matthieu 5,39 et la non-résistance," *RHPR* 37 (1957): 44–57; S. Currie, "Matthew 5.39f. – Resistance or Protest?" *HTR* 57 (1964): 140–45; J. Rausch, "The Principle of Nonresistance and Love of Enemy in Mt 5,38–48," *CBQ* 28 (1966): 31–41; L. R. Donelson, "'Do Not Resist Evil' and the Question of Biblical Authority," *HBT* 10 (1988): 33–46; W. Wink, "Beyond Just War and Pacifism: Jesus' Nonviolent Way," *RevExp* 89 (1992): 197–214; H. D. Betz, *The Sermon on the Mount* (1995), 284: "The meaning ... is not to recommend resignation and defeatism concerning evil.... Rather, what is commanded is not non-violence in general but desistance from retaliation in specific instances." These studies point out that the antithesis on nonretaliation represents only part of the totality of biblical teaching related to the question of how to deal with violence. The point of the antithesis has to do with *retaliation*, not *violence* as such (against Wink); rightly, see C. H. Talbert, *Reading the Sermon on the Mount* (2004), 90.

him, to take whatever vengeance he wanted. He refrained from any retaliation in kind, but educated him and made a good man of him" (Epictetus, *Encheiridion* 5). See also the advice in Sextus, *Sentences* 17, "Let your neighbor take away everything except your freedom."

It is God, as the only true and just judge, who will compensate or punish humans. The disciples of Jesus are to leave the judging and the vengeance to him (cf. Rom 12:19, "Beloved, never avenge yourselves, but leave room for the wrath of God; for it is written, 'Vengeance is mine, I will repay' [Deut 32:35], says the Lord").

MATTHEW 5:43–48 – EXAMPLE FIVE: LOVE OF ENEMIES

5:43: "You have heard that it was said, 'You shall love your neighbor and hate your enemy.'

5:44: But I say to you, Love your enemies and pray for those who persecute you,

5:45: so that you may be children of your Father in heaven; for he makes his sun rise on the evil and on the good, and sends rain on the righteous and on the unrighteous.

5:46: For if you love those who love you, what reward do you have? Do not even the tax collectors do the same?

5:47: And if you greet only your brothers and sisters, what more are you doing than others? Do not even the Gentiles do the same?

5:48: Be perfect, therefore, as your heavenly Father is perfect.

The fifth and final antithesis concerns love of neighbor and enemy. The first commandment that is quoted, "You shall love your neighbor" (**v. 43**), comes from Lev 19:18, "You shall not take vengeance or bear a grudge against any of your people, but you shall love your neighbor as yourself; I am the Lord." This command not only enjoins loving one's neighbor but also forbids taking vengeance, which relates to other themes in the antithesis under consideration as well as in the previous antithesis (cf. Matt 5:38–42).[179]

On another occasion, Jesus quotes Lev 19:18 as the second part of the double commandment to love God with all that one is and has and to love one's neighbor

---

[179] For a selection of studies on this popular and much-discussed antithesis, see O. Linton, "St. Matthew 5,43," *ST* 18 (1964): 66–79; W. Bauer, "Das Gebot der Feindesliebe und die alten Christen," in *Aufsätze und kleine Schriften* (Tübingen: Mohr-Siebeck, 1967), 235–52; O. J. F. Seitz, "Love Your Enemies," *NTS* 16 (1969): 39–54; D. Lührmann, "Liebet eure Feinde (Lk 6,27–36; Mt 5,39–48)," *ZTK* 69 (1972): 412–38; P. S. Minear, *Commands of Christ* (1972), 69–82; O. Bayer, "Sprachbewegung und Weltveränderung: Ein systematischer Versuch als Auslegung von Mt 5,43–8," *EvT* 35 (1975): 309–21; J. Piper, *"Love Your Enemies": Jesus' Love Command in the Synoptic Gospels and the Early Christian Paraenesis* (SNTSMS 38; Cambridge: Cambridge University Press, 1979).

as oneself (see the commentary on Matt 22:34–40). But this time Jesus sets the command to love against a command to "hate" one's "enemy." Where are we commanded to hate our enemy? The passage from which Jesus quoted, Lev 19:18, is actually preceded by a verse that enjoins one not to hate one's brother (Lev 19:17, "You shall not hate your fellow countryman in your heart; you may surely reprove your neighbor, but shall not incur sin because of him"). If we are not to hate our brother, are we permitted, even commanded, to hate our enemy? Is this said anywhere in Scripture?[180] Again, what Jesus opposes is not Scripture (for nowhere in Scripture do we actually find the words "hate your enemy") but "an improper interpretation of Lev 19:18."[181]

Nothing in Scripture explicitly commands God's people to hate their enemy. The generation of the conquest, however, was sternly commanded to show the inhabitants of the land "no mercy" (cf. Deut 7:2, 16). An angry psalm writer cries out against those who plot against him, "I hate them with perfect hatred; I count them my enemies" (Ps 139:22), but this is no commandment.

Elsewhere in Scripture, love for some and hatred for others are juxtaposed. God says to Jacob (i.e., Israel), "'I have loved you,' says the Lord. But you say, 'How have you loved us?' 'Is not Esau Jacob's brother?' says the Lord. 'Yet I have loved Jacob but I have hated Esau; I have made his hill country a desolation and his heritage a desert for jackals'" (Mal 1:2–3). The Psalmist enjoins, "Hate evil, you who love the Lord" (Ps 97:10) and "hate the double-minded, but I love your law" (Ps 119:113), whereas, more philosophically, the Preacher asserts that there is "a time to love, and a time to hate; a time for war, and a time for peace" (Eccles 3:8), and the prophet Amos commands, "Hate evil and love good" (Amos 5:15). Even the promise to the patriarch Abraham could be construed to teach hatred for enemies: "I will bless those who bless you, and the one who curses you I will curse" (Gen 12:3).

From all of this, it is not difficult to see how some could assume that Scripture really does command God's people to "hate" their "enemy." The men of Qumran evidently assumed this. There are passages among the Dead Sea Scrolls that explicitly speak of hatred of the enemies of the Qumran community. The Instructor commands the men of the community to love what God loves and to hate what God hates. This means they are to "love all the Children of Light" (members of the community) and "hate all the Children of Darkness" (that is, those who oppose them or, more simply, their enemies). Indeed, members of the community are not only to hate the "Men of the Pit" but they also believe that God will conceal the truth from their enemies (cf. 1QS 4:6, "concealing the truth"; 9:17, "he should conceal his own insight into the Law when among perverse men"; 11Q19 61:10; Josephus, *J.W.* 2.139, the Essene "will always hate the wicked").

[180] M. Smith, "Mt v, 43: Hate Thine Enemy," *HTR* 45 (1952): 71–73.
[181] H. D. Betz, *The Sermon on the Mount* (1995), 304. See also R. A. Guelich, *The Sermon on the Mount* (1982), 225–27.

A Closer Look: Loving and Hating

According to the *Rule of the Community* the Instructor is to teach them [the members of the community] to love everything ⁴ he [God] chose and to hate everything he rejected, to distance themselves from all evil ⁵ and to hold fast to all good deeds; to practice truth, justice, and righteousness ⁶ in the land ... ⁷ He is to induct all who volunteer to live by the laws of God ⁸ into the Covenant of Mercy, so as to be joined to God's society and walk faultless before him, according to all ⁹ that has been revealed for the times appointed them. He is to teach them both to love all the "Children of Light" – each ¹⁰ commensurate with his rightful place in the council of God – and to hate all the "Children of Darkness," each commensurate with his guilt ¹¹ and the vengeance due him from God. (1QS 1:3b–11a)

These are the precepts of the Way for the Instructor in these times, as to his loving and hating: eternal hatred ²² and a concealing spirit for the "Men of the Pit"! (1QS 9:21b–22a)

Translation based on M. O. Wise, M. G. Abegg, Jr., and E. M. Cook, *The Dead Sea Scrolls: A New Translation* (1996), 127, 140. On the relevance of 1QS for understanding Matt 5:43, see V. P. Furnish, *The Love Command in the New Testament* (Nashville, TN: Abingdon, 1972), 46–47. The evidence of 1QS corrects the assertion in G. Friedlander, *The Jewish Sources of the Sermon on the Mount* (London: Bloch, 1911), 69–70.

The hatred expressed in the Rule of the Community scroll from Qumran should be understood in literal terms. But the "hating" expressed in the scriptures that have been mentioned is probably relative, if not hyperbolic. When God says through Malachi, "I have loved Jacob but I have hated Esau" (cf. Rom 9:13, "As it is written, 'I have loved Jacob, but I have hated Esau'"), what is really meant is that God loves Jacob more than he loves Esau. The same applies when Jesus demands his followers to hate family: "Whoever comes to me and does not hate father and mother, wife and children, brothers and sisters, yes, and even life itself, cannot be my disciple" (Luke 14:26). That this requirement is relative and hyperbolic is seen when comparison is made with the parallel in Matthew: "Whoever loves father or mother more than me is not worthy of me; and whoever loves son or daughter more than me is not worthy of me" (Matt 10:37). Jesus has not asked his followers to hate their families; he has asked them to love him above all else.

The scriptural commandment to which Jesus has made reference was probably understood in the same way: we are to love our neighbor, but refrain from loving our enemy. However, this was not Jesus' understanding. Rather, he commands: "Love your enemies and pray for those who persecute you" (**v. 44**). The saying is echoed in Paul: "Bless those who persecute you; bless and do not curse them" (Rom

12:14). An approximate parallel is also found in Luke: "bless those who curse you, pray for those who abuse you" (Luke 6:28).

The concept of loving one's enemy, as well as one's neighbor (which would include family and friends), challenges the interpretation of Scripture that some of Jesus' contemporaries held (as seen especially in the examples from Qumran). But Jesus' teaching of love of one's enemy is anticipated in law and wisdom from the ancient Near East, both in Israelite (Prov 24:17, "Do not rejoice when your enemy falls"; 25:21, "If your enemy is hungry, give him bread to eat") and non-Israelite tradition ("Recompense your evildoer with good").[182] In one of the versions of the popular *Wisdom of Ahiqar* (ca. 600 B.C.), the sage counsels: "My son, if your enemy meets you with evil, meet him with wisdom" (2:20 in Syriac Version A).[183] According to the *Sentences* of Sextus, a second-century collection of Greco-Roman wisdom sayings, "Consider no one to be an enemy" (*Sentences* 105); "Pray that you may be able to do good to your enemies" (*Sentences* 213). The precept is found in Jewish literature closer to the time of Jesus and his disciples (*T. Benjamin* 4:3, "And though they devise with evil intent concerning him, by doing good he overcomes evil, being shielded by God: and he loves the righteous as his own soul"; *T. Joseph* 18:2, "And if any one seeks to do evil to you, do well to him, and pray for him, and you will be redeemed of the Lord from all evil").

Sayings such as these are in some ways similar to Jesus' teaching. However, there is a pragmatism behind them, the kind of pragmatism typically encountered in the wisdom tradition. In this case, it is the pragmatism of the Golden Rule: "In everything do to others as you would have them do to you" (Matt 7:12). But Jesus' teaching "Love your enemies and pray for those who persecute you" goes beyond pragmatism.[184] Its goal is not the hope of being better treated by others, including enemies, but that Jesus' disciples "may be children" of their "Father in heaven" (**v. 45**). If one loves one's enemies, one is a child of God.

How does Jesus infer this? God also loves those who love and honor him as well as those who do not. This is proven in the simple fact of nature: "he makes his sun rise on the evil and on the good, and sends rain on the righteous and on the unrighteous." God does not withhold sun and rain from the wicked; no, he gives these benefits to the wicked and righteous alike. Some Gentile philosophers made

---

[182]   The latter text is from J. B. Pritchard, *Ancient Near Eastern Texts Relating to the Old Testament* (Princeton, NJ: Princeton University Press, 1969), 426, and is cited more fully in H. D. Betz, *The Sermon on the Mount* (1995), 309. The text is from the Babylonian Counsels of Wisdom, dating to a time before 700 B.C.

[183]   Translation based on R. H. Charles (ed.), *The Apocrypha and Pseudepigrapha of the Old Testament* (2 vols., Oxford: Clarendon Press, 1913), 2:730. It is noted that the advice here is not "overcome evil with good" but rather "get the better of him" with a wise response.

[184]   Rightly, see H. D. Betz, *The Sermon on the Mount* (1995), 311: "Jesus' demand in the SM [Sermon on the Mount] has precedent or preparation in the history of ideas, although it did represent a new step at that time."

the same observation: "If you are imitating the gods, you should say, 'then bestow benefits also upon the ungrateful; for the sun also rises upon the wicked'" (Seneca, *De Benef.* 4.26.1; cf. 7.31.2–4). If Jesus' disciples are to be "children of" their heavenly "Father," they must follow God's example (see Sextus, *Sentences* 135, "God's child is the one who values only what God also values"; cf. Matt 5:48).

Jesus introduces a second argument to justify his command to love one's enemies: "For if you love those who love you, what reward do you have? Do not even the tax collectors do the same?" (**v. 46**). "And if you greet only your brothers and sisters, what more are you doing than others? Do not even the Gentiles do the same?" (**v. 47**). Behind these comparisons is the logic of arguing from the minor to the major. That is, if people like tax collectors and Gentiles (who are not Torah-observant and God-honoring) show love to their families and friends, then how are the faithful (who are Torah-observant and God-honoring) any better if they, too, show love only to their families and friends? What distinguishes the children of God from the tax collectors and the Gentiles is love of enemies and a willingness to pray for their well-being.

Accordingly, Jesus concludes: "Be perfect, therefore, as your heavenly Father is perfect" (**v. 48**). As the context makes clear, the imperative "Be perfect" means to demonstrate a complete love, a love that expresses itself toward enemies as well as toward family and friends.[185] This is the kind of love that our heavenly Father has. Again, there are some approximate parallels to this sentiment in late antiquity. One thinks of the advice of first-century Greek ethicist Epictetus: "A rather nice part of being a Cynic comes when you have to be beaten like an ass, and throughout the beating you have to love those who are beating you as though you were father or brother to them" (*Discourses* 4.5.2) and "one must act as an imitator of God" (2.14.13). One likewise recalls first-century Latin ethicist and political commentator Seneca: "We shall never desist from working for the common good, helping one another, and even our enemies" (*De Otio* 1.4). One thinks, too, of Diogenes Laertius, who is remembered to have said, "How shall I defend myself against my enemy? By proving yourself good and honorable" (*apud* Plutarch, *Moralia* 88B: "Profit by Enemies" 5), and to behave "as not to make friends into enemies, but to turn enemies into friends" (Diogenes Laertius 8.1.23). Again we hear something similar in the *Sentences* of Sextus: "Love of humanity is the foundation stone of divine worship. Whoever is considerate of all human beings and prays for them should be considered as truly of God" (371–72). Similar ideas are found in the great historian Thucydides (4.19.1–4, in reference to Pericles). These sentiments oppose those expressed elsewhere that teach that it is appropriate to hate one's enemies and to love only one's friends (as in Hesiod, *Opera et Dies* 342; Lysias, *Pro Milite* 20).

---

[185]   H. Bruppacher, "Was sagte Jesus in Matthäus 5,48?" *ZNW* 58 (1967): 145; P. J. du Plessis, "Love and Perfection in Matt. 5:43–48," *Neot* 1 (1967): 28–34; L. Sabourin, "Why Is God Called 'Perfect' in Mt 5:48?" *BZ* 24 (1980): 266–68.

The antitheses provide several important examples of how to understand the Law of Moses and how to live in its light. But these examples do not exhaust the teaching of Jesus or the situations and dilemmas that God's people will face in life. The antitheses of Matthew 5 lay out principles that can be applied to other teachings and challenges. In the end, the twofold love commandment is to be applied: Does my application of Scripture fulfill the command to love God and to love my neighbor as I love myself?

MATTHEW 6:1–4 – ALMSGIVING

6:1: "**Beware of practicing your piety before others in order to be seen by them; for then you have no reward from your Father in heaven.**

6:2: "**So whenever you give alms, do not sound a trumpet before you, as the hypocrites do in the synagogues and in the streets, so that they may be praised by others. Truly I tell you, they have received their reward.**

6:3: **But when you give alms, do not let your left hand know what your right hand is doing,**

6:4: **so that your alms may be done in secret; and your Father who sees in secret will reward you.**

*M*atthew introduces a new section of the Sermon on the Mount. The program and its rationale were spelled out in Chapter 5. In the first half of Chapter 6, Jesus speaks to true piety, and in the second half of the chapter he speaks to the wider issue of the meaning of life and what one's motives and goals should be. The first half of Chapter 6 treats three important elements of Jewish piety: the giving of alms (vv. 2–4), prayer (vv. 5–15), and fasting (vv. 16–18). These examples lie at the heart of the Sermon on the Mount and draw heavily on the teaching of the historical Jesus.[186] The thread that runs throughout is the danger and temptation of hypocrisy, of practicing one's faith in order to be praised by people. The thread that runs throughout the second half of Chapter 6 is the danger of selling out to materialism and lack of faith in God.

Part of the backdrop to Jesus' critical references to the "hypocrites" (in vv. 2, 5, and 16 – each time in reference to that aspect of piety under review) is playacting and theater. Early in the first century A.D., Herod Antipas built the theater at

[186] P. S. Minear, *Commands of Christ* (1972), 47–68; C. Dietzfelbinger, "Die Frömmigkeitsregeln von Mt 6.1–18 als Zeugnisse frühchristlicher Geschichte," *ZNW* 75 (1984): 184–200; H. D. Betz, "A Jewish-Christian Cultic *Didache* in Matt. 6:1–18: Reflections and Questions on the Historical Jesus," in H. D. Betz, *Essays on the Sermon on the Mount* (1985), 55–69. With regard to the latter study, I agree with the emphasis on the importance of 6:1–18, though whether it should be called a "cultic *didache*" is another matter.

Sepphoris (four miles north of Nazareth), with seating for 2,500. (Later, perhaps in the late first or early second century, the theater was expanded with an upper deck.) Building a Greco-Roman style theater was not particularly strange; Herod the Great, the father of Herod Antipas, had built theaters in Jericho and Jerusalem. It is not implausible that Jesus not only knew of the theater at Sepphoris but perhaps even attended a performance. His mockery of the hypocrites, or "play-actors," is consistent with this possibility.[187]

The word "hypocrite" occurs several times in the Synoptic Gospels. The word itself originally was neutral, meaning "actor" or "play-actor" (Diododrus Siculus 37.12.1),[188] but Jesus used it to criticize those who acted out their piety in an ostentatious or insincere manner. Jesus' use of "hypocrite" in Matthew 6 (and perhaps elsewhere, such as in Matthew 23) probably reflects the presence and function of the theater, and probably the one in nearby Sepphoris. There are at least five specific parallels with theater and playacting beyond the word hypocrite itself. These parallels will be discussed in turn in the passages that follow.

A Closer Look: How the Rabbis Remember Some of the Pharisees

"Our Rabbis have taught: There are seven types of Pharisees: the *shikmi* Pharisee, the *nikpi* Pharisee, the *kizai* Pharisee, the 'pestle' Pharisee, the 'What is my duty that I may perform it?' Pharisee, the Pharisee from love (of God), and the Pharisee from fear (of God). The *shikmi* Pharisee is he who performs the action of 'the shoulder' (*shekem*). [1] The *nikpi* Pharisee is one who knocks (*nekiph*) his feet together. [2] The *kizai* Pharisee ... is one who splatters (*mekiz*) his blood against the wall. [3] The 'pestle' Pharisee ... is bowed (like a pestle)

[187] R. A. Batey, "Jesus and the Theatre," *NTS* 30 (1984): 563–74; J. F. Strange, "Some Implications of Archaeology for New Testament Studies," in J. H. Charlesworth and W. P. Weaver (eds.), *What Has Archaeology To Do with Faith?* (Faith and Scholarship Colloquies; Philadelphia: Trinity Press International, 1992), 23–59, especially 44–45. The date of the theater at Sepphoris is disputed, with some claiming it was not built until the end of the first century A.D. However, Batey, Strange, and other archaeologists point to evidence (such as pottery and coins) that support an early first-century date. See J. F. Strange, "Six Campaigns at Sepphoris: The University of South Florida Excavations, 1983–1989," in L. I. Levine (ed.), *The Galilee in Late Antiquity* (New York: Jewish Theological Seminary of America, 1992), 339–55, especially 342–43; R. A. Batey, "Did Antipas Build the Sepphoris Theater?" in J. H. Charlesworth (ed.), *Jesus and Archaeology* (Grand Rapids, MI: Eerdmans, 2006), 111–19.

[188] U. Wilckens, *TDNT* 8:559–60: The Greek word hypocrite, "which almost always means 'actor,' probably derives from the orig. sense 'to expound,' 'to interpret,' ... The actor's job is to present the drama or πρόσωπον ('face') assigned to him by artistic reciting accompanied by mime and gestures." By the turn of the era, *hypocrites* had also come to mean sanctimonious pretense. Jewish and Christian usage has underscored the negative nuance.

in a mortar. ⁴ The 'What is my duty that I may perform it?' Pharisee – what a virtue! – really means to say, 'What further duty is for me that I may perform it?' ⁵ The Pharisee from love (of God) ⁶ and the Pharisee from fear (of God) ⁷ – Do not mention (them)! ... A person should always engage himself in the Law and the commandments (out of pure motives) ... the Great Tribunal will exact punishment from those who rub themselves against the walls. ⁸ King (Alexander) Jannaeus said to his wife (on his death bed): 'Do not fear the Pharisees and the non-Pharisees but the hypocrites who ape the Pharisees ...'" (*b. Sota* 22b). Adapted from the Soncino Translation.

Explanations:

¹The *shikmi* Pharisee carries his religious duties on his "shoulder" (*shekem*), so that all may see his piety. His motives are no better than the men of Shechem (*shekem*), who accepted circumcision with impure motives.

²The *nikpi* Pharisee knocks (*nekiph*) his feet together as he walks in exaggerated humility.

³The *kizai* Pharisee averts his gaze from temptation while in public, thus bloodying his face (from *naqaz*, "bleeds") against walls. In parallel traditions, he is called the "black and blue" Pharisee because of the bruises he receives walking about in public with his eyes closed.

⁴And so is grinding away at his piety.

⁵Thus implying that he has fulfilled all his obligations. He now seeks more.

⁶The Pharisee who is supposedly religious out of love of God in reality is religious out of hope for rewards.

⁷The Pharisee who is religious out of fear of God is religious only because he hopes to avoid punishment in the day of judgment (when the Great Tribunal sits).

⁸Those "who rub themselves against the walls" are those who strike themselves against the walls (as do the *kizai* Pharisees) or lean against the walls in a show of weakness from fasting (cf. Matt 6:16, "they disfigure their faces so as to show others that they are fasting").

The first half of Chapter 6 begins with a warning: "Beware of practicing your piety before others in order to be seen by them; for then you have no reward from your Father in heaven" (**v. 1**). What the NRSV translates as "piety" is in fact "righteousness." As already noted, Matthew is concerned with the theme of righteousness, especially as seen in the beatitudes (cf. Matt 5:3–10). But how is one's righteousness practiced? Not "before others in order to be seen by them." If it is, then one can expect "no reward from" one's "Father in heaven." (On referring to God as "Father in heaven," see the commentary on Matt 5:16.)

Jesus' "to be seen by them" is literally "to be watched by them" (cf. Matt 23:5). The word "watched" (or "seen") is *theathenai*, which is from the root that gives us *theater*. This word by itself would not bring to mind the theater, but as Jesus begins piling up other terms and activities, such as "hypocrites" (or play-actors), sounding a trumpet, long prayers and speeches, coordination of the movement of one's hands, and wearing makeup, his hearers would recognize the allusions to the theater, lending an element of the comical to what is otherwise a serious matter. (On Jesus' use of comedy and hyperbole, see the commentary on Matt 7:3–5.)

The first example concerns charitable donations: "So whenever you give alms, do not sound a trumpet before you, as the hypocrites do" (v. 2). Giving "alms" became a standard feature in Jewish piety of late antiquity (cf. LXX Dan 4:24[27]; LXX Prov 15:27a; Tob 1:3, 16; 2:14; 3:2; 4:7; 12:8; 14:2, 10; Sir 3:30; 7:10, where alms and prayer are together; 12:3; 29:8; 35:2) and is attested in the early church (cf. Acts 3:2, 3, 10; 10:2, 4, 31; 24:17). Giving alms is good and fulfills Old Testament commands to be generous with the poor (e.g., Exod 22:25; Deut 15:4, 7, 11). But when one practices charity, one is not to "sound a trumpet" (or "toot one's horn," as we say nowadays). In the theater of late antiquity, trumpets often announced an action or a new scene. There are also traditions about trumpets sounding for prayer or worship (e.g., CD 11:21–22; *m. Ta'anit* 2:5), but no Jewish traditions sounding trumpets in connection with almsgiving. The sounding of the trumpet comes from the Greek theater, not the Jewish temple or synagogue.[189] Jesus has warned not to make theater of one's piety, whether in giving alms or in any other act of faith and practice. In Matthew, "hypocrites" are phonies who have no sincere regard for the Law and can almost be regarded as apostates.[190] They are examples of the pious frauds that James, the brother of Jesus, talks about in his letter: "What good is it … If a brother or sister is naked and lacks daily food, and one of you says to them, 'Go in peace; keep warm and eat your fill,' and yet you do not supply their bodily needs?" (James 2:14–16).

The play-actors, Jesus says, sound the trumpet "in the synagogues and in the streets, so that they may be praised by others." That is, they draw attention to themselves in public places, where they may be observed and praised. If their motivation for almsgiving is this, then "they have received their reward."[191] Because the

189 It is not likely that the trumpet of Matt 6:2 has anything to do with the Jewish *shofar*. Pace N. J. McEleney, "Does the Trumpet Sound or Resound? An Interpretation of Matthew 6,2," *ZNW* 76 (1985): 43–46. McEleney tries to relate Matt 6:2–4 to the *shofar*-shaped boxes for the collection of money and suggests that the coins dropping into these receptacles made the "trumpets" sound. This theory and others like it are rightly rejected by H. D. Betz, *The Sermon on the Mount* (1995), 355 n. 183.

190 I. J. W. Oakley, "'Hypocrisy' in Matthew," *IBS* 7 (1985): 118–38; D. O. Via, "The Gospel of Matthew: Hypocrisy as Self-Deception," *SBLSP* 27 (1988): 508–16. The hypocrite is more of a self-deceived person than a pretender.

191 L. J. Lawrence, "'For Truly, I Tell You, They Have Received Their Reward' (Matt 6:2): Investigating Honor Precedence and Honor Virtue," *CBQ* 64 (2002): 687–702.

play-actors have done what they have done for their own glory, not for God's, they may expect no reward from God.[192]

Therefore, Jesus instructs, "when you give alms, do not let your left hand know what your right hand is doing, so that your alms may be done in secret" (**vv. 3–4**). We often jokingly refer to an organization or institution (or government!) whose "right hand does not know what its left hand is doing." We think this means inef-ficiency or clumsiness. The actual point, however, may once again have to do with the theater, in which play-actors skillfully coordinated the motions of their hands to compliment their words and to make more vivid in the minds of the audience what they are to imagine. The hands of the actors were supposed to be synchro-nized and meaningful, drawing attention to what is being said or done (on this, see Marcus Fabian Quintillian, *Institutio Oratoria* [on stage and orations] 11.2.42; 11.3.66; 11.3.70, 85–121, especially 114: "The left hand never properly performs a ges-ture alone, but it frequently acts in agreement with the right"). Against such well-orchestrated and polished performances, Jesus says, "do not let your left hand know what your right hand is doing." There is to be nothing public in one's almsgiving; it is not a public performance, an act to be observed and acclaimed. Giving is to be "in secret" (i.e., private).[193]

Jesus explains by reminding his disciples, "your Father who sees in secret will reward you." If one's almsgiving is indeed in private (and so presumably properly motivated), then God, "who sees in secret" (that is, he sees all, whether public or private) "will reward" one.[194] On divine knowledge of what is done in secret, we have parallels in Epictetus: "God is there within you, seeing and hearing every-thing" (2.8.14) and "There is God, and he cares providentially for the universe, and we cannot hide from Him what we do or even what we think or ponder" (2.14.11).

MATTHEW 6:5–15 – PRAYER

6:5: **"And whenever you pray, do not be like the hypocrites; for they love to stand and pray in the synagogues and at the street corners, so that they may be seen by others. Truly I tell you, they have received their reward.**

6:6: **But whenever you pray, go into your room and shut the door and pray to your Father who is in secret; and your Father who sees in secret will reward you.**

---

[192]   That the play-actors sometimes behave this way in synagogues should not be understood as a criticism of the synagogue itself.

[193]   Some of the Rabbis agree (cf. *b. Pesahim* 113a, "who tithes in secret"; *b. Baba Batra* 9b, "who gives charity in secret").

[194]   W. T. Wilson, "Seen in Secret: Inconspicuous Piety and Alternative Subjectivity in Matt 6:1–6, 16–18," *CBQ* 72 (2010): 475–97.

6:7: "When you are praying, do not heap up empty phrases as the Gentiles do; for they think that they will be heard because of their many words.

6:8: Do not be like them, for your Father knows what you need before you ask him.

6:9: "Pray then in this way: Our Father in heaven, hallowed be your name.

6:10: Your kingdom come. Your will be done, on earth as it is in heaven.

6:11: Give us this day our daily bread.

6:12: And forgive us our debts, as we also have forgiven our debtors.

6:13: And do not bring us to the time of trial, but rescue us from the evil one.

6:14: For if you forgive others their trespasses, your heavenly Father will also forgive you;

6:15: but if you do not forgive others, neither will your Father forgive your trespasses.

Jesus' teaching on prayer continues his warnings against hypocrisy, or playacting (see the commentary on Matt 6:1–4).

Once again, Jesus warns his disciples not to "be like the hypocrites; for they love to stand and pray in the synagogues and at the street corners, so that they may be seen by others" (**v. 5**). This time there are no peals of the trumpet (as in v. 2), but the point is the same: "hypocrites … love to stand and pray in" public places, "that they may be seen by others" and (though it is not stated) be admired. If that is the extent of their true motive, then "they have their reward."

Standing while praying was normal in Jewish practice (e.g., Luke 18:11, "the Pharisee stood and was praying"). In fact, one of Judaism's best-known prayers is called the *Amidah* (i.e., the "standing"; it is also called the *Shemoneh Esreh* [the "eighteen"] because it contains eighteen benedictions). Standing and praying in public may once again allude to the performance of the play-actor (Greek: *hypocrites*), who in the theater stands and gives a soliloquy. It has been observed that the word *plateia*, meaning "street" (one of the words in the NRSV translation "street corners," literally "corners of streets," *en tais goniais ton plateion*), was used for the colonnaded street in nearby Sepphoris. The image may be that of a play-actor standing in a busy thoroughfare speaking loudly, hoping to attract an audience to the theater.[195]

In contrast to the ostentatious public display of some, Jesus' disciples are to go into a "room and shut the door and pray" (**v. 6**). There are examples in Scripture

---

[195] This word appears in rabbinic literature (*y. Ketubot* 1.10) as a loanword and in fact occurs in reference to the city of Sepphoris, which boasted a theater. For details, see J. F. Strange, "Some Implications of Archaeology for New Testament Studies," in J. H. Charlesworth and W. P. Weaver (eds.), *What Has Archaeology To Do with Faith?* (1992), 23–59, at 44 and 57–58 n. 83.

and Jewish literature of retiring to a room for private prayer (Dan 6:11; *T. Jacob* 1:9). The word translated as "room" (Greek: *tameion*; Latin: *cubiculum*) refers to a private room where one could spend time with intimate friends (*T. Joseph* 3:3; *Joseph and Aseneth* 10:3–17).[196] The point of such prayer is not to win the praise and admiration of the public but to humble one's self before God, a God who sees all – public and private alike – and rewards the faithful. (We may have here an allusion to Isa 26:20, "Come, my people, enter your chambers, and shut your doors behind you....")

Besides praying in private, away from the approving and admiring gaze of the public, Jesus' disciples should address God with respect and with faith: "When you are praying, do not heap up empty phrases as the Gentiles do; for they think that they will be heard because of their many words" (v. 7). We may have here an allusion to the story of the prophets of Baal crying out all day to their god – who never responded. Evidently they thought that he eventually would heed their prayer if they made enough noise and repeated themselves often (cf. 1 Kings 18:26–29, "they ... called on the name Baal from morning until noon ... and no answer ... and they raved on ... but there was no voice"). The comical failure of the prophets of Baal (remember Elijah's taunts in 1 Kings 18:27: "Cry aloud! Surely he is a god; either he is meditating, or he has wandered away, or he is on a journey, or perhaps he is asleep and must be awakened") well suits the theatrical backdrop that runs throughout Matt 6:1–18. Implicit, too, in Jesus' mocking criticism of the prayer of Gentiles is their low view of God. They cry out as if to badger or cajole God into acting. They may well pray to impress the human onlookers, without much regard for God himself. The hypocrites who love to stand in public places and offer up their oratory are as ridiculous as the prophets of Baal long ago or the pagans of the first century, who frantically tried to grab the attention of their god.[197]

There is an important element of respect in Jesus' teaching; after all, verbosity suggests that God can't hear or doesn't care. This concern is expressed in the Wisdom of Ben Sira, who advises his students: "Do not babble in the assembly of the elders, and do not repeat yourself when you pray" (Sir 7:14; cf. 20:5; Job 13:5). Similarly, in the older advice of the Preacher: "Never be rash with your mouth, nor let your heart be quick to utter a word before God, for God is in heaven, and you upon earth; therefore let your words be few" (Eccles 5:2; cf. 5:3).[198]

---

[196] C. Osiek, "'When you pray, go into your ταμεῖον' (Matthew 6:6)," *CBQ* 71 (2009): 723–40.

[197] In pagan charms and incantations from late antiquity, we find prayers addressed to an almost endless list of deities, the point of which is to take care not to overlook the one or two deities that might actually take notice of the supplicant. See E. Schweizer, *The Good News According to Matthew* (Atlanta: John Knox, 1975; reprinted 1977), 146.

[198] H. D. Betz, *The Sermon on the Mount* (1995), 365, thinks we may have here an allusion to *voces magicae* ("magical words" or "magical voices"). Perhaps, but apart from vain verbosity and the possibility mentioned in the preceding note, there is nothing in Matthew 6 that hints at magical practice or any form of pagan practice per se.

Jesus continues his teaching with the warning, "Do not be like them, for your Father knows what you need before you ask him" (**v. 8**). That is, do not be like the hypocrites, who show off in public and pile up their many words. This kind of behavior is not only hypocritical but is insulting to God, for it suggests that God can hear no better than Baal or any other god of the heathen. On the contrary, Jesus assures his disciples, God "knows what you need before you ask him." On divine awareness, we have a pagan parallel in Dio: "The gods know what we have in mind even when we speak in a tiny whisper" (39.8; cf. 12.28).

Some may well reply, if God knows what his children need before asking, why pray at all? To this question one may reply – in proper rabbinic fashion – with a counter-question: Would one pray with any confidence to a God who has no idea what one needs until one informs him? No. Rather, we turn to God in prayer, with confidence that he will hear and respond, because he already knows our needs.

With this assurance, Jesus tells his disciples: "Pray then in this way" (**v. 9**). It was customary for teachers (or Rabbis) to instruct their disciples in prayer (and in other matters of piety, such as almsgiving and fasting; on the latter, see Matt 9:14; Mark 2:18; Luke 5:33). In Luke's parallel, the disciples ask Jesus to teach them to pray, just as John taught his disciples to pray (cf. Luke 11:1). The prayer that Jesus teaches his disciples is the well-known Lord's Prayer.[199]

The Lord's Prayer is preserved in New Testament literature in two forms (Matt 6:9–13; Luke 11:2–4).[200] Of the two forms of the Lord's Prayer, Matthew's is the longer and more stylized. It consists of seven petitions, presented as imperatives, either concerning God ("hallowed be your name," "Your kingdom come," "Your will be done") or concerning the human ("Give us this day our daily bread," "forgive

---

[199]   The bibliography is enormous. For a selection, see F. H. Chase, *The Lord's Prayer in the Early Church* (Texts and Studies 1, no. 3; Cambridge: Cambridge University Press, 1891); I. Abrahams, *Studies in Pharisaism and the Gospels* (2 vols., Cambridge: Cambridge University Press, 1917–1924; repr. as one vol., with Prolegomenon by M. S. Enslin; New York: Ktav, 1967), 2:93–108; C. F. Evans, *The Lord's Prayer* (London: SPCK, 1963); J. Jeremias, *The Prayers of Jesus* (SBT 6; London: SCM Press, 1967), 82–107; D. Juel, "The Lord's Prayer in the Gospels of Matthew and Luke," *Princeton Seminary Bulletin*, Supplement 2 (1992): 56–70; M. Kiley, "The Lord's Prayer and Matthean Theology," in J. H. Charlesworth, with M. Harding and M. Kiley (eds.), *The Lord's Prayer and Other Prayer Texts from the Greco-Roman Era* (Valley Forge, PA: Trinity Press International, 1994), 15–27; D. E. Oakman, "The Lord's Prayer in Social Perspective," in B. D. Chilton and C. A. Evans (eds.), *Authenticating the Words of Jesus* (NTTS 28, no 1; Leiden: Brill, 1998), 137–86; N. T. Wright, "The Lord's Prayer as a Paradigm of Christian Prayer," in R. N. Longenecker (ed.), *Into God's Presence: Prayer in the New Testament* (MNTS 5; Grand Rapids, MI: Eerdmans, 2001), 132–54; K. W. Stevenson, *The Lord's Prayer: A Text in Tradition* (Minneapolis: Fortress, 2004).

[200]   The Lord's Prayer is also found in *Didache* 8:2 (see the Closer Look box). Although some scholars contend that it is independent of the Synoptic forms of the Lord's Prayer, it seems to be based on the form we find in Matthew. Comparison of the forms in the *Didache* and Matthew shows there are only a few, very minor differences.

us our debts," "do not bring us to the time of trial," "deliver us from the evil one").
The prayer begins by naming the addressee, "Our Father in heaven," and ends (in
later manuscripts) with a eulogy: "For the kingdom and the Power and the glory
are yours forever. Amen."

A Closer Look: The Two Lord's Prayers Side by Side

Matt 6:9–13	*Luke 11:2–4*
Our Father in heaven,	Father,
hallowed be your name.	hallowed be your name.
Your kingdom come.	Your kingdom come.
Your will be done,	
on earth as it is in heaven.	
Give us this day our daily bread.	Give us each day our daily bread.
And forgive us our debts,	And forgive us our sins,
as we also have forgiven our debtors.	for we ourselves forgive everyone indebted to us.
And do not bring us to the time of trial,	And do not bring us to the time of trial.
but rescue us from the evil one.	
[For the kingdom and the Power and the glory are yours forever. Amen.]	

In essence, the prayer is Jesus' own adaptation of an ancient Aramaic Jewish
prayer known as the Qaddish ("let be sanctified" or "hallowed"). One readily recognizes the parallels with the Lord's Prayer. The standard form of the Qaddish reads:

1. May his great *name* be glorified and *hallowed* in the world that he created
   according to his will.
2. May he establish his *kingdom* in your lifetime and during your days, and
   during the lifetime of the whole house of Israel, speedily and soon;
3. and say, "Amen." (italics added)

The two petitions of this simple prayer, which in its earliest form was probably
simpler still,[201] correspond to the first two petitions of the Lord's Prayer: the petition
that the name of God be hallowed (or sanctified) and the petition that his kingdom
come.[202] The major difference, besides length, is that whereas the petitions of the

---

[201] Perhaps no more than "May his great name be hallowed," inspired by Ezek 38:23 ("I will
display my greatness and my holiness [*qdsh*]").

[202] On the Qaddish (or Kaddish), see I. Elbogen, *Jewish Liturgy: A Comprehensive History*
(Philadelphia: The Jewish Publication Society; New York: The Jewish Theological

Qaddish are in the third person, those of the Lord's Prayer are in the second person. Jesus teaches his disciples to speak directly to God their Father.

The prayer begins, "Our Father in heaven" (v. 9). On the epithet "Father in heaven," see the commentary on Matt 5:16. On calling God "Father" in Greco-Roman literature, see Sextus, *Sentences* 59, "You call God 'Father' – remember this in your actions" (see also *Sentences* 222).[203]

The first petition, "hallowed be your name," calls for the sanctification of God's name ("hallowed be" [*hagiazein*] is old-fashioned English). The terminology derives from Scripture: "the house that I have consecrated [*hagiazein*] for my name" (1 Kings 9:7 = 2 Chron 7:20); "they will sanctify [*hagiazein*] my name; they will sanctify [*hagiazein*] the Holy One of Jacob, and will stand in awe of the God of Israel" (Isa 29:23); "I will sanctify my great name" (LXX Ezek 36:23). Closer parallels are found in some of the later intertestamental literature: "Blessed be the Lord God, and may his holy name be blessed for ever and ever" (*Jub.* 25:12); "and may your name be holy and glorious and blessed unto all the ages!" (*1 Enoch* 9:4); "every spirit of light who is able to bless, and glorify, and extol, and hallow your blessed name" (*1 Enoch* 61:12).

The verb "hallowed be" is an instance of the "divine passive"; that is, use of the passive voice of a verb so that God, who is the subject of the sentence, does not need to be mentioned, especially in a petition. Put in the active voice, the petition reads "sanctify your name," thus paralleling more closely the examples in Scripture cited earlier (e.g., where in LXX Ezek 36:23 God says, "I will sanctify my great name").

Jesus' petition that God sanctify his name is consistent with teaching elsewhere, especially as seen in the teaching regarding vows and oaths (in Matt 5:33–37). The presupposition of all that Jesus proclaims and does is the holiness of God. The proclamation of the kingdom of God loses all of its meaning when set apart from the reality of God Himself.

The second petition, "Your kingdom come" (v. 10a), speaks to the burden of Jesus' proclamation "The time is fulfilled, and the kingdom of God has come near;

Seminary of America, 1993), 80–84, 407–8. For an early study comparing the Qaddish and the Lord's Prayer, see G. Klein, *Der älteste christliche Katechismus und die jüdische Propaganda-Literatur* (Berlin: G. Reimer, 1909), 256–57. See also J. Heinemann, "The Background of Jesus' Prayer in the Jewish Liturgical Tradition," in J. J. Petuchowski and M. Brocke (eds.), *The Lord's Prayer and Jewish Liturgy* (New York: Seabury Press, 1978), 81–89; D. Baumgardt, "Kaddish and Lord's Prayer," *Jewish Bible Quarterly* 19 (1992): 164–69. For a study of the prayer as written in Aramaic, the language in which Jesus originally uttered it, see B. Chilton, "The Aramaic Lord's Prayer," in J. G. Crossley (ed.), *Judaism, Jewish Identities and the Gospel Tradition: Essays in Honour of Maurice Casey* (London: Equinox, 2010), 62–82.

203   For background, see B. D. Chilton, "God as 'Father' in the Targumim, in Non-Canonical Literatures of Early Judaism and Primitive Christianity, and in Matthew," in J. H. Charlesworth and C. A. Evans (eds.), *The Pseudepigrapha and Early Biblical Interpretation* (JSPSup 14; SSEJC 2; Sheffield: Sheffield Academic Press, 1993), 151–69.

repent, and believe in the good news" (Mark 1:15). Although the kingdom of God is at hand, Jesus still petitions God that his "kingdom come." From this we rightly infer that the kingdom of God made its appearance in the ministry of Jesus but has not yet arrived in its fullness. Jesus urges his disciples to pray to God that the kingdom arrive in its fullness soon or, in the words of the Qaddish noted earlier, "speedily and soon."

The third petition, "Your will be done, on earth as it is in heaven" (v. 10b), closely relates to the second. When the kingdom of God has come in its fullness, then God's will shall be the rule of law "on earth," just as surely as it is "in heaven" now. It must be remembered that "kingdom of God" (or "kingdom of heaven," as Matthew prefers) refers to God's reign or sphere of rule. He rules in heaven (as Jesus' vision of Satan's fall from heaven surely implies; cf. Luke 10:18), but his rule on earth is rejected and opposed. Thus God's will is yet to be accomplished as far as the human sphere is concerned.

A pertinent parallel is at hand in a rabbinic prayer, "May *your will be done in heaven* above, and grant ease to those *on earth* that fear you" (*t. Ber.* 3.11, italics added), and in the Psalms: "Whatever the Lord pleases he does, in heaven and in earth" (Ps 135:6).

The fourth petition, "Give us this day our daily bread" (v. 11), is not as clear as it would at first appear. The meaning of the word that is translated as "daily" (Greek: *epiousion*) is obscure. Some scholars follow Origen (*De oratione* 27.7) and translate it as "bread for subsistence." The phrases "his needs" and "what he lacks" in the rabbinic prayer, "May it be your will, Lord our God, to give to each and every one according to his needs, and to each and every creature what he lacks" (*t. Ber.* 3.11), may clarify the meaning of *epiousios*. In other words, Jesus asks God for the "needful" bread, the bread "that we lack" or "that we need."[204]

But another and perhaps better solution may lie in seeing an allusion to Exod 16:4: "I am going to rain bread from heaven for you, and each day the people shall go out and gather enough for that day [*debar yom beyomo*]." The Hebrew's *debar yom beyomo* (literally "thing of the day in its day") or the Aramaic equivalent *pitgam yom beyomeh* (literally "thing of the day in its day") may lie behind Matthew's Greek *epiousios*. Thus, just as God provided the wilderness generation with daily bread (i.e., the manna), so Jesus' disciples, who are also living in a time of salvation, should petition God to provide them with daily bread. Given the typological orientation of Matthew (and Jesus), this solution is very attractive and could well be correct.

The fifth petition is: "And forgive us our debts, as we also have forgiven our debtors" (v. 12). The parallel in Luke 11:4 reads "forgive us our sins." It is probable that the

---

204 B. M. Metzger, "How Many Times Does 'Epiousios' Occur Outside the Lord's Prayer?" *ExpT* 69 (1957): 52–54; E. M. Yamauchi, "The 'Daily Bread' Motif in Antiquity," *WTJ* 28 (1966): 145–56.

Aramaic word *hoba'* underlies the Lord's Prayer, for this word means both "debt" and "sin" (i.e., sin in the sense of debt owed God). This dual sense of *hoba'* is clearly at work in the story of the woman "who is a sinner" and the clarifying parable of the two debtors (Luke 7:36–50). Just as the *debtor* in the parable loves the forgiving creditor, the *sinner* loves the forgiving Jesus.

Jesus petitions God to forgive our debts, or sins, even as we have forgiven our debtors, or those who have sinned against us (cf. Matt 18:23–35). We find a close parallel in the Wisdom of ben Sira: "Forgive your neighbor the wrong he has done, and then your sins will be pardoned when you pray" (Sir 28:2).

The sixth petition, "And do not bring us to the time of trial, but rescue us from the evil one" (**v. 13**), finds a close parallel in rabbinic literature: "... do not accustom me to transgression, and bring me not into sin, or into iniquity, into temptation, or into contempt" (*b. Ber.* 60b). The idea is not that no time of trial ever come upon Jesus' follower but that God not allow his follower to be overcome by the trial (see 2 Thess 3:3, "he shall guard you from evil"). Does God ever bring his children to times of trial or into sin? According to James, he does not: "No one, when tempted, should say, 'I am being tempted by God'; for God cannot be tempted by evil and he himself tempts no one" (James 1:13). Jesus' petition should be understood in a permissive sense; that is, that God not allow his children to fall into temptation or actually bring on the temptation. The "time of trial" that Jesus has in mind may very well be apostasy, as the pressures and tribulations of the coming days press upon his disciples (cf. Matt 24:9–10, "they will hand you over to be tortured.... Then many will fall away ..."; Matt 26:41, "Stay awake and pray that you may not come into the time of trial").

What is translated as "from the evil one" (*apo tou ponerou*) could also be translated as "from evil." Does the petition ask for protection from Satan or from evil? The NRSV translates the phrase as "the evil one," and that is probably correct. This is because Satan is himself the tempter (*ho peirazon*), whose purpose is to destroy the faith and morals of God's people. Elsewhere in Matthew (cf. 13:19, 38), Satan is identified as "the evil one" (*ho poneros*). Moreover, we find a parallel to this part of the Lord's Prayer in a prayer mentioned in rabbinic literature: "Rabbi, on concluding his prayer, added the following: 'May it be your will, O Lord our God ... to deliver us from ... the destructive Accuser'" (*b. Ber.* 16b).[205]

In many manuscripts, the Lord's Prayer concludes with the familiar doxology: "For the kingdom and the power and the glory are yours forever. Amen" (**v. 13**). The oldest New Testament manuscripts omit this concluding doxology; nor does it appear in Luke's version of the Lord's Prayer. It has been suggested that it may have been inspired by 1 Chron 29:11–13, part of which (i.e., v. 11) reads: "Yours, O Lord, are the greatness, the power, the glory, the victory, and the majesty ... yours

---

[205]   Rightly, see D. C. Allison, Jr. and W. D. Davies, *A Critical and Exegetical Commentary on the Gospel According to Saint Matthew* (1988–1997), 1:614–15.

is the kingdom." The doxology appears in *Did.* 8:2, though in somewhat shorter form: "for yours is the power and the glory forever." The textually uncertain doxology concludes with "Amen," a petition ("let it be so" or "may it be sure") that concludes many Jewish prayers, including the Qaddish, which parallels the Lord's Prayer closely (see the commentary on Matt 5:18).

Appended to the Lord's Prayer is an elaboration on v. 12 ("And forgive us our debts, as we also have forgiven our debtors"), which underscores the requirement to forgive: "For if you forgive others their trespasses, your heavenly Father will also forgive you; but if you do not forgive others, neither will your Father forgive your trespasses" (**vv. 14–15**). Jesus' teaching here recaps the fifth petition of the Lord's Prayer and is illustrated by the parable of the Unforgiving Servant in Matt 18:23–35 (see also Sir 28:2). In a sense, this teaching represents an extension of the command to love one's neighbor as one loves oneself. Only in this case we might say, "Forgive your neighbor as you would like to be forgiven."

MATTHEW 6:16–18 – FASTING

6:16: "And whenever you fast, do not look dismal, like the hypocrites, for they disfigure their faces so as to show others that they are fasting. Truly I tell you, they have received their reward.

6:17: But when you fast, put oil on your head and wash your face,

6:18: so that your fasting may be seen not by others but by your Father who is in secret; and your Father who sees in secret will reward you."

The third example of religious practice concerns fasting. Fasting was and is a common religious practice.[206] Despite teaching on this subject, the only fasting that Jesus does is during the temptation (Matt 4:2). Evidently, fasting was not part of his regular ministry, for the disciples of John ask him why his disciples do not fast (Matt 9:14). Jesus' answer implies that they will not fast as long as Jesus is with them (Matt 9:15). The Pharisee in the parable of the Pharisee and the tax collector self-righteously informs God that he fasts "twice a week" (Luke 18:12; cf. *Did.* 8:1, "Let not your fasts be with the hypocrites, for they fast on Mondays and Thursdays"). The Gospels therefore provide us with little to go on.[207]

There are in the Old Testament and intertestamental literature many examples of fasting. Fasting often attended a time of mourning or hope for renewal, as we see in Judg 20:26; 1 Sam 7:6 ("They fasted that day, and said, 'We have sinned against

206   R. Arbesmann, "Fasting and Prophecy in Pagan and Christian Antiquity," *Traditio* 7 (1949–1951): 1–71.
207   J. B. Muddiman, "Jesus and Fasting," in J. Dupont (ed.), *Jesus aux origins de la christologie* (BETL 40; Gembloux: Duculot; Leuven: Leuven University Press, 1975), 271–81.

the Lord'"); 31:13; 2 Sam 1:12; 12:16; 1 Kings 21:27; Zech 7:5 (the exiles have "fasted and lamented in the fifth month and in the seventh, for these seventy years"); Ezra 8:23; Neh 1:4 ("When I heard these words I sat down and wept, and mourned for days, fasting and praying before the God of heaven"); Jth 4:13; 1 Macc 3:47; Bar 1:5 ("then they wept, and fasted, and prayed before the Lord"); *Life of Adam and Eve* 6:1; *T. Simeon* 3:4; *T. Joseph* 3:4; 4:8 ("I gave myself yet more to fasting and prayer"); *T. Benjamin* 1:4; *T. Moses* 9:6; 2 *Bar* 9:2 ("we tore our garments, we wept, and mourned, and fasted seven days"); 12:5; 43:3; 47:2; 4 Ezra 5:20 ("I fasted seven days, mourning and weeping"); 6:31, 35; 10:4; *Pss. Sol.* 3:8 ("He atones for [sins of] ignorance by fasting and humbling his soul"); Josephus, *Ant.* 20.89.

Sincere fasting is of benefit: "a pure fast ... releases sin; it heals diseases; it casts out demons. It is effective up to the throne of God for an ointment and for a release from sin by means of a pure prayer" (*Apoc. Elijah* 1:20–22). The combination with prayer is also important to observe (in several of the examples just given).

The Jewish people evidently were well known for their fasting (and Josephus in his various writings, chiefly read by the upper classes in the Roman Empire, refers to Jewish fasts many times). This is seen in a passing remark made by Emperor Augustus, who comments on his own recent fast: "Not even a Jew, my dear Tiberius, fasts so scrupulously on his sabbaths as I have today; for it was not until after the first hour of the night that I ate two mouthfuls of bread in the bath before I began to be anointed" (Suetonius, *Augustus* 76).[208]

In light of this sampling of texts, it is not difficult to understand what fasting in the context of ministry dedicated to the furtherance of God's kingdom would have brought to the minds of Jesus' disciples. They will fast in preparation for ministry, in the face of opposition, in the aftermath of calamity, or in repentance. Fasting will often accompany prayer and may sometimes involve wearing sackcloth or other marks of mourning and humility. It is the latter element that underlies Jesus' criticism of the hypocrites who fast.

Jesus teaches his disciples: "And whenever you fast, do not look dismal, like the hypocrites" (**v. 16**). Once again, we probably have an ironical reference to the theater, where the play-actors (Greek: *hypocrites*) wear makeup to fit the scene. Why do they "look dismal"? The second half of the verse will explain. For "dismal" (Greek: *skythropos*), see Gen 40:7 ("Why are your faces so sad [or gloomy] today?"); Luke 24:17 ("they stood still, looking sad [or gloomy]"); *T. Simeon* 4:1 ("he saw that I was gloomy"); Sir 25:23 ("a dejected mind, a gloomy face, and a wounded heart are caused by an evil wife"!).

---

[208]   J. A. Montgomery, "Ascetic Strains in Early Judaism," *JBL* 51 (1932): 183–213; S. Lowy, "The Motivation of Fasting in Talmudic Literature," *JJS* 9 (1958): 19–38; A. J. Saldarini, "Asceticism and the Gospel of Matthew," in L. E. Vaage and V. L. Wimbush (eds.), *Asceticism and the New Testament* (New York: Routledge, 1999), 11–27.

To look dismal, the hypocrites "disfigure their faces so as to show others that they are fasting." This is the whole point of the farce. Like play-actors who paint their faces to play the role of mimes, the hypocrites put on a gloomy face and "disfigure their faces" so that their fasting will be more obvious.[209] But such fasting is of no value.

Jesus is not alone in his criticism of such hypocrisy; insincere and hypocritical fasting is criticized in other sources: "Someone else commits adultery and is sexually promiscuous, yet is abstemious in his eating. While fasting, he is committing evil deeds. Through the power of his wealth he ravages many, and yet in spite of his excessive evil, he performs the commandments" (*T. Asher* 2:8); "Let the pure one fast, but whenever the one who fasts is not pure he has angered the Lord and also the angels; and he has grieved his soul, gathering up wrath for himself for the day of wrath" (*Apoc. Elijah* 1:18–19). For examples in rabbinic literature, see *m. Ta'anit* 2.1; *t. Ta'anit* 1.8; *b. Ta'anit* 16a; *b. Sota* 22b (for examples of playacting Pharisees, described in rabbinic literature, see A Closer Look in the commentary on Matt 6:1–4).

"Truly I tell you," Jesus says of the dismal fasting hypocrites, "they have received their reward." See the commentary on Matt 6:2. Ben Sira the sage assesses hypocrisy in the same way: "So if a man fasts for his sins, and goes again and does the same things, who will listen to his prayer? And what has he gained by humbling himself?" (Sir 34:26). Again the combination of fasting and prayer is noteworthy.

Instead of the ostentation and phoniness, Jesus tells his disciples: "But when you fast, put oil on your head and wash your face" (v. 17). A well-groomed, cheery countenance hides from the public a time of fasting and devotion. Only God will know, and he will reward his faithful disciple.

One is reminded of Ruth, who was advised by her mother-in-law, "Wash yourself therefore, and anoint yourself and put on your best clothes" (Ruth 3:3), or, perhaps more relevantly, of Judith, who, taking off her widow's mourning clothing, "anointed her face with ointment and fastened her hair with a tiara and put on a linen gown" (Jth 16:8).

A washed face and an anointed head may denote celebration (e.g., Ps 23:5, "you anoint my head with oil"; Ps 104:15, "and wine to gladden the heart, oil to make the face shine, and bread to strengthen the human heart"), but it may also have been customary good grooming in Jewish Palestine of late antiquity (e.g., 2 Sam 14:2, "Pretend to be a mourner; put on mourning garments, do not anoint yourself with oil").

---

[209] U. Wilckens, *TDNT* 8:559–60: "The actor's job is to present the drama or πρόσωπον ('face') assigned to him by artistic reciting accompanied by mime and gestures"; J. F. Strange, "Some Implications of Archaeology for New Testament Studies," in J. H. Charlesworth and W. P. Weaver (eds.), *What Has Archaeology To Do with Faith?* (1992), 23–59, at 45: "If we allow the Greek word (*hypocrites*) to mean 'actor,' then we discover we are most likely talking about mimes who paint their faces."

• Jesus tells his disciples not to look as they are fasting, "so that your fasting may be seen not by others but by your Father who is in secret; and your Father who sees in secret will reward you" (**v. 18**). Reward comes from God, who sees in secret, not from humans, who judge by what they see in public.[210] See the commentary on Matt 6:4.

MATTHEW 6:19–24 – LAYING UP TREASURE IN HEAVEN

6:19: "Do not store up for yourselves treasures on earth, where moth and rust consume and where thieves break in and steal;

6:20: but store up for yourselves treasures in heaven, where neither moth nor rust consumes and where thieves do not break in and steal.

6:21: "For where your treasure is, there your heart will be also.

6:22: "The eye is the lamp of the body. So, if your eye is healthy, your whole body will be full of light;

6:23: but if your eye is unhealthy, your whole body will be full of darkness. If then the light in you is darkness, how great is the darkness!

6:24: "No one can serve two masters; for a slave will either hate the one and love the other, or be devoted to the one and despise the other. You cannot serve God and wealth."

In Matt 6:1–18, Jesus criticized the way the hypocrites practiced almsgiving, prayer, and fasting. Jesus taught his disciples how piety should be practiced, in keeping with his earlier teaching on the true meaning of the Law (Matt 5:17–48). In Matt 6:19–34, Jesus will instruct his disciples in the true meaning and purpose of life, a life that is dedicated to God's will.

Matthew 6:19–24 is made up of three parts: (1) the exhortation to lay up treasure in heaven, not earth (vv. 19–21), (2) the eye metaphor (vv. 22–23), and (3) the warning that one cannot serve God and wealth at the same time but must choose. At first glance, the eye metaphor seems out of place, but the belief was that one with a "healthy" eye was generous and compassionate, whereas one with an "unhealthy" eye was mean-spirited and lacked compassion. In the present context, this means the one with the unhealthy eye is a slave to mammon (wealth) and is busily laying up treasures on earth.

Jesus begins his instruction by commanding his disciples: "Do not store up for yourselves treasures on earth" (**v. 19**), literally "Do not treasure up for yourselves

210   A. George, "La justice à faire dans le secret (Mat. 6,1–6. 16–18)," *Bib* 40 (1959): 590–98; P. S. Minear, *Commands of Christ* (1972), 47–68; W. T. Wilson, "Seen in Secret: Inconspicuous Piety and Alternative Subjectivity in Matt 6:1–6, 16–18," *CBQ* 72 (2010): 475–97.

treasures upon the earth." One thinks of LXX Mic 6:10, which speaks of "a house of a lawless man treasuring up lawless treasures, and with the arrogance of unrighteousness." The folly of grasping for material wealth is proverbial in late antiquity (e.g., Lucretius, *De Rerum Natura* 5.1105–42; Plutarch, *Moralia* 5D: "Education of Children" 8, "Wealth is held in high esteem, but it is a possession of fortune, since often fortune takes it away from those who possess it"; 523C–528B: "On Love of Wealth" 1–10, "money cannot buy peace of mind, greatness of spirit, serenity, confidence, and self-sufficiency"; Diogenes Laertius 6.1.11; 10.1.11).

What makes earth-bound treasure ultimately futile is that one way or another it disappears. Jesus tells his disciples not to lay up treasure on earth, "where moth and rust consume and where thieves break in and steal." What the NRSV translates as "rust" is actually "eating" (Greek: *brosis*). This translation is encouraged by the parallel in James 5:2–3, "… your gold and your silver have rusted [*katioun*]; and their rust [*ios*] will be a witness against you." One could suppose that *brosis* and *ios* are roughly parallel, in that one could say that rust eats away the metal. But *brosis* really does not mean rust; *ios* does (and the cognate verb *katioun* means "to rust"). In LXX Mal 3:11, "Then I will rebuke the devourer [*brosis*] for you, so that it may not destroy the fruits of the ground," *brosis* apparently refers to an insect (a grasshopper or worm). The parallel in the *Gospel of Thomas* also supports the hypothesis of two insects: "Seek the treasure that fails not, that endures, which no moth comes near to devour and no worm destroys" (§76). The advantage of reading "moth and worm" instead of "moth and rust" is that we do not have to explain how rust destroys "treasures." After all, rust destroys base metals (especially iron and copper) but not precious metals (gold, silver). Nor do we have to apply an unusual meaning to *brosis*.

But if the loss of precious metal through rust is not in view, what treasures have been lost to moth and worm? Most probably cloth and apparel, which when of good quality were prized (cf. Josh 7:21; Judg 14:12–13, 19; 2 Kings 5:22–23; 7:8), and their loss would be keenly felt by an average Palestinian family.

Not only is earthly treasure vulnerable to moth and worm, it can be stolen. Any house or strongbox on earth is potentially a place "where thieves break in and steal." Here Jesus may have had in mind money and precious metals and stones (along with any other valuables that are easily transportable). One is reminded of the prophetic warning: "Days are coming when all that is in your house, and that which your ancestors have stored up until this day, shall be carried to Babylon; nothing shall be left" (2 Kings 20:17). The NRSV translation is "break in" (see also Matt 24:43), but the verb (*diorussein*) can also mean "dig through" (*dia* + *orussein*). The related form *exorussein* (*ek* + *orussein*) means "dig through" (cf. Mark 2:4, "having dug through" the roof), whereas the simple form *orussein* means "hew" or "dig" (cf. Matt 21:33, "hewed a wine press"; Matt 25:18, "he dug a hole in the ground and hid his master's money"; Mark 12:1, "dug a pit"). The image is that of a thief digging through a wall or a roof (removing stones, plaster, reeds, mud, or thatch) to gain access to valuables.

Rather than laying up treasure on earth, Jesus urges his disciples to "store up for yourselves treasures in heaven, where neither moth nor rust consumes and where thieves do not break in and steal" (**v. 20**). There is scriptural background to Jesus' exhortation to store up treasure in heaven. Heaven, the dwelling of God, is sometimes thought of as a treasury or storehouse (e.g., Deut 28:12, "the Lord will open for you his rich storehouse, the heavens"). Treasure is to be laid up on earth "against the day of necessity" (Tob 4:9), but it is the heavenly treasure that is the most important, and that is laid up through true piety: "the one who does righteousness treasures up life to him for himself with the Lord" (*Pss. Sol.* 9:5). Especially pertinent to the context of Matt 6:1–18 is Tobit's wise advice to his son: "Prayer is good when accompanied by fasting, almsgiving, and righteousness. A little with righteousness is better than much with wrongdoing. It is better to give alms than to treasure up gold" (Tob 12:8). The combination of prayer, fasting, and almsgiving corresponds, though not in the same order, to Matt 6:5–15, 16–18, and 2–4. For other expressions of treasure in heaven, see 4 Ezra 7:77, "you have a treasure of works laid up with the Most High" (see also Sir 3:4; 29:10–13; 2 *Bar* 14:12; 24:1; 44:14; *T. Levi* 13:5, "do righteousness on earth, that you might find it in heaven"; *T. Naphtali* 8:5–6; *1 Enoch* 38:2; *t. Peah* 4.18, "I, through giving charity, have stored up treasures for the heavenly world above"; *Pesiqta de-Rab Kahana* 8.1, "Though the man who is concerned with Torah labors under the sun, his treasure is above the sun").

Treasure in heaven portrayed in its most graphic way is depicted in the Book of Revelation, where the saints will walk streets made of gold (Rev 21:18, 21, "the city was pure gold … the twelve gates were twelve pearls; each one of the gates was a single pearl. And the street of the city was pure gold").

Treasure in heaven, in God's care, is not subject to loss. Thieves cannot get at it: "treasures of faith were sealed" (4 Ezra 6:5). Wisdom tradition in Greco-Roman sources sometimes offered the same advice: "Acquire the things of the soul, because they are secure" (Sextus, *Sentences* 77); "Acquire those things that no one can take from you" (Sextus, *Sentences* 118).

There is another important reason to lay up treasure in heaven rather than on earth: "For where your treasure is, there your heart will be also" (**v. 21**). Preoccupation with earthly treasure will inevitably lead one's heart astray. And, conversely, the type of treasure that one accumulates is a reliable indicator of what one values. Accordingly, it is not surprising that the ancient sage warns his hearers, "Keep your heart with all vigilance, for from it flow the springs of life" (Prov 4:23), and the Psalmist counsels the faithful, "if riches increase, do not set your heart on them" (Ps 62:10b).

Jesus' saying seems proverbial, but no exact matches have been found. Greco-Roman ethicists have given expression to approximations of Jesus' teaching: "Where your mind is, there will be your good" (Sextus, *Sentences* 316); "For where one can say 'I' and 'mine,' there must the creature incline" (Epictetus, *Discourses* 2.22.19). True enough; where a person invests his time and resources, there we may expect to find his loyalties. One Jewish author describes the greedy as "those who … hoard up silver and gold, in which men trust; and there is no end to their getting" (Bar 3:17). Quite so; the treasures of earth never satisfy.

To connect the teaching about where to lay up treasure (vv. 19–21) and the teaching about choosing between God and wealth (v. 24), Matthew inserts the eye metaphor (vv. 22–23). The first part reads: "The eye is the lamp of the body. So, if your eye is healthy, your whole body will be full of light" (v. 22).[211] Jesus' metaphor is based on a widespread belief in antiquity that eyes possessed light, whose rays went forth and illuminated what could be seen (as in 2 Sam 12:11; Sir 23:19), a notion probably encouraged by the strange glow in the eyes of cats and various nocturnal creatures. Thus we hear the expression the "light of the eyes" (Prov 15:30; Tob 10:5). Poor eyesight was understood as eyes having become "dim" (as in Gen 27:1; 48:10; Deut 34:7).

There are texts that describe the eye much as Jesus does here: "his eyes like flaming torches" (Dan 10:6); "seven lamps on it, with seven lips on each of the lamps that are on the top of it … these seven are the eyes of the Lord" (Zech 4:2, 10); "my eyes, acting as lamps, were watching" (*T. Job* 18:3). Jesus is not teaching that "the eye is the window of the soul" (a modern perspective) but rather that one's eyes bring illumination to what is being viewed.[212] One can then see things and evaluate them for what they are. Strong, bright eyes illuminate and discern all, and they are a good indicator of inner well-being.

This is why Jesus says, "if your eye is healthy, your whole body will be full of light." That is, a bright, healthy eye offers proof that one's body is full of light. Bright, clear eyes indicate not only that one's being is full of light but that one can see clearly and discern well. The word "healthy" (sometimes translated "clear") literally means "simple" or "single" (Greek: *haplous*). This means eyes that are focused and see a sharp, single image; they do not see double and are not blurred.

---

[211] An allusion to this metaphor is found in a second-century Gnostic work called the *Dialogue of the Savior*, where Jesus the "Savior" says: "The lamp of the body is the mind, as long as you are upright … then your bodies are lights. As long as your mind is darkness, your light which you wait for will not be" (125.18–126.1). The shift from eye to mind is in keeping with Gnosticism's emphasis on knowledge (*gnosis*).

[212] The ancients believed that the eyes were themselves the source of light, that one in effect looked *out* at the object (called "extramission"). This idea is expressed in Hellenistic texts, as is emphasized in H. D. Betz, "Matthew vi.22f and Ancient Greek Theories of Vision," in E. Best and R. McL. Wilson (eds.), *Text and Interpretation: Studies in the New Testament Presented to Matthew Black* (Cambridge: Cambridge University Press, 1979), 43–66; H. D. Betz, *The Sermon on the Mount* (1995), 442–49. But the idea is also found in Scripture and other Jewish texts (such as Dan 10:2–9; Zech 4:1–4; *b. Shab.* 151b; 2 Enoch 42:1; *T. Job* 18:3). Matthew the evangelist was familiar with the idea as it circulated among Jews, making it unnecessary to hypothesize a Hellenistic source. See D. C. Allison, Jr., "The Eye is the Lamp of the Body (Matthew 6:22–23 = Luke 11:34–36)," *NTS* 33 (1987): 61–83.

The danger lies in having the opposite condition: "if your eye is unhealthy, your whole body will be full of darkness" (**v. 23**). An unhealthy (*poneros*, literally "evil") eye indicates not only inner darkness but also that one is not in a position to shed the light of truth outside oneself (cf. *T. Benjamin* 4:2, "a good man does not have a blind eye"). Accordingly, Jesus exclaims, "If then the light in you is darkness, how great is the darkness!" In other words, if one does not possess inner light, then one is in no position to shed light on the surrounding darkness. If what is supposed to produce light produces darkness instead, then "how great is the darkness" indeed.

The eye that is unhealthy ("evil") evokes sinister associations. In Scripture, we hear of the "hostile" eye (Deut 15:9), the "evil" eye (Prov 28:22), an evil man with a "grudging eye" (Sir 14:8; Tob 4:7), the "impudent" eye (Sir 26:11), and the "winking" eye that plans evil deeds (Sir 27:22). Similar terminology is found in rabbinic literature (e.g., in *m. 'Abot* 2:9 and 5:19, "good eye"/"evil eye"; *b. Ber.* 20a and 55b, "evil eye"; *b. Qiddushin* 82a and *b. B. Mesia* 87a, "grudging eye").[213]

Jesus concludes his teaching with a declaration that "No one can serve two masters" (**v. 24**). Jesus' statement is another instance of hyperbole, for one can in fact serve two masters, as do most Christians today (e.g., an employer, as well as God). Jesus' point is that one cannot give total loyalty to two masters, especially if they have competing and conflicting interests. This is why Jesus says that attempts to serve two masters will fail, "for a slave will either hate the one and love the other, or be devoted to the one and despise the other." The believer will have to choose between the competing masters, thus hating the one and loving the other (and again, "hate" here should be understood in a relative sense, as offering less respect, love, and loyalty compared with the master that one loves; see the commentary on Matt 5:43–48).

If one tries to serve two masters whose morals and values conflict sharply, one will "be devoted to the one and despise the other." It is unavoidable. Thus, the disciple who wishes to be faithful will have to choose. The choice, of course, is between God and earthly treasure: "You cannot serve God and wealth."

The word translated as "wealth" in the NRSV is translated as "mammon" in other translations (e.g., RSV, NASB, KJV). It comes from either Hebrew *mamon* or Aramaic *mamona*. Probably the best explanation for the meaning of the word is that it is from the root *aman*, from which "amen" is derived, meaning "firm," "sure," or "certain." Therefore, "mammon" ("wealth") is whatever one relies upon, which could be money, property, or wealth of any kind. Although not found in

---

213   For more on this interesting metaphor, see H. J. Cadbury, "The Single Eye," *HTR* 47 (1954): 69–74; R. L. Roberts, "An Evil Eye (Matthew 6:23)," *RestQ* 7 (1963): 143–47; F. C. Fensham, "The Good and Evil Eye in the Sermon on the Mount," *Neot* 1 (1967): 51–58; K. Syreeni, "A Single Eye: Aspects of the Symbolic World of Matt 6:22–23," *Studia Theologica* 53 (1999): 97–118; M. F. Whitters, "'The Eye Is the Lamp of the Body': Its Meaning in the Sermon on the Mount," *ITQ* 71 (2007): 77–88.

the Old Testament, the word occurs in a few of the Dead Sea Scrolls (1QS 6:2; CD 14:20) and in the Targum, the Aramaic paraphrase of the Old Testament (cf. *Tg. Onq.* Gen 37:26, in reference to the payment for Joseph). In Luke 16:11, we hear of "unrighteous *mamona*." The implication is clear: although mammon, or wealth, is not in itself evil, it can easily become one's master, which leads to pursuit of earthly treasure instead of heavenly treasure.[214]

MATTHEW 6:25–34 – ANXIETY

6:25: "Therefore I tell you, do not worry about your life, what you will eat or what you will drink, or about your body, what you will wear. Is not life more than food, and the body more than clothing?

6:26: Look at the birds of the air; they neither sow nor reap nor gather into barns, and yet your heavenly Father feeds them. Are you not of more value than they?

6:27: And can any of you by worrying add a single hour to your span of life?

6:28: And why do you worry about clothing? Consider the lilies of the field, how they grow; they neither toil nor spin,

6:29: yet I tell you, even Solomon in all his glory was not clothed like one of these.

6:30: But if God so clothes the grass of the field, which is alive today and tomorrow is thrown into the oven, will he not much more clothe you – you of little faith?

6:31: Therefore do not worry, saying, 'What will we eat?' or 'What will we drink?' or 'What will we wear?'

6:32: For it is the Gentiles who strive for all these things; and indeed your heavenly Father knows that you need all these things.

6:33: But strive first for the kingdom of God and his righteousness, and all these things will be given to you as well.

6:34: "So do not worry about tomorrow, for tomorrow will bring worries of its own. Today's trouble is enough for today."

*M*atthew 6:19–24 focused on treasure, arguing that the follower of Jesus should lay up treasure in heaven, not on earth. Matthew 6:25–34 centers

---

[214] For more on this theme, see E. P. Groenewald, "God and Mammon," *Neot* 1 (1967): 59–66; R. T. France, "God and Mammon," *EvQ* 51 (1979): 3–21; J. Dupont, "Dieu ou Mammon (Mt 6,24; Lc 16,13)," in F. Neirynck (ed.), *Études sur les évangiles synoptiques* (BETL 70; 2 vols., Leuven: Leuven University Press, 1985), 2:551–67; F. Beutter, "Die Rede von den zwei Herren, von Gott und dem Mammon (Mt 6,24)," in M. Lutz-Bachmann (ed.), *Und dennoch ist von Gott zu reden* (H. Vorgrimler FS; Freiburg: Herder, 1994), 69–84.

on the theme of worry, which often goes hand in hand with financial matters. If the disciple neglects the pursuit of earthly wealth, it is understandable that he should worry about food and clothing. Jesus urges his disciples not to worry about these things and draws lessons from nature, arguing that if God is mindful of birds and flowers, which are of little value, we can be sure he is mindful of humans, who are of much greater value. The disciple should pursue the kingdom and trust God to meet the earthly needs.

Jesus' exhortation that his disciples not be anxious about life's needs reflects in a general way teachings found in the Old Testament and in writings from his own time (e.g., Ps 127:2, "It is vain that you rise up early, to go late to rest, eating the bread of anxious toil; for he gives sleep to his beloved"; Philo, *On the Special Laws* 2.198, "we do not ascribe our preservation to any corruptible thing, but to God the Parent and Father and Savior of the world and all that is in it, who has the power and right to nourish and sustain us by means of these or without these").[215]

Jesus begins his teaching with an exhortation: "I tell you, do not worry about your life, what you will eat or what you will drink, or about your body, what you will wear" (**v. 25**). Compare Horace, *Odes* 2.11.4–5, "Do not be anxious for life's needs; it requires little." Quintus Horatius Flaccus lived from 65 B.C. to 8 B.C. Jesus' admonition is probably echoed in 1 Pet 5:7, "Cast all your anxiety on him, because he cares for you."

Jesus supports his argument with a rhetorical question: "Is not life more than food, and the body more than clothing?" This is an example of an argument from the major to the minor (or its reverse, from the minor to the major), an argument common in rabbinic debate. That is, if God has *given* life (the *major*), then does it not follow that he will provide that which is needed to *sustain* life (the *minor*)? Or, in the words of a rabbinic tradition: "Will not [God], who created [the human], create for him his food?" (*Pesiqta de-Rab Kahana* 8.1). In other words, God has already done the hard part – the miracle, as it were. So why are his children fretting? This kind of argument is continued in much of what follows. Consider the advice found in a second-century collection of wise sayings: "Even if someone takes away your worldly possessions, do not be vexed" (Sextus, *Sentences* 15).

Jesus provides the first of his examples on why his disciples should trust God as provider: "Look at the birds of the air; they neither sow nor reap nor gather into barns, and yet your heavenly Father feeds them" (**v. 26**). Compare Ps 147:9, "He gives to the animals their food, and to the young ravens when they cry" (cf. Luke 12:24, "Consider the ravens"), and Job 35:11, "Who teaches us more than the animals of the earth, and makes us wiser than the birds of the air?" Rabbi Simeon ben Eleazar is remembered to have argued similarly, even if his principal point was different: "Have you ever seen a wild animal or a bird practicing a trade? Yet they have their sustenance without care" (*m. Qiddushin* 4:14).

---

[215]   M. F. Olsthoorn, *The Jewish Background and the Synoptic Setting of Mt 6,25–33 and Lk 12,22–31* (SBF 10; Jerusalem: Franciscan Press, 1975).

In light of God's care of the animals, Jesus asks his disciples: "Are you not of more value than they?" Similar ideas are found in Greco-Roman wisdom: "in God's sight, a man is of more value than an angel" (Sextus, *Sentences* 32). The implication is that God will surely give more caring attention to humans than he does to birds and animals.

Besides, what good does worrying do? The reference in the verse, "And can any of you by worrying add a single hour to your span of life?" (**v. 27**), literally "to add to his lifespan [or stature] one cubit," is probably to lifespan, not stature. A "cubit" (from the word for "arm") is 18 inches, or almost 50 cm (which would be quite an addition if one's height was in view!), but it can be used, as it is here, with reference to time. According to Sextus, *Sentences* 255: "We cannot control the length of life, but we can control whether we live properly."

Jesus gives a second example, this time with reference to flora, on why his disciples should trust God as provider: "And why do you worry about clothing? Consider the lilies of the field, how they grow; they neither toil nor spin" (**v. 28**). The original reading may have spoken of "the lilies that neither card nor spin" instead of lilies that grow but do not spin. This alternate reading has been observed in a papyrus fragment (P.Oxy. 655 1.9–10) and in Codex Sinaiticus (early fourth century) using ultraviolet light. Carding or combing prepares the wool for spinning. In this reading, Jesus is saying that the lilies do not produce their attire the way humans must, by carding the wool and then spinning it.[216]

The Rabbis have pointed out that "while mortals are asleep in their beds, the Holy One causes winds to blow, clouds to rise, rains to come down, dews to glisten on plants, plants to spring up, fruits to grow plump" (*Pesiqta de-Rab Kahana* 8.1).

Jesus points out to his disciples that "even Solomon in all his glory was not clothed like one of these" lilies (**v. 29**). Solomon was considered Israel's wealthiest monarch

---

[216] This curious textual variant, which may have implications for Q and the parallel in the *Gospel of Thomas* (saying §36), has been discussed in V. Bartlet, "The Oxyrhynchus 'Sayings of Jesus,'" *Contemporary Review* 87 (1905): 116–25; C. Taylor, *The Oxyrhynchus Sayings of Jesus Found in 1903* (Oxford: Clarendon Press, 1905), 18–23; T. C. Skeat, "The Lilies of the Field," *ZNW* 37 (1938): 211–14; T. F. Glasson, "Carding and Spinning: Oxyrhynchus Papyrus No. 655," *JTS* 13 (1962): 331–32; J. E. Powell, "Those 'Lilies of the Field' Again," *JTS* 33 (1982): 490–92; J. M. Robinson and C. Heil, "Zeugnisse eines griechischen, schriftlichen vorkanonischen Textes: Mt 6,28b ℵ*, P.Oxy. 655 I,1–17 (EvTh 36) und Q 12,27," *ZNW* 89 (1998): 30–44; J. M. Robinson, "A Written Greek Sayings Cluster Older than Q: A Vestige," *HTR* 92 (1999): 61–77; J. M. Robinson, "The Pre-Q-Text of the (Ravens and) Lilies: Q 12:22–31 and P.Oxy. 655 (Gos. Thom. 36)," in S. Maser and E. Schlarb (eds.), *Text und Geschichte: Facetten historisch-theologischen Arbeitens aus dem Freundes- und Schülerkreis. Dieter Lührmann zum 60. Geburtstag* (MTS 50; Marburg: N. G. Elwert, 1999), 143–80; S. E. Porter, "P.Oxy. 655 and James Robinson's Proposals for Q: Brief Points of Clarification," *JTS* 52 (2001): 84–92. In the latter study, Porter corrects some misleading claims and inferences in the studies by Robinson. For social and theological implications of the saying, see L. A. Johnson and R. C. Tannehill, "Lilies Do Not Spin: A Challenge to Female Social Norms," *NTS* 56 (2010): 475–90.

(cf. 2 Chron 9:22, "King Solomon excelled all the kings of the earth in riches and in wisdom"; Sir 47:18, "you gathered gold like tin and amassed silver like lead"; 1 Kings 10:4–5, 21, 23; 2 Chron 9:4, 20). On a king clothed in finery, see Luke 16:19.[217]

Jesus adds to his argument with another comparison: "But if God so clothes the grass of the field, which is alive today and tomorrow is thrown into the oven, will he not much more clothe you – you of little faith?" (**v. 30**). On using grass as an illustration, compare Isa 5:24, "as the tongue of fire devours the stubble, and as dry grass sinks down in the flame" (cf. Isa 37:27; 40:6–8; Job 8:12; Pss 37:2; 90:5–6; 102:11; 103:15–16, "as for man, his days are like grass"). Grass is nothing, yet even it reflects God's provision. Is not God's care for humans much greater? Jesus calls his disciples "you of little faith" (literally "little-faith ones"). This is one of Matthew's favorite designations for the disciples (cf. Matt 8:26; 14:31; 16:8).

Jesus continues, telling the disciples: "Therefore do not worry, saying, 'What will we eat?' or 'What will we drink?' or 'What will we wear?'" (**v. 31**). Having little faith and being worried about food and drink come to expression in rabbinic sayings also: "Rabbi Elazar of Modi'im said, 'If a man has food for the day, but says, "What shall I eat tomorrow?" such a one lacks faith.' Rabbi Eliezer the Great said, 'He who still has bread in his basket and says, "What shall I eat tomorrow?" belongs to those of little faith'" (*Midrash Tanhuma, Beshallah* 117b; cf. *b. Sota* 48b). The actual Greek word (*oligopistos*) is found in the second-century A.D. collection of sayings attributed to a sage named Sextus: "A faithful man is an elect man. An elect man is a man of God … a man of little faith [*oligopistos*] is without faith" (Sextus, *Sentences* 1–2, 6).

When Jesus says, "For it is the Gentiles who strive for all these things" (**v. 32a**), he presupposes that the people of Israel, who know God, have greater faith than the Gentiles, who do not know God. If the disciples are anxious for material things, the way Gentiles are, then their faith in God is no better than the misguided and idolatrous faith of Gentiles. The disciples need to be reminded that "your heavenly Father knows that you need all these things" (**v. 32b**). The reasoning here compares to what Jesus had said about prayer and God's knowing what his children need even before they ask (cf. Matt 6:8).

Instead of pursuing earthly security, the disciples should seek above all God himself: "But strive first for the kingdom of God and his righteousness, and all these things will be given to you as well" (**v. 33**). This pithy admonition sums up the essence of Jesus' message, especially as it is heard in Matthew's Gospel, in which emphasis is placed on righteousness (as seen, for example, in Matt 5:6, 10).[218] God's

---

[217] Solomon, arrayed "in all his glory," may well not be intended in a positive sense. On this point, see W. Carter, "'Solomon in All His Glory': Intertextuality and Matthew 6.29," *JSNT* 65 (1997): 3–25.

[218] Some early manuscripts read "strive first for the kingdom and his righteousness" or "strive first for righteousness and his kingdom." Whichever reading is accepted, there is no doubt that "kingdom" refers to the "kingdom of God."

"righteousness" has been defined in the antitheses in Matt 5:21–48. See Sextus, *Sentences* 311: "A wise man shares in the kingdom of God." On eternal reward, see Sextus, *Sentences* 14: "at the judgment both your rewards and your punishments will be eternal."

The words "all these things will be given to you as well" may allude to Prov 3:2: "For length of days and years of life, and peace they will add to you." The "things" that shall be added to the disciples are those things that the Gentiles eagerly seek, things like food, drink, clothing, and shelter.[219]

Jesus rounds out the section by returning to the admonition with which the section began: "So do not worry about tomorrow, for tomorrow will bring worries of its own. Today's trouble is enough for today" (**v. 34**) (cf. v. 25, "do not worry about your life"). His language is once again reminiscent of wisdom tradition, in Scripture and in the Near East: "Do not boast about tomorrow, for you do not know what a day may bring forth" (Prov 27:1); "Do not fret over tomorrow's troubles, for you know not what a day may bring forth. Tomorrow may come and you will be no more" (*b. Sanhedrin* 100b; cf. *b. Ber.* 9b, "sufficient for the hour is the trouble [of the moment]").[220]

MATTHEW 7:1–5 – JUDGING

7:1: "Do not judge, so that you may not be judged.

7:2: For with the judgment you make you will be judged, and the measure you give will be the measure you get.

7:3: Why do you see the speck in your neighbor's eye, but do not notice the log in your own eye?

7:4: Or how can you say to your neighbor, 'Let me take the speck out of your eye,' while the log is in your own eye?

7:5: You hypocrite, first take the log out of your own eye, and then you will see clearly to take the speck out of your neighbor's eye."

The warnings of Matt 7:1–5 are mostly derived from Q, the source on which both Matthew and Luke drew (cf. Luke 6:37–42), though there is a parallel with Mark (cf. Mark 4:24–25). These warnings introduce a new topic in the Sermon on the Mount. In Chapter 5, the concern was with how to interpret and fulfill the Law, whereas in Chapter 6 the concern was with how to live in the light of the Law properly understood. The first part of Chapter 7 is concerned with judging and

---

219   G. R. Beasley-Murray, "Matthew: 6,33: The Kingdom of God and the Ethics of Jesus," in H. Merklein (ed.), *Neues Testament und Ethik* (Freiburg: Herder, 1989), 84–98.
220   J. G. Griffiths, "Wisdom about Tomorrow," *HTR* 53 (1960): 219–21; P. S. Minear, *Commands of Christ* (1972), 132–51.

criticizing others, without judging oneself. Once again, hypocrisy is in view (as it was in Matt 6:1–18).

Jesus' warnings about judgment are proverbial, with parallels in Jewish and non-Jewish sources alike. The logic of the warnings is founded upon the principle of *jus talionis* ("justice of kind"; cf. the commentary on Matt 5:43). There are few parallels in the Old Testament (e.g., Ps 18:25–26, "With the loyal you show yourself loyal; with the blameless you show yourself blameless," etc.). But in late antiquity expressions based on this principle became commonplace (e.g., Musonius, frag. 23, "How can we accuse dictators when we remain worse than they are?"; Musonius, frag. 32, "Don't try telling people what they should do when they know full well you yourself do what you should not"; Ps.-Diogenes 50, "When the Athenians do philosophy in your way they are like people promising to heal others of ills that they have been unable to cure in themselves"; Petronius, *Satyricon* 57.7, "Are you so full of business that you have no time to look behind you? You can see lice on others, but not the bugs on yourself!"; Sextus, *Sentences* 183, "Whoever judges a human being is himself judged by God"; Sextus, *Sentences* 184, "There is greater danger in judging than in being judged").

Jesus begins with the warning, "Do not judge, so that you may not be judged. For with the judgment you make you will be judged" (**vv. 1–2a**). Jesus' warning of reciprocity is echoed throughout Christian literature, though not every parallel is necessarily dependent on his words (e.g., Rom 2:1, "you have no excuse, whoever you are, when you judge others; for in passing judgment on another you condemn yourself, because you, the judge, are doing the very same things"; Rom 14:10; 1 Cor 4:5; 5:12; James 4:11–12; 5:9, "Beloved, do not grumble against one another, so that you may not be judged. See, the Judge is standing at the doors!"; *1 Clem* 13:2, "Show mercy, that you may receive mercy; forgive, that you may be forgiven. As you do, so shall it be done to you. As you give, so shall it be given to you. As you judge, so shall you be judged. As you show kindness, so shall kindness be shown to you. With the measure you use, it will be measured to you").

There are parallels in works by non-Jewish writers (e.g., Sextus, *Sentences* 183, "He who judges man is judged by God"; Seneca, *de Ira* 2.28.5–8, "It will be said that someone spoke ill of you; consider whether you spoke ill of him first.... We shall become more tolerant from self-inspection if we cause ourselves to consider: Have we ourselves never been guilty of such an act?") and in later rabbinic traditions (e.g., *b. Rosh Hashanah* 16b; *b. Shabbat* 127b, 151b, "He who is merciful to others, mercy is shown to him by Heaven [i.e., God], while he who is not merciful to others, mercy is not shown to him by Heaven").

Jesus concludes the thought with the maxim "the measure you give will be the measure you get" (**v. 2b**). This form of the principle was quite common in the rabbinic tradition from the time of the early sage Yeshua ben Sira (Sir 16:14, "He will make room for every act of mercy; every one will receive in accordance with his deeds") to the time of the Tannaitic Rabbis (*Mek.* on Exod 13:19 [*Beshallah* §1], "with what measure a man measures out it is measured to him"; *m. Sota* 1:7, "with what measure a man measures out it is measured to him again") and beyond (*t. Sota* 3.1; *b. Shabbat* 105b; *b. Sanhedrin* 100a; *Tg. Ps.-J.* Gen 38:26; *Tg. Isa* 27:8). Similar statements are found in some of the apocryphal and pseudepigraphical writings (e.g., *T. Zebulon* 5:3; *2 Enoch* 44:5).

A parallel appears in Mark 4:24 ("the measure you give will be the measure you get"), but the principle of just reward/retribution is more important to Matthew, as seen in the fourth antithesis (Matt 5:38–42) and in the parable of the unforgiving servant (Matt 18:23–35), materials that are found only in Matthew's Gospel.

Jesus asks his disciples, "Why do you see the speck in your neighbor's eye, but do not notice the log in your own eye? Or how can you say to your neighbor, 'Let me take the speck out of your eye,' while the log is in your own eye?" (vv. **3–4**). It has been suggested that Jesus' humorous illustration of hypocritical judging reflects his experience as a carpenter, in which sometimes someone got a speck of sawdust or a small woodchip in the eye. The image of someone trying to help a companion get the "speck" out of his friend's eye – all the while not noticing a "log" in his own eye – surely sparked laughter. The principle is certainly commonplace (cf. *b. Qiddushin* 70a: "He who accuses another of a fault has it himself") and may even have been proverbial (e.g., *b. 'Arakin* 16b: "Rabbi Tarfon said, 'I wonder whether there is any one in this generation who accepts reproof, for if one says to him, "Remove the *speck* from between your eyes [or teeth]," he would answer, "Remove the *log* from between your eyes [or teeth]"'" [with italics added]; cf. *b. Baba Batra* 15b). We find an apt Greco-Roman parallel in Epictetus (3.22.98, "If you censure others while you are hiding a little tart behind your arm ...") and another in Seneca (*De Vita Beata* 27.4, "are you at liberty to examine others' wickedness, and pass judgment on anyone? You take note of others' blemishes, when you yourself are a mass of sores").

Jesus rebukes his disciples, "You hypocrite, first take the log out of your own eye, and then you will see clearly to take the speck out of your neighbor's eye" (v. **5**). On "hypocrite," see the commentary on Matt 6:2. Assisting one's friend is not criticized; it is the failure to take care of one's own problems that is criticized (as in Prov 28:13: "No one who conceals transgressions will prosper, but one who confesses and forsakes them will obtain mercy"). Matthew encourages believers to help other believers, but it must be done with credibility and proper decorum (cf. Matt 18:15–20).[221]

---

[221] G. B. King, "The Mote and the Beam," *HTR* 17 (1924): 393–404; P. L. Hedley, "'The Mote and the Beam' and 'The Gates of Hades,'" *ExpT* 39 (1928): 427–28; C. A. Webster, "The Mote and the Beam (Lk vi. 41, 42 = Matt vii. 3–5)," *ExpT* 39 (1928): 91–92; G. B. King, "A Further Note on the Mote and the Beam (Matt VII.3–5; Luke VI.41–42)," *HTR* 26 (1933): 73–76; P. M. Bretscher, "Log in Your Own Eye (Matt. 7:1–5)," *CTM* 43 (1972): 645–86; J. D. M. Derrett, "Christ and Reproof (Matthew 7.1–5/Luke 6.37–42)," *NTS* 34 (1988): 271–81.

MATTHEW 7:6–12 – THE NEED FOR DISCERNMENT

7:6: "Do not give what is holy to dogs; and do not throw your pearls before swine, or they will trample them under foot and turn and maul you.

7:7: "Ask, and it will be given you; search, and you will find; knock, and the door will be opened for you.

7:8: For everyone who asks receives, and everyone who searches finds, and for everyone who knocks, the door will be opened.

7:9: Is there anyone among you who, if your child asks for bread, will give a stone?

7:10: Or if the child asks for a fish, will give a snake?

7:11: If you then, who are evil, know how to give good gifts to your children, how much more will your Father in heaven give good things to those who ask him!"

7:12: "In everything do to others as you would have them do to you; for this is the law and the prophets.

*A*fter warning his disciples about the dangers of judging others, Jesus instructs them about the need for discernment. The section is made up of three parts: (1) the warning not to give what is holy to dogs (v. 6), (2) teaching on asking of God (vv. 7–11), and (3) the famous Golden Rule (v. 12).

Jesus begins this part of his teaching with a warning: "Do not give what is holy to dogs; and do not throw your pearls before swine, or they will trample them under foot and turn and maul you" (**v. 6**). The appearance of this saying has the effect of balancing what has just been said in Matt 7:1–5, a passage that enjoined believers to be tolerant and forgiving, to take perceptions of their own moral uprightness with a grain of salt (and maybe a touch of self-deprecating humor). Nevertheless, critical discernment is necessary (though ineffective if it is hypocritical). There are some people who simply cannot be corrected, no matter how carefully and fairly one offers help. Moreover, they can be dangerous. With this danger in mind, Jesus provides his disciples with additional advice.

To what does "what is holy" refer? In the books of Moses, sacrificial meat and leaven are often called holy, things that cannot be touched by the laity or the impure (e.g., Exod 29:33, no layman "shall eat of them, because they are holy"; Lev 2:3; 22:6–7, "When the sun sets he shall be clean; and afterward he may eat of the" holy things, 22:10, "No lay person shall eat of the" holy thing, 22:11–16; Num 18:8–19). In reference to the holy things of sacrifice, we have an especially pertinent parallel in the Mishnah, where it is taught that "they do not redeem holy things to feed them to the dogs" (*m. Temurah* 6:5). Thus Jesus seems to be suggesting that anything that is truly *holy* (i.e., in that it may be offered to God) must not be given to *dogs*.

What then is "what is holy" that must not be given "to dogs"? The second-century Christian work called the *Didache* thinks "what is holy" is the Eucharist (cf. *Did.* 9:5). This work teaches that unbelievers (i.e., the "dogs" and "swine" in Jesus' saying) are not to partake of the Holy Eucharist (which is likened to the holy sacrifices). But this interpretation is anachronistic; surely this would never have occurred to Jesus' disciples during the pre-Easter ministry. The context suggests that "what is holy" is Jesus' teaching (as seen especially in the Sermon on the Mount), which presupposes his proclamation of the kingdom of God and, after Easter, perhaps the Eucharist also. Elsewhere Jesus commands his disciples to quit towns that reject the gospel, shaking the dust off their sandals as a testimony against their unbelief (cf. Matt 10:14; Mark 6:11).

Especially relevant may be Matt 10:13: "If the house is worthy, let your peace come upon it; but if it is not worthy, let your peace return to you." What we may have here in Matt 7:6 is a more extreme form of this principle: in some cases one's "greeting of peace" (with which Jesus' teaching begins), or "what is holy," should not be extended at all. Qumran, too, held to this view, but even more extremely, warning its members not to share community truths with outsiders:

The Instructor must not reprove the Men of the Pit, nor argue with them about proper biblical understanding.... He shall instruct them in every legal finding that is to regulate their works in that time, and teach them to separate from every man who fails to keep himself from perversity. These are the precepts of the Way for the Instructor in these times, as to his loving and hating: eternal hatred and a concealing spirit for the Men of the Pit! (1QS 9:16, 20–22)[222]

Who are the "dogs"? Because "dog" in Deut 23:18 ("You shall not bring the fee of a prostitute or the wages of a male prostitute into the house of the Lord your God in payment for any vow, for both of these are abhorrent to the Lord your God") refers to a Gentile, and because Jesus himself refers to Gentiles as "dogs" in his encounter with the Syro-Phoenician woman (cf. Mark 7:27–28 = Matt 15:26–27: "It is not fair to take the children's food and throw it to the dogs"), it has been thought that the dogs here in Matt 7:6 are Gentiles (cf. also *1 Enoch* 89:42–49). Thus Jesus warns his disciples not to give Gentiles things that are truly holy, much as some Rabbis warn against teaching the Torah to Gentiles (as in *b. Hagiga* 13a). But is this correct? Matthew is not only open to sharing the gospel and the teachings of Jesus to Gentiles, the risen Lord expressly commands it (Matt 28:18–20).

It has also been suggested that "dogs" refers to Cynics, whose name comes from the adjective *kynikos* (to be "doglike"). One thinks of the story that Diogenes recounts in his letter to Antisthenes: "I was going up to the city from Piraeus when some young men crossed my path ... as I drew near they said to one another, 'Let's

<hr/>

[222] Translation based on M. O. Wise, M. G. Abegg, Jr., and E. M. Cook, *The Dead Sea Scrolls* (1996), 139–40.

move away from the dog.' But when I heard this I said, 'Don't be afraid, this dog doesn't bite beets.'" After the publication of Matthew, it is probable that some readers thought of the Cynics, but it is highly improbable that Jesus had them in mind.

The negative appellation "dogs" is applied to Jews and Gentiles alike. In the Old Testament, "dog" was an insult (e.g., 1 Sam 17:43; 24:14; 2 Sam 9:8; 16:9; Ps 22:20; Prov 26:11; Isa 56:10–11; many of these examples are uttered by Jews and in reference to Jews). The picture is similar in the New Testament, where "dogs" may refer to Judaizers (as in Phil 3:2), the wicked (as in Rev 22:15), or apostates (as in 2 Pet 2:21–22, quoting part of Prov 26:11: "Like a dog that returns to its vomit is a fool who reverts to his folly"), or heretics (as in Ignatius, *Eph.* 7:1, "they are mad dogs that bite by stealth; you must be on your guard against them, for their bite is hard to heal"). Jesus' warning not to "give what is holy to dogs" therefore seems to have a general reference.[223]

Similarly, Jesus warns his disciples not to "throw your pearls before swine." The "pearls" are in parallel with "what is holy," so what has been said previously applies here. Pearls were highly prized in antiquity (e.g., Job 28:18, "the price of wisdom is above pearls") and are featured in the parable of the priceless pearl (Matt 13:45–46). Pearls are often likened to wise sayings (e.g., *b. Ber.* 33b; *b. Hagiga* 3a; *b. Yebamot* 94a). Consider also the advice found in one Greco-Roman source: "When you purposely throw your best possessions in the mud, then, being pure, ask for something from God" (Sextus, *Sentences* 81); "Say nothing about God to the godless" (Sextus, *Sentences* 354; cf. ibid. 365, 407, 451).

The "swine" are in parallel with the "dogs," with no distinction between them. Both are unclean animals (especially swine; cf. Lev 11:7; Deut 14:8), and both swine and dogs were insulting appellations that sometimes occur together (e.g., 1 *Enoch* 89:42; 2 Pet 2:22; *b. Shabbat* 155b).

If one throws pearls to swine, "they will trample them under foot," implying that either the swine do not know what they have heard or that they fiercely reject it. Having rejected good teaching, the swine will "turn and maul" God's people. The logic of Jesus' warning reflects the wise counsel found in Proverbs: "Do not speak in the hearing of a fool, for he will despise the wisdom of your words" (Prov 23:9). Some have suggested that the "turn and maul" danger applies better to the dogs than to the swine. But a wild pig can be as dangerous as any dog. The point is that the teachings of Jesus, which his followers regarded as sacred and as being equivalent to Scripture itself (compare Matt 24:35 = Mark 13:31 = Luke 21:33, "my words will not pass away," with Isa 40:6–9), are not to be given to wicked, and in some cases dangerous, persons.[224]

[223] J. Schwartz, "Dogs in Jewish Society in the Second Temple Period and in the Time of the Mishnah and Talmud," *JJS* 55 (2004): 246–77.

[224] For more discussion of this saying, see A. M. Perry, "Pearls before Swine," *ExpT* 46 (1935): 381–82; T. F. Glasson, "Chiasmus in St. Matthew vii.6," *ExpT* 68 (1957): 302; P. G. Maxwell-Stuart, "Do Not Give What Is Holy to the Dogs (Mt 7.6)," *ExpT* 90 (1979): 341;

In the next section (Matt 7:7–11), Jesus speaks very much like the Jewish sage; his exhortations and promises echo those of Jewish wisdom. Asking and seeking for wisdom, or truth, as we near the conclusion of the Sermon on the Mount, constitutes an invitation to ask God's wisdom and, it is implied, confirmation of the veracity of Jesus' teaching and the validity of his mission.

Jesus tells his disciples, "Ask, and it will be given you" (**v. 7a**). Jesus teaches his followers to ask of God because God will give ("be given" is an instance of the so-called divine passive, whereby if the verb were put in the active voice God would be the explicit subject: "God will give to you"). Scriptural antecedents, as well as his own experience, encourage Jesus in this conviction. To the Lord's Anointed, God says, "Ask of me, and I will make the nations your heritage, and the ends of the earth your possession" (Ps 2:8); or again, "He asked you for life; you gave it to him – length of days forever and ever" (Ps 21:4), and "One thing I asked of the Lord, that will I seek after: to live in the house of the Lord all the days of my life, to behold the beauty of the Lord, and to inquire in his temple" (Ps 27:4). The prophet Zechariah enjoins the struggling postexilic community: "Ask rain from the Lord in the season of the spring rain, from the Lord who makes the storm clouds, who gives showers of rain to you, the vegetation in the field to everyone" (Zech 10:1). All of these examples (in the Septuagint) use the verbs ask (*aitein*) and give (*didonai*), which are the verbs in Matthew's text.

Human asking and divine giving are found together in Old Testament narrative (e.g., 1 Sam 1:27, "For this child I prayed; and the Lord has granted me the petition that I made to him"; 1 Kings 3.5, "the Lord appeared to Solomon in a dream by night; and God said, 'Ask what I should give you'"), in the Apocrypha (e.g., Tob 4:19, "At all times bless the Lord God, and ask him that your ways may be made straight and that all your paths and plans may prosper. For none of the nations has understanding, but the Lord himself will give them good counsel"), and in reference to a human king (4 Ezra 4:42: "Then the king said to him, 'Ask what you wish, even beyond what is written, and we will give it to you'").

Jesus also promises his disciples, "search, and you shall find" (**v. 7b**). The idea of seeking after truth or wisdom is a favorite in Jewish wisdom: "I love those who love me, and those who seek me diligently find me" (Prov 8:17); "Then they will call upon me, but I will not answer; they will seek me diligently, but will not find me" (Prov 1:28, in reference to fools who normally do not seek wisdom); "Wisdom is radiant and unfading, and she is easily discerned by those who love her, and is found by those who seek her" (Wisd of Sol 6:12); "When you search for me, you will find me; if you seek me with all your heart" (Jer 29:13); "If a man says to you, 'I have labored

T. J. Bennett, "Matthew 7:6 – A New Interpretation," *WTJ* 49 (1987): 371–86; S. Llewelyn, "Mt 7:6a: Mistranslation or Interpretation?" *NovT* 31 (1989): 97–103; H. van de Sandt, "'Do Not Give What Is Holy to the Dogs' (Did 9:5d and Matt 7:6a): The Eucharistic Food of the Didache in Its Jewish Purity Setting," *VC* 56 (2002): 223–46.

and not found,' do not believe him. If he says, 'I have labored and found,' you may believe him.... all depends on the assistance of Heaven ...." (*b. Megillah* 6b).

Jesus adds, "knock, and the door will be opened for you" (**v. 7c**); see Song of Sol 5:2, "I slept, but my heart was awake. Listen! my beloved is knocking. 'Open to me, my sister, my love, my dove, my perfect one.'" And, from rabbinic literature, we have "he knocked at the gates of mercy and they were opened to him" (*b. Megillah* 12b) and "A man should always immerse himself in the Mishnayot, for if he knows, it will be opened to him" (*Lev. Rab.* 21.5 [on Lev 16:3]).

Jesus promises his disciples, "For everyone who asks receives" (**v. 8**). Jesus follows up his imperatives with indicative assurances that indeed everyone who asks receives, who searches finds, and who knocks has the door opened. The grounds for this assurance are provided in vv. 9–11.

Jesus asks, "Is there anyone among you who, if your child asks for bread, will give a stone?" (**v. 9**). The Lukan parallel reads egg/scorpion (Luke 11:12), but the logic is the same. A loaf of bread is a necessity for life; a stone is worthless. No father would give his child a stone instead of the requested loaf of bread. It is sometimes remarked that a stone may resemble a loaf of bread, both in shape and in color. (Recall that in Matt 4:3 the devil invited Jesus to turn stones into loaves of bread.) One thinks of the story related by Seneca: "Fabius Verrucosus used to compare a benefit conferred by a harsh man in an offensive manner to a stone loaf, which a hungry man is forced to receive, but which he cannot eat" (*De Beneficiis* 2.7).

Jesus asks again, "Or if the child asks for a fish, will give a snake?" (**v. 10**). Similarly, no father would give his child a snake, which is not only worthless but dangerous, instead of the requested fish. Like bread, fish was a staple, especially in Galilee. Recall that Jesus fed the multitude bread and fish (cf. Matt 14:17–20).

Jesus drives home his point: "If you then, who are evil, know how to give good gifts to your children, how much more will your Father in heaven give good things to those who ask him!" (**v. 11**). All humans are evil in comparison to God, who is perfect in every attribute and virtue. If imperfect, faithless, unreliable human fathers regularly "give good gifts to" their "children," then "how much more will" our "Father in heaven give good things to those who ask him." (On "good gift," see Sir 18:17.) The argument is from the minor (frail human fathers who give good gifts to their children) to the major (the heavenly Father who gives good gifts to his children). The fact of the former guarantees that of the latter. A close parallel is found in rabbinic literature, where we hear of charitable behavior on the part of an evil man. In his prayer, the rabbi reasons with God: "If this man, who is flesh and blood, cruel and not responsible for her [his divorced wife's] maintenance, was filled with compassion for her and gave her charity, how much more should you be filled with compassion for us who are the children of your children Abraham, Isaac, and Jacob, and are dependent on you for our maintenance" (*Lev. Rab.* 34.14 [on Lev 25:25]).[225]

---

[225]   For further discussion of this material, see C. H. Kraeling, "Seek and You Will Find," in A. Wikgren (ed.), *Early Christian Origins* (Chicago: Quadrangle, 1961), 24–34; P. S. Minear,

One of the best-known sayings of Jesus is the so-called Golden Rule: "In everything do to others as you would have them do to you; for this is the law and the prophets" (**v. 12**). There are many other versions of this saying, some cast in a negative form. Luke's parallel (Luke 6:31) reads much more simply: "Do to others as you would have them do to you." Matthew may very well have added "for this is the law and the prophets."

The NRSV does not translate *oun* as "therefore" at the beginning of v. 12. It should have done so, for Matthew's *therefore* may well sum up the whole of the Sermon on the Mount, especially harking back to the thesis statement in Matt 5:17–20. In Matt 5:17, Jesus declares that he has come "to fulfill" the Law and the Prophets. What follows (in Matt 5:21–7:12) shows how he understands this fulfillment to take place, ending with the Golden Rule, which sums up the whole of the Law (as even the great Rabbi Hillel would understand it; see the example that follows).

The so-called Golden Rule probably has its roots in Lev 19:18 ("you shall love your neighbor as yourself"), a passage that Jesus quotes as one of the two great commandments (cf. Matt 22:34–40). This is especially relevant when it is noted that in the Aramaic paraphrase (Targum) of Lev 19:18 a form of the Golden Rule appears. The Aramaic version reads: "You shall love your neighbor, so that what is hateful to you, you shall not do to him" (*Tg. Ps.-J.* Lev 19:18).

The Golden Rule is paralleled by many sayings, many of which cast the dictum into a negative form: "And what you hate, do not do to anyone. Do not drink wine to excess or let drunkenness go with you on your way" (Tob 4:15); "As you wish that no evil should befall you, but to be a partaker of all good things, so you should act on the same principle towards your subjects and offenders" (*Letter of Aristeas* 207); "Judge your neighbor's feelings by your own, and in every matter be thoughtful" (Sir 31:15); "Just as a man asks something for his own soul from God, so let him do to every living soul" (2 *Enoch* 61.2); "even as a man looks out for his own home, so should he look out for the home of his fellow" (*m. 'Abot* 2:11); and Hillel to a Gentile who had wanted the Torah taught in an instant, "What is hateful to you do not to your neighbor, that is the whole Torah, while the rest is comment on it; go and learn it" (*b. Shabbat* 31a).

The same sentiment is expressed in Greco-Roman ethical writings: "As you wish your neighbors to treat you, so treat them" (Sextus, *Sentences* 89) and "As you want your neighbors to treat you, so treat them" (*Sentences* 210b). A more limited form is found in *Sentences* 87, "Treat a pious person as yourself," and a negative form is

Commands of Christ (1972), 113–31; R. A. Piper, "Matthew 7,7–11 par. Lk 11,9–13: Evidence of Design and Argument in the Collection of Jesus' Sayings," in J. Delobel (ed.), *Logia: Les paroles de Jésus – The Sayings of Jesus* (BETL 59; Leuven: Peeters and Leuven University Press, 1982), 411–18; D. Goldsmith, "'Ask, and It Will Be Given …': Toward Writing the History of a Logion," *NTS* 35 (1989): 254–65; H. W. Attridge, "'Seeking' and 'Asking' in Q, Thomas, and John," in J. Asgeirsson, K. de Troyer, and M. W. Meyer (eds.), *From Quest to Q. Festschrift James M. Robinson* (BETL 146; Leuven: Leuven University Press, 2000), 295–302.

found in *Sentences* 90, "Whatever you criticize, do not do," and in *Sentences* 179, "What you do not want to experience, do not do"). Other examples include: "If you want to be loved, love" (Seneca, *Moral Epistles* 9.6); "Take care not to harm others, so others will not harm you" (Seneca, *Moral Epistles* 103.3–4); and "All that is hateful to you, you should not wish to do that to your neighbor" (Sentences of Syriac Menander 250–51).

Jesus' explanation, "for this is the law and the prophets," implies that the Golden Rule fulfills the essence of the requirements found in Scripture. The "Law and the Prophets" are the two major parts of the Hebrew Bible, mentioned in Matt 5:17. They will reappear in Matt 11:13 and 22:40 ("On these two commandments depend the whole Law and the Prophets"; see the commentary on Matt 5:17).[226]

MATTHEW 7:13–14 – THE TWO GATES

7:13: "Enter through the narrow gate; for the gate is wide and the road is easy that leads to destruction, and there are many who take it.

7:14: For the gate is narrow and the road is hard that leads to life, and there are few who find it.

*J*esus sets before his disciples two alternatives: a narrow gate that leads to life and a wide gate that leads to destruction. The two alternatives presuppose what has been taught in Matt 5:7–6:34. That is, one can either interpret the Law according to what it really teaches and what it really requires, or one can make a sham of it (Matt 5:17–48); one can practice one's piety with integrity and sincerity, or one can play the role of an actor whose piety is intended to win the praise of humans, not God

---

[226] The bibliography on the Golden Rule is enormous; for a selection of studies, see W. H. P. Hatch, "A Syriac Parallel to the Golden Rule," *HTR* 14 (1921): 193–95; G. B. King, "The 'Negative' Golden Rule," *JR* 8 (1928): 268–79; R. H. Connolly, "A Negative Form of the Golden Rule in the Diatessaron?" *JTS* 35 (1934): 351–57; O. E. Evans, "The Negative Form of the Golden Rule in the Diatessaron," *ExpT* 63 (1951): 31–32; B. M. Metzger, "The Designation 'The Golden Rule,'" *ExpT* 69 (1958): 304; A. Dihle, *Die 'Goldene Regel': Eine Einführung in die Geschichte der antiken und frühchristlichen Vulgäethik* (Göttingen: Vandenhoeck & Ruprecht, 1962); P. Borgen, "The Golden Rule, with Emphasis on Its Usage in the Gospels," in *Paul Preaches Circumcision and Pleases Men: And Other Essays on Christian Origins* (Dragvoll: TAPIR, 1983), 99–114; J. I. H. McDonald, "The Great Commandment and the Golden Rule," in A. G. Auld (ed.), *Understanding Poets and Prophets* (G. Wishart FS; JSOTSup 152; Sheffield: Sheffield Academic Press, 1993), 213–26; B. D. Chilton, "'Do not do what you hate': Where there is not Gold, there Might be Brass. The Case of the Thomaean 'Golden Rule' (6.3)," in *Judaic Approaches to the Gospels* (USF International Studies in Formative Christianity and Judaism 2; Atlanta: Scholars Press, 1994), 123–49; P. S. Alexander, "Jesus and the Golden Rule," in J. H. Charlesworth and L. L. Johns (eds.), *Hillel and Jesus: Comparisons of Two Major Religious Leaders* (Minneapolis: Fortress, 1997), 363–88.

(Matt 6:1–18); one can lay up treasure in heaven and strive for God's kingdom, or one can pursue material wealth and earthly security (Matt 6:19–34). The one gate is narrow and difficult, the other wide and easy. Which gate will one choose? The two-ways sayings also introduce the conclusion to the Sermon on the Mount (Matt 7:15–29), where Jesus invites his hearers to heed his teaching and become his followers. Will they follow him, or will they follow someone else?

Jesus urges his disciples, "Enter through the narrow gate; for the gate is wide and the road is easy that leads to destruction, and there are many who take it" (**v. 13**).[227] The contrast between the "narrow" gate and the "wide" gate reflects the architectural realities of first-century Galilee.[228] The "narrow gate" implies that Jesus has in mind a walled city, not a village, for villages usually did not have walls or gates. Cities were walled and had various gates, some wider than others, and roads, some wider than others.[229] Perhaps the analogy implies the contrast between the broad, paved, and colonnaded roads and impressive gates built by Herod the Great and his sons and the narrow, uneven, winding paths that linked many of the small villages.

The saying is part of a wisdom theme sometimes referred to as the "two ways." It has its roots in Scripture, such as Moses' warnings to Israel: "See, I am setting before you today a blessing and a curse" (Deut 11:26); "See, I have set before you today life and prosperity, death and adversity" (Deut 30:15). These two alternatives are picked up in Jeremiah and become the two "ways": "And to this people you shall say: 'Thus says the Lord: "See, I am setting before you the way of life and the way of death"'" (Jer 21:8). It is Jeremiah's "way of life" and "way of death" alternatives and the wisdom tradition that later grew out of them that form the background to Jesus' pithy saying in Matt 7:13–14.

Intertestamental expressions of the two ways include: "Two ways has God given to the sons of men … for there are two ways of good and evil" (*T. Asher* 1:3–5); God "showed him [Adam] the two ways, the light and the darkness, and I told him: This is good, and that bad" (*2 Enoch* 30:15); "Before each person are life and death, and whichever one chooses will be given" (Sir 15:17); God appointed "for them two spirits in which to walk until the time ordained for His visitation. These are the spirits

---

[227]   The parallel in Luke 13:24 reads: "Strive to enter through the narrow door; for many, I tell you, will try to enter and will not be able." Luke's simpler form of the two-ways saying may be closer to Jesus' Aramaic original. The Lukan saying is found in the context of accepting or rejecting the kingdom of God. In Luke 13:22–23, Jesus is asked if it is true that only "a few are to be saved?" Jesus' reply is the two-ways saying in v. 24. The saying is followed by a parable about those who try to get in after the door has been shut and locked. They will not be admitted but instead will be locked out (Luke 13:25–30).

[228]   See M. Knowles, "'Wide Is the Gate and Spacious the Road that Leads to Destruction': Matthew 7.13 in Light of Archaeological Evidence," *JGRChJ* 1 (2000): 176–213.

[229]   J. F. Strange, "Some Implications of Archaeology for New Testament Studies," in J. H. Charlesworth and W. P. Weaver (eds.), *What Has Archaeology To Do with Faith?* (1992), 23–59, especially 45.

of truth and falsehood" (1QS 3:18–19; cf. 4 Ezra 7:3–9; Wisd of Sol 5:6–7; Sir 2:12; 15:11–17; 21:10).

The two ways are also expressed in various ways in Rabbinic sources (*Mek.* on Exod 14:28 [*Beshallah* §7]; *Sipre Deut.* §53 [on Deut 11:26]: "A person was sitting at crossroads, with two paths before him, one which started out smoothly but ended amidst thorns, and one which started out amidst thorns but ended smoothly"; *b. Ber.* 28b, "There are two ways before me, one leading to Paradise and the other to Gehenna, and I dare not know by which I shall be taken"; *b. Hagiga* 3b), the Targums (on Deut 30:15, 19),[230] and Greco-Roman sources (Hesiod, *Opera et Dies* 287–92; Xenophon, *Memorabilia Socratis* 2.21–34; Diogenes of Sinope, *Epistles* 30; Seneca, *Epistles to Lucilius* 8.3; 27.4; Ps.-Diogenes, frag. 30.2: "He pointed out two ways leading upwards not far from us. One was quite short, but steep and difficult. The other was a long one, smooth and easy").

The two ways theme is paradigmatic in second-century Christian literature, especially the *Didache* (1:1–2, "There are two ways, one of life and one of death, and there is a great difference between these two ways. Now this is the way of life ..."; cf. *Barn.* 18:1, "There are two ways of teaching and power, one of light and one of darkness, and there is a great difference between these two ways").

Jesus tells his disciples to "Enter through the narrow gate" (**v. 13a**). In two-ways wisdom tradition, the "narrow gate" may be depicted as steep, difficult, or unpopular. We are reminded of another of Jesus' sayings: "it is easier for a camel to go through the eye of a needle than for someone who is rich to enter the kingdom of God" (Matt 19:24).

The narrow gate is preferred, "for the gate is wide and the road is easy that leads to destruction, and there are many who take it" (**v. 13b**). Warnings about taking the easy way abound in the wisdom tradition: "Sometimes there is a way that seems to be right, but in the end it is the way to death" (Prov 16:25); "The way of sinners is paved with smooth stones, but at its end is the pit of Hades" (Sir 21:10). And outside of Scripture we hear similar warnings: "There is the sentence of corruption, the way of fire, and the path that leads to Gehenna" (2 *Bar* 85:13); "The road that leads to Hades is easy to follow" (Diogenes Laertius 4.49).

Jesus further explains that "the gate is narrow and the road is hard that leads to life" (**v. 14a**); see Ps 16:11, "You will show me the path of life." Recall also Jer 21:8, "See, I am setting before you the way of life and the way of death." In the fourth Gospel, it is Jesus himself who becomes the "door" and the "way" that leads to life and to the Father (cf. John 10:7, 9; 14:4–9); and in later Christian expression,

---

[230] The evidence for the appearance of the two-way theme in pre-Christian Jewish tradition is ably surveyed in S. Brock, "The Two Ways and the Palestinian Targum," in P. R. Davies and R. T. White (eds.), *A Tribute to Geza Vermes: Essays on Jewish and Christian Literature and History* (JSOTSup 100; Sheffield: JSOT Press, 1990), 139–52.

"I am the gate of life: the one entering through me enters into life" (*Ps.-Clementine Homilies* 3.52.2).

The difficulty in choosing rightly is seen in the warning that "there are few who find it" (**v. 14b**). Jesus' "few" is relative and stands somewhat in tension with the assurance that "many will come from east and west and will eat with Abraham and Isaac and Jacob in the kingdom of heaven" (cf. Matt 8:11) or that Jesus' death on the cross will be "a ransom for many" (cf. Matt 20:28). The "fewness" of those who find the small gate and narrow way only underscores the smallness of the gate and the narrowness of the way; that is, the difficulty of doing the right thing. It is therefore so difficult that apart from divine enabling it would be impossible. Recall the disciples' astonishment that not even the rich, who are apparently blessed (as conventional thinking would have it), will enter the kingdom of God. They ask, "Then who can be saved?" Jesus replies, "For mortals it is impossible, but for God all things are possible" (Matt 19:25–26). Jesus' saying about the two ways should be interpreted in this light.[231]

MATTHEW 7:15–20 – KNOWN BY ONE'S FRUIT

7:15: "Beware of false prophets, who come to you in sheep's clothing but inwardly are ravenous wolves.

7:16: You will know them by their fruits. Are grapes gathered from thorns, or figs from thistles?

7:17: In the same way, every good tree bears good fruit, but the bad tree bears bad fruit.

7:18: A good tree cannot bear bad fruit, nor can a bad tree bear good fruit.

7:19: Every tree that does not bear good fruit is cut down and thrown into the fire.

7:20: Thus you will know them by their fruits."

Jesus' teaching concerning two ways naturally leads to a warning about false prophets. As the true Prophet and Messiah, Jesus teaches his disciples the way that leads to life. He had warned them not to be seduced by the broad way that leads

[231] For further discussion, see M. J. Suggs, "The Christian Two Ways Tradition: Its Antiquity, Form, and Function," in D. E. Aune (ed.), *Studies in the New Testament and Early Christian Literature: Essays in Honor of Allen P. Wikgren* (NovTSup 33; Leiden: Brill, 1972), 60–74; A. Denaux, "Der Spruch von den zwei Wegen im Rahmen des Epilogs der Bergpredigt," in J. Delobel (ed.), *Logia: Les paroles de Jésus – The Sayings of Jesus* (BETL 59; Leuven: Leuven University Press, 1982), 305–35; J. D. M. Derrett, "The Merits of the Narrow Gate," *JSNT* 15 (1982): 20–29.

to destruction. He now warns them that there are false prophets who will encourage them to follow false paths. Matthew has again drawn upon Q, the source also used by Luke (cf. Luke 6:43–45), but not without significant editing.

Jesus warns his disciples, "Beware of false prophets" (**v. 15a**). Warnings regarding "false prophets" appear frequently in the New Testament. They make an appearance in Luke's woes that stand opposite the beatitudes, where Jesus warns that people speak well of the wicked, just as they did of the false prophets long ago (Luke 6:26). In the eschatological discourse, Jesus will warn his disciples of the appearance of false prophets and false messiahs (cf. Matt 24:11, 24; Mark 13:22). The apostle Paul will encounter a false prophet on the island of Cyprus (Acts 13:6: "they met a certain magician, a Jewish false prophet, named Bar-jesus"). The author of 2 Peter warns believers: "But false prophets also arose among the people, just as there will be false teachers among you, who will secretly bring in destructive opinions. They will even deny the Master who bought them – bringing swift destruction on themselves" (2 Pet 2:1). The Johannine writings contain similar warnings: "Beloved, do not believe every spirit, but test the spirits to see whether they are from God; for many false prophets have gone out into the world" (1 John 4:1; cf. Rev 16:13; 19:20, "the beast was captured, and with it the false prophet who had performed in its presence the signs by which he deceived those who had received the mark of the beast"; 20:10).

False prophets are mentioned in the Old Testament. In the Greek version (i.e., the Septuagint, abbreviated as LXX) the word *pseudoprophetes* occurs ten times (usually with no exact equivalent in the Hebrew), all ten in the prophets Jeremiah and Zechariah: "everyone is greedy for unjust gain; and from prophet to priest, everyone deals falsely" (Jer 6:13); "And the priests and the pseudo-prophets and all the people heard Jeremiah speaking these words in the house of the Lord" (LXX Jer 33:7 = Heb 26:7); "when Jeremiah had stopped speaking all that the Lord had instructed him to speak to all the people, then the priests and the pseudo-prophets and all the people laid hold of him, saying, 'You shall die by death!'" (LXX Jer 33:8 = Heb 26:11); "And the priests and the pseudo-prophets said to the rulers and to all the people, 'A sentence of death on this person!'" (LXX Jer 33:11 = Heb 26:11; cf. LXX Jer 33:16 = Heb 26:16; LXX Jer 34:9 = Heb 27:9; LXX Jer 35:1 = Heb 28:1; LXX Jer 36:1 = Heb 29:1; LXX Jer 36:8 = Heb 29:8); in the day of judgment, God "will remove from the land the pseudo-prophets and the unclean spirit" (LXX Zech 13:2).

Intertestamental texts speak of false prophets, complaining of how "they prophesied falsehood to turn Israel from following God" (CD 6:1–2). This they did, despite righteous kings like Josiah who tried to stamp out evil in Israel: "their polluted ones he burned in the fire, and the lying prophets which deceived the people, these also he burned in the fire" (2 Bar 66:4).

Perhaps one of the most sensational encounters since the days of Elijah and his contest with the prophets of Baal was that between Isaiah and the Samaritan prophet Belkira, "a false prophet whose dwelling was in Bethlehem" (*Martyrdom and Ascension of Isaiah* 2:12). He and his colleagues "prophesied falsely in Jerusalem"

(3:1) and plotted against righteous Isaiah, accusing him of prophesying lies against Israel and Judah (3:7). Through their machinations, Isaiah falls into the hands of the wicked Manasseh, who orders the great prophet sawed in two: "And when Isaiah was being sawn asunder Belkira stood up, accusing him, and all the false prophets stood up, laughing and rejoicing because of Isaiah.... And Manasseh and Belkira and the false prophets and the princes and the people all stood looking on" (5:2, 12).

False prophets continue to be a problem, even in more recent times: "With a willful heart they look about and seek you in idols. They have set the stumbling block of their iniquity before themselves, and they come to seek you through the words of lying prophets corrupted by error. With mocking lips and a strange tongue they speak to your people so as to make a mockery of all their works by deceit. For they did not choose the wa[y of] your [heart] nor attend to your word" (1QHa 12:16–18). More false prophets in the end time are foretold: "And there shall be false prophets like tempests, and they shall persecute all righteous men" (*T. Judah* 21:9). Qumran expects Israel to deal with false prophets severely: "But any prophet who arises to urge you [to apostasy, to turn you] from following your God, must be put to death" (4Q375 frag. 1, col. i, lines 4–5). Josephus refers to false prophets and charlatans in his time (*J.W.* 2.261; 6.285; *Ant.* 20.97, 160, 167).

It is against such a background that Jesus' warning of false prophets would have been understood. In what follows, Jesus informs his disciples how they will be able to recognize false prophets.[232]

These false prophets, Jesus avers, are those "who come to you in sheep's clothing but inwardly are ravenous wolves" (**v. 15b**). Aesop tells a fable of a wolf dressed in a sheepskin. The illustration is apt, given the depiction of Israel as sheep (as in Num 27:17; Ps 78:52), who are sometimes abused and neglected by false shepherds (as in Ezek 34:2, 8, 10; *1 Enoch* 89–90). One is reminded of Jesus' teaching in John's Gospel, where he warns that the hireling, not being a true shepherd, will abandon the sheep at the first sighting of the wolf (cf. John 10:12–13). Jesus' warning about wolves in "sheep's clothing" may reflect the negative side of the prophetic vision that the day will come when "the wolf shall live with the lamb" (Isa 11:6) and "the wolf and the lamb shall feed together" (Isa 65:25). Before that time comes, false prophets, pretending to be members of the flock, perhaps even shepherds of the sheep, will in fact be "ravenous wolves" who have come to devour the sheep. Rabbinic literature also speaks of Israel as sheep in the midst of wolves (cf. *Esther Rab.* 10.11 [on Esther 9:2], quoting Mic 5:8: "like a lion among the animals of the forest, like a young lion

---

[232] P. S. Minear, "False Prophecy and Hypocrisy in the Gospel of Matthew," in J. Gnilka (ed.), *Neues Testament und Kirche* (R. Schnackenburg FS; Freiburg: Herder, 1974), 76–93; D. Hill, "False Prophets and Charismatics: Structure and Interpretation in Matthew 7,15–23," *Bib* 57 (1976): 327–48; M. Krämer, "Hütet euch vor den falschen Propheten: Eine überlieferungsgeschichtliche Untersuchung zu Mt 7,15–23/Lk 6,43–46/Mt 12,33–37," *Bib* 57 (1976): 349–77.

among the flocks of sheep, which, when it goes through, treads down and tears in pieces, with no one to deliver").[233]

Jesus assures his disciples that they will recognize the false prophets: "You will know them by their fruits" (**vv. 16a, 20**). This was probably a well-known proverb. Variations of it include: "The fruit discloses the cultivation of a tree; so a person's speech discloses the cultivation of his mind" (Sir 27:6); "This accords with the popular saying, 'Every pumpkin can be told from its stalk'" (*b. Ber.* 48a).

The truth of the proverb is illustrated with two examples: "Are grapes gathered from thorns, or figs from thistles?" (**v. 16b**). Again, we have well-known proverbs that elaborate on the principle that people are known by their fruits. James, the brother of Jesus, knows the saying, which he repeats with an elaboration of his own: "Can a fig tree, my brothers and sisters, yield olives, or a grapevine figs? No more can salt water yield fresh" (James 3:12). The combination of "grapes" and "figs" is common in Scripture (e.g., Num 13:23; Ps 105:33; Isa 34:4; Jer 8:13; Mic 7:1). The combination of "grapes" and "thistles" may have been suggested by LXX Isa 5:2, 4: "I waited for it to produce a cluster of grapes, but it produced thorns" (the Hebrew does not mention thorns or thistles). Similar proverbs circulated among Greco-Roman writers and thinkers: "How can a vine be made to stop behaving like a vine and start behaving like an olive tree; or, for that matter, an olive tree like a vine?" (Epictetus 2.20.18); "Evil no more gives birth to good than an olive tree produces figs" (Seneca, *Moral Epistles* 87.25). We have in rabbinic literature a similar analogy: "From the thorn bush comes the rose" (*Song Rab.* 1:1 §6).

Accordingly, "every good tree bears good fruit, but the bad tree bears bad fruit" (**v. 17**), Jesus sums up the implications of his proverb. To give another example: "I saw all the Lord's works, how they are right, while the works of man are some good, and others bad, and in their works are known those who lie wickedly" (2 *Enoch* 42:14). Seneca may also be cited again: "Who would think to be surprised at finding no apples on the brambles in the woods? or be astonished because thorns and briars are not covered in useful fruits?" (*De Ira* 2.10.6).

An interesting version appears in the *Gospel of Thomas*: "Grapes are not harvested from thorns, nor are figs gathered from thistles, for they do not produce fruit. A good man brings forth good from his storehouse; an evil man brings forth evil things from his evil storehouse, which is his heart" (§45).

Jesus drives home his point with an observation that restates the principles of vv. 16–17: "A good tree cannot bear bad fruit, nor can a bad tree bear good fruit" (**v. 18**). Invariably one's true character is reflected in how one lives and treats others.

The section concludes with a warning: "Every tree that does not bear good fruit is cut down and thrown into the fire" (**v. 19**). Jesus' language at this point recalls

---

[233]   O. Böcher, "Wölfe in Schafspelzen: Zum religionsgeschichtlichen Hintergrund von Mt 7,15," *TZ* 24 (1968): 405–26; R. Uro, *Sheep among the Wolves: A Study on the Mission Instructions of Q* (Annales Academiae Scientiarum Fennicae. Dissertationes humanarum litterarum 47; Helsinki: Suomalainen Tiedeakatemia, 1987).

John the Baptist's warning: "Even now the ax is lying at the root of the trees; every tree therefore that does not bear good fruit is cut down and thrown into the fire" (Matt 3:10 = Luke 3:9). Cutting down a tree and throwing it into the fire also recalls language in Jeremiah: "they shall cut down your choicest cedars and cast them into the fire" (Jer 22:7).

On **v. 20**, see the commentary on v. 16.

MATTHEW 7:21–23 – FALSE DISCIPLES

7:21: "Not everyone who says to me, 'Lord, Lord,' will enter the kingdom of heaven, but only the one who does the will of my Father in heaven.

7:22: On that day many will say to me, 'Lord, Lord, did we not prophesy in your name, and cast out demons in your name, and do many deeds of power in your name?'

7:23: Then I will declare to them, 'I never knew you; go away from me, you evildoers.'"

*T*aken in context, those who say "Lord, Lord" (cf. Luke 6:46) are among the false prophets who hope to lead the church astray and even plunder it (cf. Matt 7:15–20). They will have prophesied in Jesus' name and will have cast out demons in his name; yet they never really were true members of the church (as their fruits gave evidence); in the day of judgment they will be cast out.

Double vocatives such as in "Not everyone who says to me, 'Lord, Lord'" (**v. 21a**) are common in Scripture (e.g., in the Old Testament, Gen 22:11, "Abraham, Abraham!"; Gen 46:2, "Jacob, Jacob!"; Exod 3:4, "Moses, Moses!"; 1 Sam 3:10, "Samuel! Samuel!"; and, in the New Testament, Matt 23:37, "O Jerusalem, Jerusalem"; Luke 8:24, "Master, Master"; Luke 10:41, "Martha, Martha"; Acts 9:4, "Saul, Saul"); and in other sources (e.g., 2 *Bar* 22:2, "Baruch, Baruch"; *T. Abraham* 14:14, "Abraham, Abraham!"). There are also a few examples of "Lord, Lord" (*kurie, kurie*) in the Greek Bible (e.g., LXX Ps 108:21 [109:21 in the Hebrew]; 140:8 [141:8 in the Hebrew]; and Addition to LXX Esther 4:17) and a few in rabbinic literature as well (e.g., *b. Makkot* 24a, "every time he beheld a scholar he rose from his throne and embraced and kissed him, calling him 'Father, Father; Rabbi, Rabbi; Mari, Mari'" [Mari = "my master"]; *b. Hullin* 139b: "Lord, Lord" [= *qiyri, qiyri*, from the Greek *kurie*, but written in Hebrew letters]).

One may address Jesus with apparent reverence, "Lord, Lord," but that does not mean one will "enter the kingdom of heaven" (**v. 21b**). Being unqualified to enter the kingdom of heaven recalls Jesus' thesis statement near the beginning of the Sermon on the Mount: "For I tell you, unless your righteousness exceeds that of the scribes and Pharisees, you will never enter the kingdom of heaven" (Matt 5:20). Those who say to Jesus, "Lord, Lord," but whose righteousness has not exceeded that of the scribes and Pharisees, will not enter the kingdom. The other sayings in Matthew on entering the kingdom are helpful in clarifying the meaning (cf. Matt 18:3; 19:23, 24; 23:13).

The one who enters the kingdom of heaven is "the one who does the will of my Father in heaven" (**v. 21c**). Jesus' language here again alludes to previous teaching in the Sermon on the Mount, this time to the Lord's Prayer: "Your kingdom come. Your will be done, on earth as it is in heaven" (Matt 6:10). Elsewhere in Matthew, the will of God is linked to the kingdom of heaven (cf. Matt 18:14; 21:31). There are a few texts in the Greek Old Testament that speak of God's will (e.g., Ps 39:9 [= 40:8 in the Hebrew], "To do your will, O my God, I desired"; Ps 142:10 [= 143:10 in the Hebrew], "Teach me that I do your will, because you are my God"; 1 Esd 8:16, "perform it in accordance with the will of your God").

In the day of judgment,[234] the false prophets will appeal to Jesus and ask, "did we not prophesy in your name?" (**v. 22a**). This language recalls the language of prophecy in the Old Testament: "the prophets, Haggai and Zechariah … prophesied to the Jews who were in Judah and Jerusalem, in the name of the God of Israel" (Ezra 5:1 = 1 Esd 6:1); "You shall not live, for you speak lies in the name of the Lord" (Zech 13:3); "The prophets are prophesying lies in my name; I did not send them, nor did I command them or speak to them. They are prophesying to you a lying vision, worthless divination, and the deceit of their own minds" (Jer 14:14). Jeremiah frequently complains of prophets who falsely prophesy in the name of God. This language coheres with the Matthean context, for in Matt 7:15 Jesus had warned of false prophets.

During Jesus' ministry, his disciples were able to cast out demons in the name of Jesus: "Lord, in your name even the demons submit to us!" (Luke 10:17). During one of his missionary journeys, Paul casts out a spirit of divination: "'I order you in the name of Jesus Christ to come out of her.' And it came out that very hour" (Acts 16:18). This is remarkable, given the Old Testament tradition of not speaking in the name of God.

The false prophets not only speak in the name of Jesus but will say that they "cast out demons in" his "name" (**v. 22b**). Evidently, there were people who cast out demons in the name of Jesus who were not disciples of Jesus or (later) members of the church. During Jesus' ministry, his disciples complain: "Teacher, we saw someone casting out demons in your name" (Mark 9:38 = Luke 9:49). In the Book of Acts, we hear of a bizarre episode in which "some itinerant Jewish exorcists," "Seven sons of a Jewish high priest named Sceva," were attempting exorcisms in the name of Jesus: "I adjure you by the Jesus whom Paul proclaims" (Acts 19:13–14). The evil spirit recognized the name of Jesus, and the name of Paul as well, but he did not recognize the sons of Sceva (Acts 19:16).

---

[234] See H. D. Betz, "An Episode in the Last Judgment (Matt. 7:21–23)," in H. D. Betz, *Essays on the Sermon on the Mount* (1985), 125–57; H. D. Betz, *The Sermon on the Mount* (1995), 549–56.

The false prophets will also ask Jesus the judge, did they not "do many deeds of power in your name?" (**v. 22c**). Shortly after the Day of Pentecost and the birth of the Christian Church, Peter raises up the man who had been lame from birth (Acts 3:2–10). Peter says, "in the name of Jesus Christ of Nazareth, stand up and walk" (Acts 3:6). There is an interesting tradition in rabbinic literature that tells of one Jacob (evidently a first-century Christian) who healed in the name of Jesus: "It once happened that ben Dama, the son of Rabbi Ishmael's sister, was bitten by a snake; and Jacob, a native Kefar Sekaniah, came to him in the name of Jesus ben Pantera. But Rabbi Ishmael did not permit him" (*t. Hullin* 2.22, the "ben Pantera" sobriquet being an insult, suggesting that Jesus was the illegitimate son of a Roman soldier of the name Pantera, or "panther" in Latin; cf. Origen, *Against Celsus* 1.32–33). Healing in the name of Jesus became controversial among Rabbis (cf. *b. 'Abodah Zarah* 27b). We also think of Simon Magus, who wished to purchase the Holy Spirit, that he might confer it upon whomever he wished (Acts 8:9–24).[235] Nothing is said about miracles, but they may have been in view.

Jesus the judge will not be impressed by the claims of the false prophets. He will say to them on that day: "I never knew you" (**v. 23a**). We may have an allusion to LXX Amos 3:2, "Only you have I known of all the tribes of the earth." This is said in reference to Israel. But Jesus puts these words in the negative form, "I never knew you," which is not to say that he knows nothing of them; it means only that those who will say, "Lord, Lord," were never recognized as his followers, despite the miracles and the exorcisms.

Jesus the judge will banish the wicked from his presence with the words "go away from me, you evildoers" (**v. 23b**). This language echoes several Old Testament passages (Job 21:14; 22:17; Pss 6:8; 139:19), but it is almost in exact agreement with Ps 6:8 in the Greek Bible : "Depart from me, all you who practice lawlessness" (LXX Ps 6:9). Because Jesus has come to fulfill the Law, not abolish it, he takes umbrage at the "evildoers." Here again, the Jewish perspective is evident.[236]

MATTHEW 7:24–27 – PARABLE OF THE BUILDERS

7:24: "Everyone then who hears these words of mine and acts on them will be like a wise man who built his house on rock.

---

[235] The name of Jesus came to be invoked in pagan magical papyri, lamellae, and bowls. Best known is *PGM* IV.3019–20, where the exorcist is instructed to say, "I adjure you by the god of the Hebrews, Jesus." See also *PGM* XII.385–89 ("I call upon you, great god … Jesus").

[236] M. Mees, "Ausserkanonische Parallelstellen zu den Gerichtsworten Mt 7,21–23; Lk 6,46; 13,26–28 und ihre Bedeutung für die Formung der Jesusworte," *Vetera Christianorum* 10 (1973): 79–102; M. Krämer, "Hütet euch vor den falschen Propheten: Eine überlieferungsgeschichtliche Untersuchung zu Mt 7,15–23/Lk 6,43–46/Mt 12,33–37," *Bib* 57 (1976): 349–77.

7:25: The rain fell, the floods came, and the winds blew and beat on that house, but it did not fall, because it had been founded on rock.

7:26: And everyone who hears these words of mine and does not act on them will be like a foolish man who built his house on sand.

7:27: The rain fell, and the floods came, and the winds blew and beat against that house, and it fell – and great was its fall!"

*T*he Sermon on the Mount concludes with the parable of the wise man and the fool (cf. Luke 6:47–49), which continues the wisdom theme that characterizes the second half of the discourse (i.e., Matt 6:19–7:24). This parable is the first of many that Jesus will present in the course of his ministry.

Jesus' parable is quite similar to a parable found in the rabbinic tradition:

One in whom there are good works, who has studied much Torah, to what may he be likened? To lime poured over stones: even when any number of rains fall on it, they cannot push it out of place. One in whom there are no good works, though he studied much Torah, is like lime poured over bricks: even when a little rain falls on it, it softens immediately and is washed away. (*'Abot de Rabbi Nathan* 24.3)

Another parable about wise and foolish students suggests itself:

He whose wisdom is more abundant than his works, to what is he like? To a tree whose branches are abundant but whose roots are few; and the wind comes and uproots it and overturns it.... But he whose works are more abundant than his wisdom, to what is he like? To a tree whose branches are few but whose roots are many; so that even if all the winds in the world come and blow against it, it cannot be stirred from its place. (*m. 'Abot* 3:18)

A similar comparison is found in Seneca: "Imagine that two buildings have been put up, each just as high and as splendid as the other, but each with different foundations. One is given an ideal site, and the work goes ahead without delay. But at the other site the foundations have already disappeared into the soft wet ground ..." (*Moral Epistles* 52.5).

Jesus' opening words, "Everyone then who hears these words of mine and acts on them" (**v. 24a**), refers to the whole of the Sermon on the Mount. Hearing and doing the words of Jesus recalls the language of Scripture: "If you will listen carefully to the voice of the Lord your God, and do what is right in his sight, and give heed to his commandments and keep all his statutes ..." (Exod 15:26); "And all the people with one accord answered and said, 'All that God said we will do and heed'" (LXX Exod 19:8); "If by paying attention you listen to my voice and do all that I tell you ..." (LXX Exod 23:22; cf. Exod 24:3, 7; Deut 5:27; 6:3; 7:12). Jesus has set his words alongside those of God. His words are to be heard and done, just as the words of God are to be heard and done.

Those who heed the words of Jesus "will be like a wise man who built his house on rock" (**v. 24b**). Hearing wise words is, of course, a standard feature in wisdom literature (e.g., Job 34:2, "Hear my words, you wise men, and give ear to me, you who know"; Prov 1:5, "Let the wise also hear and gain in learning"). He who heeds the words of Jesus will indeed "be like a wise man." Building one's house upon the rock, rather than upon soft ground, makes good sense. One is reminded of David's praise of God: "He brought me up out of the pit of destruction, out of the miry clay; and He set my feet upon a rock making my footsteps firm" (Ps 40:2).

Every person will be tested in life; every house will be battered by storms. Jesus' folksy parable makes this point clear. In simple but vivid detail, he describes the storm: "The rain fell, the floods came, and the winds blew and beat on that house, but it did not fall, because it had been founded on rock" (**v. 25**). Although the details of Jesus' parable are true to life, the words, phrases, and themes in a general sense reflect those of the wisdom tradition: "When the tempest passes, the wicked are no more, but the righteous are established forever" (Prov 10:25). One is also reminded of God's assurance in Isaiah: "See, I am laying in Zion a foundation stone, a tested stone, a precious cornerstone, a sure foundation: 'One who trusts will not panic'" (Isa 28:16).

The one who does not heed the words of Jesus "will be like a foolish man who built his house on the sand" (**v. 26**). This detail again parallels ideas and pictures in the wisdom tradition: "how much more those who live in houses of clay, whose foundation is in the dust, who are crushed like a moth" (Job 4:19).

Once again, the storm is described (**v. 27a**), but this time the house, which had no foundation but had been built on sand, "fell – and great was its fall!" (**v. 27b**). See Isa 28:17 ("… hail will sweep away the refuge of lies, and waters will overwhelm the shelter"). The theme of the fall of the foolish and wicked frequently finds expression in the wisdom tradition: "They were snatched away before their time; their foundation was washed away by a flood" (Job 22:16); "The wise of heart will heed commandments, but a babbling fool will come to ruin" (Prov 10:8); "The wicked are overthrown and are no more, but the house of the righteous will stand" (Prov 12:7); "The house of the wicked is destroyed, but the tent of the upright flourishes" (Prov 14:11); "The wise are cautious and turn away from evil, but the fool throws off restraint and is careless" (Prov 14:16). The storm that destroys the foolish man's house may allude to final judgment.[237]

In the commentary on v. 24, it was observed that the theme of hearing and doing the word of God is rooted in the Mosaic covenant and then later is developed in various ways in the wisdom tradition. Jesus' parable of the two houses, one built on rock and the other built on sand, coheres with the command to obey the Law: "if you will not obey the Lord your God by diligently observing all his commandments and decrees, which I am commanding you today, then all these curses shall come

---

[237]   J. A. Gibbs, *Matthew 1:1–11:1* (2006), 395.

upon you and overtake you.... You shall build a house, but not live in it" (Deut 28:15, 30). In the Greek version (the LXX) we have the verbs "hear" and "do" in v. 15 and then the warning that failure to hear and do will result in building a house in which one will not live.[238]

A similar theme is found in Ezekiel: "when the people build a wall, these prophets smear whitewash on it. Say to those who smear whitewash on it that it shall fall. 'There will be a deluge of rain, great hailstones will fall, and a stormy wind will break out'" (Ezek 13:10–11). The prophet goes on to warn that this is what God will do when he judges his people (cf. Ezek 13:12–16, "I will make a stormy wind break out, and in my anger there shall be a deluge of rain.... I will break down the wall that you have smeared with whitewash, and bring it to the ground"), who have been misled by false prophets (cf. Ezek 13:10, 16; recall Matt 7:15, which had warned of false prophets).

MATTHEW 7:28–29 – ASTOUNDING AUTHORITY

7:28: Now when Jesus had finished saying these things, the crowds were astounded at his teaching,

7:29: for he taught them as one having authority, and not as their scribes.

*M*atthew marks the conclusion of Jesus' Sermon on the Mount by saying "when Jesus finished saying these things" (**v. 28a**). This exact phrase (literally "when Jesus finished"; Greek: *egeneto hote etelesen ho Iesous*) occurs five times in Matthew, each time at the conclusion of a major discourse. The four other concluding notations are found in Matt 11:1 ("when Jesus finished giving instructions"), at the conclusion of the missionary discourse; in Matt 13:53 ("when Jesus finished these parables"), at the conclusion of the kingdom discourse; in Matt 19:1 ("when Jesus finished these words"), at the conclusion of the community discipline discourse; and in Matt 26:1 ("when Jesus finished all these words"), at the conclusion of the eschatological discourse.

It is probable that Matthew has deliberately imitated the language of the Pentateuch: "when Moses finished [Greek: *sunetelesen*] writing the words of this law in a book" (Deut 31:24); "when Moses finished [Greek: *sunetelesen*] speaking all these words to all Israel" (Deut 32:45). (Note that both *sunetelesen* and *etelesen*

---

[238]   For further study, see R. Pesch and R. Kratz, "Auf Fels oder auf Sand gebaut?" in *So liest man synoptisch: Anleitung und Kommentar zum Studium der synoptischen Evangelien. V. Gleichnisse und Bildreden* (Frankfurt am Main: Knecht, 1978), 25–37; K. Abou-Chaar, "The Two Builders: A Study of the Parable in Luke 6:47–49," *Near Eastern School of Theology Theological Review* 5 (1982): 44–58; I. H. Jones, *The Matthean Parables: A Literary and Historical Commentary* (NovTSup 80; Leiden: Brill, 1995), 173–89.

are from the verb *telein*, meaning "to finish"; see also Num 16:31; Deut 31:1; Jer 26:8; 2 *Bar* 87:1.)

Coming at the end of Deuteronomy – indeed, at the end of the Pentateuch itself – the words "when Moses finished all these words" were seen by Matthew as a fitting conclusion to each one of Jesus' major discourses. This Pentateuchal phrase, appearing at the end of these discourses and occurring nowhere else in Matthew's Gospel, provides conclusive evidence that the evangelist has indeed arranged Jesus' teaching into five major blocks of material, probably as part of a Moses typology.

When Jesus finished speaking, "the crowds were astounded at his teaching" (**v. 28b**). Jesus will amaze (Greek: *ekplessein*) audiences again in Matthew: "He came to his hometown and began to teach the people in their synagogue, so that they were astounded [*ekplessein*]" (Matt 13:54); "the disciples ... were greatly astounded" (Matt 19:25); "And when the crowd heard it, they were astounded at his teaching" (Matt 22:33). The tyrant Antiochus IV was amazed (*ekplessein*) at the grace and courage with which the martyrs endured their torture (2 Macc 7:12; 4 *Macc* 8:4).

Matthew explains why the crowds were astounded at Jesus' teaching. It was because "he taught them as one having authority, and not as their scribes" (**v. 29**). This is the first mention of Jesus' authority (Greek: *exousia*). See the commentary on Matt 9:1–8. The word occurs ten times in Matthew. Its association with the "son of man" (cf. Matt 9:6) indicates that the Old Testament background is to be found in Dan 7:13–14, where "one like a son of man" is presented to God and then is given the kingdom and authority.

Matthew observes that Jesus taught "not as their scribes."[239] How is this to be understood? Jesus did not appeal to any authority other than God himself. The pertinence of this point is seen in the story told about the great sage Hillel, who taught on a "matter all day, but they did not receive his teaching until he said, 'Thus I heard from Shemaiah and Abtalion'" (*y. Pesahim* 6.1). In Mark 1:22, 27, we see Jesus' authority related to his amazing ability to cast out demons without incantations or rigmarole of any kind. However, here in Matt 7:28–29 the crowd's amazement rests squarely on the power and authority of Jesus' teaching – his interpretation of the Law and his wisdom.

MATTHEW 8:1–4 – HEALING A LEPER

8:1: **When Jesus had come down from the mountain, great crowds followed him;**

8:2: **and there was a leper who came to him and knelt before him, saying, "Lord, if you choose, you can make me clean."**

---

[239] For more on scribes, see A. J. Saldarini, *Pharisees, Scribes and Sadducees in Palestinian Society: A Sociological Approach* (Wilmington, DE: Glazier, 1988), 144–73, 241–76.

8:3: He stretched out his hand and touched him, saying, "I do choose. Be made clean!" Immediately his leprosy was cleansed.

8:4: Then Jesus said to him, "See that you say nothing to anyone; but go, show yourself to the priest, and offer the gift that Moses commanded, as a testimony to them."

*I*n Matthew, the healing of the leper takes place after the Sermon on the Mount (Matthew 5–7), whereas in Mark's Gospel, Matthew's narrative source, it takes place closer to the beginning of Jesus' public ministry (cf. Mark 1:40–45). It thus provides Jesus the opportunity to extend to this ostracized and desperate man the compassion that he had only shortly before commanded of his disciples, to do to others as they would like to have done to themselves (cf. Matt 7:12). It is also a miracle in which Jesus is able to demonstrate his fidelity to the Law of Moses.[240]

Matthew begins by saying, "When Jesus had come down from the mountain, great crowds followed him" (**v. 1**). Mention of the descent from the mountain, for which there is no parallel in Mark, links the healing of the leper to the Sermon on the Mount that has just been delivered. Matthew's "When Jesus had come down from the mountain" closely matches LXX Exod 34:29, which refers to Moses' descent from the mount. Matthew does this to strengthen his Moses-Jesus typology. The sermon's concluding phrase, "when Jesus had finished saying these things" (Matt 7:28), is a deliberate allusion to phrases in the Pentateuch that read "when Moses finished [Greek: *sunetelesen*] speaking all these words" (Deut 31:24; 32:45; see the commentary on Matt 7:28–29).

Matthew also adds "great crowds followed him" to compensate for the omission at the end of the narrative of Mark's reference to the press of people that made it impossible for Jesus to move about freely in populated areas (cf. Mark 1:45b). Matthew's "great crowds" had also been noted before the Sermon on the Mount, in Matt 4:25.

The story begins with the notice that "there was a leper who came to him and knelt before him, saying, 'Lord, if you choose, you can make me clean'" (**v. 2**). This is the first time in Matthew's Gospel that someone has addressed Jesus as "Lord" (earlier, in Matt 7:21–22, Jesus refers to false disciples who say to him, "Lord, Lord," but there are no actual reports of people addressing him this way). When the leper says "Lord," he implies nothing about Jesus' divinity or messianic identity. This is nothing more than a title of respect. In today's parlance, we would say "sir."

In response to the leper's request, Jesus "stretched out his hand and touched him, saying, 'I do choose. Be made clean!'" (**v. 3a**). In Jesus' day, touching a leper was unthinkable, for the leper was viewed as unclean. To touch a leper was to be defiled.

[240] R. Pesch, "Die matthäische Fassung der Erzählung Mt 8,2–4," in *Jesu ureigene Taten? Ein Beitrag zur Wunderfrage* (Freiburg: Herder, 1970), 87–98; J. K. Elliott, "The Healing of the Leper in the Synoptic Parallels," *TZ* 34 (1978): 175–76.

But purity flows from Jesus to the leper, healing the disease and restoring the man to a state of purity. The man's recovery does not take long. Under orders from Elisha the prophet, Naaman the Syrian, the soldier with leprosy, dipped himself in the Jordan River seven times and was healed (2 Kings 5:10–14). No such procedure was needed with Jesus, as Matthew notes: "Immediately his leprosy was cleansed" (**v. 3b**).

The former leper is now healed, but his cleansing must be officially recognized by the local village priest. Jesus respects the Law and so instructs the man: "See that you say nothing to anyone; but go, show yourself to the priest, and offer the gift that Moses commanded, as a testimony to them" (**v. 4**). Mark says, "offer for your cleansing what Moses commanded" (Mark 1:44). Matthew replaces Mark's "for your cleansing" with "the gift." The phrase "offer the gift" recalls Jesus' instruction to leave the gift at the altar (cf. Matt 5:23–24). The addition of the offering probably once again reflects Matthew's fidelity to the Law. The healed man cannot be reintegrated into Jewish society until he receives a certificate from a priest, as required in Lev 14:2–32.

MATTHEW 8:5–13 – HEALING THE CENTURION'S SON

8:5: When he entered Capernaum, a centurion came to him, appealing to him

8:6: and saying, "Lord, my servant is lying at home paralyzed, in terrible distress."

8:7: And he said to him, "I will come and cure him."

8:8: The centurion answered, "Lord, I am not worthy to have you come under my roof; but only speak the word, and my servant will be healed.

8:9: For I also am a man under authority, with soldiers under me; and I say to one, 'Go,' and he goes, and to another, 'Come,' and he comes, and to my slave, 'Do this,' and the slave does it."

8:10: When Jesus heard him, he was amazed and said to those who followed him, "Truly I tell you, in no one in Israel have I found such faith.

8:11: I tell you, many will come from east and west and will eat with Abraham and Isaac and Jacob in the kingdom of heaven,

8:12: while the heirs of the kingdom will be thrown into the outer darkness, where there will be weeping and gnashing of teeth."

8:13: And to the centurion Jesus said, "Go; let it be done for you according to your faith." And the servant was healed in that hour.

*B*ecause both Matthew and Luke narrate the story of the healing of the centurion's servant shortly after their respective versions of the Sermon on the Mount/Plain (Matt 5:1–7:29; Luke 6:20–49), and because this healing story only occurs in Matthew and Luke, it is probable that in the Q source it directly followed the sermon. The centurion thus typifies the type of person Jesus called for in his sermon: a person of faith and one who "does" what someone "says" (compare Matt 8:9, "I say … to my slave, 'Do this!' and the slave does it," with Matt 7:21, "Not everyone who says … but only the one who does the will of my Father"). However, Matthew inserts his version of the healing of the leper (Matt 8:1–4), which he derived from Mark 1:40–45, between the ending of the sermon and the story of the centurion's servant. In Luke, there is no interruption; Jesus finishes the Sermon on the Plain, enters Capernaum in 7:1, and then encounters the worried centurion in 7:2–10.

Archaeologists and historians believe that Capernaum was an active lakeside village in Jesus' time. Fishing and agriculture were the principal businesses (see the commentary on Matt 4:12–17). Given its strategic location, both geographically and politically (on the shore of an important body of water and near the boundary separating the tetrarchies of Philip and Antipas), it is not surprising that an official, perhaps a Roman, was stationed in Capernaum. Recent excavations in the Greek section of Capernaum have uncovered second- and third-century Roman baths, beneath which are ruins of another Roman structure (perhaps another bath) dating to the first century.[241] These finds are consistent with the literary witness of both Synoptic and Johannine traditions, which speak of the presence of an official, who perhaps was a Roman. The word "centurion" comes from the Latin *centurio* (i.e., a commander of a *centuria*, a "hundred") though in reality a centurion normally commanded only eighty men. (In Matthew's text, we have not the Latin but the Greek equivalent *hekatonarchos*, "ruler of one hundred.")

The story of the healing of the centurion's servant is attested in two, perhaps three, Gospels. But there are variants in these versions of the story. Matthew and Luke mention a "centurion" (*hekatonarchos*) who resides in Capernaum and whose *servant* is seriously ill (Matt 8:6; Luke 7:2). John speaks of a "royal official" (*basilikos*) whose *son* is ill (John 4:46). Commentators debate whether we have here two versions of one story or two similar stories. It was probably one story that was passed along in two independent streams. There is no reason that the centurion of Matthew and Luke cannot also be the royal official of John. And the *pais* of Matt 8:6 can refer either to a servant (as in Luke, who uses the word *doulos*, which means "servant" or "slave") or a child (as in John, who uses the word *huios*, which means "son"). There are other variants, too, such as whether delegations were sent to Jesus (as in Luke) or the worried official came to Jesus himself (as in Matthew and John).[242] Notwithstanding these variant details in the three versions of the story, there is no

[241]   J. C. H. Laughlin, "Capernaum from Jesus' Time and After," *BAR* 19, no. 5 (1993): 54–61, 90; J. J. Rousseau and R. Arav, *Jesus and His World: An Archaeological and Cultural Dictionary* (Minneapolis: Fortress, 1995), 43. Laughlin states: "New evidence indicates that Romans indeed lived in Capernaum in the first century A.D." (p. 55). For a photograph and discussion of the Roman bathhouse, see pp. 58–59.

[242]   For a further discussion of this question, see R. A. J. Gagnon, "The Shape of Matthew's Q Text of the Centurion at Capernaum: Did It Mention Delegations?" *NTS* 40 (1994): 133–42.

compelling reason to conclude that there must have been two (or even three) separate yet very similar stories.

Matthew speaks of a "centurion" (**v. 5**). However, this officer is not necessarily a Roman soldier, for Galilee was not a Roman province until 44 A.D. He may well be a captain in Antipas' provincial militia. He seems to have been a Gentile – as Luke 7:5 ("he loves our people") seems to imply. This would be an odd thing to say if the man were Jewish. If he was an auxiliary, he could have been part of the Roman Army without being a Roman citizen. Even as a centurion, he could be called a "royal official," as in John 4:46, but this designation points equally to an officer under the command of Antipas, the tetrarch of Galilee.

The servant is quite ill; he is "lying at home paralyzed, in terrible distress" (**v. 6**). What is translated as "in terrible distress" could also be translated as "tormented" or "tortured." The man is in a bad way; hearers and readers would have assumed that he was nearing death (and, indeed, in John 4:47 he is said to be "at the point of death").

Jesus grants the centurion his request and tells him, "I will come and cure him" (**v. 7**). The Greek is not as clear as the NRSV renders it. More literally, it reads either "coming, I will heal him" or "coming, shall I heal him?" The centurion's response in vv. 8–9 suggests that Jesus' reply be understood as a question. Moreover, Jesus' response to the petition of the Canaanite (or Syro-Phoenician) mother (Matt 15:21–28), where he initially expresses reluctance to extend messianic blessings to a Gentile, as well as his instructions to the disciples to "go nowhere among the Gentiles" in their mission (Matt 10:5), supports this suggestion.

It is possible that the centurion sensed some hesitation on Jesus' part, for he declares, "Lord, I am not worthy to have you come under my roof" (**v. 8a**). That is, the centurion in effect says, "No, I do not expect you to come to my house!" He knows full well that as a Gentile, and perhaps even as a servant of a government that imprisoned John the Baptist, he may expect little help from the Jewish prophet. He certainly cannot expect Jesus to make a house call.

Jesus need not come to the centurion's house, but "only speak the word, and my servant will be healed" (**v. 8b**). The centurion may have been alluding to Ps 107:20: "He sent out his word and healed them." Is this plausible? Could this centurion have alluded to Jewish Scripture? According to the parallel story in Luke, the centurion built Capernaum's synagogue (Luke 7:5; on the archaeological work on the Capernaum synagogue, see the commentary on Matt 4:12–17).[243] In all probability, he regularly attended this synagogue (as a "God-fearer"; cf. Acts 10:22, "Cornelius, a centurion, an upright and God-fearing man, who is well spoken of by the whole Jewish nation"; Acts 13:43, "When the meeting of the synagogue broke up, many Jews and devout converts to Judaism ...") and heard the Scriptures read and

---

[243] S. Safrai, "The Synagogue the Centurion Built," *Jerusalem Perspective* 55 (1998): 12–14. The black basalt stone beneath the white synagogue dates to the time of Jesus. Safrai believes it could well be the foundation of the synagogue built by the centurion.

interpreted. Therefore, it should occasion no surprise that he used a biblical phrase when addressing a Jewish teacher and prophet.

The centurion elaborates on what he said in v. 8, adding, "For I also am a man under authority" (**v. 9**). He is himself "a man under authority" and so knows full well what it is to say a word and have it obeyed. If he can do it in the earthly realm, then Jesus should be able to do the same thing in the heavenly realm. Behind his logic is the principle of the argument from the minor to the major, but also behind his argument is a great deal of faith in Jesus.

The centurion's remarkable statement impresses Jesus, causing him to remark: "Truly I tell you, in no one in Israel have I found such faith" (**v. 10**). Jesus' saying reflects his disappointing experience in the land of Israel (cf. Matt 11:20–24, "Then he began to reproach the cities in which most of his deeds of power had been done, because they did not repent …"). Recall, too, that Jesus responded with amazement at the faith of the Canaanite woman (Matt 15:28, "Woman, great is your faith! Let it be done for you as you wish").

The faith of the centurion prompts Jesus to speak about those who come from afar and sit with the patriarchs and those who are near who are cast out. This statement, found in vv. 11–12, is a Matthean insertion. In the Lukan parallel, the story goes immediately from Jesus' marveling at the centurion's faith (Luke 7:9 = Matt 8:10) to the conclusion of the story (Luke 7:10 = Matt 8:13). The inserted material has been drawn from Q, but from a different location, as the parallel with Luke shows (cf. Luke 13:28–30). The insertion gives Matthew the opportunity to elaborate on Jesus' remark that the centurion's faith exceeds the faith found in Israel. Matthew can now hint at the mission to the Gentiles that will later be developed more explicitly (cf. Matt 10:16–23; 28:19–20). The evangelist may well have caught the allusion to Psalm 107, both in the centurion's statement and in Jesus' saying. This would have provided another reason for bringing the two verses from elsewhere in Q into the exchange with the centurion.

Jesus declares, "I tell you, many will come from east and west and will eat with Abraham and Isaac and Jacob in the kingdom of heaven" (**v. 11a**). Jesus' words allude to Ps 107:1–3, "O give thanks to the Lord … he redeemed … and gathered in from the lands, from the east and from the west, from the north and from the south," implying that those gathered are Jews of the Diaspora (or Dispersion). This is expressed in Bar 4:36–37, "Look toward the east, O Jerusalem, and see the joy that is coming to you from God. Look, your children are coming, whom you sent away; they are coming, gathered from east and west, at the word of the Holy One, rejoicing in the glory of God," and 2 Macc 1:27–29, "Gather together our scattered people, set free those who are slaves among the Gentiles.… Plant your people in your holy place, as Moses promised." According to the Targum, Israel's exiles will be gathered by the Messiah (e.g., *Tg.* Isa 28:1–6; 53:8, the Messiah "will bring our exiles near"; *Tg.* Hos 14:8, "they shall be gathered from among their exiles, they shall dwell in the shade of their Messiah"; *Tg.* Mic 5:1–3, "from you shall come forth before Me the Messiah … and they shall be gathered in from among their exiles").

Those who come from afar will "eat with Abraham and Isaac and Jacob in the kingdom of heaven" (**v. 11b**). What is translated as "eat" in the NRSV is actually "recline at table," in the Middle Eastern fashion. The parallel at Luke 13:29 reads more simply that they "will eat in the kingdom of God." "Abraham and Isaac and Jacob" are mentioned in Luke 13:28, but Matthew's relocating them to the banqueting table itself heightens the expected bitterness of the scene. Those far away, who have "come from east and west," will sit at the table, but those close by will miss out.

The imagery of the banquet is part of messianism and eschatology, which envisioned many blessings for Israel. On banquets and eating and drinking in the kingdom of God, see Matt 5:6 ("those who hunger and thirst … they will be filled"; Ps 107:1–9; Isa 25:6–8; Ezek 39:17–20; *1 Enoch* 62:14; *2 Bar* 29:4).

Those from other places will eat with the patriarchs, "while the heirs of the kingdom will be thrown" out (**v. 12a**). The "heirs of the kingdom" (literally "sons of the kingdom") are the Jewish people who live in Israel, to whom, it was supposed, belongs the kingdom of God. Because they live in the land, which in itself was thought to be a blessing, surely they would be the very first to benefit in the restoration of Israel. But no, Jesus says, those far away are more likely to benefit than those right in the land itself. This is consistent with Jesus' teaching elsewhere that the first will be last and the last first (cf. Matt 19:30; 20:16).

This interpretation helps us better understand some of the material that is unique to the Gospel of Matthew, such as the parable of the wise and foolish maids (Matt 25:1–13), the parable of the wheat and weeds (Matt 13:24–30, 36–43), and the parable of the drag net (Matt 13:47–50). In Matthew, the kingdom of God (or heaven) is identified with Israel – to whom belongs the kingdom (as in 1QSb 5:21, "He shall … establish the kingdom of his people"; cf. 4Q252 5:4, "the kingdom of his people") – but not all Israel will in fact enter the kingdom (or, as Paul puts it in Rom 9:6, "not all Israelites truly belong to Israel [i.e., belong to the patriarch Jacob]"). Repentance and faith, in response to Jesus' message, are the determining factors. Those who respond in faith will be included; those who do not will be excluded. The irony, Jesus says, is that those far away – those one thinks enjoy no advantages – will be included in the kingdom in greater numbers than those who have the privilege of living in the Holy Land itself.[244]

Jesus warns that the heirs of the kingdom will be thrown "into the outer darkness, where there will be weeping and gnashing of teeth" (**v. 12b**). This is the first

---

[244] W. Grimm, "Zum Hintergrund von Mt 8.11f./Lk 13.28f.," *BZ* 16 (1972): 255–56; D. C. Allison, Jr., "Who Will Come from East and West? Observations on Matt 8.11–12/Luke 13.28–29," *IBS* 11 (1989): 158–70; B. Witherington III, *Matthew* (2006), 184.

of three passages in which we hear of "outer darkness," "weeping," and "gnashing of teeth" (cf. Matt 22:13; 25:30). These graphic depictions of hell are only found in Matthew. That the allusion is to hell is confirmed by the parallel with *1 Enoch* 10:4a, "And he said to Raphael, 'Go, Raphael, and bind Azael hand and foot, and cast him into the darkness.'" In the context of *1 Enoch*, it is clear that the archangel Raphael has been ordered to bind the evil angel Azael and to cast him into hell (see the commentary on Matt 22:1–14). Similar language is found in the Dead Sea Scrolls, where we are told that the wicked face "everlasting damnation in the wrath of God's furious vengeance, never-ending terror and reproach for all eternity, with a shameful extinction in *the fire of Hell's outer darkness*" (1QS 4:12–13, italics added).

Jesus then says to the centurion, "Go; let it be done for you according to your faith" (**v. 13a**). Reference to the centurion's faith resumes the thread of faith (v. 10), which the evangelist interrupted with the insertion of vv. 11–12. This word of assurance is not found in Luke's version of the story. It may have been added by Matthew to underscore the importance of faith, a theme that is very important to him (cf. Matt 8:26; 9:28–29; 14:31; 15:28; 23:23).

Of course, in saying "let it be done," Jesus lives up to the centurion's earlier assertion that all Jesus need do is speak the word (v. 8). Matthew reports: "And the servant was healed in that hour" (**v. 13b**). Luke's version implies the same thing: "When those who had been sent returned to the house, they found the slave in good health" (Luke 7:10). The notation that the servant was healed "in that hour" recalls the similar miracle story in John 4:45–54.[245] The immediacy of the healing corresponds to the centurion's faith.

MATTHEW 8:14–17 – THE HEALING OF PETER'S MOTHER-IN-LAW

8:14: When Jesus entered Peter's house, he saw his mother-in-law lying in bed with a fever;

8:15: he touched her hand, and the fever left her, and she got up and began to serve him.

8:16: That evening they brought to him many who were possessed with demons; and he cast out the spirits with a word, and cured all who were sick.

8:17: This was to fulfill what had been spoken through the prophet Isaiah, "He took our infirmities and bore our diseases."

---

[245]   For more on the story of the centurion, see G. Zuntz, "The 'Centurion' of Capernaum and His Authority (Matt. viii.5–13)," *JTS* 46 (1945): 183–90; R. P. Martin, "The Pericope of the Healing of the 'Centurion's' Servant/Son (Matt 8:5–13 par. Luke 7:1–10): Some Exegetical Notes," in R. A. Guelich (ed.), *Unity and Diversity in New Testament Theology* (G. E. Ladd Festschrift; Grand Rapids, MI: Eerdmans, 1978), 14–22; T. W. Jennings, "Mistaken Identities but Model Faith: Rereading the Centurion," *JBL* 123 (2004): 467–94; D. B. Saddington, "The Centurion in Matthew 8:5–13," *JBL* 125 (2006): 140–42.

*M*atthew simplifies the Markan story, omitting Mark 1:29 and half of vv. 30 and 31. In Matthew, the healing of Simon Peter's mother-in-law takes place right after the healing of the centurion's servant (Matt 8:5–13). The story takes place in Capernaum, in Peter's house.[246]

After healing the centurion's servant, Jesus goes home with Peter. Entering the house, he saw Peter's mother-in-law "lying in bed with a fever" (**v. 14**). Fever may not sound threatening to people today, but in antiquity it was very serious, often the prelude to death.

Whereas in Matthew's account Jesus "touched her hand" (**v. 15a**), Mark says "taking her by the hand" (Mark 1:31), as though Jesus helped her up. Matthew may perhaps be implying that she got up unassisted. Touching or being touched is common in the Synoptic Gospels (occurring nine times in Matthew, eleven times in Mark, and thirteen times in Luke). In Matthew, Jesus touches people, including lepers and unseeing eyes (Matt 8:3; 9:29; 17:7; 20:34), and is touched by people (Matt 9:20, 21; and especially 14:36, where they "begged him that they might touch even the fringe of his cloak; and all who touched it were healed").

When Jesus touched Peter's mother-in-law, the "fever left her, and she got up and began to serve him" (**v. 15b**). Mark says that "she waited on them." Matthew places Jesus in the spotlight and also underscores the woman's gratitude to Jesus. The fact that the woman was able to get out of bed and serve Jesus and Peter suggests that her recovery was complete. She has been returned to robust health.

The reputation of Jesus as healer has spread: "That evening they brought to him many who were possessed with demons; and he cast out the spirits with a word, and cured all who were sick" (**v. 16**). Matthew omits Mark's redundant "at sundown" (Mark 1:32). The healing power of Jesus is so great that he is able to "cast out the spirits with a word." Jesus requires no incantation formulas or gimmickry; he simply speaks the word and the evil spirit is gone. Of course, "with a word" recalls the earlier faith of the centurion, who had said, "only speak the word" (Matt 8:8).[247]

Matthew tells us that Jesus' healing ministry "was to fulfill what had been spoken through the prophet Isaiah" (**v. 17a**). This matches Matthew's earlier explanation, "so that what had been spoken through the prophet Isaiah might be fulfilled" (Matt 4:14) and later "This was to fulfill what had been spoken through the prophet

---

[246] V. C. Corbo, *The House of St. Peter at Capharnaum: A Preliminary Report of the First Two Campaigns of Excavations, April 16–June 19, Sept. 12–Nov. 26, 1968* (Publications of the Studium Biblicum Franciscanum Collectio Minor 5; Jerusalem: Franciscan Printing Press, 1969); J. F. Strange and H. Shanks, "Has the House Where Jesus Stayed in Capernaum Been Found?" *BAR* 8, no. 6 (1982): 26–37; B. Bagatti, "Capharnaum, la ville de Pierre," *Monde de la Bible* 27 (1983): 8–16; J. J. Rousseau and R. Arav, *Jesus and His World: An Archaeological and Cultural Dictionary* (Minneapolis: Fortress, 1995), 39–47. For more on the archaeology of Capernaum, see the commentary on Matt 4:12–17.

[247] A. Fuchs, "Entwicklungsgeschichtliche Studie zu Mk 1,29-31 par Mt 8,14-15 par Lk 4,38-39," *SNTU* 6 (1981): 21–76; J. Nolland, *The Gospel of Matthew* (2005), 361.

Isaiah" (Matt 12:17), and parallels several other fulfillment introductions in Matthew (e.g., Matt 1:22; 2:15, 17, 23; 13:14, 35; 21:4; 27:9).

Speaking of the Servant, the great prophet Isaiah foretold: "He took our infirmities and bore our diseases" (**v. 17b**). Matthew has loosely quoted part of Hebrew (not LXX) Isa 53:4, "Surely he has borne our infirmities, and carried our diseases...."[248]

MATTHEW 8:18–22 – FOLLOWING JESUS

8:18: Now when Jesus saw great crowds around him, he gave orders to go over to the other side.

8:19: A scribe then approached and said, "Teacher, I will follow you wherever you go."

8:20: And Jesus said to him, "Foxes have holes, and birds of the air have nests; but the Son of Man has nowhere to lay his head."

8:21: Another of his disciples said to him, "Lord, first let me go and bury my father."

8:22: But Jesus said to him, "Follow me, and let the dead bury their own dead."

*M*atthew once again draws upon Q, the source of Jesus' teachings that the evangelist Luke also used (cf. Luke 9:57–60). The stringency of Jesus' demands for discipleship is underscored in these encounters with two potential followers (there are three in Luke's parallel passage). The opening verse alludes to Mark 4:35, the first verse of the story of the stilling of the storm. Matthew, however, will not narrate his version of this story until 8:23–27.

These encounters drive home the point that there is a *cost* to following Jesus. In the first encounter (vv. 19–20), a scribe offers to follow Jesus wherever he goes. Jesus tells him that he has little to offer by way of material security: "Foxes have holes, and birds of the air have nests; but the Son of Man has nowhere to lay his head." To follow Jesus requires radical commitment. In the second encounter (vv. 21–22), "another of his disciples" requests that he "first" be permitted to "bury" his "father." In view of the commandment to honor one's mother and father (Exod 20:12) and the importance placed upon loyalty to one's parents in Jewish society (including by Jesus himself; cf. Matt 15:3–6; Mark 7:9–13), the man's request would have seemed only reasonable. But Jesus tells him to "let the dead bury their own dead." Again the point is made that following Jesus requires radical commitment.

Matthew says a "scribe" approached Jesus (**v. 19**). Luke reads simply "a man" (Luke 9:57). Matthew may have wished to identify this man as a scribe (literally

---

[248] On the messianic implications of this quotation in Matthew, see L. Novakovic, *Messiah, the Healer of the Sick: A Study of Jesus as the Son of David in the Gospel of Matthew* (WUNT 2, no.170; Tübingen: Mohr Siebeck, 2003), 125–32.

"one scribe") because of his own interest in these professionals, who so often are critical of him. In Matt 5:20, Jesus told his disciples that "unless [their] righteousness exceeds that of the scribes and Pharisees," they cannot enter the kingdom of heaven. This passage seems to teach that unless one's commitment to discipleship surpasses that of the scribes, one cannot become a disciple of Jesus.

The scribe addresses Jesus as "teacher." Teacher (Greek: *didaskale*) is the equivalent of the Hebrew "Rabbi." He tells Jesus, "I will follow you wherever you go." The scribe has offered to become a disciple of Jesus. Disciples follow their masters (or teachers) and even imitate their behavior (e.g., *m. 'Erubin* 2:6; *m. 'Abot* 1:6; *b. 'Erubin* 30a; *'Abot R. Nathan* 4.2–3). By promising to go where Jesus goes, the scribe is implying that he will be able to live as Jesus lives. Can he?

Jesus points out that "Foxes have holes [Greek: *pholeos*], and birds of the air have nests, but the Son of Man has nowhere to lay his head" (v. 20). Plutarch comments: "The wild beasts grazing in Italy have dens [Greek: *pholeos*], and there is for each of them a lair and a hiding place; but those fighting and dying for Italy have no share in such things, only air and light, and they are forced to wander unsettled with their wives and children" (*Tiberius et Caius Gracchus* 9.5). A Cynic warns a would-be follower: "It's not how you think it is. . . . I sleep on a hard bed. . . . If you think that is how it is, stay well clear of the whole business; there is nothing in it for you. . . ." (Epictetus 3.22.9–11). Says another Cynic, "I have travelled around for so long, not only without hearth or home, but without even a single attendant to take round with me" (Dio 40.2), and "The whole earth is my bed" (Ps.-Anarchasis 5). We are not told, but readers will assume, that this nameless scribe decided not to follow Jesus after all.[249]

Next comes a man who apparently already is numbered among his disciples. He, too, is willing to follow Jesus, but there is something he first must do: "Lord, first let me go and bury my father" (v. 21). Given the great importance that the Jewish people attached to attending to the dead, this man's request is quite reasonable.

Jesus' reply is startling: "Follow me, and let the dead bury their own dead" (v. 22). Even though the Old Testament did not permit a Nazirite to bury anyone, including his own parents (Num 6:6–7; Lev 21:1–3 makes allowance for one's parents in the case of the high priest, but Lev 21:11 seems to forbid it), later rabbinic tradition came to view burial of a relative as obligatory, even for the Nazirite, and indeed came to view it as an act of meritorious service (see Tob 4:3; 6:15, where burial of the dead is viewed as one of Tobit's great demonstrations of piety). In view of this high regard for the necessity of the burial of parents by their children, what could Jesus have meant? Some interpreters have suggested that he must have meant something like this: "Allow the (spiritually) dead to bury the (physically) dead." This interpretation

---

[249] J. D. Kingsbury, "On Following Jesus: The 'Eager' Scribe and the 'Reluctant' Disciple (Matthew 8.18–22)," *NTS* 34 (1988): 45–59; R. H. Gundry, "On True and False Disciples in Matthew 8.18–22," *NTS* 40 (1994): 433–41.

could be supported by a saying of a sage: "A faithless man is a dead man in a living body" (Sextus, *Sentences* 7b). In rabbinic literature, we find: "Is it the way of the dead to be sought for among the living, or are the living among the dead?" (*Exod. Rab.* 5.14 [on Exod 5:2]; cf. *Lev. Rab.* 6.6 [on Lev 5:1]).

However, it is more likely that the would-be follower and Jesus are talking about ossilegium; that is, the Jewish custom of gathering and reburying the bones of the deceased one year after death and primary burial. We are not to imagine a dying father attended by a loving son who will see to his proper and honorable burial when he dies, but rather a son who cannot follow Jesus until the anniversary of his father's death arrives and he gathers and reburies his bones. Accordingly, Jesus has told the man to let the dead relatives who are in the tomb take care of secondary burial. Proclaiming the kingdom of God to the living takes precedence.[250]

MATTHEW 8:23–27 – STILLING THE STORM

8:23: And when he got into the boat, his disciples followed him.

8:24: A windstorm arose on the sea, so great that the boat was being swamped by the waves; but he was asleep.

8:25: And they went and woke him up, saying, "Lord, save us! We are perishing!"

8:26: And he said to them, "Why are you afraid, you of little faith?" Then he got up and rebuked the winds and the sea; and there was a dead calm.

8:27: They were amazed, saying, "What sort of man is this, that even the winds and the sea obey him?"

Matthew's account of the stilling of the storm is derived from Mark 4:35–41. Matthew delayed telling this story until after he narrated the encounters with the two would-be followers in 8:18–22. The point of these encounters is that following Jesus is difficult, even dangerous. The story of the stilling of the storm makes this point. The story begins, "when he got into the boat, his disciples followed him" (v. 23). These disciples are those who, unlike those in Matt 8:18–22, could follow Jesus. But it also makes the point that Jesus is powerful and able to save, as the name Jesus ("the Lord saves") implies (cf. Matt 1:21).

There is some possible Old Testament background against which we could read the stilling of the storm, as seen in Pss 65:7; 89:9; 104:6–7; and 107:23–30. Just as the Lord God was Lord over the sea, so Jesus is its Lord. In ancient Israel, the violent sea sometimes symbolized the forces of chaos, forces that the Lord subdued.

---

[250] B. R. McCane, "'Let the Dead Bury Their Own Dead': Secondary Burial and Matt 8:21–22," *HTR* 83 (1990): 31–43.

Sometimes ancient Israel likened its enemies to a flood of water that threatened to overwhelm the small kingdom (see Isa 28:2, 17). There is also a certain amount of correspondence with Jon 1:4–6: Jonah embarked on a boat, then fell asleep, a great storm then arose, and Jonah was aroused by a frightened crew who feared that they were about to perish.[251]

Whereas Matthew's account reads, "And when he got into the boat, his disciples followed him" (v. 23), Mark introduces his version of this story in an awkward and unusual manner: "leaving the crowd behind, they took him with them in the boat, just as he was" (Mark 4:36). Mark's version is strange and leaves the reader with the impression that the disciples loaded Jesus into the boat, "just as he was"(!). Matthew's version is much more dignified: Jesus got into the boat without assistance and "his disciples followed him," as disciples should follow their master and Rabbi (and in contrast to those in Matt 8:18–22, who were unable to meet Jesus' demands).

A violent storm suddenly came upon the disciples, and their boat was in danger of being swamped (v. 24). The Sea of Galilee is known for sudden, violent storms. In the 1980s, when the level of the lake was low, a fishing boat was discovered. With great difficulty and ingenuity, the boat was salvaged, cleaned, and preserved, and is now on display. When in service, the boat could have accommodated six men on each side and one at the stern.[252]

The frightened disciples awake Jesus and cry out, "Lord, save us! We are perishing!" (v. 25). Again, Matthew's version reads with greater dignity. Mark reads: "Teacher, do you not care that we are perishing?" (Mark 4:38). The disciples' panicked question borders on disrespect. Luke also paraphrases the disciples' question to read with more dignity: "Master, Master, we are perishing!" (Luke 8:24).

---

[251] For an assessment of interpretive traditions concerned with Jonah, as well as stories related to Julius Caesar's attempt to cross the Adriatic Sea and how they may have colored the story of the stilling of the storm, see R. D. Aus, *The Stilling of the Storm: Studies in Early Palestinian Judaic Traditions* (International Studies in Formative Christianity and Judaism; Binghamton, NY: Global Publications, 2000), 1–87. It may be conceded that some of this material may well have influenced the telling of the story, but it is unlikely that these traditions created the story.

[252] For studies on the Galilee boat, see R. Riesner, "Das Boot vom See Gennesaret," *Bibel und Kirche* 41 (1986): 135–38; S. Wachsmann, "The Excavation of the Kinneret Boat," *Bulletin of the Anglo-Israel Archaeological Society* 6 (1986): 50–52; D. Adan-Bayewitz, "Dating the Pottery from the Galilee Boat Excavation," *BAR* 14, no. 5 (1988): 24–29; I. Carmi, "How Old Is the Galilee Boat?" *BAR* 14, no. 5 (1988): 30–33; A. Raban, "The Boat from Migdal Nunia and the Anchorages of the Sea of Galilee from the Time of Jesus," *The International Journal of Nautical Archaeology and Underwater Exploration* 17 (1988): 311–29; S. Wachsmann, "The Galilee Boat: 2,000-Year-Old Hull Recovered Intact," *BAR* 14, no. 5 (1988): 18–23; C. Peachey, "Model Building in Nautical Archaeology: The Kinneret Boat," *BA* 53 (1990): 46–53; S. Wachsmann et al., *The Excavations of an Ancient Boat in the Sea of Galilee (Lake Kinneret)* ('Atiqot 19; Jerusalem: Israel Antiquities Authority, 1990); S. Wachsmann, *The Sea of Galilee Boat: A 2000-Year-Old Discovery from the Sea of Legends* (Cambridge, MA: Perseus, 2000).

Jesus asks his disciples, "Why are you afraid, you of little faith?" (**v. 26**). Matthew's version of Jesus' reply to the frightened disciples is much gentler than Mark's "How is it that you have no faith?" (Mark 4:40). Luke's version (Luke 8:25) is gentler also. Matthew is fond of the expression "you of little faith" (cf. Matt 6:30; 14:31; 16:8). The Greek (*oligopistoi*) is literally "little-faith ones." According to a Greco-Roman sage, "a man of little faith [*oligopistos*] is without faith" (Sextus, *Sentences* 6); see the commentary on Matt 6:30. Jesus then "got up and rebuked the winds and the sea; and there was a dead calm." Once again, Jesus speaks and his word is obeyed.

The astonished disciples ask, "What sort of man is this, that even the winds and the sea obey him?" (**v. 27**). The disciples' question is reminiscent of the scornful remark made in reference to the stricken Antiochus IV Epiphanes, the Syrian Greek ruler who had severely persecuted the Jews in the second century B.C.: "Thus he who had just been thinking that he could command the waves of the sea, in his superhuman arrogance, and imagining that he could weigh the high mountains in a balance, was brought down to earth and carried in a litter, making the power of God manifest to all" (2 Macc 9:8).

In contrast to the Greco-Roman despots, like Antiochus IV and the later Roman emperors, about whom all sorts of hyperbole were inscribed in public notices and official documents, Jesus is the genuine article. He speaks the word, and it happens. It is further evidence of the divine authority entrusted to this human, this "son of man."[253] Jesus displays an authority that lives up to the expectation of the Messiah in 4Q521, whom "heaven and earth will obey."

MATTHEW 8:28–34 – HEALING THE GADARENE MEN

8:28: When he came to the other side, to the country of the Gadarenes, two demoniacs coming out of the tombs met him. They were so fierce that no one could pass that way.

8:29: Suddenly they shouted, "What have you to do with us, Son of God? Have you come here to torment us before the time?"

8:30: Now a large herd of swine was feeding at some distance from them.

8:31: The demons begged him, "If you cast us out, send us into the herd of swine."

8:32: And he said to them, "Go!" So they came out and entered the swine; and suddenly, the whole herd rushed down the steep bank into the sea and perished in the water.

---

[253] G. Bornkamm, "The Stilling of the Storm in Matthew," in G. Bornkamm, G. Barth, and H. J. Held, *Tradition and Interpretation in Matthew* (Philadelphia: Westminster, 1963), 52–57; B. M. F. van Iersel and A. J. M. Linmans, "The Storm on the Lake, Mk 4.35–41 and Mt 8.18–27 in the Light of Form Criticism," in T. Baarda et al. (eds.), *Miscellanea Neotestamentica* (NovTSup 48; Leiden: Brill, 1978), 17–48.

8:33: The swineherds ran off, and on going into the town, they told the whole story about what had happened to the demoniacs.

8:34: Then the whole town came out to meet Jesus; and when they saw him, they begged him to leave their neighborhood.

*T*he encounter with the Gadarene (or Gerasene or Gergasene) demoniacs surely ranks as the eeriest episode in the life of Jesus. Matthew has again derived the story from Mark (Mark 5:1–14). In the Markan (and Lukan) account, we hear of only one man. Mark's description of this possessed and tormented man is shocking and disgusting. He lives in a cemetery, which from a Jewish perspective is wholly unclean (cf. *m. Baba Mesia* 2:10; *b. Hullin* 74b, "if it passed through a cemetery it has thereby become unclean"; *b. Temurah* 22a; Matt 23:21) and from both Jewish and Gentile perspectives is frightening. This man possesses superhuman strength, as seen in the fact that no one can bind him and when fettered he breaks the chains. He howls in the night and bruises himself with stones. The man is not only insane; he is demon-possessed.[254]

Matthew drastically trims Mark's version of the story. Most of the gruesome details have been omitted. Matthew tells us of "two demoniacs coming out of the tombs" and that these men "were so fierce that no one could pass that way" (8:28). But they were not too fierce for Jesus. In the case of the stilling of the storm (Matt 8:23–27), Jesus showed his power over nature; in the encounter with the two demon-possessed men, Jesus shows his power over the very worst of the evil spirits. Jesus' exorcism of the two demoniacs is the first of five exorcisms that Matthew will narrate (the four others are recounted in Matt 9:32–33; 12:22; 15:21–28; and 17:14–20).

Matthew understands the story to have taken place in "the country of the Gadarenes" (**v. 28a**), the vicinity of Gadara (or Gadera), which is about five miles southeast of the Sea of Galilee, another one of the cities of the Decapolis. The population of Gadara was predominantly Gentile (cf. Josephus, *Ant.* 17.320, "one of the Greek cities"), which explains the presence of a herd of swine. Some manuscripts read "Gazarenes," "Gergasenes," or (in agreement with Mark) "Gerasenes." The similar sounds, as well as the perceived problem of proximity to the Sea of Galilee, account for the variants and the confusion.

In Matthew's account of Jesus' encounter, "Two demoniacs coming out of the tombs met him" (**v. 28b**). The most noticeable difference between the Matthean and Markan stories is the appearance of "two demoniacs" in Matthew's account, not one as in Mark's. Because Luke only mentions one man (Luke 8:27) and because people

---

[254] For rich historical and traditional background material, see R. D. Aus, *My Name Is "Legion": Palestinian Judaic Traditions in Mark 5:1–20 and Other Gospel Texts* (Studies in Judaism; Lanham, MD: University Press of America, 2003), 1–99. There probably are allusions to Samson and other traditions, but the old stories and traditions did not generate the story of Jesus' encounter with the possessed man/men in the country of the Gadarenes.

and things double up elsewhere in Matthew (e.g., two animals in the entrance narrative in Matt 21:2–7, and two blind men, not once but twice, in Matt 9:27–31 and again in 20:29–34; in Luke, there is but one animal and one blind man), it is suspected that here again Matthew, for whatever reason, has portrayed Mark's one demoniac as two.[255] The demoniacs are said to have come "out of the tombs." In antiquity, it was believed that evil spirits haunted graveyards. Indeed, some believed that demons were in fact the spirits of the wicked dead.[256]

Matthew's account of the demons' question to Jesus, "What have you to do with us, Son of God?" (**v. 29**), replaces Mark's "Son of the Most High God" (Mark 5:7) with the simpler "Son of God," perhaps because this appellation is almost always used by Gentiles (whether in Scripture or in other sources) and so perhaps there are unwelcome pagan associations with it. In any event, Matthew never uses it (but both Mark and Luke do). The evil spirits that possess the two men readily recognize the presence of God's Son, and his presence terrifies them: "Have you come here to torment us before the time?" The evil spirits know that a day of judgment awaits them, but in their encounter with Jesus they wonder if they face persecution now. Their question implies that Jesus himself will play a role in the future judgment.

The demons beg Jesus to send them into the herd of swine (**vv. 30–31**). The evil spirits know that Jesus has come to deliver humans. They therefore know that they face eviction. The best they can hope for is to be sent into the swine. Jesus acquiesces with the word "Go!" (v. 32). Once again, we see the power of Jesus in that what he says happens. Matthew says nothing about "Legion" being the name of the demonic host or that the herd numbered two thousand.

The unusual story ends with the swineherds running into town and the whole town coming out to meet Jesus and begging him to leave their neighborhood (**vv. 33–34**). In contrast to Mark, Matthew says nothing about the healed men spreading the news as though they had become evangelists (cf. Mark 5:15–20). It may have struck Matthew as odd that Jesus would refuse someone who wished to follow him (recall the encounters with would-be followers in Matt 8:18–22). Of course, in Matthew it is the twelve apostles, properly trained and commissioned, who will carry the good news of the kingdom of God to Gentiles, such as those who live east of the Sea of Galilee and the Jordan River in the Decapolis (cf. Matt 10:18, "testimony to them and the Gentiles"; Matt 28:19, "make disciples of all nations [or Gentiles]").[257]

[255]   W. R. G. Loader, "Son of David, Blindness, Possession, and Duality in Matthew," *CBQ* 44 (1982): 570–85.
[256]   P. G. Bolt, "Jesus, the Daimons and the Dead," in A. N. S. Lane (ed.), *The Unseen World: Christian Reflections on Angels, Demons and the Heavenly Realm* (Carlisle, PA: Paternoster; Grand Rapids, MI: Baker Academic, 1996), 75–102.
[257]   C. H. Cave, "The Obedience of Unclean Spirits," *NTS* 11 (1964): 93–97; J. M. Hull, *Hellenistic Magic and the Synoptic Tradition* (SBT 2/28; London: SCM Press, 1974), 116–41; J. D. M. Derrett, "Contributions to the Study of the Gerasene Demoniac," *JSNT* 3 (1979): 2–17;

MATTHEW 9:1–8 – HEALING THE PARALYZED MAN

9:1: And after getting into a boat he crossed the sea and came to his own town.

9:2: And just then some people were carrying a paralyzed man lying on a bed. When Jesus saw their faith, he said to the paralytic, "Take heart, son; your sins are forgiven."

9:3: Then some of the scribes said to themselves, "This man is blaspheming."

9:4: But Jesus, perceiving their thoughts, said, "Why do you think evil in your hearts?

9:5: For which is easier, to say, 'Your sins are forgiven,' or to say, 'Stand up and walk'?

9:6: But so that you may know that the Son of Man has authority on earth to forgive sins" – he then said to the paralytic – "Stand up, take your bed and go to your home."

9:7: And he stood up and went to his home.

9:8: When the crowds saw it, they were filled with awe, and they glorified God, who had given such authority to human beings.

*M*atthew has rearranged the narrative sequence that he had before him in the Gospel of Mark, a sequence that Luke for the most part follows. Because the episode that immediately precedes the healing of the paralytic is the healing of the Gadarene (or Gerasene) demoniacs in Matt 8:28–34, it is necessary to mention Jesus' crossing of the Sea of Galilee before the new story can begin. Matthew has trimmed Mark's version of the healing of the paralytic (cf. Mark 2:1–12).

Matthew's account begins, "And after getting into a boat he crossed the sea and came to his own town" (v. 1). He does not say Capernaum (as in Mark 2:1), but there is little doubt that Matthew's "his own town" is the equivalent of Mark's "at home." The Greek word translated as "town" is *polis*, which is usually translated as "city." The difference between a town and a city (or a town and village) is somewhat subjective. Very few of the towns in Galilee should be called "cities."

When Matthew states, "When Jesus saw their faith" (v. 2a), he once again condenses Mark's version of the story. However, in omitting mention of digging through the roof and lowering the paralyzed man through it on a pallet (along with the omission of other details, such as how crowded the room was; see Mark 2:1–4), Matthew has left his readers wondering what Jesus saw when he "saw their faith." Because we have Mark's fuller version, we know. When Matthew recounts

J. Ådna, "The Encounter of Jesus with the Gerasene Demoniac," in B. D. Chilton and C. A. Evans (eds.), *Authenticating the Activities of Jesus* (NTTS 28, no.2; Leiden: Brill, 1998), 279–301.

Jesus' statement, "Take heart, son; your sins are forgiven" (**v. 2b**), he adds "take heart" (Greek: *tharsei*). He likes this word of comfort, adding it to 9:22 ("Take heart, daughter"; cf. Mark 5:34) and retaining it in 14:27 ("Take heart, it is I; do not be afraid"), where he found it in Mark 6:50 (which may have prompted Matthew's use of it in the two other passages). See Jth 11:1, "Take courage [*tharseson*], woman, and do not be afraid in your heart, for I have never hurt any one"; Tob 7:18, "Be brave [*tharsei*], my child; the Lord of heaven and earth grant you joy in place of this sorrow of yours. Be brave [*tharsei*], my daughter"; and Bar 4:30, "Take courage [*tharsei*], O Jerusalem."

Assuring the paralyzed man that his "sins are forgiven" would have been comforting indeed when it is remembered that sin and sickness were often associated. The man had come for healing; he will be healed and forgiven.

Jesus' claim that the paralyzed man's sins were forgiven prompts some of the scribes to say to themselves, "This man is blaspheming" (**v. 3**). Because Matthew writes to and has in mind Jewish readers who know Jewish religious beliefs, he does not need to explain the grounds for blasphemy; that is, that only God can forgive sins (as in Mark 2:7, followed by Luke 5:21).

Jesus' challenging question, "Why do you think evil in your hearts?" (**v. 4**), adds a moral element to the form of the question in Mark (cf. Mark 2:8, "Why do you raise such questions in your hearts?"). For examples of evil (*poneros*) in the heart (*kardia*) in the Greek Old Testament, see Ezek 38:10, "it shall be in that day, words shall come up into your heart, and you will scheme a wicked scheme," and Bar 2:8, "Yet we have not entreated the favor of the Lord by turning away, each of us, from the thoughts of our wicked hearts."

To prove that the thoughts of the scribes (that Jesus is committing blasphemy) are evil (indeed, that it is their thoughts that are blasphemy), Jesus asks another question: "For which is easier, to say, 'Your sins are forgiven,' or to say, 'Stand up and walk'?" (**v. 5**). The word of healing is harder because it can be verified; the word of forgiveness is easier because it cannot be verified. Therefore, to prove that he really can do the easier (i.e., forgive the man's sins), Jesus does the harder (i.e., heal the man's paralysis).[258]

When Jesus says, "But so that you may know that the Son of Man has authority on earth to forgive sins" (**v. 6a**), the self-designation "son of man" and the qualifier "on earth" point to Daniel 7, where a human ("one like a son of man"), coming with the clouds of heaven, approaches God (the "Ancient of Days") and from him receives authority (Dan 7:9–14). The "clouds of heaven" are antithetical to "on earth," with the latter presupposing the former. That is to say, because the "son of man" receives authority from heaven, he possesses the authority on earth to, among other things, forgive sins.

---

[258] Rightly, see D. A. Hagner, *Matthew* (1993–1995), 1:233; J. Nolland, *The Gospel of Matthew* (2005), 381–82; R. T. France, *The Gospel of Matthew* (2007), 346–47; and others.

Jesus has thrown down the challenge. It is time to demonstrate his authority: "he then said to the paralytic – 'Stand up, take your bed and go to your home'" (**v. 6b**). Jesus does not offer up prayer for the paralyzed man. He prescribes no medicine or treatment. He does not announce that, given rest and proper nourishment, the man will recover in a few days or weeks. No, he orders the man to get up, now, in front of everyone, including the scribes who a moment ago were accusing Jesus of blasphemy.

In obedience to the word of Jesus, the paralyzed man "stood up and went to his home" (**v. 7**). The healing is instantaneous and complete. The healed man is able to get up, take up his bed (as implied from v. 6; it is explicit in Mark 2:11–12), and go home, presumably without assistance. Not surprisingly, "When the crowds saw it, they were filled with awe, and they glorified God, who had given such authority to human beings" (**v. 8**). The reference to God's giving "authority" (*exousia*) "to human beings" (actually singular; Greek: *anthropos*) demonstrates that the people who witnessed the miracle recognized that Jesus, as Son of Man (*anthropos*), indeed has authority (*exousia*) from heaven to forgive sins on earth (as in v. 6).[259]

MATTHEW 9:9–13 – THE CALL OF MATTHEW AND EATING WITH SINNERS

9:9: As Jesus was walking along, he saw a man called Matthew sitting at the tax booth; and he said to him, "Follow me." And he got up and followed him.

9:10: And as he sat at dinner in the house, many tax collectors and sinners came and were sitting with him and his disciples.

9:11: When the Pharisees saw this, they said to his disciples, "Why does your teacher eat with tax collectors and sinners?"

9:12: But when he heard this, he said, "Those who are well have no need of a physician, but those who are sick.

9:13: Go and learn what this means, 'I desire mercy, not sacrifice.' For I have come to call not the righteous but sinners."

The story of the call of Matthew (or Levi) the tax collector and the feast that follows is derived from Mark 2:14–17. In Mark, the name of the man whom Jesus calls is "Levi the son of Alphaeus" (Mark 2:14), which is followed in Luke 5:27. In Matthew's version, the name is "Matthew." In Mark's version, we are told that Jesus

---

[259] H. Greeven, "Die Heilung des Gelähmten nach Matthäus," *WD* 4 (1955): 65–78; B. Reicke, "The Synoptic Reports on the Healing of the Paralytic: Matthew 9,1–8 with Parallels," in J. K. Elliott (ed.), *Studies in New Testament Language and Text* (G. D. Kilpatrick Festschrift; Leiden: Brill, 1976), 319–29; A. J. Hultgren, *Jesus and His Adversaries* (Minneapolis: Augsburg, 1979), 106–9.

had dinner (or "sat at table") "in his house." Whose house? Peter's (cf. Mark 1:29)? In Mark 2:1, Jesus has returned to Capernaum, but in Mark 2:14 Jesus has "passed on." Has he left Capernaum (and Peter's house) and walked to another village? Or has he simply moved from one house to another? In any case, it is not clear whose house is in view. Luke thinks it is Levi's house. In fact, according to Luke 5:19, Levi is the host of the banquet. Matthew is not sure whose house it is, so he simply says "in the house" (v. 10).[260]

Walking along, Jesus "saw a man called Matthew sitting at the tax booth" (**v. 9a**). Early church fathers came to identify this Matthew as a tax (or toll) collector because he was "sitting at the tax booth" (and because of Luke 5:27: "he saw a tax collector, named Levi"). Because Matthew the evangelist changed Mark's "Levi the son of Alphaeus" (Mark 2:14) into "Matthew," early church fathers also speculated that perhaps the author himself was this Matthew and substituted his preferred name.[261] As a tax collector, Matthew would have collected taxes, or tolls, for Antipas, tetrarch of Galilee. Jesus summoned Matthew with the familiar words "Follow me," and the tax collector got up (from his seated position in the tax booth) and followed him (**v. 9b**).

We probably should assume, along with Luke (cf. Luke 5:29), that the dinner that is described in **v. 10**, at which a number of tax collectors were present, had something to do with Matthew's decision to become a follower and disciple of Jesus of Nazareth. Perhaps he has invited friends and colleagues – that is, "tax collectors and sinners" – to meet and hear Jesus.

Jesus' actions provoke a response from the Pharisees: "When the Pharisees saw this, they said to his disciples, 'Why does your teacher eat with tax collectors and sinners?'" (**v. 11**). Tax collectors and "sinners" were regarded as non–Torah-observant persons. Many of them probably were nonobservant. They not only failed to live up to the written commands of Moses but also failed to observe many of the oral traditions that were so important to the Pharisees (note that Matthew omits reference to the scribes, who are present in Mark 2:16 and Luke 5:30). The Pharisees object to Jesus' eating with non–Torah-observant Jews because as a religious teacher Jesus would have been expected to avoid ritual impurity. By eating with nonobservant people, Jesus ran the risk of eating food that failed to meet the requirements of the food laws (especially as understood by Pharisees) and of coming into contact with impure persons (e.g., improperly washed hands and other aspects of uncleanness). The Pharisees may also have registered their objections out of consideration for

---

[260] A. J. Hultgren, *Jesus and His Adversaries* (1979), 109–11.

[261] Another explanation is that the name was changed from Levi to Matthew because the name Levi does not appear in any of the lists of the apostles, whereas the name Matthew does (e.g., Matt 10:2–4; Mark 3:16–19; Luke 6:14–16; Acts 1:13). On this point, see R. Pesch, "Levi/Matthaeus (Mc 2.14/Mt 9.9, 19.3): Ein Beitrag zur Lösung eines alten Problems," *ZNW* 59 (1968): 40–56.

Jesus' message and ministry (to which they probably attached some importance, at least initially). If Jesus really were the herald of the approaching kingdom of God, to which some or all of these men would have been sympathetic, then one should expect his standards of purity to be exemplary. Why then does he eat with nonobservant people?

To the question posed by the critical Pharisees, Jesus replies: "Those who are well have no need of a physician, but those who are sick" (**v. 12**). In response to these criticisms, Jesus compares himself to a physician: doctors are sent to the sick, not to the healthy.[262] Jesus' comparison has its counterparts in the Greco-Roman world. One is reminded of the story about the philosopher Antisthenes: "One day when he was censured for keeping company with evil men, the reply was made, 'Well, physicians are in attendance on their patients without getting the fever themselves'" (Diogenes Laertius, *Lives of the Philosophers*, "Antisthenes" 6.6). It is important to note that Jesus does indeed regard these people as sinners. He does not take their sin lightly. He summons sinners to repentance and admonishes Torah-observant Jews to appreciate his mission.

The most significant change that Matthew makes in the story is to replace Mark's "I have come to call not the righteous but sinners" with "Go and learn what this means, 'I desire mercy, not sacrifice.' For I have come to call not the righteous but sinners" (**v. 13**). Matthew has quoted part of Hos 6:6, "For I desire steadfast love and not sacrifice [LXX: "I desire mercy and not sacrifice"], the knowledge of God rather than burnt offerings."[263] "Go and learn" is a rabbinic idiom (e.g., *Num. Rab.* 8.4 [on Num 5:6], "Go and learn from Joshua, your master" [and then Josh 10:6 is quoted]; *b. Hullin* 50a; *b. Ketubot* 64b; *b. Menahot* 44a; *b. Qiddushin* 37a; *b. Sanhedrin* 86a; *b. Shabbat* 31a, "Hillel said to him, 'What is hateful to you, do not do to your neighbor. That is the whole Torah; the rest is commentary. Go and learn it.'").

MATTHEW 9:14–17 – NEW AND OLD

9:14: Then the disciples of John came to him, saying, "Why do we and the Pharisees fast often, but your disciples do not fast?"

9:15: And Jesus said to them, "The wedding guests cannot mourn as long as the bridegroom is with them, can they? The days will come when the bridegroom is taken away from them, and then they will fast.

9:16: No one sews a piece of unshrunk cloth on an old cloak, for the patch pulls away from the cloak, and a worse tear is made.

---

[262]   G. M. Lee, "They That Are Whole Need Not a Physician," *ExpT* 76 (1965): 254.

[263]   D. Hill, "The Use and Meaning of Hosea 6,6 in Matthew's Gospel," *NTS* 24 (1977): 107–19.

9:17: **Neither is new wine put into old wineskins; otherwise, the skins burst, and the wine is spilled, and the skins are destroyed; but new wine is put into fresh wineskins, and so both are preserved."**

*M*atthew again follows Mark (cf. Mark 2:18–22). In the previous passage, Jesus was criticized for fellowshipping with tax collectors and sinners; now he is asked why he does not require his disciples to fast (they feast but they don't fast). After all, fasting is usually observed at times of repentance (Judg 20:26; 1 Sam 7:6; 1 Kings 21:27; Ezra 8:21, 23; Neh 9:1; Jon 3:5) or in times of mourning (1 Sam 31:13; 2 Sam 1:12; Neh 1:4), in times of great distress (2 Sam 12:16, 21, 22, 23; Esther 4:3), or in preparation for a time of trial or special mission (Esther 4:16; Dan 9:3; Matt 17:21; Acts 13:2, 3; 14:23; 27:33). It was self-effacing and self-humiliating, the antithesis to pride and presumption. If God's rule is breaking into the world and if judgment comes with it, then the devout should be fasting, as are the Pharisees and the disciples of John the Baptist. The question put to Jesus is not necessarily critical. But the lack of fasting on the part of Jesus' disciples is viewed as exceptional and in need of explanation.

Matthew then states, "Then the disciples of John came to him" (**v. 14a**). Mark's beginning of this narrative is ambiguous: "Now John's disciples and the Pharisees were fasting; and people came and said to him …" (Mark 2:18). Does Mark mean to say that it was the disciples, of both John and the Pharisees, that came to Jesus with the question about fasting? Because the "they" who ask the question refers to the disciples of John and the Pharisees in the third person ("Why do John's disciples and the disciples of the Pharisees fast…?"), it may be that no disciples of either John or of the Pharisees actually put the question to Jesus. In any event, Matthew says that it was "the disciples of John" who came to Jesus with the question.

They ask Jesus, "Why do we and the Pharisees fast often, but your disciples do not fast?" (**v. 14b**). The question about fasting is now put directly to Jesus by friendly allies – John's disciples. The disciples of John are fasting for two reasons: (1) for general principles – that is, mourning, repentance, and the fasting that must precede Israel's redemption – and (2) for the very specific reason that John has been imprisoned and his life is in danger (and will eventually be taken; cf. Matt 14:1–12; Mark 6:14–29).

That mourning is in view is made clear in Jesus' reply: "The wedding guests cannot mourn as long as the bridegroom is with them, can they? The days will come when the bridegroom is taken away from them, and then they will fast" (**v. 15**). Jesus' figurative reply implies that his presence is a cause for celebration. The same idea is present in the comparison Jesus makes between John's earlier ministry and his own: "For John came neither eating nor drinking, and they say, 'He has a demon'; the Son of Man came eating and drinking, and they say, 'Look, a glutton and a drunkard, a friend of tax collectors and sinners!'" (Matt 11:18–19 = Luke 7:33–34). The wedding celebration is consistent with some of the imagery of Jewish eschatological hopes. Jesus' implied self-identification as the "bridegroom" coheres with his earlier and later self-identification as the "son of man" of Daniel 7. While he is present, announcing the good news of the kingdom of God and extending forgiveness and salvation to Israel, there can be no mourning. When he suffers and is taken from his disciples, then there will be mourning and fasting.[264]

Jesus explains his position further: "No one sews a piece of unshrunk cloth on an old cloak, for the patch pulls away from the cloak, and a worse tear is made. Neither is new wine put into old wineskins; otherwise, the skins burst, and the wine is spilled, and the skins are destroyed; but new wine is put into fresh wineskins, and so both are preserved" (vv. 16–17). Jesus illustrates his point with two more figures of speech. Both figures (old and new cloth; old and new wineskins) underscore the incompatibility of the (old) age of John and the (new) age of Jesus. Up until the close of John's preaching, it was an era of mourning, fasting, and preparation. With the presence of Jesus, it is now an era of celebration. Jesus' conduct (no fasting; rather, eating and drinking with sinners) cannot be made to fit within the context of the Baptist's earlier ministry of austerity any more than a new piece of cloth can repair an old garment or new wine can be placed in old wineskins.[265]

Jesus eats with tax collectors and sinners; he does not fast. Jesus is celebrating the rule of God now breaking into the world and the grace that reaches out to sinners, inviting them to return to a loving and forgiving God. Jesus' understanding of God does not fit old concepts and assumptions. His new teaching will not fit into the old ways of thinking any more than new wine will fit in old, no longer flexible wineskins.

MATTHEW 9:18–26 – RESTORING A DAUGHTER AND A WOMAN

9:18: **While he was saying these things to them, suddenly a leader of the synagogue came in and knelt before him, saying, "My daughter has just died; but come and lay your hand on her, and she will live."**

9:19: **And Jesus got up and followed him, with his disciples.**

9:20: **Then suddenly a woman who had been suffering from hemorrhages for twelve years came up behind him and touched the fringe of his cloak,**

9:21: **for she said to herself, "If I only touch his cloak, I will be made well."**

---

[264] H. C. Kee, "The Question about Fasting," *NovT* 11 (1969): 161–73; J. B. Muddiman, "Jesus and Fasting," in J. Dupont (ed.), *Jésus aux origenes de la christologie* (BETL 40; Gembloux: Duculot, 1975), 283–301.

[265] H. C. Kee, "The Old Coat and the New Wine," *NovT* 12 (1970): 13–21; M. G. Steinhauser, "The Patch of Unshrunk Cloth," *ExpT* 87 (1976): 312–13; A. J. Hultgren, *Jesus and His Adversaries* (1979), 78–82; R. T. Beckwith, "The Feast of New Wine and the Question of Fasting," *ExpT* 95 (1984): 334–35; G. J. Brooke, "The Feast of New Wine and the Question of Fasting," *ExpT* 95 (1984): 175–76.

9:22: Jesus turned, and seeing her he said, "Take heart, daughter; your faith has made you well." And instantly the woman was made well.

9:23: When Jesus came to the leader's house and saw the flute players and the crowd making a commotion,

9:24: he said, "Go away; for the girl is not dead but sleeping." And they laughed at him.

9:25: But when the crowd had been put outside, he went in and took her by the hand, and the girl got up.

9:26: And the report of this spread throughout that district.

Once again, Matthew streamlines a story from Mark (Mark 5:21–43), and because of his rearrangement of other materials has placed the story in a different context. In the Matthean sequence, the question of fasting (Matt 9:14–17 = Mark 2:18–22) immediately preceded this story, not the encounter with the Gerasene (or Gadarene) demoniac (cf. Matt 8:28–33; Mark 5:1–20). Matthew's story of the two restored daughters is followed by the healing of the blind men (Matt 9:27–31), which is again out of step with Mark's sequence (cf. Mark 10:46–52).

Matthew does not merely economize, using only about half the words that Mark uses, but also expurgates elements of the story that are somewhat awkward, such as all the details about the physicians who had failed the woman with the hemorrhage (cf. Mark 5:26), her healing and Jesus' uncertainty as to what had happened (cf. Mark 5:29–30, 32), or the disrespectful rejoinder of his disciples, "You see the crowd pressing in on you; how can you say, 'Who touched me?'" (Mark 5:31). Matthew also omits details of the second miracle, such as the report that the girl had died and the uncalled for question, "why trouble the teacher any further?" (Mark 5:35), and Mark's Aramaic *talitha koum* (Mark 5:41), as well as the command to feed her and to keep her healing a secret (Mark 5:42).

In Mark, the desperate father urges Jesus to hurry, for his daughter "is at the point of death" (Mark 5:23). Matthew, knowing that by the time Jesus and the father arrive they will find the girl dead (as is implied by the public lamentation; cf. Mark 5:38), has the father say, "My daughter has just died; but come and lay your hand on her, and she will live" (v. 18). The alteration displays remarkable faith on the part of the father. Although his daughter has died, he believes that Jesus will be able to restore her.

On the way to the man's house, "suddenly a woman who had been suffering from hemorrhages for twelve years came up behind him and touched the fringe of his cloak, for she said to herself, "If I only touch his cloak, I will be made well" (vv. 19–20). Mark only says that the woman "touched his cloak" (Mark 5:27). Matthew adds that she "touched the fringe of his cloak" (in agreement with Luke 8:44). Jewish men wore fringes on the corners of their cloaks, in keeping with Num 15:38–40. In late antiquity, it was believed that the fringe of the clothes of holy men, such as Honi the Circle-Drawer or Hanina ben Dosa, could convey benefit: "Hanan ha-Nehba was the son of the daughter of Honi the Circle-Drawer. When the world was in need of rain the Rabbis would send to him school children and they would take hold of the hem [or fringe] of his garment and say to him, 'Father, Father, give us rain'" (*b. Ta'anit* 23b).

The woman with the hemorrhage believes that if she does no more than touch Jesus' cloak, she will "be made well" (**v. 21**). She, too, displays remarkable faith in Jesus. Jesus sees the woman and tells her, "Take heart, daughter; your faith has made you well" (**v. 22**). Matthew has omitted the awkward scene in Mark, where Jesus inquires who touched him and the disciples respond in a way almost bordering on disrespect (Mark 5:30–33). It is interesting to note that Matthew says it is after Jesus spoke that "instantly the woman was made well." In Mark, the woman was healed before Jesus spoke; indeed, before Jesus knew who had touched him. Matthew has again shown the power of Jesus' word – he speaks and what he says happens.[266]

When Matthew reports, "When Jesus came to the leader's house and saw the flute players and the crowd making a commotion" (**v. 23**), he adds "flute players." The girl has indeed died, as the father reported earlier (v. 18), and now the funeral, complete with flute players and wailing mourners, is under way. This was part of Jewish funeral rites: "Even a poor man in Israel will not have fewer than two flute players and one wailing woman" (*m. Ketubot* 4:4; cf. *m. Shab.* 23:4; Josephus, *J.W.* 3.437).

When Jesus says, "Go away; for the girl is not dead but sleeping" (**v. 24**), he means that there is still hope. Matthew is not suggesting that the girl is merely comatose and may yet awaken. "Jesus does not deny the girl's death but rather the finality of that death."[267] The people who had gathered at the ruler's house – and we should assume this included the flute players and the wailing women – "laughed at" Jesus. They have taken his reference to "sleep" literally and know that he is wrong; they know death when they see it.[268]

Jesus puts the crowd outside, then takes the girl by the hand (recall Matt 8:15), and she arises (**v. 25**). No spells, no rigmarole, no gimmicks.[269] Matthew ends the

---

[266] J. T. Cummings, "The Tassel of His Cloak: Mark, Luke, Matthew and Zechariah," in E. A. Livingstone (ed.), *Studia Biblica 1978: II. Papers on the Gospels* (JSNTSup 2; Sheffield: JSOT Press, 1980), 47–61; V. K. Robbins, "The Woman Who Touched Jesus' Garment: Socio-Rhetorical Analysis of the Synoptic Accounts," *NTS* 33 (1987): 502–15.

[267] D. A. Hagner, *Matthew* (1993–1995), 1:250. Hagner notes that "sleep" was a euphemism in Jewish thought (cf. Dan 12:2) and became a standard euphemism for death in early Christianity, probably as an expression of faith and hope in the resurrection (cf. 1 Thess 4:13; Eph 5:14).

[268] It was the practice to prepare a body for burial immediately upon death. When the flute players and mourners arrived at the house, the girl's body was in the process of being washed, perfumed, and wrapped for burial, which would take place that very day.

[269] M. J. Harris, "'The Dead Are Restored to Life': Miracles or Revivification in the Gospels," in D. Wenham and C. L. Blomberg (eds.), *The Miracles of Jesus* (Gospel Perspectives 6; Sheffield: JSOT Press, 1986), 295–326, especially 304–10.

story with the terse remark that "the report of this spread throughout that district" (i.e., that part of the country) (**v. 26**). In Mark's account, Jesus had asked the family to keep quiet (cf. Mark 5:43), but Matthew omits this.

MATTHEW 9:27–31 – HEALING OF TWO BLIND MEN

9:27: As Jesus went on from there, two blind men followed him, crying loudly, "Have mercy on us, Son of David!"

9:28: When he entered the house, the blind men came to him; and Jesus said to them, "Do you believe that I am able to do this?" They said to him, "Yes, Lord."

9:29: Then he touched their eyes and said, "According to your faith let it be done to you."

9:30: And their eyes were opened. Then Jesus sternly ordered them, "See that no one knows of this."

9:31: But they went away and spread the news about him throughout that district.

*M*atthew's story of the healing of the two blind men seems to be based on Mark's story of the healing of blind Bartimaeus (cf. Mark 10:46–52). What complicates matters is that later in Matthew's narrative he, too, recounts a story of healing blindness in Jericho, just before Jesus journeys to Jerusalem (cf. Matt 20:29–34). Most commentators believe that Mark's story of blind Bartimaeus provides some of the details for Matthew's otherwise unattested story.

Matthew must tell a story of the healing of the blind (and more than one blind person at that) because after the discourse coming up in Chapter 10 Jesus will refer to restoring sight to the "blind" (plural) in his reply to the imprisoned John the Baptist (cf. Matt 11:5). The evangelist cannot wait until the healing of the blind mute (Matt 12:22) or the blind men of Jericho (cf. Matt 20:29–34) if the reply to John is to be made in Chapter 11. Luke does the same thing, saying Jesus "granted sight to many who were blind" (Luke 7:21) just before replying to John (Luke 7:22).

There was no need, of course, for Matthew simply to invent a story. Jesus' reply to John makes it clear that Jesus had healed several blind people. But it is also probable that in the telling of this particular story Matthew has made use of the language found in Mark's story of Bartimaeus.

Matthew's account of Jesus' encounter with the two blind men begins, "Two blind men followed him" (**v. 27a**). As elsewhere in Matthew, there are two people involved (cf. Matt 8:28, where we have two demoniacs, instead of one, or Matt 20:30, where we have two blind men at Jericho, instead of one, namely Bartimaeus). In the triumphal entry, there are two animals (cf. Matt 21:1–11).[270]

---

[270]   W. R. G. Loader, "Son of David, Blindness and Duality in Matthew," *CBQ* 44 (1982): 570–85.

The two blind men follow Jesus and cry out, "Have mercy on us, Son of David!" (**v. 27b**). To this point in the Matthean narrative, we have twice heard the words "son of David." It first appears in the opening verse, in reference to Jesus: "An account of the genealogy of Jesus the Messiah, the son of David, the son of Abraham" (Matt 1:1). It then reappears a bit later in the infancy narrative, in reference to Joseph, the husband of Mary: "an angel of the Lord appeared to him in a dream and said, 'Joseph, son of David'" (Matt 1:20). Jesus will again be called "Son of David" in Matt 12:22–24, in connection with his healing of the blind mute.[271] On the significance of the epithet for Jesus, see the commentary on Matt 20:29–34.

As the story continues, Matthew emphasizes faith in Jesus and not simply faith in God: "Do you believe that I am able to do this?" (**v. 28**). The blind men reply, "Yes, Lord" (see the commentary on the next verse). Once again, Matthew tells us that Jesus "entered the house," but it is not clear whose house (cf. Matt 9:10).

When the blind men said they believe Jesus can heal them, "he touched their eyes and said, 'According to your faith let it be done to you'" (**v. 29**). Faith is very important in the Matthean Gospel. Several times Jesus chastises his disciples for being "of little faith" (Matt 6:30; 8:26; 14:31; 16:8) or having difficulties "because of [their] little faith" (Matt 17:20). Jesus praises the centurion, probably a Gentile, for having greater faith than most in Israel (Matt 8:10, 13). He is impressed by the faith of the men who bring the paralyzed man to him (Matt 9:22). The woman with the hemorrhage is healed because of her faith (Matt 9:22). The daughter of the Gentile woman is healed because of her mother's faith (Matt 15:28). If Jesus' disciples "have faith and do not doubt," they can throw mountains into the sea (Matt 21:21). The wicked, of course, do not have faith, having believed neither in John's message (Matt 21:25, 32) nor in Jesus (Matt 27:42).

Once again, Jesus heals with a touch, as in touching the leper (Matt 8:3), Peter's mother-in-law (8:15), the woman who touches Jesus' cloak (9:20–21), the people of Gennesaret (who touch Jesus' garments; 14:36), and the blind men of Jericho (20:34).

The men regain their sight and Jesus orders them, "See that no one knows of this" (**v. 30**). Matthew retains some of Jesus' demands for secrecy found in the Gospel of Mark. This is one of them. The remarkable feature is that the healed men do not obey Jesus (**v. 31**: "they went away and spread the news about him throughout

---

[271] Lying behind the epithet "son of David" and the expectation of healing may have been a tradition of Solomon as master exorcist and healer. See J. M. Gibbs, "Purpose and Pattern in Matthew's Use of the Title 'Son of David,'" *NTS* 10 (1964): 446–64; D. C. Duling, "The Therapeutic Son of David: An Element in Matthew's Christological Apologetic," *NTS* 24 (1978): 392–410; K. Paffenroth, "Jesus as Anointed and Healing Son of David in the Gospel of Matthew," *Bib* 80 (1999): 547–54; L. Novakovic, *Messiah, the Healer of the Sick* (2003). It has also been suggested that Matthew's understanding of Jesus as Son of David who heals has more to do with Ezekiel's prophecy of a healing and restoring Davidic shepherd. See W. Baxter, "Healing and the 'Son of David': Matthew's Warrant," *NovT* 48 (2006): 36–50.

that district"), whom only a moment earlier they had addressed as "Son of David" (v. 27). How is this to be understood? First, it suggests that the joy and excitement of humans, for whom regaining sight was almost unheard of, cannot be contained; they simply have to tell everybody. Second, it underscores the fecklessness of human beings, among whom and for whom Jesus ministers. Not only do members of the general public disregard his commands; even his own disciples will fail him.

Why did Jesus ask people to keep quiet? There were probably several reasons over the course of his ministry. But probably the main reason was Jesus' desire that his proclamation of the kingdom of God and his call to national repentance and renewal not be overshadowed by the miracles themselves. The miracles were intended to demonstrate the reality of the rule of God, not compete with it.

In the ancient world, blindness was thought to be especially difficult, if not impossible, to cure (cf. Hippocrates, *Prorrhetica* 2.19: the blind "cannot with time or technique be helped to see"). There is a story told of how the newly enthroned emperor Vespasian healed a blind man by applying spittle on his cheeks and eyes (cf. Suetonius, *Vespasian* 7.2–3; Tacitus, *Histories* 4.81). A similar story is told of Emperor Hadrian, in the face of skeptics who think blindness cannot be healed (Aelius Spartianus, *On the Life of Hadrian* 25.3–4). In Matt 9:27–31, there is no mention of spittle (as there is in Mark 8:22–26).

MATTHEW 9:32–34 – HEALING OF A MUTE DEMONIAC

9:32: After they had gone away, a demoniac who was mute was brought to him.

9:33: And when the demon had been cast out, the one who had been mute spoke; and the crowds were amazed and said, "Never has anything like this been seen in Israel."

9:34: But the Pharisees said, "By the ruler of the demons he casts out the demons."

*M*atthew presents us with an edited story from Q. Luke's version is found in Luke 11:14–15. The charge made by the Pharisees in v. 34 parallels Luke 11:15 but has been influenced by the last part of Mark 3:22. A parallel form of this story will reappear in Matt 12:22–24. Matthew's version of the story here in 9:32–34 anticipates the allusion to Isa 35:5 in Matt 11:5.

Matthew tells us that "a demoniac who was mute was brought to" Jesus (**v. 32**). The Greek word for "mute" is *kophos*, and probably implies deafness as well as inability to speak. It was commonly believed that demons were causes of various ailments, such as blindness, deafness (and muteness), and a host of other maladies. In the late first-century pseudepigraphon called the *Testament of Solomon*, the wise monarch asks a demon what evils he inflicts on humans. The demon replies, "I turn their ears around backward and make them dumb and deaf" (*T. Sol.* 12:2).

Jesus cast out the demon, and "the one who had been mute spoke" (**v. 33**). The proof of the exorcism is seen in the man's ability to speak. The crowds that witnessed the miracle were amazed and said, "Never has anything like this been seen in Israel." This exclamation may allude to Judg 19:30: "Has such a thing ever happened since the day that the Israelites came up from the land of Egypt until this day?"

The Pharisees, however, are not impressed. They cannot deny the miracle, but they can attribute the power to Satan: "By the ruler of the demons he casts out the demons" (**v. 34**). This charge will be explored more fully in Matt 12:22–37. Its mention here provides an antecedent for Jesus' saying in Matt 10:25: "If they have called the master of the house Beelzebul, how much more will they malign those of his household!"[272]

MATTHEW 9:35–38 – LABORERS FOR THE HARVEST

9:35: Then Jesus went about all the cities and villages, teaching in their synagogues, and proclaiming the good news of the kingdom, and curing every disease and every sickness.

9:36: When he saw the crowds, he had compassion for them, because they were harassed and helpless, like sheep without a shepherd.

9:37: Then he said to his disciples, "The harvest is plentiful, but the laborers are few;

9:38: therefore ask the Lord of the harvest to send out laborers into his harvest."

*P*ortions of Matt 9:35–36 are drawn from phrases in Mark 1:39 and Mark 6:6, 34, and Matt 9:37–38 is drawn from Q. Matthew here has followed Q closely (cf. Luke 10:2). Matthew 9:35–38 provides a succinct summary of Jesus' ministry to this point and paves the way for the commission of the twelve and the missionary discourse that follows in Chapter 10.

Matthew's summary statement that "Jesus went about all the cities and villages, teaching in their synagogues" (**v. 35a**) recaps the earlier summary in Matt 4:23, "Jesus went throughout Galilee, teaching in their synagogues...." On "city" (*polis*), see Matt 9:1; 10:11; 11:1, 20. On "synagogue," see Matt 12:9; 13:54. On "village" (*kome*),

[272] G. N. Stanton, "Jesus of Nazareth: A Magician and a False Prophet Who Deceived God's People?" in J. B. Green and M. Turner (eds.), *Jesus of Nazareth Lord and Christ: Essays on the Historical Jesus and New Testament Christology* (I. H. Marshall Festschrift; Grand Rapids, MI: Eerdmans, 1994), 164–80, edited and reprinted in G. N. Stanton, *Jesus and Gospel* (Cambridge: Cambridge University Press, 2004), 127–47; D. D. Sheets, "Jesus as Demon-Possessed," in S. McKnight and J. B. Modica (eds.), *Who Do My Opponents Say that I Am?* (2008), 27–49.

see Matt 10:11; 14:15; 21:2. On "teaching" (*didaskein*), see Matt 5:2; 7:29; 13:54; 21:23; 22:16.

"Proclaiming the good news of the kingdom" (**v. 35b**) also alludes to the earlier summary in Matt 4.23: "… and proclaiming the gospel of the kingdom…." On "proclaiming" (*kerussein*), see Matt 3:1 (in reference to John the Baptist); 4:17, 23; 10:7. Besides Matt 9:35 and 4:23, the Matthean summaries, in only one other place do we find teaching and proclaiming in the same verse in Matthew: "He departed from there to teach and preach in their cities" (Matt 11:1). The ministry of Jesus is not limited to proclaiming but entails doing, and in evidence of the reality of what is proclaimed, it entails "curing every disease and every sickness" (**v. 35c**). Here again, we have a repeat of the earlier summary in Matt 4:23: "… and curing every disease and every sickness among the people." On disease (*nosos*), see Matt 4:24; 10:1. On "sickness" (*malakia*), see Matt 10:1.

When Jesus saw the crowds, "he had compassion for them, because they were harassed and helpless, like sheep without a shepherd" (**v. 36**). Matthew alludes to Num 27:17; 1 Kings 22:17; and/or 2 Chron 18:16, all three of which refer to Israel in distress "like sheep without a shepherd" (see also Zech 10:2: "Therefore the people wander like sheep; they suffer for lack of a shepherd"). The sheep/shepherd imagery, where the sheep represents Israel and the shepherd(s) its leader(s), is further developed in Ezekiel (especially Ezek 34:6, 12) and later in the intertestamental work *1 Enoch* (especially 90:1, 3). It will occur several more times in Matthew (e.g., Matt 10:6, 16; 14:14; 15:24, 32; 18:12–14; 25:32).[273] In the New Testament Gospels, the theme is treated more fully in John 10, where Jesus is identified as the "Good Shepherd" and his followers are identified as the "sheep" (cf. Heb 13:20; 1 Pet 2:25; 5:4; Rev 7:17). In what ways were the people "harassed and helpless"? The imagery of *1 Enoch* suggests exploitation at the hands of the leadership. Perhaps Matthew also has in mind the religious burdens placed upon the people by unsympathetic and judgmental scribes and Pharisees (cf. Matt 23:4).

After considering the condition of the people, Jesus says to his disciples, "The harvest is plentiful, but the laborers are few; therefore ask the Lord of the harvest to send out laborers into his harvest" (**vv. 37–38**). Jesus' saying seems to be proverbial in light of this parallel in the Sayings of the Fathers: "Rabbi Tarfon said, 'The day is short and the task is great and the laborers are idle and the wage is abundant and the master of the house is urgent'" (*m. 'Abot* 2.15). Jesus' reference to God as "the Lord of the harvest," who is requested to send out workers, may allude to 1 Sam 12:17: "Is it not the wheat harvest today? I will call upon the Lord, that he may send thunder and rain." Sometimes in Scripture and related literature, harvest is used as a metaphor for coming judgment (e.g., Isa 18:4; Jer 9:22, "Human corpses shall fall like

---

[273] On the importance of the shepherd theme in Matthew, see J. P. Heil, "Ezekiel 34 and the Narrative Strategy of the Shepherd and Sheep Metaphor in Matthew," *CBQ* 55 (1993): 698–708.

dung upon the open field, and like sheaves behind the reaper"; Hos 6:11; Joel 3:13; 4 Ezra 4:26–37; *2 Bar* 70:1–2).[274]

MATTHEW 10:1–4 – AUTHORIZING THE TWELVE

10:1: Then Jesus summoned his twelve disciples and gave them authority over unclean spirits, to cast them out, and to cure every disease and every sickness.

10:2: These are the names of the twelve apostles: first, Simon, also known as Peter, and his brother Andrew; James son of Zebedee, and his brother John;

10:3: Philip and Bartholomew; Thomas and Matthew the tax collector; James son of Alphaeus, and Thaddaeus;

10:4: Simon the Cananaean, and Judas Iscariot, the one who betrayed him.

*M*atthew delays Mark's narrative of the appointment of the twelve (Mark 3:13–19), combines it with Mark's narrative of the sending of the twelve (cf. Mark 6:7–13), and presents this combined and edited material as the introduction to Jesus' second major discourse, the missionary discourse that comprises Matthew 10. The discourse will be introduced in the commentary on Matt 10:5–15.

Previously Matthew has referred to disciples (Matt 5:1; 8:21, 23; 9:10, 11, 14, 19, 20, 37), but when he states "Then Jesus summoned his twelve disciples" (**v. 1a**), this is the first time in his Gospel that we hear of "twelve disciples." They will be mentioned elsewhere (Matt 10:5; 11:1; 19:28 [by inference]; 20:17; 26:14, 20, 47). Matthew presupposes Mark 3:14, where it is stated that Jesus "named twelve, whom he also named apostles." In v. 2, the twelve disciples will be called "apostles."

In Greek (*apostolos*) and in Hebrew (*shaliah*), "apostle" means one who is sent, usually as a messenger, agent, deputy, or ambassador. It was understood that an apostle was commissioned by a higher authority and acted on behalf of this authority. This is the meaning here. Jesus appoints twelve apostles, sends them out to preach his message, and grants them authority.

The appointment of "twelve" apostles symbolizes the regathering and reconstitution of the twelve tribes of Israel. The twelve apostles do not, of course, come from all twelve tribes (because some of them are brothers, this would not be possible). The association is made clearer in a passage Matthew and Luke derived from Q: "you who have followed me will also sit on twelve thrones, judging the twelve tribes of Israel" (Matt 19:28 = Luke 22:30; cf. Matt 10:6: "Go nowhere among the

---

[274] L. Legrand, "The Harvest Is Plentiful (Mt 9.37)," *Scripture* 17 (1965): 1–9; H. Lichtenberger, "'Bittet den Herrn der Ernte, daß er Arbeiter in seine Ernte sende' (Mt 9,38/Lk 10,2)," in J. Ådna et al. (eds.), *Evangelium – Schriftauslegung – Kirche: Festschrift für Peter Stuhlmacher zum 65. Geburtstag* (Göttingen: Vandenhoeck & Ruprecht, 1997), 269–78; D. W. Ulrich, "The Missional Audience of the Gospel of Matthew," *CBQ* 69 (2007): 64–83.

Gentiles ... but go rather to the lost sheep of the house of Israel"). The symbolism of the twelve is so powerful that it is necessary to replace the apostate Judas Iscariot (Acts 1:15–26).[275] Its power is also witnessed by the myriad of legendary and apocryphal writings attributed to the apostles. Some of them will be mentioned later as each apostle is briefly considered.[276]

Jesus gave the twelve apostles "authority over unclean spirits, to cast them out, and to cure every disease and every sickness" (**v. 1b**). To Mark's "authority to cast out demons" (Mark 3:15) Matthew adds the authority to "cure every disease and every sickness." The language here closely matches the summary statements in Matt 4:23 and 9:35. Jesus has imparted to his disciples, now appointed and named as apostles, the same powers that have been at work in his ministry since its inception.

Jesus has commissioned the twelve to preach his kingdom message, and he has given them the authority (or power) to cast out demons. In effect, Jesus has delegated to these chosen disciples his own special power and authority. Through them his mission to Israel has been significantly expanded.[277] The discourse in Matt 10:5–42 will spell out the nature of this mission, both for Israel and for the Gentile nations.

Matthew begins his enumeration of the twelve apostles with "These are the names of the twelve apostles: first, Simon, also known as Peter ..." (**v. 2**). "Simon," whom Jesus named Peter (Greek) or Cephas (Aramaic), both of which mean "rock," figures prominently in the first half of the Book of Acts, is mentioned a few times in Paul's letters (e.g., 1 Cor 1:12; Gal 2:9), and is given credit for two letters in the New Testament (i.e., 1 and 2 Peter). The apostle Peter is distinguished in the Gospel of Matthew for his confession of Jesus, "You are the Messiah, the Son of the living God," and the blessing and promise of the "keys of the kingdom of heaven" (Matt 16:16–19), as well as the remarkable episode where he walks on water (and then suddenly sinks) to meet Jesus (Matt 14:28–33). A number of apocryphal writings are attributed to Peter, including a Gospel, a book of Acts, an apocalypse, and a series of proclamations or *kerygmata*. The great church historian Eusebius regarded 2 Peter as apocryphal as well.

After beginning his enumeration with Peter, Matthew next lists "His brother Andrew." In his list, the evangelist Mark does not name Andrew as Simon Peter's

---

[275]   R. P. Meye, *Jesus and the Twelve: Discipleship and Revelation in Mark's Gospel* (Grand Rapids, MI: Eerdmans, 1968), 192–209; W. Horbury, "The Twelve and the Phylarchs," *NTS* 32 (1986): 503–27; J. P. Meier, "The Circle of the Twelve: Did It Exist During Jesus' Public Ministry?" *JBL* 116 (1997): 635–72; S. McKnight, "Jesus and the Twelve," *BBR* 11 (2001): 203–31.

[276]   For archaeological attestation of the names of the apostles (but not of the apostles themselves), see C. A. Evans, *Jesus and the Ossuaries* (Waco, TX: Baylor University Press, 2003), 68–80.

[277]   U. Luz, "The Disciples in the Gospel According to Matthew," in G. N. Stanton (ed.), *The Interpretation of Matthew* (IRT 3; London: SPCK; Philadelphia: Fortress, 1983), 98–128.

brother; in fact, Andrew's name appears after mention of the two sons of Zebedee (Mark 3:18). Andrew's relationship to Peter was previously indicated in Mark 1:16 (and Matt 4:18). Little is known about Andrew. On one occasion, he is with Jesus and the inner circle of James, John, and Peter, but only in Mark's Gospel (Mark 13:3). An apocryphal *Acts of Andrew* was composed sometime in the third century and was widely circulated on into the ninth century.

After the brothers Peter and Andrew, Matthew next lists "James son of Zebedee." In Mark, the sons of Zebedee are dubbed the "sons of Thunder" (*boanerges*). The etymology of this strange epithet is uncertain. The story of the martyrdom of James at the hands of Agrippa I is narrated in Acts 12:1–2. James and John are with Jesus on the Mount of Transfiguration (Matt 17:1). A legendary *Acts of James of Zebedee* appeared in Coptic sometime in the early Middle Ages. A Latin *Passion of James of Zebedee* also appeared.

Following James on Matthew's list of the apostles is "His brother John." The early church speculated that John might have been the "disciple whom Jesus loved" (John 13:23; 19:26; 20:2) and possibly the author of the fourth Gospel, or perhaps the John exiled on the island of Patmos, who wrote the Book of Revelation. An apocryphal *Acts of John* appeared in the second century.

After the two pairs of brothers on Matthew's list comes "Philip" (**v. 3**). Apart from the appearance of his name in the apostolic lists, nothing is known of "Philip" in the Synoptic Gospels, but in the fourth Gospel he plays a prominent role (John 1:43–48; 6:5–7; 12:21–22; 14:8–9). He should not be confused with Philip the deacon, who became an evangelist (Acts 6:5; 8:5–40; 21:8). A Gnostic *Gospel of Philip* began to circulate in the second century. In the Middle Ages, an *Acts of Philip* appeared.

Matthew next names "Bartholomew." Nothing is known of Bartholomew (from Aramaic, meaning "son of Tolmai"); his name appears only in the apostolic lists (Matt 10:3; Mark 3:18; Luke 14; Acts 1:13). Although some have suggested that he is the Nathanael of John 1:45–46, there is no evidence of this. In the early Middle Ages, an apocryphal *Acts of Andrew and Bartholomew* appeared.

The seventh apostle listed in Matthew 10 is "Thomas." Thomas is perhaps the most interesting figure among the twelve. He plays a prominent, if at times dubious, role in the fourth Gospel (John 11:16; 20:24; 21:2). He is understood as the twin brother of Jesus Christ in Gnostic circles, and the author of the *Gospel of Thomas*, composed in second-century Syria. Other writings are attributed to him, including the fanciful *Infancy Gospel of Thomas* and the Gnostic works *Acts of Thomas* and *Book of Thomas the Contender*.

The Gospel of Matthew next lists "Matthew the tax collector" as one of the twelve. Mark only says "Matthew" (Mark 3:18); the evangelist Matthew adds "the tax collector," which will remind readers of Matthew's call in Matt 9:9 (but in Mark 2:14 and Luke 5:27 the tax collector's name is Levi). Apart from the call itself, nothing is known of this person. The early church thought that he might have authored the

Gospel of Matthew. In the Middle Ages, a legendary *Martyrdom of Matthew* began to circulate.

The ninth apostle on Matthew's list is "James son of Alphaeus." Nothing is known of him. He is not to be confused with "James the Lord's brother" (Matt 13:55; 1 Cor 15:7; Gal 1:19) or with "James the Smaller" (Mark 15:40; cf. Matt 27:56). Because Levi (Matthew) in Mark 2:14 is called the "son of Alphaeus," it is possible that James and Levi were brothers.

Next, Matthew mentions "Thaddaeus." Thaddeus appears only in the apostolic lists of Mark 3:18 and Matt 10:3. Nothing is known of him. A Greek *Acts of Thaddaeus* and a Coptic *Acts of Thaddaeus* made their respective appearances in the early Middle Ages.

Following Thaddeus is "Simon the Cananaean" (**v. 4**). He appears as "Simon who was called the Zealot" in Luke's parallel passage (Luke 6:15) and in the list that appears in Acts 1:12–14. "Zealot" is probably meant as the Greek equivalent of the Aramaic *cananaean* (which means "zealous"). A Coptic *Acts of Simon the Cananaean* appeared in the fifth or sixth century.

Last on Matthew's list of apostles is "Judas Iscariot, the one who betrayed him." Judas is infamous as the betrayer of Jesus. Two evangelists believed that Satan influenced Judas (Luke 22:3; John 13:26–27), but little is known of the man's actual motives (see the commentary on Matt 26:14–16, 47–56). Some think Iscariot means "man from Kariot." Others wonder if the name is a form of *sicarii* (Latin plural of *sicarus*, "assassin"), the dagger-men infamous for assassinating their opponents. It has also been suggested that it means "choked," perhaps as a grim reference to his hanging and suffocation.[278]

A Closer Look: The Disciples in the Talmud

There is a rabbinic tradition that disparages Jesus' disciples by giving them names that resemble words in certain passages of Scripture: "Jesus had five disciples: Matthai, Nakai, Nezer, Buni, and Todah. When Matthai was brought [before the court] he said to them [the judges], 'Shall Matthai be executed? Is it not written, "Matthai [when] shall I come and appear before God?"' (Ps 42:3). Then they replied, 'Yes, Matthai shall be executed, because it is written, "Matthai [when] shall he die and his name perish"' (Ps 41:6)" (*b. Sanh.* 43a; cf. *b. Shab.* 104b). In similar fashion, the four other disciples are condemned. These five names only vaguely resemble some of the names of the twelve apostles. "Matthai" is surely meant to refer to Matthew. "Todah" might be Thaddaeus. "Buni" might refer to James and John, sons of Zebedee,

---

[278]   D. J. Williams, "Judas Iscariot," *DJG* (1992): 406–8; J. E. Taylor, "The Name '*Iskarioth*' (Iscariot)," *JBL* 129 (2010): 367–83.

whom Jesus nicknamed "Boanerges" ("sons of thunder"). "Nakai" might refer to Nicodemus, one of the secret disciples of the fourth Gospel. "Nezer" probably does not refer to a person but to the Christian belief that Jesus is the Branch (Hebrew *nezer*) of Isa 11:1, to which Matt 2:23 ("He shall be called a Nazarene") probably refers. There is no historical value in this tradition, but it does attest to the critical and sometimes polemical contact between Christianity (probably Jewish Christianity) and the synagogue that had long before rejected Christian faith in Jesus as Israel's Messiah.[279]

MATTHEW 10:5–15 – MISSION INSTRUCTIONS

10:5: These twelve Jesus sent out with the following instructions: "Go nowhere among the Gentiles, and enter no town of the Samaritans,

10:6: but go rather to the lost sheep of the house of Israel.

10:7: As you go, proclaim the good news, 'The kingdom of heaven has come near.'

10:8: Cure the sick, raise the dead, cleanse the lepers, cast out demons. You received without payment; give without payment.

10:9: Take no gold, or silver, or copper in your belts,

10:10: no bag for your journey, or two tunics, or sandals, or a staff; for laborers deserve their food.

10:11: Whatever town or village you enter, find out who in it is worthy, and stay there until you leave.

10:12: As you enter the house, greet it.

10:13: If the house is worthy, let your peace come upon it; but if it is not worthy, let your peace return to you.

10:14: If anyone will not welcome you or listen to your words, shake off the dust from your feet as you leave that house or town.

10:15: Truly I tell you, it will be more tolerable for the land of Sodom and Gomorrah on the day of judgment than for that town.

*M*atthew 10:5–15 is prefaced by Matthew's version of the calling of the twelve apostles (cf. Matt 10:1–4). He has developed a discourse on the missionary theme (Matt 10:5–42) by pulling together related materials from Mark (especially Mark 3:13–19; 6:7–13; 13:9–13; 8:34–35) and Q (as seen in Luke 6:40; 12:1–12,

---

[279] For a critical discussion of this Talmudic tradition, see P. Schäfer, *Jesus in the Talmud* (Princeton, NJ: Princeton University Press, 2007), 75–81.

48, 49–53). This discourse is preparation for the much shorter, confessional Great Commission in Matt 28:18–20. The discourse begins with a charge to the newly appointed apostles to go to the "lost sheep of the house of Israel" (vv. 5–15). The apostles are to proclaim the good news of the kingdom of God (or heaven) and are to heal and exorcise. But the discourse goes on to warn the disciples of being dragged before Gentiles while offering assurance that they will know what to say when the time comes (vv. 16–23). The tensions between these two parts of the discourse are obvious, indicating its composite nature. The discourse concludes with words of encouragement (vv. 24–33), warnings of conflict (vv. 34–39), and promises of reward (vv. 40–42). These disparate materials were uttered on different occasions and have been assembled and edited by the evangelist, so that he may clarify important principles of Christian mission.[280]

Matthew says, "These twelve Jesus sent out" (**v. 5**), in contrast to Mark 6:7, because in Matthew's arrangement the twelve had just been appointed (in Matt 10:1–4). Jesus commands the twelve: "Go nowhere among the Gentiles, and enter no town of the Samaritans." Israel's priority is emphasized. This is the only mention of Samaritans in Matthew (there are no references in Mark but three in Luke). Exclusion of the Gentiles is interesting, given the earlier quotation of Isa 9:1–2 in Matt 4:15–17: "The land of Zebulun, the land of Naphtali, on the road by the sea, across the Jordan, Galilee of the Gentiles...." Galilee may be the land of the Gentiles, but Jesus' apostles are to go to the Israelites, not to the Gentiles who may live among them.[281]

Rather than going to the Gentiles, the apostles are to go "to the lost sheep of the house of Israel" (**v. 6**). The description harks back to Matt 9:36 ("sheep without a shepherd"; see the commentary there). On a sheep that is lost and then retrieved, see the parable of the lost sheep (Matt 18:12–14; Luke 15:3–7). The epithet "house of Israel" is commonplace in Scripture (e.g., Exod 16:31; 40:38; Lev 10:6; Num 20:29; Josh 21:45; Ruth 4:11; Pss 98:3; 115:12; 135:19; Isa 5:7).

The apostles are to "proclaim the good news, 'The kingdom of heaven has come near.' Cure the sick, raise the dead, cleanse the lepers, cast out demons" (**vv. 7–8a**). The importance of the link between the preaching of the "kingdom of heaven" (i.e., of God) and healing and exorcism is not to be missed. The healing and exorcism provide tangible evidence of the reality of the proclamation that the kingdom of God (i.e., the rule of God) is truly present. If the rule of God is present, then the rule of Satan will be in retreat. The healings that will be performed anticipate the report that will be sent to the imprisoned John the Baptist in Matt 11:2–6 (see the commentary there).

---

[280] S. Brown, "The Matthean Community and the Gentile Mission," *NovT* 22 (1980): 193–221.

[281] M. D. Hooker, "Uncomfortable Words: X. The Prohibition of Foreign Missions (Mt 10.5–6)," *ExpT* 82 (1971): 361–65.

Jesus instructs his apostles to refuse payment: "You received without payment; give without payment. Take no gold, or silver, or copper in your belts, no bag for your journey, or two tunics, or sandals, or a staff; for laborers deserve their food" (**vv. 8b–10**). The apostles are not to reap any financial rewards. The powers they have to impart were freely given to them; they may not give them in turn to others for "gold, or silver, or copper" (i.e., monetary values in descending order). According to Sextus, *Sentences* 242: "What you freely receive from God, freely give." In rabbinic literature, we have: "Just as you received it [Torah] without payment, so teach it without payment" (*b. Bekorot* 29a; *Derek 'Erets Zuta* 2.4).

Jesus also commands his disciples to take "no bag for your journey, or two tunics, or sandals, or a staff." It has been fashionable in recent years to compare Jesus with the Cynics of late antiquity. Although at points Jesus' teaching and lifestyle resemble those of the Cynics (in that both eschew materialism, vanity, and power, instead urging trust in God, a simple lifestyle, generosity, and forgiveness), there are profound differences. Jesus believed in God as a loving Father who cares about his children; Cynics held to no such views. Jesus believed in the restoration and renewal of Israel; Cynics entertained no such ideas, instead believing that such hopes were futile and misguided. On a cruder level, but one that is quite revealing, Cynics were unkempt and coarse, sometimes relieving themselves in public places. (It was not without cause that they were called "Cynics," from the Greek adjective *kynikos*, meaning "doglike.") Such behavior would have been viewed as shocking and totally unacceptable. The criticism directed against Jesus never implied that Jesus was personally coarse or ill-mannered. He was criticized for associating with "sinners," but his purpose was redemptive.

A telling factor against comparing Jesus with the Cynics is that there is no evidence of a Cynic presence in early first-century Galilee or Judea. Indeed, nearby Sepphoris was thoroughly Jewish in culture in the pre-70 period (as recent archaeology has shown). It is highly improbable that this city supported a Cynic presence that might have influenced Jesus in a significant way.[282]

This brings us back to Jesus' command not to take a "bag" (*pera*) or a "staff." These two items, along with a coarse cloak, were the emblems of the Cynic. If Jesus had Cynic leanings, then why did he forbid his disciples to travel in the Cynic fashion? Crates the Cynic tells his students: "do not fear the name [Cynic], nor for this reason shun the cloak and bag [*pera*], which are the weapons of the gods. For they are quickly displayed by those who are honored for their character ..." (*Epistles* 16). Diogenes the Cynic pleads with his worried and disappointed father: "Do not be upset, Father, that I am called a dog (i.e., "Cynic") and put on a double, coarse cloak, carry a bag [*pera*] over my shoulders, and have a staff in my hand ..." (*Epistles* 7).

---

[282]   See the brief summary of the evidence in C. S. Keener, *A Commentary on the Gospel of Matthew* (Grand Rapids, MI: Eerdmans, 1999), 317; R. T. France, *The Gospel of Matthew* (2007), 384–85.

Diogenes also writes to Antipater: "I am doing nothing unusual in wearing a double, ragged cloak and carrying a bag [*pera*] …" (*Epistles* 15).[283] Given the importance of the bag and staff, it is odd – if Jesus were really a Cynic – that the disciples are not to take them on their journey.[284]

Matthew quotes Jesus as instructing his apostles, "Whatever town or village you enter, find out who in it is worthy, and stay there until you leave" (**v. 11**). The NRSV's translation "town or village" (Greek: *polis e kome*) is appropriate. The Greek *polis* can be translated as "city," but the apostles of Jesus entered no city that we know of. Only two in their general vicinity qualified as true cities: Tiberias, on the Sea of Galilee (a few miles southwest of Capernaum), and Sepphoris, four miles north of Nazareth. Yet there is no evidence that Jesus or his disciples ever entered these cities. The Greek *kome*, meaning "village," is the correct word and applies to most places in Galilee. The word occurs more than two dozen times in the Gospels and Acts. Jesus tells his disciples to stay in the home of someone "worthy"; that is, receptive to their message. The disciples are not to move from house to house in a given village, skimming the cream as it were. (On this point, see *Did.* 11:4–5, "if he stays three days, he is a false prophet," meaning a freeloader. Paul was sensitive with regard to this topic; see 1 Cor 4:12; Eph 4:28; 1 Thess 4:11.)

"As you enter the house, greet it. If the house is worthy, let your peace come upon it; but if it is not worthy, let your peace return to you" (**vv. 12–13**) probably refers to a blessing that in some sense brings peace. But if the house is not worthy (the people in the house is meant, of course), then the peace of Jesus, mediated through his apostles, will not remain with it.

Jesus continues, "If anyone will not welcome you or listen to your words, shake off the dust from your feet as you leave that house or town. Truly I tell you, it will be more tolerable for the land of Sodom and Gomorrah on the day of judgment than for that town" (**vv. 14–15**). If the message of Jesus is rejected, then those who rejected it are rejected. Jews shook the dust off their shoes after passing through Gentile territory (cf. *m. Tohor.* 4:5; *b. Sanh.* 12a). It is probable then that in shaking off the dust from their feet the apostles are suggesting that the Israelites of a given village are no better than Gentiles (as implied in Matt 5:47; 6:7, 32).[285]

---

[283]   The translations are based on A. J. Malherbe, *The Cynic Epistles* (SBLSBS 12; Missoula, MT: Scholars Press, 1977).

[284]   For criticism of the hypothesis that Jesus and his disciples were Cynics or similar to Cynics, see P. R. Eddy, "Jesus as Diogenes? Reflections on the Cynic Jesus Thesis," *JBL* 115 (1996): 449–69; D. E. Aune, "Jesus and Cynics in First-Century Palestine: Some Critical Considerations," in J. H. Charlesworth and L. L. Johns (eds.), *Hillel and Jesus: Comparisons of Two Major Religious Leaders* (Minneapolis: Fortress, 1997), 176–92; H. D. Betz, "Jesus and the Cynics: Survey and Analysis of a Hypothesis," *JR* 74 (1994): 453–75, reprinted in H. D. Betz, *Antike und Christentum: Gesammelte Aufsätze IV* (Tübingen: Mohr-Siebeck, 1998), 32–56.

[285]   G. B. Caird, "Uncomfortable Words: II. 'Shake off the dust from your feet,'" *ExpT* 81 (1969): 40–43.

More worrisome is the warning that the village or town that rejects the saving message of Jesus faces a fate worse than what befell the notorious cities of Sodom and Gomorrah. Sodom and Gomorrah became the archetypes of wickedness and fearful judgment: "Now the people of Sodom were wicked, great sinners against the Lord" (Gen 13:13; cf. 18:20). God "rained on Sodom and Gomorrah sulfur and fire … out of heaven" (Gen 19:24), which from a distance looked "like the smoke of a furnace" (Gen 19:28). Years later, the land of Sodom and Gomorrah is described as "burned out by sulfur and salt, nothing planted, nothing sprouting, unable to support any vegetation" (Deut 29:23). So terrible was the judgment on these two cities that their names became a byword for sin and/or destruction in Scripture (e.g., Deut 32:32; Isa 1:9–10; 3:9; 13:19; Jer 23:14; 49:18; 50:40; Amos 4:11; Zeph 2:9) and in later writings (e.g., *Jub.* 13:17; *Martyrdom of Isaiah* 3:10; *T. Levi* 14:6; *T. Naphtali* 3:4; *T. Asher* 7:1; *T. Benj.* 9:1). The judgment that befell the cities of Sodom and Gomorrah was considered the worst in history; Jesus has declared that an even heavier judgment will befall the cities that reject the message of the kingdom of God.

MATTHEW 10:16–23 – COMING PERSECUTION

10:16: "See, I am sending you out like sheep into the midst of wolves; so be wise as serpents and innocent as doves.

10:17: Beware of them, for they will hand you over to councils and flog you in their synagogues;

10:18: and you will be dragged before governors and kings because of me, as a testimony to them and the Gentiles.

10:19: When they hand you over, do not worry about how you are to speak or what you are to say; for what you are to say will be given to you at that time;

10:20: for it is not you who speak, but the Spirit of your Father speaking through you.

10:21: Brother will betray brother to death, and a father his child, and children will rise against parents and have them put to death;

10:22: and you will be hated by all because of my name. But the one who endures to the end will be saved.

10:23: When they persecute you in one town, flee to the next; for truly I tell you, you will not have gone through all the towns of Israel before the Son of Man comes."

The first part of the missionary discourse is comprised of the appointment of the twelve (Matt 10:1–4) and instructions concerning what to preach and what to do and not do (Matt 10:5–15). In the next section of the discourse, the perspective changes. Whereas in v. 5 the disciples were to avoid contact with Gentiles, now the disciples are told that they will in fact be brought before Gentiles and foreign rulers (vv. 17–18). This suggests that the second section of the discourse originally applied to the post-Easter setting in the life of the church, not to a time in the ministry of Jesus.[286] Matthew has pulled together these diverse materials because they focus on the task of evangelism, whether in the time of Jesus' ministry or in the time of the church entrusted with the Great Commission (Matt 28:18–20).[287] For more on the composition and meaning of the discourse, see the commentary on Matt 10:5–15.

Jesus warns his disciples: "I am sending you out like sheep into the midst of wolves" (**v. 16a**). Sometimes God's people are likened to sheep, who face the threat of being attacked by "wolves" or other vicious animals (e.g., *1 Enoch* 89:42, 46; cf. Jer 23:1; 50:17; Ezek 34:8, 10, 22). Therefore, the disciples are to "be wise as serpents and innocent as doves" (**v. 16b**). The idea that serpents are "wise" (or "shrewd" or "prudent"; Greek *phronimos*) reaches back to the very beginnings of the biblical story: "Now the serpent was more crafty [LXX: shrewder] than any other wild animal" (Gen 3:1). The idea that doves are "innocent" is much harder to trace. However, a later rabbinic saying that offers a very close parallel to Jesus' saying may also explain the origin of the idea. According to Rabbi Judah, God has this to say about Israel: "With me they are innocent as doves, but with the nations they are cunning as serpents" (*Song Rab.* 2:14 §1). This saying is based on the observation that it is written in Scripture that "Ephraim has become like a dove, silly and without sense" (Hos 7:11). This "silly dove" (Hebrew: "simple dove"; Greek: "dove without understanding") stands in contrast to the patriarch Dan, who "shall be a snake by the roadside" (Gen 49:17). The Rabbis inferred from these contrasting comparisons that when it came to its dealings with God, Israel was "innocent" (i.e., open, honest, and simple), like the dove, but when it came to dealings with the nations (or Gentiles), Israel was "cunning," like the serpent. What we have in Jesus' words is the earliest attestation of this saying. But the exegetical basis for this saying is not attested until its appearance in a much later rabbinic tradition.

The admonition to be wise is consistent with *T. Naphtali* 8:10, in which the dying patriarch tells his descendants to "be wise in the Lord and discerning." It may also be relevant that according to the Mishnah most animals render water unclean. The snake (or serpent) renders water unclean "because it vomits," but the dove does not render water unclean because it sucks water up and does not drool into the water (*m. Para* 9:3). Finally, we may also recall that Jesus addressed his critics, the scribes and Pharisees, as "serpents" (Matt 23:33; earlier, in Matt 3:7, John the Baptist had

---

[286]   On this transition, see M. Konradt, "Die Sendung zu Israel und zu den Völkern im Matthäusevangelium im Lichte seiner narrativen Christologie," *ZTK* 101 (2004): 397–425. Konradt rightly concludes that the eventual inclusion of Gentiles in the mission envisioned by Matthew should not be seen as the result of Jewish rejection of the gospel.

[287]   See E. C. Park, *The Mission Discourse in Matthew's Interpretation* (WUNT 2, no. 81; Tübingen: Mohr Siebeck, 1995).

called the Pharisees and Sadducees a "brood of vipers"). Jesus' saying may be ech-oed in Paul's admonition to the Roman Christians: "I want you to be wise in what is good, and guileless [or innocent] in what is evil" (Rom 16:19).

Jesus warns his disciples that the wolves "will hand you over to councils and flog you in their synagogues" (**v. 17**). These very things happen to the apostles in the Book of Acts; for example, Peter and the apostles are hauled before the Sanhedrin and ordered to desist (Acts 4:1–22; 5:27–39), Peter is imprisoned (Acts 5:17–26), the apostles are beaten (Acts 5:40), Stephen is martyred (Acts 7:54–60), Paul and Silas are beaten by city magistrates (Acts 16:19–23) and are imprisoned (Acts 16:24), Paul is seized in the temple precincts and then beaten (Acts 21:30–32), and Paul is left to languish in prison (Acts 24:27).

Jesus warns and assures them: "you will be dragged before governors and kings because of me, as a testimony to them and the Gentiles … do not worry about how you are to speak or what you are to say; for what you are to say will be given to you at that time" (**vv. 18–19**). This promise is also fulfilled, as seen in the stories in the Book of Acts: Paul speaks to a Roman tribune in his defense (Acts 21:37–22.29), speaks to the Jewish council (or Sanhedrin) in his defense (Acts 23:1–10), defends himself before the Roman governor Felix (Acts 24:10–21) and his successor Festus (Acts 25:8–12), and defends himself before Festus and the Jewish royals Agrippa and Berenice (Acts 26:1–29). The idea that God will supply his faithful with the right words is part of the wisdom tradition; for example, the wise man Ahiqar assures us, "If he is beloved of the gods they will give him something worthwhile to say" (*Ahiqar* 32).

The disciples need not worry about what they need to say because it is "the Spirit of your Father speaking through you" (**v. 20**). Peter is filled with the Holy Spirit and then is enabled to speak to the "Rulers of the people and elders …" (Acts 4:8). Stephen is filled with the Holy Spirit and is able to defend himself eloquently and die with grace (Acts 7:55). On the phrase "speaking through you," see LXX 1 Kings 22:24, where Zedekiah asks rival prophet Micaiah, "What kind of Spirit of the Lord has spoken in you?"

The response to the message of the good news will divide families: "Brother will betray brother to death, and a father his child, and children will rise against par-ents and have them put to death" (**v. 21**). This is a grim allusion to Mic 7:6, "for the son treats the father with contempt, the daughter rises up against her mother, the daughter-in-law against her mother-in-law; your enemies are members of your own household." This verse is quoted in a section of the Mishnah (ca. 220 A.D.) that describes the woes that take place shortly before the Messiah comes (*m. Sota* 9:15; *b. Sota* 49b).

What Jesus foretells is grim: "you will be hated by all because of my name. But the one who endures to the end will be saved" (**v. 22**), meaning the one who endures the suffering "to the end" of the period of persecution and tribulation, a period that will end when the Son of Man comes (v. 23). On enduring persecution, see *4 Macc*

1:11: "All people, even their torturers, marveled at their courage and endurance, and they became the cause of the downfall of tyranny over their nation. By their endurance they conquered the tyrant, and thus their native land was purified through them."

Jesus lends urgency to his instruction; there is no time to waste: "When they persecute you in one town, flee to the next; for truly I tell you, you will not have gone through all the towns of Israel before the Son of Man comes" (**v. 23**). This is one of the most debated verses in the Gospel of Matthew.[288] Matthew views the mission to Israel as still incomplete. The tour of Israel that Jesus initiated was but the beginning of messianic outreach to Israel and the nations (cf. Matt 28:18–20). Neither the original disciples nor their successors will complete the task of evangelization before the Son of Man comes and, with him, the fullness of the kingdom of God. On "Son of Man," see the commentary on Matt 9:6.

MATTHEW 10:24–25 – LIKE TEACHER, LIKE DISCIPLE

10:24: "A disciple is not above the teacher, nor a slave above the master;

10:25: it is enough for the disciple to be like the teacher, and the slave like the master. If they have called the master of the house Beelzebul, how much more will they malign those of his household!"

*T*his brief unit constitutes a transition between the warnings of persecution in Matt 10:16–23 and its consolations in Matt 10:26–33. The transition continues the theme of persecution (they will call you, the members of the master's household, an even worse name than Beelzebul) but anticipates the coming consolation, for to be persecuted in this manner is to be treated as Jesus himself was. To be treated as Jesus was is to be a member "of his household."

Jesus' teaching that "A disciple is not above the teacher, nor a slave above the master; it is enough for the disciple to be like the teacher, and the slave like the master" (**vv. 24–25a**) is similar to sayings in the fourth Gospel: "Very truly, I tell you, servants are not greater than their master, nor are messengers greater than the one

---

[288] For a sample of scholarly discussion, see R. Clark, "Eschatology and Matthew 10:23," *RestQ* 7 (1963): 73–81; C. H. Giblin, "Theological Perspective and Matthew 10:23," *TS* 29 (1968): 637–61; M. E. Boring, "Christian Prophecy and Matthew 10.23 – A Test Case," *SBL 1976 Seminar Papers* (1976): 127–33; L. Sabourin, "'You Will Not Have Gone through all the Towns of Israel, before the Son of Man Comes' (Mt 10:23b)," *BTB* 7 (1977): 5–11; J. M. McDermott, "Mt 10:23 in Context," *BZ* 28 (1984): 230–40; S. McKnight, "Jesus and the End-Time: Matthew 10:23," *SBL 1986 Seminar Papers* (1986): 501–20; A. J. M. Wedderburn, "Matthew 10,23b and the Eschatology of Jesus," in M. Becker and W. Fenske (eds.), *Das Ende der Tage und die Gegenwart des Heils: Begegnungen mit dem Neuen Testament und seiner Umwelt. Festschrift für Heinz-Wolfgang Kuhn zum 65. Geburtstag* (AGJU 44; Leiden: Brill, 1999), 165–82. See the concise summary of interpretive options in D. A. Hagner, *Matthew* (1993–1995), 1:278–80.

who sent them" (John 13:16); "'Servants are not greater than their master.' If they persecuted me, they will persecute you; if they kept my word, they will keep yours also" (John 15:20). The saying in Matthew seems to have been drawn from Q, the source also used by Luke: "A disciple is not above the teacher, but everyone who is fully qualified will be like the teacher" (Luke 6:40).

One may compare the idea of "a slave above his master" to what Philo says: "To be the slave of God is the highest boast of man, a treasure more precious not only than freedom, but than wealth and power and all that mortals most cherish" (*On the Cherubim* 107). The saying "It is enough for the disciple to be like the teacher" finds a close parallel in early rabbinic literature: "It is enough for a slave that he be like his master" (*Sipra Lev.* §251 [on Lev 25:18–24]; cf. *b. Ber.* 58b; *Aggadat Bereshit* 16.2, "It is enough for a slave to be equal to his owner").

After all, Jesus reasons, "If they have called the master of the house Beelzebul, how much more will they malign those of his household!" (**v. 25b**). In the first century A.D. pseudepigraphon called the *Testament of Solomon*, Israel's famous king overpowers demons, including Beezebul (or Beelzeboul). Solomon demands the demon's identity, and the demon replies, "I am Beelzeboul, the ruler of the demons." Defeated by Solomon and his powerful ring, Beelzeboul agrees to bring before the king "all the unclean spirits bound" (*T. Sol.* 3:6). For more on "Beelzebul," see the commentary on Matt 12:22–37.

MATTHEW 10:26–31 – DO NOT FEAR

10:26: "So have no fear of them; for nothing is covered up that will not be uncovered, and nothing secret that will not become known.

10:27: What I say to you in the dark, tell in the light; and what you hear whispered, proclaim from the housetops.

10:28: Do not fear those who kill the body but cannot kill the soul; rather fear him who can destroy both soul and body in hell.

10:29: Are not two sparrows sold for a penny? Yet not one of them will fall to the ground apart from your Father.

10:30: And even the hairs of your head are all counted.

10:31: So do not be afraid; you are of more value than many sparrows."

Jesus assures his disciples that in due course all will be revealed, all will be made known. In the meantime, his disciples must remain faithful, not fearing those who can do physical harm (alluding to the prophesied persecutions in Matt 10:16–25). Rather, the disciples should fear God, who is the ultimate judge. With this in mind, the trials and tribulations experienced in this life are not as overwhelming. The evangelist has drawn upon Q (cf. Luke 12:1–7), though the saying in v. 26 parallels Mark 4:22.

Jesus' command, "So have no fear of them" (**v. 26a**) (Greek: *me phobethete autous*, literally "do not fear them"), is found verbatim in LXX Num 14:9: "But do not depart from the Lord; and do not fear the people of the land, for they shall be our prey. Their time has been removed from them, and the Lord is among us; do not fear them (*me phobethete autous*)." This command, in the same words, occurs several times in the apocryphal Letter of Jeremiah [= Bar 6], in which the prophet impresses upon Israel: "Since you know by these things that they are not gods, do not fear them [*me phobethete autous*]" (Ep Jer 29 [= Bar 6:29]; cf. vv. 65 and 69).

The verse continues, "For nothing is covered up that will not be uncovered, and nothing secret that will not become known" (**v. 26b**). God "will visit in truth all things by means of all their hidden works. And He will assuredly examine the secret thoughts, and that which is laid up in the secret chambers of all the members of man, and will make [them] manifest in the presence of all with reproof" (2 *Bar* 83:2–3; cf. 2 Esd 16:63–66). Humans may try to suppress the truth, even kill the messengers, but in the end God will reveal all. Therefore, the disciples are to proclaim publicly what they have been told in private (**v. 27**). On privacy in Matthew, see Matt 17:19 and 24:3.

Jesus continues his consolation: "Do not fear [*me phobeisthai*] those who kill [*apokteinein*] the body but cannot kill the soul" (**v. 28a**). Said the righteous in the face of tyranny: "Let us not fear [*me phobeisthai*] him who thinks he is killing [*apokteinein*] us" (4 *Macc* 13:14). On those who "kill" [*apokteinein*] the "body"[*soma*], see Tob 1:8, "if Sennacherib the king killed [*apokteinein*] any who came fleeing from Judea, I buried them secretly. For in his anger he killed many. When the bodies [*somata*] were sought by the king, they were not found." On "killing" [*apokteinein*] the "soul" [*psuche*], see Ezekiel 13, where God expresses anger against his corrupt and perverted people, who "kill souls" (Greek: *apokteinein psuchas*) of people who should not be put to death but keep alive those who should be executed (LXX Ezek 13:19); see also *T. Job* 20:3; *Martyrdom of Isaiah* 5:10.

Cynics, Stoics, and others recommended that humans not fear death: "If the body weakens and dies, the soul will enter heaven, for it is immortal" (Ps.-Heraclitus 5.2); "Untroubled by fears, unsullied by desires, we shall not be afraid of death, nor of the gods" (Seneca, *Moral Epistles* 75.16); "As a lion has power over the body of a sage, so too does a tyrant, but only over the body" (Sextus, *Sentences* 363).

Jesus continues, "Rather fear him who can destroy both soul and body in hell" (**v. 28b**). What is translated as "hell" is *gehenna*, an Aramaic loanword that is found in the Greek New Testament a dozen times, all instances but one in the Synoptic Gospels (the other is in James 3:6).[289] For examples in Matthew, see Matt 5:22, 29, 30; 18:9; 32:15, 33.

---

[289]   I. H. Marshall, "Uncomfortable Words: VI. 'Fear Him Who Can Destroy Both Soul and Body in Hell' (Mt 10,28 RSV)," *ExpT* 81 (1970): 276–80; C. Milikowsky, "Which Gehenna? Retribution and Eschatology in the Synoptic Gospels and in Early Jewish Texts," *NTS* 34 (1988): 238–49.

Compare Luke 12:6 "Are not five sparrows sold for two cents?" with Matthew's "Are not two sparrows sold for a penny?" (**v. 29a**). The difference is slight but may actually reflect the going rates (i.e., one cent will buy two sparrows but two cents will buy five). The sparrow was the poor man's food, just as the pigeon was the poor man's offering. The point of Jesus' question will become clear in v. 31.

The statement "Yet not one of them will fall to the ground apart from your Father" (**v. 29b**) is proverbial: "Even a bird is not caught without the permission of Heaven; how much more then the soul of a human being" (*Gen. Rab.* 79.6 [on Gen 33:18]). See also Amos 3:5, "Does a bird fall into a snare on the earth, when there is no trap for it? Does a snare spring up from the ground, when it has taken nothing?"[290]

"And even the hairs of your head are all counted" (**v. 30**) reflects the fact that knowing the number of hairs on a human's head testifies to God's omniscience and providence, a point driven home in a pseudepigraphical text: "Since I created everything, how many people have been born, and how many have died and how many shall die and how many hairs do they have? Tell me, Sedrach, since the heaven and the earth have been created, how many trees have been made ... ?" (*Apoc. of Sedrach* 8:6–7).

"So do not be afraid; you are of more value than many sparrows" (**v. 31**) is another example of the argument from the minor to the major. If God is aware of the fate of a sparrow, whose worth is but half a penny, and if God knows how many hairs one has on one's head, then the disciples of Jesus should not be afraid – after all, they are worth more than many sparrows! See also Ps 84:3: "Even the sparrow finds a home, and the swallow a nest for herself, where she may lay her young...."[291]

MATTHEW 10:32–33 – CONFESSING OR DENYING

10:32: "Everyone therefore who acknowledges me before others, I also will acknowledge before my Father in heaven;

10:33: but whoever denies me before others, I also will deny before my Father in heaven."

*T*he saying of confessing or denying Matt 10:32–33 derives from Q (cf. Luke 12:8–9), though we also find a vague parallel in Mark 8:38 and Luke 9:26. (See also 2 *Clem* 3:2.) The order of Q is being followed here, which serves Matthew's purpose well. The saying provides motivation for the disciples in light of what has been said in Matt 10:26–31.[292]

---

[290]   J. G. Cook, "The Sparrow's Fall in Mt 10.29b," *ZNW* 79 (1988): 138–44.

[291]   D. C. Allison, Jr., "The Hairs of Your Head Are All Numbered," *ExpT* 101 (1990): 334–36; J. D. M. Derrett, "Light on Sparrows and Hairs (Mt 10,29–31)," *Estudios bíblicos* 55 (1997): 341–53.

[292]   H. J. de Jonge, "The Sayings on Confessing and Denying Jesus in Q 12:8–9 and Mark 8:38," in W. L. Petersen et al. (eds.), *Sayings of Jesus: Canonical and Non-Canonical. Essays in Honour of Tjitze Baarda* (NovTSup 89; Leiden: Brill, 1997), 105–21.

When Jesus says "Everyone therefore who acknowledges me before others, I also will acknowledge before my Father in heaven; but whoever denies me before others, I also will deny before my Father in heaven" (**v. 32–33**), one hears an echo of 1 Sam 2:30, "the Lord declares: 'Far be it from me; for those who honor me I will honor, and those who despise me shall be treated with contempt.'" What we have here is another example of the principle of *jus talionis* ("justice of kind"), as in "whatever you measure out to others will be measured out to you" (cf. Matt 7:2 = Luke 6:38; Mark 4:24). The Rabbis were guided by the same principle (*m. Sota* 1:7; *Frag. Tg.* Gen 38:26).

What Jesus has affirmed is a bargain for humans, who only have to confess Jesus before other humans. In return, Jesus will confess the faithful before God the Father. The same idea is expressed in the parallel found in Mark 8:38: "Those who are ashamed of me and of my words in this adulterous and sinful generation, of them the Son of Man will also be ashamed when he comes in the glory of his Father with the holy angels."

MATTHEW 10:34–39 – DISCIPLESHIP AND DIVISION

10:34: "Do not think that I have come to bring peace to the earth; I have not come to bring peace, but a sword.

10:35: For I have come to set a man against his father, and a daughter against her mother, and a daughter-in-law against her mother-in-law;

10:36: and one's foes will be members of one's own household.

10:37: Whoever loves father or mother more than me is not worthy of me; and whoever loves son or daughter more than me is not worthy of me;

10:38: and whoever does not take up the cross and follow me is not worthy of me.

10:39: Those who find their life will lose it, and those who lose their life for my sake will find it."

*T*he missionary discourse intensifies with warnings of serious and personal divisions to come. Although v. 39 is to some extent rhetorical, there was the very real danger of suffering death in following Jesus.

When Jesus says "Do not think that I have come to bring peace to the earth; I have not come to bring peace, but a sword" (**v. 34**), "Do not think" recalls his thesis statement in the Sermon on the Mount: "Do not think that I have come to abolish the law or the prophets; I have come not to abolish but to fulfill" (Matt 5:17). Jesus has "not come to bring peace"; he has instead brought a "sword." Jesus' language is hyperbolic, of course. Earlier in the missionary discourse, Jesus commands his disciples to extend greetings of peace: "If the house is worthy, let your peace come upon it" (Matt 10:13). What Jesus has in mind is the actual impact his message will have: it will be divisive. This was very true in the first several decades of the young church, for in its infancy the church was made up entirely of Jewish people. Yet most religious leaders opposed the faith, especially as it reached out to Gentiles and did not require the adoption of Jewish law. The result was division in Jewish families and in synagogues. Jesus' message brings with it no compromise. His aim is not to please but rather to proclaim the truth and fulfill his Father's will. Sometimes the sword is a symbol of division, as in Heb 4:12: "Indeed, the word of God is living and active, sharper than any two-edged sword, piercing until it divides soul from spirit...."[293]

"For I have come to set a man against his father, and a daughter against her mother, and a daughter-in-law against her mother-in-law; and one's foes will be members of one's own household" (**vv. 35–36**) represents the second time in Matthew's missionary discourse that an allusion has been made to Mic 7:6. The first allusion is found in Matt 10:21 and is derived from Mark 13:12. The second example, here in v. 35, is probably derived from Q (cf. Luke 12:53). For Jewish background (especially *m. Sota* 9:15), see the commentary on Matt 10:21.

Jesus' statement that "Whoever loves father or mother more than me is not worthy of me" (**v. 37**) elaborates on vv. 34–36. One who is not willing to lose the love of a family member, even that of a father or mother, for the sake of Jesus is not worthy of him.

A similar point is made when Jesus says "And whoever does not take up the cross and follow me is not worthy of me" (**v. 38**). With v. 28 in mind, if the disciples fear people (who can only kill the body) more than they fear God (who can condemn the soul to Gehenna), then they are not worthy of Jesus.

Jesus' declaration that "Those who find their life will lose it, and those who lose their life for my sake will find it" (**v. 39**) logically follows the teaching of vv. 37–38. Those who think they have "found their life" by ignoring God's claim will in fact lose it. But those who "lose their life" – whether figuratively or literally – for Jesus will find it. This is a variant form of a saying that appears in identical form in Matt 16:25 ("those who want to save their life will lose it ..."), Mark 8:35, and Luke 9:24, and in slightly altered form in Luke 17:33 ("Those who try to make their life secure will lose it, but those who lose their life will keep [or save; Greek: *sozein*] it"). What we have here is an instance of overlap between the Markan tradition and the tradition preserved in Q.

[293] R. C. Tannehill, *The Sword of His Mouth* (Philadelphia: Fortress, 1975), 140–47; O. L. Cope, *Matthew: A Scribe Trained for the Kingdom of Heaven* (CBQMS 5; Washington, DC: Catholic Biblical Association, 1976), 77–81; M. Black, "Not Peace but a Sword," in E. Bammel and C. F. D. Moule (eds.), *Jesus and the Politics of His Day* (Cambridge: Cambridge University Press, 1984), 287–94; D. C. Sim, "The Sword Motif in Matthew 10:34," *Hervormde Teologiese Studies* 56 (2000): 84–104.

Jesus' saying is proverbial, as is seen in Jewish sources: "He [Alexander the Great] asked them [the Jewish elders], 'What shall a man do to live?' They replied, 'Let him kill [i.e., deny] himself.' [He asked,] 'What should a man do to kill himself?' They replied, 'Let him keep himself alive'" (*b. Tamid* 32a); "If it be your will that you should not die, die that you may not die. If it be your will that you should live, live not, so that you may live. It is better for you to die in this world against your will than to die in the world to come" (*'Abot deRabbi Natan* B §32 [attributed to Judah the Prince]). It also appears in Greco-Roman sources: "Socrates does not save [*sozein*] his life with dishonor … this man cannot be saved by dishonor, but by dying [*apothneskein*] he is saved, not in fleeing" (Epictetus 4.1.164–165).[294]

MATTHEW 10:40–11:1 – RECEIVING JESUS

10:40: "Whoever welcomes you welcomes me, and whoever welcomes me welcomes the one who sent me.

10:41: Whoever welcomes a prophet in the name of a prophet will receive a prophet's reward; and whoever welcomes a righteous person in the name of a righteous person will receive the reward of the righteous;

10:42: and whoever gives even a cup of cold water to one of these little ones in the name of a disciple – truly I tell you, none of these will lose their reward."

11:1: Now when Jesus had finished instructing his twelve disciples, he went on from there to teach and proclaim his message in their cities.

Jesus concludes his missionary discourse with sayings about rewards for those who receive and treat well his disciples and apostles who go forth and proclaim the gospel. Anyone who extends the least kindness to one of Jesus' own will not "lose their reward."

Compare Matthew's "Whoever welcomes you welcomes me" (**v. 40a**) with Luke 10:16, "Whoever listens to you listens to me, and whoever rejects you rejects me, and whoever rejects me rejects the one who sent me." This is apostolic or ambassadorial language. The word "apostle" is from the Greek and means one who is sent (from the verb *apostellein*, "to send"). In Hebrew literature, the apostle is called a *shaliah*, also meaning one who is "sent" (from *shalah*, "to send"). There are several passages that can be cited, such as Moses' response to God's summons: "You are the Lord of the world. Do you really wish that I be your apostle [*shaliah*]? Behold, I am not a man of words" (*Exod. Rab.* 3.14 [on Exod 4:10]). To receive the ambassador or the apostle is to receive the potentate that sent him; to reject the ambassador is to reject the one who sent him: "speaking against the shepherd of Israel [i.e., Moses]

---

294   For additional details, see U. Luz, *Matthew* (2001–2007), 2:113–16.

is like speaking against him who spoke and the world came into being" (*Mekilta* on Exod 14:31 [*Beshallah* §7]). This concept of rejecting an apostle is illustrated in a rabbinic parable: "The matter may be compared to the case of a mortal king who had a trustee of state. The citizens were speaking against him. The king said to them, 'You have not spoken against him but against me'" (*Sipre Num.* §103 [on Num 12:8]). Josephus narrates a violent story in which King Rehoboam's ambassador, sent to appease the ten northern tribes, which were on the verge of rebellion, is attacked and killed before he can deliver his master's speech: "Rehoboam, seeing this and imagining himself the target of the stones with which the crowd had killed his min-ister, was afraid that he might actually suffer this dreadful fate and immediately mounted his chariot and fled to Jerusalem" (*Ant.* 8.221).

Compare Matthew's "And whoever welcomes me welcomes the one who sent me" (**v. 40b**) with John 13:20, "Truly, truly, I say to you, he who receives whomever I send receives Me; and he who receives Me receives Him who sent Me." Another rabbinic parallel should be noted: "'… and Aaron came with all the elders of Israel to eat a meal with Moses' father-in-law before God' [Exod 18:12]. Why does it say, 'before God'? It is to teach that when one welcomes his fellow, it is considered as if he had welcomed the Divine Presence (i.e., God Himself)" (*Mekilta* on Exod. 18:12 [*Amalek* §3]). Again, this is ambassadorial language.

The reward envisioned in "Whoever welcomes a prophet in the name of a prophet will receive a prophet's reward" (**v. 41a**) could be eschatological; that is, if one receives the prophet (i.e., receives his message), one will receive his reward (i.e., the reward the prophet has promised), which in the context of Jesus' message is entry into the kingdom of God.[295] It is also possible that the reward one receives for receiving the prophet is the benefit of hearing his words, which are from God Himself.

"And whoever welcomes a righteous person in the name of a righteous person will receive the reward of the righteous" (**v. 41b**), the second saying of the couplet that makes up v. 41, matches the first, except that the second speaks of a "righteous person" rather than a prophet. Because we find righteous ones sometimes linked with prophets, the former may be synonymous with the latter. For example, in Matt 13:17, Jesus says, "Truly I tell you, many prophets and righteous people longed to see what you see, but did not see it …," or in Matt 23:29, "Woe to you, scribes and Pharisees, hypocrites! For you build the tombs of the prophets and decorate the graves of the righteous."[296] The juxtaposition of prophets and righteous is found in rabbinic literature as well: "God said, 'My children have been guided through the world by the righteous and the prophets like a swarm of bees'" (*Deut. Rab.* 1.6 [on Deut 1:1]). It also appears in the Dead Sea Scrolls: "He must not be executed, for he is a righteous man, he is a [trus]tworthy prophet" (4Q375 frag. 1, col. i, lines 6–7).

---

[295]   G. de Ru, "The Conception of Reward in the Teaching of Jesus," *NovT* 8 (1966): 202–22.
[296]   D. Hill, "Δίκαιοι as a Quasi-technical Term," *NTS* 11 (1965): 296–302.

"And whoever gives even a cup of cold water to one of these little ones in the name of a disciple – truly I tell you, none of these will lose their reward" (**v. 42**) reflects the fact that a "cup of cold water" was considered a small gift in the Greco-Roman world. The Roman emperor Claudius (ruled 41–54 A.D.) "gave as one of his reasons for supporting a candidate for the quaetorship, that the man's father had once given him cold water when he was ill and in need" (Suetonius, *Claudius* 40.2). Suetonius cites the incident not in praise of the late emperor but as an example of "heedlessness in word and act" (*Claudius* 40.1). Claudius' appreciation for this small gift runs parallel to Jesus' sentiment.

On "little ones," see Matt 18:6, "If any of you put a stumbling block before one of these little ones who believe in me, it would be better for you if a great millstone were fastened around your neck and you were drowned in the depth of the sea"; Matt 18:10, "Take care that you do not despise one of these little ones; for, I tell you, in heaven their angels continually see the face of my Father in heaven"; and Matt 18:14, "So it is not the will of your Father in heaven that one of these little ones should be lost."[297]

The prophet Jeremiah laments: "No one shall break bread for the mourner, to offer comfort for the dead; nor shall anyone give them the cup of consolation to drink for their fathers or their mothers" (Jer 16:7). See also *T. Isaac* 6:21 ("all who … showed mercy if only a cup of cold water"); *T. Jacob* 2:23 ("Blessed be the one who will perform acts of mercy … and will give someone a cup of water to drink"); and "He who gives a piece of bread to a righteous man, it is as though he has fulfilled the whole Law" (*Gen. Rab.* 58.8 [on Gen 23:17]).

With the verse "Now when Jesus had finished instructing his twelve disciples" (**11:1**), Matthew concludes Jesus' second major discourse as he did the first one (cf. Matt 7:28), with a phrase from the Pentateuch (e.g., Deut 32:45: "When Moses had finished reciting all these words"), thus giving a Mosaic ring to Jesus' teaching. See the commentary on Matt 7:28–29. The evangelist completes the transition to the next major section of his Gospel by saying that Jesus "went on from there to teach and proclaim his message in their cities." This Jesus will do in Chapters 11 and 12 before giving his third major discourse in Chapter 13.

MATTHEW 11:2–6 – JOHN'S QUESTION

11:2: When John heard in prison what the Messiah was doing, he sent word by his disciples

11:3: and said to him, "Are you the one who is to come, or are we to wait for another?"

11:4: Jesus answered them, "Go and tell John what you hear and see:

---

[297]   O. Michel, "'Diese Kleinen' – Eine Jüngerbezeichnung Jesu," *TSK* 108 (1938): 401–15.

11:5: the blind receive their sight, the lame walk, the lepers are cleansed, the deaf hear, the dead are raised, and the poor have good news brought to them.

11:6: And blessed is anyone who takes no offense at me."

*T*his is a remarkable story, not least because of its candor. The imprisoned John has come to doubt whether Jesus is truly the "one who is to come" (literally "Coming One"). This doubt argues against the view that the story may have been invented. Moreover, Jesus' indirect affirmation of his identity also tells against fabrication, for we would expect an invented story to have Jesus affirm more directly and emphatically his messianic identity. A close parallel appears in Luke 7:18–23. This material is derived from Q.

Matthew has placed this episode in a good location. Jesus has already announced the good news of God's rule, he has healed and has empowered his disciples to do likewise, and he has made twelve of his disciples apostles and has instructed them in matters related to proclaiming the good news. Accordingly, when John inquires about Jesus' identity and mission, Jesus can give a convincing answer.

A Closer Look: The Imprisoned John

According to Josephus (*Ant.* 18.118–19), the popular preacher and baptizer John had been imprisoned in Machaerus (on the eastern side of the Dead Sea) by Herod Antipas. During his imprisonment, he had heard of the ministry of his associate Jesus but evidently began to have doubts about him. Why was this? Perhaps the answer lies in Isaiah 61, to which Jesus will make appeal in his reply. According to Isa 61:1, the anointed of the Lord is "to proclaim liberty to captives, and freedom to prisoners" (see also Isa 42:7, "to bring out prisoners from the dungeon"). But John remains imprisoned, so is Jesus really the fulfillment of prophetic expectation? If Jesus really was the "Coming One," would he not liberate John? Where is the promised "vengeance" (against God's enemies) of which Isa 61:2 speaks?

The Synoptic Gospels also tell part of John's story (see Mark 6:14–29; Matt 14:1–12; Luke 9:7–9).

Matthew begins the episode, "When John heard in prison what the Messiah was doing ..." (**v. 2**). The Greek actually reads: "John having heard of the works of the Messiah" (*ta erga tou christou*). The Lukan parallel does not introduce the passage this way. The words "works of the Messiah" are from Matthew, but as the following parallel will show, the evangelist understands accurately the implications of both John's question and Jesus' interesting reply. "Messiah" translates as the Greek word "Christ" (*christos*), the Greek equivalent of the Hebrew *meshiah* ("anointed one").

In Matthew's account, John then asks: "Are you the one who is to come" (v. 3). The "one who is to come " or "Coming One" (Greek: *ho erchomenos*) alludes to several Old Testament passages: Ps 118:26, "the one who comes in the name of the Lord"; Zech 9:9, "your king comes [Greek: *erchei*] to you"; and Zech 14:5, "then the Lord my God will come [*hexei*]." Hope of the coming of the Messiah is expressed in the Dead Sea Scrolls: "until the Righteous Messiah, the Branch of David, has come" (4Q252 5:3, interpreting Gen 49:10 "until he comes" [RSV]).

Jesus reassures John by alluding to words and phrases from Isaiah (in v. 5): "the blind receive their sight" (Isa 29:18b; 35:5a; LXX 61:1), "the lame walk" (cf. Isa 35:6), "the deaf hear" (cf. Isa 29:18a; 35:5b; 42:18a), "the dead are raised" (cf. Isa 26:19), and "the poor have the gospel preached to them" (cf. Isa 61:1; LXX 29:19, "the poor shall rejoice"). Isaiah 61, a passage associated with the Jubilee promise of Lev 25:13 (and understood in an eschatological sense in 11QMelchizedek, where phrases from Lev 25:13 and Isa 61:1–3 are cited in clarification of one another[298]), probably played an important role in the fulfillment theology shared by John and Jesus. Thus, it would have been especially comforting to the imprisoned John to be assured that the promises of Isaiah were in the process of being fulfilled.

But who is this "one who is to come" who fulfills the prophecies of Isaiah? Is he the Messiah? Matthew thinks so, which is why he refers to the "works of the Messiah" (in v. 2). A scroll from Qumran suggests that the fulfiller of the prophecies of Isaiah is the Messiah: "[... For the hea]vens and the earth shall obey his Messiah.... He will honor the pious upon the th[ro]ne of his eternal kingdom, setting prisoners free, opening the eyes of the blind, raising up those bo[wed down].... For he shall heal the critically wounded, he shall revive the dead, he shall send the gospel to the poor" (4Q521 frags. 2 and 4, col. ii, lines 1, 7–8, 12). Here we have similar, in fact sometimes identical, allusions to the same words and phrases from Isaiah. However, in this context, these events are associated with "his" (i.e., God's) Messiah, whom heaven and earth will obey.

Because of the fragmentary condition of 4Q521, we are not sure who opens the eyes of the blind, revives the dead, and so forth. Perhaps it is God, or perhaps it is the Messiah himself. This point is not important, for even if these things do take place at the hands of the Messiah, all would understand that they take place through the power of God. Jesus takes the same view, declaring that he "cast[s] out demons by the finger [i.e., power or Spirit] of God" (Luke 11:20).

The linkage of the ministry of the Messiah (or Christ) with the miracles foretold in Isaiah is attested explicitly by Matthew, as we see in the way he introduces the passage: "When John heard in prison what the Messiah was doing" (v. 2). 4Q521 shows that Matthew's messianic contextualization of the passage is not unique to early Christianity but reflects a wider Jewish understanding and expectation.[299]

---

[298]   M. P. Miller, "The Function of Isa 61:1–2 in 11QMelchizedek," *JBL* 88 (1969): 467–69.

[299]   For a selection of studies that discuss 4Q521 and Matt 11:2–6, see J. J. Collins, "The Works of the Messiah," *DSD* 1 (1994): 98–112; M. Becker, "4Q521 und die Gesalbten," *RevQ* 18

It also shows that he rightly recognized the significance of John's question and Jesus' reply.

Jesus also says that the "lepers are cleansed" (v. 5). This idea finds no obvious counterpart in Isaiah. We do read of Elisha, the successor of the great Elijah, who · in 2 Kings 5:14 was able to cleanse Naaman of leprosy. This story probably contrib- ‿ uted to the expectation that in the messianic days the cleansing of leprosy would be among the various healing and restorative miracles that would take place. Recall Luke 4:16–30, where Jesus quotes Isa 61:1–2, declaring that it has been fulfilled and that his ministry may be illustrated by the example of Elishah, who healed Naaman the Syrian (cf. Luke 4:27).

However, the cleansing of lepers may be hinted at in Isaiah, at least as some read it in antiquity. Two verses in the Suffering Servant Song speak of the servant being "stricken" or receiving a stroke: "Surely he has borne our infirmities, and carried our diseases; yet we accounted him stricken [*nagua'*], struck down by God, and afflicted" (Isa 53.4); "By a perversion of justice he was taken away. Who could have imagined his future? For he was cut off from the land of the living, stricken [*nega'*] 𝕗 for the transgression of my people" (Isa 53:8). The words "stricken" (*nagua'* or *nega'*) are from the same root (*naga'*), which appears several times in Leviticus 13, a pas- sage that discusses the signs of leprosy and what to do about them (e.g., Lev 13:9, "a leprous disease [*nega' tzara'at*]," which literally is a "stroke of leprosy"). Because the word *naga'* could refer to leprosy, a rabbinic interpretation arose in which the Messiah was associated with either the disease itself or those suffering from it: "What is the Messiah's name? ... The Rabbis said, 'His name is "The Leper Scholar," ↙ as it is written, "Surely he has borne our infirmities, and carried our diseases; yet we accounted him stricken [*nagua'*], struck down by God, and afflicted" (Isa 53:4)'" (*b. Sanh.* 98b); "He then asked him, 'When will the Messiah come?' He replied, 'Go and ask him yourself.' 'Where is he sitting?' 'At the entrance.' 'And by what sign may I recognize him?' 'He is sitting among the poor lepers' [helping them]" (*b. Sanh.* 98a). If this interpretation has ancient roots, then Jesus' reference to

(1997): 73–96; K.-W. Niebuhr, "Die Werke des eschatologischen Freudenboten (4Q521 und die Jesusüberlieferung)," in C. M. Tuckett (ed.), *The Scriptures in the Gospels* (BETL 131; Leuven: Peeters and Leuven University Press, 1997), 637–46; H. Kvalbein, "The Wonders of the End-Time: Metaphoric Language in 4Q521 and the Interpretation of Matthew 11.5 par.," *JSP* 18 (1998): 87–110; É. Puech, "Some Remarks on 4Q246 and 4Q521 and Qumran Messianism," in D. W. Parry and E. Ulrich (eds.), *The Provo International Conference on the Dead Sea Scrolls: Technological Innovations, New Texts, and Reformulated Issues* (STDJ 30; Leiden: Brill, 1998), 545–65; L. Novakovic, *Messiah, the Healer of the Sick* (2003), 169–79; M. Labahn, "The Significance of Signs in Luke 7:22–23 in the Light of Isaiah 61 and the *Messianic Apocalypse*," in C. A. Evans (ed.), *From Prophecy to Testament: The Function of the Old Testament in the New* (Peabody, MA: Hendrickson, 2004), 146–68; H. Stettler, "Die Bedeutung der Täuferanfrage in Matthäus 11,2–6 par Lk 7,18–23 für die Christologie," *Bib* 89 (2008): 173–200. Stettler rightly finds that comparison with 5Q521 leads to the conclusion that Jesus saw himself as Israel's Messiah, empowered by God to 𝑓 fulfill the prophecies of the Old Testament.

cleansing lepers, set in the context of a series of healing benefits– all derived from words and phrases from Isaiah– may also have been derived from Isaiah, in a manner along the lines of what we have seen in the later rabbinic tradition. Finally, there is a rabbinic tradition that says, in reference to the "law of the leper" (Lev 14:2), that in the world to come "all the deformed [including lepers] will be healed" (*Midrash Tanhuma, Mesora'* §7; cf. *Mesora'* §9 "in the world to come I [God] am the One who will cleanse you from on high").

Jesus concludes his reply to John's disciples by uttering a beatitude, "And blessed is anyone who takes no offense at me" (**v. 6**) (on beatitudes, see the commentary on Matt 5:3–12). In some of his other beatitudes, Jesus alludes to Isaiah 61 (as in Matt 5:3–6, 8, 12). On "offense" (literally "scandalize"), see Matt 13:57, "And they took offense [or were scandalized] at him," and John 6:61, "Does this offend [or cause you to stumble]?" The blessings foretold by Isaiah are in the process of fulfillment in the ministry of Jesus, but the judgment, the "day of vengeance of our God" (Isa 61:2), for which John the Baptist longed, was still in the future. John found this difficult to accept (so did Peter; cf. Matt 16:21–23). The one who accepts Jesus' understanding and fulfillment of prophecy is blessed.

MATTHEW 11:7–15 – JESUS ON JOHN

11:7: As they went away, Jesus began to speak to the crowds about John: "What did you go out into the wilderness to look at? A reed shaken by the wind?

11:8: What then did you go out to see? Someone dressed in soft robes? Look, those who wear soft robes are in royal palaces.

11:9: What then did you go out to see? A prophet? Yes, I tell you, and more than a prophet.

11:10: This is the one about whom it is written, 'See, I am sending my messenger ahead of you, who will prepare your way before you.'

11:11: Truly I tell you, among those born of women no one has arisen greater than John the Baptist; yet the least in the kingdom of heaven is greater than he.

11:12: From the days of John the Baptist until now the kingdom of heaven has suffered violence, and the violent take it by force.

11:13: For all the prophets and the law prophesied until John came;

11:14: and if you are willing to accept it, he is Elijah who is to come.

11:15: Let anyone with ears listen!"

John's doubts about Jesus (see the preceding commentary on Matt 11:2–6) lead Jesus to discuss him. John's imprisonment has been a setback for the John-Jesus campaign. Did his imprisonment call into question the validity of John's ministry?

Did it call into question Jesus' ministry? Some of John's followers, if not John himself, may have thought that John's ongoing imprisonment and Jesus' failure to secure his release justified doubts about Jesus. Jesus replied to these doubts in Matt 11:2–6 (cf. Luke 7:18–23). He will now speak in positive terms about John's ministry and, by implication, its validity.

Jesus asks, "What did you go out into the wilderness to look at?" (**v. 7**). To see John, the people had gone out to the wilderness (cf. Matt 3:1, 3). Jesus himself went into the wilderness, where he experienced the temptations (cf. Matt 4:1). Jesus asks what they went out to the wilderness to see, "A reed shaken by the wind?" Commentators have been puzzled by this image. Could it be related somehow to 3 *Macc* 2:22, "He shook him on this side and that as a *reed is shaken by the wind*, so that he lay helpless on the ground and, besides being paralyzed in his limbs, was unable even to speak, since he was smitten by a righteous judgment" (italics added)? This text describes the divine punishment that befell Ptolemy IV Philopator, the king of Egypt (reigned 221–203 B.C.), who had attempted to enter the holy of holies (3 *Macc* 1:10). By mentioning a "reed shaken by the wind," Jesus may have meant to refer to Herod Antipas in similar terms, perhaps because he had dared to imprison (and eventually execute) John the Baptist. His efforts to violate the kingdom of God will be no more successful than those of Ptolemy IV, or later his northern counterpart Antiochus IV Epiphanes (who also entered the holy of holies and also suffered divine punishment). Herod Antipas also issued coins bearing the image of the reed. It is, of course, possible that Jesus is only referring to reeds that grow along the bank of the Jordan River, which people would have seen when going out to John. Did they go out to sightsee, or did they go out to see a prophet?

Jesus continues to press home his point, asking the crowd, "What then did you go out to see? Someone dressed in soft robes? Look, those who wear soft robes are in royal palaces" (**v. 8**). A man in "soft robes" would stand in stark contrast to John, whose clothing and diet were coarse (cf. Matt 3:4, "clothing of camel's hair with a leather belt around his waist, and his food was locusts and wild honey"). No, those who are "dressed in soft robes" are not in the wilderness; they are in "royal palaces." The reference to royal palaces makes one again think of Herod Antipas as the counterpart to John. It is possible that he is the "reed shaken by the wind," who wears "soft robes" and lives in royal "palaces" (one of which is in the vicinity of Jericho and the Jordan River). Because Herod is the one who imprisoned John, he may well be the one contrasted with John.[300]

Jesus then asks, "What then did you go out to see? A prophet? Yes, I tell you, and more than a prophet" (**v. 9**). John is "more than a prophet" because he is himself the

---

[300] On the possibility of allusion to Herod Antipas, see C. S. Keener, *A Commentary on the Gospel of Matthew* (1999), 337; U. Luz, *Matthew* (2001–2007), 2:138. For a detailed defense of this view, see G. Theissen, *The Gospels in Context: Social and Political History in the Synoptic Tradition* (Minneapolis: Fortress Press, 1991), 28–41.

fulfillment of the prophecy of Mal 3:1–5 and 4:1–6, the prophet who comes in the spirit and power of Elijah (cf. Luke 1:17; Sir 48:1–12) and in fulfillment of that prophecy has prepared the way for Jesus the Messiah. His association with Jesus, indeed his baptism of Jesus, makes John the greatest of the prophets.

When Jesus says, "This is the one about whom it is written, 'See, I am sending my messenger ahead of you, who will prepare your way before you' (**v. 10**), he is quoting Mal 3:1. He is not the only one to link this verse to John the Baptist. Mark the evangelist does also, when he uses it as a preface to his quotation of Isa 40:3 (cf. Mark 1:2–3), by which he introduces his readers to the ministry and message of John the Baptist. Both Matthew and Luke omit the quotation at this point, probably because of its presence here in Q, where it is more fully explicated. John is the messenger who goes before God to prepare His way.

Later in Malachi (cf. Mal 4:5–6), this coming messenger is identified with Elijah. Jesus also understands the messenger this way, explicitly identifying John as Elijah in Matt 11:14 (cf. Mark 9:13) and in the parallel at Matt 17:13: "Then the disciples understood that he was speaking to them about John the Baptist." If John is Elijah, who comes to prepare the way of the Lord, and if Jesus is the one who comes after him (Mark 1:7, "The one who is more powerful than I is coming after me"), then Jesus stands in the place of "the Lord."[301]

Because John is the prophet foretold in Scripture, the eschatological prophet who will prepare the way of the Lord for the redemption of the Lord's people, "among those born of women no one has arisen greater than John the Baptist" (**v. 11a**). The phrase "born of women" is Semitic (e.g., LXX Job 11:12; Sir 10:18; Gal 4:4) and is the counterpart to "son of man" (e.g., Num 23:19; Job 25:6; Ps 8:4). Nevertheless, "the least in the kingdom of heaven is greater than" John (**v. 11b**). Why is this? The point is not to denigrate John; the point is to exalt the kingdom of God. It will be so great that the nobodies, the "least," within it will be greater than the greatest in the present evil age.[302]

In Matthew's account, Jesus says, "From the days of John the Baptist until now the kingdom of heaven has suffered violence, and the violent take it by force" (**v. 12**). The parallel in Luke 16:16 is somewhat different. What does the Matthean version mean? The qualifying phrase, "from the days of John the Baptist until now," suggests that Jesus has in mind the violent actions of Herod and others (such as the Roman authorities) to suppress the people of Israel and especially anyone who proclaims God's rule.[303] One of the leaders of the Qumran community, perhaps the

---

[301]   For a further discussion, see J. B. DeYoung, "The Function of Malachi 3.1 in Matthew 11.10: Kingdom Reality as the Hermeneutic of Jesus," in C. A. Evans and W. R. Stegner (eds.), *The Gospels and the Scriptures of Israel* (1994), 66–91.

[302]   The "least" (or "smaller" or "young"; Greek: *mikroteros*) does not refer to Jesus, as though to say Jesus was John's younger associate or successor.

[303]   The violent actions of Jewish revolutionaries may also be in mind.

Teacher of Righteousness himself, offers an interesting parallel to Jesus' reference to
"violent men" who "take" God's kingdom "by force" (and here "kingdom of heaven"
probably refers to Israel itself): "Brutal men seek my soul, while I hold fast to your
covenant" (1QH 10:21–22 [*olim* 2:20–21]).[304] The "violent men" (Greek: *biastai*) are
the antithesis of the "poor in spirit," to whom the kingdom belongs (Matt 5:3), the
"meek," who will inherit the earth (Matt 5:5), and the "peacemakers," who will be
called the children of God (Matt 5:9).

Matthew's account continues with Jesus saying, "For all the prophets and the
law prophesied until John came" (**v. 13**). In Luke's parallel passage, the order is the
"Law and the Prophets" (Luke 16:16). Matthew may have reversed the order, giving
emphasis to prophetic fulfillment. To say that "the law prophesied" is not strange
in Judaism of late antiquity, for all of Scripture was viewed as being in some sense
prophetic (and Abraham, Moses, and other figures in the Pentateuch were regarded
as prophets). Recall, too, that Jesus came to "fulfill" the Law, as well as the Prophets
(cf. Matt 5:17–20).

Jesus is teaching that, with the appearance of John, the prophetic history has
reached its climax, its fulfillment. All of the prophets, including John, have foretold
the coming of Jesus and the kingdom.[305] No more prophesying is necessary before
the kingdom of God (or heaven, as it is usually called in Matthew) can come in its
fullness. But Jesus is not teaching that the Prophets and the Law are no longer valid
or are no longer authoritative. He only means that what they proclaimed has now
been realized in the advent of the kingdom.

The Matthean verse "And if you are willing to accept it, he is Elijah who is to
come" (**v. 14**) is the most explicit in identifying John with the expected Elijah. John
dressed like Elijah (cf. Matt 3:3–4) and thus probably did think of himself as a
prophet like Elijah. But did he think he was Elijah *redivivus* (i.e., the reincarnation
of Elijah)? Probably not. Compare John 1:21, "And they asked him, 'What then? Are
you Elijah?' He said, 'I am not.' 'Are you the prophet?' He answered, 'No.'"

In Matthew, Jesus concludes this discussion by saying, "Let anyone with ears
listen!" (**v. 15**). That is, if one has any spiritual capacity, then listen carefully (in
contrast to those who have ears but do not hear or have eyes but do not see; cf. Isa

[304] On the verb *biazein*, "to act forcibly," see E. Moore, "Βιάζω, ἁρπάζω and Cognates in
Josephus," *NTS* 21 (1975): 519–43; *NewDocs* 7 (1994): 152–62; *NewDocs* 9 (2002): 54–56:
"the herdsmen forcibly led off the sheep." For a further discussion of this difficult
verse, see D. R. Catchpole, "On Doing Violence to the Kingdom," *IBS* 3 (1981): 77–91;
P. S. Cameron, *Violence and the Kingdom: The Interpretation of Matthew 11.12* (ANTJ 5;
Frankfurt am Main: Peter Lang, 1984); W. E. Moore, "Violence to the Kingdom," *ExpT*
100 (1989): 174–77; G. Häfner, "Gewalt gegen die Basileia? Zum Problem der Auslegung
des 'Stürmerspruches' Mt 11,12," *ZNW* 83 (1992): 21–51; L. Morris, *The Gospel According to
Matthew* (PNTC; Grand Rapids, MI: Eerdmans; Leicester: Apollos, 1992), 281–82.
[305] D. A. Carson, "Do the Prophets and the Law Quit Prophesying before John? A Note on
Matthew 11.13," in C. A. Evans and W. R. Stegner (eds.), *The Gospels and the Scriptures of
Israel* (1994), 179–94.

6:9; Jer 5:21; Ezek 12:2). Jesus' call to people to listen is also found in other contexts (e.g., Matt 13:9, 43; Mark 4:9, 23; Luke 14:35).

MATTHEW 11:16–19 – FICKLE ISRAEL

11:16: "But to what will I compare this generation? It is like children sitting in the marketplaces and calling to one another,

11:17: 'We played the flute for you, and you did not dance; we wailed, and you did not mourn.'

11:18: For John came neither eating nor drinking, and they say, 'He has a demon';

11:19: the Son of Man came eating and drinking, and they say, 'Look, a glutton and a drunkard, a friend of tax collectors and sinners!' Yet wisdom is vindicated by her deeds."

*A*fter replying to John's question (Matt 11:2–6) and then talking about John's importance and place in the history of prophecy (Matt 11:7–15), Jesus now offers a critique of his fickle and feckless generation (Matt 11:16–19). Matthew the evangelist once again draws upon Q, an early source of Jesus' teaching (cf. Luke 7:31–35).

When Jesus says "But to what will I compare this generation? It is like children sitting in the marketplaces and calling to one another" (v. 16), contempt is implied by the demonstrative "this." Josephus says that Jerusalem was destroyed (70 A.D.) because the city had "produced a generation such as that which caused her over-throw" (*J.W.* 6.408). Jesus criticized his generation for failing to hear God's voice. This generation is "like children sitting in the marketplaces and calling to one another."

Jesus' illustration, "We played the flute for you, and you did not dance; we wailed, and you did not mourn" (v. 17), anticipates the comparison between John and him-self in vv. 18–19. Jesus' generation is like fickle children who cannot be pleased: they refuse to dance to the wedding music of the flute or to mourn when they hear a funeral dirge.[306]

Jesus' saying may have been proverbial: "This is in line with what people say: 'Weep for the one who does not know, laugh for the one who does not know. Woe to him who does not know the difference between good and bad'" (*b. Sanh.* 103a); "Much as he may sing, it does not enter into the ear of the dancer. Much as he may sing, the son of the fool hears it not" (*Lam. Rab.* Proem §12). One also thinks of the man who played the flute thinking this would make fish dance out of the water onto the land. They did not, so he drew them in with a net. Once on dry land, the

---

[306]   O. Linton, "The Parable of the Children's Game," *NTS* 22 (1976): 159–79; D. Zeller, "Die Bildlogik des Gleichnisses Mt 11,16f./Lk 7,31f.," *ZNW* 68 (1977): 252–57.

fish began leaping and flopping about, so the man said: "You had best cease from your dancing now; you would not come out and dance then, when I played to you" (Herodotus, *Histories* 1.141).

Jesus states, "For John came neither eating nor drinking, and they say, 'He has a demon'" (**v. 18**). He refers to John's severe diet of locusts and wild honey (cf. Matt 3:4). Because of his strict diet, and probably because of his dress, his strident preaching, and his presence in the wilderness (thought by many to be the home of evil spirits), people say that John "has a demon."

In Matthew's Gospel, Jesus says of himself that "The Son of Man came eating and drinking, and they say, 'Look, a glutton and a drunkard, a friend of tax collectors and sinners!' Yet wisdom is vindicated by her deeds'" (**v. 19**). In contrast to John, Jesus "came eating and drinking." Jesus was willing to meet people where they live, to socialize with them, to receive them freely. But his critics call him "a glutton and a drunkard." Calling Jesus a glutton and a drunkard is ominous. We should not understand this as a petty insult. These words constitute a deliberate allusion to Deut 21:18–21, which provides legislation for dealing with a "stubborn and rebellious son who will not obey his father and mother" (Deut 21:18). Parents of such a son are to "take hold of him and bring him out to the elders of his town at the gate of that place" (Deut 21:19). Then they say to the elders of the city: "This son of ours is stubborn and rebellious. He will not obey us. He is a glutton and a drunkard" (Deut 21:20). He is then to be stoned (Deut 21:21).[307]

Jesus is not only a glutton and drunkard but also a "friend of tax collectors and sinners."[308] Jesus' critics are piling on the charges. The mere fact of the company that he keeps is an indication of questionable morals (as his critics would understand it; cf. Ps 1:1, "Happy are those who do not follow the advice of the wicked, or take the path that sinners tread, or sit in the seat of scoffers"). Jesus has reduced himself to the level of the dregs of Jewish society.

Matthew's version continues, "Yet wisdom is vindicated by her deeds" (**v. 19**), whereas Luke's version of this saying reads "vindicated by her children" (cf. Luke 7:35).[309] Earlier, in Matt 11:2, Matthew referred to John's hearing of the "deeds of the Messiah." Wisdom's "deeds" here probably refer to these same deeds, only now Jesus includes John. Both Jesus and John, whose styles of ministry differ sharply, are justified by their deeds. In the end, "wisdom" is "always justified by what she does."[310]

---

[307] H. C. Kee, "Jesus: A Glutton and Drunkard," in B. D. Chilton and C. A. Evans (eds.), *Authenticating the Words of Jesus* (NTTS 28, no. 1; Leiden: Brill, 1998), 311–32; J. B. Modica, "Jesus as Glutton and Drunkard: The 'Excesses' of Jesus," in S. McKnight and J. B. Modica (eds.), *Who Do My Opponents Say that I Am?* (2008), 50–75.

[308] J. R. Donahue, "Tax Collectors and Sinners," *CBQ* 33 (1971): 39–61.

[309] D. A. Carson, "Matthew 11:19b/Luke 7:35: A Test Case for the Bearing of Q Christology on the Synoptic Problem," in J. B. Green and M. Turner (eds.), *Jesus of Nazareth: Lord and Christ* (I. H. Marshall Festschrift; Grand Rapids, MI: Eerdmans, 1994), 128–46.

[310] D. A. Carson, "Do the Prophets and the Law Quit Prophesying before John?" in C. A. Evans and W. R. Stegner (eds.), *The Gospels and the Scriptures of Israel* (1994), 189.

Regrettably, many in "this generation" (v. 16) do not appreciate the deeds of John and Jesus. Those who have "ears to hear" (cf. Matt 11:15) recognize these deeds for what they are; those who cannot hear and cannot see (cf. Matt 11:4) do not recognize them.

MATTHEW 11:20–24 – WOES ON UNREPENTANT CITIES

11:20: Then he began to reproach the cities in which most of his deeds of power had been done, because they did not repent.

11:21: "Woe to you, Chorazin! Woe to you, Bethsaida! For if the deeds of power done in you had been done in Tyre and Sidon, they would have repented long ago in sackcloth and ashes.

11:22: But I tell you, on the day of judgment it will be more tolerable for Tyre and Sidon than for you.

11:23: And you, Capernaum, will you be exalted to heaven? No, you will be brought down to Hades. For if the deeds of power done in you had been done in Sodom, it would have remained until this day.

11:24: But I tell you that on the day of judgment it will be more tolerable for the land of Sodom than for you."

*I*n the Matthean context, Jesus has just finished his teaching about John the Baptist (cf. Matt 11:2–19). That teaching had ended on a note of frustration, with the people of "this generation" behaving like children who are unwilling to mourn with John, who called for repentance, or celebrate with Jesus, who has announced the arrival of the kingdom of God. Jesus' frustration now gives way to a prophetic oracle of woe pronounced upon various cities in which Jesus had ministered and worked miracles but that had rejected him.[311]

In Matt 11:19, Jesus had referred to his and John's deeds (i.e., "wisdom's deeds," which have been performed through John and Jesus). In prison, John had heard of Jesus' deeds (Matt 11:2). Now Matthew states, "Then he began to reproach the cities in which most of his deeds of power had been done, because they did not repent" (v. 20). In the light of these deeds, the refusal to repent and embrace the proclamation of the kingdom is not only inexcusable but will lead to judgment.

Hence the woes that follow: "Woe to you ..." (v. 21). Woes are given expression in the Old Testament dozens of times, sometimes in series. Many of these woes are directed against the wicked or the foolish: "Woe to the guilty!" (Isa 3:11); "Alas [or woe] for those who are at ease in Zion" (Amos 6:1). Sometimes they are directed

---

[311]   J. A. Comber, "The Composition and Literary Characteristics of Matt 11:20–24," *CBQ* 39 (1977): 497–504.

against the wealthy who oppress the poor: "Woe to him who builds his house by unrighteousness, and his upper rooms by injustice, who makes his neighbors work for nothing, and does not give them their wages" (Jer 22:13). There are strings of woes that criticize the wealthy, often for oppressing the poor and/or perverting justice (e.g., Isa 5:8–22; Hab 2:6–19; cf. Luke 6:24–26).

Three cities of Galilee and Gaulanitis (Chorazin, Bethsaida, and Capernaum) are singled out for special mention, for apparently in them Jesus had performed "deeds of power" that should have led these cities to repentance but had not. The Gentile cities "Tyre and Sidon," in contrast, would have responded by repenting and therefore will receive more mercy "on the day of judgment." It is interesting to observe that all three cities of Galilee and Gaulanitis are today uninhabited.

The "deeds of power" (or "miracles"; Greek: *dunameis*) appeared in Matt 7:22, but in reference to false disciples who have worked miracles in Jesus' name. The word will occur again in Matt 13:54–58, this time in reference to Jesus. But in this instance Jesus "did not do many deeds of power there [Nazareth], because of their unbelief." Later, a worried Herod Antipas will wonder whether such impressive miracles are being done because Jesus is John the Baptist risen from the dead (cf. Matt 14:2).

"Chorazin" was a small town in Galilee (*t. Makkoth* 3.8) noted for its production of wheat (*b. Menahoth* 85a) and located a few miles north of Lake Gennesaret (or the Sea of Galilee) and about two miles north of Capernaum. The city has been excavated. In building materials, architectural style, and other features, it is not much different from but somewhat larger than Capernaum, the city that apparently served as Jesus' base of operations.[312]

"Bethsaida" (Aramaic for "house of hunting" or "fishing") is on the northern shore of Lake Gennesaret, just east of the Jordan River. It is the town from which the "Galilean" disciples Peter, Andrew, and Philip come (according to John 1:44). It is actually not in Galilee as John 12:21 states but rather in the neighboring province of Gaulanitis, at that time ruled by Philip the tetrarch. Archaeological excavations in recent years may have identified New Testament Bethsaida, but the identification is disputed.[313]

The reference to "sackcloth and ashes" refers to the fact that in times of mourning and/or repentance, Israelites (and other peoples of the ancient Near East) would wear sackcloth (a coarse material usually made of camel's hair, comparable to modern burlap) and either sit in ashes (Esther 4:3; Job 2:8; Jon 3:6) or place ashes upon their heads (2 Sam 13:19; Matt 6:16).

---

[312]   Z. Yeivin, "Ancient Chorazin Comes Back to Life," *BAR* 13, no. 5 (1987): 22–39; R. W. Smith, "Chorazin," *ABD* (1992), 1:911–12.

[313]   R. Arav and R. A. Freund (eds.), *Bethsaida: A City by the North Shore of the Sea of Galilee* (4 vols., Kirksville, MO: Truman State University Press, 1995–2009); M. Bockmuehl, "Simon Peter and Bethsaida," in B. D. Chilton and C. A. Evans (eds.), *The Missions of James, Peter, and Paul: Tensions in Early Christianity* (NovTSup 115; Leiden: Brill, 2004), 53–90 + plate.

"Tyre and Sidon" (**v. 22**) are two famous cities of antiquity (situated on the southern coast of modern-day Lebanon) upon which prophetic oracles of doom were pronounced (Isa 23:1–18; Jer 47:4; Ezek 26:3–28:24).

On "Capernaum" (**v. 23**), see the commentary on Matt 4:13. The image of being "exalted" (literally "lifted up") and then made to "be brought down" (or "thrown down") probably is an intentional allusion to Isa 14:13, 15, part of a prophetic oracle pronounced against the city of Babylon (Isa 14:4). The suggestion is confirmed when it is noted that Satan's "fall from heaven like a flash of lightning" (Luke 10:18) is a certain allusion to Isa 14:12, a passage sometimes understood as describing Lucifer's (Satan's) fall from heaven (see Rev 12:7–10, 13).

Jesus' language is quite harsh, explicitly comparing these Jewish cities to pagan cities like Tyre and Sidon, even to Sodom (**vv. 23–24**), the archetype of wickedness, and implicitly comparing Capernaum, the town in which Jesus ministered so much, to Babylon, the city that overthrew Jerusalem, ended Israel's monarchy, and brought on Israel seventy years of exile.

"Hades" is a Greek word that in pagan circles referred to the god of the underworld. The word usually translates as the Hebrew word *sheol*, a place where all humans went at death (cf. Ps 89:49). In later Judaism, it was understood that there were two regions in Hades, one for the righteous and the other for the unrighteous (cf. Luke 16:22–25). The negative part of Sheol eventually came to be called "Gehenna" (after the infamous Valley of Hinnom, a place where the heathen offered human sacrifices to the god Molech), which is usually translated as "hell." The fires of Gehenna burn forever (from Isa 66:24). See the similar sayings in Matt 18:5; Mark 9:37; and John 5:23; 13:20.[314]

The prophetic indictment ends on an ominous note with the declaration "that on the day of judgment it will be more tolerable for the land of Sodom than for" Capernaum, the very headquarters of Jesus' ministry in Galilee. In the next passage (Matt 11:25–30), Jesus will thank God for those who have responded in faith.

MATTHEW 11:25–30 – ALL IS REVEALED TO THE SON

11:25: At that time Jesus said, "I thank you, Father, Lord of heaven and earth, because you have hidden these things from the wise and the intelligent and have revealed them to infants;

11:26: yes, Father, for such was your gracious will.

11:27: All things have been handed over to me by my Father; and no one knows the Son except the Father, and no one knows the Father except the Son and anyone to whom the Son chooses to reveal him."

---

[314]   R. Bauckham, "Early Jewish Visions of Hell," *JTS* 41 (1990): 355–85; R. Bauckham, "Hades, Hell," *ABD* (1992), 3:14–15.

11:28: "Come to me, all you that are weary and are carrying heavy burdens, and I will give you rest.

11:29: Take my yoke upon you, and learn from me; for I am gentle and humble in heart, and you will find rest for your souls.

11:30: For my yoke is easy, and my burden is light."

*I*n Matt 11:7–19, Jesus criticized his generation for its fickleness in response to the preaching of John and himself. In Matt 11:20–24, Jesus pronounced woes on several cities in Galilee (Chorazin, Bethsaida, and Capernaum) for their failure to repent. Now, in Matt 11:25–30, Jesus thanks God for revealing himself not to the professionals (some of whom lived in the aforementioned cities) but to the innocent and unsophisticated. (This material has been taken from Q; cf. Luke 10:21–22.) The section concludes with an open invitation to all who will take upon themselves Jesus' discipleship.

"At that time Jesus said" (**v. 25a**) links vv. 25–30 to the preceding woes on the cities. Luke introduces this Q material differently, saying, "At that same hour Jesus rejoiced in the Holy Spirit and said" (Luke 10:21). Evidently Q lacked an introduction, beginning with Jesus' words "I thank you, Father" and so on. We find in Matt 11:25–30 a pronounced wisdom theme whereby Jesus is presented as God's very wisdom.[315]

Jesus' prayer, "I thank you, Father, Lord of heaven and earth, because you have hidden these things from the wise and the intelligent and have revealed them to infants" (**v. 25b**), seems to be a counterpoint to Daniel's prayer, "he gives wisdom to the wise and knowledge to those who have understanding. . . . To you, O God of my ancestors, I give thanks and praise, for you have given me wisdom and power, and have now revealed to me what we asked of you" (Dan 2:21, 23). Jesus' prayer parallels these components, but in reverse order (i.e., Matt 11:25 = Dan 2:23 and 21) and in an opposite sense: Daniel thanks God for giving wisdom to the wise and knowledge to the understanding; Jesus thanks God for withholding wisdom from the wise and understanding, giving it instead to "infants" (i.e., the unsophisticated and unprofessional; cf. Ps 8:2; Matt 21:16) and thereby making "wise the simple" (Ps 19:7).[316] Note, too, that the epithet "Lord of heaven" also appears in Dan 5:23.

Jesus has not contradicted Scripture, nor has he corrected it. He finds in it the "other side of the coin," as it were. It is true that in the past God has given wisdom to the wise and knowledge to those who have understanding; that is, to people like

---

[315] On this point, see C. Deutsch, *Hidden Wisdom and the Easy Yoke: Wisdom, Torah and Discipleship in Matthew 11.25–30* (JSNTSup 18; Sheffield: JSOT Press, 1987); B. Witherington III, *Jesus the Sage: The Pilgrimage of Wisdom* (Minneapolis: Fortress, 1994), 201–8.

[316] W. Grimm, *Jesus und das Danielbuch: I. Jesu Einspruch gegen das Offenbarungs-system Daniels (Mt 11,25; Lk 17,20–21)* (ANTJ 6; Frankfurt am Main: Peter Lang, 1984).

Daniel and his companions, who function as wise men in the court of the king. But in the time of fulfillment, in the time of the arrival of the kingdom of God, the Lord has graciously revealed his truths to simple plain-folk, to people who respond in faith (see also Paul's argument in 1 Cor 1:19 and his quotation of Isa 29:14, "The wisdom of their wise shall perish, and the discernment of the discerning shall be hidden").

In fact, this is not the only time Jesus finds the other side of Scripture. One might compare Mark 10:45 ("the Son of Man came not to be served but to serve") and Dan 7:14 ("to him [i.e., the Son of Man] was given dominion, and glory and kingship, that all peoples, nations, and languages should serve him"). See the commentary on Matt 20:24–28.

On "infants" (Greek: *nepioi*), see LXX Ps 18:8, "the testimony of the Lord is sure, making wise the simple" (= Heb 19:7); Ps 114:6, "the Lord preserves the simple" (= Heb 116:6); and Ps 118:130, God's Word "instructs the simple" (= Heb 119:130), where the word is used of the righteous and faithful.

Jesus continues, "Yes, Father" (**v. 26**). On Jesus' addressing God as "Father," see the commentary on Matt 5:16. Revealing truth to the innocent was according to God's "gracious will" (*eudokia*). See 1 Cor 1:21, where we find wisdom linked with what is *eudokia* to God: "For since, in the wisdom of God, the world did not know God through wisdom, God decided [*eudokesen*], through the foolishness of our proclamation, to save those who believe."

Compare "All things have been handed over to me by my Father" (**v. 27a**) with the opening words of the Great Commission: "All authority in heaven and on earth has been given to me" (Matt 28:18). Many interpreters have noted the Johannine flavor of this verse as seen, for example, in John 3:35: "The Father loves the Son and has placed all things in his hands." However, the "all things" to which Jesus refers here are the things of revelation, to which he referred in v. 25, the things hidden from the wise but revealed to the simple.

"No one knows the Son except the Father, and no one knows the Father except the Son" (**v. 27b**) again leads us to hear a Johannine echo: "as the Father knows me and I know the Father" (John 10:15). The "knowing" being talked about here is the Semitic idea of knowing someone intimately, to be concerned with someone's welfare. This idea is seen in Tob 5:2, but in that case in the sense of not knowing someone: "he does not know me and I do not know him." These are the words of young Tobias, addressed to his father, Tobit. Tobias is not sure that he will be able to obtain the needed money from a relative he does not know and has never met.

In the verse "And anyone to whom the Son chooses to reveal him" (**v. 27c**), we again have coherence with the fourth Gospel, not so much in wording as in theme: "No one has ever seen God. It is God the only Son … has made him known" (John 1:18). Both the words of Jesus in Matt 11:26–27 and the words of John the evangelist's Prologue allude to the exchange between God and Moses, on Sinai, just before God writes out another set of tablets: "Moses said to the Lord, "See, you have said to me,

'Bring up this people'; but you have not let me know whom you will send with me. Yet you have said, "I *know* you by name, and you have also *found favor* in my sight." Now if I have *found favor* in your sight, show me your ways, so that I may *know* you and *find favor* in your sight"" (Exod 33:12–13, italics added). God grants Moses' request by revealing himself to him (cf. Exod 33:17–34:9).

Jesus' words presuppose this language, if not this very passage of Scripture. What is interesting is that Jesus has an authority that is even greater than that of Moses. Moses had to plead with God that he might know him. In contrast, Jesus knows his heavenly Father and may make him known to whomever he wishes.

The well-known invitation "Come to me, all you that are weary and are carrying heavy burdens, and I will give you rest" (**v. 28**) mimics wisdom language, as seen in many texts. In Sir 24:19, Dame Wisdom bids us all: "Come to me!" Or again, "Draw near to me, you who are uneducated" (Sir 51:23); "Come, eat of my bread, and drink of the wine I have mixed" (Prov 9:5); "Come, therefore, let us enjoy the good things" (Wisd of Sol 2:6); "Come, O children, listen to me, I will teach you the fear of the Lord" (LXX Ps 33:12 [Heb 34:11]).

Just as Jesus promises "rest," rest is also promised in the wisdom tradition: "and find rest for your souls" (Jer 6:16); "I ... found for myself much serenity" (Sir 51:27); "I will give you rest" (Exod 33:14).

Jesus also invites his hearers, "Take my yoke upon you, and learn from me; for I am gentle and humble in heart, and you will find rest for your souls" (**v. 29**). The invitation to the "weary" to "come" (v. 28) and to find "rest for your souls" finds a number of important parallels in Sir 51:23–27 (with italics added):

51:23 Draw near *to me*, you who are untaught, and lodge in my school.

51:24 Why do you say you are lacking in these things, and why are your *souls* very thirsty?

51:25 I opened my mouth and said, Get these things for yourselves without money.

51:26 Put your neck under the *yoke*, and let *your souls* receive instruction; it is to be found close by.

51:27 See with your eyes that I have *labored* little and found myself much *rest*.

The numerous parallels that have been observed indicate that Jesus is speaking as God's wisdom, inviting weary sinners to come to him, to take his yoke upon them (see the commentary on v. 30), to learn from him, and to find rest for their souls.[317]

[317] D. J. Harrington, *The Gospel of Matthew* (Sacra Pagina 1; Collegeville, MN: Liturgical Press, 1991), 168–70; J. Nolland, *The Gospel of Matthew* (2005), 475–78; B. Witherington III, *Matthew* (2006), 237–40. Witherington has pursued the sapiential tradition in great detail, both in his commentary on Matthew and in a scholarly monograph. See B. Witherington III, *Jesus the Sage* (1994). The promise of rest may also intersect with the prophetic promise of liberty. See B. Charette, "'To Proclaim Liberty to the Captives': Matthew 11.28–30 in the Light of OT Prophetic Expectation," *NTS* 38 (1992): 290–97.

The description of Jesus as "gentle" (or "meek"; Greek: *praus*) recalls the beatitude (Matt 5:5), but more importantly may allude to the tradition of Moses as a man who "was very meek" (LXX Num 12:3). Matthew has presented Jesus as a new Moses, who has given his Law, as did Moses, in five major teaching blocks (i.e., Matt 5–7, 10, 13, 18, and 24–25). See also 2 Cor 10:1, "I myself, Paul, appeal to you by the meekness and gentleness of Christ."

When Jesus says, "For My yoke is easy, and my burden is light" (**v. 30**), the yoke symbolizes discipleship, the taking upon oneself the teaching of a scholar or rabbi; for example, it has been taught that "one may first accept upon himself the yoke of the kingdom of heaven and afterwards may accept the yoke of the commandments" (*m. Ber.* 2:2). The Rabbis also speak of "the yoke of Torah" (*m. 'Abot* 3:5). Cleanthes, a student of Zeno, the Cynic philosopher, said that he did not mind the insults for claiming that "he alone was strong enough to carry the load of Zeno" (Diogenes Laertius, *Lives of Eminent Philosophers* 7.170).[318]

Paradoxically, Jesus asserts that his yoke (normally carved from wood, often linking up two oxen for purposes of plowing or hauling) is "easy" (or "comfortable"; i.e., "easy to wear") and that his "load" (or "burden") is in fact "light." In what sense can Jesus' yoke be easy? It is easy in comparison with the alternatives: suffering under the yokes of humans who do not care for one's well-being. The one who places himself under the yoke of Jesus will in fact find rest and will be enabled by the Spirit. Jesus' load is in fact quite light compared with the heavy burdens the scribes and Pharisees place upon themselves and others: "They tie up heavy burdens, hard to bear, and lay them on the shoulders of others; but they themselves are unwilling to lift a finger to move them" (Matt 23:4).

MATTHEW 12:1–8 – PLUCKING GRAIN ON THE SABBATH

12:1: At that time Jesus went through the grainfields on the sabbath; his disciples were hungry, and they began to pluck heads of grain and to eat.

12:2: When the Pharisees saw it, they said to him, "Look, your disciples are doing what is not lawful to do on the sabbath."

12:3: He said to them, "Have you not read what David did when he and his companions were hungry?

12:4: He entered the house of God and ate the bread of the Presence, which it was not lawful for him or his companions to eat, but only for the priests.

12:5: Or have you not read in the law that on the sabbath the priests in the temple break the sabbath and yet are guiltless?

[318] H. D. Betz, "The Logion of the Easy Yoke and of Rest (Matt 11:28–30)," *JBL* 86 (1967): 10–24; M. Maher, "'Take My Yoke upon You' (Matt xi.29)," *NTS* 22 (1975): 97–102.

12:6: I tell you, something greater than the temple is here.

12:7: But if you had known what this means, 'I desire mercy and not sacrifice,' you would not have condemned the guiltless.

12:8: For the Son of Man is lord of the sabbath."

*M*atthew's version of the controversy generated by plucking grain on the Sabbath immediately follows Jesus' invitation to take his yoke of teaching upon oneself, to learn from him, and to find rest (cf. Matt 11:28–30). Set in this context, the Sabbath controversy illustrates the heavy and unreasonable burden that the yoke of the Pharisees places on people.

Chapter 12 of Matthew's Gospel begins, "At that time Jesus went through the grainfields on the sabbath; his disciples were hungry, and they began to pluck heads of grain and to eat" (**v. 1**). Lest there be any doubt as to why the disciples were picking heads of grain, Matthew adds that the disciples were hungry and were eating the heads of grain that they were picking. Work was not permitted on the Sabbath, but eating was. Gleaning fields was permitted, too. But what constituted "work"?

The Pharisees cannot let this pass without comment: "When the Pharisees saw it, they said to him, 'Look, your disciples are doing what is not lawful to do on the sabbath'" (**v. 2**). Of all the Sabbath controversy stories, Matt 12:1–8 is unique in that a healing is not involved. The disciples of Jesus pluck heads of grain and eat them. The charge that they are doing something not permitted on the Sabbath has nothing to do with theft (and we assume that the fields through which they passed were not their own), for this sort of gleaning was permitted in the Law (Deut 23:25). The charge has to do with "reaping"; that is, working on the Sabbath (Exod 20:10; 34:21; Deut 5:14), at least according to oral tradition (e.g. *m. Shab.* 7:2; CD 10:14–11:18). This is why the Pharisees tell Jesus that his disciples are doing "what is not lawful to do on the sabbath."

Jesus counters the criticism with an example from the life of David, at a time of danger and hardship: "He said to them, 'Have you not read what David did when he and his companions were hungry? He entered the house of God and ate the bread of the Presence, which it was not lawful for him or his companions to eat, but only for the priests'" (**vv. 3–4**). David and his men entered the house of God and ate the bread of the Presence (1 Sam 21:1–6), which was supposed to be eaten by the priests only (Lev 24:5–9). The comparison is an important one, and it may provide evidence that Jesus did indeed see himself in Davidic terms. The logic of Jesus' reply suggests that the Pharisees can no more criticize his disciples who gleaned and ate on the Sabbath than they can criticize David and his men who ate the consecrated bread of the Presence.[319]

---

[319] In Mark's account, we are told that David entered the house of God and ate the bread "when Abiathar was high priest" (Mark 2:26). According to 1 Sam 21:1–6, Ahimelech was

Jesus continues, "Or have you not read in the law that on the sabbath the priests in the temple break the sabbath and yet are guiltless?" (**v. 5**). There is no equivalent to this verse in Mark's version. On the question "have you not read in the law," see LXX Neh 8:3 ("they have read in the book of the law"); Matt 21:42 ("Have you never read in the scriptures"); and Josephus, *Ant.* 4.209 ("let him read the laws"). How do "the priests in the temple break the sabbath" but "are guiltless"? Jesus is referring to the priestly responsibilities spelled out in Num 28:9–10; that is, the duties (or work) that priests must do "on the sabbath" (Num 28:9).[320] The Rabbis wrestle with this problem, deciding that "temple service takes precedence over the sabbath" (*b. Shab.* 132b). Other activities also take precedence over the Sabbath (cf. *m. 'Erubin* 10:11–15; *m. Nedarim* 3:11; *m. Pesahim* 6:1–2; *t. Pesahim* 4.13). Why? Because it is the work of God. So Jesus reasons that because he and his disciples are doing the work of God, plucking grain (which is necessary if one is to have the strength to continue) on the Sabbath is permissible.

But it is not just that Jesus and his disciples are doing the work of God, that they may, as do the priests in the temple, do work on the Sabbath. Jesus' work is "something greater than the temple" (**v. 6**). (Again, there is no equivalent in Mark.) This something "is here." Implicit is another instance of the argument from the minor to the major. That is, if the relatively less important work of the temple priests takes precedence over the Sabbath, that much more does the more important work of Jesus. Later, Jesus will say that "something greater than Jonah is here" (Matt 12:41) and that "something greater than Solomon is here" (Matt 12:42).[321]

Jesus then states, "I desire mercy and not sacrifice" (**v. 7**). To justify his remarkable claim to be something greater than the temple, Jesus appeals to the testimony of Hosea the prophet, which more fully, and according to the Hebrew, reads: "For I desire steadfast love and not sacrifice, the knowledge of God rather than burnt offerings" (Hos 6:6). Earlier in Matthew, Jesus appealed to this verse in defense of reaching out to sinners (Matt 9:13). Both here in Matt 12:7 and in the earlier citation in Matt 9:13, Matthew has followed the Septuagint: "I desire mercy and not sacrifice,

the high priest when David was given the bread. Ahimelech's son Abiathar became high priest later. (However, elsewhere in the Old Testament, the names of Ahimelech and Abiathar are reversed, suggesting that Abiathar was the high priest at the time.) Aware of the uncertainty of the tradition, Matthew (and Luke, too; cf. Luke 6:3–4) chooses to omit this unnecessary detail. See C. A. Evans, "Abiathar. II. New Testament," in *EBR* (2009), 1:77–78.

320 See D. C. Allison, Jr. and W. D. Davies, *A Critical and Exegetical Commentary on the Gospel According to Saint Matthew* (1988–1997), 2:314; L. Morris, *The Gospel According to Matthew* (1992), 302–3.

321 E. Levine, "The Sabbath Controversy According to Matthew," *NTS* 22 (1976): 480–83; J. M. Hicks, "The Sabbath Controversy in Matthew: An Exegesis of Matthew 12:1–14," *RestQ* 27 (1984): 79–91; M. Kister, "Plucking on the Sabbath and Christian-Jewish Polemic," *Immanuel* 24–25 (1990): 35–51; J. P. Meier, "The Historical Jesus and the Plucking of the Grain on the Sabbath," *CBQ* 66 (2004): 561–81.

and full knowledge of God rather than whole burnt offerings." Had the Pharisees understood the importance of Hos 6:6, they "would not have condemned the guiltless." That is, had the Pharisees understood the whole of Scripture's teaching, and how certain principles take precedence over certain laws, they would not have been so quick to condemn.[322]

Matthew's next verse reads, "For the Son of Man is Lord of the sabbath" (v. 8). Here he follows Mark but has omitted Mark's "The sabbath was made for man, and not man for the sabbath" (Mark 2:27) because it is out of step with the temple argument that has been developed in vv. 5–7. The saying in Mark 2:27 suggests that humankind in general takes precedence over the Sabbath, but Matthew has taken pains to show that it is the "Son of Man" (i.e., Jesus) who takes precedence over the Sabbath because he is "Lord" of it and of much else.

MATTHEW 12:9–14 – HEALING ON THE SABBATH

12:9: He left that place and entered their synagogue;

12:10: a man was there with a withered hand, and they asked him, "Is it lawful to cure on the sabbath?" so that they might accuse him.

12:11: He said to them, "Suppose one of you has only one sheep and it falls into a pit on the sabbath; will you not lay hold of it and lift it out?

12:12: How much more valuable is a human being than a sheep! So it is lawful to do good on the sabbath."

12:13: Then he said to the man, "Stretch out your hand." He stretched it out, and it was restored, as sound as the other.

12:14: But the Pharisees went out and conspired against him, how to destroy him.

*T*he Matthean context is the same as the Markan. Matthew derives his story of the healing of the man with the paralyzed hand from Mark 3:1–6 and presents it in the same sequence, though not without some omissions and additions. In the Matthean form of the story, Jesus is cast more obviously in the role of scholar and debater. For a discussion of synagogues, see the commentary on Matt 4:23.

The controversy begins with the presence in "their synagogue" (v. 9) of the man with a "withered hand" (v. 10). The hand has atrophied from lack of use. The Pharisees (see v. 14) know Jesus will heal the man, so they ask him: "Is it lawful to cure on the sabbath?" If he thinks it is and then cures the man, then the Pharisees can accuse him of working on the Sabbath; that is, working as a healer.

[322] D. Hill, "On the Use and Meaning of Hosea vi.6 in Matthew's Gospel," *NTS* 24 (1977): 107–19, especially 113–16; L. Morris, *The Gospel According to Matthew* (1992), 303–4; R. T. France, *The Gospel of Matthew* (2007), 461–62.

Jesus counters the question with a question of his own: "Suppose one of you has only one sheep and it falls into a pit on the sabbath; will you not lay hold of it and lift it out?" (**v. 11**). The way this example begins reminds us of the parable of the lost sheep (cf. Luke 15:4, "Which one of you, having a hundred sheep"). Compassion for an animal in trouble is probably based on texts such as Prov 12:10, "The righteous know the needs of their animals," and Deut 22:4, "You shall not see your neighbor's donkey or ox fallen on the road and ignore it; you shall help to lift it up." How much help one should be allowed to extend to an animal on the Sabbath was an item of debate in late antiquity. The Rabbis allowed for some assistance, such as provision of fodder or throwing something into the hole that might enable the animal to climb out (cf. *m. Besa* 3:4). The Essenes, however, made no such allowance: "No one should help an animal give birth on the Sabbath; and if it falls into a well or a pit, he may not lift it out on the Sabbath" (CD 11:13–14). Jesus' reply clearly presupposes the more lenient view of the Pharisees and not the stricter view of the Essenes.

If assistance can be given to a sheep, then surely it can be given to a human, for a human is more valuable than a sheep! (**v. 12**). In view of the practice outlined in v. 11 ("will you not lay hold of it and lift it out?"), then surely it is right to help a human being, who is of much more value in God's eyes than an animal. Once again, Jesus has employed the argument from the minor to the major: if it is permissible to aid an animal on the Sabbath, then surely it is permissible to aid a human on the Sabbath.

The account continues, "Then he said to the man …" (**v. 13**). Matthew omits Mark's "He looked around at them with anger; he was grieved at their hardness of heart" (Mark 3:5). Both Matthew and Luke are more reserved when it comes to describing Jesus' emotions. The man stretched out his hand, and it was restored.

Rather than rejoicing over the man's healing and commending Jesus, "the Pharisees went out and conspired against him, how to destroy him" (**v. 14**). Matthew omits Mark's reference to the "Herodians" (Mark 3:6). He may have done this because of the questions the association of the Herodians with the Pharisees would have raised in the minds of his readers. But it is also possible that by the time Matthew writes, it is only the Pharisees who present a challenge to the church. The Herodians have ceased to be of interest.[323]

MATTHEW 12:15–21 – THE SERVANT OF THE LORD

12:15: When Jesus became aware of this, he departed. Many crowds followed him, and he cured all of them,

---

[323] For further discussion, see A. J. Hultgren, *Jesus and His Adversaries* (1979), 82–84; J. M. Hicks, "The Sabbath Controversy in Matthew," *RestQ* 27 (1984): 79–91; D. Verseput, *The Rejection of the Humble Messianic King: A Study of the Composition of Matthew 11–12* (Frankfurt am Main: Peter Lang, 1986), 153–87.

12:16: and he ordered them not to make him known.

12:17: This was to fulfill what had been spoken through the prophet Isaiah:

12:18: "Here is my servant, whom I have chosen, my beloved, with whom my soul is well pleased. I will put my Spirit upon him, and he will proclaim justice to the Gentiles.

12:19: He will not wrangle or cry aloud, nor will anyone hear his voice in the streets.

12:20: He will not break a bruised reed or quench a smoldering wick until he brings justice to victory.

12:21: And in his name the Gentiles will hope."

*M*atthew reduces Mark 3:7–12 to two verses (Matt 12:15–16) and then introduces and quotes Isa 42:1–4 (Matt 12:17–21), the longest quotation of Old Testament Scripture in the Gospels. Matthew has done this in order to explain to his readers the meaning of the various injunctions to silence that we find especially in Mark's Gospel (e.g., Mark 1:25, 34, 44; and especially in the parallel to the present passage at 3:12).[324]

When Jesus became aware that the Pharisees were plotting his death (Matt 12:14), he relocated: "When Jesus became aware of this, he departed. Many crowds followed him, and he cured all of them" (**v. 15**). But his ministry of healing continued. He also "ordered" those he healed "not to make him known" (**v. 16**). Jesus was not interested in notoriety. Nor was he interested in fomenting an uprising.

Jesus' preference for "quiet ministry," Matthew explains, "was to fulfill what had been spoken through the prophet Isaiah" (**v. 17**). Isaiah 42:1–4 is then quoted (in **vv. 18–21**). Rather than stay and fight the Pharisees, or allow the rejoicing and enthusiastic crowds to create a ruckus, Jesus continues his itinerant ministry of proclaiming the rule of God and healing all who are afflicted.

In v. 18, we find reference to "my servant" (cf. Isa 42:1). The identity of the mysterious Servant (Hebrew: *ʿebed*; Greek: *pais*) in the so-called Servant Songs of the second half of Isaiah has mystified interpreters ancient and modern alike. Who this figure was supposed to be in the original oracles of Isaiah 40–55 will remain a matter of scholarly debate, but for Matthew the Servant was the Messiah, and the Messiah was Jesus. Jesus is not only Israel's redeemer and Messiah but the redeemer of Gentiles, for it is "in his name the Gentiles will hope" (v. 21).[325]

[324] This is not to say that Matthew's readers and hearers had themselves read the Gospel of Mark (though I suppose some may have) but only that some of them may have known of the injunctions to silence that we find in Mark. Two of Mark's injunctions to silence are repeated in Matthew (compare Mark 1:44 and Matt 8:4, and Mark 3:12 and Matt 12:16), so Matthew's readers and hearers at least knew of them and may well have wondered why Jesus enjoined those he healed to remain silent. The passage under consideration provides a scriptural warrant for the injunctions to silence.

[325] See B. Byrne, "The Messiah in Whose Name 'the Gentiles Will Hope' (Matt 12:21)," *ABR* 50 (2002): 55–73.

The messianic identification of this figure in Jewish interpretation of late antiquity is probably what encouraged Matthew and other early Christian theologians to see Jesus as the Servant of the Book of Isaiah. How early this messianic identification is remains a matter of speculation. The Servant of Isa 52:13–53:12 is explicitly identified as the Messiah in the Targum of Isaiah. Parts of the Aramaic text read:

> Behold, My Servant, the Messiah, shall prosper. . . . Just as the house of Israel hoped for Him many days. . . . He will beseech concerning our sins and our iniquities for His sake we will be forgiven … and He will build the sanctuary which was profaned for our sins, handed over for our iniquities; and by His teaching His peace will increase upon us, and in that we attach ourselves to His words our sins will be forgiven us. . . . All we like sheep have been scattered; we have gone into exile. . . . He will bring our exiles near. . . . He will hand over the wicked to Gehenna … they shall see the kingdom of their Messiah. . . . (*Tg.* Isa 52:13, 14; 53:4, 5, 6, 8, 9, 10)

The Lord's servant, according to v. 18, "will proclaim justice to the Gentiles." The Greek word translated as "justice" is *krisis*, which can also mean "judgment." The NRSV (as well as the RSV) rightly renders it as "justice," for Matthew's point is that Jesus the Davidic Messiah brings justice, mercy, and salvation to Jew and Gentile alike.[326]

All of the elements cited correspond with features of Jesus' teaching and/or what early Christians believed about him. Most of these items are only found in the Aramaic version of this Servant Song, not in the Hebrew. In view of the coherence between Aramaic Isaiah and Jesus' teaching in other places, one justifiably suspects that the messianic interpretation of Isaiah's Servant Songs (particularly those of Chapters 42 and 52–53) was known to Jesus and the Aramaic-speaking synagogues of his day.[227]

MATTHEW 12:22–32 – EXORCISM, BEELZEBUL, AND BLASPHEMY

12:22: Then they brought to him a demoniac who was blind and mute; and he cured him, so that the one who had been mute could speak and see.

12:23: All the crowds were amazed and said, "Can this be the Son of David?"

12:24: But when the Pharisees heard it, they said, "It is only by Beelzebul, the ruler of the demons, that this fellow casts out the demons."

---

[326] R. Beaton, "Messiah and Justice: A Key to Matthew's Use of Isaiah 42:1–4?" *JSNT* 75 (1999): 5–23.

[227] For further discussion, see J. C. M. Grindel, "Matt 12:18–21," *CBQ* 29 (1967): 110–15; J. Neyrey, "The Thematic Use of Isaiah 42:1–4 in Matthew 12," *Bib* 63 (1982): 457–73; D. Verseput, *The Rejection of the Humble Messianic King* (1986), 187–205; R. Beaton, *Isaiah's Christ in Matthew's Gospel* (2002); L. Novakovic, *Messiah, the Healer of the Sick* (2003), 133–51.

12:25: He knew what they were thinking and said to them, "Every kingdom divided against itself is laid waste, and no city or house divided against itself will stand.

12:26: If Satan casts out Satan, he is divided against himself; how then will his kingdom stand?

12:27: If I cast out demons by Beelzebul, by whom do your own exorcists cast them out? Therefore they will be your judges.

12:28: But if it is by the Spirit of God that I cast out demons, then the kingdom of God has come to you.

12:29: Or how can one enter a strong man's house and plunder his property, without first tying up the strong man? Then indeed the house can be plundered.

12:30: Whoever is not with me is against me, and whoever does not gather with me scatters.

12:31: Therefore I tell you, people will be forgiven for every sin and blasphemy, but blasphemy against the Spirit will not be forgiven.

12:32: Whoever speaks a word against the Son of Man will be forgiven, but whoever speaks against the Holy Spirit will not be forgiven, either in this age or in the age to come.

In the previous pericope (Matt 12:15–21), Matthew has shown that Jesus did not permit the demons to cry out and make him known. In doing this, Jesus fulfilled the prophecy in Isaiah 42 of the Servant of the Lord, who was expected not to cry out in the streets and make a fuss. This is preparation for the unit of material now under consideration, in which Jesus is accused of being in league with Beelzebul.[328] By already showing that it is not Jesus' intention to clamor for attention, or to try to gain notoriety or material advantage through his success as an exorcist, Matthew has further undermined the allegations of Jesus' critics (i.e., Why would Jesus be in league with Satan? What would he hope to gain?). Of course, Jesus himself will vigorously challenge these charges through logic and experience.

Matthew has derived most of his material from Mark 3:20–30, though some of it has been derived from the overlapping material of Q (cf. Luke 11:19–20, 23; 12:10; 6:43–45).

Matthew next describes Jesus' encounter with "a demoniac who was blind and mute" (**v. 22**). Matthew's version begins with a specific exorcism and healing. This kind of activity is implied in the Markan narrative, but an actual episode is not narrated. Demons sometimes were linked to particular infirmities, such as blindness,

[328] For general reference, see L. Gaston, "Beelzebul," *TZ* 18 (1962): 247–55; E. C. B. MacLaurin, "Beelzeboul," *NovT* 20 (1978): 156–60; W. A. Maier III, "Baal-zebub," *ABD* (1992), 1:554; W. Herrmann, "Baal-Zebub," *DDD*, 293–96.

deafness (and muteness, which often went with it), paralysis, and other crippling diseases. In interrogating a demon and asking it what harm it causes, King Solomon is told: "I blind children … and make them dumb and deaf" (*T. Solomon* 12:2). Jesus "cured" the man, which not only means that he is freed from the evil spirit but that he can now "speak and see."

The crowds were amazed and asked, "Can this be the Son of David?" (**v. 23**). Why do the crowds ask this question? "Son of David," of course, historically refers to Solomon, David's son and royal successor. Solomon's fame as wise man, herbalist, and student grew during the intertestamental period, so that his name also became associated with exorcism. Josephus tells of one Eleazar, an exorcist who could cast out demons with spells supposedly handed down from Solomon himself (cf. Josephus, *J.W.* 7.180–85; *Ant.* 8.45–49). Addressing Solomon as the "son of David" is found in the *Testament of Solomon*, a first-century pseudepigraphical text that is much concerned with demonology (cf. *T. Solomon* 1:7, "Solomon, son of David"; 5:10).[329]

The Pharisees do not think the exorcism and healing are evidence of a positive identity. Far from it. They suggest that Jesus is in league with "Beelzebul, the ruler of the demons," and it is through Beelzebul that Jesus "casts out the demons" (**v. 24**). Beelzebul is identified as the "Ruler (or Prince) of demons," who is overpowered by Solomon, in the *Testament of Solomon* (cf. *T. Solomon* 2:9–3:6, "I am Beelzebul, the ruler of the demons"; 6:1–11). It is a serious charge; Jesus must answer it.[330]

Jesus begins his rebuttal by pointing out the lack of logic in the accusation. Everyone knows that "Every kingdom divided against itself is laid waste, and no city or house divided against itself will stand" (**v. 25**). Likewise, "If Satan casts out Satan, he is divided against himself; how then will his kingdom stand?" (**v. 26**).[331] If Satan is divided against himself, his power will come to an end. This is self-evident. Therefore, why would he enable Jesus to cast out his allies?

Jesus continues his rebuttal by inquiring about the exorcists, of whom the Pharisees are not critical: "If I cast out demons by Beelzebul, by whom do your own exorcists cast them out?" (**v. 27**). This argument is not found in Mark's parallel account; it is taken from Q (cf. Luke 11:19). Jesus' logic is again quite clear: If his exorcisms are to be explained as the result of Beelzebul's assistance, then how are the exorcisms performed by the Pharisees' students (literally "your sons") to be explained? To say Jesus' exorcisms are the work of the devil but the exorcisms of others are not is simply gratuitous. This is especially so if the students of the Pharisees make use of the spells and paraphernalia that many exorcists of late antiquity used:

[329] D. C. Duling, "The Therapeutic Son of David," *NTS* 24 (1978): 392–409.

[330] M. Limbeck, "Beelzebul – eine ursprüngliche Bezeichnung für Jesus?" in *Wort Gottes in der Zeit* (H. Schelkle Festschrift; Düsseldorf: Patmos, 1973), 31–42; A. J. Hultgren, *Jesus and His Adversaries* (1979), 100–6; D. D. Sheets, "Jesus as Demon-Possessed," in S. McKnight and J. B. Modica (eds.), *Who Do My Opponents Say that I Am?* (2008), 27–49.

[331] H. Kruse, "Das Reich Satans," *Bib* 58 (1977): 29–61.

they look more like magicians than does Jesus, who simply speaks the word and the exorcism takes place. The logic of the Pharisees is so badly formed that their students "will be your judges."[332]

Jesus now makes clear the significance of his exorcisms: "But if it is by the Spirit of God that I cast out demons, then the kingdom of God has come to you" (**v. 28**). Jesus' "if" should be understood grammatically as the equivalent of "since." There is no doubt that Jesus casts out demons by the Spirit of God. It is by the "Spirit of God" ("finger of God" in Luke 11:20)[333] that the demons are cast out, not by the power of Beelzebul. Casting out demons is proof that "the kingdom of God has" indeed "come to" Israel. This is why throughout Jesus' ministry, including the preaching mission of his apostles, we find the link between the proclamation of the kingdom and exorcism (e.g., Matt 10:7–8). The latter demonstrates the reality and power of the former.[334]

Jesus returns to his rebuttal of the charge that he is in league with Satan. Not only is Jesus not empowered by Satan to cast him out, he has in fact bound Satan, "the strong man," and is now in the process of looting his house, setting free his captives (**v. 29**).

The passage concludes with a severe warning: First, if one chooses not to be "with" Jesus, he is "against" Jesus. Whoever refuses to "gather" the lost and scattered of Israel in fact "scatters" (**v. 30**). Second, people "will be forgiven for every sin and blasphemy," even criticizing Jesus the "Son of Man," but speaking "against the Holy Spirit" of God, who reveals truth and acts and works on behalf of humankind, "will not be forgiven" (**vv. 31–32**).[335] Many interpreters point out, rightly, that intentional sin against God was a very serious matter in the Jewish world (Deut 29:18–20; 1QS 7:15–17; *Jub.* 15:34; *1 Enoch* 96:7). Interpreters reason that it is one thing to speak against Jesus, who is God's Son but not yet exalted, but to speak against God's Holy Spirit is altogether something else. Whereas the former is forgivable, the latter is not.[336]

Nevertheless, a number of interpreters remain troubled by v. 32. It seems odd that those who speak against the "Son of Man" (i.e., Jesus) can be forgiven but those who speak against the "Holy Spirit" will never be forgiven. How is it forgivable to blaspheme Jesus, God's Son, while it is not forgivable to blaspheme God's Spirit? The

[332] R. Shirock, "Whose Exorcists Are They? The Referents of οἱ υἱοὶ ὑμῶν at Matthew 12.27/ Luke 11.19," *JSNT* 46 (1992): 41–51.
[333] C. S. Rodd, "Spirit or Finger," *ExpT* 72 (1961): 157–58.
[334] R. H. Hiers, "Satan, Demons, and Kingdom of God," *SJT* 27 (1974): 35–47.
[335] J. G. Williams, "A Note on the 'Unforgivable Sin' Logion," *NTS* 12 (1965): 75–77; M. E. Boring, "The Unforgivable Sin Logion, Mark iii 28–29/Matt xii 31–32/Luke xii 10: Formal Analysis and History of the Tradition," *NovT* 18 (1976): 258–79; J. C. O'Neil, "The Unforgivable Sin," *JSNT* 19 (1983): 37–42.
[336] D. A. Hagner, *Matthew* (1993–1995), 1:347–48; C. S. Keener, *A Commentary on the Gospel of Matthew* (1999), 365–66; B. Witherington III, *Matthew* (2006), 247–48; R. T. France, *The Gospel of Matthew* (2007), 483–84.

solution may be found in the idiom "Son of Man." Jesus normally refers to himself as "Son of Man" (and when he does, the NRSV capitalizes the words). But Jesus' saying originally may have referred not to himself, the "Son of Man," but to human beings, which in Hebrew and Aramaic idioms are called "sons of men," or in the singular "son of man" (e.g., Ps 8:4). Thus understood, the saying originally went like this: "Whoever speaks a word against a fellow (imperfect, sinful) human will be forgiven, but whoever speaks against the (perfect, sinless) Holy Spirit will not be forgiven." Trashing humans is one thing, but trashing the Holy Spirit is another matter. The saying in v. 32 thus expands on the previous saying in v. 31: Humans will be forgiven for all kinds of sin and blasphemy, but not against the Holy Spirit; humans will be forgiven for blaspheming against fellow humans, but not for blaspheming against the Holy Spirit. By the time Matthew composed his Gospel, the reference to "son of man" had come to be understood as a reference to Jesus, "the Son of Man."

The saying about gathering and scattering (v. 30) is drawn from Q (cf. Luke 11:23) and reflects Jewish tradition. According to the *Psalms of Solomon*, the wicked scatter, but the coming Messiah, son of David, will gather (cf. *Pss. Sol.* 4:10, "he did not stop until he scattered them"; 17:21, "their king, the son of David"; 17:26, "he will gather a holy people"; 17:32, "their king shall be the Lord Messiah"; 18:5, "when His Messiah will reign"; 18:7, "the Lord Messiah"). In the Targum of Isaiah's Suffering Servant Song (i.e., Isa 52:13–53:12), the Servant of the Lord is identified as the Messiah. But Israel "like sheep have been scattered; we have gone into exile … [but the Messiah] will bring our exiles near" (*Tg.* Isa 53:6, 8). There is a parallel proverb in rabbinic literature: "At the time when one gathers – scatter; and at the time when one scatters – gather" (*t. Ber.* 6.24; *y. Ber.* 9.5 [attributed to Hillel]; *b. Ber.* 63a).

MATTHEW 12:33–37 – WATCH WHAT YOU SAY

12:33: "Either make the tree good, and its fruit good; or make the tree bad, and its fruit bad; for the tree is known by its fruit.

12:34: You brood of vipers! How can you speak good things, when you are evil? For out of the abundance of the heart the mouth speaks.

12:35: The good person brings good things out of a good treasure, and the evil person brings evil things out of an evil treasure.

12:36: I tell you, on the day of judgment you will have to give an account for every careless word you utter;

12:37: for by your words you will be justified, and by your words you will be condemned."

The warning about blasphemy against the Holy Spirit in the previous passage (Matt 12:22–32) prompts Jesus to caution his opponents about what they say, especially with regard to insincerity and hypocrisy.

The saying "Either make the tree good, and its fruit good; or make the tree bad, and its fruit bad; for the tree is known by its fruit" (**v. 33**) is proverbial: "This accords with the popular saying, 'Every pumpkin can be told from its stalk'" (*b. Ber.* 48a). See the commentary on Matt 7:16, 20. The point is to have integrity and to be honest. Jesus tells his critics to judge something for what it is (if it is good, then it is good; if it is bad, then it is bad). Don't make something good that is in fact bad.

The words "You brood of vipers!" (**v. 34**) are the words John the Baptist had used; see the commentary on Matt 3:7–10. Jesus asks the Pharisees, "How can you speak good things, when you are evil? For out of the abundance of the heart the mouth speaks." Jesus' question is consistent with the saying mentioned in 1 Sam 24:13, "As the ancient proverb says, 'Out of the wicked comes forth wickedness.'" This saying about speaking "out of the abundance of the heart" resembles Jesus' teaching on what really defiles (cf. Matt 15:11 = Mark 7:20) and ideas found in rabbinic literature: "the Rabbis hold, 'We require his mouth and his heart [to be] the same'" (*b. Pesahim* 63a; cf. *b. Pesahim* 113b; *b. Ber.* 17a); "What was in their hearts was also in their mouths" (*Midr. Ps.* 28.4 [on Ps 28:3]; *Gen. Rab.* 84.9 [on Gen 37:4]). "If the heart has not revealed [the secret] to the mouth, to whom can the mouth reveal it?" (*Eccl. Rab.* 7:2 §1). The phrase the mouth speaks is found in Old Testament Scripture (e.g., Gen 45:12; Isa 1:20; 40:5).

Jesus presses home his argument about consistency by observing: "The good person brings good things out of a good treasure, and the evil person brings evil things out of an evil treasure" (**v. 35**). See Matt 6:21, "where your treasure is, there your heart will be also," and Matt 13:52, "Therefore every scribe who has been trained for the kingdom of heaven is like the master of a household who brings out of his treasure what is new and what is old." Jesus' saying may echo LXX Deut 28:12, "The Lord will open for you his good treasure."[337] Older contemporary Philo of Alexandria speaks of treasure of good and treasure of evil (*Fug.* 79). Matthew 12:35 and 13:52 may be versions of the same saying, a saying that reflects a disciple who is a student and scribe, perhaps even the evangelist Matthew himself.[338]

Jesus' warning about "every careless word" his critics "utter" (**v. 36**) brings to mind the earlier warning about blasphemy (Matt 12:31–32). It also recalls one of the antitheses: "if you say, 'You fool,' you will be liable to the hell of fire" (Matt 5:22). Jesus concludes his warning: "by your words you will be justified, and by your words you will be condemned" (**v. 37**). These words may allude to LXX Ps 50:6,[339] a verse

---

[337] P. S. Minear, "False Prophecy and Hypocrisy in the Gospel of Matthew," in J. Gnilka (ed.), *Neues Testament und Kirche: Für Rudolf Schnackenburg* (Freiburg: Herder, 1974), 76–93; M. Krämer, "Hüet euch vor den falschen Propheten: Eine überlieferungsgeschichtliche Untersuchung zu Mt 7,15–23 / Lk 6,43–46 / Mt 12, 33–37," *Bib* 57 (1976): 349–77; B. Gerhardsson, "'An ihren Fruchten sollt ihr sie erkennen': Die Legitimitätsfrage in der Matthäischen Christologie," *EvT* 42 (1982): 113–26.

[338] On the relationship of Matt 12:35 and 13:52, see D. E. Orton, *The Understanding Scribe: Matthew and the Apocalyptic Ideal* (JSNTSup 25; Sheffield: JSOT Press, 1989), 152, 173.

[339] R. H. Gundry, *Matthew* (1982), 241.

quoted by Paul in Rom 3:4, "so that you may be justified in your words" (Heb 51:4), and may have contributed to Paul's bold affirmation, "if you confess with your lips that Jesus is Lord and believe in your heart that God raised him from the dead, you will be saved" (Rom 10:9; cf. Rom 10:8, which quotes Deut 30:14, "the word is very near to you; it is in your mouth and in your heart"; and Rom 10:13, which quotes Joel 2:32, "everyone who calls on the name of the Lord shall be saved").

MATTHEW 12:38–42 – SOMETHING GREATER IS HERE

12:38: Then some of the scribes and Pharisees said to him, "Teacher, we wish to see a sign from you."

12:39: But he answered them, "An evil and adulterous generation asks for a sign, but no sign will be given to it except the sign of the prophet Jonah.

12:40: For just as Jonah was three days and three nights in the belly of the sea monster, so for three days and three nights the Son of Man will be in the heart of the earth.

12:41: The people of Nineveh will rise up at the judgment with this generation and condemn it, because they repented at the proclamation of Jonah, and see, something greater than Jonah is here!

12:42: The queen of the South will rise up at the judgment with this generation and condemn it, because she came from the ends of the earth to listen to the wisdom of Solomon, and see, something greater than Solomon is here!"

*J*esus answered well the charges that had been laid against him to the effect that his success in exorcism was due to Satan's assistance (Matt 12:22–37). In that section, Jesus concluded with a warning that "on the day of judgment" people – like the Pharisees who had accused him and who were perilously close to blaspheming the Holy Spirit – "will have to give an account" (v. 36). In the section under consideration, the Pharisees and some of the scribes counter by asking Jesus for a sign that will prove valid his warnings of judgment, his authority for uttering them, and perhaps, still, his legitimacy as an exorcist.

When the Pharisees say, "Teacher, we wish to see a sign from you" (**v. 38**), what kind of sign do they want? It is hard to say.[340] The prophet Isaiah offered a sign to feckless and fearful Ahaz, king of Judah in the eighth century B.C.: "Ask a sign of the Lord your God; let it be deep as Sheol or high as heaven" (Isa 7:11). In Jesus' time, there were men who offered various signs to prove that God was indeed about to work deliverance through them. A man named Theudas (ca. 45 A.D.) said that at his command the waters of the Jordan River would be parted (cf. Josephus, *Ant.*

---

[340]   O. Linton, "The Demand for a Sign from Heaven," *ST* 19 (1965): 112–29.

20.97–98). A Jew from Egypt (ca. 56 A.D.) said that at his command the walls of Jerusalem would collapse (cf. Josephus, *Ant.* 20.169–70). In every case, the signs that these men offered crowds were to prove that God was working in them and was about to bring about Israel's redemption. In each case, Rome reacted militarily and brutally. In view of these parallel episodes (which postdate Jesus' ministries, but they probably were not the only such incidents), it is probable that the Pharisees were asking Jesus for a sign along similar lines.

Jesus has no interest in providing the kind of sign that has been requested. But he does speak prophetically: "An evil and adulterous generation asks for a sign" (**v. 39a**). Jesus' refusal to fall into the category of men like Theudas and the Egyptian (again, these men postdate Jesus' ministry) is understandable. The healings and exorcisms, the work of the Holy Spirit, speak for themselves. Jesus' words, "An evil and adulterous generation," may allude to Isa 57:3, "But as for you, come here, you children of a sorceress, you offspring of an adulterer and a whore," especially as it is paraphrased in the Aramaic: "But you, draw near, *people of the generation whose deeds are evil, whose plant was from a holy plant, and they are* adulterers and *harlots*" (italics indicate important departures from the Hebrew). The Aramaic supplies *generation* and *evil*, whereas the Hebrew supplies *adulterers*. These three words correspond to the words that Jesus uses to describe his faithless generation: "An evil and adulterous generation." One should also note that in Isa 57:4 the prophet asks, "Whom are you mocking? Against whom do you open your mouth wide and stick out your tongue?" This may correspond to the question that "some of the scribes and Pharisees" put to Jesus. That is, an evil and adulterous generation sticks out its tongue and jests with the revelation of God.

Note the possible parallel in the Talmud: "The disciples of Rabbi Yose ben Kisma asked him, 'When will the Messiah come?' He answered, 'I fear [giving an answer], lest you demand a sign of me [to prove that my answer is correct].' They assured him, 'We will demand no sign of you.' So he answered them, 'When this gate [of the city of Caesarea Philippi] falls down, is rebuilt, falls again, and is again rebuilt, and then falls a third time, before it can be rebuilt the son of David will come.' They said to him, 'Master, give us a sign.' He protested, 'Did you not assure me that you would not demand a sign?'" (*b. Sanh.* 98a).

Matthew's account continues, "But no sign will be given to it except the sign of the prophet Jonah" (**v. 39b**). Even the faithless Ahaz was promised a sign (Isa 7:10–14), but no sign will be given to the evil and adulterous generation of Jesus' day. It was one thing to despise God's word as given by Isaiah but quite another to despise God's word as given by His Son. But Jesus does say "the sign of Jonah" will be given. Jonah the prophet was the son of Amittai of Gath-hepher (2 Kings 14:25; Jon 1:1). God sent him to proclaim judgment on Nineveh. Fearing that the people would repent and that God would forgive them and not destroy the city, the prophet fled by sea, was thrown overboard by the frightened seamen, was swallowed by a large fish, was thrown up onto the shore, went to Nineveh, where he preached as he had been commanded, and saw the city repent and judgment averted (cf. Jonah 1–4).

What exactly was the "sign of Jonah"? Commentators have wrestled with this question. In Mark's parallel to this passage (Mark 8:11–12), no sign of Jonah is mentioned. But the "sign of Jonah" is mentioned in the parallel passage in Luke 11:30, in material that Matthew and Luke have drawn from Q. The sign of Jonah may have referred to the prophet's preaching that Nineveh repent.[341] But in Matthew the sign refers to Jonah's miraculous deliverance from the "belly of the sea monster" (**v. 40**). Thus the only "sign" concerning Jesus that will be given to the scribes and Pharisees will be his resurrection after three days "in the heart of the earth."[342]

Jesus continues with his comparison. Because the men of Nineveh repented, they "will rise up at the judgment" and condemn "this generation" (i.e., the "evil and adulterous generation" that asks for a sign but rejects the evidence of God before their very eyes). They will condemn Jesus' generation because someone far greater than Jonah had preached repentance to them (**v. 41**).

Likewise in the case of the "queen of the South" (**v. 42**). She, too, "will rise up at the judgment" and will condemn "this generation," for "she came from the ends of the earth to listen to the wisdom of Solomon." Yet "this generation" had the opportunity to hear one far greater than Solomon but chose not to listen.[343]

The scribes and Pharisees are without excuse. The power of God is clearly at work in Jesus, but they request signs, complain that some of his amazing miracles take place on the Sabbath (Matt 12:9–14), and complain of his association with sinners and tax collectors (Matt 9:11; 11:19). Such a generation will be condemned on the day of judgment.

MATTHEW 12:43–45 – THE PARABLE OF THE EVICTED
AND RETURNING DEMON

12:43: "When the unclean spirit has gone out of a person, it wanders through waterless regions looking for a resting place, but it finds none.

---

[341] According to the pseudepigraphical "Life of Jonah," the prophet Jonah "gave a portent concerning Jerusalem and the whole land, that whenever they should see a stone crying out piteously the end was at hand" (*Lives of the Prophets* 10:10). Thus the "sign of Jonah" may have been understood as a warning of impending judgment (as in the original prophecy concerning Nineveh).

[342] J. Howton, "The Sign of Jonah," *SJT* 15 (1962): 288–304; R. A. Edwards, *The Sign of Jonah in the Theology of the Evangelists and Q* (SBT 2, no. 18; London: SCM Press, 1971); G. M. Landes, "Matthew 12.40 as an Interpretation of 'The Sign of Jonah' against its Biblical Background," in C. L. Meyers and M. O'Connor (eds.), *The Word of the Lord Shall Go Forth: Essays in Honor of David Noel Freedman in Celebration of His Sixtieth Birthday* (Winona Lake, IN: Eisenbrauns, 1983), 665–84.

[343] For more on Jesus as exorcist and greater than Solomon, see D. C. Duling, "Solomon, Exorcism, and the Son of David," *HTR* 68 (1975): 235–52.

12:44: Then it says, 'I will return to my house from which I came.' When it comes, it finds it empty, swept, and put in order.

12:45: Then it goes and brings along seven other spirits more evil than itself, and they enter and live there; and the last state of that person is worse than the first. So will it be also with this evil generation."

*I*n the Matthean context, Jesus' teaching on evil spirits comes right after the demand for a sign (Matt 12:38–42), which in turn had been preceded by the accusation that Jesus cast out demons by the power of Beelzebul (Matt 12:22–37). The concluding reference to "this evil generation" (v. 45; not in the parallel at Luke 11:26) links the passage to the previous passage, in which a sign from Jesus is demanded, resulting in Jesus' comment that "an evil and adulterous generation asks for a sign" (Matt 12:39). Twice more, Jesus will critically speak of "this generation" (Matt 12:41, 42). The present passage (vv. 43–45) returns to the topic of evil spirits, which was inaugurated by the exorcism in Matt 12:22–32.

The passage begins, "When the unclean spirit has gone out of a person, it wanders through waterless regions looking for a resting place, but it finds none" (**v. 43**). The demon usually seeks a "resting place" (literally "rest"; Greek: *anapausis*) in a human host: "we who are demons are exhausted from not having a way station from which to ascend or on which to rest [*anapausis*] …" (*T. Solomon* 20:16). Some evil spirits prefer dry regions. Therefore they avoid water (which is why the drowning of the demon-filled swine in the abyss, in Matt 8:32, signifies annihilation for the demons). In late antiquity, waterless places were often synonymous with desert places (which is why Jesus encounters Satan in the wilderness in the temptation narrative). On such places, see Tob 8:3; *1 Enoch* 10:4–5; *2 Bar* 10:8; *4 Macc* 18:8. In the *Testament of Solomon*, the wicked demon Asmodeus entreats Israel's famous monarch: "I beg you, King Solomon, do not condemn me to water." But Solomon shows no mercy toward the evil being, surrounding it with barrels of water and ordering it to make clay (*T. Solomon* 5:11–12). Other evil spirits prefer water. One commentator calls attention to incantations against evil spirits: "Neither with sea water, nor with sweet water, nor with bad water … shalt thou be covered …" and "O evil spirit – to the desert. O evil demon – to the desert. O evil ghost – to the desert. O evil devil – to the desert…."[344] The first incantation warns the demon that it shall find no water of any kind, and the second incantation threatens demons, evil spirits, and ghosts with banishment to the desert (where no water shall be found). Of course, "waterless regions" usually have no humans, so an evil spirit searching for a human host may not find a new home.

---

[344]   W. Allen, *A Critical and Exegetical Commentary on the Gospel According to St. Matthew*, 3rd edition (ICC; Edinburgh: T & T Clark, 1912), 140–41, quoting R. C. Thompson, *The Devils and Evil Spirits of Babylonia* (2 vols., Luzac's Semitic Text and Translation Series 14–15; London: Luzac; New York: AMS Press, 1903–1904), 1:61, 167.

If a demon that has left someone cannot find a new place of rest, it decides to return "home"; that is, to the person whom the evil spirit had originally possessed (**v. 44**). On the return of an evil spirit, see Josephus (*Ant.* 8.47), where Eleazar "adjured the demon never to come back into him," and Philostratus (*Life of Apollonius* 4.20), who tells us that "the ghost [i.e., the demon] swore that he would leave the young man alone and never take possession of any man again." On a human host as "house," see *T. Naphtali* 8:6, "the devil will inhabit him [the evil doer]"; *b. Gittin* 52a, "he heard Satan say, 'Alas for this man [i.e., Satan himself] whom Rabbi Meir has driven from his house!'"; *b. Hullin* 105b, "he then heard it [the demon] exclaiming, 'Alas, he has driven me out of his house!'" (It is interesting to observe that Meir, like Jesus, was known for his parables; cf. *m. Sota* 9.15.)

But if the demon returns to its former residence and "finds it empty, swept, and put in order," it then "goes and brings along seven other spirits more evil than itself, and they enter and live there; and the last state of that person is worse than the first" (**vv. 44b–45a**). The former home is more attractive than ever to the evil spirit whose quest for a new residence has been futile. A person who has had the evil spirit evicted is in danger of having it return. If the returning spirit finds his old home "empty, swept, and put in order," he will bring along some friends. We think of the demoniac with the "legion" of demons (Mark 5:1–20), or even Mary Magdalene, from whom seven demons went forth (cf. Luke 8:2; Mark 16:9). The number seven often signifies severity, sometimes with the connotation of revenge (e.g., Gen 4:15, "Whoever kills Cain will suffer a sevenfold vengeance"; Gen 4:24, "If Cain is avenged sevenfold, truly Lamech seventy-sevenfold"; Ps 79:12; Prov 6:31).

If the demon returns with seven friends who are more evil than itself, "the last state of that person is worse than the first. So will it be also with this evil generation" (**v. 45b**). By failing to respond to Jesus' message in repentance and faith, even his exorcisms ultimately will be of little help to Israel. The wicked powers that plague the beleaguered nation will return for a season of even heavier oppression.[345]

MATTHEW 12:46–50 – THE TRUE FAMILY OF JESUS

12:46: While he was still speaking to the crowds, his mother and his brothers were standing outside, wanting to speak to him.

---

[345] A. Plummer, "The Parable of the Demon's Return," *ExpT* 3 (1892): 349–51; O. Böcher, *Das Neue Testament und die dämonischen Mächte* (SBS 58; Stuttgart: Katholisches Bibelwerk, 1972), 9–11. R. T. France, *The Gospel of Matthew* (2007), 494, cautions against treating Jesus' "folksy parable" as a "guide to demonology." The purpose of the parable is "to illustrate the danger facing 'this generation.'"

12:47: Someone told him, "Look, your mother and your brothers are standing outside, wanting to speak to you."

12:48: But to the one who had told him this, Jesus replied, "Who is my mother, and who are my brothers?"

12:49: And pointing to his disciples, he said, "Here are my mother and my brothers!

12:50: For whoever does the will of my Father in heaven is my brother and sister and mother."

*M*atthew's context for this story is approximately the same as Mark's, with the exception of the addition of the teaching about the return of an evil spirit (Matt 12:43–45), for which Mark has no parallel. As he often does, Matthew has streamlined Mark's account. It has been pointed out that Jesus' family – consisting of two or more brothers and two or more sisters – fits the typical pattern of the Mediterranean world of late antiquity.[346]

Matthew's account begins, "His mother and his brothers were standing outside, wanting to speak to him" (v. 46). Mark's version only says, "they sent to him and called Him" (Mark 3:31) and "Your mother and your brothers and sisters are outside, asking for you" (Mark 3:32). Mark's readers may well assume that once again Jesus' family wants to "take him into custody" (Mark 3:21). Matthew's version, however, says nothing about Jesus' family hoping to seize him, and here in v. 46 we are told that they only want to speak to him.

Jesus responds by "pointing to his disciples" and saying, "Here are my mother and my brothers! For whoever does the will of my Father in heaven is my brother and sister and mother" (vv. 49–50). Mark's version has "whoever does the will of God" (Mark 3:35). Matthew's version is consistent with his preference for "Father" and "heaven," in place of "God."

This story lightens the somber tone of the material that had preceded it. Standing in stark contrast to those who criticize Jesus, accusing him of violating the Sabbath and even of being in league with Satan, is his "family," a family that is made up not simply of blood relatives (his mother and his brothers) but of anyone who "does the will" of the heavenly Father.

---

[346] R. S. Kraemer, "Typical and Atypical Jewish Family Dynamics: The Case of Babatha and Berenice," in D. L. Balch and C. Osiek (eds.), *Early Christian Families in Context: An Interdisciplinary Dialogue* (Grand Rapids, MI: Eerdmans, 2003), 130–56, at 142. For further discussion, see J. Blinzler, *Die Brüder und Schwester Jesu* (SBS 21; Stuttgart: Katholisches Bibelwerk, 1967); C. A. Evans, "Context, Family and Formation," in M. Bockmuehl (ed.), *The Cambridge Companion to Jesus* (Cambridge Companions to Religion; Cambridge: Cambridge University Press, 2001), 11–24.

MATTHEW 13:1–9 – THE PARABLE OF THE SOWER

13:1: That same day Jesus went out of the house and sat beside the sea.

13:2: Such great crowds gathered around him that he got into a boat and sat there, while the whole crowd stood on the beach.

13:3: And he told them many things in parables, saying: "Listen! A sower went out to sow.

13:4: And as he sowed, some seeds fell on the path, and the birds came and ate them up.

13:5: Other seeds fell on rocky ground, where they did not have much soil, and they sprang up quickly, since they had no depth of soil.

13:6: But when the sun rose, they were scorched; and since they had no root, they withered away.

13:7: Other seeds fell among thorns, and the thorns grew up and choked them.

13:8: Other seeds fell on good soil and brought forth grain, some a hundredfold, some sixty, some thirty.

13:9: Let anyone with ears listen!"

*M*atthew's context is the same as Mark's. Teaching the crowds from the boat sets the stage for the parable of the sower (or soils) that follows in Matt 13:3–9 (cf. Mark 4:3–9; Luke 8:4–8). Matthew streamlines the parable, abbreviating Mark's introduction (compare Mark 4:2–3 with Matt 13:3) and omitting a few phrases, such as "Listen to this!" (Mark 4:3; cf. Matt 13:3), "and it yielded no crop" (Mark 4:7; cf. Matt 13:7), "as they grew up and increased" (Mark 4:8; cf. Matt 13:8), and "to hear" (Mark 4:9; cf. Matt 13:9).

Jesus has gone outside to teach "beside the sea" (**v. 1**). The crowds that gathered to hear Jesus were so large that it was necessary to sit in a boat and push away from the shore (**v. 2**). Although it is not stated, it is probable that this was necessary not simply so the crowds sitting on the inclining shore could better see and hear Jesus but to shield Jesus from people who wanted to touch him for healing or blessing (Matt 9:20; 14:36). To teach unmolested and undistracted, Jesus had to create a barrier between himself and those he taught.

The well-known parable describes four types of soil, in which the sown seed reacts in various ways (**vv. 3–8**). The parable is allegorical, and the meaning of its details will be explained in Matt 13:18–23. It recalls words and imagery from the Old Testament. God's word is likened to rain and snow that give seed to the sower and does not fail to accomplish the divine purpose (Isa 55:10–11).[347] Through the prophet

---

[347] C. A. Evans, "On the Isaianic Background of the Sower Parable," *CBQ* 47 (1985): 464–68.

Jeremiah, the Lord enjoins the men of Judah and the inhabitants of Jerusalem, "Break up your fallow ground, and do not sow among thorns" (Jer 4:3). The closest parallel is found in 4 Ezra: "For just as the farmer sows many seeds in the ground and plants a multitude of seedlings, and yet not all that have been sown will come up in due season, and not all that were planted will take root; so also those who have been sown in the world will not all be saved" (8:41; cf. 3:20; 9:17, 31–37).

The seed that falls in good soil bears fruit, though in varying amounts: "some a hundredfold, some sixty, some thirty." Curiously, Matthew presents the yields in descending order (cf. Mark 4:8, "thirty and sixty and a hundredfold"). Why the reversal? He may assume a correlation of the yields with the status and effectiveness of Jesus' followers (i.e., the most effective produce a hundredfold, less effective followers produce thirtyfold, and so on). Support for this is seen in the emphasis on order and rank in some Jewish traditions, especially as seen in the Dead Sea Scrolls:

The procedure for the meeting of the men of reputation when they are called to the banquet ... the Priest, as head of the entire congregation of Israel, shall enter first, trailed by all his brothers, the sons of Aaron ... then the Messiah of Israel may enter, and the head of thousands of Israel are to sit before him by rank.... Last of all, the heads of the congregation's clans.... (1QSa 2:11–16)

Jesus concludes his parable with the challenge, "Let anyone with ears listen!" (**v. 9**). This challenge functions almost as a refrain in Jesus' teaching (cf. Matt 11:15; 13:43). For further commentary on the parable of the sower, see the commentary on Matt 13:18–23.

MATTHEW 13:10–17 – THE PURPOSE OF PARABLES

13:10: Then the disciples came and asked him, "Why do you speak to them in parables?"

13:11: He answered, "To you it has been given to know the secrets of the kingdom of heaven, but to them it has not been given.

13:12: For to those who have, more will be given, and they will have an abundance; but from those who have nothing, even what they have will be taken away.

13:13: The reason I speak to them in parables is that 'seeing they do not perceive, and hearing they do not listen, nor do they understand.'

13:14: With them indeed is fulfilled the prophecy of Isaiah that says: 'You will indeed listen, but never understand, and you will indeed look, but never perceive.

13:15: For this people's heart has grown dull, and their ears are hard of hearing, and they have shut their eyes; so that they might not look with their eyes, and listen with their ears, and understand with their heart and turn – and I would heal them.'

13:16: But blessed are your eyes, for they see, and your ears, for they hear.

13:17: Truly I tell you, many prophets and righteous people longed to see what you see, but did not see it, and to hear what you hear, but did not hear it."

*I*n all three of the Synoptic Gospels, a discussion of parables appears between the parable of the sower and its explanation. This was Mark's doing, and both Matthew and Luke have followed him; however, not without some changes. Mark's discussion is awkward, both in context and in content (cf. Mark 4:10–13). How exactly it relates to the parable (Mark 4:3–9) or its explanation (Mark 4:14–20) is not clear. The evangelists Matthew and Luke seek to smooth out these difficulties.

Matthew makes several changes in his version of the explanation of parables. He simplifies the introduction (v. 10) and then expands the explanation proper, making it speak more clearly to the purpose of the parables. Matthew also prefers the Greek version of Isa 6:9–10, which as we shall see reads differently from both the Hebrew and the Aramaic.[348]

Matthew's "the disciples came and asked him" (**v. 10**) is much less difficult than Mark's "When he was alone, those who were around him along with the twelve asked him about the parables" (Mark 4:10). Because private explanation elsewhere is given to the disciples (and not the general following), Matthew narrows the scope accordingly. The disciples ask Jesus, "Why do you speak to them in parables?" Matthew's form of the question (which is framed as direct speech) is more clearly focused than Mark's indirect and somewhat vague "asked him about the parables" (Mark 4:10).

Jesus tells his disciples, "To you it has been given to know the secrets of the kingdom of heaven" (**v. 11a**). Matthew explains in what sense the disciples have been given the secrets (literally "mysteries") of the kingdom: they have been given (or granted) to know them. Note, too, that Matthew uses the plural "mysteries," not the singular "mystery" as in Mark 4:11. By saying "mysteries," Matthew has in mind various aspects of the kingdom (as the larger number of kingdom parables in Matthew 13 will illustrate). To what Mark's singular "mystery" refers is not clear (i.e., that the kingdom of God has arrived? or that not all will respond to it? or not all will be equally fruitful?). Matthew's plural allows for all of these aspects.[349] Matthew also

---

[348] For details, see J. Schmid, *Das Evangelium nach Matthäus* (RNT 1; Regensburg: Pustet, 1959), 218–20; A. Sand, *Das Evangelium nach Matthäus*, 5th edition (RNT; Regensburg: Pustet, 1965), 279–81; R. Schnackenburg, *The Gospel of Matthew* (Grand Rapids, MI: Eerdmans, 2002), 125–26.

[349] L. Cerfaux, "La connaissance des secrets du royaume d'après Matt. xiii.11 et par.," *NTS* 2 (1956): 238–49.

has his customary "kingdom of heaven" instead of "kingdom of God."[350] Matthew's "but to them it has not been given" is much less harsh than Mark's "those who are outside" (Mark 4:11).

Jesus then says, "For to those who have, more will be given" (**v. 12**). One of the most helpful aspects of Matthew's editing has been the relocation of Mark 4:25 to this point in the explanation of why Jesus speaks in parables. The meaning is the same, but the confusion is reduced. Insiders are granted the mysteries of the king-dom because spiritual "haves" receive more ("they will have an abundance"). But outsiders are not given these mysteries because spiritual "have-nots" receive less, and even face the danger of losing what they have ("even what they have will be taken away"). There is simply no neutral ground: either one accepts Jesus' message and acts on it, or one rejects it and suffers the consequences.

Jesus answers the disciples' question, saying, "The reason I speak to them in parables is that 'seeing they do not perceive, and hearing they do not listen, nor do they understand'" (**v. 13**). Here is another important editorial change in Matthew's version. Jesus speaks to outsiders in parables *because* (NRSV: "is that") they will not see and *because* they will not listen or understand. Mark says "in order that" (*hina*) the outsiders not see and hear; Matthew says "because" (*hoti*) they will not see. Matthew is careful to lay the blame on those who will not see or hear, not on divine capriciousness, as some might conclude.

Because outsiders will not perceive, listen, or understand, the prophecy of Isaiah is fulfilled in them: "You will indeed listen, but never understand, and you will indeed look, but never perceive," and so on (**v. 14**). Consistent with this change in orientation, Matthew quotes the Greek version (the Septuagint) of Isa 6:9–10 verba-tim. The Greek version predicts the obduracy of the people: "You will indeed listen, but never understand, and you will indeed look, but never perceive" (= Isa 6:9), in contrast to the Hebrew, which has the prophet not predicting obduracy but causing it: "Keep on hearing, but do not perceive; keep on seeing, but do not understand" (literal translation). Moreover, the prophet is not to render the heart of the people insensitive; it already is: "For this people's heart has grown dull, and their ears are hard of hearing, and they have shut their eyes; so that they might not look with their eyes, and listen with their ears, and understand with their heart and turn – and I would heal them" (**v. 15** = Isa 6:10). The people have allowed their hearts to become dull, they have stopped hearing, they have closed their eyes. Why have they done

---

[350] "Kingdom of God/heaven" means the rule of God. The association of mystery (or secret; Greek: *musterion*) to the rule of God finds an interesting parallel in rabbinic literature: "This is what Scripture says: 'The secret of the Lord is for those who fear him' (Ps 25:14). What is the secret of the Holy One? This is circumcision, because the Holy One did not reveal the secret [*misteryon*] of circumcision from Adam until the twentieth generation; until Abraham stood up" (*Aggadat Bereshit* 16.2), adapted from L. M. Teugels, *Aggadat Bereshit: Translated from the Hebrew with an Introduction and Notes* (JCP 4; Leiden: Brill, 2001), 51. The Hebrew text has used the Greek word *musterion* as a loanword.

this? Because they do not want to see, hear, understand, or repent, and then allow God to heal them. God's people have become hopelessly hardened and are headed for unavoidable judgment.

In contrast to those who have rejected Jesus' message and therefore do not have eyes that see or ears that hear are the disciples: "But blessed are your eyes, for they see, and your ears, for they hear" (**v. 16**). Because they have eyes to see and ears to hear (cf. Matt 13:9), they are seeing and hearing what God's servants had hoped to witness: "many prophets and righteous people longed to see what you see, but did not see it, and to hear what you hear, but did not hear it" (**v. 17**). On the combination of "prophets and righteous," see the commentary on Matt 10:41.

There are parallels in rabbinic and intertestamental literature: "Blessed are my eyes that have seen thus" (*b. Hagiga* 14b); "Blessed are those born in those days (i.e., when the Messiah will appear) to see the good fortune of Israel, which God will bring to pass in the assembly of the tribes" (*Pss. Sol.* 17:44); "Rabbi Eliezer says: 'Whence can you say that a maid-servant saw at the sea what Isaiah and Ezekiel and all the prophets never saw? It says about them: "And by the hand of prophets have I given parables" [Hos 12:11, in English 12:10]'" (*Mekilta* on Exod 15:2 [*Shirata'* §3]; cf. *Mekilta* on Exod 19:11 [*Bahodesh* §3]).[351]

MATTHEW 13:18–23 – EXPLANATION OF THE PARABLE OF THE SOWER

13:18: "Hear then the parable of the sower.

13:19: When anyone hears the word of the kingdom and does not understand it, the evil one comes and snatches away what is sown in the heart; this is what was sown on the path.

13:20: As for what was sown on rocky ground, this is the one who hears the word and immediately receives it with joy;

13:21: yet such a person has no root, but endures only for a while, and when trouble or persecution arises on account of the word, that person immediately falls away.

13:22: As for what was sown among thorns, this is the one who hears the word, but the cares of the world and the lure of wealth choke the word, and it yields nothing.

13:23: But as for what was sown on good soil, this is the one who hears the word and understands it, who indeed bears fruit and yields, in one case a hundredfold, in another sixty, and in another thirty."

---

[351] B. van Elderen, "The Purpose of the Parables According to Matthew 13:10–17," in R. N. Longenecker and M. C. Tenney (eds.), *New Dimensions in New Testament Study* (Grand Rapids, MI: Zondervan, 1974), 180–90; C. A. Evans, *To See and Not Perceive: Isaiah 6.9–10 in Early Jewish and Christian Interpretation* (JSOTSup 64; Sheffield: JSOT Press, 1989), 107–13, 208–10.

*M*atthew dramatically alters the context of the explanation of the parable of the soils. In Mark, the explanation begins with two almost disparaging questions of the disciples: "Do you not understand this parable? Then how will you understand all the parables?" (Mark 4:13). Matthew drops both of these questions and begins the explanation with the straightforward declaration: "Hear then the parable of the sower" (Matt 13:18). There are other changes in Matthew's version, most of them streamlining Mark.

Jesus begins his explanation by saying, "Hear then the parable of the sower" (**v. 18**). "Hear" means understand, but it also means heed. It is spoken in light of the positive note on which the explanation in Matt 13:10–17 concludes. Jesus' disciples are blessed for what they have seen and heard. Now they must listen carefully and take to heart the meaning of the parable of the sower.

The seeds that fell on the path and were eaten by the birds (v. 4) signify people who do not understand the "word of the kingdom." In their case, "the evil one comes and snatches away what is sown in the heart" (**v. 19**). The seeds that fell on "rocky ground," which sprang up quickly but withered in the heat of the sun (vv. 5–6), signify the person who "hears the word" and initially "receives it with joy" but "falls away" in the face of "persecution" (**vv. 20–21**). The seeds that fell "among thorns" and were choked by the thorns (v. 7) signify the person "who hears the word, but the cares of the world and the lure of wealth choke the word, and it yields nothing" (**v. 22**).

The seeds that fell "on good soil and brought forth grain" (v. 8) signify "the one who hears the word and understands it, who indeed bears fruit" (**v. 23**). The fruitfulness varies, "in one case a hundredfold, in another sixty, and in another thirty." Once again, Matthew presents the yields in descending order (cf. Mark 4:20 "thirty and sixty and a hundredfold"). See the commentary on Matt 13:8.[352]

The parable of the sower creates an important context for the parables that follow in Chapter 13. The parable makes it clear that people respond in different ways to the message of the kingdom. Not all respond in faith and obedience; and of those who do, not all endure and bear fruit. But there are other ways of explaining the diverse responses and their causes. The parables that follow offer these explanations.

MATTHEW 13:24–30 – THE PARABLE OF THE WHEAT AND WEEDS

13:24: He put before them another parable: "The kingdom of heaven may be compared to someone who sowed good seed in his field;

13:25: but while everybody was asleep, an enemy came and sowed weeds among the wheat, and then went away.

[352]   B. Gerhardsson, "The Parable of the Sower and Its Interpretation," *NTS* 14 (1968): 165–93; D. Wenham, "The Interpretation of the Parable of the Sower," *NTS* 20 (1974): 299–318; P. B. Payne, "The Seeming Inconsistency of the Interpretation of the Parable of the Sower," *NTS* 26 (1980): 564–68.

13:26: So when the plants came up and bore grain, then the weeds appeared as well.

13:27: And the slaves of the householder came and said to him, 'Master, did you not sow good seed in your field? Where, then, did these weeds come from?'

13:28: He answered, 'An enemy has done this.' The slaves said to him, 'Then do you want us to go and gather them?'

13:29: But he replied, 'No; for in gathering the weeds you would uproot the wheat along with them.

13:30: Let both of them grow together until the harvest; and at harvest time I will tell the reapers, Collect the weeds first and bind them in bundles to be burned, but gather the wheat into my barn.'"

The parable of the wheat and weeds is the second allegorical parable in the collection that Matthew has assembled in Chapter 13, an assemblage based on Mark 4. The parable of the wheat and weeds appears only in Matthew. This parable, like the parable of the soils (which appears in all three Synoptic Gospels) and the parable of the seed and harvest (which appears only in Mark), makes symbolic use of seed and sowing. Like the parable of the soils, the parable of the wheat and weeds will also be explained privately to the disciples (cf. Matt 13:36–43).

Whereas the parable of the soils focused on human response to the word (and therefore human responsibility), the parable of the wheat and weeds focuses on the role played by evil. Of course, within the parable of the soils, evil plays a role (in snatching away the word shortly after it is heard), but it plays a much more prominent role in the parable of the wheat and weeds. Together, the parables of the soils and the wheat and weeds tell us about why people respond to Jesus' word differently and what negative role evil plays in this response.[353]

Matthew's parable of the wheat and weeds (or "tares") is the first of several parables found only in Matthew that distinguish good from bad, righteous from unrighteous. The parables of the drag net (Matt 13:47–48), the unforgiving slave (Matt 18:23–35), the maidens (Matt 25:1–13), and the sheep and goats (Matt 25:31–46) are prime examples.

A version of the parable appears in the *Gospel of Thomas* §57:

Jesus says: "The kingdom of the Father is like a person who has [good] seed. His enemy came by night; he sowed a weed among the good seed. The man did not permit them to pull up the weed. He says to them: 'Lest perhaps you go forth saying,

---

[353]   R. H. Gundry, *Matthew* (1982), 262: "true and false disciples"; A. Sand, *Das Evangelium nach Matthäus* (RNT; Regensburg: Pustet, 1986), 285: "good and evil in the community"; D. C. Allison, Jr. and W. D. Davies, *A Critical and Exegetical Commentary on the Gospel According to Saint Matthew* (1988–1997), 2:408; D. J. Harrington, *The Gospel of Matthew* (1991), 208: "separation between the just and unjust."

"We shall pull up the weed" – and you pull up the wheat along with it.' For on the day of harvest the weeds will appear; they pull them and burn them."

The version in *Thomas* is probably not independent or early but a compressed form of the Matthean parable.

There is a similar parable in rabbinic tradition:

This can be compared to weeds that said to the wheat: "We are as beautiful as you, because on you and on us the rain falls, and on both of us the sun shines." The wheat said: "Not what you say, and not what we say [matters], but the winnowing fan comes and separates us for the storehouse and you for the birds to eat. Likewise the nations of the world and Israel are intermingled in this world.... But behold, the day will come that you will know that he makes the righteous enter the Garden of Eden and the wicked Gehenna." (*Aggadat Bereshit* 23.4)[354]

Jesus compares the "kingdom of heaven" to "good seed" that is sowed (**v. 24**). This was also the meaning of the "word" in the parable of the sower (Matt 13:19). In the world of the parable, the "good seed" is seed that is made up entirely of grain, free from weed seed. LXX Isa 1:4 speaks of "evil seed" (Hebrew: "seed of evil doers").

"An enemy came and sowed weeds among the wheat" (**v. 25**) while "everybody was asleep" makes it clear that the enemy did his wicked deed at night. It is not implied that the workers were asleep on the job. The enemy often works under cover of darkness. The "weeds" (or "tares") may refer to a type of plant (perhaps rye) that resembles wheat, at least in its early stages of growth.[355] To illustrate the utter corruption of the world, necessitating the judgment of the flood, some Rabbis speak of the misbehavior of the ground itself: "Wheat was sown, and it produced rye grass, for the rye grass we now find came from the age of the flood" (*Gen. Rab.* 28.8 [on Gen 6:7]). The principal point is different, but the illustration itself is similar.

In due season, "the plants came up and bore grain" (**v. 26**); literally, "the blade sprouted up and produced fruit." The language is similar to LXX Gen 1:11: "Let the earth put forth vegetation: plants yielding seed...." However, as the wheat came up, "the weeds appeared as well." The absence of heads of grain exposed the weeds for what they were. The details of the parable imply that the landowner is not acquainted with the condition of his field on a day-to-day basis. Perhaps we should imagine a man who lives in a nearby city who only on occasion inspects his fields.[356]

[354] Translation based on L. M. Teugels, *Aggadat Bereshit* (2001), 74.
[355] "Weeds" can also be translated as "darnel" (Greek: *zizania*), a noxious weed native to the Middle East. See BAGD ad loc.
[356] As suggested by J. F. Strange, "Some Implications of Archaeology for New Testament Studies," in J. H. Charlesworth and W. P. Weaver (eds.), *What Has Archaeology To Do with Faith?* (1992), 23–59, at 46. The "slaves of the householder" (in v. 27) implies a large farm, which is consistent with Strange's suggestion.

The slaves of the householder wonder if they should pluck out the weeds (**v. 28**), but the suggestion is rejected, "for in gathering the weeds you would uproot the wheat along with them" (**v. 29**). Instead, both the wheat and weeds can grow alongside one another. When the harvest comes, the reapers will be told, "Collect the weeds first and bind them in bundles to be burned, but gather the wheat into my barn" (**v. 30**). What probably is envisioned here is the usual cutting and winnowing to separate the wheat from the chaff (cf. Matt 3:12, "His winnowing fork is in his hand, and he will clear his threshing floor and will gather his wheat into the granary; but the chaff he will burn with unquenchable fire"). The wind blows aside the chaff, allowing the heavier grain to drop to the ground (e.g., Hos 13:3, "like chaff that swirls from the threshing floor"; Ps 1:4, "like chaff which the wind drives away"; Ps 35:5, "like chaff before the wind"; Ps 83:13, "like chaff before the wind"; Job 21:18). The chaff is then bundled and burned, which again is a phrase sometimes used metaphorically in Scripture (e.g., Exod 15:7, "you sent out your fury, it consumed them like stubble"; Mal 4:1, "See, the day is coming, burning like an oven, when all the arrogant and all evildoers will be stubble; the day that comes shall burn them up"). But the "wheat" will be gathered into the farmer's "barn" (which closely parallels Matt 3:12, he "will gather his wheat into the granary"). The imagery of wheat gathered into the barn and the chaff thrown into the fire is a colorful way of speaking of the day of judgment.[357] The allegorical details of the parable will be spelled out in Matt 13:36–43.

MATTHEW 13:31–32 – THE PARABLE OF THE MUSTARD SEED

13:31: He put before them another parable: "The kingdom of heaven is like a mustard seed that someone took and sowed in his field;

13:32: it is the smallest of all the seeds, but when it has grown it is the greatest of shrubs and becomes a tree, so that the birds of the air come and make nests in its branches."

*M*atthew's version of the parable of the mustard seed combines the Markan version (Mark 4:30–32) with an independent version found in Q (cf. Luke 13:18–19).

Matthew reads, "The kingdom of heaven is like a mustard seed that someone took and sowed in his field" (**v. 31**), whereas Mark says "sown upon the soil" (Mark 4:31). Matthew's "sowed in his field" coheres with the rabbinic law that requires mustard to be sown in fields, not in gardens (contrast Luke 13:19, "threw into his own garden"): "… they may flank a field of vegetables with mustard seed … not every kind of seed may be sown in a garden-bed … mustard and small beans are deemed a kind of seed …" (*m. Kilaim* 2:8–9; 3:2). Perhaps Matthew reads "field" in light of this law (or Luke, not being influenced by rabbinic law, changed Q to read "garden").

---

[357] W. G. Doty, "An Interpretation of the Weeds and Wheat," *Int* 25 (1971): 185–93; D. R. Catchpole, "John the Baptist, Jesus and the Parable of the Tares," *SJT* 31 (1978): 557–70.

Although the mustard is the "smallest of all the seeds" regularly used in the farming of Jesus' day (and botanists will inevitably qualify this), "when it has grown it is the greatest of shrubs and becomes a tree" (**v. 32**). Mark's version does not say this, but this detail is in Luke 13:19, so presumably this is a detail from the version Matthew and Luke found in Q. Proof that the mustard shrub really has grown to such a size that it can be called a tree is seen in the fact that "the birds of the air come and make nests in its branches."

The point of the parable seems clear enough: The kingdom may seem small now, but in time it will grow. Unlike the previous parables of Matthew 13, this parable is not an allegory. But the details of "birds" and "branches" seem to allude to Ezek 17:23 ("... a noble cedar.... Under it every kind of bird will live; in the shade of its branches will nest winged creatures of every kind") and Dan 4:20–22 ("The tree ... in whose branches the birds of the air had nests"). Given the allegorical potential of these details, it is possible that Matthew sees in the parable hints of the entry of Gentiles into the kingdom of God (cf. *1 Enoch* 90:30, where the "birds of heaven" [Gentiles] do homage to and obey the "sheep" [people of Israel]), which the risen Jesus in fact commands his disciples to seek to do (cf. Matt 28:18–20). There is no warrant, however, for interpreting the birds as heretics in the church (as in some patristic interpretations).[358]

MATTHEW 13:33–35 – THE PARABLE OF THE YEAST

13:33: He told them another parable: "The kingdom of heaven is like yeast that a woman took and mixed in with three measures of flour until all of it was leavened."

13:34: Jesus told the crowds all these things in parables; without a parable he told them nothing.

13:35: This was to fulfill what had been spoken through the prophet: "I will open my mouth to speak in parables; I will proclaim what has been hidden from the foundation of the world."

This is Matthew's fourth kingdom parable in the discourse that makes up Chapter 13, a discourse derived from Mark 4 but significantly expanded and enriched (e.g., with quotations at Matt 13:14–15, 34–35, and an interesting saying at Matt 13:51–52). The parable of the yeast (or leaven) is a simple parable, with no allegorical elements.

A version of the parable appears in the *Gospel of Thomas* §96: "Jesus says: 'The kingdom of the Father is like [a] woman. She has taken a little yeast; she [has hidden] it in dough. She produced large loaves of it. Whoever has ears, let him hear!'"

[358]   H. K. McArthur, "The Parable of the Mustard Seed," *CBQ* 33 (1971): 198–201; J. Dupont, "Les paraboles du sénevé et du levain (Mt 13,31–33; Lc 13,18–21)," in F. Neirynck (ed.), *Études sur les Évangiles synoptiques* (1985), 2:592–608.

"The kingdom of heaven is like yeast" (**v. 33**) is a curious choice for comparison, given the negative associations of yeast (or leaven) in the Old Testament. Yeast is first mentioned on the eve of the first Passover. To commemorate the Passover, when the Israelites packed unleavened bread (which would last longer during a journey, when baking fresh bread was impractical), in anticipation of a hasty departure from Egypt, no leavened bread was to be eaten. According to the Law of Moses: "Seven days you shall eat unleavened bread; on the first day you shall remove leaven from your houses, for whoever eats leavened bread from the first day until the seventh day shall be cut off from Israel" (Exod 12:15; cf. 12:19). Indeed, yeast was not to be found within Israel's borders (cf. Exod 13:7; Deut 16:4, "all your territory"). Certain offerings are not to have yeast (cf. Lev 2:11; 6:17).

By the time we reach the New Testament period, yeast is readily used for negative metaphors and examples. Paul warns an arrogant Corinthian congregation, "Your boasting is not a good thing. Do you not know that a little yeast leavens the whole batch of dough?" (1 Cor 5:6; Gal 5:9), and admonishes them to "Clean out the old yeast so that you may be a new batch, as you really are unleavened.... Therefore, let us celebrate the festival, not with the old yeast, the yeast of malice and evil, but with the unleavened bread of sincerity and truth" (1 Cor 5:7–8). Jesus himself warned of the "leaven of the Pharisees" and of others (e.g., Matt 16:11; Mark 8:15; Luke 12:1). Negative associations are also seen in Greco-Roman writers (e.g., Plutarch, *Moralia* 289F, "Roman Questions" 109: "Yeast is itself also the product of corruption, and produces corruption in the dough with which it is mixed").

The negative applications of yeast notwithstanding, the substance can be used in a positive sense (as in Philo, *Special Laws* 2.184–85, "But yeast is also a symbol for … food in its most complete and perfect form … and joy …"; Lev 7:13–14; 23:17), or in a purely neutral sense, as here in Jesus' parable.

Jesus' parable of the yeast is not an allegory. The "woman" of the parable has no symbolic value; she is not Mary, the Holy Spirit, or anyone or anything else. The woman's mixing in "three measures of flour" is not a reference to the Trinity or to the concept of perfection. To be sure, three measures is a goodly amount of flour, which is probably better translated as "wheat dough" (Greek: *aleuron*). The three measures (Greek: *sata*, an Aramaic loanword), perhaps alluding to Gen 18:6 ("Make ready quickly three measures of choice flour, knead it, and make cakes"), probably equal one ephah (cf. Ruth 2:17), or about a dozen pints, valued at about three shekels (cf. Josephus, *Ant.* 9.85). The dough that would result should be sufficient for several loaves of bread, perhaps enough to serve one hundred or more. Accordingly, the amount of flour is probably hyperbolic, thus underscoring the pervasiveness of the leaven and making the lesson that much clearer: a little bit of yeast can leaven a very large lump of dough.[359]

---

[359]   On leaven, literally and metaphorically, see C. L. Mitton, "Leaven," *ExpT* 84 (1972–1973): 339–43.

What the NRSV translates as "mixed" in Greek is actually "hid" (*enekrupsen*). The verb "hid" implies nothing special. It is used probably because the yeast, when kneaded into the dough, is hidden from view. Even though it is out of sight, it is very much at work.

Matthew follows the yeast parable with the statement, "Jesus told the crowds all these things in parables; without a parable he told them nothing" (**v. 34**). Matthew transforms Mark's summary in order to cite a passage of Scripture as fulfilled, as he does in the infancy narrative (e.g., Matt 1:22), the inauguration of public ministry in Galilee (Matt 4:14), the healing ministry (Matt 8:17), and the refusal to quarrel in public (Matt 12:17). All are said to fulfill this or that prophecy (especially those in Isaiah).

Jesus' habit of teaching in parables is said "to fulfill what had been spoken through the prophet: 'I will open my mouth to speak in parables; I will proclaim what has been hidden from the foundation of the world'" (**v. 35**). Matthew has quoted Ps 78:2 [LXX 77:2]. He follows the LXX closely, though there are a few differences worth mentioning. Matthew says (literally), "I will open my mouth in parables; I will declare [Greek: *ereugesthai*] things hidden [Greek: *kekrummena*] from the foundation [Greek: *kataboles*] of the world [Greek: *kosmos*]," whereas the Greek Old Testament reads (literally), "I will open my mouth in parables; I will utter [Greek: *phtheggesthai*] riddles [Greek: *problemata*] from the beginning [Greek: *arche*]."

Matthew may have altered his quotation (especially "things hidden") to fit Jesus' teaching about what is hidden and what is revealed; for example, Matt 10:26, "for nothing is covered up that will not be uncovered, and nothing secret that will not become known." This language is also well attested among the Dead Sea Scrolls: "Bless the One who performs majestic wonders, and makes known the strength of His hand, sealing up mysteries and revealing hidden things, raising up those who stumble and fall" (4Q427 frag. 7, col. i, lines 18–19); "You have opened within me knowledge in the mystery of Your insight …" (1QHa 20:13). A revealer of hidden things casts Jesus into the role of the authoritative teacher of the end times.[360]

MATTHEW 13:36–43 – EXPLANATION OF THE PARABLE OF THE WHEAT AND WEEDS

13:36: Then he left the crowds and went into the house. And his disciples approached him, saying, "Explain to us the parable of the weeds of the field."

13:37: He answered, "The one who sows the good seed is the Son of Man;

---

[360] F. van Segbroeck, "Le scandale de l'incroyance: La signification de Mt 13,35," *ETL* 41 (1965): 344–72; R. Q. Ford, "Body Language: Jesus' Parables of the Woman with the Yeast, the Woman with the Jar, and the Man with the Sword," *Int* 56 (2002): 295–306.

13:38: the field is the world, and the good seed are the children of the kingdom; the weeds are the children of the evil one,

13:39: and the enemy who sowed them is the devil; the harvest is the end of the age, and the reapers are angels.

13:40: Just as the weeds are collected and burned up with fire, so will it be at the end of the age.

13:41: The Son of Man will send his angels, and they will collect out of his kingdom all causes of sin and all evildoers,

13:42: and they will throw them into the furnace of fire, where there will be weeping and gnashing of teeth.

13:43: Then the righteous will shine like the sun in the kingdom of their Father. Let anyone with ears listen!"

*M*atthew has postponed Jesus' private explanation of the parable of the wheat and weeds (Matt 13:24–30) so as not to interrupt his account of Jesus' ongoing public teaching (Matt 13:31–33). With his public teaching completed (noted in Matt 13:34–35), Jesus leaves the crowds and retires to the privacy of a house.

The disciples desire private clarification: "Explain to us the parable of the weeds of the field" (**v. 36**). Jesus explains that the "one who sows the good seed is the Son of Man; the field is the world, and the good seed are the children of the kingdom" (**vv. 37–38a**). The imagery recalls the parable of the sower (Matt 13:3). The seed that the sower sowed was the "word of the kingdom" in Matt 13:19. On "Son of Man," see the commentary on Matt 9:6. The word "world" (Greek: *kosmos*) occurs fifteen times in the Synoptic Gospels, nine of those occurrences in Matthew. In the temptation narrative, the devil shows Jesus "all the kingdoms of the world" and offers them to him if he will worship him (Matt 4:8). Jesus tells his disciples that they "are the light of the world" (Matt 5:14). Jesus expects his gospel to be "proclaimed in the whole world" (Matt 26:13). It is to this that the "field" or "world" in the parable refers. Everywhere that humans live is the world; it is the field into which the message of the kingdom has been sown.

The "good seed are the children of the kingdom"; that is, the children of the kingdom, who will not be "thrown into the outer darkness," as in Matt 8:12. We should infer that the good seed represents those children of the kingdom that do respond to the kingdom message and are not among those "children" (Israelites) who are cast out of the kingdom. See the commentary on Matt 8:12. There are some suggestive parallels with 1QS 3:13–4:26, in which the children of light and the children of darkness, along with their eternal destinies, are contrasted.[361] The parable

---

[361] See D. Marguerat, "L'église et le monde in Matthieu 13,36–43," *Revue de théologie et de philosophie* 110 (1978): 111–29, especially 127–28.

of the wheat and weeds and its interpretation authentically reflect pre-Christian Jewish thought.

The "weeds," Jesus continues to explain, "are the children of the evil one" (**v. 38b**). If the good seed are the children of the kingdom, then the reverse is true: the weed seed are the "children of the evil one" (Greek: *tou ponerou*). Jesus does not mean they are literal offspring but that their character is defined by and consistent with the evil one. The "evil one" could be translated as abstract "evil." But it is probable that evil one is personal and that it refers to the devil himself, named in the next verse. The designation "sons of the evil one" is one among many in the literature of the period. At Qumran, the most common negative appellation is "children of darkness" (e.g., 1QM 1:1, 7, 10), who are assisted by Belial (e.g., 1QM 17:11, "When [Belial] prepares himself to assist the Children of Darkness"); these are also called "children of Belial" (e.g., 4Q174 3:8; 4Q286 frag. 7, col. ii, line 6; 4Q287 frag. 6, line 5). Matthew himself refers to the Pharisees as "sons of hell" (Matt 23:15).

And, of course, the "enemy who sowed [the weed seeds] is the devil" (**v. 39a**). Another popular appellation for the wicked is "children of the devil" (1 John 3:10) or, as Jesus in the fourth Gospel puts it, "You are from your father the devil" (John 8:44). Satan, or the devil, is sometimes referred to as the "enemy." Jesus tells his disciples, "See, I have given you authority to tread on snakes and scorpions, and over all the power of the enemy" (Luke 10:19). Paul says to the magician who opposed the gospel: "You son of the devil, you enemy of all righteousness ..." (Acts 13:10). Satan is called the "enemy" several times in the pseudepigraphical *Life of Adam and Eve*, and in the *Testaments of the Patriarchs* it is said "that upon the day on which Israel shall repent, the kingdom of the enemy shall be brought to an end" (*T. Dan* 6:4).

As Jesus' hearers would have suspected, "the harvest is the end of the age, and the reapers are angels" (**v. 39**). Harvest is sometimes a symbol of coming judgment: "Daughter Babylon is like a threshing floor at the time when it is trodden; yet a little while and the time of her harvest will come" (Jer 51:33); "Put in the sickle, for the harvest is ripe. Go in, tread, for the wine press is full" (Joel 3:13); and 2 *Bar* 70:2. See Mark 4:26–29. But the harvest may also signify a judgment of blessing, as in Hos 6:11, "For you also, O Judah, a harvest is appointed, when I would restore the fortunes of my people."

Jesus identifies the "reapers" of the parable as angels. This is a standard feature in Jewish eschatology; for example, *1 Enoch* 54:6, "And Michael, and Gabriel, and Raphael, and Phanuel shall take hold of them on that great day, and cast them on that day into the burning furnace, that the Lord of Spirits may take vengeance on them for their unrighteousness in becoming subject to Satan and leading astray those who dwell on the earth." See also *1 Enoch* 63:1; Rev 14:15, 17–19; Matt 24:31.

On the topic of the day of judgment, Jesus says, "Just as the weeds are collected and burned up with fire, so will it be at the end of the age" (**v. 40**). One must recall the words of John the Baptist, who proclaimed the coming of one who will baptize the people with fire: "His winnowing fork is in his hand, and he will clear his threshing floor and will gather his wheat into the granary; but the chaff he will burn with unquenchable fire" (Matt 3:12). Fiery judgment is the expectation in Malachi, the very prophecy that informed much of John's preaching (cf. Mal 3:2; 4:1; Zeph 3:8).

As "Son of Man," Jesus will play a role in the day of judgment, for he "will send his angels, and they will collect out of his kingdom all causes of sin and all evildoers, and they will throw them into the furnace of fire, where there will be weeping and gnashing of teeth" (**vv. 41–42**). Angels have played a part in Matthew's narrative, making appearances in the infancy narrative and at the conclusion of the temptation in the wilderness (cf. Matt 4:11). However, this is the first mention of angels in the command of the Son of Man. This feature will occur later in Matt 16:27: "For the Son of Man is to come with his angels in the glory of his Father, and then he will repay everyone for what has been done" (see also Matt 24:31; 25:31; 26:53). It may be that Matthew's understanding of Jesus as the "Son of Man" is based on the interesting reading of Daniel 7 in the Old Greek (OG) version, in which the Son of Man figure seems to be identified with the Ancient of Days (i.e., God), sits on a throne, and is attended by angels.

In Matthew, the kingdom of God is linked to Israel in the sense that by right of Abrahamic descent and by right of covenant Israelites are "children of the kingdom." But in the last days the people of this kingdom will be culled, weeded out, as it were. Some of the "children of the kingdom" will be cast out (Matt 8:12), others will be gathered in (Matt 13:38). All wicked people and wickedness, including "causes of sin" and "evildoers," will be removed. What will be left will be a purified and refined people of God (see Isa 4:2–6; 6:13); this will make up Jesus' church (see Matt 16:18–19).

In Matthew, "causes of sin" (or "stumbling blocks"; Greek: *skandala*) are things, people, or impulses that lead to sin (e.g., Matt 5:29–30; 18:6–9, especially v. 7, "Woe to the world because of stumbling blocks!") or to unbelief (e.g., Matt 11:6; 13:57). In the great tribulation that will precede the return of the Son of Man, many will stumble (cf. Matt 24:10). Even the disciples themselves, Jesus warns, will stumble when Jesus is arrested and condemned (cf. Matt 26:31). For the present context, perhaps Matt 13:21 (in reference to the person who may be compared to shallow soil) offers the most helpful guidance: "yet such a person has no root, but endures only for a while, and when trouble or persecution arises on account of the word, that person immediately falls away [or stumbles]."

Jesus' words, "the furnace of fire," allude to Dan 3:6, where Nebuchadnezzar threatens to throw into a blazing furnace anyone who does not worship his image. Warning of fiery judgment has already been heard in Matthew, from John the Baptist (Matt 3:10, 12) and from Jesus (Matt 7:19). In the fires of hell, "there will be weeping and gnashing of teeth." Earlier, Jesus warned that even "children of the kingdom" will "be cast into the outer darkness; in that place there shall be weeping and gnashing of teeth" (Matt 8:12). The image will appear again in the parable of the drag net (Matt 13:50) and in other judgment passages in Matthew (cf. 22:13; 24:51; 25:30).

In contrast to the wicked, who have been cast into darkness, "the righteous will shine like the sun in the kingdom of their Father" (**v. 43**). We probably have an allusion to Dan 12:3, especially when it is remembered that Dan 12:2 speaks of resurrection: "Those who are wise shall shine like the brightness of the sky, and those who lead many to righteousness, like the stars forever and ever" (Dan 12:3). The explanation of the parable of the wheat and weeds concludes with the familiar admonition, "Let anyone with ears listen!" See the commentary on Matt 11:15.[362]

There are a few approximate parallels in Greco-Roman philosophy and ethics. Antisthenes is remembered to have remarked, at the expense of politicians: "But it is very odd that we weed out tares from the wheat, and we weed out those unfit for war; but in city politics the misfits have no exemption" (Diogenes, *Lives of Eminent Philosophers* 6.6). Seneca opines: "Divine seeds are sown in our human bodies. If a good farmer receives them, they spring up in the likeness of their source and of a parity with those from which they came. If, however, the farmer be bad, like a barren or marshy soil, he kills the seeds, and causes tares to grow up instead of wheat" (*Moral Epistles* 73.16).

MATTHEW 13:44–46 – THE PARABLES OF THE TREASURE AND THE PEARL

13:44: "**The kingdom of heaven is like treasure hidden in a field, which someone found and hid; then in his joy he goes and sells all that he has and buys that field.**

13:45: "**Again, the kingdom of heaven is like a merchant in search of fine pearls;**

13:46: on finding one pearl of great value, he went and sold all that he had and bought it."

*M*atthew's parable of the treasure (Matt 13:44) has no parallels in Mark or Luke. The point of the parable is quite straightforward: the kingdom of heaven is so precious that to gain it one should be willing to give up all else. Its lesson is the same as in the parable of the pearl that follows (Matt 13:45–46). The question of the legality of buying a field in order to acquire a hidden treasure is treated later.

---

[362] M. de Goedt, "L'explication de la parabole de l'ivraie (Mt 13,36–43)," *RB* 66 (1959): 32–54; C. W. F. Smith, "The Mixed State of the Church in Matthew's Gospel," *JBL* 82 (1963): 149–68; W. G. Doty, "An Interpretation of the Weeds and Wheat," *Int* 25 (1971): 185–93; D. R. Catchpole, "John the Baptist, Jesus and the Parable of the Tares," *SJT* 31 (1978): 557–70.

Jesus' comparison that "The kingdom of heaven is like treasure hidden in a field" (**v. 44a**) is apt (cf. Isa 33:6, "he will be the stability of your times, abundance of salvation, wisdom, and knowledge; the fear of the Lord is Zion's treasure").

It was not uncommon in antiquity to hide money and valuables underground, especially in times of war. In the aftermath of the capture of Jerusalem, according to Josephus, the Romans found Jewish treasures: "Of the vast wealth of the city no small portion was still being discovered among the ruins. Much of this the Romans dug up, but the greater part they became possessed of through the information of the prisoners, gold and silver and other most precious articles, which the owners in view of the uncertain fortunes of war had stored underground" (Josephus, *J.W.* 7.114–15). According to *2 Bar* 6:7–9 and *4 Bar* 3:6–11, cultic treasures of the temple were stored underground, to be retrieved at a later time. See also Sir 20:30, which speaks of "hidden wisdom and unseen treasure."

The verse continues, "which someone found and hid." The man who discovers the treasure rehides it, lest someone else (perhaps the owner of the field) find it, too. The lucky finder rejoices ("in his joy"). In another parable found only in Matthew, the faithful slave is invited to "enter into the joy of your master" (Matt 25:21, 23). Scripture sometimes speaks of joy (Greek: *chara*) in connection with God or with God's kingdom itself, such as in Sir 1:12, "The fear of the Lord delights the heart, and gives gladness and joy and long life"; see also Rom 14:17.

The statement "He goes and sells all that he has and buys that field" (**v. 44b**) points out an ambiguity in Jewish law. According to the Mishna, which is Jewish law and oral tradition edited and published at the beginning of the third century A.D.: "If a man sold a field he has sold also the stones that are necessary to it, and the canes in a vineyard that are necessary to it..." (*m. Baba Batra* 4:8). However, the passage goes on to discuss various items that are not "necessary" to the field and therefore are excluded from the purchase (4:9). On the basis of this ruling, one could argue that the treasure was not necessary to the field and therefore the purchaser would not be entitled to it. But that is not a universal opinion.

We find in a parable, part of which follows, a conversation between Alexander the Great and two men in dispute: "While they were sitting, two men came before the king for judgment. One said, 'Your majesty, I bought a deserted building from this man; and when I cleaned it out, I found a treasure in it.' So I said to him, "Take your treasure, because I [only] bought a deserted building. I did not buy a treasure."' But the other said, 'Just as you are afraid of punishment for robbery, so I am afraid of punishment for robbery; for when I sold you the deserted building, I sold you whatever was in it from under the ground up to the heavens'" (*Midrash Tanhuma, Emor* §9 [on Lev 22:26–27]; cf. *Lev. Rab.* 27.1 [on Lev 22:27] and *Pesiqta deRab Kahana* 9.1, which repeat the story, only in these versions we hear of a tree with golden fruit rather than a building with a hidden treasure).[363]

---

[363]   For more examples, see C. S. Keener, *A Commentary on the Gospel of Matthew* (1999), 391–92.

Jesus' parable does not intend to teach law pertaining to real estate, nor does the parable teach us anything about ethics (and the ethics of the treasure seeker are indeed dubious); the point of the parable is that the kingdom of God is like a treasure (and a treasure laid up in heaven, at that; cf. Matt 6:19–21) that should be acquired at whatever cost.

There are legends from antiquity about hidden treasures. The Roman poet Virgil (70–19 B.C.) speaks of "ancient treasures in the earth, a hoard of gold and silver known to none" (*Aeneid* 1.358–59). Better known today is the Copper Scroll from Qumran (i.e., 3Q15), which provides directions to the locations of hidden gold, silver, and other valuables, whose worth today would be enormous.

The *Gospel of Thomas* §109 preserves an interesting version of the parable of the treasure: "Jesus says: 'The kingdom is like a person who has a treasure [hidden] in his field without knowing it. And [after] he died, he bequeathed it to his [son. The] son did not know (about it), he accepted that field, he sold [it]. And he came who purchased it; he plowed it, [he found] the treasure. He began to lend money at interest to whomever he wishes.'"

The lesson of the parable of the pearl is essentially the same as the lesson taught by the preceding parable of the treasure. The parable of the pearl is not found in Mark or Luke.

In the next verse, Jesus once again returns to the subject of pearls: "Again, the kingdom of heaven is like a merchant in search of fine pearls" (**v. 45**). In the Sermon on the Mount, Jesus had advised his disciples not to throw their "pearls before swine" (Matt 7:6). Here pearls (Greek: *margaritas*) once again represent precious things. In antiquity, pearls were greatly prized (much as diamonds are today); see, for example, Job 28:18; Rev 21:21. In the *Gospel of Philip*, a second-century Gnostic writing, we are told: "When the pearl is cast down into the mud, it becomes greatly despised; nor if it is anointed with balsamic oil will it become more precious. But it always has value in the eyes of its owner" (§48). The *Acts of Peter and the Twelve Apostles*, another Gnostic writing, perhaps also dating to the second century, tells of a pearl merchant walking the streets, crying out, "Pearls! Pearls!" (NHC VI 2.29–32; 3.11–13). Facing martyrdom, early second-century church father Ignatius referred to the chains with which he was bound as "my spiritual pearls" (*Letter to the Ephesians* 11:2).

The story continues, "on finding one pearl of great value, he went and sold all that he had and bought it" (**v. 46**). On "great value" (Greek: *polutimos*), which does not occur in the Greek Old Testament (the Septuagint), see John 12:3; 1 Pet 1:7. One thinks of a story in rabbinic literature that tells of a man who "went and sold all his property and bought a precious stone with the proceeds …" (*b. Sanh.* 119a). In a conversation with a wealthy Roman (of "consular rank"), Epictetus asks him if he takes care of his various possessions, such as his prized horses, his money and valuables, and even his own body. The Roman affirms that he does indeed. Epictetus then asks him what his most prized possession is. The Roman is not sure at first, but then guesses correctly that it must be his soul: "I do really think it a much better possession than all the rest" (Epictetus 2.12.21–22).

When the merchant realizes what he has found, he sells everything he has so he can buy the pearl. This part of the parable is similar to a rabbinic parable that at one point reads: "He went, sold all this property, and bought a precious stone with the proceeds" (*b. Shab.* 119a).[364] So it is with the kingdom of God; to possess it is worth everything one has.

> **A Closer Look: Parallels to the Parable of the Pearl**
>
> The *Gospel of Thomas* §76 contains a version of the parable of the pearl, though it also draws upon elements from Matthew 6: "Jesus says, 'The king-dom of the Father is like a merchant possessing a fortune, who found a pearl. That merchant was shrewd. He sold the fortune, he bought the one pearl for himself. You yourselves, seek for [the treasure of his face], which perishes not, which endures – the place where no moth comes near to devour nor worm ravages.'"
>
> There are approximate parallels to the parable of the pearl that make the same basic point. Job says in the pseudepigraphical *Testament of Job* (first century A.D.): "And I became as one wishing to enter a certain city to discover its wealth and gain a portion of its splendor, and as one embarked with cargo in a seagoing ship. Seeing at mid-ocean the third wave and the opposition of the wind, he threw the cargo into the sea, saying, 'I am willing to lose every-thing in order to enter this city so that I might gain both the ship and things better than the payload.' Thus, I also considered my goods as nothing com-pared to the city about which the angel spoke to me" (*T. Job* 18:6–8).
>
> The closest parallel is found in a rabbinic writing: "[It is like] one to whom there fell [as] an inheritance a residence in a seaport city and he sold it for a small sum and the purchaser went and dug through it and found in it trea-sures of silver and treasures of gold and precious stones and pearls. The seller almost choked [for rage and grief]. So did Egypt because they sent away [Israel] and did not know what they sent away" (*Mekilta deRabbi Simeon ben Yohai* 14.5).

MATTHEW 13:47–50 – THE PARABLE OF THE NET

13:47: "Again, the kingdom of heaven is like a net that was thrown into the sea and caught fish of every kind;

[364] J. C. Fenton, "Expounding the Parables: IV. The Parables of the Treasure and the Pearl," *ExpT* 77 (1966): 178–80; J. Dupont, "Les paraboles du trésor et de la perle," *NTS* 14 (1968): 408–18; J. D. Crossan, "Hidden Treasure Parables in Late Antiquity," *SBL 1976 Seminar Papers* (1976): 359–79.

13:48: when it was full, they drew it ashore, sat down, and put the good into baskets but threw out the bad.

13:49: So it will be at the end of the age. The angels will come out and separate the evil from the righteous

13:50: and throw them into the furnace of fire, where there will be weeping and gnashing of teeth.

*T*he parable of the net (or drag net) is another parable found only in Matthew. It does not, however, make the same point made in the parables of the treasure and the pearl (Matt 13:44–46). In those parables, the point has to do with the incomparable value of the kingdom: sell all – do what it takes – to gain the kingdom. But the parable of the net returns to the theme of varying responses to the kingdom, as in the parable of the sower (Matt 13:3–9) or, even better, the parable of the wheat and weeds (Matt 13:24–30). The parables of the net and the wheat and weeds teach that in the day of judgment, when the true membership of God's kingdom is finally settled, the good will be separated from the bad, the sheep from the goats (as in Matt 25:31–46), or the wise from the foolish (as in Matt 25:1–13). Because the parable of the net teaches approximately the same lesson as the parables of the sower and the wheat and weeds, Matthew is able to conclude the kingdom discourse on the theme with which it had begun. The parable of the net also makes a fitting conclusion to the discourse because of its warning of judgment to come.

Jesus' analogy, "The kingdom of heaven is like a net that was thrown into the sea and caught fish of every kind" (**v. 47**), has its counterpart in rabbinic literature, where people are sometimes compared to fish. Commenting on Hab 1:14 ("You have made people like the fish of the sea"), Rab Judah asks, "Why is a human here compared to the fishes of the sea? To tell you, just as the fishes of the sea, as soon as they come on to dry land, die, so also a human, as soon as he abandons Torah and the precepts [falls into judgment]" (*b. 'Abodah Zarah* 3b). The Talmud goes on to make another comparison: "Just as among the fish of the sea, the greater swallow up the smaller ones, so with humans" (*b. 'Abodah Zarah* 4a). The variety of fish is illustrated in this example: "On the subject of disciples Rabban Gamaliel the Elder spoke of four kinds: An unclean fish, a clean fish, a fish from the Jordan, a fish from the Great Sea. An unclean fish – who is that? A poor youth who studies … without understanding. A clean fish – who is that? That's a rich youth who studies … with understanding. A fish from the Jordan – who is that? A scholar who studies … and is without the talent for give and take. A fish from the Great Sea – who is that? A scholar who studies … and has the talent for give and take" (*'Abot deRabbi Nathan* 40.9).

The net (Greek: *sagene*) is mentioned a few times in the Greek version of the Old Testament (LXX). One passage is interesting: "On this account he will sacrifice to his seine [net] and burn incense to his fishing net, because by them he made his portion fat and his food choice" (LXX Hab 1:16). The net is secured between two boats, which then drag the net through the water, and sometimes to the shore.

In the verse that follows, "When it was full, they drew it ashore, sat down, and put the good into baskets but threw out the bad" (**v. 48**), we again have the good/bad (or saved/lost) distinction of which Matthew is fond. The "good" fish are kosher (Lev 11:9, "that has fins and scales, whether in the seas or in the streams"). The "bad" fish are probably unclean from a Jewish perspective (cf. Lev 11:12, "that does not have fins and scales is detestable to you"; *b. Hullin* 63b, on what characteristics "distinguish [clean and unclean] fish").[365]

Jesus draws the analogy with the good and bad fish by saying, "So it will be at the end of the age" (**v. 49a**). Once again, we probably have an allusion to Dan 12:13, "But you, go your way, and rest; you shall rise for your reward at the end of the days." See Matt 13:43 and the comment there. The phrase "the end of the days" appears twice in the explanation of the parable of the wheat and the weeds (cf. Matt 13:39, 40).

Jesus then discusses the part angels will play at the judgment: "The angels will come out and separate the evil from the righteous and throw them into the furnace of fire, where there will be weeping and gnashing of teeth" (**vv. 49b–50**). On the role of angels in the day of judgment, see the commentary on Matt 13:41. On the imagery of hell, weeping, and gnashing of teeth, see the commentaries on Matt 8:12 and 13:42.

A version of this parable appears in the *Gospel of Thomas* §8: "And he says: 'The [kingdom] is like a wise fisherman who cast his net into the sea. He drew it up from the sea full of small fish. Among them he found a large good fish. That wise fisherman, he threw all the small fish back into the sea, he chose the large fish without hesitation. Whoever has ears to hear, let him hear!'" This form of the parable may have been influenced by the parable of the pearl (because of the focus on *one* fish and the lack of hesitation in choosing it above all others). Note that the fisherman is twice described as "wise," which may reflect a gnosticizing tendency.[366]

MATTHEW 13:51–53 – THE SCRIBE TRAINED FOR THE KINGDOM

13:51: **"Have you understood all this?" They answered, "Yes."**

13:52: **And he said to them, "Therefore every scribe who has been trained for the kingdom of heaven is like the master of a household who brings out of his treasure what is new and what is old."**

13:53: **When Jesus had finished these parables, he left that place.**

---

[365] J. D. M. Derrett, "ἦσαν γὰρ ἁλιεῖς (Mk i 16): Jesus's Fishermen and the Parable of the Net," *NovT* 22 (1980): 108–37; P. Archbald, "Interpretation of the Parable of the Dragnet (Matthew 13:47–50)," *Vox Reformata* 48 (1987): 3–14.

[366] W. G. Morrice, "The Parable of the Dragnet and the Gospel of Thomas," *ExpT* 95 (1984): 269–73.

$\mathcal{E}$xpanding Mark 4, Matthew in Chapter 13 has produced a third discourse on the kingdom of God (the first discourse is the Sermon on the Mount, Matt 5:3–7:27, the second the missionary discourse, Matt 10:1–42). The kingdom discourse is made up of seven parables: the sower (vv. 3–9), the wheat and weeds (vv. 24–30), the mustard seed (vv. 31–32), the yeast (v. 33), the hidden treasure (v. 44), the pearl (vv. 45–46), and the net (vv. 47–50). Here in vv. 51–53 Matthew brings the discourse to a conclusion with an interesting comment about the "scribe who has been trained for the kingdom of heaven."

Jesus wants to make sure that his disciples have understood all these parables: "'Have you understood all this?' They answered, 'Yes'" (**v. 51**). To *understand* (Greek: *sunienai*) is very important in the Gospel of Matthew. The word occurs eighteen times in the Synoptic Gospels; half of those occurrences are in Matthew. Jesus speaks parables to those who do not see and do not understand (Matt 13:13). In the parable of the sower, those who hear the word of the gospel but have it snatched from their hearts are those who have not understood it (Matt 13:19). Those who hear it and are fruitful are those who did understand it (Matt 13:23). Later in Matthew's narrative, a point will be made that the disciples understand Jesus' teaching, even in contexts where Mark leaves the reader in doubt (e.g., Matt 16:12 = Mark 8:21; Matt 17:13 = Mark 9:13). "All this" takes the reader back to Matt 13:34 "… all these things in parables.…"

The disciples affirm that, "yes," they do understand Jesus' parables and his reason for using them. This affirmation places the disciples squarely among those to whom the mysteries (or secrets) of the kingdom of heaven are given. They are not among those upon whom the dreadful word of Isaiah falls (cf. Matt 13:11–17 and quotation of Isa 6:9–10).

Jesus finishes his discourse of seven parables with a comparison that in a sense is a parable itself: "Therefore every scribe who has been trained for the kingdom of heaven is like the master of a household who brings out of his treasure what is new and what is old" (**v. 52**). The positive usage of "scribe" is surprising, given its consistently negative associations everywhere else (e.g., Matt 23:13: "But woe to you, scribes and Pharisees, hypocrites! For you lock people out of the kingdom of heaven"). However, a scribe converted, "who has been trained for the kingdom of heaven," would be well qualified to research and teach the gospel story and the teachings of Jesus. Could this be an autobiographical reference?[367] It has been suggested that the author (whether the traditional Matthew – the former tax collector – or someone else) was a member of a group of Christian scribes who saw themselves as scribes with expertise in matters of eschatology, such as the authors of *1 Enoch*, *4 Ezra*, *2 Baruch*, and other writings, who were thought to have been scribes also. The words attributed to Enoch should be quoted: "Fear not, Enoch, righteous man

[367] Even if autobiographical, it nevertheless applies to other scholars in the early Christian movement. See R. Schnackenburg, *The Gospel of Matthew* (2002), 135–36.

and scribe of righteousness" (*1 Enoch* 15:1). Note, too, the autobiographical comment of Yeshua ben Sira, the second-century sage: "He seeks out the wisdom of
all the ancients, and is concerned with prophecies; he preserves the sayings of the
famous and penetrates the subtleties of parables; he seeks out the hidden meanings
of proverbs and is at home with the obscurities of parables" (Sir 39:1–3). A major
part of this scribe's work was bound up with parables and in studying the "sayings
of the famous." This description fits the evangelist Matthew. The scribe "who has
been trained" (literally "having been discipled"; Greek: *matheteuein*) complies with
an essential element of the Great Commission: "Go therefore and make disciples
[*matheteuein*] of all nations, baptizing them … teaching them …." (Matt 28:19–20).

The discipled scribe is compared to a "master of a household." Jesus had referred
to himself as a "the master of the house" (Greek: *oikodespotes*) in reference to the
Beelzebul controversy: "It is enough for the disciple to be like the teacher, and the
slave like the master. If they have called the master of the house Beelzebul, how
much more will they malign those of his household!" (Matt 10:25). Epictetus
applies *oikodespotes* to God, who "is a master of the house who orders everything"
(3.22.4).

The discipled scribe, like a master of a household, "brings out of his treasure what
is new and what is old." We find treasure (Greek: *thesauros*) and parables linked in
Sir 1:25: "In the treasuries [*thesauroi*] of wisdom are parables." The juxtaposition
of "new" and "old" may have been suggested by Lev 26:10: "You shall eat old grain
long stored, and you shall have to clear out the old to make way for the new." *Gospel
of Thomas* §70 seems to be loosely based on Matt 13:51–52: "Jesus says: 'When you
bring forth that which is within you, this that you have shall save you. If you do not
have that within you, this which you do not have within you will kill you.'"[368]

When Matthew states, "When Jesus had finished these parables, he left that place"
(**v. 53**), it marks the third time that he concludes a major discourse with words from
the Pentateuch. See the commentaries on Matt 7:28 and 11:1.

MATTHEW 13:54–58 – UNBELIEF AT NAZARETH

**13:54: He came to his hometown and began to teach the people in their syna-
gogue, so that they were astounded and said, "Where did this man get this wisdom and these deeds of power?**

---

[368] For further discussion of this important passage, see O. L. Cope, *Matthew* (1976),
especially 13–31; J. Dupont, "Nova et vetera (Mt 13,52)," in F. Neirynck (ed.), *Études
sur les Évangiles synoptiques* (1985), 2:920–28; D. E. Orton, *The Understanding Scribe*
(1989), especially 137–53; R. Schnackenburg, "'Jeder Schriftgelehrte, der ein Jünger des
Himmelreiches geworden ist' (Mt 13.52)," in K. Aland and S. Meurer (eds.), *Wissenschaft
und Kirche: Festschrft für Eduard Lohse* (Texte und Arbeiten zur Bibel 4; Bielefeld: Luther,
1989), 57–69; P. Philips, "Casting Out the Treasure: A New Reading of Matthew 13.52,"
JSNT 31 (2008): 3–24.

13:55: Is not this the carpenter's son? Is not his mother called Mary? And are not his brothers James and Joseph and Simon and Judas?

13:56: And are not all his sisters with us? Where then did this man get all this?"

13:57: And they took offense at him. But Jesus said to them, "Prophets are not without honor except in their own country and in their own house."

13:58: And he did not do many deeds of power there, because of their unbelief.

The Matthean context is quite different from the Markan context. Whereas Mark's account of Jesus' rebuff in Nazareth followed works of power on both sides of the Sea of Galilee (cf. Mark 5), Matthew's account of the Nazareth visit is almost appended, as it were, to the conclusion of the discourse that is made up of parables about the kingdom of heaven (i.e., Matt 13:3–52). It seems to function as a link between the discourse and the story about the death of John the Baptist (cf. Matt 14:1–14). Perhaps this is Matthew's point: Jesus' rejection at the hands of the people of Nazareth, followed by the tragic story of John's death, may be intended to prepare the reader for the shift in the narrative that will soon take place, from a public ministry characterized by miracle and promise to a sobering journey toward Jerusalem characterized by predictions of passion and suffering.

Matthew's report of Jesus' travels continues with a homecoming: "He came to his hometown and began to teach the people in their synagogue" (**v. 54**). Jesus regularly taught in synagogues; see the commentary on Matt 4:23. When the people of Nazareth (as implied by "hometown")[369] heard Jesus, "they were astounded and said, 'Where did this man get this wisdom and these deeds of power?'" The immediate context suggests that the "wisdom" refers to the teaching of the parables as well as the idea that Jesus himself has drawn new truth from old tradition (cf. Matt 13:52). Of course, readers of Matthew will assume that reference to teaching includes everything from Chapter 3 to Chapter 13. Jesus' teaching in Nazareth is spelled out more fully in Luke 4:16–30.

The people of Nazareth ask, "Is not this the carpenter's son? Is not his mother called Mary? And are not his brothers James and Joseph and Simon and Judas? And are not all his sisters with us? Where then did this man get all this?" (**vv. 55–56**). Mark's version of the question reads "Is not this the carpenter, the son of Mary . . . ?" (Mark 6:3). Matthew's change eliminates the reference to Jesus himself as a carpenter, and the potentially awkward reference to Jesus as the "son of Mary." The reference to Jesus' mother, brothers, and sisters implies that Jesus is no better than they; he is one of them. He is not special; he is the son of a carpenter. The people wonder where he has studied; see John 7:15, "How does this man have such learning, when he has never been taught?"

---

[369]   R. L. Sturch, "The 'πατρίς' of Jesus," *JTS* 28 (1977): 94–96.

Not surprisingly, the people of Nazareth "took offense at him" (**v. 57**). In response, Jesus remarks: "Prophets are not without honor except in their own country and in their own house." The parallel found in the *Gospel of Thomas* §31 ("No prophet is accepted in his hometown; no doctor cures those who know him") does not derive from independent tradition but is better explained as a conflation of sayings taken from Luke's version of Jesus' experience in Nazareth (Luke 4:23, "Doctor, cure yourself!"; Luke 4:24, "no prophet is accepted in the prophet's hometown"). In the late first century, Apollonius of Tyana complains to his brother: "Other men regard me as the equal of the gods, and some of them even as a god, but until now my own country alone ignores me, my country for which in particular I have striven to be distinguished" (*Letters to Hestiaeus* 44).

Matthew's account of Jesus' homecoming concludes: "And he did not do many deeds of power there, because of their unbelief" (**v. 58**). On the importance of faith for healing in Matthew, see Matt 8:13; 9:2, 22, 28, 29; 15:28. Matthew revises Mark's "he could do no deed of power there" (Mark 6:5), perhaps to avoid the inference that Jesus was not in control of the situation.[370]

MATTHEW 14:1–12 – THE EXECUTION OF JOHN THE BAPTIST

14:1: At that time Herod the ruler heard reports about Jesus;

14:2: and he said to his servants, "This is John the Baptist; he has been raised from the dead, and for this reason these powers are at work in him."

14:3: For Herod had arrested John, bound him, and put him in prison on account of Herodias, his brother Philip's wife,

14:4: because John had been telling him, "It is not lawful for you to have her."

14:5: Though Herod wanted to put him to death, he feared the crowd, because they regarded him as a prophet.

14:6: But when Herod's birthday came, the daughter of Herodias danced before the company, and she pleased Herod

14:7: so much that he promised on oath to grant her whatever she might ask.

14:8: Prompted by her mother, she said, "Give me the head of John the Baptist here on a platter."

14:9: The king was grieved, yet out of regard for his oaths and for the guests, he commanded it to be given;

14:10: he sent and had John beheaded in the prison.

---

[370] P. J. Temple, "The Rejection at Nazareth," *CBQ* 17 (1955): 229–42; F. van Segbroeck, "Jésus rejeté par sa patrie (Mt 13,54–58)," *Bib* 48 (1968): 167–98; R. A. Batey, "'Is Not This the Carpenter?'," *NTS* 30 (1984): 249–58.

14:11: The head was brought on a platter and given to the girl, who brought it to her mother.

14:12: His disciples came and took the body and buried it; then they went and told Jesus.

*M*atthew has again condensed Mark's version, this time by about one hundred words. Matthew omits the speculation about who Jesus is (as in Mark 6:15) and deletes many other details, corrects Mark's reference to Herod as "king" (Mark 6:14) to the more strictly accurate "tetrarch" (NRSV: "ruler"), and adds at the end of the story that the disciples of John notified Jesus of Herod's death.

"At that time Herod the ruler heard reports about Jesus; and he said to his servants, 'This is John the Baptist; he has been raised from the dead, and for this reason these powers are at work in him'" (**vv. 1–2**). Herod Antipas (not to be confused with his father, Herod the Great, who died in 4 B.C.) has heard reports of Jesus' powerful preaching and miracles. He can only assume that the "powers" at work in Jesus have been brought into this world from a powerful otherworldly source. He wonders if Jesus could be the recently executed John the Baptist, "raised from the dead." Readers should note the irony here. In Matt 13:53–58, Jesus' family and friends who live in Nazareth show Jesus no respect. The tetrarch Herod respects, even fears, him.

The balance of the passage is given over to an explanation of what had happened to John. John had baptized Jesus (Matt 3:13–15) and had been arrested (Matt 4:12), John's disciples had asked Jesus about fasting (Matt 9:14), John had sent messengers to Jesus (Matt 11:2), and Jesus had talked about him (Matt 11:7–19). But up to this point nothing had been said about John's fate. We now learn in Matt 14:3–11 that Herod had executed him. He did so because John had condemned Herod for marrying Herodias, the wife of Herod's brother Philip, tetrarch of Gaulanitis and Perea. Herod did not execute John right away, on account of his fear of the populace, for "they regarded him as a prophet" (**v. 5**). Mark says that "Herod feared John, knowing that he was a righteous and holy man" (Mark 6:20a). Matthew is less charitable. Herod was reluctant to kill John only because the people regarded him as a prophet. Matthew also omits Mark's statement that "When he heard him, he was greatly perplexed; and yet he liked to listen to him" (Mark 6:20b).

The imprisonment comes to an end when Herod rashly promises "on oath" to give the daughter of Herodias whatever she wants (**v. 7**). Matthew has omitted Mark's hyperbolic "even half of my kingdom" (Mark 6:23), perhaps because readers would have wondered in what sense Herod could possibly have made good on such a ridiculous offer, which, in any event, would have had to be approved by Rome, at whose pleasure Herod the "tetrarch" ruled over a quarter of his father's kingdom. Perhaps we should not press this question too closely; after all, Herod's offer, however edited, was reckless enough, and it may have been the wine talking. "Prompted by her mother," the girl requested "the head of John the Baptist here on a platter" (**v. 8**). With regret but having no way out on account of his pompous oaths, Herod had John beheaded and the head brought on a platter and given to the girl, "who brought it to her mother" (**vv. 9–11**).[371]

The Synoptic accounts of John's imprisonment and death are at points either unattested or somewhat at variance with the account in Josephus (*Ant.* 18.116–19). But at most points the accounts can be reconciled and there is no good reason to give Josephus priority. Although Josephus chooses to emphasize the political dangers that John posed to Herod, and Mark chose to emphasize the moral dimension, the two accounts are in essential agreement. Herod's disgraceful dismissal of his wife, the daughter of Aretas IV, the king of Nabatea, and his unlawful marriage to Herodias, his sister-in-law, prompted John's condemnation, which focused on the immoral and unlawful aspects (which the Synoptics emphasize), while Herod's fears focused on the political dangers (which Josephus narrates). Later, Josephus himself mentions the inappropriateness of Herod's divorce and remarriage (*Ant.* 18.136).

MATTHEW 14:13–21 – FEEDING THE FIVE THOUSAND

14:13: Now when Jesus heard this, he withdrew from there in a boat to a deserted place by himself. But when the crowds heard it, they followed him on foot from the towns.

14:14: When he went ashore, he saw a great crowd; and he had compassion for them and cured their sick.

14:15: When it was evening, the disciples came to him and said, "This is a deserted place, and the hour is now late; send the crowds away so that they may go into the villages and buy food for themselves."

14:16: Jesus said to them, "They need not go away; you give them something to eat."

14:17: They replied, "We have nothing here but five loaves and two fish."

---

[371]   J. D. M. Derrett, "Herod's Oath and the Baptist's Head," *BZ* 9 (1965): 49–59, 233–46; H. W. Hoehner, *Herod Antipas* (SNTSMS 17; Cambridge: Cambridge University Press, 1972), 112–22, 149–65; O. L. Cope, "The Death of John the Baptist in the Gospel of Matthew," *CBQ* 38 (1976): 515–19; J. P. Meier, "John the Baptist in Matthew's Gospel," *JBL* 99 (1980): 383–405; G. Yamasaki, *John the Baptist in Life and Death: Audience-Oriented Criticism of Matthew's Narrative* (JSNTSup 167; Sheffield: Sheffield Academic Press, 1998), 129–42; B. D. Chilton, "John the Baptist: His Immersion and His Death," in S. E. Porter and A. R. Cross (eds.), *Dimensions of Baptism: Biblical and Theological Studies* (JSNTSup 234; London: Sheffield Academic Press, 2002), 25–44; M. H. Jensen, *Herod Antipas in Galilee*, 2nd edition (WUNT 2, no. 215; Tübingen: Mohr Siebeck, 2010), especially 109–11.

14:18: And he said, "Bring them here to me."

14:19: Then he ordered the crowds to sit down on the grass. Taking the five loaves and the two fish, he looked up to heaven, and blessed and broke the loaves, and gave them to the disciples, and the disciples gave them to the crowds.

14:20: And all ate and were filled; and they took up what was left over of the broken pieces, twelve baskets full.

14:21: And those who ate were about five thousand men, besides women and children.

As he has elsewhere, Matthew condenses Mark's wordier account (Mark 6:30–44). He also omits mention of the disciples' report (Mark 6:30, "The apostles … told him all that they had done and taught"), the lack of opportunity to eat, being anticipated and preceded by the multitudes, and the comparison of the people to sheep lacking a shepherd. Matthew also enhances the links between Jesus' words and actions in the distribution of the food and his words and actions at the Lord's Supper (Matt 26:20–29). The context and meaning are otherwise essentially the same as found in Mark.

The phrase "Now when Jesus heard this" (**v. 13**) refers to news of John's death, which had been relayed to him by John's disciples (Matt 14:12). Although Jesus "withdrew from there in a boat to a deserted place by himself," the crowds "followed him on foot from the towns." Jesus' fame as healer and teacher drew crowds, which he found difficult to escape, even for brief periods of solitude. So it is in this case; Jesus is unable to avoid the crowds. "When he went ashore," there they were. So, out of "compassion for them," he "cured their sick" (**v. 14**). Mark says nothing about healing. Matthew, however, misses no opportunity to portray Jesus as healer. See Matt 4:23–24; 9:35; 12:15; 15:30; 19:2; 21:14.[372] What happens next is that Jesus will also "cure" their hunger.

Matthew's version of the feeding of the five thousand reduces Mark's version by about 20 percent. Matthew enhances the links between Jesus' words and actions in the distribution of the food and his words and actions at the Lord's Supper (Matt 26:20–29), as does Luke (see Luke 9:12–17).

When evening comes, the disciples ask Jesus to dismiss the crowds. They cannot stay together as a group, for they are in an uninhabited area, so food for the evening is not available. Everyone will have to make his own way to the various villages in the vicinity and obtain what food he can (**v. 15**). But Jesus says to his disciples, "They need not go away; you give them something to eat" (**v. 16**). They respond, "We have nothing here but five loaves and two fish" (**v. 17**). Mark's details about the disciples wondering if they should spend 200 denarii to buy food and Jesus' question about

---

[372] L. Novakovic, *Messiah, Healer of the Sick* (2003); U. Luz, *Matthew* (2001–2007), 2:314: "The mercy of Israel's Messiah … can be seen almost always in his healings."

what food they have on hand are omitted (Mark 6:37–38). In Matthew, the disciples simply state that they have "nothing but five loaves and two fish" (in John 6:9, the disciples obtain this food from a boy). In other words, they cannot possibly feed the multitude. So Jesus takes charge: "Bring them here to me" (v. 18).

Jesus has the crowd recline (the normal posture for eating). He took the bread and fish, "looked up to heaven, and blessed and broke the loaves, and gave them to the disciples, and the disciples gave them to the crowds" (v. 19). Everyone ate and was satisfied, and twelve baskets of what was left over were filled (v. 20). Those who were fed numbered "about five thousand men, besides women and children" (v. 21), a considerable crowd. Elisha had been able to multiply twenty loaves for one hundred men (2 Kings 4:42–44), but now Jesus will multiply a mere five loaves for five thousand! The abundance of bread may have called to mind traditions about the giving of manna in the eschatological age (cf. *2 Bar* 29:1–8). The fourth Gospel develops this typology (cf. John 6:1–59).[373] In the context of the Gospel of Matthew, which emphasizes Jesus' role as a Moses-like teacher of the way of righteousness, feeding the multitude in the wilderness would have made many readers and hearers think of the bread God provided his people in the wilderness (Exodus 16).

MATTHEW 14:22–33 – WALKING ON THE WATER

14:22: Immediately he made the disciples get into the boat and go on ahead to the other side, while he dismissed the crowds.

14:23: And after he had dismissed the crowds, he went up the mountain by himself to pray. When evening came, he was there alone,

14:24: but by this time the boat, battered by the waves, was far from the land, for the wind was against them.

14:25: And early in the morning he came walking toward them on the sea.

14:26: But when the disciples saw him walking on the sea, they were terrified, saying, "It is a ghost!" And they cried out in fear.

14:27: But immediately Jesus spoke to them and said, "Take heart, it is I; do not be afraid."

14:28: Peter answered him, "Lord, if it is you, command me to come to you on the water."

---

[373] S. Masuda, "The Good News of the Miracle of the Bread," *NTS* 28 (1982): 191–219; E. Bammel, "The Feeding of the Multitude," in E. Bammel and C. F. D. Moule (eds.), *Jesus and the Politics of His Day* (Cambridge: Cambridge University Press, 1984), 211–40; R. I. Pervo, "Panta Koina: The Feeding Stories in the Light of Economic Data and Social Practice," in Lukas Bormann, Kelly Del Tredici, and Angela Standhartinger (eds.), *Religious Propaganda and Missionary Competition in the New Testament World: Essays Honoring Dieter Georgi* (NovTSup 74; Leiden: Brill, 1994), 163–94.

14:29: He said, "Come." So Peter got out of the boat, started walking on the water, and came toward Jesus.

14:30: But when he noticed the strong wind, he became frightened, and beginning to sink, he cried out, "Lord, save me!"

14:31: Jesus immediately reached out his hand and caught him, saying to him, "You of little faith, why did you doubt?"

14:32: When they got into the boat, the wind ceased.

14:33: And those in the boat worshiped him, saying, "Truly you are the Son of God."

*M*atthew places his version of the walk on the sea in essentially the same context as what we find in Mark (i.e., Mark 6:47–52), but he shortens the story by about 20 percent and then adds a short story about Peter venturing forth on the water himself (Matt 14:28–33). Part of Mark's story appears near the end of this addition (cf. Mark 6:51 and Matt 14:32). Matthew's addition contains important confessional material.

Jesus has dismissed the crowds, now ministered to and well fed, and has sent his disciples on ahead in their boat. Jesus himself goes up on a mountain to pray (vv. 22–23). In the meantime, the disciples are having a rough time, for their boat is "battered by the waves" and the "wind was against them" (v. 24). The windy, choppy conditions set the stage for their fear and at the same time highlight the awesomeness of Jesus.

Matthew begins his account of Jesus' rescue of his disciples with the timing of the event: "And early in the morning he came walking toward them on the sea" (v. 25). Jesus did not simply walk on water; he walked some distance (recall from v. 24 that the boat "was far from the land") and walked across a stormy sea. One might compare the story of the rescue at sea recounted by the dying patriarch Naphtali:

And our father said to us: "Come, let us embark on our ship." And when he had gone on board, there arose a vehement storm, and a mighty tempest of wind; and our father, who was holding the helm, departed from us. And we, being tossed with the tempest, were borne along over the sea; and the ship was filled with water, pounded by mighty waves, until it was broken up. And Joseph fled away upon a little boat, and we were all divided upon nine planks, and Levi and Judah were together. And we were all scattered unto the ends of the earth. Then Levi, girt about with sackcloth, prayed for us all unto the Lord. And when the storm ceased, the ship reached the land as it were in peace. (*T. Naphtali* 6:3–9)

The disciples are terrified and imagine that they have seen a ghost: "But when the disciples saw him walking on the sea, they were terrified, saying, 'It is a ghost!' And they cried out in fear" (v. 26). It was believed that only a spirit or divine being could walk on water. No human being could do this. We find this belief in biblical literature (cf. Job 9:8 [especially in the Septuagint]; 38:16; Ps 77:19; 2 Macc 5:21) and in extrabiblical literature: "Hesiod says that [Orion] was the son of Euryale, the daughter of Minos, and of Poseidon, and that there was given him as a gift the power of walking upon the waves as though upon the land" (Eratosthenes, frag. 182). The disciples' fear subsides when Jesus identifies himself: "Take heart, it is I; do not be afraid" (v. 27).

Mark's version concludes with a remark about the disciples' utter astonishment caused by their failure to understand "about the loaves," all because "their hearts were hardened" (Mark 6:51–52). It is no surprise that Matthew elects to omit this confusing material. Nevertheless, the addition of the story of Peter's attempt to walk on the water serves in some sense as a substitute for the material omitted from Mark, for it ends in failure and a rebuke for lack of faith.

Responding to Jesus' presence, Peter asked his master to command him to go to him on the water (v. 28). Jesus bade Peter to come to him, so "Peter got out of the boat, started walking on the water, and came toward Jesus" (v. 29).[374] Frightened by the wind, Peter loses his faith (as should be inferred, given what is said in v. 31) and begins to sink, crying out, "Lord, save me!" (v. 30). Peter's cry reminds us of "Lord, save us! We are perishing!" (Matt 8:25; cf. Mark 4:38, "Teacher, do you not care that we are perishing?"). But Peter's cry for help in the present context reminds us of Ps 69:1–3: "Save me, O God, for the waters have come up to my neck. I sink in deep mire, where there is no foothold; I have come into deep waters, and the flood sweeps over me. I am weary with my crying; my throat is parched. My eyes grow dim with waiting for my God."

Matthew then details Peter's rescue: "Jesus immediately reached out his hand and caught him" (v. 31). See LXX 2 Sam 15:5, "he stretched out his hand and took hold of him." Jesus says to Peter, "You of little faith, why did you doubt?" Matthew is fond of the expression "little faith" (Greek: *oligopistos*), often in reference to all of the disciples (see, e.g., Matt 8:26; 16:8). According to a Greco-Roman sage, "a person of little faith [*oligopistos*] is without faith" (Sextus, *Sentences* 6); see the commentary on Matt 6:30. When Jesus and Peter climbed aboard, "the wind stopped" (v. 32). This detail, drawn from Mark 6:51a, once again reveals Jesus' power over nature itself (cf. Matt 8:35–41).

Matthew's story of the walk on the water ends very differently from the ending found in Mark 6:51b–52. In Mark, the disciples are confused, ignorant, and hard-hearted. But in Matthew they recognized Jesus and "worshiped him, saying, 'Truly you are the Son of God'" (v. 33). Instead of bewilderment and obduracy, the disciples react with reverence and awe, confessing Jesus' divinity. The actual wording,

---

374 Some have compared Peter's experience to that of a Buddhist who could walk on water while meditating upon the teaching of Buddha but sank when he did not (*Jâtaka* 190). The parallel is interesting, but it is unlikely that this Buddhist story was known in the eastern Mediterranean in late antiquity. See C. S. Keener, *A Commentary on the Gospel of Matthew* (1999), 407 n. 30.

"Truly you are the Son of God," parallels Mark's form of the centurion's confession in Mark 15:39 ("Truly this man was the Son of God!"). In the Matthean context, the disciples' exclamation anticipates Peter's confession, "You are the Messiah, the Son of the living God" (Matt 16:16).[375]

MATTHEW 14:34–36 – CROWDS REACH OUT TO JESUS

14:34: When they had crossed over, they came to land at Gennesaret.

14:35: After the people of that place recognized him, they sent word throughout the region and brought all who were sick to him,

14:36: and begged him that they might touch even the fringe of his cloak; and all who touched it were healed.

*M*atthew again condenses Mark, but does not pass up the opportunity to provide a summary of Jesus' ministry, emphasizing the healing. With this aspect in mind, Matthew supplements Mark's version at one point, adding v. 35b.

Matthew then reports on the conclusion of the voyage: "When they had crossed over, they came to land at Gennesaret" (**v. 34**). In Matt 14:13, Jesus and his disciples had traveled by boat to a "deserted place." Nevertheless, they encountered crowds of people, to whom Jesus ministered. Before dismissing them, Jesus fed them by multiplying the loaves. The disciples got into their boat and began to recross the lake. Jesus joined them in the remarkable walking on the water episode. In v. 34, Matthew tells us that Jesus and his disciples have reached "Gennesaret," which is probably Ginosar,[376] some three miles southwest of Capernaum.

Jesus continues to heal, for as soon as "the people of that place recognized him, they sent word throughout the region and brought all who were sick to him, and

---

[375] On the meaning of "Son of God" in Matthew (cf. Matt 27:43, 54), see R. L. Mowery, "Son of God in Roman Imperial Titles and Matthew," *Bib* 83 (2002): 100–10. For further discussion of Matt 14:22–33, see J. P. Heil, *Jesus Walking on the Sea: Meaning and Gospel Functions of Matt 14:22–33, Mark 6:45–52 and John 6:15b–21* (AnBib 87; Rome: Pontifical Biblical Institute Press, 1981), 31–67; J. Smit-Sibinga, "Matthew 14,22–33: Text and Composition," in E. J. Epp and G. D. Fee (eds.), *New Testament Textual Criticism: Its Significance for Exegesis. Essays in Honour of Bruce M. Metzger* (Oxford: Clarendon Press, 1981), 15–33; C. R. Carlisle, "Jesus' Walking on the Water: A Note on Matthew 14:22–33," *NTS* 31 (1985): 151–55; J. M. C. Scott, "Jesus Walking on the Sea: The Significance of Matthew 14,22–33 for the Narrative Development of the Gospel," in G. J. Brooke and J.-D. Kaestli (eds.), *Narrativity in Biblical and Related Texts* (BETL 149; Leuven: Peeters and Leuven University Press, 2000), 91–104.

[376] See D. C. Allison, Jr. and W. D. Davies, *A Critical and Exegetical Commentary on the Gospel According to Saint Matthew* (1988–1997), 2:511; R. T. France, *The Gospel of Matthew* (2007), 572, and others. Modern Ginosar is where the 2000-year-old fishing boat is preserved and on display.

begged him that they might touch even the fringe of his cloak; and all who touched it were healed" (**vv. 35–36**). To touch or be touched by Jesus and to be healed was not an opportunity to be missed (cf. Matt 8:3, 15; 9:20–21, 29; 20:34).[377]

MATTHEW 15:1–11 – ON WHAT DEFILES

15:1: Then Pharisees and scribes came to Jesus from Jerusalem and said,

15:2: "Why do your disciples break the tradition of the elders? For they do not wash their hands before they eat."

15:3: He answered them, "And why do you break the commandment of God for the sake of your tradition?

15:4: For God said, 'Honor your father and your mother,' and, 'Whoever speaks evil of father or mother must surely die.'

15:5: But you say that whoever tells father or mother, 'Whatever support you might have had from me is given to God,' then that person need not honor the father.

15:6: So, for the sake of your tradition, you make void the word of God.

15:7: You hypocrites! Isaiah prophesied rightly about you when he said:

15:8: 'This people honors me with their lips, but their hearts are far from me;

15:9: in vain do they worship me, teaching human precepts as doctrines.'"

15:10: Then he called the crowd to him and said to them, "Listen and understand:

15:11: it is not what goes into the mouth that defiles a person, but it is what comes out of the mouth that defiles."

*M*atthew's condensing (by almost half) and revising of this passage reflect his Jewish orientation and his sensitivity with respect to the written Law and aspects of the oral Law as it was emerging in the first century. For one, Matthew omits Mark's explanation of impure hands (Mark 7:3–4), either because he assumes that his readers already know or perhaps because some of his readers might find it somewhat disrespectful. Again, Matthew omits reference to "corban" and what it means, probably because his readers already know the subject. Finally, Matthew has rearranged the episode so that it concludes in vv. 7–9 with the quotation of Isa 29:3 (whereas in Mark the quotation appears in the middle of the debate; cf. Mark 7:6–8).

Matthew's account begins, "Then Pharisees and scribes came to Jesus from Jerusalem" (**v. 1**). The excitement and large crowds attract Pharisees and scribes

377   W. Carter, "The Crowds in Matthew's Gospel," *CBQ* 55 (1993): 54–67; J. R. Cousland, *The Crowds in the Gospel of Matthew* (NovTSup 102; Leiden: Brill, 2002).

from Jerusalem. Jesus' activities on previous occasions had attracted the attention of these men (Matt 9:3, 9; 12:2, 14, 24), and they will again (Matt 16:1; 19:3; 22:15).

The Pharisees and scribes ask Jesus, "Why do your disciples break the tradition of the elders? For they do not wash their hands before they eat" (**v. 2**). Mark states that they had observed that Jesus' disciples ate with "unwashed hands" (Mark 7:2) and then explains to his readers who are unfamiliar with this Jewish sect its great concern with matters of purity (Mark 7:3–5). It is possible that the food that the disciples ate was the food left over from the feeding of the five thousand (Matt 14:20). According to Josephus, "The Pharisees have imposed on the people many laws from the tradition of the fathers not written in the Law of Moses" (*Ant.* 13.297). Earlier, some Pharisees had objected to Jesus' free association with "sinners and tax collectors" (Matt 9:11). This time they ask Jesus why his disciples do not eat with washed hands. Both of these concerns have to do with the Pharisees' understanding of purity.

Jesus counters with a question of his own: "And why do you break the command-ment of God for the sake of your tradition? For God said, 'Honor your father and your mother,' and, 'Whoever speaks evil of father or mother must surely die.' But you say that whoever tells father or mother, 'Whatever support you might have had from me is given to God,' then that person need not honor the father" (**vv. 3–5**). Jesus does not answer the question directly; he does not say that eating with unwashed hands is permissible or that concerns with purity are unnecessary. Rather, he cuts to the heart of the matter: Pharisaic teachings often go beyond the requirements of Scripture; indeed, these teachings sometimes nullify Scripture itself. Jesus appeals to Isa 29:13 (cited in **vv. 8–9**), where the prophet of old leveled a similar complaint against the religious authorities of his day. With biting irony, Jesus chides his critics: "So, for the sake of your tradition, you make void the word of God" (**v. 6**). By way of illustration, Jesus alludes to Exod 20:12 (= Deut 5:16) and Lev 20:9 (cf. Exod 21:17), Scriptures that enjoin grown children to care for their parents. But the tradition of "corban" (Greek *doron*, meaning "gift"), whereby something is dedicated to God and so is no longer available for secular use, was sometimes invoked with the result that substance needed by elderly parents was denied them (v. 5).[378]

Having silenced the Pharisees, Jesus "called the crowd to him and said to them, 'Listen and understand: it is not what goes into the mouth that defiles a person, but it is what comes out of the mouth that defiles'" (**vv. 10–11**). Through editing

---

[378] For readers unfamiliar with Jewish religious customs, the evangelist Mark explains that corban means "given to God" (Mark 7:11). Josephus understands it similarly: "'Corban' to God – meaning what Greeks would call a 'gift'" (*Ant.* 4.73); "Now this oath [i.e., Corban] will be found in no other nation except [that of] the Jews, and, translated from the Hebrew, one may interpret it as meaning "God's gift" (*Against Apion* 1.167). A first-century ossuary inscription reads: "All that a man may find to his profit in this ossuary is an offering to God from him who is within it." See J. A. Fitzmyer, "The Aramaic Qorban Inscription from Jebel Hallet Et-Turi and Mk 7:11/Mt 15:5," *JBL* 78 (1959): 60–65.

and omission, Matthew softens Mark's severe criticism of the Pharisees. Matthew omits Mark's "You have a fine way of rejecting the commandment of God in order to keep your tradition!" (Mark 7:9), as well as his "you no longer permit doing anything" (Mark 7:12) and "through your tradition that you have handed on. And you do many things like this" (Mark 7:13). A similar softening will be seen in Matt 15:12–20.[379]

MATTHEW 15:12–20 – EXPLANATION OF WHAT DEFILES

15:12: Then the disciples approached and said to him, "Do you know that the Pharisees took offense when they heard what you said?"

15:13: He answered, "Every plant that my heavenly Father has not planted will be uprooted.

15:14: Let them alone; they are blind guides of the blind. And if one blind person guides another, both will fall into a pit."

15:15: But Peter said to him, "Explain this parable to us."

15:16: Then he said, "Are you also still without understanding?

15:17: Do you not see that whatever goes into the mouth enters the stomach, and goes out into the sewer?

15:18: But what comes out of the mouth proceeds from the heart, and this is what defiles.

15:19: For out of the heart come evil intentions, murder, adultery, fornication, theft, false witness, slander.

15:20: These are what defile a person, but to eat with unwashed hands does not defile."

Matthew condenses and omits some of the material he finds in Mark, but he also freely supplements it. Perhaps the most noticeable omission is Mark's editorial comment "Thus He declared all foods clean" (Mark 7:19). Such a categorical statement would have been far too controversial in Matthean circles, which were very much engaged in debate with the Jewish people and Jewish teachers. It is Matthew's Jesus, after all, who said, "Do not think that I have come to abolish the law or the prophets; I have come not to abolish but to fulfill" (Matt 5:17), and "Therefore, whoever breaks one of the least of these commandments, and teaches others to do the same, will be called least in the kingdom of heaven" (Matt 5:19).

---

[379] C. E. Carlston, "The Things that Defile (Mark 7,14) and the Law in Matthew and Mark," *NTS* 15 (1968): 75–96; A. J. Hultgren, *Jesus and His Adversaries* (1979), 115–19; R. P. Booth, *Jesus and the Laws of Purity: Tradition History and Legal History in Mark 7* (JSNTSup 13; Sheffield: JSOT Press, 1986).

How the "least of" God's "commandments" can be fulfilled (commandments that declare some foods unclean) and at the same time "all foods" are "clean" is not easily reconciled. Of course, for Christians all foods do become clean, as Peter learns through a vision in Acts 10, but in the time of Jesus, well before Peter's experience and the launch of the Gentile mission, not all foods were clean. Mark's bold declaration is simply ahead of its (or Matthew's) time and will have to wait.

Matthew's most important addition is found in **vv. 12–14**, which begins with the disciples' report that the Pharisees are offended by Jesus' statement (especially if at the time of Matthew's writing they had heard the declaration in Mark 7:19). Jesus replies to his disciples with a proverb: "Every plant that my heavenly Father has not planted will be uprooted" (Matt 5:13). What does this mean? One immediately thinks of the parable of the wheat and weeds and its interpretation (Matt 13:24–30, 36–43). In this parable and explanation, the servants offer to gather the weeds before the harvest time, but the farmer says no, lest they "uproot the wheat along with them" (cf. Matt 13:29). The saying in Matt 15:13 relates to the same idea. Those plants (or seeds) not planted by God (but planted by Satan instead) will be rooted up. In context, Jesus is referring to the Pharisees and scribes who have disputed his teaching. They run the risk of being identified as bad seed, as plants not planted by God and that on the day of judgment (or "harvest") will be rooted up.

John the Baptist had offered a similar warning, again reflecting the agrarian orientation of the Jewish people in Israel in late antiquity: "Even now the ax is lying at the root of the trees; every tree therefore that does not bear good fruit is cut down and thrown into the fire" (Matt 3:10). No one should assume that physical descent from Abraham guarantees life in the world to come (cf. Matt 3:7–9). Evidently, both John and Jesus saw in passages like Isa 60:21 ("Your people shall all be righteous ... the shoot that I planted, the work of my hands ...") no guarantee of being regarded as God's plant. Their skepticism on this point stands in tension with rabbinic interpretation, which appeals to this passage from Isaiah 60 and finds in it assurance of salvation for every Israelite: "All Israelites have a share in the world to come, as it is said, 'Then all your people will be righteous ... the branch of My planting, the work of My hands ...'" (*m. Sanh.* 10:1).

Jesus sees no point in further argument with the Pharisees, advising his disciples: "Let them alone; they are blind guides of the blind. And if one blind person guides another, both will fall into a pit" (**v. 14**). This criticism here anticipates the diatribe in Chapter 23 (see especially Matt 23:16, 24, which refer to the scribes and Pharisees as "blind guides").

Jesus explains to his disciples that "what comes out of the mouth proceeds from the heart, and this is what defiles. For out of the heart come evil intentions, murder, adultery, fornication, theft, false witness, slander. These are what defile a person, but to eat with unwashed hands does not defile" (**vv. 18–20**). Matthew's paraphrase of Mark 7:21 may hark back to Matt 12:34: "You brood of vipers! How can you speak good things, when you are evil? For out of the abundance of the heart the mouth speaks." The "vipers" Jesus castigates are the Pharisees (cf. Matt 12:24). In the context of Matt 15:1–20, "what comes out of the mouth," the things that "defile," may well include corban vows that deny support to one's parents (cf. Matt 15:4–6). What comes out of the mouth can potentially defile, but eating with unwashed hands does not.[380]

MATTHEW 15:21–28 – THE FAITH OF THE CANAANITE WOMAN

15:21: Jesus left that place and went away to the district of Tyre and Sidon.

15:22: Just then a Canaanite woman from that region came out and started shouting, "Have mercy on me, Lord, Son of David; my daughter is tormented by a demon."

15:23: But he did not answer her at all. And his disciples came and urged him, saying, "Send her away, for she keeps shouting after us."

15:24: He answered, "I was sent only to the lost sheep of the house of Israel."

15:25: But she came and knelt before him, saying, "Lord, help me."

15:26: He answered, "It is not fair to take the children's food and throw it to the dogs."

15:27: She said, "Yes, Lord, yet even the dogs eat the crumbs that fall from their masters' table."

15:28: Then Jesus answered her, "Woman, great is your faith! Let it be done for you as you wish." And her daughter was healed instantly.

There are so many verbal differences between the Matthean and Markan accounts of Jesus' encounter with the woman from the region of Tyre that some think Matthew may have had access to another version of the story. Again we see differences in Matthew's narrative that are consistent with his interest in the Jewish mission. The story fits into the context in an interesting way. Jesus has just declared that eating with unwashed hands does not defile, that what defiles is what comes out of the mouth, from the heart (Matt 15:17–18). From a Pharisaic point of view, of course, socializing with Gentiles (such as eating with them) causes defilement. Almost as a demonstration of his teaching, Jesus converses with a Gentile woman and acquiesces to her request.

In Matthew's Gospel, Jesus next visits "the district of Tyre and Sidon" (**v. 21**) (in modern-day Lebanon). Two times in the Old Testament we have the exact phrase

---

[380]   S. Zeitlin, "The Halaka in the Gospels and Its Relation to the Jewish Law at the Time of Jesus," *HUCA* 1 (1924): 357–73; H. Räisänen, "Jesus and the Food Laws: Reflections on Mark 7.15," *JSNT* 16 (1982): 79–100; T. Kazen, *Jesus and Purity Halakhah: Was Jesus Indifferent to Impurity?* (ConBNT 38; Stockholm: Almqvist & Wiksells, 2002).

"Tyre and Sidon" (Jer 47:4; Zech 9:2), though the two cities appear together in other passages (e.g., Jer 25:22; 27:3; Ezek 27:8; Joel 3:4).[381] Jesus refers to the cities in a woe pronounced upon unbelieving cities: "Woe to you, Chorazin! Woe to you, Bethsaida! For if the deeds of power done in you had been done in Tyre and Sidon, they would have repented long ago in sackcloth and ashes. But I tell you, on the day of judgment it will be more tolerable for Tyre and Sidon than for you" (Matt 11:21–22 = Luke 10:13–14). Tyre and Sidon compare favorably to Chorazin and Bethsaida, but the inference is clear that they, too, face judgment.

During his time in Tyre and Sidon, Jesus meets "a Canaanite woman from that region" (**v. 22**). Why does Matthew change Mark's "woman was a Gentile, of Syrophoenician origin" (Mark 7:26) to "a Canaanite woman"? He does this once again to give his version a biblical flavor that will be appreciated by his Jewish readers. Twice in the Old Testament, Tyre and Sidon are linked to Philistia, the nation that plagued Israel as it tried to occupy and consolidate its hold on the land of Canaan (cf. Jer 47:4; Joel 3:4). But the most significant passage may be 2 Sam 24:7, where Tyre is linked to the "Canaanites." Thus, a Canaanite woman in the region of Tyre and Sidon carries strong biblical associations. This is a person who represents a people historically antagonistic toward Israel and clearly outside the covenant and with no expectations of messianic blessings.[382]

The woman's cry, "Have mercy on me, Lord, Son of David," anticipates the cry of the blind men at Jericho (Matt 20:29–30; or one blind man, Bartimaeus, according to Mark 10:46), who cried out: "Lord, have mercy on us, Son of David!" (Matt 20:30–31 = Mark 10:47–48). In Mark's version, there is no reported speech. All we are told is that the woman "begged him to cast the demon out of her daughter" (Mark 7:26). Her cry for help in Matthew's version carries with it confessional value. She has addressed Jesus as "Lord" and as "Son of David." One should also remember that Hiram, king of Tyre, was said to have been a good friend of King David and contributed to the building of the royal residence in Jerusalem (cf. 2 Sam 5:11: "Then Hiram king of Tyre sent messengers to David with cedar trees and carpenters and stonemasons; and they built a house for David"). Perhaps, then, it is not so strange that a person from the region of Tyre would respectfully hail Jesus as "Son of David."

The disciples, however, urge Jesus, saying, "Send her away, for she keeps shouting after us" (**v. 23**). There is no parallel to this plea in Mark's account. The disciples have grown weary of this persistent woman who follows Jesus and continues to shout for help. Perhaps the disciples recalled Jesus' instructions in the missionary discourse in Chapter 10. Apparently Jesus did, for he remarks, "I was sent only to the lost

[381]   J. Schmid, *Das Evangelium nach Matthäus* (1959), 240; R. T. France, *The Gospel of Matthew* (2007), 592.
[382]   R. H. Gundry, *Matthew* (1982), 310–11; U. Luz, *Matthew* (2001–2007), 2:338; J. Nolland, *The Gospel of Matthew* (2005), 631–32.

sheep of the house of Israel" (**v. 24**). Jesus' words do not contradict or correct the disposition of the disciples; they are in agreement. He is doing what they requested; he is sending the woman away by explaining to her that he has been sent "only to the lost sheep of the house of Israel," the very words of instruction in the missionary discourse in Matt 10:5–6, "Go nowhere among the Gentiles, and enter no town of the Samaritans, but go rather to the lost sheep of the house of Israel."

But the woman does not give up: "… she came and knelt before him, saying, 'Lord, help me'" (**v. 25**). She had been following Jesus and his disciples, crying out. Now she has placed herself in front of him, blocking his progress, and "knelt before him." Jesus explains why his mission is directed primarily to Israel, not to Gentiles: "It is not fair to take the children's food and throw it to the dogs" (**v. 26**). He explains that the bread (of the kingdom; cf. Isa 25:6; 1QSa 2:17–21; Luke 14:15, "Blessed is anyone who will eat bread in the kingdom of God!") is not to be thrown to the dogs. She does not disagree, but counters that "even the dogs eat the crumbs that fall from their masters' table" (**v. 27**). Matthew's version adds "fall" and "masters," additions that enhance important elements in the story. The addition of the word "fall" clarifies Mark's version in that it explains how the dogs "under the table" (Mark 7:28) get at the crumbs.[383] The addition of "masters'" makes it clear that the Canaanite woman knows her place; she is not attempting to put herself on an equal footing with the people of Israel. Implicit in her reply is the conviction that God's grace is so great that there is more than enough to go around, even while it is being extended to Israel first.

Impressed, Jesus responds, "Woman, great is your faith! Let it be done for you as you wish" (**v. 28**). Jesus has encountered a great faith (and Mark 7:29 only says "For saying that"), reminiscent of the faith of the centurion, which had prompted him to say: "Truly I say to you, I have not found such great faith with anyone in Israel" (Matt 8:10 = Luke 7:9). Her "great" faith contrasts with the "little faith" that the disciples themselves have on occasion displayed (Matt 6:30; 8:26; 14:31; 16:8; 17:20).[384] Because of her confession of Jesus as Son of David, her acceptance of the priority of Israel, and her faith, Jesus gives her what she has requested: "And her daughter was healed instantly" (cf. Matt 8:13, "And the servant was healed in that hour").[385]

---

[383]   One recalls the parable of the rich man and the poor man (Luke 16:19–31), in which the poor man, lying at the gate of the rich man, ate, presumably along with the dogs, "what fell from the rich man's table" (Luke 16:21). The poor man of the parable seems to be doing what the Canaanite woman suggests in her expansion of Jesus' analogy.

[384]   D. J. Harrington, *The Gospel of Matthew* (1991), 236: "Matthew portrays the mother as another model of praying faith."

[385]   R. A. Harrisville, "The Woman of Canaan: A Chapter in the History of Exegesis," *Int* 20 (1960): 274–87; T. A. Burkill, "The Historical Development of the Story of the Syrophoenician Woman," *NovT* 9 (1967): 161–77; E. A. Russell, "The Canaanite Woman and the Gospels (Mt 15,21–28; cf. Mark 7,24–30)," in E. A. Livingstone (ed.), *Studia Biblica 1978 II. Papers on the Gospels* (JSNTSup 2; Sheffield: JSOT Press, 1979), 263–300; G. Jackson, *'Have Mercy on Me': The Story of the Canaanite Woman in Matthew 15.21–28* (JSNTSup 228; CIS 10; London: Sheffield Academic Press, 2002).

MATTHEW 15:29–31 – HEALINGS ON THE MOUNTAIN

15:29: After Jesus had left that place, he passed along the Sea of Galilee, and he went up the mountain, where he sat down.

15:30: Great crowds came to him, bringing with them the lame, the maimed, the blind, the mute, and many others. They put them at his feet, and he cured them,

15:31: so that the crowd was amazed when they saw the mute speaking, the maimed whole, the lame walking, and the blind seeing. And they praised the God of Israel.

*M*atthew omits the specific story of the healing of the deaf-mute, deletes most of Mark's somewhat confusing geographical details (for Mark's sweep from Tyre and Sidon to the Sea of Galilee and on into the region of the Decapolis is quite a journey), and expands what is implied in the crowd's comment that Jesus "has done everything well" (Mark 7:37) into a much fuller summary of Jesus' healing ministry, something that Matthew does elsewhere (e.g., Matt 4:23–24; 8:16; 9:35; 12:15; 14:14; 19:2; 21:14).

Jesus "went up the mountain, where he sat down" (**v. 29**), which depicts his authority as a teacher and recalls the giving of the Sermon on the Mount (Matt 5:1–2). Once again, large crowds of people bring to him the ill and the physically challenged, and Jesus heals them all (**v. 30**). Matthew expands the list of infirmities healed by Jesus, probably to show that Jesus has indeed fulfilled the expectations foretold by Isaiah: "Then the eyes of the blind shall be opened, and the ears of the deaf unstopped; then the lame shall leap like a deer, and the tongue of the speechless sing for joy" (Isa 35:5–6; cf. LXX Isa 61:1–2, where recovery of sight for the blind is mentioned). We may also have important typology at work here. These healings, of every kind of infirmity, may have been understood as signaling the era of salvation, being modeled after patterns found in the giving of the Law at Sinai and the wilderness wanderings, where God performed miracles. According to one rabbinic interpretation, at Sinai there were "no blind ones among them," "no deaf ones among them," and "no lame ones among them" (cf. *Mekilta* on Exod 20:15–19 [*Bahodesh* §9]). The same was expected in the time of restoration.

When the crowd saw "the mute speaking, the maimed whole, the lame walking, and the blind seeing," they "praised the God of Israel" (**v. 31**). In Matt 9:8, "the crowds ... glorified God," but here they glorified "the God of Israel." This epithet is common in the Old Testament (e.g., Exod 5:1; 1 Kings 1:48; Pss 41:13; 68:35; 69:6; Isa 29:23), in the Dead Sea Scrolls (e.g., 1QS 3:24; 1QM 6:6; 10:8; 13:1–2; 14:4; 4Q177 3:9; 4Q502 passim), and in other Jewish literature (e.g., *T. Solomon* 1:13; *m. Ber.* 7:3; *m. Sanh.* 6:2; *m. Tamid* 3:7; *t. Hagiga* 2.1). Matthew sees in these acclamations credit to Israel's historic faith, a credit that Jesus is bringing to the attention of the world at large. Far from bringing disgrace to the God of Israel, as some Jews in the first century would have argued in their criticism of Jesus and Christian faith, Jesus' ministry in fact brought great glory to Israel's God.[386]

MATTHEW 15:32–39 – FEEDING THE FOUR THOUSAND

15:32: Then Jesus called his disciples to him and said, "I have compassion for the crowd, because they have been with me now for three days and have nothing to eat; and I do not want to send them away hungry, for they might faint on the way."

15:33: The disciples said to him, "Where are we to get enough bread in the desert to feed so great a crowd?"

15:34: Jesus asked them, "How many loaves have you?" They said, "Seven, and a few small fish."

15:35: Then ordering the crowd to sit down on the ground,

15:36: he took the seven loaves and the fish; and after giving thanks he broke them and gave them to the disciples, and the disciples gave them to the crowds.

15:37: And all of them ate and were filled; and they took up the broken pieces left over, seven baskets full.

15:38: Those who had eaten were four thousand men, besides women and children.

15:39: After sending away the crowds, he got into the boat and went to the region of Magadan.

*M*atthew has condensed Mark's version of the feeding of the four thousand, noticeably toning down the Elisha typology that is present in the first feeding story (cf. 2 Kings 4:42–44 and the commentary on Matt 14:15–21). What is distinctive about Matthew's account is the context that he provides. Immediately preceding the feeding of the four thousand is the report of Jesus healing many people of various infirmities, with the result that the crowds "glorified the God of Israel" (Matt 15:31). This distinctive appellation occurs only here in Matthew (and apart from Luke 1:68, it appears nowhere else in the New Testament). The reference to the "God of Israel," followed by a wilderness feast ("bread in the desert," v. 33), is probably a deliberate allusion to the Exodus: "Afterward Moses and Aaron went to Pharaoh and said, 'Thus says the Lord, the God of Israel, "Let my people go, so that they may celebrate a festival to me in the wilderness"'" (Exod 5:1). Thus Matthew

---

[386] T. J. Ryan, "Matthew 15.29–31: An Overlooked Summary," *Horizons* 5 (1978): 31–42; B. Gerhardsson, *The Mighty Acts of Jesus According to Matthew* (Scripta Minora Regiae Societatis Humaniorum Litterarum Lundensis 5; Lund: Gleerup, 1979), 28; T. L. Donaldson, *Jesus on the Mountain* (1985), 122–35.

redirects the second feeding miracle away from the Elisha typology to that of the wilderness typology.[387]

The baskets (Greek: *spuris*) referred to as "seven baskets full" (**v. 37**) are probably larger than the baskets (Greek: *kophinos*) in the feeding of the five thousand in Matt 14:20. The two words for "basket" appear in Matt 16:9–10, where the two feeding miracles are recalled. Different details such as these argue in favor of there originally being two feedings and not simply two versions of one feeding. There is no symbolic meaning behind the number "seven." In Matt 14:20, the "twelve" baskets may have been twelve in number simply because each of the twelve disciples oversaw the filling of his basket. Here, in Matt 15:37, there were seven larger baskets, not because "seven" means something but simply because that was all that was needed to gather the leftover portions of food.

After dispersing the crowd, Jesus departs for "the region of Magadan" (**v. 39**). The location of Magadan today is unknown. Many scribes understandably altered the name to Magdala, suspecting that this better-known village had been intended. Nevertheless, the name "Magadan" is read in several early and important manuscripts.

MATTHEW 16:1–4 – DEMAND FOR A SIGN FROM HEAVEN

16:1: The Pharisees and Sadducees came, and to test Jesus they asked him to show them a sign from heaven.

16:2: He answered them, ["When it is evening, you say, 'It will be fair weather, for the sky is red.'

16:3: And in the morning, 'It will be stormy today, for the sky is red and threatening.' You know how to interpret the appearance of the sky, but you cannot interpret the signs of the times.]

16:4: An evil and adulterous generation asks for a sign, but no sign will be given to it except the sign of Jonah." Then he left them and went away.

*M*atthew draws upon Mark (especially in v. 1, which is from Mark 8:11) and Q (v. 4, which parallels Matt 12:39 = Luke 11:29, and vv. 2–3, which parallel Luke 12:54–56). In context, Matt 16:1–4 prepares more fully for Jesus' warning about the "teaching" of the Pharisees and Sadducees in Matt 16:5–12, which the disciples in Matthew will understand (cf. Matt 16:12 with Mark 8:14–21). The parallel in the *Gospel of Thomas* §91 ("You test the face of heaven and earth, and you have not known what is before you, nor do you know how to test this time") derives from Luke 12:56.

---

[387] T. L. Donaldson, *Jesus on the Mountain* (1985), 122–35; A. Seethaler, "Die Brotvermehrung – Ein Kirchenspiegel?" *BZ* 34 (1990): 108–12; J. R. C. Cousland, "The Feeding of the Four Thousand Gentiles in Matthew? Matthew 15:29–39 as a Test Case," *NovT* 41 (1999): 1–23.

Several early manuscripts (such as Codex Sinaiticus and Codex Vaticanus) omit Jesus' words in vv. 2–3, the material that loosely parallels Luke 12:54–56. If the material is omitted, then Jesus' reply is limited to v. 4, which amounts to nothing more than a repeat of the question and reply in Matt 12:38–39. The view taken here is that vv. 2–3 are probably original, for it is easier to explain their deliberate omission by scribes than their addition. Throughout his Gospel, Matthew creatively combines and edits material from Q, and this is probably another instance of this practice.[388]

Matthew states that "The Pharisees and Sadducees came, and to test Jesus ..." (v. 1). He includes the Sadducees, which he does elsewhere (cf. Matt 3:7; 16:1, 6, 11, 12), whereas Mark 8:11 mentions the Pharisees only. In Matt 12:38, we have "scribes and Pharisees." As in Matt 12:38, a sign is requested of Jesus. On "sign," see the commentary on Matt 12:38–42.

A Closer Look: Josephus on the Pharisees

[12]The Pharisees simplify their standard of living, making no concession to luxury. They follow the guidance of that which their doctrine has selected and transmitted as good, attaching the chief importance to the observance of those commandments which it has seen fit to dictate to them. They show respect and deference to their elders, nor do they rashly presume to contradict their proposals. [13]Though they postulate that everything is brought about by fate, still they do not deprive the human will of the pursuit of what is in man's power, since it was God's good pleasure that there should be a fusion and that the will of man with his virtue and vice should be admitted to the council-chamber of fate. [14]They believe that souls have power to survive death and that there are rewards and punishments under the earth for those who have led lives of virtue or vice: eternal imprisonment is the lot of evil souls, while the good souls receive an easy passage to a new life. [15]Because of these views they are, as a matter of fact, extremely influential among the townsfolk; and all prayers and sacred rites of divine worship are performed according to their exposition. This is the great tribute that the inhabitants of the cities, by practising the highest ideals both in their way of living and in their discourse, have paid to the excellence of the Pharisees. (*Ant.* 18.12–15)

Translation is based on L. H. Feldman, *Josephus IX* (LCL 433; London: Heinemann, 1969), 11, 13. See A. J. Saldarini, "Pharisees," *ABD* (1992), 5:289–303.

---

[388] T. Hirunima, "Matthew 16,2b–3," in E. J. Epp and G. D. Fee (eds.), *New Testament Textual Criticism: Its Significance for Exegesis. Essays in Honour of Bruce M. Metzger* (Oxford: Clarendon Press, 1981), 35–45. Also see comments in D. C. Allison, Jr. and W. D. Davies, *A Critical and Exegetical Commentary on the Gospel According to Saint Matthew* (1988–1997), 2:581; D. A. Hagner, *Matthew* (1993–1995), 2:453; J. Nolland, *The Gospel of Matthew* (2005), 646; R. T. France, *The Gospel of Matthew* (2007), 604–6. Nolland remarks that the passage "is best seen as authentic."

Jesus responds to the request for a sign with a weather analogy: "When it is evening, you say, 'It will be fair weather, for the sky is red.' And in the morning, 'It will be stormy today, for the sky is red and threatening.' You know how to interpret the appearance of the sky, but you cannot interpret the signs of the times" (vv. 2–3). Predicting the weather on the basis of the color of the sky was proverbial in late antiquity. If the wind inclined northward, then the coming rains would be abundant; if they inclined southward, there would be little rain (*b. Yoma* 21b); "is not the sun red at sunrise and at sunset?" (*b. Baba Batra* 84a); "Rabbi Yohanan said, 'Clouds are a sign of coming rain.' ... Rab Judah said, 'Should fine rain come down before the heavy rain then the rain will continue for some time ...'" (*b. Ta'anit* 9b).

A Closer Look: Josephus on the Sadducees

[16]The Sadducees hold that the soul perishes along with the body. They own no observance of any sort apart from the laws; in fact, they reckon it a virtue to dispute with the teachers of the path of wisdom that they pursue. [17]There are but few men to whom this doctrine has been made known, but these are men of the highest standing. They accomplish practically nothing, however. For whenever they assume some office, though they submit unwillingly and perforce, yet submit they do to the formulas of the Pharisees, since otherwise the masses would not tolerate them. (*Ant.* 18.16–17)

Translation is based on L. H. Feldman, *Josephus IX* (LCL 433; London: Heinemann, 1969), 13, 15. See G. G. Porton, "Sadducees," *ABD* (1992), 5:892–95.

Jesus continues, "An evil and adulterous generation asks for a sign, but no sign will be given to it except the sign of Jonah" (v. 4). See the commentary on Matt 12:38–42; Luke 11:29–32. See also John 4:48, "Unless you see signs and wonders, you will not believe."

The reference to an unbelieving and "evil and adulterous generation," in response to a request from Pharisees and Sadducees for "a sign from heaven," creates the context for Matt 16:5–12, where Jesus will warn his disciples of the "yeast of the Pharisees and Sadducees" (Matt 16:6).

MATTHEW 16:5–12 – WARNING OF FALSE TEACHING

16:5: When the disciples reached the other side, they had forgotten to bring any bread.

16:6: Jesus said to them, "Watch out, and beware of the yeast of the Pharisees and Sadducees."

16:7: They said to one another, "It is because we have brought no bread."

16:8: And becoming aware of it, Jesus said, "You of little faith, why are you talking about having no bread?

16:9: Do you still not perceive? Do you not remember the five loaves for the five thousand, and how many baskets you gathered?

16:10: Or the seven loaves for the four thousand, and how many baskets you gathered?

16:11: How could you fail to perceive that I was not speaking about bread? Beware of the yeast of the Pharisees and Sadducees!"

16:12: Then they understood that he had not told them to beware of the yeast of bread, but of the teaching of the Pharisees and Sadducees.

*M*atthew's version of the warning against the Pharisees follows Mark in context and contents (cf. Mark 8:14–21), though there is some abbreviation and a few interesting changes. It has been prepared for contextually by the reference to the "evil and adulterous generation" in the immediately preceding passage (cf. Matt 16:1–4).

The passage begins with the observation that the disciples "had forgotten to bring any bread" (v. 5). Matthew omits Mark's unnecessary "they had only one loaf with them in the boat" (Mark 8:14b). The reference to no bread, of course, occasions the disciples' misunderstanding following Jesus' warning.

Jesus cautions, "Watch out, and beware of the yeast of the Pharisees and Sadducees" (v. 6). Mark's version speaks of "the yeast of the Pharisees and the yeast of Herod" (Mark 8:15). The juxtaposition of Pharisees and Herod is odd. Not surprisingly, Matthew replaces "yeast of Herod" with "Sadducees." Matthew retains the "Herodians" at Matt 22:16 (which he derives from Mark 12:13) but omits them at Matt 12:14, where, according to Mark 3:6, they are once again in the company of the Pharisees. Elsewhere, Matthew adds Sadducees to the scene (e.g., Matt 3:7; 16:1, 11, 12). Matthew therefore understands the warning to be more focused on religious ideas. The disciples assume that Jesus' warning about yeast has something to do with their having no bread (v. 7).

Jesus then asks, "You of little faith, why are you talking about having no bread?" (v. 8). As noted previously, Matthew is fond of the expression "little faith" (*oligopistos*), which he derived from Q (cf. Matt 6:30 = Luke 12:28). Luke only uses "little faith" the one time, but Matthew uses it three more times (cf. Matt 8:26; 14:31; 16:8); see the commentary on Matt 6:30. According to a Greco-Roman sage, "a person of little faith [*oligopistos*] is without faith" (Sextus, *Sentences* 6).

Jesus continues, "Do you still not perceive? Do you not remember ..." (v. 9a). Matthew tones down the severity of the rebuke by omitting most of it (cf. Mark 8:17–18, "Do you still not perceive or understand? Are your hearts hardened? Do you have eyes, and fail to see? Do you have ears, and fail to hear? And do you not remember?"). Jesus asks them if they remember "how many baskets" of leftovers the disciples gathered when the five thousand were fed (v. 9b) and when the four thousand were fed (**v. 10**). In light of Jesus' ability to multiply loaves, how could the disciples think that he was talking of literal bread (**v. 11**)? In light of Jesus' remarkable power, a short supply of bread is nothing to worry about. No warning is required. But the "yeast" of false teachers is another matter.

Eventually, the disciples get Jesus' point: "Then they understood that he had not told them to beware of the yeast of bread, but of the teaching of the Pharisees and Sadducees" (**v. 12**). Readers of Mark's version would recognize that Jesus' reference to "the leaven of the Pharisees and the leaven of Herod" (Mark 8:15) was figurative, but figurative of what? Mark's version is not clear on this point. The meaning of the exchange between Jesus and his disciples is made quite clear in Matthew's version. "Then they understood that he had not told them to beware of the yeast of bread" (that is, *literal bread*) makes it clear that the disciples did indeed understand what Jesus meant (in contrast to Mark's account, in which the reader is left wondering if the disciples ever did grasp the meaning). They rightly recognized that Jesus was warning them "of the teaching of the Pharisees and Sadducees." This is a teaching that insists on signs (cf. Matt 16:1–4) instead of a believing response in what was clearly at work in Jesus' ministry.[389] It has been suggested that we may have here an Aramaic wordplay between *yeast* (*hamir'a*) and *teaching* (*'amir'a*). For another possible wordplay in Aramaic, see the commentaries on Matt 23:24, 27.

MATTHEW 16:13–20 – THE IDENTITY OF JESUS CONFESSED

16:13: Now when Jesus came into the district of Caesarea Philippi, he asked his disciples, "Who do people say that the Son of Man is?"

16:14: And they said, "Some say John the Baptist, but others Elijah, and still others Jeremiah or one of the prophets."

16:15: He said to them, "But who do you say that I am?"

16:16: Simon Peter answered, "You are the Messiah, the Son of the living God."

16:17: And Jesus answered him, "Blessed are you, Simon son of Jonah! For flesh and blood has not revealed this to you, but my Father in heaven.

16:18: And I tell you, you are Peter, and on this rock I will build my church, and the gates of Hades will not prevail against it.

16:19: I will give you the keys of the kingdom of heaven, and whatever you bind on earth will be bound in heaven, and whatever you loose on earth will be loosed in heaven."

---

[389] C. L. Mitton, "Leaven," *ExpT* 84 (1973): 339–43; N. A. Beck, "Reclaiming a Biblical Text: The Mark 8.14–21 Discussion about Bread in a Boat," *CBQ* 43 (1981): 49–56; P. J. Williams, "Bread and the Peshitta in Matthew 16:11–12 and 12:4," *NovT* 43 (2001): 331–33.

16:20: Then he sternly ordered the disciples not to tell anyone that he was the Messiah.

*M*atthew's context is the same as Mark's, but Matthew makes some interesting changes. For one, he has omitted Mark's story of the healing of the blind man (Mark 8:22–26), probably because of the awkward details (spitting in the man's eyes, two stages in the process of healing) and because he wanted to move directly from the warning regarding the false teaching of the Pharisees and Sadducees (Matt 16:5–12) to the truth of Jesus' identity in Matt 16:13–20.

The "district of Caesarea Philippi" (**v. 13**) simplifies Mark's somewhat confusing "villages of Caesarea Philippi" (Mark 8:27). Caesarea Philippi (not to be confused with Caesarea Maritima, seat of the Roman governor Pontius Pilate) is located in northern Galilee, not far from Dan. The city was known for its pagan temples and its association with the god Pan. It is near this city that Jesus asks his disciples, "Who do people say that the Son of Man is?" The disciples' report, "Some say John the Baptist, but others Elijah, and still others Jeremiah or one of the prophets" (**v. 14**), recalls the earlier opinion expressed by Antipas, "This is John the Baptist; he has been raised from the dead, and for this reason these powers are at work in him" (Matt 14:2). Public speculation that Jesus might in some sense be "John the Baptist," whether in spirit or in some sense *redivivus* (as in Mark 6:16), pays a significant compliment to Jesus. The popular wilderness prophet had been put to death by Herod Antipas, as much for political reasons as for personal ones (see the commentary on Matt 14:1–12).

Matthew adds "Jeremiah" to the list of possible candidates for identification of Jesus. Matthew, more than the other Gospel writers, is especially interested in the prophet Jeremiah. It has been suggested that he has presented the rejection of Jesus in the light of the suffering and rejection that Jeremiah of old experienced. Jesus' appeal to Jer 7:11 ("cave of robbers") in the temple action (cf. Matt 21:13) encouraged this typology. The prophecies of Jeremiah are explicitly cited in Matt 2:17–18 (Jer 31:15) and 27:9–10 (Jer 19:1–13; cf. Zech 11:12–13).[390]

Jesus asks his disciples, "But who do you say that I am?" (**v. 15**). Public opinion has been polled. What do the disciples think? Peter answers, "You are the Messiah, the Son of the living God" (**v. 16**). In Mark, Peter simply affirms, "You are the Messiah" (Mark 8:29). See LXX 2 Sam 23:1, "Messiah of God" (Hebrew: "anointed of God"). The epithet "living God" is common in the Old Testament (Deut 5:26; Josh 3:10; 1 Sam 17:26 [on the lips of David]; Ps 42:2; Jer 10:10) and other Jewish literature (*Jub.* 1:25; *Sibylline Oracles* 3:763; *T. Job* 37:2; *T. Solomon* 1:13).

---

[390] On this theme, see M. Knowles, *Jeremiah in Matthew's Gospel: The Rejected Prophet Motif in Matthaean Redaction* (JSNTSup 68; Sheffield: JSOT Press, 1993). Many commentators have been puzzled by the inclusion of Jeremiah in Matt 16:14. See, e.g., T. Zahn, *Das Evangelium des Matthäus*, 3rd edition (Leipzig: Deichert, 1910), 538; J. Schmid, *Das Evangelium nach Matthäus* (1959), 245; A. Sand, *Das Evangelium nach Matthäus* (1986), 325.

Compare the preceding with Nathanael's exclamation: "Rabbi, you are the Son of God! You are the King of Israel!" (John 1:49). This parallelism equates the two epithets, as one would infer from Old Testament Scriptures like 2 Sam 7:14 ("I will be a father to him, and he shall be a son to me") and Ps 2:7 ("You are my son; today I have begotten you"). The description "living God" may allude to Hos 1:10 (= LXX Hos 2:1): "sons of the living God."[391] Here again, the plural "sons" or collective singular "son" (cf. Matt 2:15, in reference to Hos 11:1) has been applied to Jesus, the singular Son of God. According to Cyril of Alexandria (early fifth century), Peter called Jesus the Son of the *living* God because "Christ himself is life and that death has no authority over him" (frag. 190).

In response to Peter's declaration, Jesus pronounces, "Blessed are you, Simon son of Jonah! For flesh and blood has not revealed this to you, but my Father in heaven" (**v. 17**). This blessing and what follows are not derived from Mark 8. The antiquity of the beatitude is seen in referring to Peter as *Simon* and in using his Aramaic "last name," "son of Jonah." (The Aramaic, transliterated in Matthew's Greek text, is *barjona.*) The phrase "flesh and blood" (= Hebrew: *basar we-dam*) is a Semitic idiom, meaning a human being, as opposed to an angel or to God. (This idiom occurs in rabbinic literature frequently and is usually translated as "mortal." It also occurs in Gal 1:16, "I did not consult with flesh and blood"; Ignatius, *Philippians* 7:2, "human flesh"; cf. 1 Cor 15:50; Eph 6:12; Heb 2:14.) In other words, the truth of Jesus' identity was not disclosed to Simon Peter through human knowledge (on his part) or through someone else's teaching. What revealed to Peter the true identity of Jesus was Jesus' "Father in heaven." For this reason, Peter is indeed blessed, for he has been the recipient of divine revelation. Compare 4 Ezra 10:57: "For you are more blessed than many, and you have been called before the Most High, as but few have been."

To the blessing, Jesus adds a pronouncement: "And I tell you, you are Peter, and on this rock I will build my church, and the gates of Hades will not prevail against it" (**v. 18**). Here we have the well-known wordplay on *Peter* (Greek: *Petros*; Aramaic: *kepha'*), whose name means "rock" (Greek: *petra*). It has been suggested that the naming of Simon and the declaration that he was the foundation of a new people of God follow an Old Testament pattern. Abram and Jacob are the only persons in the Hebrew Bible whose names are changed (Abram to Abraham [Gen 17:1–8] and Jacob to Israel [Gen 32:22–32]). Of special interest is that the change of their names was related to their role as founders of a new nation, or new people. Of the two, only Abraham is later associated with a rock foundation. According to Isa 51:1–2, "Listen to me, you that pursue righteousness, you that seek the Lord. Look to the rock from which you were hewn, and to the quarry from which you were dug. Look to Abraham your father and to Sarah who bore you; for he was but one when I

---

[391]　R. H. Gundry, *Matthew* (1982), 330; M. J. Goodwin, "Hosea and 'the Son of the Living God' in Matthew 16:16b," *CBQ* 67 (2005): 265–83.

called him, but I blessed him and made him many." The parallel suggests that Jesus foresees founding a new people, his "church," on the bedrock of Peter's confession and leadership. (See also the commentary on Matt 3:9, where John the Baptist links Abraham with stones.)

Jesus' promise to "build" his "church" recalls God's promise in Jer 31:4, "Again I will build you, and you shall be built, O virgin Israel!" and in Amos 9:11, "On that day I will raise the booth of David that is fallen, and repair its breaches, and raise up its ruins, and rebuild it as in the days of old" (cf. Acts 15:15–18). The word church (Greek: *ekklesia*) means "assembly" or "congregation" and is the equivalent of the Hebrew word *qahal*, which occurs frequently in the Old Testament (often in reference to the "assembly of God" or "assembly of the Lord"; cf. Num 16:3; 20:4; Deut 23:2, 3, 4, 9).[392]

Jesus assures Peter and the other disciples that the very "gates of Hades will not prevail against" this church founded on the rock. The "gates of Hades" are not the realm of the dead (as in Job 38:17 or Ps 9:13, which speak of the "gates of death," or Isa 38:10, which speaks of the "gates of Sheol") or death by martyrdom but the powers of evil that attempt to overwhelm the church. But because the church is built on the rock, it will withstand the attack (much as the house built on the rock withstands the storm in the parable in Matt 7:24–27). In view of this parallel, it has been suggested that the saying originally referred to "storm" (Aramaic: *sa'ar*) instead of "gate" (Aramaic: *sha'ar*); that is, the storms of Hades will not overpower the church.[393]

Jesus has blessed Peter, has promised that the church will be built and will withstand the worst that Hades can throw at it, and now promises Peter even more: "I will give you the keys of the kingdom of heaven, and whatever you bind on earth will be bound in heaven, and whatever you loose on earth will be loosed in heaven" (**v. 19**). Jesus' saying is in some way related to Isa 22:22: "I will place on his shoulder the key of the house of David; he shall open, and no one shall shut; he shall shut, and no one shall open." As the representative of the "house of David," Jesus has given the key to his principal disciple Peter, who will exercise authority "on earth", even as Jesus as the Son of Man exercised authority "on earth" (see Matt 9:6). As

---

[392]   M. Wilcox, "Peter and the Rock: A Fresh Look at Matthew 16:17–19," *NTS* 22 (1975): 73–88; J. A. Fitzmyer, "Aramaic *Kepha'* and Peter's Name in the New Testament," in E. Best and R. McL. Wilson (eds.), *Text and Interpretation: Studies in the New Testament Presented to Matthew Black* (Cambridge: Cambridge University Press, 1979), 121–32; T. Finley, "'Upon This Rock': Matthew 16.18 and the Aramaic Evidence," *Aramaic Studies* 4 (2006): 133–51.

[393]   S. Gero, "The Gates or the Bars of Hades? A Note on Matthew 16.18," *NTS* 27 (1981): 411–14; C. Brown, "The Gates of Hell and the Church," in J. Bradley and R. Muller (eds.), *Church, Word, and Spirit: Historical and Theological Essays in Honor of Geoffrey W. Bromiley* (Grand Rapids, MI: Eerdmans, 1987), 15–43; J. Marcus, "The Gates of Hades and the Keys of the Kingdom (Matt 16:18–19)," *CBQ* 50 (1988): 443–55.

chief apostle, Peter will unlock the doors that will allow true Israel to enter the kingdom (be they Jews or Gentiles), a role we see him play at Pentecost (Acts 2) and later with respect to the salvation of Gentiles (Acts 10–11).[394]

To have the "keys of the kingdom" is to have the power to "bind on earth" what "will be bound in heaven" and "loose on earth" what will be "loosed in heaven." The binding and loosing mentioned here clarify what was said earlier about the keys, especially in light of the parallel in Isa 22:22. That is, binding and loosing is the equivalent of shutting and opening – shutting the door on some, opening the door for others; or less figuratively, of deciding what is permitted and what is not permitted. A similar idea is found in the parallel in Matt 18:18, but with reference to questions of discipline within the church itself. Saying that what Peter binds *on earth* will be bound *in heaven* is to assure the apostle that he has heaven's backing (compare Luke 11:52, where legal experts misuse their expertise and take away the "key of knowledge," shutting people out of the kingdom and not entering themselves).[395]

For rabbinic examples of permit/not permit (or forbid), see *m. 'Eduyyot* 4:8, "the House of Shammai permit levirate marriage between the co-wives and the surviving brothers, but the House of Hillel forbid it"; *Terumot* 5:4, "the House of Shammai declare it forbidden, but the House of Hillel permit"; and other examples in *m. Peah* 7:5; *Demai* 2:4; *Ta'anit* 2:7; *Megillah* 1:11; *Temurah* 7:6.

MATTHEW 16:21–23 – FIRST PREDICTION OF SUFFERING AND DEATH

16:21: From that time on, Jesus began to show his disciples that he must go to Jerusalem and undergo great suffering at the hands of the elders and chief priests and scribes, and be killed, and on the third day be raised.

16:22: And Peter took him aside and began to rebuke him, saying, "God forbid it, Lord! This must never happen to you."

16:23: But he turned and said to Peter, "Get behind me, Satan! You are a stumbling block to me; for you are setting your mind not on divine things but on human things."

[394] B. D. Chilton, "Shebna, Eliakim, and the Promise to Peter," in B. D. Chilton and C. A. Evans, *Jesus in Context: Temple, Purity, and Restoration* (AGJU 39; Leiden: Brill, 1997), 319–37.

[395] J. A. Emerton, "Binding and Loosing – Forgiving and Retaining," *JTS* 13 (1962): 325–31; G. Bornkamm, "The Authority to 'Bind' and 'Loose' in the Church in Matthew's Gospel: The Problem of Sources in Matthew's Gospel," *Perspective* 11 (1970): 37–50; R. H. Hiers, "'Binding and Loosing': The Matthean Authorizations," *JBL* 104 (1985): 233–50; D. C. Duling, "Binding and Loosing: Matthew 16:19; Matthew 18:18; John 20:23," *Forum* 3, no. 4 (1987): 3–31.

*J*esus' first formal prediction of his suffering and death is based on Mark 8:31–33. We see again some editing in Matthew's version, mostly to ameliorate Peter's objection and the rebuke Jesus gives his anxious disciple.

Matthew then relates, "From that time on, Jesus[396] began to show his disciples that he must go to Jerusalem and undergo great suffering" (**v. 21a**). Jesus will predict his suffering again in Matt 17:22–23 and Matt 20:18–19. Did Jesus really predict his death, or did Matthew or tradents before him create the tradition? The probability that Jesus did in fact anticipate his death is seen in his prayer in the Garden of Gethsemane: "Abba, Father, all things are possible for you. Take this cup from me! But not what I want, but what you want!" (Matt 26:39). This scene, in which Jesus expresses his dread (cf. Matt 26:37–38) and in which his disciples fail to keep watch and pray with him, is so potentially embarrassing for the early church that its authenticity is virtually guaranteed (see the commentary on Matt 26:36–46). Jesus' prayer implies that he anticipates his death and would like somehow to avoid it. The violent fate of John the Baptist probably influenced Jesus' thinking as well. But did Jesus anticipate his resurrection also? Very probably. For him not to have anticipated it would have been strange, for pious Jews very much believed in the resurrection (Dan 12:1–3; *1 Enoch* 22–27; 92–105; *Jub.* 23:11–31; *4 Macc* 7:3; Josephus, *Ant.* 18.14, 16, 18). Would Jesus have faced death and then, having on another occasion affirmed his belief in the resurrection (Matt 22:23–33), have expressed no faith in his own vindication? It seems unlikely.

The qualifying phrase, "on the third day be raised," probably owes its inspiration to Hos 6:2, "on the third day he will raise us up." The allusion to this passage in all probability derives from Jesus himself. But his allusion may have meant no more than his expectation that his resurrection would be soon, perhaps as part of the general resurrection (see *Tg.* Hos 6:2, which reads "on the day of the resurrection of the dead he will raise us up"), because the kingdom itself was soon to appear in its fullness, and with it judgment. Perhaps we should think that when the tomb was found empty the morning of the first day of the week, his followers interpreted the phrase in a literal fashion.[397]

---

[396]   The NASB reads "Jesus Christ," but the NRSV reads only "Jesus" (as do the KJV, ASV, and RSV). Our two oldest Greek New Testaments (i.e., Codex Sinaiticus and Codex Vaticanus) read *Iesous Christos*, but the vast majority read only *Iesous*. Textual scholars agree that it is easier to explain the addition of *Christos* than its omission. Accordingly, most think "Christ" is a scribal addition, probably inspired by the previous passage, in which Peter confesses that Jesus is indeed "the Christ" (cf. Matt 16:16).

[397]   B. Willaert, "La connexion littéraire entre la première prediction de la passion et la confession de Pierre chez les synoptiques," *ETL* 32 (1956): 24–45; M. Black, "The 'Son of Man' Passion Sayings in the Gospel Tradition," *ZNW* 60 (1977): 1–8; J. Schaberg, "Daniel 7,12 and the New Testament Passion-Resurrection Predictions," *NTS* 31 (1985): 208–22; H. F. Bayer, *Jesus' Predictions of Vindication and Resurrection: The Provenance, Meaning and Correlation of the Synoptic Predictions* (WUNT 2, no. 20; Tübingen: Mohr [Siebeck], 1986).

Shocked by what he has just heard, Peter takes Jesus aside and begins to "rebuke him, saying, 'God forbid it, Lord! This must never happen to you'" (**v. 22**). Mark does not tell us what Peter actually said. Peter's "God forbid it, Lord!" (literally "Be it far from you, Lord"; Greek: *heleos soi, kurie*) echoes similar interjections in the Greek version of the Old Testament. These include 2 Sam 23:17, "Be it far from me, O Lord [*heleos moi, kurie*], that I should do this," and 1 Chron 11:19, "Be it far from me before my God [*heleos moi, ho theos*] that I should do this." The addition of Peter's words clarifies "rebuke," which Mark does not do (cf. Mark 8:32). Being "killed" is exactly the anticipated fate of messianic pretenders. Peter fervently believes that no such thing will happen to Jesus.

Jesus responds by rebuking Peter: "Get behind me, Satan! You are a stumbling block to me; for you are setting your mind not on divine things but on human things" (**v. 23**). Matthew has added "You are a stumbling block [Greek: *skandalon*] to me," which he did not derive from Mark (Mark 8:32). Matthew frequently refers to a "stumbling block" or to the verb "to stumble" (Greek: *skandalizein*); see Matt 5:29. For more on the theme of stumbling, see the commentary on Matt 18:5–9. The prospects of crucifixion and death are troubling enough (cf. Matt 26:37–42) without having one's principal disciple opposing one's mission. The rebuke of Peter is not the end of the matter; the disciple will have to hear more on the theme of suffering. See the commentary on Matt 16:24–28.

MATTHEW 16:24–28 – FOLLOWING JESUS

16:24: Then Jesus told his disciples, "If any want to become my followers, let them deny themselves and take up their cross and follow me.

16:25: For those who want to save their life will lose it, and those who lose their life for my sake will find it.

16:26: For what will it profit them if they gain the whole world but forfeit their life? Or what will they give in return for their life?

16:27: "For the Son of Man is to come with his angels in the glory of his Father, and then he will repay everyone for what has been done.

16:28: Truly I tell you, there are some standing here who will not taste death before they see the Son of Man coming in his kingdom."

*M*atthew's version of Jesus' teaching on discipleship derives from Mark 8:34–9:1 and falls in the same context as Mark's version. Matthew edits the material he has inherited from Mark, mostly through deletion.

Matthew continues, "Then Jesus told his disciples ..." (**v. 24**), omitting Mark's reference to the "crowd" (Mark 8:34, "the crowd with the disciples"). Jesus tells his disciples, "If any want to become my followers, let them deny themselves and take up their cross and follow me." Peter's opposition to Jesus' predicted fate leads to teaching on suffering. The disciples of Jesus must be prepared to face martyrdom. But the loss of everything, even one's life, is to gain eternal reward if it is in the service of the Son of Man. Jesus' saying about taking up the cross finds an interesting parallel in Epictetus, who warns the nonconformist: "If you want to be crucified, just wait. The cross will come" (*Discourses* 2.2.20). Jesus' saying about saving and losing one's life also finds a parallel in a late first-century source: "Because of what have men lost their life and for what have those who were on the earth exchanged their soul?" (*2 Bar* 51:15).[398]

Jesus' saying about saving and losing one's life (**v. 25**) also finds a parallel in a later rabbinic tractate: "Everyone who preserves one thing from the Torah preserves his life, and everyone who loses one thing from the Torah will lose his life" (*'Abot R. Nat.* B §35). The saying here is proverbial (and quite rare). The saying in John 12:25 is similar: "Those who love their life lose it, and those who hate their life in this world will keep it for eternal life."[399]

The rhetorical questions about the futility of gaining the whole world only to lose one's life (**v. 26**) have approximate counterparts in the Hebrew Bible (e.g., Eccles 1:3; Ps 49:7–9) and the ethicists of late antiquity (e.g., Menander, *Sentences* 843: "Nothing is more valuable than [one's] life"). Jesus' saying is distinctive for succinctness and clarity, but not for its originality.

In Matthew's account, Jesus tells his disciples, "For the Son of Man is to come with his angels in the glory of his Father . . ." (**v. 27**). Matthew omits Mark's reference to "an adulterous and sinful generation" (Mark 8:38), for these words were used earlier in Matt 16:4 and earlier still in Matt 12:39 (see the commentary there). On the reference to "his angels," see the commentary on Matt 26:53. The saying "he will repay everyone for what has been done" is proverbial and sometimes appears in eschatological contexts. Examples include LXX Ps 61:13, "you will recompense every man according to his deeds"; Prov 24:12, "he will recompense every man according to his deeds"; Sir 35:22, "till he repays the man according to his deeds, and the works of men according to their devices"; *T. Job* 17:3, "I will repay him according to what he has done"; Rom 2:6, "who will render to every man according to his deeds"; Rev 2:23, "I will give to each one of you according to your deeds"; Rev 22:12, "Behold, I am coming quickly, and My reward is with Me, to render to every man according to what he has done."

---

[398] D. R. Fletcher, "Condemned to Die: The Logion on Cross-Bearing. What Does It Mean?" *Int* 18 (1964): 156–64; J. G. Griffiths, "The Disciples' Cross," *NTS* 16 (1970): 358–64; J. D. Kingsbury, "The Significance of the Cross within the Plot of Matthew's Gospel. A Study in Narrative Criticism," in C. Focant (ed.), *The Synoptic Gospels: Source Criticism and the New Literary Criticism* (BETL 110; Leuven: Peeters and Leuven University Press, 1993), 263–79.

[399] W. A. Beardslee, "Saving One's Life by Losing It," *JAAR* 47 (1979): 57–72.

Jesus continues, "There are some standing here who will not taste death before they see the Son of Man coming in his kingdom" (**v. 28**). Mark's version reads, "… until they see that the kingdom of God has come with power" (Mark 9:1), but Matthew's version places the emphasis on Jesus himself, not the kingdom of God, for it is Jesus whom the disciples will see transfigured six days hence (cf. Matt 17:1–8).[400]

MATTHEW 17:1–8 – TRANSFIGURATION OF JESUS

17:1: Six days later, Jesus took with him Peter and James and his brother John and led them up a high mountain, by themselves.

17:2: And he was transfigured before them, and his face shone like the sun, and his clothes became dazzling white.

17:3: Suddenly there appeared to them Moses and Elijah, talking with him.

17:4: Then Peter said to Jesus, "Lord, it is good for us to be here; if you wish, I will make three dwellings here, one for you, one for Moses, and one for Elijah."

17:5: While he was still speaking, suddenly a bright cloud overshadowed them, and from the cloud a voice said, "This is my Son, the Beloved; with him I am well pleased; listen to him!"

17:6: When the disciples heard this, they fell to the ground and were overcome by fear.

17:7: But Jesus came and touched them, saying, "Get up and do not be afraid."

17:8: And when they looked up, they saw no one except Jesus himself alone.

Several scholars have argued that the Transfiguration story was originally a resurrection appearance story.[401] In some second-century Gnostic traditions, the resurrection of Jesus is described in language that clearly parallels the Transfiguration account; e.g., "Then a great light appeared so that the mountain shone from the sight of him who had appeared. And a voice called out to them, saying, 'Listen to my words that I may speak to you'" (*Letter of Peter to Philip* [NHC VIII] 134.9–16). Another significant example is seen here: "What then is the resurrection? It is always

---

[400] W. G. Kümmel, "Eschatological Expectation in the Proclamation of Jesus," in J. M. Robinson (ed.), *The Future of Our Religious Past* (R. Bultmann Festschrift; New York: Harper & Row, 1971), 29–48; B. D. Chilton, "'Not to Taste Death': A Jewish, Christian and Gnostic Usage," in E. A. Livingstone (ed.), *Studia Biblica 1978: II. Papers on the Gospels* (JSNTSup 2; Sheffield: JSOT Press, 1979), 29–36; B. S. Crawford, "Near Expectation in the Sayings of Jesus," *JBL* 101 (1982): 225–44; L. Sabourin, "Matthieu 10.23 et 16.28 dans la perspective apocalyptique," *ScEs* 37 (1985): 353–64.

[401] For example, C. E. Carlston, "Transfiguration and Resurrection," *JBL* 80 (1961): 233–40.

the disclosure of those who have risen. For if you remember reading in the Gospel that Elijah appeared and Moses was with him, do not think the resurrection is an illusion" (*Treatise on the Resurrection* [NHC I] 48.3–11). The phrase "Elijah appeared and Moses was with him" comes right out of Mark 9:4. Yet this Gnostic text speaks of the post-Easter Resurrection, not the pre-Easter Transfiguration. Nevertheless, there are problems with the theory that the Transfiguration story originated as an Easter story.[402] Among other things, it has been observed that at many points the Transfiguration account differs from the Resurrection accounts found in the New Testament Gospels. It is not at all clear that the earliest accounts of Jesus' resurrection involved the kind of luminosity depicted in the Transfiguration.

There are many features about the Transfiguration that have led commentators to conclude that this episode is intended to have some sort of typological connection to Exodus 24 and 33–34, passages that describe Moses' ascent up Mount Sinai, where he meets God and then descends with the tablets of the Law and with a shining face. The following specific parallels between Matthew's account (Matt 17:1–8) and Exodus are evident: (1) the reference to "six days" (Matt 17:1; Exod 24:16), (2) the cloud that covers the mountain (Matt 17:5; Exod 24:16), (3) God's voice from the cloud (Matt 17:5; Exod 24:16), (4) three companions (Matt 17:1; Exod 24:1, 9), (5) a transformed appearance (Matt 17:2; Exod 34:30), and (6) the reaction of awe and fear (Matt 17:6, 7; Exod 34:30).[403] Another suggestive item that should be mentioned is that in Exod 24:13 Joshua is singled out and taken up the mountain with Moses. Because "Joshua" in the Greek Old Testament is frequently rendered "Jesus," the early church may have seen in Exod 24:13 a veiled prophecy, or typology, that came to fulfillment in the Transfiguration, where once again Moses and Jesus are together. Matthew continues to follow Mark's sequence and context. Few changes are made in this passage, and these mostly comprise deletions or simplifications.

Matthew says Jesus "was transfigured before them, and his face shone like the sun, and his clothes became dazzling white" (**v. 2**). Mark's version reads, "his clothes became dazzling white, such as no one on earth could bleach them" (Mark 9:3). Matthew drops the homespun comparison with bleaching. Rather, he draws attention to Jesus himself, noting that his "face shone like the sun" and that his clothing "became dazzling white." Matthew prefers to compare Jesus' clothing to "light" itself rather than to the best efforts of a launderer ("on earth"! Are there launderers in

---

402   See R. H. Stein, "Is the Transfiguration (Mark 9:2–8) a Misplaced Resurrection-Account?" *JBL* 95 (1976): 79–96.

403   R. H. Gundry, *Matthew* (1982), 342–44; D. C. Allison, Jr. and W. D. Davies, *A Critical and Exegetical Commentary on the Gospel According to Saint Matthew* (1988–1997), 2:685–87; D. J. Harrington, *The Gospel of Matthew* (1991), 253–55; D. A. Hagner, *Matthew* (1993–1995), 2:492–93; R. Schnackenburg, *The Gospel of Matthew* (2002), 165–66; R. T. France, *The Gospel of Matthew* (2007), 644.

heaven?). According to *T. Levi* 18:40, the Messiah will "shine forth as the sun." In one tradition, it is said that, when Elijah was born, "men of shining white appearance greeted him and wrapped him in fire" (*Lives of the Prophets* 21:2). According to Philo, Moses gave off light like "rays of the sun" (*Life of Moses* 1.70), and in rabbinic interpretation we are told that the "face of Moses was as the face of the sun" (*Sipre Num.* §140 [on Num 27:1–11]; see also Ps.-Philo, *Biblical Antiquities* 12:1, where we are told that Moses' "face surpassed the splendor of the sun and moon"). Matthew has described Jesus in terms of Mosaic tradition, placing him in the very company of Moses, to enhance Jesus' law-giving authority.

There are similar stories in Greco-Roman traditions. One thinks of Servius, thought to have been begotten by a god, whose "head shone with the radiance very like the gleam of lightning ... his face was seen by the women to be surrounded by the gleam of fire. This was a token of his birth from fire and an excellent sign pointing to his unexpected accession to the kingship" (Plutarch, *Moralia* 323CD: "The Fortune of the Romans," 10).

Matthew then reports, "Suddenly there appeared to them Moses and Elijah, talking with him" (**v. 3**). Mark says "there appeared to them Elijah with Moses" (Mark 9:4). By placing Moses first, Matthew once again emphasizes the great lawgiver. According to one rabbinic midrash, God promises in the future to bring Moses with Elijah (*Deut. Rab.* 3.17 [on Deut 10:1]; cf. *Pesiq. R.* 4.2). Both Moses and Elijah had revelatory experiences on mountaintops (Exodus 20–34; 1 Kings 19:8), and biblical and extrabiblical sources preserve traditions of translation to heaven prior to resurrection (Josephus, *Ant.* 4.326, "while [Moses] bade farewell to Eleazar and Joshua and was yet communicating with them, a cloud suddenly descended upon him and he disappeared").[404]

Whereas in Matthew's account "Peter said to Jesus, 'Lord'" (**v. 4**), Mark's version reads "Rabbi" (Mark 9:5). Matthew's use of Lord (*kurios*) heightens the respect for Jesus; perhaps it also indicates a heightened Christology. Peter's offer to "make three dwellings here" may have in mind the booths or huts erected for seven days as part of the celebration of the Feast of Booths (Lev 23:42–44; Neh 8:14–17), a celebration that in time came to look forward to future deliverance as much as it looked to the past deliverance from Egypt.

When Matthew states, "Suddenly a bright cloud overshadowed them" (**v. 5**), he adds "bright" to heighten the revelatory context. We see this feature in Ezek 1:4, "a great cloud with fire flashing forth continually and a bright light around it" (cf. *T. Abraham* [A] 9:8, "a cloud of light"). The overshadowing cloud recalls Exodus tradition: "Moses was not able to enter the tent of meeting because the cloud settled upon it, and the glory of the Lord filled the tabernacle" (Exod 40:35; cf. 19:19). From this bright cloud, the heavenly voice declares: "This is my Son, the Beloved; with

---

[404] M. E. Thrall, "Elijah and Moses in Mark's Account of the Transfiguration," *NTS* 16 (1970): 305–17.

him I am well pleased; listen to him!" Matthew adds "with him I am well pleased," thus recalling fully the words spoken at the baptism of Jesus (cf. Matt 3:17).

According to Mark 9:6, the disciples "were terrified." Matthew changes this to "When the disciples heard this, they fell to the ground and were overcome by fear" (**v. 6**). This reaction conforms to the expected behavior in the presence of the divine, as we see in Gen 17:3: "And Abram fell on his face, and God talked with him ..." (cf. Josh 5:14: "And Joshua fell on his face to the earth, and bowed down ...").

Ever the master of the situation, "Jesus came and touched them, saying, 'Get up and do not be afraid'" (**v. 7**). Jesus will approach his disciples in Matt 28:18, again as an exalted and transfigured being.[405]

MATTHEW 17:9–13 – ELIJAH HAS ALREADY COME

17:9: As they were coming down the mountain, Jesus ordered them, "Tell no one about the vision until after the Son of Man has been raised from the dead."

17:10: And the disciples asked him, "Why, then, do the scribes say that Elijah must come first?"

17:11: He replied, "Elijah is indeed coming and will restore all things;

17:12: but I tell you that Elijah has already come, and they did not recognize him, but they did to him whatever they pleased. So also the Son of Man is about to suffer at their hands."

17:13: Then the disciples understood that he was speaking to them about John the Baptist.

*F*ollowing the remarkable experience of the Transfiguration (Matt 17:1–8), the disciples ask Jesus about the view held by scribes that Elijah is to "come first," presumably before the consummation of the kingdom of God. Jesus agrees with the interpretation, but applies it in a way the scribes would not. Matthew continues to follow Mark's sequence and context (Mark 9:9–13). He will, however, introduce some much-needed clarification and will again omit details that he finds unhelpful (such as Mark 9:10).

Following the remarkable experience of the Transfiguration, Jesus orders his disciples: "Tell no one about the vision" (**v. 9**). Mark's version reads "tell no one about

---

[405]   P. Dabeck, "Siehe, es erschienen Moses und Elia (Mt 17,3)," *Bib* 23 (1942): 175–89; W. L. Liefeld, "Theological Motifs in the Transfiguration Narrative," in R. N. Longenecker and M. C. Tenney (eds.), *New Dimensions in New Testament Study* (Grand Rapids, MI: Zondervan, 1974), 162–79; S. Pedersen, "Die Proklamation Jesu als des eschatologischen Offenbarungsträgers (Mt. xvii.1–13)," *NovT* 17 (1975): 241–64; B. D. Chilton, "The Transfiguration: Dominical Assurance and Apostolic Vision," *NTS* 27 (1981): 115–24; M. Pamment, "Moses and Elijah in the Story of the Transfiguration," *ExpT* 92 (1981): 338–39.

what they had seen" (Mark 9:9). But in Matthew it becomes "a vision" (Greek: *to horama*), which is consistent with a divine epiphany, or a vision of God. The disciples are not to tell others about this vision "until after the Son of Man has been raised from the dead." The Transfiguration, a foreshadowing of Jesus' resurrection and of the kingdom's power, is to be proclaimed when Jesus is resurrected. It is at this time that the disciples will proclaim Jesus' messiahship, not before (as earlier commanded by Jesus in Matt 16:20).

The disciples' question, "Why, then, do the scribes say that Elijah must come first?" (v. 10), reflects interpretation at least as old as the sage Yeshua ben Sira (Sirach), who committed his wisdom to writing ca. 180 B.C. It is seen in his praise of Elijah, who says that the great prophet is "ready at the appointed time ... to restore the tribes of Jacob" (Sir 48:10). Sirach's hope of the restoration of the tribes finds expression in Jesus' appointment of the twelve apostles (see the commentary on Matt 10:1–4). This interpretive opinion is probably based on Mal 4:5–6, which in part reads: "Lo, I will send you the prophet Elijah *before* the great and terrible day of the Lord comes. He will turn the hearts of parents to their children and the hearts of children to their parents" (RSV; emphasis added).[406]

Jesus agrees with what the scribes say: "Elijah is indeed coming and will restore all things" (v. 11). Of course the scribes have not recognized the martyred John the Baptist as the prophesied Elijah, but Jesus has: "I tell you that Elijah has already come, and they did not recognize him, but they did to him whatever they pleased" (v. 12). Jesus, the "Son of Man," will experience the same fate: "So also the Son of Man is about to suffer at their hands." Matthew has removed the ambiguity of Mark's text ("How then is it written about the Son of Man, that he is to go through many sufferings ... ?"). He also makes it clear to his readers that the "disciples understood" that Jesus was indeed "speaking to them about John the Baptist" (v. 13). The ambiguity is removed not only for the readers of Matthew's Gospel but for the disciples themselves.

MATTHEW 17:14–21 – HEALING A DEMONIZED BOY

17:14: When they came to the crowd, a man came to him, knelt before him,

17:15: and said, "Lord, have mercy on my son, for he is an epileptic and he suffers terribly; he often falls into the fire and often into the water.

17:16: And I brought him to your disciples, but they could not cure him."

---

[406] In what sense Elijah comes "first" is debated. See M. M. Faierstein, "Why Do the Scribes Say that Elijah Must Come First?" *JBL* 100 (1981): 75–86; D. C. Allison, Jr., "'Elijah Must Come First,'" *JBL* 103 (1984): 256–58; J. A. Fitzmyer, "More about Elijah Coming First," *JBL* 104 (1985): 295–96; J. Taylor, "The Coming of Elijah, Mt 17,10–13 and Mk 9,11–13: The Development of the Texts," *RB* 98 (1991): 107–19.

17:17: Jesus answered, "You faithless and perverse generation, how much longer must I be with you? How much longer must I put up with you? Bring him here to me."

17:18: And Jesus rebuked the demon, and it came out of him, and the boy was cured instantly.

17:19: Then the disciples came to Jesus privately and said, "Why could we not cast it out?"

17:20: He said to them, "Because of your little faith. For truly I tell you, if you have faith the size of a mustard seed, you will say to this mountain, 'Move from here to there,' and it will move; and nothing will be impossible for you."

17:21: [Omitted from the NRSV; see the commentary that follows]

*M*atthew derives the story of the healing of the demonized boy from Mark 9:14–19. He abbreviates the story but enhances the theme of faith (especially in Matt 17:20, where we find material taken from Mark 11:22–23). He also increases the respect shown for Jesus, for the man kneels before Jesus and addresses him as "Lord" (Matt 17:15) rather than "teacher" as in Mark's account. The exorcism of the demonized boy provides Jesus the opportunity to demonstrate a power far beyond that of his disciples, who had earlier received authority over demons (Matt 10:1).

The story begins with the notice that a man "came to" Jesus and "knelt before him" (**v. 14**). He then respectfully petitions Jesus: "Lord, have mercy on my son, for he is an epileptic and he suffers terribly; he often falls into the fire and often into the water" (**v. 15**). Matthew's version of the story greatly simplifies Mark's complicated and chaotic version (see Mark 9:14–18a). Falling to the ground, foaming at the mouth, and grinding one's teeth are all symptomatic of epilepsy, or the "falling down" syndrome, as people in late antiquity thought of it. One of the more famous persons with this affliction was Alexander the Great. The condition was sometimes thought to be the result of contact with spirits or deities. The case of the stricken boy falls loosely into this category, though Jesus' contemporaries regard it as demonic possession.

The distraught father goes on to tell Jesus, "I brought him to your disciples, but they could not cure him" (**v. 16**). The disciples' inability sets the stage for Jesus' superior display of strength, as the "stronger one" (Matt 12:29) whom John had predicted (Matt 3:11). It also occasions Jesus' expression of disappointment.

Jesus' outburst, "You faithless and perverse generation" (**v. 17**), underscores the need for faith, a theme touched upon elsewhere in Matthew (cf. Matt 9:2, 22, 28–29; 15:28; 21:21–22). The implication is that this generation is not only a generation of skeptics but one that has failed to respond to the good news of the presence of the kingdom, a presence attested by Jesus' power over Satan and his unholy allies. The rhetorical questions "How much longer must I be with you?" and "How much longer must I put up with you?" show how antithetical unbelief is to Jesus' message and his own faith in God. Jesus wonders how long he must put up with this unbelief, which may hint at his expectation of death.

Jesus ordered the boy to be brought to him and "rebuked the demon, and it came out of him, and the boy was cured instantly" (**v. 18**). The contrast between Jesus, who heals with a word and heals instantly, and his disciples, who fail, is striking. Matthew highlights this feature by omitting the discussion between Jesus and the anxious and doubting father (cf. Mark 9:20–24).

In private, the disciples ask Jesus why they could not cast out the evil spirit (**v. 19**). Their question is understandable, given the fact that Jesus had earlier given them "authority over unclean spirits" (Matt 10:1). We know of no other case where the disciples failed. Their question gives Matthew the opportunity to have Jesus speak about the importance of faith.

Jesus' answer, "Because of your little faith. For truly I tell you, if you have faith the size of a mustard seed, you will say to this mountain, 'Move from here to there,' and it will move; and nothing will be impossible for you" (**v. 20**), derived in part from Mark 11:22–23, is one of those rare occasions when Matthew actually expands Mark's version of a story. He cannot pass up an opportunity to drive home a lesson related to faith. The disciples could not cast out the demon because of their "little faith" (Greek: *oligopistia*). This had been the disciples' problem on other occasions when Jesus called them "you of little faith" (literally "little-faith [ones]"; Greek: *oligopistoi*); see Matt 6:30; 8:26; 14:31; 16:8. Indeed, if the disciples have even a little faith, they can do great things, such as – in proverbial language – move mountains. Matthew's form of the saying parallels Luke 17:6 (which mentions a "mustard seed" but speaks of a mulberry tree, not a mountain) and Mark 11:23 (which speaks of a "mountain" but does not mention a mustard seed).[407]

Verse 21 ("But this kind does not go out except by prayer and fasting") is omitted in the NRSV because the translators rightly recognize that this verse, which is not found in the oldest manuscripts of Matthew (e.g., the Codex Sinaiticus and Codex Vaticanus), was probably imported into the text by a scribe familiar with Mark's parallel version. The verse is not consistent with Matthew's theme. The disciples failed not because they did not fast or pray but because of their lack of faith.

MATTHEW 17:22–23 – SECOND PREDICTION OF THE PASSION

17:22: As they were gathering in Galilee, Jesus said to them, "The Son of Man is going to be betrayed into human hands,

17:23: and they will kill him, and on the third day he will be raised." And they were greatly distressed.

[407] J. Wilkinson, "The Case of the Epileptic Boy," *ExpT* 79 (1967): 39–42; G. E. Sterling, "Jesus as Exorcist: An Analysis of Matthew 17:14–21; Mark 9:14–29; Luke 9:37–43a," *CBQ* 55 (1993): 467–93.

*I*n Matt 17:22–23, Jesus predicts his Passion a second time. Matthew again draws upon Mark, but has simplified the material, omitting Mark's "He did not want anyone to know it" (Mark 9:30) and the statement that the disciples "did not understand …" (Mark 9:32). For a discussion of the first Passion prediction, see the commentary on Matt 16:21–23.

Matthew introduces the second Passion prediction by saying, "As they were gathering in Galilee" (**v. 22a**), whereas Mark says, "They went on from there and passed through Galilee" (Mark 9:30). Matthew's revision may be intended to suggest that Jesus and his disciples "were gathering in Galilee" in preparation for the final journey to Jerusalem to celebrate Passover and to proclaim God's rule. This activity, of course, stands in tension with Mark's secretive "He did not want anyone to know it" (Mark 9:30), and so Matthew omits it.

In contrast to the first Passion prediction (Matt 16:21; following Mark 8:31), the second prediction is presented in Jesus' own words: "The Son of Man is going to be betrayed into human hands, and they will kill him, and on the third day he will be raised" (**vv. 22b–23a**). This prediction has few details. The third prediction (Matt 20:18–19) is far more detailed.

Matthew's "they were greatly distressed" (**v. 23b**) replaces Mark's "they did not understand what he was saying and were afraid to ask him" (Mark 9:32). Throughout his narrative, Matthew tones down or eliminates Mark's references to the disciples' obduracy and lack of understanding.[408]

MATTHEW 17:24–27 – ON PAYING THE TEMPLE TAX

17:24: **When they reached Capernaum, the collectors of the temple tax came to Peter and said, "Does your teacher not pay the temple tax?"**

17:25: **He said, "Yes, he does." And when he came home, Jesus spoke of it first, asking, "What do you think, Simon? From whom do kings of the earth take toll or tribute? From their children or from others?"**

17:26: **When Peter said, "From others," Jesus said to him, "Then the children are free.**

17:27: **However, so that we do not give offense to them, go to the sea and cast a hook; take the first fish that comes up; and when you open its mouth, you will find a coin; take that and give it to them for you and me."**

*T*he story of finding a shekel in the mouth of a fish, whereby Peter could pay the half-shekel temple tax for himself and Jesus, is one of the best-known stories

---

[408]   W. G. Thompson, *Matthew's Advice to a Divided Community: Matt 17:22–18:35* (AnBib 44; Rome: Biblical Institute Press, 1970), 16–49; D. J. Verseput, "Jesus' Pilgrimage to Jerusalem and Encounter in the Temple: A Geographical Motif in Matthew's Gospel," *NovT* 36 (1994): 105–21, especially 109–14.

found only in Matthew.[409] It has been suggested that the debate originally centered on a Roman or civil tax,[410] but the point of the story ("Then the children [of God] are free"), as well as the monetary value involved, cohere with the controversial temple tax.

The tax collectors ask Peter, "Does your teacher not pay the temple tax?" (**v. 24**). Although disputed by some, the tax in view is probably the half-shekel temple tax prescribed by Exod 30:11–16 (the so-called Ransom).[411] This tax was controversial in Jesus' day, with some contending that it was to be paid annually and others contending that it should be paid but once in one's lifetime; for example, "… concerning the Ransom: the money of the valuation which a man gives as ransom for his life shall be half a shekel in accordance with the shekel of the sanctuary. He shall give it only once in his life" (4Q159 frag. 1, col. ii, lines 6–7). Peter's response to the tax collectors' question is, "Yes, he does" (**v. 25**).

When Peter says that rulers receive tribute "from others," not from children, Jesus replies, "Then the children are free" (**v. 26**). Because in secular life kings do not collect tax from their own sons, one may infer that the king of heaven (i.e., God) does not collect taxes from his own children. The temple tax is therefore illegitimate. Because it is very unlikely that Jesus opposed what Moses taught in Exod 30:11–16, he probably opposed the interpretation that called for annual payment. Accordingly, Jesus' view of the matter was probably the same as that held at Qumran (as seen in the excerpt from 4Q159 quoted earlier).[412]

Although Jesus argues that the king's sons are exempt from the annual tax, he is nevertheless willing to pay it: "So that we do not give offense to them … you will find a coin; take that and give it to them for you and me" (**v. 27**). The coin (or stater) will cover both Peter and Jesus. Jesus' willingness to pay what he believes he really does not owe is consistent with his willingness to be baptized, "for it is proper for us in this way to fulfill all righteousness" (Matt 3:15). The great church scholar Jerome

---

[409] On the authenticity of the story, see D. Daube, "Temple Tax," in E. P. Sanders (ed.), *Jesus, the Gospels, and the Church: Essays in Honor of William R. Farmer* (Macon, GA: Mercer University Press, 1987), 121–34; G. Harb, "Matthew 17.24–27 and Its Value for Historical Jesus Research," *JSHJ* 8 (2010): 254–74.

[410] As argued by R. J. Cassidy, "Matthew 17:24–27 – A Word on Civil Taxes," *CBQ* 41 (1979): 571–80.

[411] For a discussion of the options, see D. C. Allison, Jr. and W. D. Davies, *A Critical and Exegetical Commentary on the Gospel According to Saint Matthew* (1988–1997), 2:738–51; A. Sand (1986), 362. Allison and Davies conclude that it is the Ransom tax, as do D. A. Carson, "Matthew," in F. E. Gaebelien (ed.), *The Expositor's Bible Commentary*, vol. 8 (Grand Rapids, MI: Zondervan, 1984), 393; D. J. Harrington, *The Gospel of Matthew* (1991), 261–62; R. T. France, *The Gospel of Matthew* (2007), 665–66; and others.

[412] W. Horbury, "The Temple Tax," in E. Bammel and C. F. D. Moule (eds.), *Jesus and the Politics of His Day* (Cambridge: Cambridge University Press, 1984), 265–86; D. E. Garland, "Matthew's Understanding of the Temple Tax," in D. R. Bauer (ed.), *Treasures New and Old* (1996), 69–98; M. Tellbe, "The Temple Tax as a Pre-70 CE Identity Marker," in J. Ådna (ed.), *The Formation of the Early Church* (WUNT 183; Tübingen: Mohr Siebeck, 2005), 19–44.

(late fourth to early fifth century) commented: "Therefore as the son of a king he [Jesus] did not owe tax, but as one who had assumed the humility of the flesh he has to fulfill all justice" (*Commentary on Matthew* 3.17.26 [on Matt 17:24–27]).

We find approximate parallels in the rabbinic tradition. A certain Gentile

> went and sold all his property and bought a precious stone with the proceeds, which he set in his turban. As he was crossing a bridge, the wind blew it off and cast it into the water; a fish swallowed it. The fish was hauled up and brought [to the market-place] on the Sabbath eve toward sunset. They said, "Who will buy at this hour?" They said to them, "Go and take it to Joseph who honors the sabbath, as he is in the habit of buying" [to stop commerce before the Sabbath]. So they took it to him. He bought it, opened it, and found the jewel therein, and sold it for thirteen roomfuls of gold denarii. A certain old man met him and said, "He who lends to the Sabbath, the Sabbath will repay him." (*b. Sanh.* 119a)

In another story, "It is related of a certain man who every day took a loaf of bread and threw it into the sea. One day he went and bought a fish; on cutting it open he found a valuable object in it" (*Eccl. Rab.* 11:1 §1, commenting on Eccles 11:1: "Send out your bread upon the waters"). A man's "wife gave birth to a son, so he bought for her a fish. Opening it he found within it a pearl" (*b. Baba Batra* 133b). Finally, there is also the tailor whom God "caused to find in the fish a gem of purest ray, a pearl, and on the money he got for it he sustained himself all the rest of his days" (*Pesiqta Rabbati* 23.6).

In all of these stories, the point is that a person is rewarded for his or her righteousness, for honoring the Sabbath, for honesty, for charity, or the like. The genre of this type of story and the lessons it typically teaches suggest that the story of Peter, the tax, and the fish teaches that Jesus' decision not to give offense but instead pay the temple tax was honored by heaven with the provision of the needed money.[413]

MATTHEW 18:1–5 – ON GREATNESS IN THE KINGDOM

18:1: At that time the disciples came to Jesus and asked, "Who is the greatest in the kingdom of heaven?"

18:2: He called a child, whom he put among them,

413   R. Bauckham, "The Coin in the Fish's Mouth," in D. Wenham and C. L. Blomberg (eds.), *The Miracles of Jesus* (Gospel Perspectives 6; Sheffield: JSOT Press, 1986), 219–52; T. Brodie, "Fish, Temple Tithe, and Remission: The God-Based Generosity of Deuteronomy 14–15 as One Component of Matt. 17:22–18:35," *RB* 99 (1992): 697–718; B. D. Chilton, "A Coin of Three Realms (Matthew 17:24–27)," in B. D. Chilton and C. A. Evans, *Jesus in Context: Temple, Purity, and Restoration* (AGJU 39; Leiden: Brill, 1997), 339–51; W. G. Thompson, *Matthew's Advice to a Divided Community* (1970), 50–68; W. Carter, "Paying the Tax to Rome as Subversive Praxis: Matt. 17.24–27," *JSNT* 76 (1999): 3–31; W. Carter, *Matthew and Empire: Initial Explorations* (Harrisburg, PA: Trinity Press International, 2001), 130–44.

18:3: and said, "Truly I tell you, unless you change and become like children, you will never enter the kingdom of heaven.

18:4: Whoever becomes humble like this child is the greatest in the kingdom of heaven.

18:5: Whoever welcomes one such child in my name welcomes me.

*I*n Matt 18:1–5, Jesus answers his disciples' question, "Who is the greatest in the kingdom of heaven?" This question and the answer that is provided introduce the fourth of Matthew's five discourses. The fourth discourse provides teaching on community life, attitudes, values, and discipline. In the passage at hand, Matthew continues to follow Mark's sequence (cf. Mark 9:33–37, 42), but, as usual, not without some abbreviation and revision. The most noticeable feature is the omission of Mark 9:38–41 (the report of the exorcist outside of Jesus' following).

In Mark 9:33–34, Jesus overhears his disciples discussing with one another who is the greatest; that is, the greatest of the twelve. The incident hardly puts the disciples in a good light. In Matthew's version, the question, which the disciples put to Jesus directly, takes on a more academic tone: "Who is the greatest in the kingdom of heaven?" (v. 1). There is no suggestion of rivalry or conceit among the disciples. Stated this way, the question presents Jesus with the opportunity to teach on what truly constitutes greatness.

Putting a child before the disciples (v. 2), Jesus answers their question: "Truly I tell you, unless you change and become like children, you will never enter the kingdom of heaven" (v. 3). Matthew's version emphasizes the need to be humble and to be converted, "like children." Jesus answers the disciples' question by saying, "Whoever becomes humble like this child is the greatest in the kingdom of heaven" (v. 4). Humility is what achieves greatness, not grasping for power or asserting oneself. Plutarch (died ca. 120 A.D.) warns his contemporaries to flee the vice of the love of fame and the "desire to be first and greatest" (*Moralia* 788E, "Public Affairs" 8). On humility, see the commentary on Matt 23:12. Jesus makes yet another pronouncement: "Whoever welcomes one such child in my name welcomes me" (v. 5). Here "child" may be literal as well as figurative (i.e., in reference to a powerless, socially unimportant person). Thus, the greatest in the kingdom are those who are humble, like children, and therefore welcome a child.[414]

---

[414] For background and context, see J. Dupont, "Matthieu 18.3," in E. E. Ellis and M. Wilcox (eds.), *Neotestamentica et Semitica: Studies in Honour of Matthew Black* (Edinburgh: T & T Clark, 1969), 50–60; D. Wenham, "A Note on Mark 9.33–42/Matt 18.1–6/Luke 9.46–50," *JSNT* 14 (1982): 113–18; W. G. Thompson, *Matthew's Advice to a Divided Community* (1970), 50–68; A. Tropper, "Children and Childhood in Light of the Demographics of the Jewish Family in Late Antiquity," *JSJ* 37 (2006): 299–343; K. J. White, "'He Placed a Little Child in the Midst': Jesus, the Kingdom, and Children," in M. J. Bunge et al. (eds.), *The Child in the Bible* (Grand Rapids, MI: Eerdmans, 2008), 353–74.

MATTHEW 18:6–9 – WARNING AGAINST CAUSING OFFENSE

18:6: "If any of you put a stumbling block before one of these little ones who believe in me, it would be better for you if a great millstone were fastened around your neck and you were drowned in the depth of the sea.

18:7: Woe to the world because of stumbling blocks! Occasions for stumbling are bound to come, but woe to the one by whom the stumbling block comes!

18:8: "If your hand or your foot causes you to stumble, cut it off and throw it away; it is better for you to enter life maimed or lame than to have two hands or two feet and to be thrown into the eternal fire.

18:9: And if your eye causes you to stumble, tear it out and throw it away; it is better for you to enter life with one eye than to have two eyes and to be thrown into the hell of fire.

*I*n Matt 18:6–9, Jesus warns his disciples of the danger and consequences of causing "little ones" to stumble. The passage is made up primarily of Mark 9:42–47, though Matthew may have drawn upon parallel material in Q.[415] The importance of the teaching is underscored by the graphic hyperbole that is employed. The passage makes a significant contribution to Chapter 18, which makes up Jesus' fourth discourse in Matthew.

Jesus warns against putting "a stumbling block before one of these little ones who believe in me" (**v. 6**). How does one cause a little one to stumble? If we take our lead from Matt 18:1–5, failure to treat the little one as important and as significant as the powerful and influential may indeed be the cause of stumbling that Jesus has in mind. The danger consists of those who, self-absorbed, fail to have consideration for the weaker and more vulnerable. Paul's advice to the Christians at Corinth (1 Corinthians 8–9; cf. Romans 14) may very well represent an extrapolation of this dominical tradition. Rather than face judgment for harming someone, it would be better "if a great millstone were fastened around" one's neck and to be "drowned in the depth of the sea." The "millstone" (literally a "donkey[-driven] millstone") of which Jesus speaks is much larger than the stones of the common hand-mills. The latter would be more than heavy enough to take one to the bottom quickly; the heavier stone would sink one like an anchor. Some of these stones have been uncovered in and around Capernaum. Hanging the stone around one's neck would make the situation as deadly as possible. Jesus uses hyperbolic language here to underscore the great importance of the point that he is making. Matthew's version has the added detail "in the depth," which intensifies the picture of judgment, as seen in

---

[415] J. Lambrecht, "Scandal and Salt (Mark 9,42–50 and Q)," in J. Lambrecht, *Understanding What One Reads: New Testament Essays* (ed. V. Koperski; Annua Nuntia Lovaniensia 46; Leuven: Peeters, 2003), 68–79.

Scripture. Examples include Exod 15:5, "The floods covered them; they went down into the depths like a stone" (in reference to the destruction of Pharaoh's army in the sea); Neh 9:11, "And you divided the sea before them, so that they passed through the sea on dry land, but you threw their pursuers into the depths, like a stone into mighty waters"; and Ps 63:9, "But those who seek to destroy my life, shall go down into the depths of the earth."

"Woe to the world because of stumbling blocks!" (**v. 7a**) is the first, and more general, of the two interesting woes in Matthew's version. He adds a second, more specific, woe to the man who occasions stumbling blocks: "Occasions for stumbling are bound to come, but woe to the one by whom the stumbling block comes!" (**v. 7b**). Matthew's woe does not derive from Mark 9 but from Q (cf. Luke 17:1). The inevitable stumbling blocks to which Jesus refers are those that will take place in the dark days of the tribulation that precedes the coming of the Son of Man.

In **vv. 8–9**, Jesus again uses hyperbole to stress the importance of ridding oneself of temptations to sin: "… it is better for you to enter life maimed or lame than to have two hands or two feet and to be thrown into the eternal fire" (cf. Mark 9:43–47). Jesus' grotesque recommendations, of course, are not to be taken literally. But they do make an important point. In 2 Macc 7:4, Antiochus IV had the hands and feet of the Jewish woman's eldest son chopped off (and inflicted similar punishment on some of the boy's brothers). Several of the dying sons warned the tyrant of hell that awaits him. The examples of the seven brothers illustrate Jesus' point: It is better to enter life maimed than to be cast into hell whole.[416]

MATTHEW 18:10–14 – NONE SHOULD BE LOST

18:10: "Take care that you do not despise one of these little ones; for, I tell you, in heaven their angels continually see the face of my Father in heaven.

18:11: [Omitted from the NRSV; see the commentary that follows]

18:12: What do you think? If a shepherd has a hundred sheep, and one of them has gone astray, does he not leave the ninety-nine on the mountains and go in search of the one that went astray?

18:13: And if he finds it, truly I tell you, he rejoices over it more than over the ninety-nine that never went astray.

18:14: So it is not the will of your Father in heaven that one of these little ones should be lost.

---

[416] J. D. M. Derrett, "Cutting Off the Hand that Causes Offense," in *Jesus' Audience: The Social Psychological Environment in which He Worked. Prolegomena to a Restatement of the Teaching of Jesus* (London: Darton, Longman & Todd, 1973), 201–4; W. G. Thompson, *Matthew's Advice to a Divided Community* (1970), 100–20.

*J*esus has warned his disciples not to cause the little ones to stumble because in the sight of heaven they are greatly valued (even if not by humans). Matthew 18:10–14 appears to be a reworking of material drawn from Q (cf. Luke 15:3–7), introduced by an utterance found only in Matthew (v. 10). The passage makes an important contribution to the fourth discourse (Matthew 18), which is centered on community life.

To underscore the value of "these little ones," Jesus makes the remarkable claim that "in heaven their angels continually see the face of my Father in heaven" (**v. 10**). On the idea of seeing God, compare Matt 5:8, "Blessed are the pure in heart, for they will see God." Although much disputed, in ancient sources as well as modern ones, the words "in heaven their angels" are probably what in time gave rise to the idea of "guardian angels." The protection that the angel Raphael provided young Tobias (in the Book of Tobit) offers a classic pre-Christian example: "I am Raphael, one of the seven angels who stand ready and enter before the glory of the Lord" (Tob 12:15). See also Job 33:23, "Then, if there should be for one of them an angel, a mediator, one of a thousand, one who declares a person upright"; *1 Enoch* 40:6, "intercede for those who dwell on the earth" (see also 40:9; 104:1); Heb 1:14, "Are not all angels spirits in the divine service, sent to serve for the sake of those who are to inherit salvation?"[417]

Similar ideas may have circulated in Greco-Roman speculation: "Hesiod calls the worthy and good demigods 'holy deities' and 'guardians of mortals' and 'givers of wealth, and having therein a reward that is kingly.' Plato calls this class of beings an interpretive and ministering class, midway between gods and men, in that they convey thither the prayers and petitions of men, and thence they bring hither the oracles and gifts of good things" (Plutarch, *Moralia* 361 BC: "Isis and Osiris" 26).

Verse 11 ("For the Son of Man came to seek and to save the Lost") is rightly omitted in the NRSV. The verse is not found in the oldest Greek manuscripts (such as the great codices Sinaiticus and Vaticanus). The verse is a scribal gloss inspired by Luke 19:10.

The parable of the lost sheep (**vv. 12–13**) in the Matthean context appears right after the teaching in Matt 18:1–10 on receiving and respecting children and "little ones" in the faith and on avoiding causes of offense (or "stumbling blocks"). The parable underscores the importance of the "little ones" (vv. 6, 10). One not only must not cause one of these to stumble but must also seek to restore one that is lost.

Jesus' parable of the lost sheep may have been inspired by Ezek 34:11–16, part of which reads: "For thus says the Lord God, 'I myself will search for my sheep, and will seek them out. As shepherds seek out their flocks when they are among their scattered sheep, so I will seek out my sheep.... I will seek the lost, and I will bring back the strayed....'" See also Isa 40:11: "He will feed his flock like a shepherd; he will gather the lambs in his arms, and carry them in his bosom, and gently lead the mother sheep."

---

[417] E. Koskenniemi, "Forgotten Guardians and Matthew 18:10," *TynBul* 61 (2010): 119–29.

The sheep imagery in the Old Testament is rich and illustrative (e.g., Ps 23:1, "The Lord is my shepherd"; Ps 119:176, "I have gone astray like a lost sheep"; Isa 53:6, "All we like sheep have gone astray; we have all turned to our own way"; Jer 50:6, "My people have been lost sheep; their shepherds have led them astray"). See also *1 Enoch* 89–90 and John 10. In *Pss. Sol.* 17:40, the Davidic Messiah is expected to shepherd Israel (i.e., the "Lord's flock") faithfully.

A shepherd who has a "hundred sheep" would be relatively well off in first-century Palestine. It was in search of a stray goat that a Palestinian goatherd discovered the first cave in the Dead Sea region, containing the now-famous Dead Sea Scrolls. Although the shepherd of the parable has "ninety-nine" other sheep, his concern for the one sheep that has "gone astray" impels him to search.[418]

Approximate parallels to the point of Jesus' parallel are found in Greco-Roman ethics: "[T]he true Cynic, when he is thus prepared, cannot rest contented … but he must know that he has been sent by Zeus to men, partly as a messenger, in order to show them that in questions of good and evil they have gone astray…." (Epictetus 3.22.23); "If one has lost his way and is roaming across our fields, it is better to put him on the right path than to drive him out" (Seneca, *On Anger* 1.14.3; cf. Seneca, *Moral Epistles* 34.1). The version of the parable in *Gospel of Thomas* §107, in which the lost sheep is valued above the ninety-nine, is secondary to the Synoptic tradition.

MATTHEW 18:15–20 – COMMUNITY DISCIPLINE

18:15: "If another member of the church sins against you, go and point out the fault when the two of you are alone. If the member listens to you, you have regained that one.

18:16: But if you are not listened to, take one or two others along with you, so that every word may be confirmed by the evidence of two or three witnesses.

18:17: If the member refuses to listen to them, tell it to the church; and if the offender refuses to listen even to the church, let such a one be to you as a Gentile and a tax collector.

18:18: Truly I tell you, whatever you bind on earth will be bound in heaven, and whatever you loose on earth will be loosed in heaven.

18:19: Again, truly I tell you, if two of you agree on earth about anything you ask, it will be done for you by my Father in heaven.

18:20: For where two or three are gathered in my name, I am there among them."

[418] E. F. F. Bishop, "The Parable of the Lost or Wandering Sheep," *ATR* 44 (1962): 44–57; W. L. Petersen, "The Parable of the Lost Sheep in the Gospel of Thomas and the Synoptics," *NovT* 23 (1981): 128–47; B. B. Scott, *Hear Then the Parable: A Commentary on the Parables of Jesus* (Minneapolis: Fortress, 1989), 405–17.

*T*his unit of material continues Matthew's discourse on discipline in the life of the church. Teaching on humility, avoiding offense, and restoring the lost now moves into teaching dealing with an errant brother or sister who perhaps is resistant to correction. Proper process is taught, as well as the willingness to forgive – repeatedly if necessary.

The goal of discipline is to restore right relationships and fellowship: "If another member of the church sins against you, go and point out the fault when the two of you are alone. If the member listens to you, you have regained that one" (**v. 15**). Compare the advice in *T. Gad* 6:3: "Love, therefore, one another from the heart; and if one sin against you, cast forth the poison of hate and speak peaceably to him, and in your soul hold not guile; and if he confess and repent, forgive him." On the instruction "go and point out the fault when the two of you are alone," see Prov 3:12, "the Lord reproves the one he loves," and Prov 25:9, "Argue your case with your neighbor directly."

When Jesus instructs his disciples, "But if you are not listened to, take one or two others along with you" (**v. 16**), he alludes to Deut 19:15, "... on the evidence of two or three witnesses shall a charge be sustained." See also 2 Cor 13:1 and 1 Tim 5:19. However, "If the member refuses to listen to them, tell it to the church" (or assembly; Greek: *ekklesia*) (**v. 17a**). See Deut 4:10: "Assemble [*ekklesiazein*] the people for me, and I will let them hear my words, so that they may learn to fear me as long as they live on the earth, and may teach their children so." Moses is reminding the second wilderness generation of Israelites of their being assembled (where in the Septuagint the word used is *ekklesia*, meaning "church") that they might hear what God had to say. See also 1 Chron 28:2, "Then King David rose in the midst of the assembly [*ekklesia*] and said, 'Listen to me, my brethren and my people'"; Sir 33:18, "Hear me, you who are great among the people, and you leaders of the congregation [*ekklesia*], hearken."

But "if the offender refuses to listen even to the church, let such a one be to you as a Gentile and a tax collector" (**v. 17b**). The Jewish orientation of Matthew is clearly seen here. The person who refuses to acknowledge the authority of the church is to be regarded as a Gentile or tax collector, much as a synagogue would regard him if he showed contempt for its authority. See Matt 5:46–47: "Do not even the tax gatherers do the same? ... Do not even the Gentiles do the same?"

Jesus tells his disciples, "Truly I tell you, whatever you bind on earth will be bound in heaven, and whatever you loose on earth will be loosed in heaven" (**v. 18**); see the commentary on Matt 16:19. In this context, however, the emphasis falls on decisions related to discipline.[419] "Binding and loosing" normally refer to forbidding and permitting. In the present case (which is now plural and not singular, as in Matt 16:19), the reference is to convicting and acquitting.

---

[419]   D. C. Duling, "Binding and Loosing: Matthew 16:19; Matthew 18:18; John 20:23," *Forum* 3, no. 4 (1987): 3–31.

Jesus continues, "Again, truly I tell you, if two of you agree on earth about anything you ask, it will be done for you by my Father in heaven" (**v. 19**). It was believed that the united prayer of many was much more effective than the prayer of one (cf. *b. Ber.* 8a, where we hear that God "does not despise the prayer of the congregation"). God will heed the prayers of his people, for Jesus himself is among them (**v. 20**). There is an interesting parallel in 1 Cor 5:3–5, where Paul says that he is "present in spirit" when the Corinthians are assembled to pass judgment on an unrepentant sinner. Paul's idea seems to be based on Matt 18:20. Jesus' saying also seems to reflect the belief that God himself is present among the faithful or, in rabbinic idiom: "But if two sit together and words of the Law [are spoken] between them, the Divine Presence rests between them" (*m. 'Abot* 3:2).[420]

The teaching of Jesus is meant to assure a small and struggling community that faces opposition from the synagogue establishment. The Jesus who conferred upon his disciples the authority to preach and heal in his name (10:1–15) has also conferred upon his disciples authority in all matters of teaching and discipline.[421]

MATTHEW 18:21–35 – ON FORGIVENESS

18:21: Then Peter came and said to him, "Lord, if another member of the church sins against me, how often should I forgive? As many as seven times?"

18:22: Jesus said to him, "Not seven times, but, I tell you, seventy-seven times.

18:23: "For this reason the kingdom of heaven may be compared to a king who wished to settle accounts with his slaves.

18:24: When he began the reckoning, one who owed him ten thousand talents was brought to him;

18:25: and, as he could not pay, his lord ordered him to be sold, together with his wife and children and all his possessions, and payment to be made.

18:26: So the slave fell on his knees before him, saying, 'Have patience with me, and I will pay you everything.'

18:27: And out of pity for him, the lord of that slave released him and forgave him the debt.

---

[420] J. Sievers, "'Where Two or Three …': The Rabbinic Concept of Shekinah and Matthew 18:20," in A. Finkel and L. Frizzell (eds.), *Standing before God: Studies on Prayer in Scriptures and in Tradition with Essays in Honor of John M. Oesterreicher* (New York: Ktav, 1981), 171–82.

[421] W. G. Thompson, *Matthew's Advice to a Divided Community* (1970), 175–202; D. R. Catchpole, "Reproof and Reconciliation in the Q Community: A Study of the Tradition-History of Matthew 18.15–17, 21–2/Lk 17.3–4," *SNTU* 8 (1983): 79–90.

18:28: But that same slave, as he went out, came upon one of his fellow slaves who owed him a hundred denarii; and seizing him by the throat, he said, 'Pay what you owe.'

18:29: Then his fellow slave fell down and pleaded with him, 'Have patience with me, and I will pay you.'

18:30: But he refused; then he went and threw him into prison until he would pay the debt.

18:31: When his fellow slaves saw what had happened, they were greatly distressed, and they went and reported to their lord all that had taken place.

18:32: Then his lord summoned him and said to him, 'You wicked slave! I forgave you all that debt because you pleaded with me.

18:33: Should you not have had mercy on your fellow slave, as I had mercy on you?'

18:34: And in anger his lord handed him over to be tortured until he would pay his entire debt.

18:35: So my heavenly Father will also do to every one of you, if you do not forgive your brother or sister from your heart."

The discourse on community life and discipline (Chapter 18) concludes with Peter's question about forgiveness and Jesus' parable that warns his disciples that they must be willing to forgive others, even as God has forgiven them. Humans' refusal to forgive cannot be excused in light of the enormity of human sin that God has forgiven.

Peter's offer to forgive someone up to seven times, "Lord, if another member of the church sins against me, how often should I forgive? As many as seven times?" (**v. 21**), may rest on biblical precedent (e.g., Gen 4:15, "Whoever kills Cain will suffer a sevenfold vengeance"; Lev 16:14, "... before the mercy seat he shall sprinkle the blood with his finger seven times"; Lev 26:18, "I will continue to punish you sevenfold for your sins"; Prov 24:16, "though they fall seven times, they will rise again"; 4Q511 frag. 35, lines 1–3, "... God with all flesh, and a judgment of vengeance to wipe out wickedness and by the fierce anger of God among those who have been refined sevenfold. But God will consecrate some of the holy ones for Himself as an eternal sanctuary; a refining among those who are purified"). From a human point of view, Peter's suggestion of sevenfold forgiveness is rather generous. But it is not enough from a divine perspective, as Jesus tells him: "Not seven times, but, I tell you, seventy-seven times" (**v. 22**). Jesus' demand of forgiveness "seventy-seven times" may allude to and intentionally reverse the angry sentiment expressed in Gen 4:24: "If Cain is avenged sevenfold, then Lamech seventy-sevenfold."[422]

---

[422] On the theme in Matthew, see T. Buckley, *Seventy Times Seven: Sin, Judgment, and Forgiveness in Matthew* (Zacchaeus Studies: New Testament; Collegeville, MN: The Liturgical Press, 1991).

Matthew brings the discourse on community life to a close with the parable of the unforgiving slave. Its point is to warn those who would be part of Jesus' assembly (or church) to be ready and willing to forgive, which completes the discussion with Peter in vv. 21–22. If one is not willing to forgive a brother or sister, who is a fellow sinner, then why should those persons think God, who is sinless, will be willing to forgive them?

Jesus continues with the analogy that "The kingdom of heaven may be compared to a king" (**v. 23**). Many rabbinic parables speak of God as a human king. For other examples in Matthew, see 17:25; 22:2, 7, 11, 13; 25:34, 40. The parable tells of two debtors (which in Aramaic could also mean two "sinners"). The first owes the king "ten thousand talents" (**v. 24**), an enormous sum. A talent was worth about 6,000 drachmas. According to Josephus, the sum total of Judea's tax revenue for one year during the reign of Archelaus, son of Herod the Great, was 600 talents (*Ant.* 17.320). The church father Jerome (late fourth to early fifth century) says that all of Egypt's annual revenue in his time was 14,800 talents. The amount of the debt is beyond realistic possibilities. But then that is the point of the parable. Human sin against God is incalculable. On the possibility that in the original form of the parable the debt was more realistic, see the commentary on Matt 18:25.

The story continues, "And, as he could not pay, his lord ordered him to be sold, together with his wife and children and all his possessions, and payment to be made" (**v. 25**). In antiquity, individuals and sometimes whole families were sold into slavery in order to repay debts. It is thought that Jesus' parable originally referred to a smaller debt, one that actually could be recovered through the sale of one's estate and family (as in the parable of the two debtors in Luke 7:41–42, whose debts were "five hundred denarii, and the other fifty"). Matthew himself may well have exaggerated the amount of debt to underscore the gravity of human sin and the magnitude of God's grace. On this point, compare the parable of the talents (Matt 25:14–30) with Luke's parallel parable of the minas (Luke 19:11–27). Matthew and Luke seem to be giving two versions of the same parable, but in Matthew's version the servants trade with talents, which are worth much more than the minas in Luke's version.[423]

For biblical and extrabiblical examples of individuals and families sold into slavery to repay debts or where children inherit their parents' debts, see Exod 22:2; 1 Sam 22:2; 2 Kings 4:1; Neh 5:1–13; Isa 50:1; Amos 2:6; Diogenes Laertius, *Lives of Eminent Philosophers* 4.46–58.

The indebted slave begged for mercy (**v. 26**) and the "lord of that slave released him and forgave him the debt" (**v. 27**). It is important to know that the Aramaic word for "debt" is *hoba'*, which also may be translated as "sin" (see the parable in Luke 7:41–42). Thus, the parable is not simply about a generous king who

---

[423] M. C. de Boer, "Ten Thousand Talents? Matthew's Interpretation and Redaction of the Parable of the Unforgiving Servant (Mt 18:23–35)," *CBQ* 50 (1988): 214–32.

forgives his servants large sums but about God, who forgives people their many and grievous sins.

Unfortunately, the forgiven slave seems to have learned nothing about mercy. He seeks out "one of his fellow slaves who owed him a hundred denarii; and seizing him by the throat, he said, 'Pay what you owe'" (**v. 28**). A denarius (plural: denarii) was one day's wage (see Matt 20:2, "the usual daily wage," literally "a denarius a day"). Accordingly, a debt of one hundred denarii was not a trifling amount. Nevertheless, compared to the ten thousand talents the first slave owed, it is almost nothing. Like the first slave, the second slave begged for mercy (**v. 29**). But the second slave, unlike the first slave, received none. The first slave threw the second slave into debtor's prison "until he would pay the debt" (**v. 30**). The matter is reported to the king, who then summons the first slave and says to him: "You wicked slave! I forgave you all that debt because you pleaded with me. Should you not have had mercy on your fellow slave, as I had mercy on you?" (**vv. 32–33**).[424]

Because the first slave had refused to extend mercy to the second slave, the mercy the first slave had received has now been rescinded. Accordingly, the king "handed him over to be tortured until he would pay his entire debt" (**v. 34**). It may be that those who do the torturing are expected to extract information from the wicked slave as to where some of the borrowed wealth has gone (cf. Livy, *Annals of the Roman People* 3.13.8; 25.4.8–10; Appian, *Roman History* 2.8.2).[425] The hapless servant, of course, will never be able to repay his enormous debt. He has hardly exemplified the virtue of the greater debtor in the parable of the two debtors, who loved the forgiving moneylender more (Luke 7:41–42).

Jesus concludes both the parable and his teaching on forgiveness with a warning that God will not forgive those who refuse to forgive others (cf. Matt 6:14–15). Forgiveness, of course, is to be "from your heart" (**v. 35**), which is consistent with Jesus' general teaching but as seen especially in the antitheses (cf. Matt 5:21–48).[426]

MATTHEW 19:1–2 – HEALING THE CROWDS

19:1: When Jesus had finished saying these things, he left Galilee and went to the region of Judea beyond the Jordan.

19:2: Large crowds followed him, and he cured them there.

---

[424] We have an interesting parallel in *b. Rosh Hashanah* 17b–18a, where in a parable a king tells an unforgiving subject: "For the wrong done to me I excuse you, but go and obtain forgiveness from your neighbor."

[425] For a discussion of the tension between violent judgment, on the one hand, and loving enemies, turning the other cheek, and the like, see B. E. Reid, "Violent Endings in Matthew's Parables and Christian Nonviolence," *CBQ* 66 (2004): 237–55.

[426] W. G. Thompson, *Matthew's Advice to a Divided Community* (1970), 203–37; T. Deidun, "The Parable of the Unmerciful Servant (Mt 18:23–35)," *BTB* 6 (1976): 203–24; B. B. Scott, "The King's Accounting: Matthew 18:23–34," *JBL* 104 (1985): 429–42; B. Weber, "Vergeltung oder Vergebung!? Matthäus 18,21–35 auf dem Hintergrund des 'Erlassjahres'," *TZ* 50 (1994): 124–51.

$\mathcal{M}$atthew again ends a major discourse (in this case the fourth) with a phrase from the Pentateuch (cf. Deut 32:45, "When Moses had finished reciting all these words to all Israel"; see the commentary on Matt 7:28–29), thus giving Jesus' teaching a Mosaic flavor. These two verses not only bring the discourse on community life and discipline (Chapter 18) formally to a close but provide a transition to the narrative material that follows.[427]

The "large crowds followed" Jesus into "the region of Judea beyond the Jordan," where again they could be cured of their illnesses and diseases (see Matt 4:23). On large "crowds" that follow or gather to Jesus, see Matt 4:25; 8:1, 18; 12:15; 13:2.

MATTHEW 19:3–12 – ON DIVORCE

19:3: Some Pharisees came to him, and to test him they asked, "Is it lawful for a man to divorce his wife for any cause?"

19:4: He answered, "Have you not read that the one who made them at the beginning 'made them male and female,'

19:5: and said, 'For this reason a man shall leave his father and mother and be joined to his wife, and the two shall become one flesh'?

19:6: So they are no longer two, but one flesh. Therefore what God has joined together, let no one separate."

19:7: They said to him, "Why then did Moses command us to give a certificate of dismissal and to divorce her?"

19:8: He said to them, "It was because you were so hard-hearted that Moses allowed you to divorce your wives, but from the beginning it was not so.

19:9: And I say to you, whoever divorces his wife, except for unchastity, and marries another commits adultery."

19:10: His disciples said to him, "If such is the case of a man with his wife, it is better not to marry."

19:11: But he said to them, "Not everyone can accept this teaching, but only those to whom it is given.

19:12: For there are eunuchs who have been so from birth, and there are eunuchs who have been made eunuchs by others, and there are eunuchs who have made themselves eunuchs for the sake of the kingdom of heaven. Let anyone accept this who can."

$\mathcal{M}$atthew's version of the debate over the permissibility of divorce differs from Mark's version (Mark 10:2–12) in several interesting and sometimes subtle

---

[427] H. D. Slingerland, "The Transjordanian Origin of St. Matthew's Gospel," *JSNT* 3 (1979): 18–28; A. Van Den Branden, "Mt. 19,1–2 dans une perspective historique," *BO* 34 (1992): 65–82.

ways. Divorce and remarriage were as controversial among Jews in the time of Jesus as they are in the church today.

The debate begins when the Pharisees ask Jesus, "Is it lawful for a man to divorce his wife for any cause?" (**v. 3**). Matthew's version adds "for any cause" (Greek: *kata pasan aitian*). The addition of this qualification anticipates the exception clause that appears in v. 9. In other words, divorce is certainly allowed in cases of "immorality," but is it allowed for other reasons?

Why did the Pharisees put this question to Jesus? Jesus was known as a healer, exorcist, and proclaimer of the rule of God. His call for repentance and embracing the rule of God brought with it ethical teaching, to be sure, but not a focus on domestic life. There was nothing about Jesus' ministry and proclamation, in themselves, that called for comment on divorce and remarriage. The most likely reason for questioning Jesus about this topic was due to his association with John the Baptist.[428] John had condemned Antipas, the tetrarch of Galilee, for divorcing his wife and taking up with his sister-in-law Herodias, wife of his brother Philip (see the commentary on Matt 14:1–12). Jesus was known as an associate of John's and in fact had been compared to John. Antipas even thought that Jesus was John "raised from the dead" (Matt 14:2).

John had been highly critical of Antipas. We are not told why the tetrarch turned away from his wife, the daughter of Aretas IV, king of the Nabateans, to take up with his former sister-in-law. Perhaps we should assume that John had understood marriage as permanent and that divorce should not take place. In any case, the Pharisees want to know Jesus' opinion, perhaps to see if he took a hard line, as John had. Of course, if Jesus held to the same view that John had, perhaps he could be drawn into making comments that might prompt Antipas to take malevolent interest in him (as may well have been the case; cf. Luke 13:31, "Herod wants to kill you"; Luke 23:7–8).

Jesus begins his reply (**vv. 4–5**) with quotations of Gen 1:27 ("made them male and female") and Gen 2:24 ("For this reason a man shall leave his father and mother and be joined to his wife, and the two shall become one flesh"). Matthew has omitted Mark's counterquestion and postponed the reference to Deut 24:1–4. This way, he can cut to the chase with the stinging rhetorical question, "Have you not read?"[429] If marriage is permanent, reason the Pharisees, "Why then did Moses command us to give a certificate of dismissal and to divorce her?" (**v. 7**). If marriage is permanent, if divorce is to be avoided, then why the presence of divorce legislation?

The reason Moses permitted divorce was because of his people's "hard-heartedness," not because it was what God wanted for them. Or, as Jesus puts it, "but from the beginning it was not so" (**v. 8**), where "beginning" alludes to Genesis and

---

[428] John baptized Jesus (Matt 3:13–15); John inquired of Jesus (Matt 11:2–6); and Jesus spoke of John on more than one occasion (Matt 11:7–15, 16–19; 17:9–13; 21:23–27, 28–32).
[429] Jesus challenges his opponents this way elsewhere in Matthew (cf. Matt 12:5; 21:42).

the passages cited in vv. 4–5.[430] Divorce may be permitted, but a man who "divorces his wife, except for unchastity, and marries another commits adultery" (**v. 9**); see the commentary on Matt 5:27–32. Because Matthew has omitted Mark 10:10 ("in the house the disciples asked him again about this matter"), what is said in Matt 19:9 is now said in the presence of the Pharisees. On the meaning of "except for unchastity," see the commentary on Matt 5:32.[431]

A Closer Look: Divorce in the Dead Sea Scrolls

Qumran provides an important parallel to Jesus' thought. Expanding on Deut 17:17 ("he shall not multiply wives for himself, lest his heart turn away"), the Temple Scroll teaches: "He is not to take another wife in addition to her; no, she alone will be with him as long as she lives. If she dies, then he may take himself another wife from his father's house, that is, his family" (11QTemple 57:17–19). One might object to the relevance of this passage because it is referring to Israel's king. But the next text shows that the Essenes evidently did apply this teaching universally: "They [Qumran's opponents] are caught in two traps: fornication, by taking two wives in their lifetimes although the principle of creation is 'male and female he created them' [Gen 1:27] and those who went into the ark 'went into the ark two by two' [Gen 7:9]. Concerning the Leader it is written 'he shall not multiply wives to himself' [Deut 17:17]; but David had not read the sealed book of the Law ...'" (CD 4:20–5:2). And finally, in 4Q416 we find reference to Gen 2:24: "When you are united, live together with your fleshly helper [... For as the verse says, "A man should leave] his father and his mother [and adhere to his wife and they will become one flesh]" (frag. 2, col. iii, line 21–col. iv, line 1).

Translations based on M. O. Wise, M. G. Abegg, and E. Cook, *The Dead Sea Scrolls* (1996), 485, 55, 385.

Matthew appends vv. 10–12, which do not derive from Mark (or Q). This section forms an appendix to the discussion of divorce in vv. 3–9.

In light of Jesus' teaching, the disciples remark, "If such is the case of a man with his wife, it is better not to marry" (**v. 10**). That is, if divorce is contrary to the will of God, then perhaps it is wise not to marry at all. The response of the disciples is disappointing. If Jesus has ruled against divorce, which therefore means a lifetime commitment to the same woman (cf. Sir 25:16–26), then marriage should be

---

[430] A. E. Harvey, "Genesis versus Deuteronomy? Jesus on Marriage and Divorce," in C. A. Evans and W. R. Stegner, *The Gospels and the Scriptures of Israel* (1994), 55–65.

[431] B. Witherington III, "Matthew 5.32 and 19.19 – Exception or Exceptional Situation?" *NTS* 31 (1985): 571–75; M. N. A. Bockmuehl, "Matthew 5.32; 19.9 in the Light of Pre-Rabbinic Halakhah," *NTS* 35 (1989): 291–95.

avoided. Of course, if one is not prepared to make a proper commitment, then one should not marry. Indeed, this is the conclusion that many in antiquity reached (e.g., Josephus, *Ant.* 18.21, in reference to Essenes: "They neither bring wives into the community nor do they own slaves, since they believe that the latter practice contributes to injustice and that the former opens the way to a source of dissension"; *J.W.* 2.120, "Marriage they disdain"; and the ethicist Epictetus, 3.22.37, 47, "Was it not great gain to lose a frail and adulterous wife? ... I have neither wife nor children ... Yet what do I lack? Am I not free from pain and fear?").

Jesus agrees with his disciples only in part. If a man cannot commit to his marriage, then he should not marry. If a man is divorced in cases where there has been no infidelity on the part of his wife, then he should not marry. Of course, "for the sake of the kingdom of heaven," (**v. 12**) some will choose to remain single (i.e., "have made themselves eunuchs").[432] But not everyone "can accept this teaching, but only those to whom it is given" (**v. 11**). Jesus' teaching surfaces in Paul's instructions to the Corinthian Christians: "I wish that all were as I myself am [i.e., single].... To the unmarried and the widows I say that it is well for them to remain unmarried as I am. But if they are not practicing self-control, they should marry. For it is better to marry than to be aflame with passion.... However that may be, let each of you lead the life that the Lord has assigned, to which God called you" (1 Cor 7:7–9, 17).[433]

MATTHEW 19:13–15 – JESUS AND CHILDREN

19:13: Then little children were being brought to him in order that he might lay his hands on them and pray. The disciples spoke sternly to those who brought them;

19:14: but Jesus said, "Let the little children come to me, and do not stop them; for it is to such as these that the kingdom of heaven belongs."

19:15: And he laid his hands on them and went on his way.

*M*atthew follows Mark 10:13–16, except for the omission of Mark 10:15 (which Luke preserves at Luke 18:17). Matthew probably omitted it because it had

---

[432]   R. C. Tannehill, *The Sword of His Mouth* (1975), 134–40.

[433]   For further discussion, see A. J. Hultgren, *Jesus and His Adversaries* (1979), 119–23; G. J. Wenham, "Matthew and Divorce: An Old Crux Revisited," *JSNT* 22 (1984): 95–107; W. C. Carter, *Households and Discipleship: A Study of Matthew 19–20* (JSNTSup 103; Sheffield: Sheffield Academic Press, 1994), 56–89; J. Kampen, "The Matthean Divorce Texts Reexamined," in G. J. Brooke (ed.), *New Qumran Texts and Studies: Proceedings of the First Meeting of the International Organization for Qumran Studies, Paris 1992* (STDJ 15; Leiden: Brill, 1994), 149–67; J. Nolland, "The Gospel Prohibition of Divorce: Tradition History and Meaning," *JSNT* 58 (1995): 19–35; J. A. Fitzmyer, "The Matthean Divorce Texts and Some New Palestinian Evidence," in *To Advance the Gospel: New Testament Studies*, revised edition (Grand Rapids, MI: Eerdmans, 1998), 79–111.

already been used in Matt 18:3. But Matthew adds a few details. He changes Mark's "that he might touch them" (Mark 10:13) to "that he might lay his hands on them and pray" (v. 13). Reference to laying hands on the children anticipates v. 15, which also appears in Mark 10:16. Reference to praying is unique to Matthew, lending an important element to the story. Matthew also adds "Let the children alone" in place of Mark's "Let the little children come to me" (Mark 10:14).

Matthew states, "Then little children were being brought to him in order that he might lay his hands on them and pray" (**v. 13**), but we are not told who was bringing children to Jesus; presumably it was their parents, hoping for some benefit or blessing. In late antiquity, it was believed that touching a holy man, even his clothing, or being touched by him would confer blessing, perhaps healing (cf. Matt 9:20–21). The disciples, however, "spoke sternly" to them for trying to do this.

Jesus, however, welcomes the children, declaring, "for it is to such as these that the kingdom of heaven belongs" (**v. 14**). In later rabbinic literature, there are some approximate parallels. According to *b. Sanh.* 110b, Israelite children will enter the world to come: "Rabbi Aqiba said: 'They [the children] will enter the world to come, as it is written, "The Lord preserves the simple" [Ps 116:6].'" In some rabbinic traditions, children are regarded as pure, even without sin (*b. Yoma* 22b; *b. Nid.* 30b).[434]

MATTHEW 19:16–22 – ON INHERITING ETERNAL LIFE

19:16: Then someone came to him and said, "Teacher, what good deed must I do to have eternal life?"

19:17: And he said to him, "Why do you ask me about what is good? There is only one who is good. If you wish to enter into life, keep the commandments."

19:18: He said to him, "Which ones?" And Jesus said, "You shall not murder; You shall not commit adultery; You shall not steal; You shall not bear false witness;

19:19: Honor your father and mother; also, You shall love your neighbor as yourself."

19:20: The young man said to him, "I have kept all these; what do I still lack?"

19:21: Jesus said to him, "If you wish to be perfect, go, sell your possessions, and give the money to the poor, and you will have treasure in heaven; then come, follow me."

19:22: When the young man heard this word, he went away grieving, for he had many possessions.

---

[434] R. Brown, "Jesus and the Child as a Model of Spirituality," *IBS* 4 (1982): 178–92; J. D. Crossan, "Kingdom and Children: A Study in the Aphoristic Tradition," *Semeia* 29 (1983): 75–95; V. K. Robbins, "Pronouncement Stories and Jesus' Blessing of the Children: A Rhetorical Approach," *Semeia* 29 (1983): 43–74; W. C. Carter, *Households and Discipleship* (1994), 90–114.

*M*atthew follows Mark in content and in context (Mark 10:17–22), but does make a few interesting changes. The story is a classic; the young man keeps the commandments but cannot part with his wealth and so cannot receive assurance about life in the world to come.

The question put to Jesus, "Teacher, what good deed must I do to have eternal life?" (**v. 16**), is related to the question about the greatest commandment (cf. Luke 10:25–28). The verb "do" (Greek: *poieso*) comes from the command in Lev 18:5 to keep the statutes of the Law; if one does (*poiei*) so, this person will live. In the Aramaic paraphrase, Lev 18:5 was understood to promise eternal life, which is the concern of the man (who is "young" according to vv. 20 and 22) who has questioned Jesus. As the dialogue shows, the young man has kept many of the commandments, but which "good deed" (*agathon*) must he do to guarantee eternal life?

Matthew has altered the exchange where Jesus asks, "Why do you ask me about what is good? There is only one who is good" (**v. 17a**). In Mark's version, the man asks, "Good Teacher, what must I do . . ." But in Matthew the man asks Jesus, ". . .what *good deed* must I do?" Jesus responds, "Why do you ask me about what is good?" Matthew may be trying to avoid the implication that Jesus denied goodness to himself. See how Matthew presents Jesus' baptism (cf. Matt 3:13–15).

Jesus' statement, "If you wish to enter into life, keep the commandments" (**v. 17b**), is not found in Mark's parallel. The added statement makes explicit what is implicit in the exchange here and elsewhere. Matthew has emphasized, with a skeptical synagogue in mind, that Jesus respects the law of Moses; indeed, he has come to fulfill it (Matt 5:17–18) and expects his disciples to follow his teaching and therefore exhibit a righteousness that "exceeds that of the scribes and Pharisees" (Matt 5:20).

The link between *life* and the *commandments* is commonplace in Scripture and early Judaism (e.g., Deut 30:11–20; Lev 18.5; Bar 3:9; *Pss. Sol.* 14:2; *m. 'Abot* 2:7). One thinks especially of 4QMMT, a letter that spells out what "works of the law" must be observed so one will "rejoice at the end time" (cf. 4Q398 frags. 14–17, col. ii, lines 2–8).

The man now inquires, "Which ones?" (**v. 18a**). In other words, which of the commandments does Jesus have in mind? There are hundreds of commandments in the books of Moses. Best known, of course, are the Ten Commandments of Exodus 20 and Deuteronomy 5. In **vv. 18b–19**, Jesus cites five of the Ten Commandments and the command to love one's neighbor (Lev 19:18; cf. Matt 22:34–40). Mark's "Do not defraud" (Mark 10:19), which is not one of the Ten Commandments, is omitted.

Matthew reports that "The young man said to him, 'I have kept all these; what do I still lack?'" (**v. 20**). In Mark's version, we hear nothing about the man being "young." There it was Jesus who pointed out that the man lacked "one thing" (Mark 10:21). In Matthew's version, however, the man rightly recognized himself that although he had kept these important commandments something was missing.

On the phrase "If you wish to be perfect" (**v. 21**) or "complete," see Matt 5:48: "Be perfect, therefore, as your heavenly Father is perfect." If the man is to be perfect, lacking nothing in God's sight, he must follow Jesus ("follow me"). This means setting aside his treasure on earth (by giving it to the poor), which will result in his having "treasure in heaven" (cf. Matt 6:19–21).

Matthew then describes the young man's reaction to Jesus' instructions: "When the young man heard this word, he went away grieving, for he had many possessions" (**v. 22**). As in the parable of the sower (Matt 13:18), the young man has heard the "word." But he could not embrace it, "for he had many possessions," by which is implied that he values his treasure on earth more highly than his treasure in heaven (Matt 13:22, "but the cares of the world and the lure of wealth choke the word").[435]

MATTHEW 19:23–26 – ON THE SALVATION OF THE RICH

19:23: Then Jesus said to his disciples, "Truly I tell you, it will be hard for a rich person to enter the kingdom of heaven.

19:24: Again I tell you, it is easier for a camel to go through the eye of a needle than for someone who is rich to enter the kingdom of God."

19:25: When the disciples heard this, they were greatly astounded and said, "Then who can be saved?"

19:26: But Jesus looked at them and said, "For mortals it is impossible, but for God all things are possible."

*I*n 19:23–27, Matthew offers an edited and slightly shortened version of Mark 10:23–27. The refusal of the young man to follow Jesus occasions additional teaching on the dangers of wealth and questions about election.

The failure of what perhaps had looked like a promising recruit prompts Jesus to say to his disciples, "Truly I tell you, it will be hard for a rich person to enter the kingdom of heaven" (**v. 23**). Matthew adds "truly" (literally "amen") to underscore the importance of the point being made. Consistent with his custom, Matthew changes Mark's "kingdom of God" to "kingdom of heaven" (see also Matt 3:2; 4:17; 5:3). However, he will not make this change in v. 24. Because wealth competes for loyalty with God, those who have it will find it very difficult to receive God's rule. Jesus' pronouncement here is in step with his teaching elsewhere about the need to choose between love of God and love of money: "No one can serve two masters; for a slave will either hate the one and love the other, or be devoted to the one and despise the other. You cannot serve God and wealth" (Matt 6:24).

The difficulty the rich have in heeding the call of discipleship is such that Jesus declares that "it is easier for a camel to go through the eye of a needle than for

---

[435] O. L. Cope, *Matthew* (1976), 111–19; J. W. Wenham, "Why Do You Ask about the Good? A Study of the Relation between Text and Source Criticism," *NTS* 28 (1982): 116–25; W. C. Carter, *Households and Discipleship* (1994), 115–45.

someone who is rich to enter the kingdom of God" (**v. 24**). When Jesus says "eye of a needle," he means just that. He is not talking about a small gate somewhere in the walls of Jerusalem through which camels may pass but with great difficulty. The "Needle Gate" that the locals show to gullible pilgrims to the Holy Land cannot be dated any earlier than the Middle Ages (usually to Theophylact). Similar extreme comparisons are found in rabbinic literature (*b. Ber.* 55b, which speaks of "a palm of gold or an elephant which goes through the eye of a needle"; *b. B. Mes.* 38b; *Song Rab.* 5:2 §2: "The Holy One, blessed be He, said to Israel: 'My sons, present to me an opening no bigger than the eye of a needle, and I will widen it into openings through which wagons and carriages can pass'"). There really is no need to reduce the severity of the comparison. The last rabbinic parable anticipates the point that Jesus will make in v. 26.

The disciples are astounded by Jesus' statement and wonder "who can be saved?" (**v. 25**). As did many in their time, the disciples assume that wealth is a sign of divine blessing,[436] whereas disease and poverty were signs of judgment. It was further assumed that because God is fair, the blessed surely are righteous, whereas the judged surely are sinners. These generalizing assumptions (and exceptions, of course, would be allowed) are rooted in Deuteronomy, which promises blessings for obedient Israel but judgment for disobedient Israel (see the summary in Deuteronomy 30). If it is very difficult for the wealthy – and therefore the apparently blessed – to be saved, can anyone be saved?[437]

In answer, Jesus declares, "For mortals it is impossible, but for God all things are possible (**v. 26**). According to Jesus, people cannot save themselves; only God can (see Philo, *Life of Moses* 1.174, "What is impossible to all created beings is possible to [God] only"; *Virtues* 27; cf. *Creation of the World* 47; *Abraham* 175; *Special Laws* 4.127). This theology can be traced to the Torah itself: "Is anything too wonderful for the Lord?" (Gen 18:14). The implication, of course, is that no, nothing is impossible for God.[438]

MATTHEW 19:27–30 – REWARD FOR FAITHFUL SERVICE

19:27: Then Peter said in reply, "Look, we have left everything and followed you. What then will we have?"

---

[436] T. Zahn, *Das Evangelium des Matthäus* (1910), 600; L. Morris, *The Gospel According to Matthew* (1992), 494.

[437] To "be saved" means, of course, to enter heaven; see Sand, *Das Evangelium nach Matthäus* (1986), 398.

[438] P. S. Minear, "The Needle's Eye: A Study in Form Criticism," *JBL* 61 (1942): 157–69; P. S. Minear, *Commands of Christ* (1972), 98–112; J. D. M. Derrett, "A Camel through the Eye of a Needle," *NTS* 32 (1986): 465–70; W. C. Carter, *Households and Discipleship* (1994), 115–45.

19:28: Jesus said to them, "Truly I tell you, at the renewal of all things, when the Son of Man is seated on the throne of his glory, you who have followed me will also sit on twelve thrones, judging the twelve tribes of Israel.

19:29: And everyone who has left houses or brothers or sisters or father or mother or children or fields, for my name's sake, will receive a hundredfold, and will inherit eternal life.

19:30: But many who are first will be last, and the last will be first.

*T*he failure of the wealthy young man to accept Jesus' discipleship (Matt 19:16–22) and Jesus' startling assertion that human beings, including and especially the wealthy, cannot save themselves (Matt 19:23–26) lead to further teaching that promises reward for the disciples who have in fact left behind possessions to follow Jesus. Matthew edits and simplifies Mark's account in several places. The major change is seen in the insertion of a Q saying (cf. Luke 22:28–30) in v. 28.

When Peter says, "Look, we have left everything and followed you. What then will we have?" (**v. 27**), his point is that they have in fact done what Jesus asked the rich man to do: they have given up property and have followed him. Jesus' startling saying about the difficulty of a camel trying to pass through the eye of a needle may have jarred the disciples. Surely their sacrifices have been sufficient. Jesus' reply in the next verse suggests that Peter's exclamation may have carried with it a note of complaint: The disciples have left everything to follow Jesus; what will they get out of it?

Jesus' promise in **v. 28** ("you who have followed me will also sit on twelve thrones") is based on two passages of Old Testament Scripture: Daniel 7 and Psalm 122. A third passage, Psalm 110, is also presupposed, though not alluded to here. According to Daniel's vision, "thrones were set in place, and an Ancient One took his throne" (Dan 7:9). Then the "court sat in judgment, and the books were opened" (Dan 7:10). Judgment is rendered against God's and Israel's enemies, and then appeared "one like a human being coming with the clouds of heaven. And he came to the Ancient One and was presented before him. To him was given dominion and glory and kingship, that all the peoples, nations, and languages should serve him" (Dan 7:13–14).

It is to this vision that Jesus refers when he says that "the Son of Man is seated on the throne of his glory." Jesus, the Son of Man, will sit on one of the "thrones" set up in Dan 7:9. It will be a throne "at the right hand" of God (cf. Ps 110:1; Mark 14:62). At that time, "at the renewal of all things,"[439] he will receive "dominion and glory

---

[439]   Probably in the sense of the renewal of the cosmos and not simply the restoration of the nation of Israel. See F. W. Burnett, "παλιγγενεσία in Matt 19.28: A Window on the Matthean Community?" *JSNT* 17 (1983): 60–72; and especially D. C. Sim, "The Meaning of παλιγγενεσία in Matthew 19.28," *JSNT* 50 (1993): 3–12.

and kingship" (Dan 7:14).[440] But Jesus goes on to say that his disciples "will also sit on twelve thrones, judging the twelve tribes of Israel." We again have allusion to Dan 7:9 and the plural "thrones," but there is more. The reference to judging the twelve tribes alludes to Ps 122:3–5: "Jerusalem – built as a city that is bound firmly together. To it the tribes go up, the tribes of the Lord, as was decreed for Israel, to give thanks to the name of the Lord. For there the thrones for judgment were set up, the thrones of the house of David." Here we have "thrones," "tribes," and "judgment," the vocabulary that makes up the second part of Jesus' saying. The number *twelve* is an inference from the number of the tribes of Israel and, of course, is the number of Jesus' inner circle. Jesus appointed twelve disciples in order to make this correlation.

In what sense do the twelve disciples, sitting on the twelve thrones, *judge* the twelve tribes of Israel? Although some church fathers understood it as "condemn" (as though the Greek word was *katakrinein*, which means "condemn," instead of *krinein*, meaning "judge," which is how it reads – admittedly ambiguously – here in v. 28). But that is not what Jesus meant. He meant it in the sense of the judges of the Book of Judges. That is, judges functioned as leaders and administrators who ruled Israel's tribes with justice, and who on occasion defended the tribes from foreign aggression. It is in this sense that the twelve disciples will judge the twelve tribes – not to punish them but to shepherd them (cf. *Pss. Sol.* 17:26). For more on this theme, see the commentary on Matt 20:20–23.[441]

The placement of **v. 30** ("many who are first will be last, and the last will be first") here links the present passage, where we have disciples who "have left everything" to follow Jesus (v. 27), and the earlier passage where the rich young man, because of his wealth, is unable to do so (Matt 19:16–22).

MATTHEW 20:1–16 – THE PARABLE OF THE VINEYARD WORKERS

20:1: "For the kingdom of heaven is like a landowner who went out early in the morning to hire laborers for his vineyard.

20:2: After agreeing with the laborers for the usual daily wage, he sent them into his vineyard.

20:3: When he went out about nine o'clock, he saw others standing idle in the marketplace;

---

[440] In some Old Greek (OG) texts, the Son of Man figure seems to be identified with the Ancient of Days, who sits on his throne. Matthew may be acquainted with this distinctive tradition. See the commentary on Matt 13:41.

[441] J. Dupont, "Le logion des douze trônes (Mt 19,28; Lc 22.28–30)," *Bib* 45 (1964): 335–92; C. A. Evans, "The Twelve Thrones of Israel: Scripture and Politics in Luke 22:24–30," in *Luke and Scripture* (1993), 154–70; W. C. Carter, *Households and Discipleship* (1994), 115–45.

20:4: and he said to them, 'You also go into the vineyard, and I will pay you whatever is right.' So they went.

20:5: When he went out again about noon and about three o'clock, he did the same.

20:6: And about five o'clock he went out and found others standing around; and he said to them, 'Why are you standing here idle all day?'

20:7: They said to him, 'Because no one has hired us.' He said to them, 'You also go into the vineyard.'

20:8: When evening came, the owner of the vineyard said to his manager, 'Call the laborers and give them their pay, beginning with the last and then going to the first.'

20:9: When those hired about five o'clock came, each of them received the usual daily wage.

20:10: Now when the first came, they thought they would receive more; but each of them also received the usual daily wage.

20:11: And when they received it, they grumbled against the landowner,

20:12: saying, 'These last worked only one hour, and you have made them equal to us who have borne the burden of the day and the scorching heat.'

20:13: But he replied to one of them, 'Friend, I am doing you no wrong; did you not agree with me for the usual daily wage?

20:14: Take what belongs to you and go; I choose to give to this last the same as I give to you.

20:15: Am I not allowed to do what I choose with what belongs to me? Or are you envious because I am generous?'

20:16: So the last will be first, and the first will be last."

*M*atthew extends Jesus' teaching on wealth and priorities by adding the parable of the vineyard workers, a parable found only in Matthew's Gospel. The parable illustrates one of the lessons of Jesus' well-known dictum "the last shall be first, and the first last" (v. 16; cf. Matt 19:30).

The parable involves "… a landowner who went out early in the morning to hire laborers for his vineyard" (v. 1) and reflects the hard economic realities in Jesus' day. Hiring day laborers at any time of the day and men standing idle in town or out near fields, hoping to find work, indicates widespread unemployment. It also testifies to the trouble in which many small farmers found themselves. In many cases, they had lost their land and found themselves looking for day labor.[442]

---

[442] On the social and economic realism reflected in the parable, see C. S. Keener, *A Commentary on the Gospel of Matthew* (1999), 481–82.

There were many vineyards in Israel and the eastern Mediterranean. Grapes as fruit and, of course, grapes for making wine were in high demand. To meet this need, many commercial vineyards were developed that required varying numbers of laborers depending on the time of the year. Dressing the vines and maintaining irrigation ditches were among the most demanding chores. Of course, when it was harvest time, additional workers were needed to gather in the clusters and take them to the press. The words "early in the morning" indicate that the first workers hired went to work at the beginning of the day; that is, at 6 A.M.

Matthew continues, "After agreeing with the laborers for the usual daily wage, he sent them into his vineyard" (**v. 2**). The "usual daily wage" is one denarius, which in the first century was a standard day's wage. These men have agreed to work the full day; that is, from 6 A.M. until 6 P.M., twelve full hours. This was a normal workday at that time. To appreciate the conclusion of the parable, this detail needs to be kept in mind. The landowner goes out again at "nine o'clock" (literally "the third hour") and finds "others standing idle in the marketplace" (**v. 3**). He tells these new recruits that he will pay them "whatever is right" (**v. 4**). Had the owner of the vineyard told these men that he was going to pay them a denarius for part of a day's work, the anticipation at the conclusion of the parable would have been spoiled. In saying "whatever is right," the workers (and the hearers of the parable) would have assumed that their pay was to be prorated; that is, three-quarters of a denarius for three-quarters of a day's work. The owner of the vineyard goes out again and again (**vv. 5–7**), hiring more workers, some at noon (literally "the sixth hour"), some at three o'clock (literally "the ninth hour"), and some even as late as five o'clock (literally "the eleventh hour"), leaving only one hour of work time.

At the day's end (i.e., 6 P.M.), the workers receive their wages, beginning with those hired last (**v. 8**). Those hired last receive a denarius, the "usual daily wage" (**v. 9**). The last ones hired are the first ones paid. This superficially conforms to the concluding dictum "the last will be first" (v. 16), but the function in the parable is to create anticipation, as it does in the workers who are paid last. The parable would not work if the first workers hired were the first paid.

Anticipation is created when these men, who had worked but one hour, are paid a full day's wage. The owner of this vineyard is indeed generous! If he paid these men a denarius, what will he pay those who worked the whole day? So goes their thinking (as becomes clear in vv. 11–12).

The parable continues, "Now when the first came, they thought they would receive more" (**v. 10a**). For the parable to work, it is necessary to skip over the men hired at nine o'clock, at noon, and at three o'clock. Had the parable mentioned that they, too, had received only a denarius, the surprise ending of the parable would have been given away.

Contrary to their eager expectation, those hired first "also received the usual daily wage" (**v. 10b**). Both the workers and the hearers of the parable are surprised. The full denarius paid to the workers who had only worked part of the day had raised the expectations of those men who had worked twelve hours. These workers are understandably annoyed (**v. 11**) and complain, "These last worked only one hour, and you have made them equal to us who have borne the burden of the day and the scorching heat" (**v. 12**). After all, they have done a full day's work and have labored right through the hottest part of the day. The implication is that this is summer work, which in Palestine can be hot indeed. Surely they deserve more payment than those who worked fewer hours.

But the owner of the vineyard replies that he has done no wrong to those hired first. Did they not agree to work the whole day for the usual wage (**v. 13**)? As for the other workers, cannot the owner be as generous with his money as he wishes (**vv. 14–15**)? His generosity, even if extravagant, does not mean that others have been cheated. Or are those hired first envious because of the owner's generosity? The employer has raised the question of evil motives on the part of the complaining workers. What the NRSV translates as "are you envious" is literally "is your eye evil" (Greek: *ho ophthalmos sou poneros*). See Matt 6:23, where an evil eye (or "your eye is unhealthy," as in the NRSV) keeps a person in darkness. See the commentary on Matt 6:22–23.

There is in the rabbinic tradition a very similar parable that makes essentially the same point:

Sweet is the sleep of the laborer whether he has eaten much or little. Like a king who had hired many laborers, one of whom so distinguished himself by industry and skill that the king took him by the hand and walked up and down with him. In the evening the laborers came, and the skillful one among them, to receive their pay. The king gave them all the same pay. Therefore those who had worked the whole day murmured, and said, "We have worked the whole day, and this man only two hours, and yet he also has received his whole pay." The king answered, "This man has done more in two hours than you in the whole day." (*y. Ber.* 2.8)

It is speculated that this parable is either dependent upon Jesus' parable or, more likely, dependent upon the same images and motifs on which Jesus' earlier parable is based.

The parable concludes with the well-known saying, "So the last will be first, and the first will be last" (**v. 16**). It is probable that Matthew has added this floating saying to the conclusion of the parable. In ancient Greek manuscripts, there are no quotation marks (and rarely any kind of punctuation), so we do not always know where Jesus' words end and editorial comments of the evangelist begin.

The point of the parable for Jesus is that God is generous ("to a fault"!) with all human beings and that those who respond to God's call sooner than others, and so labor for God longer and harder than do others, should not be envious of others who receive equal rewards. The point is quite similar to the point of the parable of the lost son (see Luke 15:11–32), where the older son resents the grand treatment extended to his returned and repentant younger brother. Just as the father admonished the older son to rejoice in the recovery of the lost brother, so the laborers in the field should rejoice that fellow workers, as hard-pressed as any, have had the good fortune of receiving a full reward.[443]

MATTHEW 20:17–19 – THIRD PREDICTION OF THE PASSION

20:17: While Jesus was going up to Jerusalem, he took the twelve disciples aside by themselves, and said to them on the way,

20:18: "See, we are going up to Jerusalem, and the Son of Man will be handed over to the chief priests and scribes, and they will condemn him to death;

20:19: then they will hand him over to the Gentiles to be mocked and flogged and crucified; and on the third day he will be raised."

In Matt 16:21–23 and 17:22–23, Jesus previously predicted his suffering and death. In Matt 20:17–19, he predicts it a third time. Matthew slightly condenses Mark's account, omitting most of Mark 10:32 and replacing "kill him" and "after three days" (Mark 10:34) with "crucified" and "on the third day," respectively. Matthew states explicitly that Jesus "took the twelve disciples aside by themselves" (**v. 17**), indicating private instruction, whereas Mark only says, "He took the twelve aside" (Mark 10:32). For a discussion of the difference in the phrases "after three days" (in Mark) and "on the third day" (in Matthew), and their reflection of Hos 6:2 ("After two days he will revive us; on the third day he will raise us up that we may live before him"), see the commentary on Matt 16:21–23.

The third prediction of the Passion sets the stage for the request of James and John, the sons of Zebedee, in the next passage (Matt 20:20–23), and Jesus' teaching that his life will be given as a "ransom for many" in the passage after that (Matt 20:24–28). Jesus will suffer in Jerusalem. Will his disciples accept this? Can they understand it?[444]

[443] P. S. Minear, *Commands of Christ* (1972), 83–97; J. D. M. Derrett, "Workers in the Vineyard: A Parable of Jesus," *JJS* 25 (1974): 64–91; M. Lowe, "A Hebraic Approach to the Parable of the Laborers in the Vineyard," *Immanuel* 24–25 (1990): 109–17; J. H. Elliott, "Matthew 20:1–15: A Parable of Invidious Comparison and Evil Eye Accusation," *BTB* 22 (1992): 52–65; J. M. Tevel, "The Labourers in the Vineyard: The Exegesis of Matthew 20,1–7 in the Early Church," *VC* 46 (1992): 356–80; W. C. Carter, *Households and Discipleship* (1994), 146–60; E. K. Vearncombe, "Redistribution and Reciprocity: A Socio-economic Interpretation of the Parable of the Labourers in the Vineyard (Matthew 20.1–15)," *JSHJ* 8 (2010): 199–236.

[444] M. Black, "The 'Son of Man' Passion Sayings in the Gospel Tradition," *ZNW* 60 (1977): 1–8; J. Schaberg, "Daniel 7,12 and the New Testament Passion-Resurrection Predictions," *NTS* 31 (1985): 208–22; W. C. Carter, *Households and Discipleship* (1994), 161–92.

MATTHEW 20:20–28 – A REQUEST FOR POSITIONS OF HONOR

20:20: Then the mother of the sons of Zebedee came to him with her sons, and kneeling before him, she asked a favor of him.

20:21: And he said to her, "What do you want?" She said to him, "Declare that these two sons of mine will sit, one at your right hand and one at your left, in your kingdom."

20:22: But Jesus answered, "You do not know what you are asking. Are you able to drink the cup that I am about to drink?" They said to him, "We are able."

20:23: He said to them, "You will indeed drink my cup, but to sit at my right hand and at my left, this is not mine to grant, but it is for those for whom it has been prepared by my Father."

20:24: When the ten heard it, they were angry with the two brothers.

20:25: But Jesus called them to him and said, "You know that the rulers of the Gentiles lord it over them, and their great ones are tyrants over them.

20:26: It will not be so among you; but whoever wishes to be great among you must be your servant,

20:27: and whoever wishes to be first among you must be your slave;

20:28: just as the Son of Man came not to be served but to serve, and to give his life a ransom for many."

*T*he story of the request for the seats of honor and the angry, quarrelsome reaction of the disciples could well have been occasioned by Jesus' promise that someday the twelve would sit on thrones judging the twelve tribes of Israel (Matt 19:28). The two sons of Zebedee would like to sit on the thrones adjacent to the throne on which Jesus will sit. The other disciples resent their ambitions. The quarrel itself occasions Jesus' important remark about giving his life as a "ransom for many." Matthew condenses Mark's account (Mark 10:35–40) in places but does add a few interesting details.

Matthew's account continues, "Then the mother of the sons of Zebedee came to him with her sons" (**v. 20**). According to Mark, it is "James and John," the sons of Zebedee, themselves who make a request of Jesus to sit at his right and left in his glory. Because their request arouses the indignation of the other disciples (v. 24), we should not be surprised that the scene is mitigated by Matthew, who in various ways seeks to put the disciples in a better light. According to **vv. 20–21**, it is the *mother* of James and John who makes the request. But it is clear that Matthew knows Mark's version, for he has Jesus reply: "You [pl.] do not know what you [pl.] are asking" (cf. Mark 10:38). The use of "they" in the next sentence clearly indicates that the "you" in Jesus' response is plural – that Jesus was addressing James and John, not their mother.

Jesus asks the disciples if they are "able to drink the cup" that Jesus will drink
(**v. 22**). The disciples assure him that indeed they are able. The cup refers, of course,
to suffering, even death. The authenticity of this exchange is strongly supported
by the observation that Jesus himself was reluctant to drink the cup, as seen in his
agonized prayer in Gethsemane (Matt 26:39, 42), and by the observation that the
disciples themselves will run away when Jesus is arrested (Matt 26:56), showing that
they had no interest whatsoever in sharing Jesus' fate.

Whether or not the disciples are up to the challenge, Jesus cannot in fact grant their
request. Where people sit, or the positions they hold, "is for those for whom it has
been prepared by my Father" (**v. 23**). This unexpected admission on the part of Jesus
is yet another indication of the antiquity and authenticity of the conversation.

When the other disciples hear of the Zebedees' request, they are angry (**v. 24**).
This anger provides Jesus with the opportunity to teach his disciples what true leadership is all about. Jesus reminds his disciples of the conventions of leadership in
their day: in essence it was tyranny (**v. 25**). (One will be surprised how frequently
Josephus uses the words "tyrant" and "to act as tyrant" in his descriptions of Greek
rulers and various Jewish rebels who hoped to seize power.) In the Greco-Roman
world, "great ones" are those who rule over others, who "lord it over" others. These
great ones were eulogized (see Virgil's flattery of Augustus). In other words, greatness in Jesus' day was defined as coercive power. The more power one had, the
"greater" one was.

"It will not be so among you," Jesus tells his disciples; "but whoever wishes to
be great among you must be your servant, and whoever wishes to be first among
you must be your slave" (**vv. 26–27**). Here again, we hear Jesus teaching of reversal,
how the first will be last and the last first (cf. Matt 18:4; 19:30; 20:16; 23:11–12). What
Jesus commands from his disciples could not possibly be more at odds with conventional wisdom. In the Greek world, service was the opposite of happiness, as
Plato says: "How can one be happy when he has to serve someone?" (*Gorg.* 491e).
But the Jewish world had a higher appreciation of service (e.g., *Mek.* on Exod 18:12
[*Amalek* §3]; *b. Qid.* 32b). Jesus, however, draws his contrast not between himself and Israel's religious heritage but between his style of leadership and that of
the Roman world, which of course would include Roman influences in the land
of Israel also (such as seen in the Herodian dynasty, which was closely aligned
with Rome).

Jesus concludes his teaching with a reference to himself. The principle of service is seen in the example of the Son of Man, who "came not to be served but to
serve, and to give his life a ransom for many" (**v. 28**). The first part of this statement
inverts what is said of the Son of Man in Dan 7:13–14, who approaches God (the
Ancient of Days) and receives from him royal power, "that all peoples, nations, and
languages should serve him." But according to Jesus, the Son of Man did not come
to be served but to serve. On what grounds does Jesus invert the vision of Daniel 7?
The second part of the statement answers our question. The Son of Man serves and

gives "his life a ransom for many" in his capacity as the Suffering Servant of Isaiah 53: "my servant, shall make many righteous, and he shall bear their iniquities … [H]e bore the sin of many, and made intercession for the transgressors" (vv. 11–12). By blending together Daniel 7 (which speaks of royal power and struggle) and Isaiah 53 (which speaks of suffering service and vindication), Jesus teaches that he, as the Son of Man, must first undergo suffering on behalf of his people before he experiences vindication and glory.

The "ransom" of which Jesus speaks is a payment. There is a price to be paid for Israel's sin (indeed, for the sin of all humanity), and the Son of Man will pay the price (in his suffering and death). In doing so, he will redeem his people (pay the ransom, as it were), thus freeing them from the consequences of judgment. This is how the Son of Man serves the "many," the great many people who will be redeemed, who will be saved "from their sins" (Matt 1:21).[445]

MATTHEW 20:29–34 – SIGHT FOR TWO BLIND MEN

20:29: As they were leaving Jericho, a large crowd followed him.

20:30: There were two blind men sitting by the roadside. When they heard that Jesus was passing by, they shouted, "Lord, have mercy on us, Son of David!"

20:31: The crowd sternly ordered them to be quiet; but they shouted even more loudly, "Have mercy on us, Lord, Son of David!"

20:32: Jesus stood still and called them, saying, "What do you want me to do for you?"

20:33: They said to him, "Lord, let our eyes be opened."

20:34: Moved with compassion, Jesus touched their eyes. Immediately they regained their sight and followed him.

*M*atthew draws upon Mark 10:46–52, editing and simplifying as he usually does. However, Matthew, as he does elsewhere (Matt 9:27–28), speaks of *two* blind men, not one blind man named Bartimaeus. Matthew's version of the story is also different from Mark's in that Jesus touches the eyes of the blind men (Matt 20:34). In Matthew, Jesus often touches or is touched to convey healing (e.g., Matt 8:3, 15; 9:20, 21, 29; 14:36).

---

[445] C. K. Barrett, "The Background of Mark 10.45," in A. J. B. Higgins (ed.), *New Testament Essays: Studies in Memory of Thomas Walter Manson 1893–1958* (Manchester: Manchester University Press, 1959), 1–18; P. Stuhlmacher, "Vicariously Giving His Life for Many: Mark 10:45 (Matt. 20:28)," in *Reconciliation, Law, and Righteousness: Essays in Biblical Theology* (Philadelphia: Fortress, 1986), 16–29; W. C. Carter, *Households and Discipleship* (1994), 161–92; R. T. France, "The Servant of the Lord in the Teaching of Jesus," *TynBul* 19 (1996): 26–52.

Matthew's account of the healing of the blind men begins, "As they were leaving Jericho, a large crowd followed him" (**v. 29**). The southward journey at last takes Jesus and his followers to Jericho, some fifteen miles northeast of Jerusalem. The next major leg of the journey will take them to Jerusalem itself, a wearisome uphill trek. When Jesus leaves Jericho, he is, as almost always, accompanied by crowds of people.

Founded perhaps as early as 8,000 B.C., Jericho is the oldest known continually inhabited city on earth. It is situated five miles to the west of the Jordan River and about fifteen miles northeast of Jerusalem. The ancient site conquered by Joshua would have been in Jesus' day not much different from the tel that Kathleen Kenyon excavated a half century ago. Nearby (at the mouth of the Wadi Qelt) is the newer city that Herod the Great enhanced and expanded with various official buildings, including a hippodrome and royal palace, the ruins of which are clearly visible today. Herod himself later died at Jericho. A century earlier, the Maccabean priest King Janneus had a royal residence at Jericho. Qumran is some miles to the south, on the northwestern shore of the Dead Sea.

When the blind men hear that Jesus is passing by, they shout out, "Lord, have mercy on us, Son of David!" (**v. 30**). We are not told that they were beggars (as we are told Bartimaeus was in Mark 10:46). Hailing Jesus as "Son of David" is authentic, pre-Easter tradition. Some have contended that the tradition of Jesus' Davidic descent arose only later, in the aftermath of the early church's proclamation of Jesus as Messiah. To proclaim Jesus as Israel's Messiah, so the argument goes, would require Davidic descent. Moreover, it is claimed that there were no records of Davidic descent extant in the time of Jesus. This claim, however, is dubious. Eusebius reports that Emperors Vespasian (*Eccl. Hist.* 3.12), Domitian (3.19–20), and Trajan (3.32.5–6) persecuted the family of David, so that no royal claimant might arise and challenge the authority of Rome. Not long ago, an ossuary dating from the first century B.C. was found in Jerusalem bearing the inscription: "of the house of David." According to early rabbinic literature, "the family of David" brought the wood offering of the priests to temple on the twentieth of Tammuz (cf. *m. Ta'an.* 4:5; *t. Ta'an.* 3.5).

The evidence of a recognized Davidic lineage in the time of Jesus is compelling. Early Christianity accepted Jesus' Davidic descent, but apparently made little of it (see Paul's remarks in Rom 1:3–4). Indeed, Jesus himself challenges the adequacy of understanding the Messiah in terms of the epithet "son of David" (Mark 12:35–37). Moreover, there is no evidence in early sources that anyone challenged Jesus' Davidic descent. In short, New Testament Christology is founded on other, more important traditions than mere Davidic descent.

Despite the rebuke of the crowd, the blind men persist in crying out to Jesus (**v. 31**). The crowd tried to silence the men, probably for the same reason the disciples rebuked parents for bringing their children to Jesus (see Matt 19:13–14): Jesus had more important things to do. But Jesus does have time for them (**vv. 32–33**) and heals them (**v. 34**).[446]

MATTHEW 21:1–11 – ENTRY INTO JERUSALEM

21:1: When they had come near Jerusalem and had reached Bethphage, at the Mount of Olives, Jesus sent two disciples,

21:2: saying to them, "Go into the village ahead of you, and immediately you will find a donkey tied, and a colt with her; untie them and bring them to me.

21:3: If anyone says anything to you, just say this, 'The Lord needs them.' And he will send them immediately."

21:4: This took place to fulfill what had been spoken through the prophet, saying,

21:5: "Tell the daughter of Zion, Look, your king is coming to you, humble, and mounted on a donkey, and on a colt, the foal of a donkey."

21:6: The disciples went and did as Jesus had directed them;

21:7: they brought the donkey and the colt, and put their cloaks on them, and he sat on them.

21:8: A very large crowd spread their cloaks on the road, and others cut branches from the trees and spread them on the road.

21:9: The crowds that went ahead of him and that followed were shouting, "Hosanna to the Son of David! Blessed is the one who comes in the name of the Lord! Hosanna in the highest heaven!"

21:10: When he entered Jerusalem, the whole city was in turmoil, asking, "Who is this?"

21:11: The crowds were saying, "This is the prophet Jesus from Nazareth in Galilee."

*J*esus' celebrated entry is one of as many as twelve similar entries, as recorded in 1 and 2 Maccabees and in Josephus. These entries follow a more or less fixed pattern. Entries involving major figures include Alexander, who enters Jerusalem, is greeted with ceremony, and is escorted into the city, where he participates in

---

[446] C. Burger, *Jesus als Davidssohn* (FRLANT 98; Göttingen: Vandenhoeck & Ruprecht, 1970), 72–106; J. D. Kingsbury, "The Title 'Son of David' in Matthew's Gospel," *JBL* 95 (1976): 591–602; D. C. Duling, "The Therapeutic Son of David: An Element in Matthew's Christological Apologetic," *NTS* 24 (1978): 392–410; B. D. Chilton, "Jesus *ben David*: Reflections on the *Davidssohnfrage*," *JSNT* 14 (1982): 88–112; W. R. G. Loader, "Son of David, Blindness, Possession, and Duality in Matthew," *CBQ* 44 (1982): 570–85.

cultic activity (*Ant.* 11.325–39); Apollonius, who enters Jerusalem accompanied by torches and shouts (2 Macc 4:21–22); Judas Maccabeus, who returns home from a military victory and is greeted with hymns and "praising God" (1 Macc 4:19–25; Josephus, *Ant.* 12.312); Judas Maccabeus again, this time returning from battle and entering Jerusalem amidst singing and merrymaking, followed by sacrifice (1 Macc 5:45–54; *Ant.* 12.348–49); Jonathan, brother of Judas Maccabeus, who is greeted by the men of Askalon "with great pomp" (1 Macc 10:86); Simon, brother of Judas Maccabeus, who enters Gaza, expels idolatrous inhabitants, cleanses idolatrous houses, and enters the city "with hymns and praise" (1 Macc 13:43–48); Simon, brother of Judas Maccabeus, again, this time entering Jerusalem, where he is met by crowds "with praise and palm branches, and with harps and cymbals and stringed instruments and with hymns and songs" (1 Macc 13:49–51); Antigonus, who with pomp enters Jerusalem and then the temple precincts, but with so much pomp and self-importance he is criticized by some for imagining that he himself was "king" (*J.W.* 1.73–74; *Ant.* 13.304–6); Marcus Agrippa, who enters Jerusalem, is met by Herod, and is welcomed by the people with acclamations (*Ant.* 16.12–15); and Archelaus, who, hoping to confirm his kingship, journeys to and enters Jerusalem amidst acclamation of his procession (*Ant.* 17.194–239).[447]

Matthew follows Mark in chronology and basic content (cf. Mark 11:1–11) but adds several important details, all designed to enhance Christology. Matthew's unusual feature is the mention of *two* animals, the donkey and her colt. The entrance into Jerusalem marks the beginning of Passion Week. Jesus directs his disciples to enter a nearby village, where they will find the animals. If anyone questions the disciples, they are to reply as Jesus instructed them. They follow Jesus' instructions and all works out as planned. Jesus mounts the donkey, and his disciples and others create a procession, with garments and branches paving the way. Amidst shouts of "Hosanna" and "Son of David," Jesus and his disciples wend their way into the ancient city of Jerusalem.

The manner of the entry, Matthew tells us, "took place to fulfill what had been spoken through the prophet" (**v. 4**), namely to fulfill the prophecy of Zech 9:9: "Tell the daughter of Zion, Look, your king is coming to you, humble, and mounted on a donkey, and on a colt, the foal of a donkey" (**v. 5**). Matthew's quotation matches neither the Hebrew nor the Greek exactly, but it does capture the thrust of the prophetic passage, in which Israel's king returns to Zion. In riding the donkey into the city, as did David's son Solomon centuries earlier, Jesus fulfills prophecy. Because the prophecy seems to mention two animals, a donkey and a colt, the foal of the donkey, Matthew speaks of two animals (in contrast to Mark's one). The language of the Hebrew and the Greek does not require two animals but does allow for it.

---

[447]   D. R. Catchpole, "The 'Triumphal' Entry," in E. Bammel and C. F. D. Moule (eds.), *Jesus and the Politics of His Day* (Cambridge: Cambridge University Press, 1984), 319–34.

Although some commentators have thought that Matthew has misunderstood the synonymous parallelism of Zech 9:9 in thinking that the text speaks of two animals, others rightly recognize that it is highly unlikely that the evangelist, who can work with Greek and probably Aramaic and Hebrew, would not recognize synonymous parallelism. As with other texts that are cited as "fulfilled," Matthew may well have seen a correspondence between an event in the life of Jesus and the details of a prophetic text. Matthew would have read Mark's reference to the colt as "never been ridden" (Mark 11:2) and so would have assumed that the mother of the young colt was present and would have accompanied it. Matthew either assumed this from the practice of his time or actually knew that this had been the case. The presence of both the mother and the foal, seen through the eyes of typology, would have drawn a close correspondence with the prophetic text.[448]

When Matthew writes that "The disciples went and did as Jesus had directed them" (**v. 6**), he expands and enhances Mark's "They went away and found a colt tied near a door ..." (Mark 11:4). Matthew takes the opportunity to portray Jesus as very much in control of the situation. He also portrays the disciples as reliable.

The disciples "put their cloaks on them, and he sat on them" (**v. 7**). Jesus sat on the garments of one of the animals (we should assume the colt, the never-before-ridden animal, with its mother trotting alongside); we are not supposed to think that he rode the animals successively (or at the same time!). The presence of the colt's mother attests to the newness of the colt and justifies the claim that no one had yet sat on it (cf. Mark 11:2).

The spreading of "cloaks on the road" and "branches from trees" (**v. 8**) is part of the custom of celebrating the approach of an honored guest; see the introductory paragraph to this pericope.

Matthew's "Hosanna to the Son of David" (**v. 9**) places the focus squarely on Jesus. In Mark, the people shouted, "Blessed is the coming kingdom of our ancestor David!" (Mark 11:10). The people rejoice not because the kingdom of David is coming but because Jesus, the "Son of David," is coming.

Matthew reports that "The whole city was in turmoil, asking, 'Who is this?' The crowds were saying, 'This is the prophet Jesus from Nazareth in Galilee'" (**vv. 10–11**). Instead of Mark's faltering and uncertain conclusion, "when he had looked around at everything, as it was already late" (Mark 11:11), Matthew narrates a rousing reception. Again, the focus is on who Jesus is. He is "the prophet Jesus from Nazareth in Galilee." (The "in Galilee" is added because Nazareth is not well known in Judea.) This identification may be adequate, but it does not compete with his disciples' better-informed exclamations of "Son of David" (v. 9), for David himself

---

[448] The point is well made in R. H. Gundry, *Matthew: A Commentary on His Handbook for a Mixed Church under Persecution*, revised edition (Grand Rapids, MI: Eerdmans, 1994), 408–10; D. A. Hagner, *Matthew* (1993–1995), 2:594–95; C. S. Keener, *A Commentary on the Gospel of Matthew* (1999), 491–92.

was viewed as a prophet (cf. Acts 1:16; 4:25; 11QPs[a] 27:11, "All these he [David] spoke through prophecy, which was given him from before the Most High"). Thus, Jesus, both Son of David and prophet, has arrived in Jerusalem on the eve of the Passover celebration.[449]

MATTHEW 21:12–17 – A DEMONSTRATION IN THE TEMPLE

21:12: Then Jesus entered the temple and drove out all who were selling and buying in the temple, and he overturned the tables of the money changers and the seats of those who sold doves.

21:13: He said to them, "It is written, 'My house shall be called a house of prayer'; but you are making it a den of robbers.'"

21:14: The blind and the lame came to him in the temple, and he cured them.

21:15: But when the chief priests and the scribes saw the amazing things that he did, and heard the children crying out in the temple, "Hosanna to the Son of David," they became angry

21:16: and said to him, "Do you hear what these are saying?" Jesus said to them, "Yes; have you never read, 'Out of the mouths of infants and nursing babies you have prepared praise for yourself'?"

21:17: He left them, went out of the city to Bethany, and spent the night there.

*M*atthew's version of Jesus' demonstration in the temple precincts is made up of two parts: the demonstration itself (vv. 12–13), which is derived from Mark 11:15–18, and the reception of the blind and lame (vv. 14–16), which is unique to Matthew. The concluding verse (v. 19) is based on Mark's conclusion (Mark 11:19).

Matthew's account begins, "Then Jesus entered the temple and drove out all who were selling and buying in the temple" (**v. 12**). On a historical level, it is possible that Jesus was pursuing a line of action that arose out of his understanding of Zechariah (as seen in mounting the colt and entering the city, and now in the action he has taken in the temple). The temple action, traditionally known as a "cleansing" (though cleansing language occurs nowhere in the passage), may have been prompted by Zech 14:20–21, a passage that anticipates the day when every vessel in the temple will be pure and there shall no longer be any trader in the precincts.[450]

---

[449]   J. D. M. Derrett, "Law in the New Testament: The Palm Sunday Colt," *NovT* 13 (1971): 241–58; C.-P. März, *"Siehe, dein König kommt zu dir …": Eine traditionsgeschichtliche Untersuchung zur Einzugsperikope* (ETS 43; Leipzig: St. Benno, 1980); J. A. Fitzmyer, "Aramaic Evidence Affecting the Interpretation of Hosanna in the New Testament," in G. F. Hawthorne and O. Betz (eds.), *Tradition and Interpretation in the New Testament* (E. E. Ellis Festschrift; Grand Rapids, MI: Eerdmans, 1987), 110–18.

[450]   C. Roth, "The Cleansing of the Temple and Zechariah xiv.21," *NovT* 4 (1960): 174–81; B. D. Chilton, *The Temple of Jesus: His Sacrificial Program within a Cultural History of Sacrifice*

Did Jesus encounter policies or activities that he regarded as corrupt, and if so, what were they? From rabbinic tradition, we hear of a first-century protest against a policy of overcharging for doves, the poor person's sacrifice (*m. Ker.* 1:7). Josephus tells us of shameful strong-armed actions of the ruling priests against the lower-ranking priests in the years before the great revolt of 66–70 A.D. in an effort to steal the tithes (*Ant.* 20.181; 20.206–7). Josephus relates stories of religious teachers inciting crowds to take action in the temple precincts over questions of purity (*Ant.* 13.372–73; *J.W.* 1.648–55; *Ant.* 17.149–67). These incidents suggest a range of disputes and practices, any one or more of which may have been at issue the year that Jesus visited Jerusalem at Passover time.[451]

When Jesus clears the temple, he tells the buyers and sellers that "It is written, 'My house shall be called a house of prayer'; but you are making it a den of robbers" (**v. 13**). The first part of the statement quotes a portion of Isa 56:7, part of a larger oracle (Isa 56:1–8) that looks forward to the day when people from all over the world, including Gentiles, come to the temple to worship God. It will be a time when their sacrifices will be acceptable and their prayers heard. The prophetic oracle is itself alluding to Solomon's dedication of the temple (1 Kings 8:41–43). In Jesus' view, however, the temple establishment has failed to live up to this standard; it is not prepared for the new order that will come with the kingdom of God. Instead of a house of prayer, the temple has become a "den of robbers." Here Jesus has alluded to Jer 7:11, part of a passage in which the prophet Jeremiah indicted the temple establishment of his day, warning that it would be destroyed.[452]

Matthew condenses Mark's version of the temple action to two verses (vv. 12–13), but then supplements it with the story of the healing of the blind and lame in the temple precincts. He says of Jesus that the "blind and the lame came to him in the temple, and he cured them" (**v. 14**). As has been mentioned, this story is found only in Matthew. He has rewritten the last part of Mark's verse, "And when the chief priests and the scribes heard it, they kept looking for a way to kill him; for they were afraid of him, because the whole crowd was spellbound by his teaching" (Mark 11:18), retaining "the chief priests and the scribes," who may not have heard Jesus' words (cf. Matt 21:13 = Mark 11:17) but have seen the "amazing things that he

(University Park, PA: Penn State Press, 1992), 91–111; C. Ham, *The Coming King and the Rejected Shepherd: Matthew's Reading of Zechariah's Messianic Hope* (New Testament Monographs 4; Sheffield: Sheffield Phoenix, 2005), 90–91.

[451] For more on the temple demonstration, see R. Bauckham, "Jesus' Demonstration in the Temple," in B. Lindars (ed.), *Law and Religion: Essays on the Place of the Law in Israel and Early Christianity* (Cambridge: Clarke, 1988), 72–89, 171–76; C. A. Evans, "Jesus and the 'Cave of Robbers': Toward a Jewish Context for the Temple Action," *BBR* 3 (1993): 93–110; J. Ådna, *Jesu Stellung zum Tempel: Die Tempelaktion und das Tempelwort Jesu als Ausdruck seiner messianischen Sendung* (WUNT 2, no. 119; Tübingen: Mohr Siebeck, 2000).

[452] M. Hengel, *Was Jesus a Revolutionist?* (FBBS 28; Philadelphia: Fortress, 1971), 15–18; C. A. Evans, "Jesus' Action in the Temple: Cleansing or Portent of Destruction?" *CBQ* 51 (1989): 237–70; M. Knowles, *Jeremiah in Matthew's Gospel* (1993), 173–76.

did" and have heard "the children crying out in the temple, 'Hosanna to the Son of David'" (**v. 15**). Accordingly, the chief priests did not take offense at what Jesus said about them and the implied threat against the temple, something that would have in all probability offended many Jews, whether sympathetic to the Jesus movement or not; they took offense at the things taking place in the temple precincts: the approach of the blind and lame and the shouts of the children.

The cry "Hosanna to the Son of David" coheres with Matthew's desire to present Jesus as the Davidic Messiah, the fulfillment of prophetic Scripture (cf. Matt 1:1, 17, 20–25; 2:1–6; 12:23; 15:22). The shout repeats the shout of the crowds when Jesus entered the city (Matt 21:9), which in accordance with Matthean chronology – unlike the Markan – takes place the *same day* as the demonstration in the temple. Having the demonstration immediately follow the entry, and having Jesus on both occasions hailed as the "Son of David" (cf. Matt 21:9, 15), not only strengthens the Davidic identity of Jesus but clarifies the nature of his action in the temple precincts in an important way. Jesus is portrayed as the royal reformer of Israel's faith and as such stands in the tradition of Israel's righteous kings; David, who moved the ark of the covenant to Jerusalem and planned the construction of the temple (2 Sam 6–7; 1 Chron 15–17), Solomon, the son of David, who built and dedicated the temple (1 Kings 5–8; 2 Chron 1–7), Hezekiah, who reformed temple practice (2 Kings 18–20; 2 Chron 29–31), and Josiah, who also reformed temple practice (2 Kings 22–23; 2 Chron 35–36; 1 Esd 1), are among the most conspicuous.

The appearance of the "blind and the lame" at the temple also recalls Davidic tradition. One immediately thinks of 2 Sam 5:8, where David commanded, "The blind and the lame shall not come into the house." This was retaliation for an insult, for the inhabitants of Jerusalem had boasted that the blind and lame could offer sufficient force to prevent David from taking the city (2 Sam 5:6). But Jesus, the "Son of David," now welcomes the blind and lame to the temple and heals them, thus underscoring the redemptive mission of the Messiah. In the Aramaic paraphrase, it is "sinners and the guilty" who are denied entry into the temple. If this understanding were current in the time of Jesus, then an allusion to 2 Sam 5:8 would be quite appropriate, signifying that Jesus had begun to "save his people from their sins" (Matt 1:21; cf. 9:2, 5; 15:31).[453]

Those with defects, such as the blind, deaf, mute, and lame, were suspected of being not only under the judgment of God but quite possibly under demonic influence (Matt 9:32; 12:22; cf. *T. Solomon* 12:2). Such persons would not be welcome in the holy precincts or in any setting where angels were thought to be present.[454]

[453]   C. A. Evans, "A Note on Targum 2 Samuel 5.8 and Jesus' Ministry to the 'Maimed, Halt, and Blind," *JSP* 15 (1997): 79–82.

[454]   For a further discussion, see C. Wassen, "What Do Angels Have against the Blind and the Deaf? Rules of Exclusion in the Dead Sea Scrolls," in W. O. McCready and A. Reinhartz (eds.), *Common Judaism: Explorations in Second-Temple Judaism* (Minneapolis: Fortress Press, 2008), 115–29, 270–80.

Jesus' critics are outraged by what they hear and wonder if Jesus is listening. Jesus cuts short the complaints of his critics by citing part of Ps 8:2 (v. 3 in the Septuagint and the Masoretic Text, the standard Hebrew version of the Old Testament): "Yes; have you never read, 'Out of the mouths of infants and nursing babies you have prepared praise for yourself'?" (**v. 16**). The quotation is taken from the Septuagint verbatim, so it is probably the work of the Greek-speaking church, if not Matthew himself (the Masoretic Text reads: "Out of the mouths of babes and infants you have founded a bulwark because of your foes"). Rabbinic exegesis links Ps 8:3 with Exod 15:2, the Song of Moses, suggesting that at the Red Sea children praised God (cf. *Mekilta* on Exod 15:1 [*Shirata* §1], attributed to Yose the Galilean). This tradition is ancient, as attested in Wisd of Sol 10:18–21, and so it is not implausible that it clarifies Matthew's intended meaning: children have responded to Jesus' saving work in song and praise, just as they did in response to Moses' great work at the Red Sea. Comparing Jesus with Moses is a favorite theme in Matthew (as seen, for example, in the infancy narrative and in the Sermon on the Mount) and does not compete with the presentation of Jesus as David's messianic descendant.

MATTHEW 21:18–22 – THE LESSON OF THE FIG TREE

21:18: In the morning, when he returned to the city, he was hungry.

21:19: And seeing a fig tree by the side of the road, he went to it and found nothing at all on it but leaves. Then he said to it, "May no fruit ever come from you again!" And the fig tree withered at once.

21:20: When the disciples saw it, they were amazed, saying, "How did the fig tree wither at once?"

21:21: Jesus answered them, "Truly I tell you, if you have faith and do not doubt, not only will you do what has been done to the fig tree, but even if you say to this mountain, 'Be lifted up and thrown into the sea,' it will be done.

21:22: Whatever you ask for in prayer with faith, you will receive."

*M*atthew follows Mark's basic contents, but not his sequence. Whereas Mark presents the temple action (Mark 11:15–19) "sandwiched" between the cursing of the fig tree (Mark 11:12–14) and its discovery withered (Mark 11:20–21), Matthew presents the temple action (Matt 21:12–17) and then the fig tree episode (Matt 21:18–20). There is nothing sandwiched into the Matthean sequence: the fig tree withered "at once" (Matt 21:19). Finally, Matthew takes pains to link the appended lessons on faith more closely to the remarkable episode of the fig tree (Matt 21:21–22).

Matthew's report, "And seeing a fig tree by the side of the road, he went to it and found nothing at all on it but leaves" (**v. 19a**), condenses and simplifies Mark 11:12–13, 20. Matthew also omits Mark's comment that it was not the season for figs. It is probable that Matthew understood what Mark meant, but he views it as unnecessary and as potentially confusing to his readers. Finding no fruit, Jesus exclaims, "May no fruit ever come from you again!" (**v. 19b**). Here Matthew has slightly reworded Mark's "May no one ever eat fruit from you again" (Mark 11:14). The imprecation as it is found in Mark could be understood to mean simply that no one will eat fruit from this fig tree; that is, they will avoid it. Matthew's form of the saying clarifies what Jesus really meant: people will not eat fruit from this fig tree because it will no longer produce any.

In patristic interpretation, the fig tree has been compared to the tree from which Adam and Eve ate, with Jesus' imprecation seen as an allusion to God's utterance against Adam, lest he "reach out his hand and take also from the tree of life, and eat, and live forever" (Gen 3:22; cf. Ephrem the Syrian, *Commentary on the Diatessaron* 21.20–21). But the comparison is strained. (After all, there are two trees in the Garden of Eden, the tree of knowledge, from which Adam and Eve ate, and the tree of life, from which God would not permit them to eat. Moreover, God speaks against Adam and Eve, not against the tree itself.)

Matthew continues, "And the fig tree withered at once" (**v. 19c**). The most dramatic difference in Matthew's account is the immediate withering of the tree. It does not take a day to die, as Mark's readers would have supposed; it dies right before the eyes of the astonished disciples. There are similar stories in Judaism and Christianity. One will recall Paul's bringing blindness upon the false prophet Bar-Jesus (Acts 13:9–11). The Talmud tells us that merely by looking at a person Rabbi Yohanan could reduce someone to a heap of bones (*b. B. Bat.* 75a = *b. Sanh.* 100a).

The astounded disciples ask their master, "How did the fig tree wither at once?" (**v. 20**). In Mark's Gospel, Peter exclaims to Jesus, "Rabbi, look! The fig tree that you cursed has withered" (Mark 11:21). But in Matthew the disciples ask "how" the fig tree withered "at once," thus providing Jesus the opportunity to teach them about faith.

Jesus tells his disciples, "Truly I tell you, if you have faith and do not doubt, not only will you do what has been done to the fig tree, but even if you say to this mountain, 'Be lifted up and thrown into the sea,' it will be done" (**v. 21**). Jesus' reply explicitly links what happened to the fig tree to the saying about hurling the mountain into the sea. Given the location of Jesus and his disciples, "this mountain" may well have referred to the Mount of Olives and may again reflect the prophetic imagery of Zech 14:4.[455]

Jesus concludes his teaching by assuring his disciples, "Whatever you ask for in prayer with faith, you will receive" (**v. 22**). There is no "blank check" here; the followers of Jesus are to pray for God's will to be done on earth as it is in heaven (cf. Matt 6:9–13). Personal interests and gratification are not in view.[456]

---

[455]   J. Nolland, *The Gospel of Matthew* (2005), 853.
[456]   For further discussion, see J. G. Kahn, "La parabole du figuier sterile et les arbres récalcitrants de la Genèse," *NovT* 13 (1971): 38–45; W. R. Telford, *The Barren Temple and the*

MATTHEW 21:23–27 – THE QUESTION OF AUTHORITY

21:23: When he entered the temple, the chief priests and the elders of the people came to him as he was teaching, and said, "By what authority are you doing these things, and who gave you this authority?"

21:24: Jesus said to them, "I will also ask you one question; if you tell me the answer, then I will also tell you by what authority I do these things.

21:25: Did the baptism of John come from heaven, or was it of human origin?" And they argued with one another, "If we say, 'From heaven,' he will say to us, 'Why then did you not believe him?'

21:26: But if we say, 'Of human origin,' we are afraid of the crowd; for all regard John as a prophet."

21:27: So they answered Jesus, "We do not know." And he said to them, "Neither will I tell you by what authority I am doing these things."

*I*n the story in which Jesus is asked about his authority, Matthew continues to follow Mark (cf. Mark 11:27–33), this time with a minimum of editing. The story follows the temple demonstration (Matt 21:12–17) and the fig tree incident (Matt 21:18–22).

Matthew's account of the incident begins, "When he entered the temple, the chief priests and the elders of the people came to him" (**v. 23a**). The temple precincts are vast, stretching some 480 meters from north to south and about 300 meters from east to west. In the center is the sanctuary itself, but there are a series of buildings and colonnades within the precincts. While teaching in the precincts, Jesus is approached by powerful critics. Several times in Matthew, the "chief priests and elders" appear together (cf. Matt 16:21; 26:3, 47; 27:3, 12, 20, 41; 28:12). They constitute Jesus' deadly foes in the Passion narrative. Some of these men may have been members of the Sanhedrin, or Jewish council. They approach Jesus in order to question him.

The priests and elders ask Jesus, "By what authority are you doing these things, and who gave you this authority?" (**v. 23b**). Their question is in response to the temple action in Matt 21:12–17, though it is possible that some of Matthew's readers may have thought of the fig tree as well. The chief priests and elders approach Jesus and demand to know by what authority he does what he does and who gave him this authority.[457] Jesus does not answer their question, at least not directly. Rather,

---

Withered Fig Tree (JSNTSup 1; Sheffield: JSOT Press, 1980), 69–204; J. D. M. Derrett, "Moving Mountains and Uprooting Trees (Mk 11.22; Mt 17.20; 21.21; Lk 17.6)," *BibOr* 30 (1988): 231–44; C. Böttrich, "Jesus und der Feigenbaum Mk 11,12–14.20–25 in der Diskussion," *NovT* 39 (1997): 328–59.

457 On the Jewish background, see D. Daube, *The New Testament and Rabbinic Judaism* (Jordan Lectures 1952; London: Athlone, 1956), 205–23, especially 217–23.

he counters defiantly with a question of his own: "I will also ask you one question; if you tell me the answer, then I will also tell you by what authority I do these things" (v. 24). Countering a question with a question has Socratic roots and was well known in Jewish circles in the time of Jesus.[458]

The chief priests had every right to question Jesus or anyone else in the temple precincts who created a disturbance and made comments critical of this sacred institution. The chief priests had sole jurisdiction over the temple. From them people derived authority to conduct business in the temple precincts. The Sanhedrin had a broader legislative and judicial jurisdiction, but the high priest and his ranking priestly associates possessed ultimate authority on the temple mount, an authority that the Romans themselves respected.

The high priest's authority over the Sanhedrin itself is illustrated by the late rabbinic tradition that the latter was ejected from the "Chamber of Hewn Stone" within the temple precincts, evidently by order of the high priest (cf. *b. Rosh Hashanah* 31a; *b. Shabbat* 15a; *b. Sanh.* 41a). Now this tradition is admittedly late, and the refrain that this event took place "forty years" before the destruction of the temple (i.e., 30 A.D.) must be taken with a grain of salt, but it probably does accurately reflect the actual authority of the high priest within the temple precincts themselves. Josephus himself draws attention to the strict prohibition against trespassing in restricted areas, which resulted in summary execution (*J.W.* 5.193–94; note that Josephus says the inscribed warning was written "in Greek and Roman letters," implying that this warning was as much for Gentiles as for Israelites; fragments of this stone inscription have been found).

Because the chief priests had exclusive jurisdiction over the temple, their question, which had no acceptable answer so far as they were concerned, was more a move to incriminate Jesus than an attempt to gain information from him. Either Jesus would admit his conduct was "unauthorized," which would make him publicly vulnerable, or claim an authority or "right" superseding that of the chief priests, a claim that could make him politically vulnerable. In either case, his conduct would then have provided a basis for a more formal proceeding against him.

Jesus' counterquestion, "Did the baptism of John come from heaven, or was it of human origin?" (v. 25a), creates a problem for the chief priests and elders. They clearly perceive the difficulty. Just as their question put to Jesus could not be answered without jeopardy, so likewise the question Jesus put to them: "If we say, 'From heaven,' he will say to us, 'Why then did you not believe him?' But if we say, 'Of human origin,' we are afraid of the crowd; for all regard John as a prophet" (vv. 25b–26).

The significance of Jesus' counterquestion is what it implies about himself. Of course, what Jesus believes is the correct answer is quite clear: John's authority was from heaven; that is, from God. Likewise, Jesus' authority was from God, not from himself, the people, or a political party. The chief priests and elders refuse to answer

---

[458]   D. Daube, *The New Testament and Rabbinic Judaism* (1956), 151–57, 219–20.

the question put to them and therefore avoid the dilemma. Therefore, Jesus can refuse to answer their question, directly at least, and avoid losing face or placing himself in a predicament. However, he will answer the question soon, in the parable of the vineyard (Matt 21:33–46).[459]

MATTHEW 21:28–32 – THE PARABLE OF THE TWO SONS

21:28: "What do you think? A man had two sons; he went to the first and said, 'Son, go and work in the vineyard today.'

21:29: He answered, 'I will not'; but later he changed his mind and went.

21:30: The father went to the second and said the same; and he answered, 'I go, sir'; but he did not go.

21:31: Which of the two did the will of his father?" They said, "The first." Jesus said to them, "Truly I tell you, the tax collectors and the prostitutes are going into the kingdom of God ahead of you.

21:32: For John came to you in the way of righteousness and you did not believe him, but the tax collectors and the prostitutes believed him; and even after you saw it, you did not change your minds and believe him."

The parable of the two sons is found only in Matthew and right after the exchange with the chief priests over the question of Jesus' (and John's) authority. The Matthean context makes it clear that the son in the parable who says "I go, sir," and then does not do the work represents the chief priests (who questioned Jesus' authority in Matt 21:23–27), whereas the son who says, "'I will not'; but later he changed his mind and went," represents the "tax collectors and the prostitutes" who believed John's preaching. But the chief priests "did not change their minds and believe" his message. (In some manuscripts, the order of the sons in the parable is reversed, with the first son saying no and then repenting and the second son saying yes and then failing to follow through.)

In the parable of the wicked vineyard tenants (Matt 21:33–46), the tenant farmers represent the chief priests. In this parable, they do indeed go into the vineyard to work, but they plunder the vineyard and refuse to recognize the rights and authority of the owner and his son.

---

[459] For further discussion of Matt 21:23–27, see G. S. Shae, "The Question on the Authority of Jesus," *NovT* 16 (1974): 1–29; A. J. Hultgren, *Jesus and His Adversaries* (1979), 68–75; J.-G. Mudiso Mbâ Mundla, *Jesus und die Führer Israels. Studien zu den sogenannten Jerusalemer Streitgesprächen* (NTAbh 17; Münster: Aschendorff, 1984), 5–40; W. Weiss, *"Eine neue Lehre in Vollmacht": Die Streit- und Schulgespräche des Markus-Evangeliums* (BZNW 52; Berlin: de Gruyter, 1989), 143–62; A. Fuchs, "Die Frage nach der Vollmacht Jesu: Mk 11,27–33 par Mt 21,23–27 par Lk 20,1–8," *SNTU* 26 (2001): 27–58.

There are parables in the rabbinic literature that are similar to Jesus' parable of the two sons. We have the parable of the two workers:

When God was about to give the Torah, no other nation but Israel would accept it. It can be compared to a man who had a field that he wished to entrust to tillers. Calling the first of these, he inquired, "Will you take over this field?" He replied, "I have no strength; the work is too hard for me." In the same way the second, third, and fourth declined to undertake the work. He called the fifth and asked him, "Will you take over this field?" He replied, "Yes." "On condition that you till it?" Then the reply was again, "Yes." But as soon as he took possession of it, he let it lie fallow. With whom is the king angry? With those who declare, "We cannot undertake it," or with him who did undertake it, but no sooner undertook it than he left it lying fallow? Surely, with him who undertook it. (*Exod. Rab.* 27.9 [on Exod 18:1])

The second is the parable of the two tenants:

If one learns the words of the Torah and does not fulfill them, his punishment is more severe than that of him who has not learned at all. It is like the case of a king who had a garden, which he let out to two tenants, one of whom planted trees and cut them down, while the other neither planted any [trees] nor cut any down. With whom is the king angry? Surely with him who planted [trees] and cut them down. Likewise, whosoever learns the words of Torah and does not fulfill them, his punishment is more severe than that of him who has never learned at all. (*Deut. Rab.* 7.4 [on Deut 28:1])

The "two sons" parable motif would in all probability bring to mind issues of election. Jesus' use of this tradition in his parable subverts what were probably widely held assumptions. That is, the issue is not the election of Israel over the Gentiles but the election of the obedient and responsive on the one hand and the nonelection of the obdurate and disobedient on the other. Jews and Gentiles will find themselves in both camps, segregated on the basis of faith and obedience, not ethnicity or religious affiliation.[460]

MATTHEW 21:33–46 – THE PARABLE OF THE VINEYARD

21:33: "Listen to another parable. There was a landowner who planted a vineyard, put a fence around it, dug a wine press in it, and built a watchtower. Then he leased it to tenants and went to another country.

---

[460]   For further study, see J. D. M. Derrett, "The Parable of the Two Sons," *ST* 25 (1971): 109–16; H. Merkel, "Das Gleichnis von den 'ungleichen Söhnen' (Matth. xxi.28–32)," *NTS* 20 (1974): 254–62; H. Weder, *Die Gleichnisse Jesu als Metaphern* (FRLANT 120; Göttingen: Vandenhoeck & Ruprecht, 1978), 230–38; B. Przybylski, *Righteousness in Matthew and His World of Thought* (SNTSMS 41; Cambridge: Cambridge University Press, 1980), 94–96; P. Foster, "A Tale of Two Sons: But Which One Did the Far, Far Better Thing? A Study of Matt 21.28–32," *NTS* 47 (2001): 26–37.

21:34: When the harvest time had come, he sent his slaves to the tenants to collect his produce.

21:35: But the tenants seized his slaves and beat one, killed another, and stoned another.

21:36: Again he sent other slaves, more than the first; and they treated them in the same way.

21:37: Finally he sent his son to them, saying, 'They will respect my son.'

21:38: But when the tenants saw the son, they said to themselves, 'This is the heir; come, let us kill him and get his inheritance.'

21:39: So they seized him, threw him out of the vineyard, and killed him.

21:40: Now when the owner of the vineyard comes, what will he do to those tenants?"

21:41: They said to him, "He will put those wretches to a miserable death, and lease the vineyard to other tenants who will give him the produce at the harvest time."

21:42: Jesus said to them, "Have you never read in the scriptures: 'The stone that the builders rejected has become the cornerstone; this was the Lord's doing, and it is amazing in our eyes'?

21:43: Therefore I tell you, the kingdom of God will be taken away from you and given to a people that produces the fruits of the kingdom.

21:44: The one who falls on this stone will be broken to pieces; and it will crush anyone on whom it falls."

21:45: When the chief priests and the Pharisees heard his parables, they realized that he was speaking about them.

21:46: They wanted to arrest him, but they feared the crowds, because they regarded him as a prophet.

Matthew derives the parable of the vineyard from Mark 12:1–12 and makes some very interesting changes. However, whereas Mark's form of the parable immediately follows the question of authority (see Mark 11:27–33 and then 12:1–12), Matthew has inserted the parable of the two sons (Matt 21:28–32) between the question of authority (Matt 21:23–27) and the parable of the vineyard (Matt 21:33–46). The parable of the two sons in effect serves as a bridge between the debate over authority and the parable of the vineyard, thereby defining and identifying more clearly the chief priests. In the parable of the two sons, the chief priests are defined by the son who says he will obey his father and then does not. In the vineyard parable, they are further defined by the tenants who flout the vineyard owner's authority, molesting his servants and then murdering his son.[461]

---

[461]   C. E. Carlston, *The Parables of the Triple Tradition* (Philadelphia: Fortress, 1975), 40–45.

Jesus' parable of the vineyard is based on Isaiah's Song of the Vineyard (cf. Isa 5:1–7). Speaking for the Lord, the prophet Isaiah complained that, despite loving care, the vineyard planted and nurtured on the hill produced worthless grapes. The parable is an allegory and is a juridical parable, a parable that induces the hearers to pass judgment on themselves. The vineyard is Israel, its owner is God, and the fruit is the behavior of Israel, as seen in economics and justice. Israel has no excuse: "What more could God do for his people?" Therefore, the nation may expect judgment. Jesus' parable presupposes these allegorical features but adds tenant farmers to the story and reassigns the guilt (Israel is not at fault; its religious leaders are) and redirects the judgment (the religious leaders will lose their stewardship).

Matthew's account of the parable begins, "There was a landowner who planted a vineyard, put a fence around it, dug a wine press in it, and built a watchtower. Then he leased it to tenants and went to another country" (**v. 33**). The shift of focus from the nation as a whole to the religious leaders, specifically the ruling priests, was not unique to Jesus. A small fragment from Qumran (4Q500), which dates to the first century B.C., alludes to Isaiah's Song of the Vineyard (Isa 5:1–7) and identifies it with the temple. This identification is made explicit in the later Aramaic paraphrase of Isaiah (the Targum). This is seen clearly in vv. 1–2 and 5, with departures from the Hebrew Bible placed in italics:

The prophet said, I will sing now for *Israel – which is like a vineyard, the seed of Abraham, my friend – my friend's* song for his vineyard: *My people*, my beloved *Israel, I gave them a heritage on a high* hill *in* fertile *land.* ² And I *sanctified* them and I *glorified* them and I *established them as the plant of a* choice vine; and *I* built *my sanctuary* in *their* midst, and I even *gave my altar to atone for their sins; I thought that they would do good deeds, but they made their deeds evil.* ⁵ And now I will tell you what I *am about to do* to my *people.* I will *take up my Shekinah from them*, and *they* shall be for *plundering*; I will break down *the place of their sanctuaries*, and *they will be* for *trampling.*⁴⁶²

The "watch tower" of Hebrew Isaiah has become God's "sanctuary" in the Aramaic, and the "wine vat" of Hebrew Isaiah has become the "altar to atone for their sins" in the Aramaic. Because of Israel's sin, God's presence, or "Shekinah," will be withdrawn (an allusion to God's departure from the temple described in Ezek 10:1–22; 11:22–25) and the "sanctuaries" (i.e., the temple and other buildings in the temple precincts, perhaps also synagogues) will be destroyed. In later rabbinic literature, the watchtower and wine vat are explicitly equated with the temple and altar, respectively (cf. *t. Meʿila* 1.16; *t. Sukkah* 3.15).

---

⁴⁶² The translation is based on B. D. Chilton, *The Isaiah Targum* (ArBib 11; Wilmington, DE: Glazier, 1987), 10–11.

Jesus' use of Isaiah's Song of the Vineyard presupposed aspects of this interpretive orientation. However, his introduction of tenant farmers, which he identified with the chief priests, was innovative but readily understood and deeply resented.

Jesus' parable immediately calls to mind several rabbinic parables. A parable attributed to Rabbi Simeon ben Halafta begins: "To what may this be compared? To one man living in Galilee and owning a vineyard in Judea, and another man living in Judea and owning a vineyard in Galilee" (*Midr. Tanhuma* B: *Qedoshin* §6 [on Lev 19:1]). One also thinks of the parable applied to Egypt, which had once enslaved Israel: "They were like robbers who had broken into the king's vineyard and destroyed the vines. When the king discovered that his vineyards had been destroyed, he was filled with wrath, and descending upon the robbers, without help from anything or anyone, he cut them down and uprooted them as they had done to his vineyard" (*Exod. Rab.* 30.17 [on Exod 21:18]). Another parable, attributed to Rabbi Simeon ben Yohai (ca. 140 A.D.), equates Israel to a vineyard and appeals to Isa 5:7:

Rabbi Simeon ben Yohai said: "Why was Israel likened to a vineyard? In the case of a vineyard, in the beginning one must hoe it, then weed it, and then erect supports when he sees the clusters [forming]. Then he must return to pluck the grapes and press them in order to extract the wine from them. So also Israel – each and every shepherd who oversees them must tend them [as he would tend a vineyard]. Where [in Scripture] is Israel called a vineyard? In the verse, 'For the vineyard of the Lord of Hosts is the House of Israel, and the seedling he lovingly tended are the men of Judah' [Isa 5:7]." (*Sipre Deut.* §312 [on Deut 32:9])

The parable of the unworthy tenants is sometimes cited as an illustrative parallel. In it we have an example of problems between the owner of a vineyard (God) and the tenants of his vineyard (the Canaanites), whom he evicts to make room for his son (Israel).

Another parable that has nothing to do with a vineyard or farming nevertheless well illustrates betrayal of a trust and the exaggerated naivete of the protagonist. This parable illustrates how in parables people sometimes behave in extraordinary ways:

The parable, as told by Rabbi Yose the Galilean, concerned a mortal king who had set out for a city far across the sea. As he was about to entrust his son to the care of a wicked guardian, his friends and servants said to him: My lord king, do not entrust your son to this wicked guardian. Nevertheless the king, ignoring the counsel of his friends and servants, entrusted his son to the wicked guardian. What did the guardian do? He proceeded to destroy the king's city, have his house consumed by fire, and slay his son with the sword. After a while the king returned. When he saw his city destroyed and desolate, his house consumed by fire, his son slain with the sword, he pulled out the hair of his head and his beard and broke out into wild weeping, saying: Woe is me! How foolish I have been, how sense-lessly I acted in this kingdom of mine in entrusting my son to a wicked guardian! (*Seder Elijah Rab.* §28)

These parables parallel at many points the principal elements that make up Jesus' parable of the wicked vineyard tenants. Rabbi Simeon's parable speaks of absentee vineyard owners. The next parable talks of an angry king who takes vengeance on men who had violated his vineyard. The third parable is based on Isaiah 5, as is Jesus' parable of the vineyard. Note, too, how Simeon ben Yohai mixes his metaphors by introducing "shepherds." Jesus likewise introduces a new metaphor by appending a scriptural proof text about "builders" (i.e., Ps 118:22–23). The fourth parable, attrib-uted to Yose the Galilean (second century A.D.), describes a remarkably foolish and incautious king who entrusts his son to a villain.

Several details of this parable have significance for Jesus' parable of the vineyard. In Yose's parable, we have a man who appears to utterly lack common sense. Against the advice of friends and counselors, he entrusts his son to a man known to be a "wicked guardian." But the actions of the guardian are just as difficult to compre-hend. We are not told that he stole anything or profited in any way by his actions. He destroys the king's city, burns down his house, and murders his son. What could he possibly have hoped to gain? Did he imagine that he could get away with these crimes? Would not every hearer of this parable suppose that the king would send troops after the guardian and have him executed? How could the owner of the vine-yard be so foolish and so reckless with the lives of his servants and especially the life of his son? What could the tenants realistically have hoped to gain? Did they not know that the owner had the power to come and destroy them? Did they really imagine that they could inherit the vineyard?[463]

---

[463] Some scholars believe that the Markan form of the parable, followed by Matthew and Luke, has been allegorized and updated by Greek-speaking, Septuagint-reading Christians and that an older, independent form of the parable has been preserved in the *Gospel of Thomas* §§65–66. For a detailed defense of this view, see J. S. Kloppenborg, *The Tenants in the Vineyard* (WUNT 195; Tübingen: Mohr Siebeck, 2006). The major weakness of this interpretation is its failure to sufficiently account for the Judaic parallels and back-ground of the Synoptic form(s) of the parable of the vineyard on the one hand and the thoroughly redacted form of the parable and its context as found in *Thomas* on the other. In keeping with its second-century Syrian asceticism, *Thomas* presents the parable of the vineyard, along with edited Synoptic materials in §§63–64, as a challenge to wealth and materialism. The perspective of *Thomas* coheres with second-century Syrian Christianity, not with the first-century Palestinian Jesus, whose parable is much more accurately and realistically reflected in the first-century Synoptic Gospels. For criticism of arguments for the antiquity and independence of the parable in *Thomas*, see K. R. Snodgrass, "The Parable of the Wicked Husbandmen: Is the Gospel of Thomas Version the Original?" *NTS* 21 (1974): 142–44; K. R. Snodgrass, *Stories with Intent: A Comprehensive Guide to the Parables of Jesus* (Grand Rapids, MI: Eerdmans, 2007), 276–99, 677–86.

Matthew's account of the vineyard parable begins, "There was a landowner who planted a vineyard.... Then he leased it to tenants and went to another country" (**v. 33**). Borrowing details from Isaiah's Song of the Vineyard (Isa 5:1–7), Jesus creates a parable about leased land and tenant vinedressers. In doing this, Jesus has followed a common theme we see in rabbinic parables, some of which were reviewed earlier, and has presupposed business practices common in his day, as we see in the papyri and other types of literature. There is nothing about this verse or the next (**v. 34**) that would have seemed unusual to his hearers. The chief priests and others standing by who knew well the Book of Isaiah probably heard the allusions to Isaiah 5. Aware of its judgmental nature, especially as seen in later interpretations (4Q500; *Tg.* Isa 5:1–7; *t. Me'ila* 1.16; *t. Sukkah* 3.15), in which the passage is more directly aimed at the temple establishment, the chief priests may well have anticipated the parable's dramatic conclusion. Of course, Jesus has not only introduced "tenants" of the vineyard but will also introduce a "son" of the vineyard owner.[464]

The tenants prove to be utter rascals (**vv. 35–36**), not only refusing to abide by the terms of the lease agreement but beating and murdering the servants of the vineyard owner who have been sent to collect payment.[465] It is not likely that the hearers of Jesus' parable shared the owner's optimism in thinking that the tenants would respect his son (**v. 37**). No indeed, "when the tenants saw the son, they said to themselves, 'This is the heir; come, let us kill him and get his inheritance'" (**v. 38**). The nefarious plan of the tenants mimics a theme in the rabbinic parables considered earlier. But the tenants of Jesus' parable have no more chance of succeeding than the tenants in the parables of the Rabbis.

Matthew continues, "So they seized him, threw him out of the vineyard, and killed him" (**v. 39**). We find in the correspondence of a man named Zenon, which dates to the middle of the third century B.C., an actual parallel to Jesus' parable. Zenon's agent, a man named Alexandros, sent a servant with another man named Straton in order to collect a debt from a Jewish man named Jeddous. The mission was a failure, and Alexandros writes to a colleague to explain:

I have received your letter, to which you added a copy of the letter written by Zenon to Jeddous saying that unless he gave the money to Straton, Zenon's man, we were to

---

[464] On the Judaic background of the parable of the vineyard, see K. R. Snodgrass, *The Parable of the Wicked Tenants* (WUNT 27; Tübingen: Mohr-Siebeck, 1983); C. A. Evans, "God's Vineyard and Its Caretakers," in *Jesus and His Contemporaries: Comparative Studies* (AGJU 25; Leiden: Brill, 1995), 381–406.

[465] In v. 35, Matthew adds "and stoned another." Mark's version of the parable says nothing about servants being stoned. Matthew may have introduced this detail to draw the description of the persecution and murder of the servants (who in the allegory are understood as God's prophets) closer to Jesus' saying about Jerusalem's tragic history of opposing and sometimes killing God's prophets: "Jerusalem, Jerusalem, the city that kills the prophets and stones those who are sent to it!" (Matt 23:37). For this reason, Matthew increases the number of servants sent to collect the fruit of the vineyard.

hand over his pledge to him [Straton]. I happened to be unwell as a result of taking some medicine, so I sent a young man, a servant of mine, to Straton, and wrote a letter to Jeddous. When they returned they said that he had taken no notice of my letter, but had attacked them and thrown them out of the village. So I am writing to you. (P.Cair.Zen. 59.018, 258 B.C.)

The reference to having been "attacked and thrown out [*egbalein*] of the village" closely parallels Matt 21:39: "they seized him, threw [*ekballein*] him out of the vineyard." What is amazing is that Zenon was the chief steward for Apollonius, the minister of finance for the king of Egypt (Ptolemy III), who at that time controlled Israel. Jeddous' treatment of the servants of Zenon, himself a servant of the king, is no more surprising than the vineyard tenants' treatment of the servants and son in Jesus' parable.

According to Mark's version, the vineyard tenants seized the son and "killed him, and threw him out of the vineyard" (Mark 12:8). Matthew has reversed the order of the killing and throwing to throwing and *then* killing. Why? Probably for two reasons: (1) to keep with Jewish custom of not executing someone within a city, and (2) to mirror what actually happened to Jesus (who is the "son" of the parable), for he was led out of the city and then put to death.

Jesus asks his audience, "Now when the owner of the vineyard comes, what will he do to those tenants?" (**v. 40**). The question is rhetorical, of course. Everyone knows what the owner of the vineyard will do. Accordingly, the crowd responds, "He will put those wretches to a miserable death, and lease the vineyard to other tenants who will give him the produce at the harvest time" (**v. 41**). In Mark, it is not clear that anyone speaks up in answer to Jesus' question, "What will the owner of the vineyard do?" (Mark 12:9). In Matthew, the crowd, perhaps including some of the chief priests themselves, is so caught up in the story that they burst out in condemnation of the wickedness of the tenant farmers.

With the chief priests and elders in mind (Matt 21:23), Jesus asks, "Have you never read in the scriptures: 'The stone that the builders rejected has become the cornerstone; this was the Lord's doing, and it is amazing in our eyes'?" (**v. 42**). The question is again rhetorical; of course they have read this passage of Scripture, which is Ps 118:22–23. What drew a passage about a rejected *stone* to a parable about a rejected *son*? Once again, the Aramaic paraphrase of Scripture may provide an important clue. According to the Targum to the Psalms: "The boy [or son] which the builders abandoned was among the sons of Jesse and he is worthy to be appointed king and ruler." The Aramaic version understands the rejected stone to be none other than David, the son of Jesse, who is "worthy to be appointed king and ruler." The equation of stone with boy or son is probably based on a play on words, for in Hebrew "the stone" is *haeben* and "the son" is *haben*. This play on words is likely what lies behind John the Baptist's assertion, "God is able from these stones to raise up children [or sons] to Abraham" (Matt 3:9 = Luke 3:8). The "builders" would in all probability have been identified with Israel's religious leaders, in either positive or negative colors (cf. CD 4:19; 8:12, 18; Acts 4:11; 1 Cor 3:10; *Song Rab.* 1:5 §3; *Exod. Rab.* 23.10 [on Exod 15:11]; *b. Ber.* 64a; *b. Shabbat* 114a).

In Matthew (but not in Mark), Jesus warns the chief priests and elders (which includes Pharisees; see v. 45): "Therefore I tell you, the kingdom of God will be taken away from you and given to a people that produces the fruits of the kingdom" (**v. 43**). This verse is sometimes mistakenly thought to mean that the kingdom of God will be taken away from the Jewish people and will be given to Gentiles (or to the Christian church). This interpretation points to the word "nation" (Greek: *ethne*). However, such an interpretation is inconsistent with Matthew's very pro-Jewish stance. Jesus' words allude to Dan 7:27: "The kingship and dominion and the greatness of the kingdoms under the whole heaven shall be given to the people of the holy ones of the Most High." The kingdom of God, which in Matthew is closely related to the nation of Israel, will be taken away from the ruling priests and will be given to a people (made up of true believers, which will include Jews and Gentiles) whose leadership will result in the "fruits" that God expects.[466]

Matthew then has Jesus adding, "The one who falls on this stone will be broken to pieces; and it will crush anyone on whom it falls" (**v. 44**). This verse is omitted by some ancient manuscripts and some modern translations (such as the RSV). Although it is present in many manuscripts, including our earliest codices (i.e., Codex Sinaiticus and Codex Vaticanus), many interpreters suspect that it is an early scribal addition to Matthew based on Luke 20:18.

In Matthew, Jesus' words induce the following reaction: "When the chief priests and the Pharisees heard his parables, they realized that he was speaking about them" (**v. 45**). In Mark 12:12, the chief priests perceive that Jesus "had told this parable against them." Because Matthew has included the parable of the two sons (Matt 21:28–32), he notes that "chief priests and the Pharisees" understood (rightly) that both parables were speaking "against them." The sudden appearance of the Pharisees is a bit of a surprise. They were not mentioned previously in the immediate context, nor are they present in Mark's account. It may be that Matthew is anticipating their appearance in Matt 22:15–22, where they will ask Jesus about paying taxes. We should assume that they are among "the elders" (v. 23; cf. Matt 16:21).

Matthew continues, "They wanted to arrest him, but they feared the crowds, because they regarded him as a prophet" (**v. 46**). The meaning of Isa 5:1–7 (outlined earlier) was known to the ruling priests. Therefore they readily appreciated the point Jesus was making and resented it. They would have seized Jesus on the spot but did not dare out of fear of how the crowds might react. Moreover, Matthew's

---

[466] See also 1 Sam 15:28: "Samuel said to him [i.e., Saul], 'The Lord has torn the kingdom of Israel from you this very day, and has given it to a neighbor [i.e., David] of yours, who is better than you.'"

statement here echoes what was said earlier about John the Baptist in Matt 21:26: "we are afraid of the crowd; for all regard John as a prophet." John was a prophet, whose authority was from heaven; Jesus, too, is a prophet, whose authority is from heaven.

MATTHEW 22:1–14 – THE PARABLE OF THE WEDDING BANQUET

22:1: Once more Jesus spoke to them in parables, saying:

22:2: "The kingdom of heaven may be compared to a king who gave a wedding banquet for his son.

22:3: He sent his slaves to call those who had been invited to the wedding banquet, but they would not come.

22:4: Again he sent other slaves, saying, 'Tell those who have been invited: Look, I have prepared my dinner, my oxen and my fat calves have been slaughtered, and everything is ready; come to the wedding banquet.'

22:5: But they made light of it and went away, one to his farm, another to his business,

22:6: while the rest seized his slaves, mistreated them, and killed them.

22:7: The king was enraged. He sent his troops, destroyed those murderers, and burned their city.

22:8: Then he said to his slaves, 'The wedding is ready, but those invited were not worthy.

22:9: Go therefore into the main streets, and invite everyone you find to the wedding banquet.'

22:10: Those slaves went out into the streets and gathered all whom they found, both good and bad; so the wedding hall was filled with guests.

22:11: "But when the king came in to see the guests, he noticed a man there who was not wearing a wedding robe,

22:12: and he said to him, 'Friend, how did you get in here without a wedding robe?' And he was speechless.

22:13: Then the king said to the attendants, 'Bind him hand and foot, and throw him into the outer darkness, where there will be weeping and gnashing of teeth.'

22:14: For many are called, but few are chosen."

*M*atthew's parable of the wedding banquet bears an uncertain relationship to Luke's similar parable of the great banquet (Luke 14:15–24). Many commentators think that the Matthean form of the parable has been updated to reflect Christology rather than election and to reflect the destruction of the city of Jerusalem in 70 A.D.[467] In any case, the differences between the two versions will be highlighted in the commentary.

Matthew's version of the parable begins, "The kingdom of heaven may be compared to a king who gave a wedding banquet for his son" (**v. 1**). In Luke, it is simply "someone" (Luke 14:16); he is not a king. Moreover, Luke's host gave a "great dinner"; nothing is said of a wedding banquet or of a son being honored. These elements in Matthew's form of the parable may point to God's recognition of Jesus as the groom and Israel as his bride (Matt 9:15; Eph 5:25–27; Rev 21:2, 9; 22:17; see also Matt 25:1–3, the parable of the bridesmaids, who are to await the arrival of the bridegroom). The details of this parable cohere with a setting in which a wealthy man lives in a villa outside a nearby city.[468]

When the time for the banquet comes, the invited guests refuse to attend (**v. 3**). More servants are sent with a message from the king, saying, "Look, I have prepared my dinner, my oxen and my fat calves have been slaughtered, and everything is ready; come to the wedding banquet" (**v. 4**). But those invited made light of it and carried on with their routines (**v. 5**). Others mistreated the king's servants, even killing them (**v. 6**). This verse has no equivalent in Luke's form of the parable. To be sure, the invited guests are discourteous in excusing themselves from the feast (and it is assumed that they had originally agreed to attend when the invitations had been extended on an earlier occasion). Luke says this in Luke 14:18–20, and Matthew relates this in much condensed form in v. 5.

Not surprisingly, the "king was enraged. He sent his troops, destroyed those murderers, and burned their city" (**v. 7**). Again, there is no parallel in Luke's version of the parable. This Matthean detail could mirror the horrors of the capture and destruction of Jerusalem and the temple. Josephus greatly emphasizes the fiery catastrophe: "You would indeed have thought that the temple mount ... was boiling over from its base, being everywhere one mass of flame" (*J.W.* 6.275). He mentions in many places Jerusalem's fiery destruction (e.g., *J.W.* 6.165–68, 177–85, 190–92, 228–35, 250–84, 316, 346, 353–55, 407, 434).[469] Looking back on the fiery destruction of the city and temple, rabbinic interpreters applied Zech 11:1: "Open your doors, O Lebanon, so that fire may devour your cedars" (cf. *y. Sota* 6.3). The king's rage is

---

[467] See D. C. Allison, Jr. and W. D. Davies, *A Critical and Exegetical Commentary on the Gospel According to Saint Matthew* (1988–1997), 3:210; but D. A. Hagner, *Matthew* (1993–1995), 2:628, 630, expresses some doubts.

[468] J. F. Strange, "Some Implications of Archaeology for New Testament Studies," in J. H. Charlesworth and W. P. Weaver (eds.), *What Has Archaeology To Do with Faith?* (1992), 23–59, especially 46–47.

[469] The language of v. 7 may well reflect the language of the Old Testament, in which the city of Jerusalem and the temple are said to have been "burned with fire" (e.g., 2 Kings 25:9; 2 Chron 36:19; Isa 64:11; Jer 21:10). As such, it may not be a post-70 reflection.

understandable, for the behavior of those invited to the banquet is unpardonable, especially in the Middle Eastern culture of the first century.

The king now decides to invite other people because "those invited were not worthy" (**v. 8**). Their unworthiness was made evident by their refusal to answer the summons to the banquet and by their outrageous treatment of the king's servants.[470] The king's servants are now to go "into the main streets" and invite all they find (**v. 9**). The "all whom they found" is in reference to the general populace, including those that many religiously observant people would think of as "sinners." So the servants "went out into the streets and gathered all whom they found, both good and bad; so the wedding hall was filled with guests" (**v. 10**).

Gathering in "both good and bad" sets the stage for the second part of the parable (vv. 11–14), in which the king reviews his guests and identifies those who are not worthy. This added detail is in step with Matthew's interest in parables about the good and the bad (such as the parable of the wheat and the weeds, the parable of the drag net, or the parable of the wise and foolish maids). Again, this is to be explained as Matthew's close association of the kingdom of heaven with Israel itself. Not all Israel will be saved; some will have to be culled out.

The second part of the parable begins, "But when the king came in to see the guests, he noticed a man there who was not wearing a wedding robe …" (**vv. 11–12**). It finds a parallel in rabbinic literature:

Rabbi Yohanan ben Zakkai [late first century A.D.] said, "This may be compared to a king who summoned his servants to a banquet without appointing a time. The wise ones adorned themselves and sat at the door of the palace, for they said, 'Is anything lacking in a royal palace?' The fools went about their work, saying, 'Can there be a banquet without preparations?' Suddenly the king desired his servants. The wise entered adorned, while the fools entered soiled. The king rejoiced at the wise but was angry with the fools. 'Those who adorned themselves for the banquet,' he ordered, 'let them sit, eat and drink. But those who did not adorn themselves for the banquet, let them stand and watch.'" (*b. Shabbat* 153b; cf. *Eccl. Rab.* 3:9 §1)

In Matthew's parable, the man without the "wedding robe" probably represents Jewish leaders who ignore Jesus' summons to repent and embrace the kingdom of God and, possibly, faithless disciples who initially accept Jesus' summons but fail to endure.[471]

Matthew continues, "Then the king said to the attendants, 'Bind him hand and foot, and throw him into the outer darkness, where there will be weeping and gnashing of teeth'" (**v. 13**). The command of the king may be an allusion to *1 Enoch* 10:4a: "And he said to Raphael, 'Go, Raphael, and bind Azael hand and foot, and cast him

---

470   P. Ballard, "Reasons for Refusing the Great Supper," *JTS* 23 (1972): 341–50.
471   See D. C. Sim, "The Man without the Wedding Garment," *HeyJ* 31 (1990): 165–78.

into the darkness." The Greek of Matthew parallels quite closely Greek *1 Enoch*;[472] see the commentary on Matt 8:12.

Jesus' well-known dictum, "For many are called, but few are chosen" (**v. 14**), finds many parallels in Jewish literature of late antiquity: "Many have been created, but few will be saved" (4 Ezra 8:3); "There are more who perish than will be saved" (4 Ezra 9:15).[473]

MATTHEW 22:15–22 – ON TAXATION

22:15: Then the Pharisees went and plotted to entrap him in what he said.

22:16: So they sent their disciples to him, along with the Herodians, saying, "Teacher, we know that you are sincere, and teach the way of God in accordance with truth, and show deference to no one; for you do not regard people with partiality.

22:17: Tell us, then, what you think. Is it lawful to pay taxes to the emperor, or not?"

22:18: But Jesus, aware of their malice, said, "Why are you putting me to the test, you hypocrites?

22:19: Show me the coin used for the tax." And they brought him a denarius.

22:20: Then he said to them, "Whose head is this, and whose title?"

22:21: They answered, "The emperor's." Then he said to them, "Give therefore to the emperor the things that are the emperor's, and to God the things that are God's."

22:22: When they heard this, they were amazed; and they left him and went away.

In an effort to lure Jesus into making a dangerous statement, the Pharisees ask whether or not it is lawful to pay taxes to Caesar. The question is a good one; many Jews in first-century Palestine pondered it. For Jesus to say "yes" would diminish his popularity (and make it easier for the ruling priests to arrest him); to say "no" would easily lead to a charge of sedition, making Roman arrest all but inevitable

---

[472] D. C. Sim, "Matthew 22.13a and 1 Enoch 10.4a: A Case of Literary Dependence?" *JSNT* 47 (1992): 3–19.

[473] For further discussion of the parable, see J. D. M. Derrett, "The Parable of the Great Supper," in *Law in the New Testament* (London: Darton, Longman and Todd, 1970), 126–55; E. E. Lemcio, "The Parables of the Great Supper and the Wedding Feast: History, Redaction and Canon," *HBT* 8 (1986): 1–26; B. F. Meyer, "Many (= All) are Called, but Few (= Not All) are Chosen," *NTS* 36 (1990): 89–97; D. C. Sim, "The Man without the Wedding Garment (Matthew 22:11–13)," *HeyJ* 31 (1990): 165–78.

(see Josephus, *J.W.* 2.117, who tells of Judas the Galilean, ca. 6–9 A.D., who upbraided fellow Jews as cowards for paying tribute to the Romans). Matthew follows Mark's version of the story but makes a few changes that sharpen aspects of the drama.

Matthew's version emphasizes the premeditated nature of the plan against Jesus: "Then the Pharisees went and plotted to entrap him in what he said" (**v. 15**). They "plotted to entrap" Jesus before approaching him.

Matthew continues, "So they sent their disciples to him, along with the Herodians" (**v. 16**). His rearrangement now clears up the confusion in Mark's "they sent" (Mark 12:13). In Mark's narrative, it is not clear who sent the Pharisees and Herodians. Now we know that Pharisaic teachers (it would be inferred) sent some of their disciples, along with the Herodians.[474] The opening flattery, "Teacher, we know that you are sincere …," lays it on thick. But the question, "Is it lawful to pay taxes to the emperor, or not?" (**v. 17**), cuts to the chase.

In his account of Jesus' response, "But Jesus, aware of their malice, said, "Why are you putting me to the test, you hypocrites?" (**v. 18**), Matthew postpones Mark's "hypocrisy," which he will transform into "hypocrites," and adds "malice," revealing more fully the sinister nature of the plot against Jesus.

Jesus then instructs his questioners, "Show me the coin used for the tax" (**v. 19**). Mark's version reads "Bring me a coin, and let me look at it" (Mark 12:15). Matthew's version specifically requests the money used for paying the tax (which was the denarius).

As he has done on other occasions, Jesus counters with a question of his own: "Whose head is this, and whose title?" (**v. 20**) (cf. Matt 9:4–5; 19:17; 21:24–25). Most Greek and Roman coins bore the image of the ruler, along with his title. Some of these titles, "Lord," "Savior," "Son of God," and the like, were very offensive to the Jewish people.

The Pharisees' disciples and the Herodians answer the question put to them, "The emperor's" (**v. 21a**), to which Jesus gives his famous reply: "Give therefore to the emperor the things that are the emperor's, and to God the things that are God's" (**v. 21b**).

Matthew concludes the story with: "When they heard this, they were amazed; and they left him and went away" (**v. 22**). He adds that "they" (which includes the Pharisees and not just their disciples sent to question Jesus, as well as the Herodians)

---

[474] This is the only appearance of "Herodians" in the Gospel of Matthew (cf. Mark 3:6; 12:13). Nothing is known of this group or party. It is assumed that they are loyal to one or more of the Herodian rulers. See J. P. Meier, "The Historical Jesus and the Historical Herodians," *JBL* 119 (2000): 740–46. Meier suspects the combination of Pharisees and Herodians is editorial (on the part of Mark, then followed by Matthew). Perhaps. Josephus tells us that there existed a détente of sorts between Herod the Great and the Essenes (*Ant.* 15.372–78). If this was truly the case, an alliance of convenience between the Pharisees, who were at odds with the Sadducees, and supporters of the Herodians (instead of the Roman governors?) is possible.

"went away," which clears the stage for the Sadducees, who are next to take on Jesus (cf. Matt 22:23–33).

Since arriving in Jerusalem, Jesus has been rumored to be a messianic descendant of David and proclaimer of the kingdom of God. As Israel's sovereign, surely he would not authorize payment of taxes to a foreign king, would he? But, as we have seen, Jesus did not take the bait. Jesus' answer was clever to be sure, but it was more than that.[475] Lying behind it is probably the principle of conscience, a principle that will surface elsewhere in early Christian literature (for example, in Paul's letters to Corinth and Rome). As long as one gives God what is due, it matters little what is given to the emperor.[476]

MATTHEW 22:23–33 – GOD OF THE LIVING

22:23: The same day some Sadducees came to him, saying there is no resurrection; and they asked him a question, saying,

22:24: "Teacher, Moses said, 'If a man dies childless, his brother shall marry the widow, and raise up children for his brother.'

22:25: Now there were seven brothers among us; the first married, and died childless, leaving the widow to his brother.

22:26: The second did the same, so also the third, down to the seventh.

22:27: Last of all, the woman herself died.

22:28: In the resurrection, then, whose wife of the seven will she be? For all of them had married her."

22:29: Jesus answered them, "You are wrong, because you know neither the scriptures nor the power of God.

22:30: For in the resurrection they neither marry nor are given in marriage, but are like angels in heaven.

22:31: And as for the resurrection of the dead, have you not read what was said to you by God,

22:32: 'I am the God of Abraham, the God of Isaac, and the God of Jacob'? He is God not of the dead, but of the living."

22:33: And when the crowd heard it, they were astounded at his teaching.

---

[475] It is neither dissembling nor a sign of weakness; pace W. R. Herzog, "Dissembling, a Weapon of the Weak: The Case of Christ and Caesar in Mark 12:13–17 and Romans 13:1–7," *Perspectives in Religious Studies* 21 (1994): 339–60.

[476] For further discussion, see A. J. Hultgren, *Jesus and His Adversaries* (1979), 75–78; F. F. Bruce, "'Render to Caesar,'" in E. Bammel and C. F. D. Moule (eds.), *Jesus and the Politics of His Day* (Cambridge: Cambridge University Press, 1984), 249–63.

*M*atthew's account of the question about the resurrection of the dead draws upon and closely follows Mark 12:18–27, but he does make a few minor changes. Having dodged a potentially dangerous political question, Jesus is now tested with a tricky theological one. The Sadducees know that Jesus, like the Pharisees, believes in the resurrection. The Sadducees believe in no such thing (see Acts 23:8; Josephus, *J.W.* 2.154–66), which for Matthew's readers means that they would roundly reject Jesus' previous predictions of his own resurrection (Matt 16:21; 17:22–23; 20:17–19). The Sadducees attempt to show that belief in the resurrection leads to violation of the commandments of Moses. They reason that if a woman is married successively to seven brothers (in keeping with the law of levirate marriage; see Deut 25:5–6), then in the resurrection she will have seven husbands, which of course is adulterous and unlawful.

Matthew reports that "The same day some Sadducees came to him, saying there is no resurrection; and they asked him a question" (**v. 23**). Matthew adds "the same day" to heighten Jesus' prowess in defending himself against the establishment's top guns. The Sadducees have made several appearances in Matthew (Matt 3:7; 16:1, 6, 11, 12). This will be their last (cf. Matt 22:34, which refers to the present passage). The evangelist tells us that the Sadducees say "there is no resurrection." Josephus reports the same (*J.W.* 2.165, "will have none of it"; *Ant.* 18.16, "the soul perishes along with the body"). This is also mentioned in rabbinic literature, where we are told the Sadducees used to say: "It is a tradition among the Pharisees to afflict themselves in this world; yet in the world to come they will have nothing" (*Abot deRabbi Nathan* A 5.2).

The Sadducees begin by laying out their problem for Jesus: "Teacher, Moses said, 'If a man dies childless, his brother shall marry the widow, and raise up children for his brother'" (**v. 24**). Matthew has simplified Mark (cf. Mark 12:19). The Sadducees are referring to the Levirate law (cf. Deut 25:5–6). Its observance evidently predated the Law of Moses (cf. Gen 38:8: "Perform the duty of a brother-in-law to her; raise up offspring for your brother").

The Sadducees continue, "Now there were seven brothers among us …" (**vv. 25–27**). Matthew adds "among us," perhaps implying that the Sadducees' hypothetical story about a hapless woman married successively to seven brothers is not hypothetical at all but a real story![477] Perhaps as they tell it they pretend to be sincerely concerned and want insight into the eternal fate of all concerned. According to Josephus, quarreling with teachers is just the sort of thing the Sadducees enjoyed doing (*Ant.* 18.16, "they regard it a virtue to dispute with the teachers of the path of wisdom").

---

[477]   The reference to seven brothers is sometimes understood as an allusion to the seven martyred brothers in 2 Macc 7. It is more likely, however, that the reference is to the seven husbands of Tob 3:8, who married but died without issue. See P. Bolt, "What Were the Sadducees Reading? An Enquiry into the Literary Background of Mark 12:18–23," *TynBul* 45 (1994): 369–94.

After explaining the problem, the Sadducees ask Jesus: "In the resurrection, then, whose wife of the seven will she be? For all of them had married her" (**v. 28**). The conundrum is meant to show the silliness, if not impossibility, of the idea of resurrection, for if there really was a resurrection, then the Law of Moses has created a problem. Thanks to the Levirate law, there will be one woman and seven husbands in the resurrection! Therefore, given the Levirate law, which Moses himself commanded, there can be no resurrection.

Jesus begins his reply with a rhetorical retort: "You are wrong, because you know neither the scriptures nor the power of God" (**v. 29**). The Sadducees do not know the Scriptures, by which Jesus means both the Law of Moses – the only Scriptures respected by the Sadducees – and other Scriptures, such as Daniel and the Prophets. For example, it is declared in Isaiah: "Your dead shall live, their corpses shall rise. O dwellers in the dust, awake and sing for joy!" (Isa 26:19). And in Daniel, perhaps alluding to this passage in Isaiah, we read: "Many of those who sleep in the dust of the earth shall awake, some to everlasting life, and some to shame and everlasting contempt" (Dan 12:2). Of course, Jesus knows these Scriptures mean nothing to the Sadducees. In v. 32, he will appeal to a passage of Scripture that they should take seriously.

In this resurrected state, the righteous "neither marry nor are given in marriage, but are like angels in heaven" (**v. 30**). According to Dan 12:3, the righteous will be "like stars," which in Job 38:7 are compared to "heavenly beings." Other traditions compare the righteous and/or resurrected with angels (cf. *T. Isaac* 4:45–47; Philo, *Sacr.* 1.5; *2 Bar* 51:5). As angelic beings, there will be no marriage. Accordingly, the Levirate law only applies to the present age, not to the age to come, and therefore belief in the resurrection does not contradict Moses.

In **vv. 31–32**, Jesus speaks directly to the Sadducees' rejection of the resurrection. Matthew replaces Mark's "have you not read in the book of Moses" (Mark 12:26) with "have you not read what was said to you by God." This interesting change enhances the authority of the passage to which Jesus has appealed. It also personalizes it. No longer is it simply a story about what God said to Moses; it is God speaking to the Sadducees and to anyone who reads or hears. But the Sadducees do not hear God, for they "know neither the scriptures nor the power of God" (v. 29). Jesus, of course, does know the power of God, for he has healed and has raised the dead (e.g., Matt 11:5).

Because God continues to speak, his words to Moses, "I am the God of Abraham, the God of Isaac, and the God of Jacob," remain relevant and powerful. Accordingly, Jesus can affirm, "He is God not of the dead, but of the living." Death may annul a human covenant (such as marriage), but it does not annul God's covenant with the patriarchs.[478]

---

[478] On this important point, see B. R. Trick, "Death, Covenants, and the Proof of the Resurrection in Mark 12:18–27," *NovT* 49 (2007): 232–56.

The argument turns on an inference drawn from parallel truths. God is the God of the patriarchs and also the God of the living; therefore the patriarchs, though presently dead, must someday live. Jesus' argument parallels very closely an argument Philo makes, whereby the three great patriarchs are spoken of as eternal (cf. Philo, *On Abraham* 50–55). Also relevant is *4 Macc* 7:18–19, "But as men with their whole heart make righteousness their first thought, these alone are able to master the weakness of the flesh, believing that unto God they die not, as our patriarchs, Abraham and Isaac and Jacob die not, but they live unto God" (on the last phrase, see Luke 20:38), as well as *4 Macc* 16:25, "those who die for the sake of God live unto God, as do Abraham and Isaac and Jacob and all the patriarchs."

The tradition here in *4 Maccabees* complements Jesus' inference from Exod 3:6 and the truism that God is a God "of the living." Especially interesting is Rabbi Hiyya's interpretation in *y. Ber.* 2.3:

You know how to recite [Scripture] but you do not know how to interpret [the verse]: 'The living know that they will die' [Qoh 9:5] refers to the righteous who are called 'the living' even when they are dead.... And whence do we know that the righteous are called 'the living' even when dead? For it is written, 'This is the land of which I swore to Abraham, to Isaac, and to Jacob, saying' [Deut 34:4] (cf. *b. Ber.* 18a).

We have a roughly parallel argument for the resurrection in rabbinic literature, where Rabbi Simeon ben Eleazar says,

On the following basis I proved that the versions of Scripture of the Samaritans are forgeries, for they maintained that the dead do not live. I said to them, "Lo, Scripture says, '... such a person shall be utterly cut off and bear the guilt' (Num 15:31)." For Scripture says, "bear the guilt," only so as to indicate that it is destined to give a full accounting of itself on the day of judgment. (*Sipre Num.* §112 [on Num 15:27–31])

In other words, because Scripture promises the wicked a full accounting of their iniquity, they must be raised up to face it on the day of judgment (thus proving the resurrection).

Matthew adds the conclusion, "And when the crowd heard it, they were astounded at his teaching" (**v. 33**), which parallels the conclusion at the end of the debate over taxation (cf. Matt 22:22).[479]

MATTHEW 22:34–40 – WHAT IS THE GREATEST COMMANDMENT?

22:34: When the Pharisees heard that he had silenced the Sadducees, they gathered together,

---

[479]   For a defense of the historicity of the exchange between Jesus and the Sadducees, see J. P. Meier, "The Debate on the Resurrection of the Dead: An Incident from the Ministry of the Historical Jesus?" *JSNT* 77 (2000): 3–24.

22:35: and one of them, a lawyer, asked him a question to test him.

22:36: "Teacher, which commandment in the law is the greatest?"

22:37: He said to him, "'You shall love the Lord your God with all your heart, and with all your soul, and with all your mind.'

22:38: This is the greatest and first commandment.

22:39: And a second is like it: 'You shall love your neighbor as yourself.'

22:40: On these two commandments hang all the law and the prophets."

*M*atthew again follows Mark's sequence, but he abridges the narrative by omitting the response of the scribe and Jesus' rejoinder (i.e., Mark 12:32–34). Matthew also introduces and concludes the passage differently. The question put to Jesus in this instance is neither a trick nor a trap but a test (v. 35). Unlike his responses to the previous questions (Matt 21:24–25, 28; 22:18–20, 31–32), which Jesus countered with questions of his own, this time Jesus answers in a straightforward manner.

Matthew states that "When the Pharisees heard that he had silenced the Sadducees, they gathered together" (v. 34). Mark says nothing about Pharisees, stating that it was a "scribe" who put the question to Jesus (Mark 12:28). But in Matthew the Pharisees huddle, presumably to plan their next move. As it turns out, one of the Pharisees is a "lawyer" (v. 35); that is, one well studied in the Law of Moses puts a question to Jesus to test his knowledge.

The "lawyer" asks Jesus, "Teacher, which commandment in the law is the greatest?" (v. 36). Matthew adds "Teacher" (the equivalent of Rabbi), which lends greater respect to Jesus. Matthew also adds "in the law," possibly to clarify that it is the written law, not the oral law (or oral tradition), that is at issue.

Jesus replies with an abridged quotation of Deut 6:5 ("You shall love the Lord your God with all your heart, and with all your soul, and with all your mind"),[480] adding, "This is the greatest and first commandment" (v. 38). Matthew elevates the prestige of the first commandment by adding this summary and the reference to the commandment as the "first."

But Jesus adds a "second" commandment, "You shall love your neighbor as yourself" (v. 39), which is found in Lev 19:18 and sums up his understanding of the principal import of the Law of Moses: "On these two commandments hang all the law and the prophets" (v. 40). Matthew has concluded his account with a maxim that has close parallels in rabbinic literature (cf. *Sipra Lev.* §195 [on Lev 19:1–4]; §200 [on Lev 19:15–20]; *m. Hag.* 1:8, "they are the essentials of the Law"; *b. Shabbat* 31a, "that is the whole Law"; *Exod. Rab.* 30.19 [on Exod 21:1], "The whole Torah rests on justice").

---

[480] Deuteronomy 6:5 reads "might" instead of "mind." On this discrepancy, see P. Foster, "Why Did Matthew Get the *Shema* Wrong? A Study of Matt 22:37," *JBL* 122 (2003): 309–33.

MATTHEW 22:41–46 – WHOSE SON IS THE MESSIAH?

22:41: **Now while the Pharisees were gathered together, Jesus asked them this question:**

22:42: **"What do you think of the Messiah? Whose son is he?" They said to him, "The son of David."**

22:43: **He said to them, "How is it then that David by the Spirit calls him Lord, saying,**

22:44: **'The Lord said to my Lord, "Sit at my right hand, until I put your enemies under your feet" '?**

22:45: **If David thus calls him Lord, how can he be his son?"**

22:46: **No one was able to give him an answer, nor from that day did anyone dare to ask him any more questions.**

*M*atthew once again follows Mark (Mark 12:35–37), but not without a few interesting changes.

Jesus challenges the adequacy of the scribal habit of referring to the Messiah as the "son of David." The appeal to Ps 110:1, where David himself calls the Messiah his "lord," implies that Jesus regards the epithet "son of David" as insufficient as a reference to the Messiah. Evidently, Jesus holds to a higher view of the Messiah. This figure is so exalted that even the great David, the archetype of the Messiah, has "by the Spirit" addressed him as "Lord." On what basis does Jesus hold to such a lofty view of the Messiah? Probably because the Messiah is "son of God" (Matt 4:3, 6; 8:29; 14:33) and like the "son of man" figure of Dan 7:9–14 has received his kingdom and authority directly from God himself (and not from the line of David). Jesus' stunning teaching, as well as his interpretation of Ps 110:1, will come to the fore in the later hearing before the high priest and the council.

After the appeal to the testimony of David in Ps 110:1, Jesus asks the Pharisees, "If David thus calls him Lord, how can he be his son?" (**v. 45**). Modern people are sometimes baffled by Jesus' logic, as well as his point, because we do not always understand the cultural assumptions of Jesus' contemporaries. In the Middle East of late antiquity, fathers were as lords to their sons; it was not the other way around. Yet here in Ps 110:1, David himself, the father of the Messiah (which is why the scribes call the Messiah the "son of David"), calls his messianic descendant "Lord" and not "son." If David – inspired by the Holy Spirit – calls him Lord, then it really is not appropriate, or at least not adequate, to refer to the Messiah as the "son of David," as some of the Jewish teachers, including Pharisees, do.

Jesus has not denied the Davidic descent of the Messiah (and the early church accepted this descent as a given; cf. Rom 1:3–4); he has questioned the adequacy of the epithet itself. The Messiah is more than a mere "junior David"; he is the Son of

God (Matt 14:33; 26:63), the heavenly Son of Man of Daniel 7, to whom authority and kingdom have been given (cf. Matt 9:6; 12:8; 13:41; 16:27; 24:30).

So impressive is Jesus' logic that no one could reply, "nor from that day did anyone dare to ask him any more questions" (**v. 46**). The second half of this verse has been carried over from Mark 12:34b, with which Mark had concluded the discussion about the greatest commandment. Matthew had omitted it in his abridged version. He has made the point that none of the religious teachers, including and especially the Pharisees, could best Jesus in wisdom and knowledge of Scripture.[481]

MATTHEW 23:1–12 – WARNING AGAINST THE SCRIBES AND PHARISEES

23:1: Then Jesus said to the crowds and to his disciples,

23:2: "The scribes and the Pharisees sit on Moses' seat;

23:3: therefore, do whatever they teach you and follow it; but do not do as they do, for they do not practice what they teach.

23:4: They tie up heavy burdens, hard to bear, and lay them on the shoulders of others; but they themselves are unwilling to lift a finger to move them.

23:5: They do all their deeds to be seen by others; for they make their phylacteries broad and their fringes long.

23:6: They love to have the place of honor at banquets and the best seats in the synagogues,

23:7: and to be greeted with respect in the marketplaces, and to have people call them rabbi.

23:8: But you are not to be called rabbi, for you have one teacher, and you are all students.

23:9: And call no one your father on earth, for you have one Father – the one in heaven.

23:10: Nor are you to be called instructors, for you have one instructor, the Messiah.

23:11: The greatest among you will be your servant.

23:12: All who exalt themselves will be humbled, and all who humble themselves will be exalted.

*M*atthew picks up one verse of Mark's version of scribal rapacity (Mark 12:39 in Matt 23:6–7a) and then supplements it with several related sayings in order to present an extended diatribe against scribal and Pharisaic hypocrisy.

---

[481] For further discussion, see A. J. Hultgren, *Jesus and His Adversaries* (1979), 45–46; B. D. Chilton, "Jesus *ben David*: Reflections on the *Davidssohnfrage*," *JSNT* 14 (1982): 88–112.

It has been suggested that Chapter 23 should be viewed as part of the fifth discourse found in Chapters 24–25. Seen this way, Chapter 23, comprising a series of woes (see vv. 13, 15, 16, 23, 25, 27, 29), becomes a counterpart to Chapter 5, beginning with a series of beatitudes, the first chapter of the Sermon on the Mount (Chapters 5–7).[482] Because of the narrative shift in Matt 24:1–2, where Jesus leaves the temple precincts and the disciples ask him a question, the position taken here is that the fifth discourse is only made up of Chapters 24–25. Nevertheless, it is acknowledged that Chapter 23 not only looks back to the preceding materials, where resistance to and criticisms of Jesus escalate, but looks forward to the eschatological discourse where judgment upon Israel, among other things, is foretold.

Matthew writes, "The scribes and the Pharisees sit on Moses' seat" (**v. 2**). To what "Moses' seat" (or chair; Greek: *kathedra*) refers is much debated. It could be figurative; that is, the scribes and Pharisees teach with the authority of Moses or have inherited the great lawgiver's status, or something to that effect. (After all, in the next verse, Jesus tells his disciples to do and observe what they are told.) It may also refer to an actual chair or seat on which the scribes and Rabbis sit when they teach in the schools and synagogues. Special stone seats, complete with Hebrew inscriptions (usually phrases from the Bible), have been found in the ruins of old synagogues at Chorazin, Delos, Dura Europos, and Tiberias, and may be examples of what Jesus has mentioned here (cf. *Pesiqta deRab Kahana* 1.7, "'The top of the throne was rounded in the back' (1 Kings 10:19) means, according to Rabbi Aha, that the throne resembled the seat of Moses [Hebrew: *qetidra deMosheh*]"; *Exod. Rab.* 43.4 [on Exod 32:22], Moses "wrapped himself in his cloak and seated himself in the posture of a sage"; *Song Rab.* 1:3 §1, "The house of study of Rabbi Eliezer was shaped like an arena, and there was in it a stone which was reserved for him to sit on"; and perhaps *Esth. Rab.* 1.11 [on Esther 1:2], "the seat of Israel is a real seat").

With regard to the scribes and Pharisees, Jesus tells the crowd and his disciples: "Do whatever they teach you and follow it" (**v. 3a**). This is taken from Deut 17:10: "Carry out exactly the decision that they announce to you from the place that the Lord will choose, diligently observing everything they instruct you." Commenting on this verse, the Rabbis teach that "even if they [the scribes] teach you that right is left and left is right, obey them" (*Sipre Deut.* §154 [on Deut 17:10]); "No man should say, 'In matters such as these I will not obey the elders' commands, since such commands are not found in the Torah.' To a man who does such a thing, the Holy One, blessed be He, replies, 'No, My son! Whatever laws the elders decree to you, obey'" (*Pesiqta Rabbati* 3.1).

---

482 The matter has been debated in the commentaries. For a recent study in which arguments are made that Matthew 23 should be seen as part of the fifth discourse, see J. Hood, "Matthew 23–25: The Extent of Jesus' Fifth Discourse," *JBL* 128 (2009): 527–43. See in the Introduction to the commentary the section "The Structure of Matthew" for a discussion of the view that Matthew has six discourses rather than five, with Chapter 23 serving as the fifth discourse and Chapters 24–25 serving as the sixth.

Jesus cautions his audience, "But do not do as they do" (**v. 3b**). Unfortunately, the deeds of the scribes and Pharisees are not always consistent with the teaching of Moses. The rabbinic tradition agrees with Jesus: "This refers to one who learns with the intention of practicing and not to one who learns with no intention of practicing. He who learns with no intention of practicing had been better unborn" (*Lev. Rab.* 35.7, [on Lev 26:3], "keep my commandments and observe them faithfully"). Jesus is not attacking the rabbinic ideal; he is faulting some of his contemporaries for failing to live up to it.

Jesus tells his hearers that they should not do as the scribes and Pharisees do because "They do not practice what they teach" (**v. 3c**). Jesus was not the only teacher to complain of inconsistency: "… if you wish to be a proper sort of philosopher, a perfect one, consistent with your own doctrines. If not, you will be no better than we who bear the name of Stoics; for we too talk of one thing and do another" (Epictetus 3.7.17).

Jesus continues, "They tie up heavy burdens, hard to bear, and lay them on the shoulders of others; but they themselves are unwilling to lift a finger to move them" (**v. 4**). Again, Jesus' complaint is consistent with the teaching found in the rabbinic literature: "They relied on the dictum of Rabban Simeon ben Gamaliel and Rabbi Eleazar ben Zadok who declared, 'We make no decree upon the community unless the majority are able to bear it'" (*b. 'Abodah Zarah* 36a). The reference to "heavy burdens" that are laid "on the shoulders of others" is another way of referring to taking the yoke of the Torah on oneself (as in *m. 'Abot* 3:5; see the commentary on Matt 11:28–30). Making the yoke heavy was in some contexts considered a virtuous thing; see, for example, *b. Sanhedrin* 94b: "It is not as the early generations [the ten tribes] who made the yoke of Torah light; but the latter generations [king Hezekiah and others] who made the yoke of Torah heavy upon themselves and are worthy of having a miracle performed for them…." For a figurative sense of "finger," see *b. Shabbat* 13b: "He did not touch me, even with his little finger!" (cf. *'Abot deRabbi Natan* 2.2).

Jesus' observation that the scribes and Pharisees "do all their deeds to be seen by others" (**v. 5a**) will remind his readers of the earlier teaching regarding piety and motives (cf. Matt 6:1, 5, 16). The public piety of the religious teachers is seen in their making "their phylacteries broad and their fringes long" (**v. 5b**). The "phylacteries" that Jesus has in mind are the *tephillin*, two small leather pouches or boxes that contain small pieces of parchment on which certain Scriptures were written (usually passages related to the Shema', though in some cases the Ten Commandments were included). There are three of these pouches: one for the hand, one for the upper arm, and one for the forehead. Jewish males thirteen years and older are expected to wear them (cf. *m. Shebuot* 3:8, 11), based on inferences from Exod 13:9, 16; Deut 6:8; 11:18. The earliest mention of the phylactery is found in the second-century B.C. *Letter of Aristeas* 159 in reference to the one worn on the hand. Phylacteries have been found at Qumran (in Cave 4) that date to the first centuries B.C. and

A.D. According to the Talmud, wearing phylacteries distinguishes Rabbis and their students from the "people of the land"; that is, those who did not study or observe the oral laws and traditions (cf. *b. Ber.* 47b; *b. Sota* 22a). To broaden the phylacteries may mean to widen the leather straps that hold them in place, thus making them obvious, or perhaps to wear them for longer periods of time (even sleep in them). The fringes are also called tassels (see Num 15:38).

Jesus criticizes the self-importance of many of the religious teachers who "love to have the place of honor at banquets and the best seats in the synagogues, and to be greeted with respect in the marketplaces, and to have people call them rabbi" (**vv. 6–7**). The Rabbis agree with Jesus' views here, criticizing those who wish to show off their learning: "One should not say, 'I will read Scripture that I may be called a sage; I will study, that I may be called a Rabbi; I will study, to be an elder, and sit in the assembly'; but learn out of love, and honor will come in the end, as it is written, 'Bind them on your fingers; write them on the tablet of your heart' (Prov 7:3)" (*b. Nedarim* 62a). The reference to binding links this teaching to the binding and wearing of the phylacteries.

Jesus tells his disciples, "But you are not to be called rabbi, for you have one teacher, and you are all students" (**v. 8**). In the first century, the title "rabbi" did not refer to a formally trained and ordained clergyman as it would later. Late first-century inscriptions suggest that rabbi was something like "sir," signifying a man's importance and stature in the community; see, for example, Beth She'arim ossuary §61: "The grave of Leontios, father of Rabbi Paregorios and Julianus the Palatine, of the goldsmiths."

The use of rabbi in the Gospels, in reference to Jesus, suggests that the title is the equivalent of "teacher"; cf. John 1:38, "Rabbi (which translated means Teacher)." Here in Matthew, Jesus is teaching against hierarchicalism. With aspects of this, the rabbinic tradition is once again in agreement with Jesus: "… hate mastery [or lordship; Hebrew: *rabanuth*] and do not seek to be acquainted with ruling power" (*m. 'Abot* 1:10). The word *rabanuth* is from the same root that gives us the titles rab, rabbi, and rabban (all meaning "great").

Jesus continues, "And call no one your father on earth, for you have one Father – the one in heaven" (**v. 9**). Several of the great Rabbis were called "Fathers" (cf. the Mishnaic tractate *'Abot*, which means "Fathers"). Compare Dio Chrysostom's remarks on the good king who "may be called by the title 'Father' of his people and his subjects, but he may justify the title by his deeds. In the title 'master,' however, he can take no delight" (*Discourses* 1.22).

Jesus adds, "Nor are you to be called instructors, for you have one instructor, the Messiah" (**v. 10**). Jesus' teaching would have resonated with many of his contemporaries. Josephus tells us that fanatics, who resisted Rome and whose theology was essentially Pharisaic, "have a passion for liberty that is almost unconquerable, since they are convinced that God alone is their leader and master. They think little of submitting to death in unusual forms and permitting vengeance to fall on kinsmen and friends if only they may avoid calling any man master" (Josephus, *Ant.* 18.23). Or, in Greco-Roman idiom: "How can *you* be my master? Zeus has set me free. Or do you really think that he was likely to let his own son be made a slave?" (Epictetus 1.19.9). The only teacher, in the truest sense, is the Messiah.[483]

The saying "The greatest among you will be your servant" (**v. 11**) parallels Matt 20:26–27 but takes on a somewhat different nuance in the present context, finding an interesting parallel in rabbinic literature:

> Once Rabbi Eliezer, Rabbi Joshua, and Rabbi Zadok were reclining at a banquet for the son of Rabban Gamaliel. Rabban Gamaliel mixed a cup for Rabbi Eliezer, who declined it. Rabbi Joshua took it, whereupon Rabbi Eliezer said to him, 'What is this, Joshua? Is it fitting for us to be reclining while Rabban Gamaliel son of Rabbi stands and serves us?' Rabbi Joshua replied, 'Let him serve. After all, Abraham, one of the great ones of the world, served the ministering angels when he thought they were pagan Arabs.... If Abraham, one of the great ones of the world, served angels when he thought they were pagan Arabs, should not Gamaliel son of Rabbi serve us?' (*Sipre Deut.* §38 [on Deut 11:10])

Jesus concludes his lesson with the reminder that "All who exalt themselves will be humbled, and all who humble themselves will be exalted" (**v. 12**); see Matt 18:1–5; 20:24–28.[484]

MATTHEW 23:13–33 – CRITICISM OF THE PHARISEES

23:13: "But woe to you, scribes and Pharisees, hypocrites! For you lock people out of the kingdom of heaven. For you do not go in yourselves, and when others are going in, you stop them.

23:14: [Omitted from the NRSV. See the commentary that follows.]

23:15: Woe to you, scribes and Pharisees, hypocrites! For you cross sea and land to make a single convert, and you make the new convert twice as much a child of hell as yourselves.

23:16: "Woe to you, blind guides, who say, 'Whoever swears by the sanctuary is bound by nothing, but whoever swears by the gold of the sanctuary is bound by the oath.'

---

[483] What is translated as "instructor" (*kathegetes*) can also be translated as "tutor," as seen in a first-century papyrus where the word appears frequently. For a discussion of this point, see B. W. Winter, "The Messiah as the Tutor: The Meaning of καθηγητής in Matthew 23:10," *TynBul* 42 (1991): 152–57.

[484] For further discussion, see P. S. Minear, *Commands of Christ* (1972), 83–97; M. A. Powell, "Do and Keep What Moses Says (Matthew 23:2–7)," *JBL* 114 (1995): 419–35. Powell addresses important questions that ask how Matt 23:1–12 fits into the larger context of Matthew.

23:17: You blind fools! For which is greater, the gold or the sanctuary that has made the gold sacred?

23:18: And you say, 'Whoever swears by the altar is bound by nothing, but whoever swears by the gift that is on the altar is bound by the oath.'

23:19: How blind you are! For which is greater, the gift or the altar that makes the gift sacred?

23:20: So whoever swears by the altar, swears by it and by everything on it;

23:21: and whoever swears by the sanctuary, swears by it and by the one who dwells in it;

23:22: and whoever swears by heaven, swears by the throne of God and by the one who is seated upon it.

23:23: "Woe to you, scribes and Pharisees, hypocrites! For you tithe mint, dill, and cummin, and have neglected the weightier matters of the law: justice and mercy and faith. It is these you ought to have practiced without neglecting the others.

23:24: You blind guides! You strain out a gnat but swallow a camel!

23:25: "Woe to you, scribes and Pharisees, hypocrites! For you clean the outside of the cup and of the plate, but inside they are full of greed and self-indulgence.

23:26: You blind Pharisee! First clean the inside of the cup, so that the outside also may become clean.

23:27: "Woe to you, scribes and Pharisees, hypocrites! For you are like whitewashed tombs, which on the outside look beautiful, but inside they are full of the bones of the dead and of all kinds of filth.

23:28: So you also on the outside look righteous to others, but inside you are full of hypocrisy and lawlessness.

23:29: "Woe to you, scribes and Pharisees, hypocrites! For you build the tombs of the prophets and decorate the graves of the righteous,

23:30: and you say, 'If we had lived in the days of our ancestors, we would not have taken part with them in shedding the blood of the prophets.'

23:31: Thus you testify against yourselves that you are descendants of those who murdered the prophets.

23:32: Fill up, then, the measure of your ancestors.

23:33: You snakes, you brood of vipers! How can you escape being sentenced to hell?

*M*atthew's diatribe against the Pharisees and the scribes continues (see Matt 23:1–12). He has derived most of this material from Q, the source that he and Luke drew upon, in supplementing the Markan narrative.

The angry denunciation "But woe to you, scribes and Pharisees, hypocrites!" (**v. 13a**) becomes a veritable refrain in the diatribe that follows. Like the beatitude "Blessed," the woe also has a form and is given expression in the Old Testament dozens of times, sometimes in a series, as in Luke 6:24–26 (cf. Isa 5:8, 11, 18, 20–22; Hab 2:6, 9, 12, 15, 19). Many of these woes are directed against the wicked or foolish (cf. Isa 3:11; Amos 6:1) or against the wealthy who oppress the poor (Jer 21:13). For "hypocrites," see the commentary on Matt 6:2. This is the first of seven woes (assuming that v. 14 is not to be read), and the verse continues, "For you lock people out of the kingdom of heaven. For you do not go in yourselves, and when others are going in, you stop them" (**v. 13b**). All of the faults that follow illustrate and justify this charge. Luke 11:52 may present an older form of this saying: "For you have taken away the key of knowledge; you did not enter yourselves, and you hindered those who were entering." The scribes and Pharisees have shut the gates of the kingdom, thus barring entry. Compare Matt 16:19, where Jesus offers to Peter: "I will give you the keys of the kingdom of heaven."

The NRSV omits the verse "Woe to you, scribes and Pharisees, hypocrites, because you devour widows' houses" (**v. 14**) because it is not found in the earliest manuscripts but appears to have been carried over from Mark 12:40 and/or Luke 20:47.

The denunciation continues, "Woe to you, scribes and Pharisees, hypocrites! For you cross sea and land to make a single convert" (**v. 15a**). A "convert" (or "proselyte," a Greek word meaning one who "came over" to the Jewish faith; the underlying Hebrew is *ger*) is a Gentile who is converted to Judaism; for example, "... whoever brings a Gentile close [to the faith] is as if he had created him anew.... Abraham converted the men and Sarah the women" (*Gen. Rab.* 39.14 [on Gen 12:5]). Another example reads:

When a man comes in these times seeking to become a proselyte, he is asked, "What is your motive in presenting yourself to become a proselyte? Do you not know that in these times the Israelites are afflicted, distressed, downtrodden, torn to pieces, and that suffering is their lot?" If he answers, "I know; and I am unworthy (to share in these sufferings)," they accept him at once. (*b. Yebamot* 47a)

The hyperbole of crossing "sea and land" is biblical (e.g., Hag 2:6; 1 Macc 8:23, 32) and stands in ironic contrast with v. 13: though the scribes and Pharisees have shut people out of the kingdom, they go to great lengths to bring people into their fold.

The conversion of King Izates is often cited as an example of a convert made in a faraway land (cf. Josephus, *Ant.* 20.34–48). How active Jews were in evangelization in late antiquity is very much an open question.[485]

---

[485] On this question, see S. McKnight, *A Light among the Gentiles: Jewish Missionary Activity in the Second Temple Period* (Minneapolis: Fortress, 1991); M. F. Bird, *Jesus and the Origin of the Gentile Mission* (LNTS 331; London: T. & T. Clark, 2006).

Verse 15 continues, "And you make the new convert twice as much a child of hell as yourselves" (**v. 15b**). No one is more zealous than a new convert. On this point, see the comment made by Justin Martyr: "But the proselytes not only do not believe, but twofold more than yourselves blaspheme His name, and wish to torture and put to death us who believe in Him; for in all points they strive to be like you" (*Dialogue with Trypho* 122). On "child of hell" (literally "son of Gehenna"), see *b. Rosh Hashanah* 17a, which speaks of the wicked, who "will be called 'sons of Gehenna.'"

Another denunciation follows: "Woe to you, blind guides" (**v. 16a**). According to Philo, fools "choose to lean on one who lacks rather than one who has the gift of sight, and with this defective guidance to their steps must of necessity fall" (*On the Virtues* 7).

Matthew's account continues, "Whoever swears by the sanctuary is bound by nothing, but whoever swears by the gold of the sanctuary is bound by the oath" (**vv. 16b–22**). If the Mishnah (*c.* 220 A.D.) is anything to go on, the laws of vows and oaths had become quite complicated and often involved various loopholes and qualifications that allowed people to be exempt. Jesus finds inconsistencies in some of these decisions, such as swearing "by the sanctuary" and being exempt or swearing "by the gold of the sanctuary" and then being obligated. Here are a few examples from the Mishnah: "If he said, 'May it be to me as the altar … [or] as Jerusalem,' it is a vow as binding as if he had uttered the word *qorban*. Rabbi Judah says, 'If he said, "[May it be] Jerusalem!" he has said nothing'" (*m. Nedarim* 1:3); "[If a man said,] 'By heaven and earth,' he is exempt" (*m. Shebuot* 4:13).

On the verse "So whoever swears by the altar, swears by it and by everything on it" (**v. 20**), see Exod 29:37, "the altar shall be most holy; whatever touches the altar shall become holy"; *m. Zebahim* 9:1, "The altar makes holy whatsoever is prescribed as its due." Likewise, "whoever swears by the sanctuary, swears by it and by the one who dwells in it" (**v. 21**); see Ps 135:21, "Blessed be the Lord from Zion, he who resides in Jerusalem."

On the verse "Whoever swears by heaven, swears by the throne of God and by the one who is seated upon it" (**v. 22**), see Isa 66:1, "Heaven is My throne, and the earth is my footstool"; *Mekilta* on Exod 17:16 [*Amalek* §2], "the Holy One, blessed be He, swore by the throne of His glory."

Jesus continues his rebuke, "For you tithe mint, dill, and cummin, and have neglected the weightier matters of the law: justice and mercy and faith" (**v. 23**). Tithing mint, dill, and cummin would count as "lighter" provisions of the law, while justice and mercy and faith (or faithfulness), especially in view of what the prophets have to say, are the weightier or heavier provisions of the law; see, for example, Mic 6:8, "And what does the Lord require of you but to do justice, and to love kindness [LXX: mercy]" (cf. Hos 6:6). On tithing dill and cummin, see *m. Ma'aserot* 4:5 and *m. Demai* 2:1 (tithing "mint" is not mentioned in rabbinic literature). On lighter and heavier, one may review again the passage on making a proselyte: "They accept him at once [as a proselyte], and acquaint him with some of the lighter and some of the heavier commandments" (*b. Yebamot* 47a).

Jesus is not opposed to minding the minor matters; he is critical of those who neglect the greater matters. He likens this inconsistency to those who "strain out a gnat but swallow a camel!" (**v. 24**). We probably have here a humorous Aramaic wordplay involving gnat (*qalma*) and camel (*gamla*). For another possible wordplay, see v. 27. On a possible wordplay involving the Aramaic words "leaven" and "teaching," see the commentary on Matt 16:12.

Jesus provides another illustration, suggesting hypocrites "clean the outside of the cup and of the plate, but inside they are full of greed and self-indulgence" (**v. 25**). Recall Mark 7:4: "... and there are also many other traditions that they observe, the washing of cups, pots, and bronze kettles."

What should one do? Jesus urges the scribes and Pharisees to "clean the inside of the cup, so that the outside also may become clean" (**v. 26**). Rabbinic literature teaches the same principle: "Rabbi Gamaliel had issued a proclamation, 'No disciple whose inside is not as his outside may enter the House of Study.' On that day many stools were added ... Rabbi Gamaliel became alarmed and said, 'Perhaps, God forbid, I withheld Torah from Israel!' He was shown in his dream white casks full of ashes" (*b. Ber.* 28a); "Any scholar whose inside is not as his outside is no scholar" (*b. Yoma* 72b). In actual practice, Pharisees did clean the inside of the cup (cf. Lev 11:32; 15:12).

A strange version of this teaching is found in the *Gospel of Thomas* §22: "Jesus says to them, 'When you make the two one, and you make the inside as the outside and the outside as the inside and the above as the below ... then shall you enter [the kingdom].'" Here ethical integrity has been transformed into something esoteric.

Jesus tells the scribes and Pharisees, "You are like whitewashed tombs, which on the outside look beautiful, but inside they are full of the bones of the dead and of all kinds of filth" (**v. 27**). It has been suggested that we have an Aramaic wordplay on "tomb" (*qeber*) and "inside" (*qereb*). One can easily imagine the large and ornate tombs along the Kidron Valley, beneath the temple mount, which are traditionally known as the Tomb of Absalom, the Tomb of Zechariah, and the Tomb of Benei Hezir, whitewashed and neatly trimmed and dressed. These tombs would have been standing in the time of Jesus and would have been passed every time Jesus and his disciples walked from the Mount of Olives to the city or to the temple mount. To the north of the city is the Tomb of Queen Helene of Adiabene, itself a very impressive structure, with two large interior columns, an ornate lintel, and a broad expanse of steps leading down through an arch to the plaza that lies before the entrance of the crypt. As beautiful as these structures are, they contain, of course, the corrupt remains of the deceased.

These tombs were whitewashed annually, on the eve of Passover. Recently whitewashed tombs, which Jesus and his disciples would have seen as they reached Jerusalem, would have been fresh in mind.

Jesus continues, "You build the tombs of the prophets and decorate the graves of the righteous, and you say, 'If we had lived in the days of our ancestors, we would not have taken part with them in shedding the blood of the prophets'" (vv. **29–30**). The construction of various tombs and monuments (including some of those described previously) is mentioned in sources such as 1 Macc 13:27–30 (in honor of members of the Hasmonean family, the "Maccabees"); Josephus, *Ant.* 7.392–94; 13.249; and Acts 2:29. (all in reference to the Tomb of David); *Ant.* 18.108 (Tomb of Philip the tetrarch); *Ant.* 20.95 (Tomb of Queen Helena); *J.W.* 5.506 (Tomb of Annas the High Priest, which may have been identified at Akeldama). By building the tombs and adorning the monuments in memory of this prophet or that, the scribes and Pharisees wish to distance themselves from their ancestors who persecuted the prophets and in some cases martyred them.

"Thus you testify against yourselves that you are descendants of those who murdered the prophets" (v. **31**), Jesus explains. By devoting themselves to the tombs of the prophets and the righteous, the scribes and Pharisees demonstrate that they stand in continuity with those who killed them. By plotting against Jesus, they show themselves to be true sons of their ancestors (see v. **32**), who murdered the prophets.

In Jesus' rebuke "You snakes, you brood of vipers! How can you escape being sentenced to hell?" (v. **33**), we hear the words of John the Baptist; see the commentary on Matt 3:7.[486]

MATTHEW 23:34–36 – A HISTORY OF REJECTED PROPHETS

23:34: Therefore I send you prophets, sages, and scribes, some of whom you will kill and crucify, and some you will flog in your synagogues and pursue from town to town,

23:35: so that upon you may come all the righteous blood shed on earth, from the blood of righteous Abel to the blood of Zechariah son of Barachiah, whom you murdered between the sanctuary and the altar.

23:36: Truly I tell you, all this will come upon this generation.

*M*atthew's diatribe ends with a summary of Israel's history of rejecting God's prophets. In it, he has drawn upon Q (cf. Luke 11:49–51).

The promise to send apostles and missionaries, "Therefore I send you prophets, sages, and scribes, some of whom you will kill and crucify, and some you will flog

---

[486] For a further discussion, see A. J. Saldarini, "Delegitimation of Leaders in Matthew 23," *CBQ* 54 (1992): 659–80.

in your synagogues and pursue from town to town" (**v. 34**), looks back to the missionary discourse in Matthew 10 and looks forward to the Great Commission in Matt 28:18–20. The prediction of persecution and murder will be seen fulfilled in the Book of Acts.

"So that upon you may come all the righteous blood shed on earth" (**v. 35a**) refers to the fact that the sin of opposing and persecuting God's prophets and righteous ones has been building and compounding for generations. The guilt of it will fall heavily on the generation that puts to death (or crucifies, as alluded to in v. 34) God's greatest emissary – his Son – and his apostles. The idea of blood coming "upon" someone is Semitic (cf. 2 Sam 1:16; Jer 51:35). So is the expression "righteous blood" (cf. Joel 4:19; Jon 1:14; Prov 6:17).

Jesus proceeds to give some examples of those whose "righteous blood" was spilled: "From the blood of righteous Abel to the blood of Zechariah son of Barachiah, whom you murdered between the sanctuary and the altar" (**v. 35b**). Abel, of course, was the son of Adam and was murdered by his brother, Cain (cf. Gen 4:1–15, especially v. 10: "Listen; your brother's blood is crying out to me from the ground!"). The identity of "Zechariah son of Barachiah," who was "murdered between the sanctuary and the altar," is less certain. More than one candidate has been suggested: (1) Zechariah, son of the high priest Jehoiada, who was murdered in the temple precincts (cf. 2 Chron 24:20–22); (2) Zechariah, son of Bareis (or, in some manuscripts of Josephus, Bariscaeus or Baruch), a wealthy man murdered by rebels in the temple precincts in 69 A.D., not long before the capture and destruction of Jerusalem (cf. Josephus, *J.W.* 4.334–43). Of these two, it is probable that the first one is in view, but the name "son of Barachiah" has been imported from the prophet Zechariah (cf. Zech 1:1, 7: "the word of the Lord came to the prophet Zechariah son of Berechiah son of Iddo"), either deliberately, to enhance the prophetic status of this Zechariah and so throw his lot in with the lot of the other prophets who have been martyred, or as a later scribal gloss.[487]

It is sometimes suggested that Jesus refers to Abel and Zechariah in order to encompass the whole of Scripture's witness; that is, from the first book (Genesis) to the last book (2 Chronicles) as the biblical books are arranged in the Hebrew Bible. This may be true. However, we cannot be sure, for the exact contents and order of the third part of the canon, of which Chronicles is a part, were not settled in the early part of the first century. Although everyone agreed that Genesis was the first book, not all would have thought of Chronicles as the last.[488]

---

[487] The options are succinctly presented in D. A. Carson, "Matthew," in F. E. Gaebelien (ed.), *The Expositor's Bible Commentary*, vol. 8 (1984), 485–86.

[488] For more on this question, see H. G. L. Peels, "The Blood 'from Abel to Zechariah' (Matthew 23,35; Luke 11,50f.) and the Canon of the Old Testament," *ZAW* 113 (2001): 583–601.

MATTHEW 23:37–39 – A LAMENT FOR JERUSALEM

23:37: "Jerusalem, Jerusalem, the city that kills the prophets and stones those who are sent to it! How often have I desired to gather your children together as a hen gathers her brood under her wings, and you were not willing!

23:38: See, your house is left to you, desolate.

23:39: For I tell you, you will not see me again until you say, 'Blessed is the one who comes in the name of the Lord.'"

The reference to the murder of the righteous Abel and Zechariah in Matt 23:35 anticipates the lament for Jerusalem, the city that kills God's prophets. The angry denunciations are over. Now Jesus weeps for the historic city.

In Matthew's account, Jesus laments "Jerusalem, Jerusalem, the city that kills the prophets and stones those who are sent to it!" (**v. 37a**), but there are actually few clear examples in the Old Testament of prophets who were either stoned or killed by other means. In 2 Chron 24:20–21, the priest Zechariah, son of Jehoida the priest, is stoned to death for speaking the word of the Lord (a prophetic activity). This is probably the Zechariah mentioned in Matt 23:35.

Jeremiah is placed in stocks (Jer 20:1–2) and cast into a pit (Jer 38:6). There was a tradition that the prophet Isaiah was placed in a hollow log and sawed in two by order of Manasseh (cf. *Martyrdom and Ascension of Isaiah* 5:11–14), a tradition possibly alluded to in Heb 11:37: "they were sawn in two." According to Josephus, the wilderness generation wanted to stone Moses (cf. *Ant.* 2.327). The pseudepigraphical *Lives of the Prophets* (first century A.D.) tells us of several prophets who were murdered.

The general tradition of the unpopularity of the prophets' messages is seen pretty well throughout the Old Testament, from Elijah down to the postexilic prophets. In Jesus' day, the idea of the persecuted and stoned prophet had become commonplace. See also the account of the stoning of Stephen in Acts 7:47–58. Sometimes this passage is compared to Deut 17:2–7, where the Israelites are commanded to stone those who teach and practice false religion.

Jesus' statement "How often have I desired to gather your children together as a hen gathers her brood under her wings, and you were not willing!" (**v. 37b**) recalls the imagery of God's care and protection; see Deut 32:11, "As an eagle stirs up its nest, and hovers over its young; it spreads its wings, takes them up, and bears them aloft on its pinions," and Ruth 2:12, "May the Lord reward you for your deeds, and may you have a full reward from the Lord, the God of Israel, under whose wings you have come for refuge!" (cf. Pss 17:8; 36:7; 57:1; 61:4). On "you were not willing," see *1 Enoch* 42:2: "Wisdom went forth to make her dwelling among the children of men, and found no dwelling-place; Wisdom returned to her place, and took her seat among the angels."

Jesus' words "See, your house is left to you, desolate" (**v. 38**) allude to Jer 22:5, "this house shall become a desolation" (see also Jer 12:7). The word "house" may refer to Israel as a nation. But to refer to "your house" in the context of a lament for Jerusalem makes us think of the temple. Added to this is the word "desolate" (*eremos*), recalling the "abomination of desolation [*eremosis*]" (Matt 24:15; Mark 13:14), which refers to the defilement of the temple's sanctuary.

Jesus continues, "For I tell you, you will not see me again until you say ..." (**v. 39a**). Jerusalem will not see Jesus? What does this mean? In the Matthean context, it may mean that Jesus will make no more public appearances (and he does not, for his teaching in Chapters 24–25 is private). But what about his humiliating public presentation by Pilate, followed by a very public execution? It may mean that Jerusalem will not see its Savior, the redeeming Messiah and Son of David, until the city repents and is willing to receive Jesus.

Jesus now quotes a verse from the Psalms: "Blessed is the one who comes in the name of the Lord" (**v. 39b**). The evidence that the city has repented and accepted its Messiah will be seen in the welcoming words of Ps 118:26: "Blessed is the one who comes in the name of the Lord. We bless you from the house of the Lord." When we remember that in the Aramaic version (the Targum) of this psalm the stone that is rejected by the builders is none other than David, the boy fit to rule as king and who will be hailed by the priests as he enters Jerusalem, the meaning of Jesus' condition presented to the city makes better sense. It is not simply that the city will greet Jesus, as it might any pilgrim who has arrived to celebrate Passover or one of the other festivals; he is to be greeted as the Davidic king, as the Messiah. See the commentary on Matt 21:9.[489]

MATTHEW 24:1–2 – THE PROPHECY OF THE TEMPLE'S DESTRUCTION

24:1: As Jesus came out of the temple and was going away, his disciples came to point out to him the buildings of the temple.

24:2: Then he asked them, "You see all these, do you not? Truly I tell you, not one stone will be left here upon another; all will be thrown down."

*T*he hostile questioning and the angry diatribe are over. But the bad news is not. The lament of the preceding passage (Matt 23:37–39) prepares Matthew's readers for the explicit prophecy of the temple's destruction. The prophecies of Matthew 24–25 constitute Matthew's fifth and final discourse. This eschatological material draws upon and greatly expands Mark 13.

---

[489] For a further discussion, see D. C. Allison, Jr., "Matt. 23.39 = Luke 13.35b as a Conditional Prophecy," *JSNT* 18 (1983): 75–84.

Jesus was not the only one to make predictions of the doom of Jerusalem and/or its temple. Several predictions are found in intertestamental literature: "… your holy places will be made desolate" (*T. Levi* 16:4; cf. 15:1); "… destruction … slaughter … plunder … consumption of God's sanctuary by fire …" (*T. Judah* 23:3); "But again the kings of the peoples will launch an attack together against this land, bringing doom upon themselves, for they will want to destroy the Temple of the Great God and most excellent men when they enter the land. The abominable kings, each one with his throne and faithless people, will set them up around the city" (*Sibylline Oracles* 3:665); "And he [Jonah] gave a portent concerning Jerusalem and the whole land, that whenever they should see a stone crying out piteously the end was at hand. And whenever they should see all the gentiles in Jerusalem, the entire city would be razed to the ground" (*Lives of Prophets* 10:10–11 [on Jonah]); "And concerning the end of the Temple he [Habakkuk] predicted, 'By a western nation it will happen.' 'At that time,' he said, 'the curtain of the Dabeir [i.e., the holy of holies] will be torn into small pieces, and the capitals of the two pillars will be taken away, and no one will know where they are; and they will be carried away by angels into the wilderness, where the Tent of Witness was set up in the beginning'" (*Lives of Prophets* 12:11 [on Habakkuk]). Although there are some who have expressed skepticism, many, if not most, scholars accept these traditions as authentic predictions of the temple's doom.

Josephus himself claims that he foresaw the temple's destruction: "But as … Josephus overheard the threats of the hostile crowd, suddenly there came back into his mind those nightly dreams, in which God had foretold to him the impending fate of the Jews and the destinies of the Roman sovereigns … he was not ignorant of the prophecies in the sacred books" (Josephus, *J.W.* 3.351–52); "Who does not know the records of the ancient prophets and that oracle which threatens this poor city and is even now coming true? For they foretold that it would then be taken whenever one should begin to slaughter his own countrymen" (Josephus, *J.W.* 6.109); "Thus the Jews, after the demolition of Antonia, reduced the Temple to a square, although they had it recorded in their oracles that the city and the sanctuary would be taken when the Temple should become foursquare" (Josephus, *J.W.* 6.311).

Josephus, moreover, tells us of another Jesus who had predicted the coming destruction: "Four years before the war … one Jesus, son of Ananias … who, standing in the Temple, suddenly began to cry out: 'A voice from the east, a voice from the west, a voice from the four winds, a voice against Jerusalem and the Sanctuary, a voice against the bridegroom and the bride, a voice against all people … Woe to Jerusalem! … Woe once more to the city and to the people and to the Sanctuary … and woe to me also'" (*J.W.* 6.301, 306, 309; cf. Jer 7:34). What is intriguing here is that this Jesus, like Jesus of Nazareth thirty years earlier, also appealed to Jeremiah 7 to clarify, if not justify, his prophecy of the temple's fate (cf. Matt 21:13, where Jesus alludes to Jer 7:11).

Rabbinic literature also contains traditions of predictions of the temple's destruction. Of special importance is the story of Yohanan ben Zakkai: "Forty years before the destruction of the Temple the western light went out, the crimson thread remained crimson, and the lot for the Lord always came up in the left hand. They would close the gates of the Temple by night and get up in the morning and find them wide open. Said Rabban Yohanan ben Zakkai [first century A.D.] to the Temple, 'O Temple, why do you frighten us? We know that you will end up destroyed. For it has been said, "Open your doors, O Lebanon, so that fire may devour your cedars"' [Zech 11:1]" (*y. Sota* 6.3; cf. *b. Yoma* 39b; *'Abot deRabbi Natan* 4.5). "[When Vespasian objected to Yohanan ben Zakkai's greeting, 'Vive domine Imperator,' Yohanan explained:] 'If you are not the king, you will be eventually, because the Temple will only be destroyed by a king's hand; as it is said, "and Lebanon with its majestic trees will fall" [Isa 10:34]"' (*Lam. Rab.* 1:5 §31). These Scriptures were thought to pertain to the doom of the temple because of the tradition that linked "Lebanon" with the temple.[490]

Recent excavations at the southwest corner of the pavement below the Temple Mount have clearly exposed the stones that were cast down. The original, specific placements of some of these stones have been identified (such as part of the lintel of what may have been Barclay's gate and the stone bearing the inscription "to the place of trumpeting …," which was at one time at the top of the Temple Mount wall). The enormous weight of these stones and the force with which they impacted the pavement below actually caused the pavement in one place to collapse into the subterranean passages below. The enormous quantity of the building material that has been cleared away (and some of it has been intentionally left in situ) impresses one with the magnitude of the task of demolition ordered by Titus (cf. *J.W.* 7.1–4, "Caesar ordered the whole city and the temple to be razed to the ground"), which followed the capture of Jerusalem and the fiery destruction of the Sanctuary and adjacent buildings. Although it is possible that this demolition was completed in a few months, it is probable that it took considerable time, perhaps even years.

The excavation of the Western Wall has uncovered many massive Herodian stones relatively untouched by the ravages of time. One stone has gained attention owing to its enormous dimensions. It is more than fifteen meters in length and 2.5 meters in height. Because its width is unknown, estimations of its weight vary from 420 to 600 tons. What is especially remarkable is that this stone is not set at the base of the wall but has been set on the second tier above the pavement. This stone, as well as countless others, complete with their characteristic borders, attest to the magnificence and beauty to which one of the disciples meant to call Jesus' attention.

Matthew follows Mark 13:1–2, but he makes a few minor revisions. As they leave the temple precincts, the disciples point out to Jesus the "buildings of the temple"

---

[490]   C. A. Evans, "Predictions of the Destruction of the Herodian Temple in the Pseudepigrapha, Qumran Scrolls, and Related Texts," *JSP* 10 (1992): 89–147.

(**v. 1**). Herod's magnificent temple was famous in its time. The greatness, grandeur, and size of the buildings surely suggested permanence. Alas, not so.

Jesus stuns his disciples with his solemn prophecy, "Truly I tell you, not one stone will be left here upon another; all will be thrown down" (**v. 2**). The parable of the vineyard (Matt 21:33–44) threatened the ruling priesthood with regime change, anticipating that care of Israel will be given to another people "that produces the fruits of the kingdom" (Matt 21:43). The disciples anticipated receiving positions of authority and administering the affairs of the twelve tribes of Israel (Matt 19:28). They did not anticipate the complete destruction of their great temple.

MATTHEW 24:3–8 – EARLY SIGNS OF JESUS' COMING

24:3: When he was sitting on the Mount of Olives, the disciples came to him privately, saying, "Tell us, when will this be, and what will be the sign of your coming and of the end of the age?"

24:4: Jesus answered them, "Beware that no one leads you astray.

24:5: For many will come in my name, saying, 'I am the Messiah!' and they will lead many astray.

24:6: And you will hear of wars and rumors of wars; see that you are not alarmed; for this must take place, but the end is not yet.

24:7: For nation will rise against nation, and kingdom against kingdom, and there will be famines and earthquakes in various places:

24:8: all this is but the beginning of the birthpangs.

*M*atthew takes over Mark 13:3–13 and edits it in order to emphasize Christology and the mission of the church.

Jesus and his disciples have left the temple precincts, and Jesus has startled them with a prophecy of the temple's complete destruction (Matt 24:1–2). Not surprisingly, the disciples ask their master, "Tell us, when will this be, and what will be the sign of your coming and of the end of the age?" (**v. 3**). Mark's form of the question asked nothing about Jesus' coming (cf. Mark 13:4). In the aftermath of the destruction of Jerusalem and the temple, this had become a pressing question for Christians. When will Jesus return? And what will be the sign of the end of the age?

Jesus' reply begins with a warning, "Beware that no one leads you astray" (**v. 4**). Many will come in Jesus' name; that is, claiming to be the Messiah (not Jesus of Nazareth, though see the discussion that follows). They will say, "'I am the Messiah!' and they will lead many astray" (**v. 5**). Jesus warns his disciples of those who will come claiming to be the Messiah. When Jesus first uttered these words, the warning would have been understood to apply to false messiahs. But decades later, after the destruction of Jerusalem, when few who had known Jesus personally were still living, it is possible that this warning was also understood to refer to false messiahs who would actually claim to be Jesus returned. When the Jewish revolt broke out in 66 A.D., a number of men arose grasping for power. It is likely that one or more of them claimed to be Israel's new anointed king, perhaps even an eschatological messiah.

Jesus warns his disciples that they "will hear of wars and rumors of wars" (**v. 6**) and that "nation will rise against nation, and kingdom against kingdom, and there will be famines and earthquakes in various places" (**v. 7**). Some of these events could be said to have taken place in the decades following Jesus' death and resurrection. The Jewish war broke out in 66 A.D. Nero committed suicide in 68 and was followed by one failed emperor after another (Galba, Otho, and Vitellius) in 68–69. Apocalyptic literature that appeared during the first century envisioned wars and upheavals (cf. *T. Moses* 10:4; *Lives of the Prophets* 10:8; 12:2; 4 Ezra 6:13–15; 9:3; 2 Bar 27:3, 5). But these events also anticipate upheaval and catastrophes that precede the return of Israel's Messiah.

As bad as things will become, Jesus warns his disciples (in his time and in the future) that things will actually get worse. The destruction of Jerusalem's temple, the false messiahs, and the wars are "but the beginning of the birthpangs" (**v. 8**). In biblical literature, "birthpangs" are frequently taken in a figurative sense (Deut 2:25; Isa 13:8; 21:3; Jer 4:31; 6:24; cf. Gal 4:27; 1 Thess 5:3). In later rabbinic literature, the advent of the Messiah was preceded by "birthpangs" (*b. Shab.* 118a; *b. Sanh.* 98b).[491]

MATTHEW 24:9–14 – WARNINGS OF PERSECUTION

24:9: "Then they will hand you over to be tortured and will put you to death, and you will be hated by all nations because of my name.

24:10: Then many will fall away, and they will betray one another and hate one another.

24:11: And many false prophets will arise and lead many astray.

24:12: And because of the increase of lawlessness, the love of many will grow cold.

24:13: But the one who endures to the end will be saved.

24:14: And this good news of the kingdom will be proclaimed throughout the world, as a testimony to all the nations; and then the end will come.

---

[491] For a further discussion of this passage and the rest of the eschatological discourse, see D. Wenham, *The Rediscovery of Jesus' Eschatological Discourse* (Gospel Perspectives 4; Sheffield: JSOT Press, 1984); J. A. Gibbs, *Jerusalem and Parousia: Jesus' Eschatological Discourse in Matthew's Gospel* (St. Louis MO: Concordia Academic Press, 2000).

*T*he general warnings of Matt 24:3–13, which primarily applied to nations and kingdoms, give way here in vv. 9–14 to warnings of personal danger. The disciples (current and future) will be severely persecuted, even martyred; nevertheless, the missionary task must continue.

Jesus warns his disciples, "Then they will hand you over to be tortured and will put you to death, and you will be hated by all nations because of my name" (**v. 9**). Matthew's version updates Mark in the light of what has happened in the interval between Jesus' original warning and the time in which Matthew pens his Gospel. Christians have gone through tribulation, and some have been killed.

Jesus continues, "Then many will fall away, and they will betray one another and hate one another" (**v. 10**). Again, Matthew's version updates what we have in Mark because apostasy has taken place. The Jewish war (66–70 A.D.) brought out the worst in Jewish society, with severe persecutions directed against believers in Jesus who did not support the various zealots who vied for power and perhaps made messianic claims. Roman persecution of Christians intensified during the latter part of Nero's reign. According to Roman historian Tacitus (early second century): "Nero had self-acknowledged Christians arrested. Then, on their information, large numbers of others were condemned" (*Annals* 15.44).

In v. 5, Jesus warned his disciples of false messiahs. Now he warns them of false prophets: "And many false prophets will arise and lead many astray" (**v. 11**). In Josephus, we hear of a number of false prophets who offered Israel signs of one sort or another (*J. W.* 2.261; 6.285–86; *Ant.* 20.97). Early Christian authorities also warn of false teachers within the church itself (cf. Acts 20:29–30; 1 John 2:18–19; Rev 19:20; *Did.* 16:3–5).

Jesus then explains, "And because of the increase of lawlessness, the love of many will grow cold" (**v. 12**). There is no equivalent of this verse in Mark's account. In the days leading up to the coming of the Messiah, according to the Mishnah, there will be little compassion, little mercy, and little assistance (cf. *m. Sota* 9:15).[492]

When Jesus says "But the one who endures to the end will be saved" (**v. 13**), he is referring not to the eschatological end (of history as humans know it) but to enduring and not quitting or abandoning the faith. A similar idea is expressed in 4 Ezra 6:25: "[W]hoever remains after all that I have foretold to you shall be saved and shall see my salvation and the end of my world."

Jesus adds, "And this good news of the kingdom will be proclaimed throughout the world, as a testimony to all the nations; and then the end will come" (**v. 14**). This statement clarifies the added question in v. 3: "what will be the sign of Your coming, and of the end of the age?" The "end will come" when the "good news of the kingdom" has been "proclaimed throughout the world." Matthew's formulation

---

[492] See D. Wenham, "A Note on Matthew 24:10–12," *TynBul* 31 (1980): 155–62; J. Taylor, "'The Love of Many Will Grow Cold': Matt 24:9–13 and the Neronian Persecution," *RB* 96 (1989): 352–57.

anticipates the Great Commission (Matt 28:18–20), where the risen Jesus sends forth his apostles into the world to accomplish this very thing.[493]

MATTHEW 24:15–22 – WATCH FOR THE DESOLATING SACRILEGE

24:15: "So when you see the desolating sacrilege standing in the holy place, as was spoken of by the prophet Daniel (let the reader understand),

24:16: then those in Judea must flee to the mountains;

24:17: the one on the housetop must not go down to take what is in the house;

24:18: the one in the field must not turn back to get a coat.

24:19: Woe to those who are pregnant and to those who are nursing infants in those days!

24:20: Pray that your flight may not be in winter or on a sabbath.

24:21: For at that time there will be great suffering, such as has not been from the beginning of the world until now, no, and never will be.

24:22: And if those days had not been cut short, no one would be saved; but for the sake of the elect those days will be cut short.

*M*atthew continues to follow Mark's eschatological material (Mark 13:14–20), but again he makes some interesting revisions and adds material of his own.

When Matthew writes "So when you see the desolating sacrilege standing in the holy place" (**v. 15**), he is interpreting Mark 13:14, "when you see the desolating sacrilege set up where it ought not to be." Where is "set up where it ought not to be"? In "the holy place"; that is, in the temple, and probably, even more specifically, in the holy of holies (cf. Exod 28:29, 35, 43; 29:30, where the holy of holies is called the "holy place"), the most sacred place in the temple and in all of Israel. The reference to "Daniel," which is not found in Mark, makes it clear that Dan 9:17 ("O our God, listen to the prayer of your servant … let your face shine upon your desolated sanctuary") is in view, though the desolating sacrilege of the temple in the time of Antiochus IV (ca. 167 B.C.) probably exerts some influence, too (cf. 1 Macc 1:54, "they erected a desolating sacrilege on the altar of burnt offering").

Jesus instructs, "Then those in Judea must flee to the mountains … not turn back to get a coat" (**vv. 16–18**). The danger will be such that the faithful will have to flee immediately. There will be no time to pack and make arrangements. When the desolating sacrilege takes place, it is time to run.

It has been suggested that the desolating sacrilege was Caligula's attempt to erect his image in the temple precincts or perhaps Titus's entrance into the sanctuary

---

[493] On this point, see V. Balabanski, "Mission in Matthew against the Horizon of Matthew 24," *NTS* 54 (2008): 161–75.

in the summer of 70 A.D., when his army occupied the precincts and brought
the revolt to an end. But none of these events fit the prophecy of Matt 24:15–22.
Caligula's order was never carried out, and the temple was in ruins and sacrifice had
ceased before Titus entered the sanctuary. In any case, the opportunity to flee was
long past. The event Jesus envisions here is to take place in the future. It is probably
related in some way to Paul's explanation to the Thessalonian Christians, where he
says the "lawless one" will take "his seat in the temple of God, declaring himself to
be God" (2 Thess 2:3–4). Such an abomination will bring normal observance in the
temple to an end.

It will be the worst possible time for pregnant and nursing women: "Woe to
those who are pregnant and to those who are nursing infants in those days!" (**v. 19**).
Expectant women or women with a nursing infant cannot drop their burdens and
run, as implied in the instructions in vv. 16–18. They shall face an awful dilemma
and therefore even greater danger. In Old Testament literature, pregnant and nursing women sometimes figure in oracles and descriptions of national disasters or
times of divine judgment (e.g., Deut 32:25; 2 Kings 8:12; 15:16; Jer 44:7; Lam 2:11; 4:4;
Hos 13:16; Amos 1:13; 4 Ezra 6:21).

In the statement "Pray that your flight may not be in winter or on a sabbath"
(**v. 20**), the Jewish character of Matthew is again evident. Flight in winter brings with
it dangers and discomforts, but for those who scrupulously observe the Sabbath,
there is yet another problem. A Sabbath day's journey was limited to two thousand
cubits (cf. *m. 'Erubin* 4:3; 5:7). By having Jesus urge his disciples to pray that the day
of emergency not occur "on a Sabbath," Jesus is once again seen as upholding the
Law (cf. Matt 5:17–20).[494]

Jesus' warning continues, "For at that time there will be great suffering, such
as has not been from the beginning of the world until now, no, and never will be"
(**v. 21**). The tribulation will be so great that it will eclipse all crises of biblical history, which is quite a claim when we remember the flood, the Babylonian captivity,
and the war with Antiochus. The language itself echoes Daniel, "And there shall be
a time of trouble [LXX: that day of tribulation], such as never has been since there
was a nation till that time" (Dan 12:1), and may also reflect acquaintance with the
Testament of Moses, as seen in the reference to "creation" (which is lacking in the
Daniel parallel): "And there will come upon them … punishment and wrath such as
has never happened to them from the creation till that time when he stirs up against
them a king of the kings of the earth …" (*T. Mos.* 8:1).

Unless we view the statement "And if those days had not been cut short, no one
would be saved; but for the sake of the elect those days will be cut short" (**v. 22**) as

---

494   For further discussion, see G. N. Stanton, "'Pray that Your Flight May Not Be in Winter
       or on a Sabbath' (Matthew 24.20)," *JSNT* 37 (1989): 17–30; E. K.-C. Wong, "The Matthean
       Understanding of the Sabbath: A Response to G. N. Stanton," *JSNT* 44 (1991): 3–18; W. H.
       Shea, "The Sabbath in Matt 24:20," *AUSS* 40 (2002): 23–35.

unbridled hyperbole, the warning that the period of tribulation would be so severe that unless shortened it would extinguish human life argues that what is in view here is more than the Jewish war. To be sure, this war threatened all Jewish lives in Jerusalem (though, as it turned out, many thousands survived), but on no account did the fate of the whole of humanity hang in the balance. On the days being "short-ened," see 4Q385 frag. 3, lines 3–5: "[T]he days hasten in order that the children of Israel may inherit.... I shall cut short the days and the years." The idea of God short-ening time is found in some pseudepigraphical texts (e.g., *1 Enoch* 80:2; Ps.-Philo, *Bib. Ant.* 19:13; *2 Bar* 20:1; 54:1; 83:1).

MATTHEW 24:23–28 – BEWARE FALSE MESSIAHS AND FALSE PROPHETS

24:23: Then if anyone says to you, 'Look! Here is the Messiah!' or 'There he is!' – do not believe it.

24:24: For false messiahs and false prophets will appear and produce great signs and omens, to lead astray, if possible, even the elect.

24:25: Take note, I have told you beforehand.

24:26: So, if they say to you, 'Look! He is in the wilderness,' do not go out. If they say, 'Look! He is in the inner rooms,' do not believe it.

24:27: For as the lightning comes from the east and flashes as far as the west, so will be the coming of the Son of Man.

24:28: Wherever the corpse is, there the vultures will gather.

*M*atthew continues to follow Mark (Mark 13:21–23), supplementing it with a saying in vv. 27–28 that may have come from Q (cf. Luke 17:24). In contrast to the false messiahs and false prophets who promise and perhaps even produce "great signs and omens," the coming of the Son of Man will be sudden, like light-ning, which comes without warning.

The warning about false messiahs (see Matt 24:5) is now repeated: "Then if any-one says to you, 'Look! Here is the Messiah!' or 'There he is!' – do not believe it" (**vv. 23–25**). The disciples are not to believe these claims because when the real Messiah does come he will be as plain to see as the lightning (v. 27). No secret dis-closures will be necessary.

Jesus offers an example of a false claim: "Look! He is in the wilderness" (**v. 26a**). The wilderness was the theater of operations for revival movements (recall that John the Baptist appeared in the wilderness [cf. Mark 1:2–4], as did the Essenes in answer to the wilderness summons of Isa 40:3; cf. 1QS 8:12–14; 9:19–20). Charlatans and false prophets, according to Josephus, rallied the desperate in the wilderness, promising to show them confirming signs (cf. *J.W.* 2.261–63; 6.315; *Ant.* 17.278–84; 20.168, 188). See also LXX Jer 4:11, "a spirit of error in the wilderness."

Jesus continues with another example of a false claim: "Look! He is in the inner rooms" (**v. 26b**). A false messiah may be reported to be in hiding, awaiting public disclosure at the right moment. See LXX Deut 32:25: "Outside the sword shall bereave, and from the inner rooms [there will be] terror...." Matthew had used "inner" room in Matt 6:6 in reference to private prayer. It has been suggested that the Aramaic word underlying inner room has been mistranslated and that it should be council or assembly, but this is doubtful.

Jesus then offers a description of his return: "For as the lightning comes from the east and flashes as far as the west" (**v. 27**). Lightning or the like sometimes features in theophanic contexts (e.g., Exod 19:16; Isa 62:1; Pss 18:14; 97:4; 144:6). The closest parallel is probably Zech 9:14: "Then the Lord will appear over them, and his arrow will go forth like lightning; the Lord God will sound the trumpet." This passage is part of an eschatological oracle of salvation. Celestial phenomena are associated with the appearance of one who will be called "Son of God" and "Son of the Most High": "He will be called the Son of God, they will call him the Son of the Most High. And like the comets that you saw in your vision, so will be their kingdom" (4Q246 2:1–2). A story is told that a German fortune-teller told Emperor Domitian (ruled 81–96 A.D.) that recent lightning "foretold a change of rulers." Frightened and angry, the doomed emperor condemned the man to death. The following day, Domitian was assassinated (cf. Suetonius, *Domitian* 16.1).[495]

The saying "Wherever the corpse is, there the vultures will gather" (**v. 28**) has a proverbial ring to it, and there are many parallels, both in Scripture and in secular writings. See Job 9:26; 15:23; 39:27 and 30, "Is it at your command that the eagle mounts up and makes its nest on high? ... Its young ones also suck up blood; and where the slain are, there it is"; Hab 1:8; Cornutus, *De natura deorum* 21, "the birds ... gather wherever there are many corpses"; Seneca, *Epistles* 95.43, "he is a vulture awaiting a corpse."

It has been suggested that "vultures" should be understood as eagles (and the words in Greek, Latin, and Hebrew can be interchangeable), and if so they refer to the Roman standards that will be seen when Jerusalem is surrounded and finally overthrown in 69–70 A.D. This is probably not what the saying originally had in mind, but it is likely that some of Matthew's readers and hearers, in the aftermath of the destruction of Jerusalem, did make this association. See 1QpHab 3:8–12, "'... they fly like a vulture intent on food, all of them bent on violence, their faces ever forward' [Hab 1:8–9a]. [This refers to] the Kittim [i.e., the Romans] who trample the

---

[495]   For another approach, see J. A. Oñate Ojeda, "Pues, así como el relámpago," *Burgense* 32 (1991): 569–72. Oñate Ojeda thinks the reference is to the sun, not to lightning; i.e., the sun rises in the east and moves to the west. But in what sense is the movement of the sun – whose movement is slow and predictable – a suitable analogy for the coming of the Son of Man?

land with [their] horses and with their beasts. From far away they come, from the sea-coasts, to eat up all the peoples like an insatiable vulture."[496]

Jesus' saying is probably not too different from the saying "Where there is smoke, there is fire." When the day finally comes, and the Son of Man makes his appearance, there will be unmistakable signs, just as surely as one may expect to find corpses, if there are vultures circling overhead. The grim proverb is probably selected because it is consistent with the whole negative tenor of the dangers and calamities that have been described in vv. 15–28. The saying may be proverbial, but it also paints a realistic picture of what may be expected in the end times.

MATTHEW 24:29–35 – THE RETURN OF THE SON OF MAN

24:29: "Immediately after the suffering of those days the sun will be darkened, and the moon will not give its light; the stars will fall from heaven, and the powers of heaven will be shaken.

24:30: Then the sign of the Son of Man will appear in heaven, and then all the tribes of the earth will mourn, and they will see 'the Son of Man coming on the clouds of heaven' with power and great glory.

24:31: And he will send out his angels with a loud trumpet call, and they will gather his elect from the four winds, from one end of heaven to the other.

24:32: "From the fig tree learn its lesson: as soon as its branch becomes tender and puts forth its leaves, you know that summer is near.

24:33: So also, when you see all these things, you know that he is near, at the very gates.

24:34: Truly I tell you, this generation will not pass away until all these things have taken place.

24:35: Heaven and earth will pass away, but my words will not pass away.

*I*n this part of the eschatological discourse, Matthew follows Mark more closely (Mark 13:24–31), with significant differences limited to vv. 30 and 31. The previous passage ended with a prophecy of the coming of the Son of Man (vv. 27–28). The present passage will elaborate on this theme.

The expression "Those days" (**v. 29**) is biblical language and frequently introduces eschatological oracles (e.g., Jer 3:16; 5:18; 31:29; 33:15–16; Joel 3:2[2:29]; 4[3]:1;

---

[496] For an interesting and different interpretation, see W. Carter, "Are There Imperial Texts in the Class? Intertextual Eagles and Matthean Eschatology as 'Lights Out' Time for Imperial Rome (Matthew 24:27–31)," *JBL* 122 (2003): 467–87. Carter argues that the "eagles" (not vultures) signify the defeat of the Roman Empire. The eagles (perhaps the Roman legions), along with the empire, will end when the Messiah, the Son of Man, returns.

Zech 8:23) and has already appeared in Matthew 24 (vv. 19 and 22). The days of suffering will be characterized by cosmic upheaval, which in colorful biblical parlance is described in exaggerated terms: "the sun will be darkened, and the moon will not give its light; the stars will fall from heaven, and the powers of heaven will be shaken" (see Isa 13:10; 34:4; Amos 9:5; Mic 1:4; Hab 3:6).

In Matt 24:3, the disciples had asked Jesus what the sign of his coming would be. (This question is not asked in Mark 13.) The verse "Then the sign of the Son of Man will appear in heaven" (**v. 30a**) now speaks directly to this question. The Book of Revelation thrice speaks of a "great sign that appeared in heaven," the first "a woman clothed with the sun, and the moon under her feet, and on her head a crown of twelve stars" (Rev 12:1), the second "a great red dragon having seven heads and ten horns, and on his heads were seven diadems" (Rev 12:3), and the third "seven angels who had seven plagues" (Rev 15:1), but does not speak of a "sign of the Son of Man."

However, Rev 14:14–15:1 may in fact speak of a sign of the Son of Man. The seer describes the Son of Man sitting on a cloud and wielding a "sharp sickle in His hand" (Rev 14:14). He is commanded, "Use your sickle and reap, for the hour to reap has come, because the harvest of the earth is fully ripe" (Rev 14:15). He does so (Rev 14:16) and is soon assisted by an angel, also armed with a sharp sickle; together they reap the earth (Rev 14:17–20). Then we are told in Rev 15:1, "I saw another portent in heaven, great and amazing: seven angels with seven plagues, which are the last, for with them the wrath of God is ended." The seer's "another sign in heaven" implies that the earlier appearance of the Son of Man was also a sign in heaven, even though it was not explicitly identified as such.

Although we should not assume that the vision of Revelation is the same thing described in Matthew 24, the former may help us understand the latter. Furthermore, in Matt 24:32, Jesus says the putting forth of leaves is an indication of summer. But the Greek word underlying "summer" may also be translated "harvest." Thus we have another important point of contact between Revelation 14 and Matthew 24: the harvest (or summer) has come and the Son of Man appears in heaven, sitting on a cloud, with sickle in hand, ready to reap the earth, at which time the wheat and the weeds will be separated (as in Matt 13:24–30, 36–43).

There is another interpretation, and it is not necessarily in competition with the one just advanced. The "sign of the Son of Man" may well be his ensign, or standard, a standard to be carried into battle. The War Scroll of Qumran legislated the very words to be written on this standard (cf. 1QM 3:13–15). The inspiration for this is derived from the Old Testament itself, which speaks of an ensign (Isa 62:10) and links it to hopes of a new David (cf. Isa 11:10). Furthermore, in Isa 5:26–30, someone (a "king" in the Aramaic paraphrase) will raise a standard or signal and will gather people for war.[497] What this suggests is that the sign of the Son of Man will be

---

[497]   See G. D. Kirchhevel, "He that Cometh in Mark 1:7 and Matt 24:30," *BBR* 4 (1994): 105–11. Kirchhevel believes the image of the coming of the Son of Man, as a warrior king, is

his appearance in heaven, "'coming on the clouds of heaven' with power and great glory," with his battle ensign, ready to execute judgment.

When the tribes of the earth see the Son of Man, "Then all the tribes of the earth will mourn" (**v. 30b**), for they will know that judgment has come. Saying that humans "will mourn" may allude to Zech 12:10, "they look on the one whom they have pierced, they shall mourn for him, as one mourns for an only child." If so, then the tribes of the earth will mourn not simply because the day of judgment has arrived but because they realize that the coming judge is none other than he whom they had put to death. (See also Zech 12:12, 14, 17, which speak of tribes mourning and, in the LXX, "all the tribes of the earth.")

Matthew's account continues, "He will send out his angels with a loud trumpet call" (**v. 31**). Trumpets were expected to sound forth when the men of Qumran prepared to engage the enemy in the final eschatological war. The primary reference here, however, is to the shofar (the traditional Jewish horn) that will sound in the end time, when God's people will be regathered. The primary passage from the Old Testament is Isa 27:13: "And on that day a great trumpet will be blown, and those who were lost in the land of Assyria and those who were driven out to the land of Egypt will come and worship the Lord on the holy mountain at Jerusalem." This tradition appears in the New Testament (here in Matt 24:31, and in 1 Cor 15:52; 1 Thess 4:16) and in other literature, such as *Apocalypse of Abraham* 31:1: "And then I will sound the trumpet out of the air, and I will send my chosen one, having in him one measure of all my power, and he will summon my people, humiliated by the heathen." The passage goes on to describe the wrath that will be poured out on the heathen who had mocked and ruled over God's people.

It is interesting that Jesus speaks of the Son of Man as sending out *his* angels rather than *God's* angels. In the vision of Dan 7:9–14, the throne of God (a.k.a. the "Ancient One") is surrounded by a myriad of angels (v. 10). They are God's angels, who serve and attend him. Yet Jesus implies that the angels obey the Son of Man (i.e., himself). Jesus assumes this probably because in Daniel's vision authority is given to the Son of Man (vv. 13–14). As Son of Man, Jesus exercises this authority on earth (Matt 9:6), and when raised from the dead and sending his apostles forth, he declares, "All authority in heaven and on earth has been given to me" (Matt 28:18). In the time of his return, this authority will include command over the angels themselves, who "will gather his elect from the four winds."[498]

We are then told, "From the fig tree learn its lesson" (**v. 32**). The original context of the parable might now be obscure, but the basic meaning is clear enough: when one sees the green buds form and begin to sprout leaves, one knows that summer

---

informed by Isa 5:26–30, especially as it was understood in the emerging Aramaic interpretation (which in due course became the Targum).

[498] For background, see A. Schlatter, *Der Evangelist Matthäus: Seine Sprache, sein Ziel, seine Selbständigkeit*, 5th edition (Stuttgart: Calwer, 1959), 711–12; A. Sand, *Das Evangelium nach Matthäus* (1986), 490; C. S. Keener, *A Commentary on the Gospel of Matthew* (1999), 586–88.

is on its way. Accordingly, one will know that the Son of Man "is near, at the very gates" (**v. 33**). For examples from the LXX of "at the gates" (or "door[s]"), see Gen 19:11; Prov 9:14; and Wisd of Sol 19:17.

Jesus declares, "Truly I tell you, this generation will not pass away until all these things have taken place" (**v. 34**). The phrase "this generation," which in the New Testament is almost always found on the lips of Jesus (for elsewhere in Matthew, see 11:16; 12:41, 42; 23:36), is almost always in a negative or judgmental context, whether in the Old Testament or in Jesus' usage. Jesus' use of the phrase suggests that he understood his mission and message as being of the utmost importance for Israel and that rejection of his message will have dire consequences for his people. In the present context, "all these things" refer to the various predictions of the eschatological discourse (vv. 4–33), the events leading up to and including the coming of the Son of Man.

Jesus continues, "Heaven and earth will pass away, but my words will not pass away" (**v. 35**). Contrasts between God's eternal word and the temporal, created order are found in the Old Testament (e.g., Isa 40:6–8; 51:6; Ps 102:25–27). But it is only God's word that is regarded as eternal, never a human's. In later Jewish writings, the eternity of the Torah is emphasized (e.g., Bar 4:1; Wisd of Sol 18:4; 4 Ezra 9:36–37). The remarkable quality of Jesus' saying is underscored further when we remember that on another occasion Jesus used similar language with respect to the Torah itself: "For truly I tell you, until heaven and earth pass away, not one letter, not one stroke of a letter, will pass from the law until all is accomplished" (Matt 5:18). To what do Jesus' "words" refer? They may refer to all that has gone before (vv. 4–34). They may even refer to his teaching as a whole. But they may only refer to the preceding verse. Whatever the principal reference, the assertion is remarkable.

MATTHEW 24:36–44 – BE READY: NO ONE KNOWS
THE TIME OF HIS COMING

24:36: "But about that day and hour no one knows, neither the angels of heaven, nor the Son, but only the Father.

24:37: For as the days of Noah were, so will be the coming of the Son of Man.

24:38: For as in those days before the flood they were eating and drinking, marrying and giving in marriage, until the day Noah entered the ark,

24:39: and they knew nothing until the flood came and swept them all away, so too will be the coming of the Son of Man.

24:40: Then two will be in the field; one will be taken and one will be left.

24:41: Two women will be grinding meal together; one will be taken and one will be left.

24:42: Keep awake therefore, for you do not know on what day your Lord is coming.

24:43: But understand this: if the owner of the house had known in what part of the night the thief was coming, he would have stayed awake and would not have let his house be broken into.

24:44: Therefore you also must be ready, for the Son of Man is coming at an unexpected hour.

*M*atthew supplements Mark 13:32–37 with several parables and parable fragments. He will add another entire chapter (i.e., Chapter 25), most of which is unique to his Gospel. The present passage elaborates on the theme of the suddenness and unexpectedness of the coming of the Son of Man. Most people will be taken completely by surprise.

According to the saying "But about that day and hour no one knows, neither the angels of heaven, nor the Son, but only the Father" (**v. 36**), no one knows, not even "the Son," when the eschatological "that day" will come. The inclusion of the Son with those who do not know was an embarrassment for early Christians (not surprisingly, some manuscripts omit these words, and Luke omits the verse altogether). All of this suggests that the saying goes back to Jesus and not to the early community. In Jewish Scripture and tradition, it is believed that God knows everything, including the future (e.g., Isa 46:10; Zech 14:7; 4 Ezra 4:51–52). There are also traditions that declare that humans, or even angels, do not and cannot know the future (see 4 Ezra 4:44–52, where Ezra asks if he will be alive in the last days and the angel tells him, "I do not know"; *Pss. Sol.* 17:21; and also *2 Bar* 21:8, which in a prayer to God says: "You alone know the end of times before it has arrived"). In a discussion of the length of the Messiah's reign (*b. Sanh.* 99a), Rabbi Simon ben Laqish comments that Isa 63:4 ("For the day of vengeance was in my heart, and the year for my redeeming work had come") implies that God has not revealed his eschatological plans to the angels, for knowledge of this day is in God's heart only – in no one else's.[499]

"For as the days of Noah were…" (**vv. 37–39**) recalls the flood story, which was well known in the eastern Mediterranean world of late antiquity (and versions of it circulated in great antiquity). Ovid (Latin poet, 43 B.C.E–18 A.D.) tells the story of a couple from Phrygia whose piety won them the favor of the gods and spared them from the coming flood (cf. Ovid, *Metamorphoses* 8.618–724). The writings of Plutarch (45–125 A.D.) and those of the fifth-century Nonnos make mention of the flood. There are coins from Asia Minor that depict the ark, the dove, or even the name Noah (Greek: *Noe*). The *Sibylline Oracles* refer to the flood, with the Sibyl

---

[499] On the temporal and contingent nature of Matthew's eschatology, see B. Cooper, "Adaptive Eschatological Inference from the Gospel of Matthew," *JSNT* 33 (2010): 59–80.

(3:815–18: "I am Sibylla ... a prophetess of the great God") claiming to be Noah's daughter-in-law: "For when the world was deluged with waters, and a certain single approved man was left floating on the waters in a house made of hewn wood with beasts, and birds, so that the world might be filled again, I was his daughter-in-law and I was of his blood" (*Sib. Or.* 3:823–27). Many of these traditions are linked to the city of Apamea in Asia Minor, whose nickname was *kibotoi* (Greek, meaning "people of the ark"; the Septuagint translates the Hebrew word for "ark" as *kibotos*). Jesus' point is that the coming of the Son of Man will entail a worldwide judgment, the likes of which have not been seen since the great flood long ago.

The suddenness and unexpectedness of this time of judgment is given further illustration: "Then two will be in the field; one will be taken and one will be left" (**vv. 40–41**). It is not easy to understand which one is saved; the one "taken" or the one "left." The one *taken* could refer to those who are saved, as in Matt 24:31, where the angels of the Son of Man gather his elect. However, in the present context, the saved seem to be those who are *left* or remain after judgment. Those who entered the ark were saved, or "left" alive, while those who perished in the flood (v. 39) were *taken* in judgment. In view of this danger, Jesus tells his disciples, "Keep awake" (**v. 42**).

Jesus then uses an analogy to reinforce the point: "If the owner of the house had known in what part of the night the thief was coming, he would have stayed awake and would not have let his house be broken into" (**v. 43**). Very true. Here and in Matt 25:6 (in the parable of the bridesmaids), the Son of Man is envisioned as coming at *night*. This idea is consistent with Jewish messianism, which sometimes speaks of the coming of the Messiah at night, probably based on association with the night of the original Passover (cf. *Tg. Neof.* Exod 12:42: "It is a night reserved and set aside for redemption ... when the world reaches its appointed time to be redeemed: the iron yokes shall be broken and the generations of wickedness shall be blotted out ... and the King Messiah will go up ... and lead at the head of the flock [some manuscripts read "at the head of a cloud"] ... it is a night reserved and set aside for the redemption of all Israel").

This section of the discourse ends with a concluding exhortation to be ready: "Therefore you also must be ready, for the Son of Man is coming at an unexpected hour" (**v. 44**).[500]

MATTHEW 24:45–51 – THE PARABLE OF THE WISE AND WICKED SLAVES

24:45: "Who then is the faithful and wise slave, whom his master has put in charge of his household, to give the other slaves their allowance of food at the proper time?

---

[500]　P. S. Minear, *Commands of Christ* (1972), 152–77.

24:46: Blessed is that slave whom his master will find at work when he arrives.

24:47: Truly I tell you, he will put that one in charge of all his possessions.

24:48: But if that wicked slave says to himself, 'My master is delayed,'

24:49: and he begins to beat his fellow slaves, and eats and drinks with drunkards,

24:50: the master of that slave will come on a day when he does not expect him and at an hour that he does not know.

24:51: He will cut him in pieces and put him with the hypocrites, where there will be weeping and gnashing of teeth.

*T*his parable of the wise and wicked slaves elaborates on the theme of some taken (or saved) and others left behind (Matt 24:37–41). However, it narrows the focus to the followers of Jesus. Some will remain faithful, but others will not.

Jesus begins the parable by asking, "Who then is the faithful and wise slave...?" (vv. 45–51). The "faithful and wise slave" is he who continues with his master's work, though he be delayed in returning. That the master has been delayed should not lead one to conclude, foolishly, that he will not return at all and that there will be no accountability.

The details in the parable should not be allegorized, but they should not be ignored either. The parable portrays a servant (or slave) who has responsibilities. The faithful slave will go about his duties diligently and responsibly. The "wicked slave" (v. 48) will take advantage of his authority for his own lusts and benefits. Such a slave will face the music when his master finally does return. The wicked slave will find himself harshly judged and assigned a place with the "hypocrites," which in Matthew's context (recall Chapter 23) means in the place with scribes and Pharisees, who murder the prophets and face severe condemnation.[501]

MATTHEW 25:1–13 – THE PARABLE OF THE BRIDESMAIDS

25:1: "Then the kingdom of heaven will be like this. Ten bridesmaids took their lamps and went to meet the bridegroom.

---

[501] The fate of the wicked slave is portrayed graphically. The Master will "cut him in pieces" (v. 48). Literally, the text says "cut in two." On the background imagery, see T. A. Friedrichsen, "A Note on καὶ διχοτομήσει αὐτόν (Luke 12:46 and the Parallel in Matthew 24:51)," *CBQ* 63 (2001): 258–64; D. C. Sim, "The Dissection of the Wicked Servant in Matthew 24:51," *HTS Teologiese Studies/Theological Studies* 58 (2002): 172–84. Friedrichsen hears an echo of Jer 34:18–20a (MT). Sims thinks the fate of the false accusers of Susanna is in view. On the vulnerability of slaves in the first-century Mediterranean world and how this is reflected in Matthew's slave/servant parables, see J. A. Glancy, "Slaves and Slavery in the Matthean Parables," *JBL* 119 (2000): 67–90.

25:2: Five of them were foolish, and five were wise.

25:3: When the foolish took their lamps, they took no oil with them;

25:4: but the wise took flasks of oil with their lamps.

25:5: As the bridegroom was delayed, all of them became drowsy and slept.

25:6: But at midnight there was a shout, 'Look! Here is the bridegroom! Come out to meet him.'

25:7: Then all those bridesmaids got up and trimmed their lamps.

25:8: The foolish said to the wise, 'Give us some of your oil, for our lamps are going out.'

25:9: But the wise replied, 'No! there will not be enough for you and for us; you had better go to the dealers and buy some for yourselves.'

25:10: And while they went to buy it, the bridegroom came, and those who were ready went with him into the wedding banquet; and the door was shut.

25:11: Later the other bridesmaids came also, saying, 'Lord, lord, open to us.'

25:12: But he replied, 'Truly I tell you, I do not know you.'

25:13: Keep awake therefore, for you know neither the day nor the hour.

*M*atthew's parable of the bridesmaids is the first major supplement beyond his Markan source (Matthew elaborated on Mark 13:33–37 with parables of watching and faithfulness; cf. Matt 24:37–51). This parable continues the theme of the need to be alert and watching, for the bridegroom will appear at a time one least expects. The parable also adds to Matthew's interest in portraying two types of people in Israel: those who will be included in the kingdom and those who will be thrust out (as seen, for example, in the parable of the wheat and weeds; cf. Matt 13:24–30).[502]

The parable is an allegory of the return of Jesus Christ, Israel's Messiah and the church's Lord. The bridegroom is Jesus, and the wise bridesmaids are the faithful, who will be admitted into the kingdom. The foolish bridesmaids are the reprobate, who will be shut out of the kingdom. The wedding feast is the symbol for the celebration of the kingdom of God, when God's rule on earth is finally and fully established. But the allegory only goes so far; it probably does not reflect a concern over the delay of the coming of the Son of Man.

The details of the parable are true to ancient customs of the wedding feast and celebration. After the wedding feast at the house of the bride's parents, which ends well into the night, the bridegroom escorts his bride to his parents' house. A number of maids await the arrival of the bride and groom and will escort them with lamps to the bridal chamber. However, these maids do not know at what hour of the

---

[502] K. P. Donfried, "The Allegory of the Ten Virgins (Matt 25:1–13) as a Summary of Matthean Theology," *JBL* 93 (1974): 415–28.

evening the bride and groom will appear. Hence the point of the parable: the need to be vigilant and prepared.[503]

The parable begins "Ten bridesmaids took their lamps and went to meet the bridegroom" (**v. 1**). The wedding imagery recalls the parable in Matt 22:1–14, where the king gives a wedding feast for his son. The number ten is a favorite in biblical literature. In the New Testament, we have the woman and her ten silver coins (Luke 15:8), the ten lepers (Luke 17:12), and the parable of the ten slaves who were given ten minas to trade with (Luke 19:13). In the Old Testament, we have the ten plagues (Exod 7:8–11:10) and the Ten Commandments (Exod 20:3–17; Deut 5:7–21). In later times, we have ten to make a synagogue congregation (*m. 'Abot* 5:1–6; cf. CD 13:1; 1QS 6:6) and ten to make up a judicial body (see CD 10:4–5) or community council (see 1QS 6:3).

The identification of Jesus as the "bridegroom" probably started with Jesus himself (cf. Matt 9:15). In time, Jesus is viewed as the bridegroom and the church as his bride (Eph 5:27).

The maids who were prepared "trimmed their lamps" (**v. 7**), giving attention to the wicks of their lamps and adding oil as needed. But the foolish maids had not brought along extra oil for their lamps (v. 3), not anticipating a long vigil. As their lamps began flickering out, they asked the other maids for oil (**v. 8**), but there was not enough to spare (**v. 9**). Had the oil been divided up, all of the lamps may have failed.

"And while they went to buy it" (**v. 10a**) raises the question of what seller of oil would be willing to do business at midnight. Hearers of the parable would think of this and realize that, through their lack of planning, the foolish maids have indeed gotten themselves into trouble.

Matthew's account reports that "The bridegroom came, and those who were ready went with him into the wedding banquet; and the door was shut" (**v. 10b**). The very purpose of the maids with the lamps was to light the procession into the house in which the wedding celebration was to take place. Those with extinguished lamps could serve no useful purpose. They therefore abandoned their post. Those who were ready, however, were able to perform their duty and so were admitted along with the rest of the wedding party. On the shutting of the door, recall Matt 23:13: "But woe to you, scribes and Pharisees, hypocrites! For you lock people out of the kingdom of heaven. For you do not go in yourselves, and when others are going in, you stop them." See also Matt 24:33: "So also, when you see all these things, you know that he is near, at the very gates." The door to the wedding feast has been shut (perhaps for security reasons); no one will be permitted to crash the party.

The foolish maids then plead, "Lord, lord, open to us" (**v. 11**). See Matt 7:21: "Not everyone who says to me, 'Lord, Lord,' will enter the kingdom of heaven."

---

[503] On this interpretation, see R. Zimmermann, "Das Hochzeitsritual im Jungfrauengleichnis: Sozialgeschichtliche Hintergründe zu Mt 25.1–13," *NTS* 48 (2002): 48–70.

The bridegroom replies, "Truly I tell you, I do not know you" (**v. 12**). For all the bridegroom knows, these are uninvited and unwelcome souls. The maids recruited to light the procession had lit lamps. Who were these people outside in the dark? He does not know them. Recall Jesus' earlier teaching in Matt 7:23, "Then I will declare to them, 'I never knew you; go away from me, you evildoers,'" as well as Peter's tragic denial of his Lord: "I do not know the man!" (Matt 26:74).

The parable concludes with another exhortation to keep awake, for the disciples "know neither the day nor the hour" (**v. 13**) of the coming of the Son of Man (cf. Matt 24:27, 30, 37, 39, 44).

MATTHEW 25:14–30 – THE PARABLE OF THE SERVANTS

25:14: "For it is as if a man, going on a journey, summoned his slaves and entrusted his property to them;

25:15: to one he gave five talents, to another two, to another one, to each according to his ability. Then he went away.

25:16: The one who had received the five talents went off at once and traded with them, and made five more talents.

25:17: In the same way, the one who had the two talents made two more talents.

25:18: But the one who had received the one talent went off and dug a hole in the ground and hid his master's money.

25:19: After a long time the master of those slaves came and settled accounts with them.

25:20: Then the one who had received the five talents came forward, bringing five more talents, saying, 'Master, you handed over to me five talents; see, I have made five more talents.'

25:21: His master said to him, 'Well done, good and trustworthy slave; you have been trustworthy in a few things, I will put you in charge of many things; enter into the joy of your master.'

25:22: And the one with the two talents also came forward, saying, 'Master, you handed over to me two talents; see, I have made two more talents.'

25:23: His master said to him, 'Well done, good and trustworthy slave; you have been trustworthy in a few things, I will put you in charge of many things; enter into the joy of your master.'

25:24: Then the one who had received the one talent also came forward, saying, 'Master, I knew that you were a harsh man, reaping where you did not sow, and gathering where you did not scatter seed;

25:25: so I was afraid, and I went and hid your talent in the ground. Here you have what is yours.'

25:26: But his master replied, 'You wicked and lazy slave! You knew, did you, that I reap where I did not sow, and gather where I did not scatter?

25:27: Then you ought to have invested my money with the bankers, and on my return I would have received what was my own with interest.

25:28: So take the talent from him, and give it to the one with the ten talents.

25:29: For to all those who have, more will be given, and they will have an abundance; but from those who have nothing, even what they have will be taken away.

25:30: As for this worthless slave, throw him into the outer darkness, where there will be weeping and gnashing of teeth.'

*M*atthew adds a second major parable to his extension of Mark's eschatological discourse (the first one was the parable of the bridesmaids in Matt 25:1–13). The parable of the servants bears an uncertain relation to Luke 19:11–27. It is probable that these two parables derive from the same basic parable, though it is possible that Jesus himself told many of his parables over and over again, with variations in the details. Both forms of parable relate in some way to Mark 4:24–25, in which we find the principle that "For to those who have, more will be given; and from those who have nothing, even what they have will be taken away" (Mark 4:25).

The parable begins, "A man, going on a journey, summoned his slaves and entrusted his property to them" (v. 14). Envisioned here is a well-heeled man of business, doubtless off on another business trip.

The businessman gathered his slaves and "To one he gave five talents, to another two, to another one, to each according to his ability" (v. 15). A talent is a substantial sum of money.[504] Recall the parable of the unforgiving servant (Matt 18:23–35) and the commentary on Matt 18:24. The businessman prudently hands out funds according to proven track records. His judgment will be vindicated, for the man given the most will earn the most; the man given the least will earn nothing. As it turns out, the wealthy man judged correctly, for the first servant earned five talents and the second earned two (vv. 16–17).

Matthew reports, "But the one who had received the one talent went off and dug a hole in the ground and hid his master's money" (v. 18). Unlike the two other servants who doubled their master's money, the timid servant who had been given only one talent hid the money "in the ground" (cf. the parable of the treasure in Matt 13:44). This was a safe thing to do, but it was not wise.

---

[504] For discussion of the meaning of the distributed talents, see B. Chenoweth, "Identifying the Talents: Contextual Clues for the Interpretation of the Parable of the Talents (Matthew 25:14–30)," *TynBul* 56 (2005): 61–72; M. Locker, "Reading and Re-reading Matthew's Parable of the Talents in Context," *BZ* 49 (2005): 161–73.

The master commends the slaves who doubled his money, saying "Well done, good and trustworthy slave" (**vv. 19–23**). He then rewards them with additional responsibility. But it is a very different story with the man who simply hid his talent in the ground.

The servant who received only one talent and hid it explains why he took such a conservative approach: "Master, I knew that you were a harsh man, reaping where you did not sow, and gathering where you did not scatter seed" (**v. 24**). The master is unforgiving. If he severely punishes one who makes no money, how will he treat one who loses his money? So, we are to imagine, went the thinking of the timid servant. Therefore, to avoid the possibility of loss, he hid the money in the ground (**v. 25**).

The servant has every reason to fear his master; he is no nice man. He is a "harsh" man (i.e., unforgiving, unmerciful), which is illustrated in two ways: he reaps fields that he "did not sow," and he gathers in crops and fruit where he did not "scatter (or plant) seed." Either this man is an outright thief (which is probably not the case) or he is a very tough businessman and landlord. What is in view is seizure of crops because tenant farmers have fallen behind in payments. The slave's master is no friend to the local farmers or to anyone at his mercy. Jesus' audience would not have a sympathetic view of this man.[505]

The master scolds the timid servant: "You wicked and lazy slave! You knew, did you, that I reap where I did not sow, and gather where I did not scatter?" (**v. 26**). The master is not impressed with the servant's excuse (but neither does he dispute the accuracy or fairness of the servant's description of him, it is presupposed). The master's point is simple: The servant knew what kind of man he was, so why didn't he act accordingly?

The master's rebuke continues, "You ought to have invested my money with the bankers, and on my return I would have received what was my own with interest" (**v. 27**). The master is most displeased that his timid servant did not at least lend the money to a trusted banker, so that some interest might have been earned (on the illegality of lending for interest, see Exod 22:25; Deut 23:19–20; Lev 25:36–37). Jewish law permitted Jews to collect interest from Gentiles but not from fellow Jews.

The master then orders, "Take the talent from him, and give it to the one with the ten talents" (**v. 28**). Consistent with his hard-nosed policy, the master entrusts the talent of the unprofitable servant to the servant who has generated the greatest return.

The master goes on to summarize how he does business: "For to all those who have, more will be given" (**v. 29**). The principle of spiritual receptivity (as in Mark

---

[505]   Yeshua ben Sira, the sage from the second century B.C., also took a very dim view of grasping businessmen; see, e.g., Sir 13:4, "A rich man will exploit you if you can be of use to him, but if you are in need he will forsake you"; Sir 26:29, "A merchant can hardly keep from wrongdoing, and a tradesman will not be declared innocent of sin."

4:24–25) is here applied to the principle of productivity, or lack thereof. The appearance of this saying here, which may not have been part of the original parable, indicates the meaning the parable has for Matthew and his community. Originally the parable was probably told as an illustration of the selfish and oppressive policies of the pagan rulers (whose behavior the disciples are not to emulate; cf. Matt 20:25–28). But in the present context the parable serves as a warning to those who think their Lord's work is not to be taken seriously.[506]

The master continues, "As for this worthless slave, throw him into the outer darkness" (v. 30). Again, consistent with his character, the master is unmerciful in his judgment against the unproductive servant. On hell as a place of outer darkness, see 1QS 4:12–13, which speaks of "everlasting damnation in the wrath of God's furious vengeance, never-ending terror and reproach for all eternity, with a shameful extinction in the fire of Hell's outer darkness." For other examples of the imagery of "weeping and gnashing of teeth," see Matt 8:12; 13:42, 50; 22:13; 24:51. Outside of Matthew, this language occurs but once (cf. Luke 13:28).

MATTHEW 25:31–46 – REWARD FOR THE MERCIFUL

25:31: "When the Son of Man comes in his glory, and all the angels with him, then he will sit on the throne of his glory.

25:32: All the nations will be gathered before him, and he will separate people one from another as a shepherd separates the sheep from the goats,

25:33: and he will put the sheep at his right hand and the goats at the left.

25:34: Then the king will say to those at his right hand, 'Come, you that are blessed by my Father, inherit the kingdom prepared for you from the foundation of the world;

25:35: for I was hungry and you gave me food, I was thirsty and you gave me something to drink, I was a stranger and you welcomed me,

25:36: I was naked and you gave me clothing, I was sick and you took care of me, I was in prison and you visited me.'

25:37: Then the righteous will answer him, 'Lord, when was it that we saw you hungry and gave you food, or thirsty and gave you something to drink?

---

[506] For the nontraditional approach to the parable, see M. Fricke, "Wer is der Held des Gleichnisses? Kontextuelle Lesarten des Gleichnisses von den Talenten," *BK* 63 (2008): 76–80. Another suggestion is that the parable itself has been inverted in that in the original form it was the third servant, the one who did not gouge or cheat his fellow Israelites, who was praised and rewarded. For a defense of this view, which I do not find convincing, see H. Frankemölle, "Das Gleichnis von den Zentnern/Talenten (Mt 25,14–30). Zwei Lesenweisen: Jesus und Matthäus," *Orientierung* 69 (2005): 10–12.

25:38: And when was it that we saw you a stranger and welcomed you, or naked and gave you clothing?

25:39: And when was it that we saw you sick or in prison and visited you?'

25:40: And the king will answer them, 'Truly I tell you, just as you did it to one of the least of these who are members of my family, you did it to me.'

25:41: Then he will say to those at his left hand, 'You that are accursed, depart from me into the eternal fire prepared for the devil and his angels;

25:42: for I was hungry and you gave me no food, I was thirsty and you gave me nothing to drink,

25:43: I was a stranger and you did not welcome me, naked and you did not give me clothing, sick and in prison and you did not visit me.'

25:44: Then they also will answer, 'Lord, when was it that we saw you hungry or thirsty or a stranger or naked or sick or in prison, and did not take care of you?'

25:45: Then he will answer them, 'Truly I tell you, just as you did not do it to one of the least of these, you did not do it to me.'

25:46: And these will go away into eternal punishment, but the righteous into eternal life."

*M*atthew's parable of the sheep and the goats, which promises rewards for the merciful, once again underscores the division between the saved and the lost. Someday all the nations will gather before the glorified Son of Man, who will then separate them, the righteous from the unrighteous, much as a shepherd separates the sheep from the goats.[507]

The picture reflected by the verse "When the Son of Man comes in his glory, and all the angels with him, then he will sit on the throne of his glory" (**v. 31**) is that of Daniel 7, which speaks of thrones (v. 9), of "one like a Son of Man" (v. 13), "myriads" (i.e., angels, v. 10), and glory (v. 14). When the Son of Man comes, the court will convene; judgment will take place (cf. Dan 7:10: "The court sat in judgment, and the books were opened"). Once again, Jesus speaks of the angels of the Son of Man as though the Son of Man has authority over the angels (see the commentary on Matt 24:31).

The parable continues, "All the nations will be gathered before him, and he will separate people one from another" (**v. 32**). The Son of Man does not separate one nation from another (as though to say "Japan is okay, but China is in trouble"). No, all the Gentile nations (and previously Jesus had warned of a similar sifting of Israel) will now be gathered before him and the people of these nations will be

---

[507] K. Weber, "The Image of Sheep and Goats in Matthew 25:31–46," *CBQ* 59 (1997): 657–78. Weber cautions against interpreting the symbolism of sheep and goats from a modern perspective.

separated, the righteous from the wicked. Accordingly, the Son of Man "will put the sheep at his right hand and the goats at the left" (**v. 33**). The sheep are those who will be saved, as indicated by being placed on the *right*, at the place of honor (cf. Ps 110:1: "Sit at my right hand").

The saying "Then the king will say to those at his right hand, 'Come, you that are blessed by my Father, inherit the kingdom prepared for you from the foundation of the world'" (**v. 34**) is significant, for earlier in Matthew, the good news of the kingdom was to be preached only to the lost sheep of the House of Israel (cf. Matt 10:6; 15:24). Now, righteous Gentiles will be added to the flock of sheep destined for salvation (cf. Matt 28:19, "make disciples of all nations"). These Gentiles, just as surely as the righteous of Israel, will "inherit the kingdom." But on what grounds? Verses 35–45 explain.

Matthew lays out some ways by which the righteous inherit the kingdom: "For I was hungry and you gave me food, I was thirsty and you gave me something to drink, I was a stranger and you welcomed me; I was naked and you gave me clothing, I was sick and you took care of me, I was in prison and you visited me" (**vv. 35–36**). The compassion and care that people show for Jesus' disciples provide the proof of their righteousness and sincerity. It is not what is said with the mouth but what is done that proves character. Rabbinic literature agrees: "Concerning them who are merciful, who feed the hungry, give drink to the thirsty, clothe the naked, and distribute alms, Scripture declares: 'Tell the righteous that it shall be well with them' [Isa 3:10]" (*Derek 'Erets Rabba* 2.21).

The righteous will ask when it was they saw Jesus and ministered to him (**vv. 37–39**). It was whenever they extended mercy to "one of the least of these who are members of" Jesus' "family" (**v. 40**). The ministrations described in these verses reveal the desperate straits in which many found themselves in late antiquity, especially those who were persecuted, driven out of the synagogue, and hunted down by pagan authorities.[508]

The imaginary conversation is repeated in **vv. 41–45**, only this time in reverse: those on the left will be condemned for having done nothing for those in need. They "will go away into eternal punishment, but the righteous into eternal life" (**v. 46**).[509]

---

[508] For the view that the "least of these" are the followers of Jesus in general, see D. Cortés-Fuentes, "The Least of These My Brothers: Matthew 25:31–46," *Apuntes* 23 (2003): 100–9. For a different view, see J. S. Ruh, "Das Weltgericht und die Matthäische Gemeinde," *NovT* 48 (2006): 217–33. Ruh suggests the focus is on those in the mission field.

[509] On the tension between the irenic ethics of Jesus on the one hand and the anticipation of violent retribution in the future on the other, see D. J. Neville, "Toward a Teleology of Peace: Contesting Matthew's Violent Eschatology," *JSNT* 30 (2007): 131–61. See also J. P. Heil, "The Double Meaning of the Narrative of Universal Judgment in Matthew 25:31–46," *CBQ* 69 (1998): 3–14.

MATTHEW 26:1–5 – THE PLOT TO ARREST JESUS

26:1: When Jesus had finished saying all these things, he said to his disciples,

26:2: "You know that after two days the Passover is coming, and the Son of Man will be handed over to be crucified."

26:3: Then the chief priests and the elders of the people gathered in the palace of the high priest, who was called Caiaphas,

26:4: and they conspired to arrest Jesus by stealth and kill him.

26:5: But they said, "Not during the festival, or there may be a riot among the people."

*M*atthew follows Mark 14:1–2 but elaborates on a few points. The opening line, "When Jesus had finished saying all these things" (**v. 1**), refers to the eschatological discourse found in Matthew 24–25. The phrase itself is taken from the Pentateuch to remind readers of the first lawgiver, Moses (see the commentary on Matt 7:28). In **v. 2**, Jesus recaps previous Passion predictions, linking them to Mark's chronology of two days before Passover (Mark 14:1).[510] In **vv. 3–4**, Matthew more elaborately describes the "chief priests and the elders of the people" (instead of Mark's "scribes") gathered "in the palace of the high priest, who was called Caiaphas," where they plot how to seize and kill Jesus. More will be said on Caiaphas in the commentary on Matt 26:57–68.

The chief priests do not want to seize Jesus "during the festival" (that is, the Passover celebration), which could instigate "a riot among the people" (**v. 5**). The Passover festival celebrated Israel's deliverance from Egyptian slavery. Tens of thousands of Jews gathered in Jerusalem every spring to observe this festival. Among these pilgrims would be thousands of Galilean Jews. Seizing and killing Jesus (on a Roman cross no less) could very well lead to a riot.

MATTHEW 26:6–13 – THE ANOINTING OF JESUS

26:6: Now while Jesus was at Bethany in the house of Simon the leper,

26:7: a woman came to him with an alabaster jar of very costly ointment, and she poured it on his head as he sat at the table.

26:8: But when the disciples saw it, they were angry and said, "Why this waste?

---

[510]   For more discussion on how Matthew links Jesus' Passion predictions with the story of the Passion, see E. LaVerdiere, "The Passion Story as Prophecy," *Emmanuel* 93 (1987): 85–90. For an analysis of Matthew's composition of the Passion narrative, see J. G. Lodge, "Matthew's Passion-Resurrection Narrative," *Chicago Studies* 25 (1986): 3–20.

26:9: For this ointment could have been sold for a large sum, and the money given to the poor."

26:10: But Jesus, aware of this, said to them, "Why do you trouble the woman? She has performed a good service for me.

26:11: For you always have the poor with you, but you will not always have me.

26:12: By pouring this ointment on my body she has prepared me for burial.

26:13: Truly I tell you, wherever this good news is proclaimed in the whole world, what she has done will be told in remembrance of her."

*T*he present passage, based on Mark 14:3–9, narrates the story of the woman who anoints Jesus. The meaning of this Passion week anointing is a matter of debate. Anointing was a custom at feasts, including Passover (Pss 23:5; 141:5; *b. Hullin* 94a), but it seems to be too much of a coincidence that Jesus was anointed during Passover week and then days later he was crucified as "king of the Jews" (Matt 27:37; *Pss. Sol.* 17:32). It is more probable that the woman's action was intended to be messianic (cf. 1 Sam 16:12, where Samuel anoints David). The woman's act of anointing could have connoted, and probably did connote, both ideas – a holiday anointing, which was even more than a mere holiday anointing because Jesus was the Lord's Anointed.

The other question has to do with the relationship of Jesus' anointing in Matthew 26 (and Mark 14) and his anointing in Luke 7. In Matt 26:6–13, Jesus is in the house of Simon the leper (v. 6), and in Luke 7 he is in the house of Simon the Pharisee (Luke 7:40, 43, 44). In Mark 14, it is the head of Jesus that is anointed, but in Luke 7 it is his feet. What we probably have here are two separate stories, which may have shared some details over the passing of time.

The anointing takes place in the village of Bethany (**v. 6**), some three kilometers opposite Jerusalem. Bethany, along with Bethphage, is mentioned in Mark 11:1 in connection with Jesus' entrance into Jerusalem. Matthew, however, had omitted the reference to the village.[511] But it is mentioned now, for it is where Simon the leper lives and where Jesus spends his evenings during the Passover week. Who was Simon the leper? The sobriquet "the leper" does not mean that Simon was still leprous on the occasion of Jesus' visit; this is quite improbable (for the disciples and the unnamed woman would scarcely have gone into this man's house for a meal). This Simon had been a leper but now was cleansed, perhaps by Jesus. Beyond the probability that Simon numbered among Jesus' followers, we know nothing of this man.[512]

---

[511] This Bethany is not to be confused with the "Bethany beyond the Jordan" (cf. John 1:19–28), which in fact may have been the region of Batanea.

[512] In Christian legend, Simon is identified as the father of Lazarus and Martha; see D. C. Allison, Jr. and W. D. Davies, *A Critical and Exegetical Commentary on the Gospel According to Saint Matthew* (1988–1997), 3:443.

The account of the anointing begins, "A woman came to him with an alabaster jar of very costly ointment" (**v. 7**). Mark 14:3 says the ointment was "pure nard." The very best perfumes and other precious unguents were often contained in alabaster vessels (cf. Pliny the Elder, *Nat. Hist.* 13.3.19). Nard was among the most costly ointments. The unnamed woman poured the ointment on Jesus' head as he reclined at table.

The disciples respond to the woman's generous act with anger and regard it as a "waste" (**v. 8**). The disciples' reaction is oafish and betrays their lack of sensitivity for the woman in view of her great sacrifice. They point out that "this ointment could have been sold for a large sum, and the money given to the poor" (**v. 9**). Mark 14:5 specifies that the ointment could have been sold for three hundred denarii, or about one year's wages, a not insignificant sum. On the evening of Passover, the poor were remembered (cf. *m. Pesah.* 9:11). Perhaps of more pressing concern to the disciples were the financial needs of a new government that some still hoped would be inaugurated soon. Money would be needed – for the poor, as well as for other expenses.

Jesus, however, appreciates what the woman has done, saying, "She has performed a good service for me" (**v. 10**). Jesus is not indifferent to the needs of the poor – the disciples will have many opportunities to care for them – but they will not always have the opportunity to minister to Jesus (**v. 11**). But Jesus has more to say about the matter: "By pouring this ointment on my body she has prepared me for burial" (**v. 12**). Indeed, Jesus tells his disciples, "wherever this good news is proclaimed in the whole world, what she has done will be told in remembrance of her" (**v. 13**). Jesus' grim words allude to the Jewish custom of anointing the body as part of the preparation for burial: "They make ready all that is needful for the dead, and anoint it [the corpse] and wash it . . ." (*m. Shab.* 23:5). But Jesus' prophecy that what the woman has done will be told in remembrance of her anticipates his vindication and the continued proclamation of his message and ministry. Otherwise, why would anyone recall the woman's generous act? Her act of devotion has put her into the heart of the gospel story.[513]

MATTHEW 26:14–16 – A SINISTER BARGAIN

26:14: Then one of the twelve, who was called Judas Iscariot, went to the chief priests

26:15: and said, "What will you give me if I betray him to you?" They paid him thirty pieces of silver.

26:16: And from that moment he began to look for an opportunity to betray him.

---

[513] On the authenticity and transmission of the story of the woman who anointed Jesus, see K. E. Corley, "The Anointing of Jesus in the Synoptic Tradition: An Argument for Authenticity," *JSHJ* 1 (2003): 61–72. See also S. C. Barton, "Mark as Narrative: The Story of the Anointing Woman (Mk 14:3–9)," *ExpT* 102 (1991): 230–34.

atthew follows Mark 14:10–11 but supplies a few details in order to answer questions that linger. The major question has to do with Judas' motive for betraying Jesus. According to Matt 26:15–16, it is money. This is consistent with the fourth evangelist's claim that Judas used to pilfer from the money box (John 12:6). It is probable that additional factors also were in play.

Matthew's account of Jesus' betrayal begins, "Then one of the twelve, who was called Judas Iscariot …" (**v. 14**). Attentive readers will note the contrast between the unnamed woman in Matt 26:6–13, who out of devotion to Jesus gave such a generous gift, and Judas, who out of avarice betrayed his master.

Matthew continues with a report of Judas' reward for betraying Jesus: "They paid him thirty pieces of silver" (**v. 15**). Mark mentions only that the chief priests "promised to give him money" (Mark 14:11). The thirty pieces of silver probably alludes to Zech 11:12, "So they weighed out as my wages thirty shekels of silver," and perhaps also Exod 21:32, "the owner shall pay to the slave-owner thirty shekels of silver," as though Judas was seeking compensation for lost time and investment.[514] The attentive reader of Matthew may recall that in the missionary discourse Jesus commanded his apostles to take no silver (cf. Matt 10:9). By coveting silver, has Judas demonstrated that he is a false apostle whose quality, like that of a tree, has been disclosed by his fruit? See Matt 7:17–19.

Matthew continues, "And from that moment he began to look for an opportunity to betray him" (**v. 16**). Some scholars have tried to make Judas' deed into something other than a betrayal of Jesus. But these proposals struggle against the evidence. In the world of late antiquity, traitors were despised (Babrius 138.7–8; Livy 1.11.6–7; 5.27.6–10); to betray one's own people for a bribe was considered a terrible crime and a cause for great shame (cf. Demosthenes, *For the Liberty of the Rhodians* 23; Demosthenes, *On the Crown* 46–49). There is no hint in Christian tradition that Judas' deed could be interpreted in any but the darkest light. However, just as we should not exculpate or even lionize Judas and try to find something positive in his deed, neither should we demonize him. Judas Iscariot exemplifies human weakness, and all Christians should know that the discouragement and temptation that overtook him could overtake them as well.

MATTHEW 26:17–19 – PREPARATION FOR THE PASSOVER

26:17: On the first day of Unleavened Bread the disciples came to Jesus, saying, "Where do you want us to make the preparations for you to eat the Passover?"

26:18: He said, "Go into the city to a certain man, and say to him, 'The Teacher says, My time is near; I will keep the Passover at your house with my disciples.'"

---

[514] For an interesting cultural suggestion, see K. Luke, "The Thirty Pieces of Silver," *Indian Theological Studies* 31 (1994): 156–58. On the basis of ancient Middle Eastern tradition, Luke argues that "thirty pieces of silver" for someone's life implies contempt.

26:19: So the disciples did as Jesus had directed them, and they prepared the Passover meal.

*T*he evangelist Matthew's account of the preparation for the Passover meal is a simplified version of Mark 14:12–16. The major historical and interpretive question is whether or not the meal that Jesus eats with his disciples was a Passover meal. That he intended to eat the Passover seems clear enough, and Mark's version relates the preparations and the precautions undertaken. But was the meal, which has become known as the Last Supper (or Lord's Supper), the Passover Seder, as planned?

Major scholars have weighed in on both sides of the debate. The Gospels themselves appear divided on the question. Mark 14:12 ("Where do you want us to go and make the preparations for you to eat the Passover?"), followed by Matthew (26:17) and Luke (22:8), apparently understands the Last Supper (Mark 14:17–25 = Matt 26:20–29 = Luke 22:14–23) as a Passover meal, while John 18:28 (cf. John 19:14, 31, 42) seems to imply that the Last Supper took place *the day before* Passover and that Jesus in fact died the next day, on the Passover, the fifteenth of Nisan. Perhaps Johannine chronology in this instance should be preferred to the Synoptic chronology. Jesus may very well have intended to eat the Passover with his disciples, but, as it turned out, his last meal with them was a meal the day before, in which he foretold betrayal and uttered the words of institution. Recall, too, that the chief priests evidently intended to take Jesus into custody before the Passover festival, or at least not during the festival itself (Matt 26:1–2 = Mark 14:1–2).

Jesus' disciples ask him, "Where do you want us to make the preparations for you to eat the Passover?" (**v. 17**). In ancient times, if biblical legislation was observed literally, the Passover lamb would have been cooked and eaten within the temple precincts themselves (inferred from Deut 16:7, "the place that the Lord your God will choose"). In late antiquity, the much larger population made this impossible. After the slaughter and the sprinkling of blood on the altar, the celebrant and his family retired to a private setting within the city of Jerusalem (cf. *Sipre Num.* §69 [on Num 9:10], "What is the place in which it must be eaten? Within the gate of Jerusalem," and also *t. Pisha* 8.2) to cook and eat the Passover lamb. The implication of the disciples' question is that the Passover lamb has just been slaughtered, so there is now need to retire to suitable quarters. They are asking where those quarters are.

Jesus' response begins, "Go into the city to a certain man …" (**v. 18**). Matthew's version of finding the place where Jesus and his disciples will keep the Passover is much simpler than Mark's version. The details of finding a man carrying a jar, following him, asking a question, and being shown a furnished upper room are all omitted. In Matthew, the disciples simply state: "The Teacher says, My time is near; I will keep the Passover at your house with my disciples." Matthew's version places the emphasis on Jesus, not on the occasion. The time of his suffering has arrived. Thus the focus is shifted away from the Passover to the Passion of Jesus, as foretold several times (cf. Matt 16:21; 17:22–23; 20:18–19). The disciples did as Jesus instructed them and "prepared the Passover meal" (**v. 19**).[515]

MATTHEW 26:20–25 – A PROPHECY OF BETRAYAL

26:20: When it was evening, he took his place with the twelve [disciples];

26:21: and while they were eating, he said, "Truly I tell you, one of you will betray me."

26:22: And they became greatly distressed and began to say to him one after another, "Surely not I, Lord?"

26:23: He answered, "The one who has dipped his hand into the bowl with me will betray me.

26:24: The Son of Man goes as it is written of him, but woe to that one by whom the Son of Man is betrayed! It would have been better for that one not to have been born."

26:25: Judas, who betrayed him, said, "Surely not I, Rabbi?" He replied, "You have said so."

$\mathcal{M}$atthew follows Mark 14:17–21, with a few minor stylistic variations (such as the addition of "disciples"[516] in **v. 20** and "will betray me" in **v. 23**). The significant addition is seen in **v. 25**. After Jesus' grim statement, "It would have been better for that one not to have been born" (**v. 24**), Judas asks, "Surely it is not I, Rabbi?" And Jesus replies, "You have said so." Because readers have already been told about Judas' bargain with the chief priests (in Matt 26:14–16), they recognize Judas' question "Surely it is not I, Rabbi?" for the hypocrisy that it is. But the emphasis falls on Jesus' prescience. He knows that Judas is the traitor; he has not been taken by surprise.

In Matthew's account, Jesus says, "The one who has dipped his hand into the bowl with me will betray me" (**v. 23**). Mark 14:18 simply says the "one who is eating with me." Matthew's revision heightens the element of personal betrayal. The

---

[515]   For further discussion, see J. Klawans, "Was Jesus' Last Supper a Seder?" *BRev* 17 (2001): 24–33, 47; R. Routledge, "Passover and Last Supper," *TynBul* 53 (2002): 203–21. Following John 19:14, Klawans thinks the Last Supper took place the night before Passover, whereas Routledge argues that the Last Supper was in fact the Passover meal. For another approach, see B. D. Smith, "The Chronology of the Last Supper," *WTJ* 53 (1991): 29–45. For Old Testament backgrounds, see R. A. D. Clancy, "The Old Testament Roots of Remembrance in the Lord's Supper," *Concordia Journal* 19 (1993): 35–50; D. Stacey, "The Lord's Supper as Prophetic Drama," *EpReview* 21 (1994): 65–74; C. Ham, "The Last Supper in Matthew," *BBR* 10 (2000): 53–69.

[516]   "Disciples" (RSV) is read by some major witnesses to the Gospel of Matthew. It is, however, omitted by P[45] and B, two early and very important witnesses.

betrayer is not only one of the twelve in the room eating with Jesus but is actually sharing the dish with him.[517]

MATTHEW 26:26–30 – WORDS ABOUT THE EUCHARIST

26:26: While they were eating, Jesus took a loaf of bread, and after blessing it he broke it, gave it to the disciples, and said, "Take, eat; this is my body."

26:27: Then he took a cup, and after giving thanks he gave it to them, saying, "Drink from it, all of you;

26:28: for this is my blood of the covenant, which is poured out for many for the forgiveness of sins.

26:29: I tell you, I will never again drink of this fruit of the vine until that day when I drink it new with you in my Father's kingdom."

26:30: When they had sung the hymn, they went out to the Mount of Olives.

Once again, Matthew follows Mark closely (Mark 14:22–25), with a few minor additions (such as adding "disciples" in v. 26, as he may have done earlier in v. 20, Jesus' command that the disciples "Drink from" the cup in v. 27, or "my Father's" in v. 29). The most significant addition is seen in v. 28, where Jesus says, "this is my blood of the covenant, which is poured out for many for the forgiveness of sins." The last phrase, "for the forgiveness of sins," is not in Mark's parallel. The appearance of this phrase takes the attentive reader of Matthew back to Matt 1:21, where the angel tells Joseph that Mary "will bear a son, and you are to name him Jesus, for he will save his people from their sins." In the words of institution, Jesus now explains – it is implied – how he will "save his people from their sins." He does it by dying, so that their sins may be forgiven.

Jesus says, "Take, eat; this is my body" (**v. 26**). Matthew adds "eat" to Mark's "Take, this is my body" (Mark 14:22). The appearance of "eat" may have been prompted by the command to "drink" in v. 27. Luke adds "which is given for you" and "Do this in remembrance of me" (Luke 22:19b), which closely parallels Paul's form of the tradition (1 Cor 11:24). The copula "is" (Greek: *estin*) should be taken to mean "signifies" or "represents." Jesus does not mean to say that the bread is literally his body. The sense in Aramaic may have been "this (bread) represents me."[518]

---

[517] For further discussion on this aspect, see J. Bohnen, "'Watch How You're Eating': Judas and Jesus and Table Manners. An Intertextual Reading of John 13:26, Matthew 26:23 and Sirach 31:12–32:13," *Scriptura* 74 (2000): 259–83. For a priestly and cultic interpretation, which I do not find convincing, see J. D. M. Derrett, "The Upper Room and the Dish," *HeyJ* 26 (1985): 373–82.

[518] On the meaning of bread in the Passover setting, see D. B. Carmichael, "David Daube on the Eucharist and the Passover Seder," *JSNT* 42 (1991): 45–67.

Jesus continues, "This is my blood of the covenant, which is poured out for many for the forgiveness of sins" (**v. 28**). The true significance of the cup (v. 27) is now clarified. The broken bread is Jesus, who will sacrifice himself, but the cup is Jesus' "blood of the covenant." The expression "blood of the covenant" recalls Exod 24:8: "Moses took the blood and dashed it on the people, and said, 'See the blood of the covenant that the Lord has made with you in accordance with all these words.'" Although Jesus does not say "new covenant" (and some scribes add the adjective "new" to the text; cf. Luke 22:20; 1 Cor 11:25), it is quite probable that he was indeed alluding to the new covenant foretold by the prophet Jeremiah (cf. Jer 31:31). His sacrificial death will establish the promised new covenant.[519]

The reference "poured out" recalls the language of sacrificial atonement (cf. Lev 4:7, 18, 25, 30, 34),[520] while "for many" probably alludes to the Suffering Servant (cf. Isa 53:8, "stricken for the transgression of my people"; Isa 53:12, "he poured out himself to death … he bore the sin of many"). The theme of forgiveness of sins is very important.[521] Of course, human sacrifice was never part of the Jewish sacrificial system. But the near sacrifice of Isaac by his father, the great patriarch Abraham, as well as several examples of Jewish martyrs whose suffering and death benefited Israel and even in some sense atoned for Israel's sin (1 Macc 6:44; 2 Macc 7:33, 37–38; 4 *Macc* 1:11b; 17:21b–22; 18:3–4; *T. Mos.* 9:6b–10:1; Ps.-Philo, *Bib. Ant.* 18:5),[522] provides sufficient backdrop for the disciples to understand the meaning of their master's words.

Jesus then warns the disciples of his impending death: "I tell you, I will never again drink of this fruit of the vine until that day when I drink it new with you in my Father's kingdom" (**v. 29**). When Jesus drinks of the fruit of the vine (i.e., wine) in the kingdom of God, he will do so renewed. This makes good sense, especially if Jesus anticipates his death and subsequent vindication. It will not be the old Jesus who drinks wine at the next Passover but the "new" Jesus who will drink it in the kingdom.

---

[519] On the Old Testament background of Jesus' words, see C. Ham, "The Last Supper in Matthew," *BBR* 10 (2000): 53–69.

[520] Jesus is referring to the pouring out of his blood, literally, on the cross. On this point, see L. C. Boughton, "'Being Shed for You/Many': Time-Sense and Consequences in the Synoptic Cup Citations," *TynBul* 48 (1997): 249–70.

[521] As rightly underscored in the studies by E. LaVerdiere, "The Eucharist in the New Testament and the Early Church – V. For the Forgiveness of Sins: The Eucharist in Matthew's Gospel," *Emmanuel* 100 (1994): 196–206; and O. Hofius, "'Für euch gegeben zur Vergebung der Sünden': Vom Sinn des Heiligen Abendmahls," *ZTK* 95 (1998): 313–37.

[522] See M. F. Whitters, "Taxo and His Seven Sons in the Cave (*Assumption of Moses* 9–10)," *CBQ* 72 (2010): 718–31. Whitters suggests that the deaths of Taxo's seven sons (in the *Testament* [or *Assumption*] *of Moses*) may be "the missing link to the martyrological symbolism found in the death of Jesus" (p. 731).

Matthew's account of the Last Supper concludes, "When they had sung the hymn, they went out to the Mount of Olives" (**v. 30**). It has been suggested that Jesus and his disciples sang the *Hallel Hagadol* (the "Great Hallel"; i.e., Psalm 136), which recounts God's mighty acts, connecting Israel's past with Jesus' Passion.[523] However, the hymn may have been drawn from the *Hallel* (Psalms 113–118), especially if the supper had been a Passover meal (cf. *m. Pesah.* 10:7).[524] Paul and Silas sing in Acts 16:25, though it has nothing to do with a meal or celebration of a holy day. There are other allusions to singing, music, or melody elsewhere in the New Testament (cf. 1 Cor 14:26; Eph 5:19; Col 3:16; Heb 2:12[?]; James 5:13).

With the meal concluded, the disciples exit the city and go out to the Mount of Olives. It is possible that Jesus intended to return to Bethany (house of Simon the leper?) to spend the night. In any case, he and some of his disciples stop at a place for Jesus to pray (see Matt 26:31–35).

MATTHEW 26:31–35 – THREE PROPHECIES

26:31: Then Jesus said to them, "You will all become deserters because of me this night; for it is written, 'I will strike the shepherd, and the sheep of the flock will be scattered.'

26:32: But after I am raised up, I will go ahead of you to Galilee."

26:33: Peter said to him, "Though all become deserters because of you, I will never desert you."

26:34: Jesus said to him, "Truly I tell you, this very night, before the cock crows, you will deny me three times."

26:35: Peter said to him, "Even though I must die with you, I will not deny you." And so said all the disciples.

*M*atthew follows Mark 14:27–31, though in places he augments the narrative with emphasis and vividness, adding "because of me this night" and "of the flock" in v. 31, "because of You" and "never desert you" in v. 33, and, as is often done, "disciples" in v. 35.

Jesus prophesies, "You will all become deserters because of me this night" (**v. 31**). Jesus knows this not only because of his prophetic powers but because the scattering of the shepherd's flock was foretold by the prophet Zechariah (cf. Zech 13:7). Some think Mark, followed by Matthew, added the prophetic words "I will strike the shepherd, and the sheep of the flock will be scattered." But this is doubtful, for it

523   H. Rusche, "Das letzte gemeinsame Gebet Jesu mit seinen Jüngern: Der Psalm 136," *Wissenschaft und Weisheit* 51 (1988): 210–12.
524   J. du Preez, "The Missionary Significance of Psalm 117 in the Book of Psalms and in the New Testament," *Missionalia* 27 (1999): 369–76.

is unlikely that early Christians, including Mark, would appeal to Zech 13:7 as a prophetic reference to Jesus, because the prophecy speaks of divine judgment directed against the shepherd: "'Awake, O sword, against my shepherd, against the man who stands next to me,' says the Lord of hosts. 'Strike the shepherd, that the sheep may be scattered; I will turn my hand against the little ones.'" It is more likely that in a creative way Jesus adapted and applied to himself Zechariah's prophecy.

The *scattering* of the sheep is a temporary undoing of the messianic task of *gathering* the sheep, the lost, and the exiles of Israel (cf. Num 27:17; 1 Kings 22:17; 2 Chron 18:16; Ezek 34:8, 12, 15; Zech 10:2; Bar 4:26; *Pss. Sol.* 17:4, 21, 26–28; *Tg.* Isa 6:13; 8:18; 35:6; 53:8, "From chastisements and punishments he [the Messiah] will bring our exiles near"; *Tg.* Hos 14:8, "They shall be gathered from among their exiles, they shall dwell in the shade of their Messiah"; *Tg.* Mic 5:1–3).[525]

Jesus assures his disciples that, after he has been raised from the dead, he will go ahead of them to Galilee (**v. 32**). But Peter breaks the train of thought, disagreeing with Jesus' prediction of the desertion of *all* of his disciples: "Though all become deserters because of you, I will never desert you" (**v. 33**). Evidently, Peter thinks he knows better than Jesus.

To Peter's well-intended but misguided declaration, Jesus adds yet one more prophecy: "Truly I tell you, this very night, before the cock crows, you will deny me three times" (**v. 34**). Unfazed, Peter continues to affirm his courage and fidelity: "Even though I must die with you, I will not deny you" (**v. 35**). Perhaps buoyed by Peter's apparent boldness, the other disciples chime in and affirm the same thing.

MATTHEW 26:36–46 – A PLACE CALLED GETHSEMANE

26:36: Then Jesus went with them to a place called Gethsemane; and he said to his disciples, "Sit here while I go over there and pray."

26:37: He took with him Peter and the two sons of Zebedee, and began to be grieved and agitated.

26:38: Then he said to them, "I am deeply grieved, even to death; remain here, and stay awake with me."

26:39: And going a little farther, he threw himself on the ground and prayed, "My Father, if it is possible, let this cup pass from me; yet not what I want but what you want."

26:40: Then he came to the disciples and found them sleeping; and he said to Peter, "So, could you not stay awake with me one hour?

---

[525] For further discussion, see W. Tooley, "The Shepherd and Sheep Image in the Teaching of Jesus," *NovT* 7 (1964–1965): 15–25, especially 16–19; P. Foster, "The Use of Zechariah in Matthew's Gospel," in C. M. Tuckett (ed.), *The Book of Zechariah and Its Influence: Papers of the Oxford-Leiden Conference* (Aldershot: Ashgate, 2003), 65–85.

26:41: Stay awake and pray that you may not come into the time of trial; the spirit indeed is willing, but the flesh is weak."

26:42: Again he went away for the second time and prayed, "My Father, if this cannot pass unless I drink it, your will be done."

26:43: Again he came and found them sleeping, for their eyes were heavy.

26:44: So leaving them again, he went away and prayed for the third time, saying the same words.

26:45: Then he came to the disciples and said to them, "Are you still sleeping and taking your rest? See, the hour is at hand, and the Son of Man is betrayed into the hands of sinners.

26:46: Get up, let us be going. See, my betrayer is at hand."

*M*atthew's version of the prayer in Gethsemane follows Mark's account closely (Mark 14:32–42). In v. 37, Matthew says Jesus took along "the two sons of Zebedee," whereas Mark had mentioned them by name (cf. Mark 14:33, "James and John"). In that same verse, Matthew says that Jesus "began to be grieved and agitated" instead of Mark's "very distressed and troubled" (cf. Mark 14:33). Matthew has replaced Mark's "very distressed" (which in the Greek usually means "amazed" or "alarmed") with "grieved," perhaps to avoid the impression that Jesus is disturbed or surprised. In v. 42, Matthew provides the actual words of Jesus' second prayer, "My Father, if this cannot pass unless I drink it, your will be done." The wording makes it clearer than it is in Mark that Jesus is indeed willing to do his Father's will. All of these changes (and there are a few other minor stylistic changes) enhance the portrait of Jesus as master.

Jesus prayed at "a place called Gethsemane" (**v. 36**). The name "Gethsemane" comes from the Aramaic and means "oil-press." According to John 18:1, Jesus and his disciples went "across the Kidron valley to a place where there was a garden." Although it is not certain, the garden of John probably should be identified with the Gethsemane of Mark 14:32 and Matt 26:36. (Luke 22:39 says Jesus and his disciples went to the Mount of Olives but does not mention a specific place.) Jesus has most of his disciples remain at one place and then takes "Peter and the two sons of Zebedee" (**v. 37**) to another. Earlier, Jesus had taken Peter, James, and John with him to the Mount of Transfiguration (Matt 17:1). Jesus takes along these three disciples because he needs and wants their company and because he wishes to disciple them to the very end.

Jesus says, "I am deeply grieved, even to death" (**v. 38**). For Jesus to say that his soul is grieved "even to death" is remarkable and appears to be a deliberate echo of biblical language (cf. Pss 42:4–5, 11; 43:5; Jon 4:9; Sir 37:2). The latter text is especially interesting, given Jesus' knowledge of Judas' imminent betrayal: "Is it not a sorrow like that for death itself when a dear friend turns into an enemy?" Jesus' words could be understood more literally as "grieved to death" (as the RSV similarly translates Sir 37:2, "a grief to the death"), but "to the point of death," a sense the Greek will allow, seems truer to the intended meaning.

Jesus prays, "My Father, if it is possible, let this cup pass from me; yet not what I want but what you want" (**v. 39**). Jesus leaves Peter, James, and John and goes on ahead a bit farther. Now by himself – though we should assume that the three disciples are still within earshot – Jesus "threw himself on the ground and prayed" that, if possible, the "cup" may pass from him. Literally, Matthew says Jesus "fell on his face." Normally Jews pray standing and looking up to heaven (cf. Luke 18:11; recall also the name of a famous Jewish prayer, the Amidah, which means "standing"). Falling to the ground (or on one's face), though exceptional, nevertheless does reflect Middle Eastern custom in antiquity and has biblical precedents (cf. Gen 17:1–3; Lev 9:24). Several times in Numbers, Moses, Aaron, and the people fall on their faces, either in great religious distress or in the presence of God (Num 14:5; 16:4, 22, 45; 20:6). Other examples can be found outside the Bible, where praying/worshiping and falling on one's face are juxtaposed (cf. *T. Job* 40:4; *Joseph and Aseneth* 14:3).

The "cup" Jesus prefers not to drink is the cup of suffering. On "cup of wrath," see Isa 51:17, where the prophet enjoins Jerusalem: "Stand up, O Jerusalem, you who have drunk at the hand of the Lord the cup of his wrath...." On "removing," or "taking away" the cup, see Isa 51:22, where a compassionate and forgiving God says, "See, I have taken from your hand the cup of staggering; you shall drink no more from the bowl of my wrath." See also Ezek 23:32–34; Lam 4:21; Ps 11:6; and *Mart. Asc. Isa.* 5:13. There is an element of divine wrath in Jesus' suffering, in the sense of God's wrath directed against the sin of his people, on whose behalf Jesus will die. Recall, too, the reference to Zech 13:7, applied to Jesus in Matt 26:31: "I will strike the shepherd."

Addressing God as "Father" implies a personal relationship, but it is not unique to Jesus, nor is the Aramaic "Abba" (see Mark 14:36) the equivalent of "Daddy," as has been claimed.[526] Faced with a severe test, Jesus cried out "Father" and then proclaimed his willingness to seek God's will, not his own: "yet not what I want but what you want."

Jesus returns to his three disciples and finds them sleeping (v. 40). Jesus admonishes them to "Stay awake and pray that you may not come into the time of trial" (**v. 41**). His warning to "stay awake and pray" is both literal and figurative. If the disciples are alert and at prayer, they will be ready for the trials that will soon overtake

---

[526] On this debate, see D. Zeller, "God as Father in the Proclamation and in the Prayer of Jesus," in A. Finkel and L. Frizzel (eds.), *Standing before God: Studies in Prayer in Scriptures and in Tradition* (New York: Ktav, 1981), 117–29; J. A. Fitzmyer, "Abba and Jesus' Relation to God," in *À cause de l'évangile: Études sur les Synoptiques et les Actes* (LD 123; 2 vols., Paris: Cerf, 1985), 1:15–38.

them (that night and in the future). Jesus' statement that "the spirit indeed is willing, but the flesh is weak" underscores the need for prayer and the strength that God can give. On our own, we humans are not strong enough to face temptation. Jesus' warning has to do with the temptation to abandon the cause to which Jesus had called his disciples; in effect, to fall away from the faith, to go the way of Judas Iscariot, to betray Jesus and the kingdom of God.

Jesus then says, "My Father, if this cannot pass unless I drink it, your will be done" (**v. 42**), repeating his words of v. 39, though in the negative form. The same language is found in the account of the second-century martyrdom of Polycarp: "[T]hough he still could have escaped from there to another place, he refused, saying, 'May God's will be done'" (*Mart.Pol.* 7:1). It has been suggested that the Gethsemane prayer is a pious invention of Jesus' disciples[527] because, after all, they were not with Jesus (and were sleeping) and therefore could not have heard his prayer. Such an objection carries no weight. Jesus had only gone on ahead "a little farther," thus implying that the disciples were still in earshot. Moreover, prayer in antiquity was normally spoken aloud; silent prayer was exceptional (see 1 Sam 1:12–16, where Eli the high priest mistakes Hannah's silent prayer for drunkenness). Moreover, Jesus was in anguish and may have spoken quite loudly (see Heb 5:7, "Jesus offered up prayers and supplications, with loud cries and tears, to the one who was able to save him from death"). We should also assume that the disciples did not drop off to sleep so quickly that they heard nothing of what Jesus said.[528]

Jesus' declaration, "See, the hour is at hand, and the Son of Man is betrayed into the hands of sinners" (**v. 45**), harks back to his Passion predictions (Matt 16:21; 17:22–23; 20:18–19); for example, "The Son of Man is going to be betrayed into human hands" (Matt 17:22). What Jesus had predicted several times is now beginning to be fulfilled. The three disciples with Jesus would also think back to the Last Supper, concluded only a few hours earlier (Matt 26:21–25). The reference here to "sinners" is ironic, given the criticism that Jesus' opponents had leveled against him earlier in his ministry: "Why does your teacher eat with tax collectors and sinners?" (Matt 9:11). Those who had criticized Jesus for associating with "sinners" are now themselves acting as sinners in the worst way.

Jesus then instructs his disciples, "Get up, let us be going. See, my betrayer is at hand" (**v. 46**). Although the disciples have failed as sentries and fellow prayer warriors, Jesus nevertheless urges them to prepare to meet the approaching enemy.

---

[527] See M. Kiley, "'Lord, Save My Life' (Ps 116:4) as Generative Text for Jesus' Gethsemane Prayer (Mark 14:36a)," *CBQ* 48 (1986): 655–59. Kiley allows that something of Jesus' prayer was probably known, but he thinks Ps 116:1–4 gave shape to it. The language of the psalm may have been a factor for Jesus, but I doubt the disciples later composed a prayer based on it.

[528] For further discussion, see D. M. Stanley, *Jesus in Gethsemane: The Early Church Reflects on the Sufferings of Jesus* (New York: Paulist, 1980), 155–87; C. A. Smith, "A Comparative Study of the Prayer of Gethsemane," *IBS* 22 (2000): 98–122.

In military contexts, "be going" (Greek: *agein*) is used as a command, as with "Forward," "March," or "Advance!" Similarly, Jesus has ordered his men to ready themselves. He has not been taken by surprise; he knows his betrayer approaches.

MATTHEW 26:47–56 – THE ARREST OF JESUS

26:47: While he was still speaking, Judas, one of the twelve, arrived; with him was a large crowd with swords and clubs, from the chief priests and the elders of the people.

26:48: Now the betrayer had given them a sign, saying, "The one I will kiss is the man; arrest him."

26:49: At once he came up to Jesus and said, "Greetings, Rabbi!" and kissed him.

26:50: Jesus said to him, "Friend, do what you are here to do." Then they came and laid hands on Jesus and arrested him.

26:51: Suddenly, one of those with Jesus put his hand on his sword, drew it, and struck the slave of the high priest, cutting off his ear.

26:52: Then Jesus said to him, "Put your sword back into its place; for all who take the sword will perish by the sword.

26:53: Do you think that I cannot appeal to my Father, and he will at once send me more than twelve legions of angels?

26:54: But how then would the scriptures be fulfilled, which say it must happen in this way?"

26:55: At that hour Jesus said to the crowds, "Have you come out with swords and clubs to arrest me as though I were a bandit? Day after day I sat in the temple teaching, and you did not arrest me.

26:56: But all this has taken place, so that the scriptures of the prophets may be fulfilled." Then all the disciples deserted him and fled.

*M*atthew condenses part of Mark's account (cf. Mark 14:43–52), but supplements it in vv. 50 and 52–53 and adds a few words and phrases elsewhere. Matthew's supplements accentuate Jesus' authority and control over the situation.

Matthew reports that "Judas, one of the twelve, arrived; with him was a large crowd with swords and clubs, from the chief priests and the elders of the people" (v. 47). The presence of thugs armed with clubs, working for the ruling priests, is attested in the turmoil of Jerusalem in the late 50s and early 60s A.D. According to Josephus, "Such was the shamelessness and effrontery which possessed the ruling priests that they actually were so brazen as to send slaves to the threshing floors to receive the tithes that were due to the priests, with the result that the poorer priests starved to death" (*Ant.* 20.181). Later, Josephus narrates: "But Ananias had servants who were utter rascals and who, combining operations with the most reckless men, would go to the threshing floors and take by force the tithes of the priests; nor did they refrain from beating those who refused to give. The ruling priests were guilty of the same practices as his slaves, and no one could stop them" (*Ant.* 20. 206–7). Later rabbinic traditions recalled with chagrin the violence and oppression of the ruling priests in the first century A.D. (e.g., *t. Menah.* 13.19–21; *t. Zebah.* 11.16–17; *b. Pesah.* 57a; *b. Yebam.* 86a–b; *b. Ketub.* 26a). First-century priestly corruption is attested in the *Testament of Moses* (composed ca. 30 A.D.), which describes the ruling priests as avaricious, corrupt, thieving, and proud (5:3–6:1; 7:1–10). Similar criticisms are found in the Dead Sea Scrolls (e.g., 1QpHab 8:12; 9:5; 10:1; 12:10; 4QpNah 1:11). The arrest of Jesus attests to a similar strong-armed enforcement operative some twenty to thirty years earlier.

Judas now informs the priests, "The one I will kiss is the man; arrest him" (**v. 48**). In the uncertain light, it would not be easy to identify Jesus. Approaching Jesus and kissing him would do the trick. Accordingly, when Judas approaches Jesus, he salutes him with the words, "Greetings, Rabbi!" (**v. 49**). The greeting (which is not in Mark 14:45) adds to Judas' hypocrisy and villainy. The kiss is supposed to demonstrate loyalty, as well as love.

Matthew reports that "Jesus said to him, 'Friend, do what you are here to do'" (**v. 50**). The RSV reads, "Friend, why are you here?" But the NRSV adopts a reading almost identical to the New American Standard Bible (NASB): "Friend, do what you are here to do." Matthew shows that Jesus is in control, even ordering Judas to carry out his preordained betrayal. Despite the betrayal (and possibly to underscore it), Jesus addresses Judas as "friend."[529]

Matthew continues, "Suddenly, one of those with Jesus put his hand on his sword, drew it, and struck the slave of the high priest, cutting off his ear" (**v. 51**). Mark had only referred to one of those standing by. Matthew's version implies that it was one of the disciples themselves who struck the high priest's servant. Both Matthew and Luke (Luke 22:50) substitute the more appropriate verb for "strike" (Greek: *patassein*) for Mark's verb (Greek: *paiein*) meaning to hit (or "slug") with the fist. For examples of "strike [*patassein*] with the sword," see LXX Num 21:24; Deut 20:13; Josh 19:48; 2 Sam 15:14; and Isa 37:38.

Jesus' well-known saying "Put your sword back into its place; for all who take the sword will perish by the sword" (**v. 52**) appears to reflect the Aramaic paraphrase (the

---

[529] The discovery, announcement, and publication of the second-century Gnostic *Gospel of Judas* created a media sensation in 2006. However, contrary to the much publicized "Judas as hero" interpretation, ongoing study has shown that the author of the *Gospel of Judas* viewed Judaism and apostolic Christianity with disdain. When properly translated and interpreted, no hero is to be found in the *Gospel of Judas*. For further discussion, see C. A. Evans, "Understanding the Gospel of Judas," *BBR* 20 (2010): 561–74.

Targum) of Isa 50:11: "Behold, all you who kindle a fire, *who grasp a sword!* Go, *fall in the fire, which you kindled,* and on the *sword, which you grasped!*" (italics indicate departures from or additions to the Hebrew). Jesus' saying may also be alluded to in Rev 13:10, "... if anyone kills with the sword, with the sword he must be killed." On the phrase "put ... sword back into its place," see *Joseph and Aseneth* 29:4, where Levi prevents Benjamin from slaying the wounded son of Pharaoh: "And now, put your sword back into its place, and come, help me, and we will heal him of his wound...."

Jesus continues his rebuke, "Do you think that I cannot appeal to my Father, and he will at once send me more than twelve legions of angels?" (**v. 53**). In Judaism and Christianity of late antiquity, angels were thought of as warriors, as well as messengers and worshipers of the Lord (cf. especially 1QM 7:6; 13:10). According to *2 Bar* 63:5–11, Sennacherib's army was destroyed by angels sent by God in answer to Hezekiah's prayer. According to 2 Macc 3:26, angels prevent one Heliodorus, an agent of the king, from entering and looting the temple: "Two young men also appeared to him, remarkably strong, gloriously beautiful and splendidly dressed, who stood on each side of him and scourged him continuously, inflicting many blows on him." It is in the light of these traditions that Jesus' question would have been understood. Reference to "twelve legions" is probably meant to parallel the twelve disciples, who offer ineffectual resistance.

Jesus then explains, "But all this has taken place, so that the scriptures of the prophets may be fulfilled" (**v. 56**). Matthew's version expands Mark's simpler "But let the scriptures be fulfilled" (Mark 14:49). Matthew adds "of the prophets" to underscore once again the prophetic nature of Jesus' ministry (cf. Matt 2:23, "that what had been spoken through the prophets might be fulfilled"). Not only are the prophetic Scriptures fulfilled, so is Jesus' prophecy, for just as he foretold, so it happened: "Then all the disciples deserted him and fled" (cf. Matt 26:31).[530]

MATTHEW 26:57–68 – JESUS BEFORE THE JEWISH COUNCIL

26:57: Those who had arrested Jesus took him to Caiaphas the high priest, in whose house the scribes and the elders had gathered.

26:58: But Peter was following him at a distance, as far as the courtyard of the high priest; and going inside, he sat with the guards in order to see how this would end.

---

[530] In recent years, there have been efforts to rehabilitate Judas Iscariot. Probably the best effort to date is W. Klassen, *Judas: Betrayer or Friend of Jesus?* (Minneapolis: Fortress Press, 1996). Klassen argues that the verb *paradidomi* only means "hand over," not betray. Perhaps so, but Judas' handing over of Jesus to his enemies is a betrayal nevertheless. For critiques of Klassen's argument, see H. T. Fleddermann, *CBQ* 59 (1997): 771–72; R. E. Brown, *JBL* 117 (1998): 134–36; F. A. Gosling, "O Judas! What Have You Done?" *EvQ* 71 (1999): 117–25.

26:59: Now the chief priests and the whole council were looking for false testimony against Jesus so that they might put him to death,

26:60: but they found none, though many false witnesses came forward. At last two came forward

26:61: and said, "This fellow said, 'I am able to destroy the temple of God and to build it in three days.'"

26:62: The high priest stood up and said, "Have you no answer? What is it that they testify against you?"

26:63: But Jesus was silent. Then the high priest said to him, "I put you under oath before the living God, tell us if you are the Messiah, the Son of God."

26:64: Jesus said to him, "You have said so. But I tell you, From now on you will see the Son of Man seated at the right hand of Power and coming on the clouds of heaven."

26:65: Then the high priest tore his clothes and said, "He has blasphemed! Why do we still need witnesses? You have now heard his blasphemy.

26:66: What is your verdict?" They answered, "He deserves death."

26:67: Then they spat in his face and struck him; and some slapped him,

26:68: saying, "Prophesy to us, you Messiah! Who is it that struck you?"

*M*atthew again follows Mark's account closely (cf. Mark 14:53–65), but at points offers a few interesting changes. In the hands of his enemies and with his life on the line, Jesus does not lose composure. The composed Jesus, who truthfully identifies himself in v. 64, stands in stark contrast to the coward Peter, who denies his discipleship and that he even knows Jesus (see Matt 26:69–75).

Matthew states that Jesus is taken before "Caiaphas the high priest" (v. 57), correctly identifying this man as Caiaphas, whereas Mark does not name the high priest. Caiaphas is mentioned by name nine times in the Gospels of Matthew, Luke, and John, and in the Book of Acts. He is not mentioned by name in Mark. In John 18:13, he is identified as the son-in-law of Annas (a.k.a. Ananus or Hanan), whereas in Luke 3:2 we are told that the word of God came to John the Baptist "in the high-priesthood of Annas and Caiaphas." This linkage of Caiaphas, the ruling high priest, with his father-in-law attests to the enduring influence of the former high priest, who served in 6–15 A.D.

A recent archaeological discovery has renewed scholarly and popular interest in this figure. In 1990, in Jerusalem's Peace Forest, which is 1.5 km south of the Old City, two ossuaries from the first century A.D. (now in the Israel National Museum) were found on which was inscribed the name Caiaphas. On one of the boxes, two inscriptions read (on one end) "Yehoseph bar Qaipha" and (on one side) "Yehoseph bar Qapha." This ossuary contained the bones of a sixty-year-old man (and those of two infants, a toddler, a young boy, and a woman) and could be the ossuary of Caiaphas the high priest, to whom Josephus refers as "Joseph called Caiaphas" (cf. *Ant.* 18.35, "Joseph the Caiaphas," and 18.95, "the high priest Joseph called the Caiaphas"; for mention of Annas, whose five sons became high priests in turn, see *Ant.* 20.197–98). The sloppy scrawl on the side of the ossuary may be the writing of the relative who placed his bones in the box (to keep a record of whose bones were in which box). A second ossuary in the tomb bears the name Qapha.[531]

A few scholars have called into question the identification of the inscribed name with the high priest before whom Jesus stood.[532] Part of the problem is the spelling itself. Instead of Qayapha (which is how the Hebrew should read, if it is the equivalent of the Greek Caiaphas of the New Testament and of Josephus), it seems to be either Qepha (i.e., "rock," the same name that Jesus gave to Peter), Qopha, or Qupha.

Matthew's account continues, "Now the chief priests and the whole council were looking for false testimony against Jesus" (v. **59**). The chief priests are mentioned first, and then the council, because they form the real power in Jewish politics, even if subordinate to their Roman overlords (cf. Josephus, *Ant.* 20.251, "the ruling priests were entrusted with the leadership of the nation"). Nevertheless, the ruling priests, acting as prosecutors, hope to win the support of the council (or Sanhedrin). A charge brought to the Roman authorities will carry more weight if the council supports it.[533]

The ruling priests were seeking "false testimony" because from Matthew's point of view Jesus has committed no crime. Honest and fair testimony will not lead to a conviction. The priests need something incriminating that the council will condemn and that the Romans will take seriously.

A number of "false witnesses came forward," but to no effect, and then, "At last two came forward" (v. **60**). Finally, "two came forward" who had something to say that could lead to a charge. Mark had only said "some" (Mark 14:57). Matthew's "two" probably alludes to Deut 19:15, "on the evidence of two or three witnesses shall a charge be sustained." These two witnesses claim they heard Jesus say, "I am able to destroy the temple of God and to build it in three days" (v. **61**). Curiously, Matthew omits Mark's notice that the testimony of these two witnesses "did not agree" (Mark 14:56). In what sense it did not agree is not clear, which could explain the omission. (The entire exchange is omitted in Luke.)

Because Jesus gives no answer (v. **62**), the exasperated high priest demands to know who Jesus thinks he is: "I put you under oath before the living God, tell us if you are the Messiah, the Son of God" (v. **63**). The high priest's question recalls

531 See R. Reich, "Caiaphas Name Inscribed on Bone Boxes," *BAR* 18, no. 5 (1992): 38–44, 76.
532 W. Horbury, "The 'Caiaphas' Ossuaries and Joseph Caiaphas," *PEQ* 126 (1994): 32–48.
533 On the Jewish trial of Jesus, see D. R. Catchpole, *The Trial of Jesus* (SPB 18; Leiden: Brill, 1971), 183–202.

Peter's earlier confession, "You are the Messiah, the Son of the living God" (Matt 16:16). Matthew replaces Mark's circumlocution, "Son of the Blessed One" (Mark 14:61), with its literal referent, "Son of God."

When the high priest qualifies "Messiah" as "the son of God," it is clear that he is talking about the anointed *king* as opposed to an anointed prophet or anointed priest. Only the Davidic, royal descendant is talked about as being in some sense the "son of God," as seen in a number of texts (cf. 2 Sam 7:12, 14; 1 Chron 17:13; Ps 2:2, 7). At Qumran, Nathan's oracle (2 Samuel 7) is interpreted explicitly as referring to the eschatological Messiah: "'I will be a father to him, and he will be my son.' This refers to the Shoot of David, who is to arise with the Interpreter of the Law, and who will arise in Zion in the last days …" (4Q174 3:11–12); Ps 2:2, 7, moreover, is probably alluded to in the poorly preserved and controversial 1QSa 2:11–12, "… when God begets the Messiah with them …" The qualification "son of the God" distinguishes the royal Messiah from other anointed figures, such as anointed priests (Lev 16:32; 1 Chron 29:22) or anointed prophets (1 Kings 19:15–16; 1 Chron 16:22 = Ps 105:15). The texts at Qumran tell against the skepticism of some scholars who have argued that in Jewish circles the Messiah was never called "son of God."

Matthew then states that "Jesus said to him, 'You have said so …'" (**v. 64a**). In Mark, Jesus replies quite explicitly, "I am" (Mark 14:62). But here in Matthew (and in Luke 22:70), Jesus' reply is indirect. Having Jesus directly affirm his messiahship may have been perceived as problematic, for it would strike Jewish readers as presumptuous. Simon ben Kosiba, the messianic pretender in 132–135 A.D., is discredited in *b. Sanhedrin* 93b by having him claim bluntly, "I am the Messiah." Jesus goes on to say that someday his judges "will see the Son of Man seated at the right hand of Power and coming on the clouds of heaven" (**v. 64b**). Here we have unmistakable allusions to Dan 7:13, in which "one like a son of man" is presented before God, and to Ps 110:1, where Israel's king is commanded to sit at the right hand of God.

Presupposing the Jewish exegetical principle of *gezera shawa* ("an equivalent category"), Jesus has drawn together Daniel 7 and Psalm 110. Both passages envision the enthronement of God and judgment upon his enemies: "thrones were set in place, and an Ancient One took his throne … the court sat in judgment, and the books were opened" (Dan 7:9–10); "The Lord says to my lord, 'Sit at My right hand until I make your enemies your footstool.'" The plural "thrones" of Dan 7:9 and God's invitation to the Psalmist's "lord" to sit next to him create the picture that Jesus envisions: As "the Son of Man," Jesus will take his seat next to God himself (Ps 110:1), he will "come with the clouds" (Dan 7:13), the court will sit "in judgment" (Dan 7:9), and his "enemies" will become his "footstool" (Ps 110:1).[534]

---

[534]   On this important passage, see M. Hengel, "'Sit at My Right Hand!' The Enthronement of Christ at the Right Hand of God and Psalm 110:1," in *Studies in Early Christology* (Edinburgh: T. & T. Clark, 1995), 119–225.

The high priest exclaims, "He has blasphemed!" (**v. 65**). Given what Jesus has just claimed, it is not hard to see why the high priest has reacted with anger and horror. Jesus has claimed that he will share in God's power and that he will sit in judgment on Caiaphas and his colleagues. Jesus has not only affirmed his royal messiahship, his identity as Israel's king, but has affirmed a power that transcends that of the chief priests themselves. The first affirmation will be of great concern to the Roman authority (Matt 27:11), and the second will unite the council in condemning Jesus on the grounds of blasphemy (**v. 66**).[535]

With the verdict pronounced, Jesus is spat upon and struck (**v. 67**). Because Matthew has omitted Mark's reference to the covering of Jesus' face (Mark 14:65), the mocking words, "Prophesy to us, you Messiah! Who is it that struck you?" (**v. 68**), are not as clear as they could be. The idea is that if Jesus was a true prophet and therefore possessed the power of clairvoyance, he would know who struck him even if he could not see the person who did it. The irony is that outside in the high priest's courtyard (v. 58) Peter is in the act of fulfilling Jesus' prophecy by denying his master (see Matt 26:69–75).

MATTHEW 26:69–75 – PETER DENIES KNOWING JESUS

26:69: Now Peter was sitting outside in the courtyard. A servant-girl came to him and said, "You also were with Jesus the Galilean."

26:70: But he denied it before all of them, saying, "I do not know what you are talking about."

26:71: When he went out to the porch, another servant-girl saw him, and she said to the bystanders, "This man was with Jesus of Nazareth."

26:72: Again he denied it with an oath, "I do not know the man."

26:73: After a little while the bystanders came up and said to Peter, "Certainly you are also one of them, for your accent betrays you."

26:74: Then he began to curse, and he swore an oath, "I do not know the man!" At that moment the cock crowed.

26:75: Then Peter remembered what Jesus had said: "Before the cock crows, you will deny me three times." And he went out and wept bitterly.

$\mathcal{M}$atthew follows Mark fairly closely (Mark 14:66–72), though he presents a few details in a different light. The most interesting added detail is in v. 73.

---

[535]   On this topic, see D. L. Bock, *Blasphemy and Exaltation in Judaism and the Final Examination of Jesus: A Philological-Historical Study of the Key Jewish Themes Impacting Mark 14:61–64* (WUNT 2, no. 106; Tübingen: Mohr [Siebeck], 1998). On the political context of the Jewish high priest, see H. K. Bond, *Caiaphas: Friend of Rome and Judge of Jesus?* (Louisville, KY: Westminster John Knox Press, 2004).

The embarrassing story of Peter's denial of Jesus provides a dramatic demonstration of Jesus' predictive power in foretelling that the principal disciple will deny his master three times before the morning cock crows (Matt 26:34) and in providing a stark contrast between the courageous figure of Jesus, who stands before Israel's most powerful men, and the cowardly figure of Peter, who quails before a servant-girl, Israel's least powerful person.

The story begins with the reminder that Peter is "sitting outside in the courtyard" (**v. 69**; cf. v. 54). Matthew omits reference to Peter being warmed by the fire (cf. Mark 14:54, 67). A servant-girl thinks she recognizes Peter: "You also were with Jesus the Galilean." But Peter denies his association with Jesus; he claims to have no idea what she is talking about (**v. 70**). Peter moves away, but then another servant-girl sees him and says to bystanders: "This man was with Jesus of Nazareth" (**v. 71**). Again Peter, this time with an oath, denies knowing Jesus (**v. 72**). Attentive readers of Matthew will remember that Jesus told his disciples not to swear and make oaths, teaching them instead: "Let your word be 'Yes, Yes' or 'No, No'; anything more than this comes from the evil one" (Matt 5:37). Peter has lied and has sworn an oath falsely.

Unfortunately, Peter cannot catch a break, for after "a little while the bystanders came up and said to Peter, 'Certainly you are also one of them, for your accent betrays you'" (**v. 73**). According to the Talmud (cf. *b. Ber.* 32a; *b. Megillah* 24b), Galileans are said to pronounce the guttural letters in reverse: the *'aleph* as *'ayin* and the *'ayin* as *'aleph* (i.e., too much guttural for the *'aleph*, too little for the *'ayin*). One text pokes fun at Galilean pronunciation: "A certain Galilean went around saying to people, 'Who has *amar*? Who has *amar*?' They said to him, 'You Galilean fool, do you mean an ass (*hamar*) for riding, or wine (*hamar*) for drinking, wool (*'amar*) for clothing, or a lamb (*'immar*) for slaughtering?'" (*b. 'Erubin* 53b). An instance of being betrayed by one's speech is found in a fragment of the *Acts of the Pagan Martyrs*: "His non-Greek (literally barbaric) bearing and his speech show him to be a foreigner." According to Acts 2:7, the disciples are recognized as Galileans by their speech (cf. Acts 4:13).[536]

For the third time, Peter denies knowing Jesus (**v. 74**). This time he not only swears another oath but even curses, insisting, "I do not know the man!" At this point, Peter could not possibly be more unlike a disciple of Jesus. Then the cock crows and Peter remembers what Jesus had said: "Before the cock crows, you will deny me three times" (**v. 75**). No sooner were the words of the third, final, climactic denial out of his mouth when the cock crowed a second time. The ugly words of the third denial were still ringing in the ears of all. The fulfillment of Jesus' prophecy, brought to mind so suddenly and jarringly, heightens the drama and poignancy of the scene and the remarkable accuracy of the prophecy.

---

[536] For a further discussion, see J. M. Watt, "Of Gutturals and Galileans: The Two Slurs of Matthew 26.73," in S. E. Porter (ed.), *Diglossia and other Topics in New Testament Linguistics* (JSNTSup 193; Sheffield: Sheffield Academic Press, 2000), 107–20.

The tragic scene ends with Peter weeping bitterly (**v. 75**). Peter's reaction to his betrayal stands in contrast to the tragic reaction of Judas the following day (Matt 27:3–10).

MATTHEW 27:1–2 – HANDING JESUS OVER TO PILATE

27:1: When morning came, all the chief priests and the elders of the people conferred together against Jesus in order to bring about his death.

27:2: They bound him, led him away, and handed him over to Pilate the governor.

*M*atthew elaborates on Mark's description in a few places, adding that the elders were "elders of the people" and that the purpose of the council was to confer "together against Jesus in order to bring about his death" (v. 1). Matthew also explains (v. 2) that Pilate was the "governor" (Mark never mentions Pilate's title; in contrast, Matthew refers to the "governor" six more times).

Pilate normally resided in Caesarea Maritima (on the Mediterranean), but during Passover and other holidays took up residence in Jerusalem, either in the Antonia (which is doubtful), which overlooked the temple precincts, or in Herod's palace (see *J.W.* 2.301, which says Gesius Florus, the last governor before the outbreak of war, resided in Herod's palace). The Roman historian Cornelius Tacitus (ca. 56–ca. 118 A.D.) states that "Christus … had suffered the death penalty during the reign of Tiberius, by sentence of the procurator Pontius Pilate [*per procuratorem Pontium Pilatum*]" (*Annals* 15.44). Calling Pilate a "procurator" is anachronistic, for prior to the brief reign of Agrippa I (41–44 A.D.), the Roman governors of Samaria and Judea were prefects. From 44 A.D. on, the governors of Samaria and Judea (now including Galilee) held the rank of procurator. Prefect was more of a military officer (i.e., a military governor), whereas the procurator had broader civil authority and was concerned with protecting the emperor's financial interests.

Pilate's rank as prefect has been confirmed by the discovery in Caesarea Maritima (on the Mediteranean Sea, not to be confused with Caesarea Philippi, in the north of Galilee), in the vicinity of the theater, of an inscription that bears the governor's name. It has been recently restored to read:

[NAUTI]STIBERIÉVM
[PON]TIVSPILATVS
[PRAEF]ECTVSIVDA[EA]E
[REF]É[CIT]

[Seamen']s Tiberieum
[Pon]tius Pilate,
[Pref]ect of Jude[a]
[restor]e[s …]

It is speculated that the "Seamen's Tiberieum" (named in honor of Emperor Tiberius) was one of the buildings connected with the harbor of Caesarea Maritima, a harbor developed by Herod the Great and then later expanded and improved by Pilate.[537]

In the writings of two Jewish contemporaries, the portrait of Pilate is quite negative. Philo of Alexandria describes the governor of Judea as a "man of an inflexible, stubborn, and cruel disposition," adding that "briberies, insults, robberies, outrages, wanton injuries, executions without trial, and endless and supremely grievous cruelty" marked his administration (*Legatio ad Gaium* 301–2). Philo's remarks here are primarily in reference to the incident of the golden shields that Pilate had placed (or attempted to place) in Herod's palace in Jerusalem. These criticisms are politically motivated and probably exaggerate the governor's faults.

Josephus, who also has no praise for the man, relates an incident in which one night Pilate transferred from Caesarea Maritima to Jerusalem military standards bearing the image of the Roman emperor (possibly another version of the same event described by Philo). A large group of Jews went to Caesarea Maritima, imploring the governor to remove the standards. Only their willingness to die, unresisting, compelled Pilate to have the offensive standards returned to Caesarea (*J.W.* 2.171–74; *Ant.* 18.55–59). Josephus relates another incident whereby Pilate dipped into the temple treasury to secure additional funding for a municipal project. The account from which the money was taken was the "sacred treasure known as *korbonas*" (*J.W.* 2.175; *Ant.* 18.60–62). Josephus is here referring to the dedicated offering known as "qorban" (cf. Mark 7:11, "Corban [that is, an offering to God]"; Matt 27:6, "It is not lawful to put them [i.e., Judas' pieces of silver] into the treasury [literally *korbonas*]"); that is, a gift given to God (see the commentary on Matt 15:3–5). To take such consecrated items and put them to a secular use would have been highly offensive to the Jewish people. Once again, the Jewish people protest and offer no resistance. Pilate sent soldiers, dressed as civilians, among the people. At a prearranged signal, these disguised soldiers began beating the people with clubs, killing some, injuring many others, and finally dispersing the crowd.

In both of the incidents related by Josephus, the ruling priests are conspicuous by their silence. This is especially startling in the case of taking money from the *korbonas*, for Pilate could not have done this, nor would he have dared to do this, without permission and assistance from the chief priests themselves. Evidently, Caiaphas the high priest and Pilate the governor worked well together. It is not surprising that when Pilate was removed from office in early 37 A.D., after his brutal assault on the Samaritans, Caiaphas was also removed from office shortly thereafter (*Ant.* 18.88–89, 95). Luke alludes to a grisly event when Jesus is told "of the Galileans whose blood Pilate had mingled with their sacrifices" (Luke 13:1).

---

[537] For this restoration and interpretation, see G. Alföldy, "Pontius Pilatus und das Tiberieum von Caesarea Maritima," *Scripta Classica Israelica* 18 (1999): 85–108.

However, it should not be inferred from these acts, which have been portrayed in the worst possible light, that Pilate was so decisive and brutal that the portrait of him in the Gospels, as wavering and uncertain in the case of Jesus, lacks historical credibility. Critical reading of the events related by Philo and Josephus will observe the same tendency toward uncertainty and political expedience.[538]

MATTHEW 27:3–10 – JUDAS AND THE FIELD OF BLOOD

27:3: When Judas, his betrayer, saw that Jesus was condemned, he repented and brought back the thirty pieces of silver to the chief priests and the elders.

27:4: He said, "I have sinned by betraying innocent blood." But they said, "What is that to us? See to it yourself."

27:5: Throwing down the pieces of silver in the temple, he departed; and he went and hanged himself.

27:6: But the chief priests, taking the pieces of silver, said, "It is not lawful to put them into the treasury, since they are blood money."

27:7: After conferring together, they used them to buy the potter's field as a place to bury foreigners.

27:8: For this reason that field has been called the Field of Blood to this day.

27:9: Then was fulfilled what had been spoken through the prophet Jeremiah, "And they took the thirty pieces of silver, the price of the one on whom a price had been set, on whom some of the people of Israel had set a price,

27:10: and they gave them for the potter's field, as the Lord commanded me."

*B*oth Matthew and Luke know of Judas' suicide, though the versions of the story they provide differ at many points. For one, Luke does not recount the story until the first chapter of his second volume, the Book of Acts (cf. Acts 1:15–20). He makes no mention of it in his Gospel. Another major difference is that whereas Judas' death in Matthew is by suicide, in Acts it is by accident (or so it seems).

Matthew's account begins, "When Judas, his betrayer, saw that Jesus was condemned ..." (**v. 3a**). Jesus has been condemned by the Jewish council. He has not yet been condemned by Pilate, but Judas knows that in all probability he will be. Judas well knew the chief priests' intentions and their influence with the governor. But now Judas "repented and brought back the thirty pieces of silver to the chief priests and the elders" (**v. 3b**). Judas regretted his action, but it is too much to say that he repented (NASB: "felt remorse").[539] The church father Chrysostom agrees, saying,

---

[538] For more on the prefect, see H. K. Bond, *Pontius Pilate in History and Interpretation* (SNTSMS 100; Cambridge: Cambridge University Press, 1998).

[539] Matthew's (Greek) word is *metamelesthai*, "regret," whereas "repent" in the New Testament is usually *metanoein*.

For to condemn [his betrayal] and to throw down the pieces of silver and not to regard the Jewish people were all acceptable things. But to hang himself, this again was unpardonable and a work of an evil spirit. For the devil led him out of his repentance too soon, so that he should reap no fruit from it, and carried him off by a most disgraceful death, and one manifest to all, having persuaded him to destroy himself (*Gospel of Matthew, Homily* 85.2) (cf. Origen, *Commentary on Matthew* 117).

Jerome adds:

It profits nothing to do an act of penance that is incapable of correcting the sin. If a man sins against his brother in such a way that the wrong he committed can be amended, it is possible for him to be forgiven. If the consequences of his sin remain in force, however, in vain does he attempt to do penance. (*Commentary on Matthew* 4.27.5)

Judas now admits, "I have sinned by betraying innocent blood" (**v. 4a**). Later in the narrative, the Roman governor will concur, finding Jesus guilty of nothing deserving death (cf. Matt 27:18, 24). Indeed, Pilate's wife declares Jesus "righteous" (Matt 27:19). Matthew's point in reporting Judas' words is that Jesus is indeed innocent – even his betrayer acknowledges it. Judas' confession may allude to Deut 27:25: "Cursed be anyone who takes a bribe to shed innocent blood." After all, Judas had accepted payment of thirty pieces of silver (cf. Matt 26:15). On "innocent blood," see *T. Zebulon* 2:2, where Joseph cries out to his brothers, "Do not put your hands on me to pour out innocent blood, because I have not sinned against you."

The priests and elders respond to Judas' remorse with a dismissive "What is that to us? See to it yourself" (**v. 4b**). However, Jesus' innocence or guilt is no concern to the ruling priests and elders. Jesus is in the hands of the Romans. Priestly indifference hides the zeal with which Jesus had been pursued and the vehemence with which very shortly calls will be made for his crucifixion. Nor is the regret and anguish of Judas of any concern to the priests. If he has a problem, let him see to it himself. This is a remarkable betrayal of their priestly function in serving as mediator between a repentant sinner and Israel's holy God.

Judas has returned the money to its source: "Throwing down the pieces of silver in the temple, he departed" (**v. 5a**). The action alludes to Zech 11:13: "I took the thirty shekels of silver and threw them into the treasury in the house of the Lord." Matthew says *sanctuary* (Greek: *naos*), not "temple" (Greek: *hieron*) as in the NRSV, perhaps implying that the money was hurled into the inner sanctuary, either in or in the proximity of the holy of holies and the altar. If so, then this sacred place has been defiled by the presence of blood money. There may be symbolism here, hinting at the end of the temple's function of providing atonement for Israel.[540] No more

---

[540] On this possibility, see D. C. Allison, Jr. and W. D. Davies, *A Critical and Exegetical Commentary on the Gospel According to Saint Matthew* (1988–1997), 3:564–65.

sacrifices offered there will be of any value, but the sacrifice soon to be offered just outside the walls of the city (i.e., the crucifixion of Jesus) will provide the atonement (in keeping with the promise in Matt 1:21, "you are to name him Jesus, for he will save his people from their sins").

Matthew then reports Judas' suicide: "And he went and hanged himself" (**v. 5b**). This alludes to 2 Sam 17:23: "When Ahithophel saw that his counsel was not followed, he saddled his donkey and went off home to his own city. He set his house in order, and hanged himself; he died and was buried in the tomb of his father."[541]

We have a different account of Judas' death in Acts 1:18, where we are told that "falling headlong, he burst open in the middle and all his bowels gushed out." There have been attempts to harmonize the Matthean and Lukan accounts, suggesting that Judas hanged himself, but fell (or, after dying, some days later fell) and burst open on impact. Perhaps, but it is more likely that the early church had heard two separate accounts. Because Matthew and Luke wrote independently of one another, and because Mark's Gospel contains no account of the fate of Judas, Matthew and Luke had no opportunity to harmonize their respective versions.

Later church tradition provides yet two more accounts of Judas' death, each emphasizing the lapsed disciple's sinfulness, his physical problems (such as becoming horribly swollen, infested with worms, oozing), and either his suicide, after years of torment, or his accidental death when run over by a passing wagon: "crushed by the wagon, his bowels emptied out" (attributed to Papias, according to Apollinarius).[542]

Matthew reports that the priests debate over what to do with the pieces of silver that Judas has returned: "It is not lawful to put them into the treasury, since they are blood money" (**v. 6**). The fastidiousness of the priests over where the money may be legally placed stands in stark contrast to their callousness with respect to Jesus and Judas. The law they have in mind is probably Deut 23:18: "You shall not bring the fee of a prostitute or the wages of a male prostitute into the house of the Lord your God in payment for any vow, for both of these are abhorrent to the Lord your God." On "blood money" (or "price of blood"), see *T. Zebulon* 3:3, again in reference to Joseph: "We will not use the money for eating, which is the price of our brother's blood, but we will trample it underfoot...."

The chief priests decided to use the thirty pieces of silver "to buy the potter's field as a place to bury foreigners" (**v. 7**). The reference to "potter" probably reflects the

[541] D. J. Harrington, *The Gospel of Matthew* (1991), 385; C. S. Keener, *A Commentary on the Gospel of Matthew* (1999), 659.

[542] For further discussion of the death of Judas, see A. G. Moser, "The Death of Judas," *BToday* 30 (1992): 145–51 (Judas' repentance remains a possibility); R. van de Water, "The Punishment of the Wicked Priest and the Death of Judas," *DSD* 10 (2003): 395–419 (Judas' death as typology); D. A. Reed, "'Saving Judas' – A Social Scientific Approach to Judas's Suicide in Matthew 27:3–10," *BTB* 35 (2005): 51–59 (Judas' act is noble, shifting responsibility to the chief priests).

ambiguity of Zech 11:13, which the NASB translates: "So I took the thirty *shekels* of silver and threw them to the potter in the house of the Lord." "Potter" here (and also in the KJV) is "treasury" in the RSV and NRSV. We may also have an allusion to Gen 23:17–20, which speaks of a field for foreigners purchased with silver. Passages in Jeremiah may also have colored the narrative (cf. Jer 32:6–16; 18:1–11); see the commentary on v. 9.

Matthew then gives the name of the field, referring back to v. 7 for the reason: "For this reason that field has been called the Field of Blood to this day" (**v. 8**). See Acts 1:19: "This became known to all the residents of Jerusalem, so that the field was called in their language Hakeldama, that is, Field of Blood." Luke is referring to the Aramaic *haqel dema* (literally "bloody field"). The location of this place is disputed, though traditionally it has been identified as the place where the Kidron and Hinnom valleys intersect.

Matthew's quotation, "Then was fulfilled what had been spoken through the prophet Jeremiah" (**vv. 9–10**), is an admixture of Zechariah (i.e., Zech 11:13) and Jeremiah (primarily Chapters 18–19, though Jer 32:6–15 refers to the purchase of a field with silver). Matthew mentions Jeremiah because most of the details come from this prophecy and because the prophet Jeremiah is better known and has contributed to Matthew's story of Jesus in a more profound way.[543]

MATTHEW 27:11–14 – JESUS BEFORE PILATE

27:11: Now Jesus stood before the governor; and the governor asked him, "Are you the King of the Jews?" Jesus said, "You say so."

27:12: But when he was accused by the chief priests and elders, he did not answer.

27:13: Then Pilate said to him, "Do you not hear how many accusations they make against you?"

27:14: But he gave him no answer, not even to a single charge, so that the governor was greatly amazed.

*M*atthew enhances the Markan narrative (Mark 15:2–5) at several points. Matthew adds that when accused by the "chief priests and elders" (v. 12) in the presence of Pilate, before whom Jesus stands (v. 11), Jesus "did not answer."

---

[543] On the allusions to Zechariah and Jeremiah, see A. Conard, "The Fate of Judas: Matthew 27:3–10," *Toronto Journal of Theology* 7 (1991): 158–68; P. Wick, "Judas als Prophet wider Willen: Mt 27,3–10 als Midrasch," *TZ* 57 (2001): 26–35. For a further discussion of Matthew's composition of the story of Judas, see D. Senior, "Matthew's Special Material in the Passion Story: Implications for the Evangelist's Redactional Technique and Theological Perspective," *ETL* 63 (1987): 272–94.

When the governor weighs in, Jesus remains silent, providing no answer, not even to "a single charge" (v. 14).

The juridical process that is narrated here agrees with what Josephus says about Jesus, a teacher and wonder-worker "accused by the first men among" the Jews (i.e., the chief priests) and then condemned and crucified by Pilate (*Ant.* 18.63–64). It also matches the story of Jesus ben Ananias, who in the years before Jerusalem's destruction was seized and beaten by "leading citizens" and then handed over to the Roman governor (*J.W.* 6.300–309).

The exchange between Pilate and Jesus, "'Are you the King of the Jews?' Jesus said, 'You say so'" (**v. 11**), marks the first reference to Jesus as "king of the Jews" since the quest of the magi (Matt 2:2). He will be called this again in vv. 29 and 37. "King of the Jews" is a Roman designation (cf. Josephus, *J.W.* 1.282, where Mark Antony makes Herod "king of the Jews"; cf. *Ant.* 14.36; 15.373, 409; 16.291, 311). "Messiah" (Matt 1:1, 16, 17, 18; 2:4; 11:2; 16:16; 22:42; 23:10; 24:5, 23; 26:63, 68; 27:17, 22), "son of David" (Matt 1:1, 20; 9:27; 12:23; 15:22; 20:30, 31; 21:9, 15; 22:42), "king of Israel" (Matt 27:42), and perhaps even "son of God" (Matt 4:3, 6; 8:29; 14:33; 26:63; 27:40), are Jewish designations for Israel's king. Pilate's question utilizes the emphatic personal pronoun *su* ("Are *you* the King of the Jews?"). The emphatic pronoun carries with it a touch of mockery, perhaps suggesting that Pilate had anticipated meeting someone more impressive.

Jesus provides an affirmative answer, "You say so," but it is qualified. He is indeed the Messiah, God's Son and Israel's king, but is no "King of the Jews" as the Roman governor would understand it. With that, Jesus has nothing more to say to Pilate (**vv. 12–14**).[544]

MATTHEW 27:15–23 – THE PASSOVER PARDON

27:15: **Now at the festival the governor was accustomed to release a prisoner for the crowd, anyone whom they wanted.**

27:16: **At that time they had a notorious prisoner, called Jesus Barabbas.**

27:17: **So after they had gathered, Pilate said to them, "Whom do you want me to release for you, Jesus Barabbas or Jesus who is called the Messiah?"**

27:18: **For he realized that it was out of jealousy that they had handed him over.**

27:19: **While he was sitting on the judgment seat, his wife sent word to him, "Have nothing to do with that innocent man, for today I have suffered a great deal because of a dream about him."**

---

[544] For a major study, see H. K. Bond, *Pontius Pilate in History and Interpretation* (1998). See also J. E. Taylor, "Pontius Pilate and the Imperial Cult in Roman Judaea," *NTS* 52 (2006): 555–82. Taylor underscores Pilate's attempts to promote the Roman imperial cult in Samaria and Judea.

27:20: Now the chief priests and the elders persuaded the crowds to ask for Barabbas and to have Jesus killed.

27:21: The governor again said to them, "Which of the two do you want me to release for you?" And they said, "Barabbas."

27:22: Pilate said to them, "Then what should I do with Jesus who is called the Messiah?" All of them said, "Let him be crucified!"

27:23: Then he asked, "Why, what evil has he done?" But they shouted all the more, "Let him be crucified!"

*M*atthew's version of the Passover pardon draws upon Mark 15:6–14. As is his custom, Matthew edits his source, trimming a few words but also adding several elements. The three most interesting additions are found in vv. 19 and 24–25. In v. 16, Matthew tells us that Barabbas was "a notorious prisoner." In v. 17, Matthew makes the alternatives clearer: "Jesus Barabbas or Jesus who is called the Messiah?" And again in v. 21: "Which of the two do you want me to release for you?" Matthew also notes that Pilate sat on the "judgment seat" (v. 19, Greek: *bema*; cf. John 19:13; Acts 7:5; 12:21; 18:12, 16, 17; 25:6, 10, 17; Rom 14:10; 2 Cor 5:10).

Matthew states, "Now at the festival the governor was accustomed to release a prisoner" (**v. 15**). Because there is no explicit corroboration of Pilate's Passover pardon (the so-called *privilegium paschale*) outside the New Testament Gospels, some critics think it is nothing more than a literary and theological invention.[545] But the tradition is attested in at least two independent streams, Mark (followed by Matthew and Luke) and John (which is independent of the Synoptics). There is also a measure of corroborating evidence that lends credibility to Matthew's narrative. The Mishnah says that "they may slaughter [the Passover lamb] for one … whom they have promised to bring out of prison" on the Passover (*m. Pesah.* 8:6). A papyrus (P. Flor. 61, ca. 85 A.D.) "containing a report of judicial proceedings, quotes these words of the governor of Egypt, G. Septimius Vegetus (to one Phibion): 'You were worthy of scourging … but I give you to the crowds'" (lines 59–60, 64).[546] Behind the offer of a pardon on the eve of Passover is nothing more than politics and public relations. It is Pilate's way of showing respect for the most important Jewish holiday, a holiday that celebrates liberation from bondage. Pilate's offer of pardon may well have served early Christian apologetics, but nevertheless it is better understood as history, not fiction.[547]

[545] As in F. W. Beare, *The Gospel According to Matthew: A Commentary* (Oxford: Blackwell; New York: Harper & Row, 1981), 529; and, surprisingly, R. E. Brown, *The Death of the Messiah: From Gethsemane to the Grave. A Commentary on the Passion Narratives in the Four Gospels* (ABRL; 2 vols., New York: Doubleday, 1994), 1:814–20.

[546] A. Deissmann, *Light from the Ancient East* (London: Hodder & Stoughton; New York: George H. Doran, 1927), 269–70 + pl., slightly adapted.

[547] See D. C. Allison, Jr. and W. D. Davies, *A Critical and Exegetical Commentary on the Gospel According to Saint Matthew* (1988–1997), 3:583; D. A. Hagner, *Matthew* (1993–1995),

Pilate asks the crowd, "Whom do you want me to release for you, Jesus Barabbas or Jesus who is called the Messiah?" (**v. 17**). In **v. 16**, Barabbas is described as a "notorious prisoner." In John 18:40, Barabbas is described as a "robber" (or "violent" man). In Mark 15:7, we are told that Barabbas "was in prison with the rebels who had committed murder during the insurrection." Not all manuscripts read "Jesus Barabbas"; some only read "Barabbas" (as is also the case in the Gospels of Mark, Luke, and John). It is hard to understand why a scribe would add "Jesus" to the text of Matthew, even if the intention is to heighten the contrast between Barabbas, whose Semitic name means "son of the father," and Jesus of Nazareth, who was indeed the true "Son of the Father." However, it is not hard to understand why some scribes omitted "Jesus" from vv. 16 and 17. "Jesus Barabbas" is probably original.

Pilate is no fool; "he realized that it was out of jealousy that they had handed him over" (**v. 18**). This comment explains the political motivation behind the offer of pardon and placing the burden of choice on the Jewish people themselves. Pilate is not about to take the blame for ordering the execution of a popular preacher and healer. If the ruling priests want Jesus dead, then let them say so publicly (and they do in vv. 22–23).[548]

In **v. 19**, Pilate's wife becomes involved in the drama, advising her husband, "Have nothing to do with that innocent man, for today I have suffered a great deal because of a dream about him." In the infancy narrative of Matthew, dreams play an important role in disclosing the divine will (cf. Matt 1:20; 2:12, 13, 19, 22), as they do here. If Pilate knows what is good for him, he'll find Jesus innocent and release him.[549] The story could not fail to impress readers in the Roman world, who well knew the story of the death of Julius Caesar a century earlier: "Now Caesar's approaching murder was foretold to him by unmistakable signs.... In fact the very night before his murder he dreamt now that he was flying above the clouds, and now that he was clasping the hand of Jupiter; and his wife Calpurnia thought that the pediment of their house fell, and that her husband was stabbed in her arms...." (Suetonius, *Julius* 81.1, 3).

Accordingly, Pilate seeks a plebescite (**vv. 20–23**). The people may choose whom they wish to have released. They may also choose the punishment for the one they

---

2:822; U. Luz, *Matthew* (2001–2007), 3:495–96 (which provides a succinct summary of the salient factors); R. Schnackenburg, *The Gospel of Matthew* (2002), 284; and J. Nolland, *The Gospel of Matthew* (2005), 1166–67; among others.

[548] On the historical plausibility of Pilate's actions as depicted in Matthew (and in the parallel accounts in Mark, Luke, and John), see B. C. McGing, "Pontius Pilate and the Sources," *CBQ* 53 (1991): 416–38; B. C. McGing, "The Governorship of Pontius Pilate: Messiahs and Sources," *PIBA* 10 (1986): 55–71.

[549] For a critical assessment of the story of Pilate's wife's dream, see F. M. Gillman, "The Wife of Pilate (Matthew 27:19)," *Louvain Studies* 17 (1992): 152–65. For an overview of the interesting history of speculation about this woman, including her name (Claudia Procula), see R. Kany, "Die Frau des Pilatus und ihr Name: Ein Kapitel aus der Geschichte neutestamentlicher Wissenschaft," *ZNW* 86 (1995): 104–10.

chose not to have released. Matthew notes that the "chief priests and the elders persuaded the crowds to ask for Barabbas" (v. 20). Implicit here is a coalition of ruling priests and their natural allies, which included the wealthy and powerful in Jerusalem, and supporters of the insurrectionist Barabbas. These two groups were normally opposed. But the supporters of Barabbas, who would have concurred with Jesus' criticisms of the temple establishment, had little interest in a teacher who spoke of love of enemies and turning the other cheek. Similarly, the ruling priests, who had no love for Barabbas and all that he stood for, were willing to call for his release if that is what it took to persuade Pilate to do away with Jesus of Nazareth.

MATTHEW 27:24–26 – JESUS IS HANDED OVER FOR CRUCIFIXION

27:24: So when Pilate saw that he could do nothing, but rather that a riot was beginning, he took some water and washed his hands before the crowd, saying, "I am innocent of this man's blood; see to it yourselves."

27:25: Then the people as a whole answered, "His blood be on us and on our children!"

27:26: So he released Barabbas for them; and after flogging Jesus, he handed him over to be crucified.

The present passage is an expansion of Mark 15:15 ("So Pilate, wishing to satisfy the crowd, released Barabbas for them; and after flogging Jesus, he handed him over to be crucified"). The details of this expansion will be explained in the commentary that follows.

In **v. 24**, Pilate decides to bring the hearing to a close before a riot breaks out, so he washes his hands and declares to the crowd, "I am innocent of this man's blood; see to it yourselves." This recalls what the priests had shortly before said to Judas, "See to that yourself!" (Matt 27:4). In both cases, death follows. In Mark's account, Pilate says, "Why, what evil has he done?" (Mark 15:14). Matthew makes explicit what is implied in Mark.[550]

On the custom of washing one's hands as a symbol of innocence, see Deut 21:6–8 ("all the elders of that town … shall wash their hands … and declare, 'Our hands did not shed this blood …'"); Ps 26:6 ("I wash my hands in innocence, and go around your altar, O Lord"); and Ps 73:13 ("All in vain I have kept my heart clean

---

[550] For recent probings of the role Pilate plays in Matthew's version of the story, see C. Callon, "Pilate the Villain: An Alternative Reading of Matthew's Portrayal of Pilate," *BTB* 36 (2006): 62–71; B. E. Messner, "'No Friend of Caesar': Jesus, Pilate, Sejanus, and Tiberius," *Stone-Campbell Journal* 11 (2008): 47–57. Although Messner's study primarily references John 19:12, it has implications for the portaits of Pilate in the Synoptic Gospels as well.

and washed my hands in innocence"). The custom is also known in Greco-Roman sources (e.g., Herodotus 1.35; Virgil, *Aeneid* 2.719; Sophocles, *Ajax* 654).

Another significant Matthean addition is also one of the most tragic verses in the New Testament: "Then the people as a whole answered, 'His blood be on us and on our children!'" (v. 25). The cry of the people may allude to Deut 19:10 ("so that the blood of an innocent person may not be shed in the land that the Lord your God is giving you as an inheritance, thereby bringing bloodguilt upon you"), as well as 2 Sam 1:16 ("David said to him, 'Your blood be on your head; for your own mouth has testified against you, saying, "I have killed the Lord's anointed""'"). Saul, the Lord's anointed (or "messiah"), had been murdered. The murderer is now held responsible for his own death. Thus, when the people cry out, "His blood be on us and on our children!" they are assuming responsibility for Jesus' death; Pilate, as he had hoped, is off the hook.

The cry of the people is not a curse[551] and does not apply to all Jews (at the time it was uttered), and it certainly does not apply to all Jews of all time (as many church fathers have, unfortunately, taken it).[552] When Matthew's Gospel was published, it was probably related to the catastrophe in 70 A.D. that overtook the city of Jerusalem and, especially, the temple establishment. In Josephus and in later rabbinic tradition, it is noted that among the very first to suffer were the ruling priests, they who had abused their positions of authority and who (from Matthew's point of view) had called for the death of Jesus. (Recall the same idea in Josephus, who explains that Herod Antipas' army was destroyed in divine retaliation for having executed John the Baptist, also a righteous man; cf. *Ant.* 18.116: "But to some of the Jews the destruction of Herod's army seemed to be divine vengeance, and certainly a just vengeance, for his treatment of John, surnamed the Baptist.")

In the end, Pilate complies with the wishes of the crowd and so releases Barabbas and flogs Jesus in preparation for his crucifixion (v. 26). Scourging was apparently standard precrucifixion procedure in Roman times (cf. *Digesta* 48.19.8.3; Josephus, *J.W.* 2.306). It was done with a whip made of several leather straps, to which were attached sharp, abrasive items, such as nails, glass, or rocks. Scourging resulted in severe laceration of the skin and damage to the flesh beneath (cf. Josephus, *J.W.* 6.304, who refers to a man "flayed to the bone with scourges").

---

[551] For the suggestion that the words "his blood be on us and on our children" constitute a double entendre (i.e., the people are responsible for Jesus' death, but his death will provide salvation for them), see T. B. Cargal, "'His Blood Be upon Us and upon Our Children': A Matthean Double Entendre?" *NTS* 37 (1991): 101–12.

[552] On the history of interpretation, see F. Lovsky, "Comment comprendre 'Son sang sur nous et nos enfants'?" *ETR* 62 (1987): 343–62. It is probable that in Matthew's time the fateful words "his blood be on us" would have been understood in reference to the recent destruction of Jerusalem and the temple. On this point, see F. J. Matera, "'His Blood Be on Us and on Our Children'," *BToday* 27 (1989): 345–50; C. S. Hamilton, "'His Blood Be upon Us': Innocent Blood and the Death of Jesus in Matthew," *CBQ* 70 (2008): 82–100.

From a purely political point of view, Pilate has successfully extricated himself from a serious difficulty. On the one hand, he has avoided straining relations with the ruling priests, and on the other hand he has insulated himself from public outrage over executing a popular Jewish teacher and healer.

MATTHEW 27:27–31 – THE ROMANS MOCK JESUS

27:27: Then the soldiers of the governor took Jesus into the governor's headquarters, and they gathered the whole cohort around him.

27:28: They stripped him and put a scarlet robe on him,

27:29: and after twisting some thorns into a crown, they put it on his head. They put a reed in his right hand and knelt before him and mocked him, saying, "Hail, King of the Jews!"

27:30: They spat on him, and took the reed and struck him on the head.

27:31: After mocking him, they stripped him of the robe and put his own clothes on him. Then they led him away to crucify him.

*M*atthew recounts the story of the mocking of Jesus somewhat differently from the way it is told in Mark 15:16–20. Jesus is dressed in "scarlet" (v. 28) instead of purple (cf. Mark 15:17), though there may have been little difference in the color of the robe or cloak. Matthew's preference for scarlet probably reflects the assumption that Jesus was dressed in a soldier's cloak (which is probably better than the NASB's "robe"; cf. 2 Macc 12:35; Plutarch, *Philopoemen* 11). Matthew makes it clear that the crown of thorns was placed on Jesus' head but that the reed was placed "in his right hand" (like a royal scepter) before it was used to strike him on the head (vv. 29–30).

The mockery of Jesus as a Jewish king finds an approximate parallel in Philo (*In Flaccum* 36–39). It was on the occasion of King Agrippa's visit to Alexandria that the people seized a lunatic named Carabas, a street person who was often humiliated. They

put on his head a sheet of byblus spread out wide for a diadem, clothed the rest of his body with a rug for a royal robe, while someone who had noticed a piece of the native papyrus thrown away in the road gave it to him for his sceptre. And when as in some theatrical farce he had received the insignia of kingship and had been tricked out as a king, young men carrying rods on their shoulders as spearmen stood on either side of him in imitation of a bodyguard. Then others approached him, some pretending to salute him, others to sue for justice, others to consult him on state affairs. Then from the multitudes there rang out a tremendous shout hailing him as *Mari* [Aramaic: "My lord"], which is said to be the name for 'lord' with the Syrians.

Plutarch (*Pompey* 24.7–8) relates a story in which pirates mocked a prisoner who had claimed the rights of Roman citizenship. They dressed him up ("threw a toga on him"), extended to him various honors (including falling to their knees), and then finally made him walk the plank. The mockery of Jesus stands in this general tradition.

In the verse, "Then the soldiers of the governor took Jesus into the governor's headquarters" (v. 27), the "governor's headquarters" translates as *praetorium*, a Latin loanword that referred to the official residence of the governor. The Roman praetorium of Jerusalem may have been located in the fortress Antonia (at the northwest corner of the Temple Mount), in Herod's Upper Palace (near the Jaffa Gate), or somewhere on the western slope of the Tyropoeon Valley, opposite the southwest corner of the Temple Mount. Scholarly opinion remains divided.[553]

The mockery described in vv. 28–30 mimics aspects of the Roman triumph, whereby Caesar is hailed as emperor and receives homage. The purple (or scarlet) cloak, the crown of thorns (resembling the crown of ivy), the reed with which Jesus is struck on the head, and the bowing in mock homage are all components of the apparel worn and homage received by the Roman emperor, who at the triumph wore a purple robe and laurel wreath and held a scepter (see, e.g., Dio Cassius 6.23; 44.11 [Julius Caesar]; Appian, *Civil Wars* 5.130 [Augustus]; Dio Cassius 59.25.3 [Gaius Caligula]). Being dressed in purple would also recall the attire of Hellenistic kings of an earlier period (cf. 1 Macc 10:20, "purple robe and golden crown"; 10:62, "clothe him in purple"; 11:58, "to dress in purple"; 14:43–44, "clothed in purple"; Luke 16:19, "dressed in purple").[554]

When the mockery comes to an end, Jesus is taken out to be crucified (v. 31). The garments of mockery are removed, and Jesus is once again dressed in his own clothes.

MATTHEW 27:32–37 – THE CRUCIFIXION OF JESUS

27:32: As they went out, they came upon a man from Cyrene named Simon; they compelled this man to carry his cross.

27:33: And when they came to a place called Golgotha (which means Place of a Skull),

---

[553] For discussion of the praetorium and the findings of archaeology, see P. L. Maier, *Pontius Pilate* (Garden City, NY: Doubleday, 1968), 215–40; B. Pixner, "Noch einmal das Prätorium: Versuch einer neuen Lösung," *ZDPV* 95 (1979): 56–86; R. Riesner, "Das Prätorium des Pilatus," *BK* 41 (1986): 34–37; R. Riesner, "Praetorium," *NIDB* 4:577–78.

[554] For extended discussions and many more citations, see H. S. Versnel, *Triumphus* (Leiden: Brill, 1970), 56–57, 235–300; T. E. Schmidt, "Mark 15.16–32: The Crucifixion Narrative and the Roman Triumphal Procession," *NTS* 41 (1995): 1–18.

27:34: they offered him wine to drink, mixed with gall; but when he tasted it, he would not drink it.

27:35: And when they had crucified him, they divided his clothes among themselves by casting lots;

27:36: then they sat down there and kept watch over him.

27:37: Over his head they put the charge against him, which read, "This is Jesus, the King of the Jews."

*M*atthew reworks the crucifixion scene found in Mark 15:21–26. He makes a few minor changes, including the omission of the reference to the sons of Simon (v. 32). In v. 34, it is wine mixed with gall that Jesus is offered (not wine mixed with myrrh, as in Mark 15:23). Jesus actually tastes it before refusing it. In v. 36, we are told that the soldiers sat down and "kept watch over him." This addition is preparation for the story of the guard at the tomb (cf. Matt 27:62–66). In v. 37, we are told that the *titlus* is placed over Jesus' head and includes his name.

Matthew states that "As they went out, they came upon a man from Cyrene named Simon; they compelled this man to carry his cross" (**v. 32**). Matthew simplifies Mark's "They compelled a passer-by, who was coming in from the country, to carry his cross; it was Simon of Cyrene, the father of Alexander and Rufus" (Mark 15:21). It is remotely possible that the ossuary of Simon's son Alexander has been recovered. On the front and back of the ossuary, inscriptions read, "Alexander, son of Simon," and on the lid another inscription reads, "[Bones] of Alexander the Cyrenite."[555] The combination of a father named Simon (the Aramaic form of the Hebrew name Simeon) and a son named Alexander (a Greek name) who hails from Cyrene, North Africa, and has connections with Jerusalem (which is inferred by Alexander's burial in that city) suggests this identification, even if it is not enough to prove it. Matthew omits the names of Simon's sons, probably because he has no idea of their significance. (It has been suggested that Rufus in Mark 15:21 is the same person Paul mentions in Rom 16:13.) It is poignant that no disciple of Jesus was on hand to assist his master with his cross.[556]

Normally, the condemned man carried his cross (or *patibulum*, the crossbeam; cf. Plautus, *Carbonaria* 2; *Miles gloriosus* 2.4.6–7 §§359–360; Plutarch, *Mor.* 554A–B). Evidently, Jesus is too weak, which is consistent with his unexpectedly early expiration later in the day. The appearance of Simon of Cyrene in the narrative may have

---

[555] For a discussion, see C. A. Evans, *Jesus and the Ossuaries* (Waco, TX: Baylor University Press, 2003), 94–96. The ossuary was discovered by E. L. Sukenik in 1941 and the information published by N. Avigad in 1962.

[556] As observed in A. Schlatter, *Der Evangelist Matthäus* (1959), 779. Schlatter reminds us of Jesus' prophecy that when the Shepherd will be struck down, the sheep will scatter (cf. Matt 26:31).

served as an example of committed discipleship, in which one takes upon himself the cross of Jesus.[557]

Matthew reports of the arrival at the crucifixion site, "They came to a place called Golgotha (which means Place of a Skull)" (**v. 33**). "Golgotha" transliterates the Aramaic *galgata'*, which means "round stone." Some think it is better to translate this as "Place of the Head" (Latin: *capitis locus*). If so, we may have another allusion to Roman tradition related to the Roman emperor. (Recall that aspects of Jesus' treatment at the hands of the Roman soldiers in Matt 27:28–30 mocked the honor accorded Caesar.) Every Roman triumph reached its conclusion at the temple of Jupiter Capitolinus, the place of the "head" (see Livy 50.55.5–6). This meaning is possible, but *galgata'* also means "skull." The hill may have acquired this name from the legend that Adam's skull was buried there.[558]

Matthew continues, "They offered him wine to drink, mixed with gall" (**v. 34**). The offer of drink to the sufferer may have its roots in Scripture itself, especially in Prov 31:6 ("Give strong drink to one who is perishing, and wine to those in bitter distress"). Part of this verse is appealed to as justification for showing mercy to one who is executed. According to a late third-century rabbinic saying, "They give him who goes out to be executed a grain of frankincense in a cup of wine so that his mind becomes confused, as it is said, 'Give strong drink to him who is perishing, and wine to those in bitter distress' [Prov 31:6]" (*b. Sanh.* 43a).[559] But Matthew does not speak of frankincense or myrrh (as in Mark 15:23); he speaks of "gall" (*chole*). In Luke 23:36, it is "vinegar." The later evangelists may have been influenced by Ps 69:21 ("They gave me poison for food, and for my thirst they gave me vinegar to drink") and Lam 3:15 ("He has filled me with bitterness, he has sated me with wormwood"). Jesus has been offered wine, perhaps out of mercy (in keeping with Prov 31:6), but adding gall to the wine has embittered the taste.[560] When Jesus tastes the fouled wine, he refuses it.

Matthew then begins his account of the aftermath of Jesus' death: "And when they had crucified him ..." (**v. 35**). According to Cicero (*Ag. Verr.* 2.5.168) and Josephus (*J.W.* 7.203), crucifixion was the worst form of death (see also the disturbing comments in Juvenal, *Satires* 14.77–78; Suetonius, *Augustus* 13.1–2; Horace, *Epistles*

[557] On this possibility, see B. K. Blount, "A Socio-Rhetorical Analysis of Simon of Cyrene: Mark 15:21 and Its Parallels," *Semeia* 64 (1993): 171–98.

[558] For details, see L. Ginzberg, *The Legends of the Jews* (7 vols., Philadelphia: The Jewish Publication Society of America, 1909–1938), 5:125–27 n. 137.

[559] A similar teaching is found in one of the Talmud's minor tractates: the condemned are "given to drink wine containing frankincense so that they should not feel grieved" (*Semahot* 2:9).

[560] In the Septuagint, *chole* is usually associated with bitterness (either literally, in reference to taste, or metaphorically, in reference to sorrow). See LXX Deut 29:18; 32:32; Prov 5:4; Jer 8:14; 9:15.

1.16.48; Seneca, *Dialogue* 3.2.2; 6.20.3; Isidore of Seville, *Etymologia* 5.27.34; *Mek.* on Exod 15:18 [*Shirata* §10]). Indeed, the words *cross* and *crucify* actually derive from the word *torture* (Latin: *cruciare*). The primary political and social purpose of crucifixion was deterrence: "Whenever we crucify the condemned, the most crowded roads are chosen, where the most people can see and be moved by this terror. For penalties relate not so much to retribution as to their exemplary effect" (Ps.-Quintilian, *Declamations* 274; Aristophanes, *Thesmophoriazusae* 1029; cf. Josephus, *J.W.* 5.450–51).[561]

Writing in the second century B.C., Plautus refers to the crucifixion victim with "his arms and legs double-nailed" (*Mostellaria* 359–61). A third-century A.D. author described it this way: "Punished with limbs outstretched … they are fastened [and] nailed to the stake in the most bitter torment, evil food for birds of prey and grim picking for dogs" (*Apotelesmatica* 4.198–200). After his defeat at the hands of Herod and the Romans, Antigonus (ruled 40–37 B.C.) was executed. Most early writers say the last Hasmonean ruler was beheaded (Strabo, *Historica Hypomnemata*, *apud*; Josephus, *Ant.* 15.8–10; Plutarch, *Life of Antony* 36.4), but one says he was bound to a cross and scourged (Cassius Dio, *Roman History* 22.6). If Dio's account is correct, then we have another example of the crucifixion of a man who, in the eyes of Rome, wrongly claimed to be "king of the Jews."

Normally, crucifixion victims were left to die, however long that took (sometimes several days). The longer delay of death for victims of crucifixion is evident in that on occasion friends and relatives were allowed to feed their crucified loved one. It was typical protocol for guards to be stationed by the cross until the victim expired, in part to prevent possible attempts by friends or relatives to rescue the victim. The bodies of the crucified were often left unburied, to rot and be picked apart by birds and animals, though Roman law did permit bodies to be taken down and buried (cf. *Digesta* 48.24.1, 3; Josephus, *Life* 420–21). The Palatine Cross Graffito, which probably dates to the second half of the second century, depicts a Christian slave saluting the crucified Jesus (who is depicted, in insulting fashion, with the head of a donkey). The cross is drawn in the traditional † manner, which is consistent with the references in the preceding paragraph.[562]

The soldiers who crucified Jesus "divided his clothes among themselves by casting lots." The phrase comes from Ps 22:18: "they divide my clothes among themselves, and for my clothing they cast lots." The division of the crucifixion victim's property, including his clothing, was apparently customary (*Digest of Justinian* 48.20.1; Tacitus, *Annals* 6.29, "people sentenced to death forfeited their property"),

---

[561]   For background to crucifixion in the Roman Empire, see M. Hengel, *Crucifixion: In the Ancient World and the Folly of the Message of the Cross* (London: SCM Press; Philadelphia: Fortress, 1977); D. W. Chapman, *Ancient Jewish and Christian Perceptions of Crucifixion* (WUNT 2, no. 244; Tübingen: Mohr Siebeck, 2008).

[562]   For a discussion, see J. G. Cook, "Envisioning Crucifixion: Light from Several Inscriptions and the Palatine Graffito," *NovT* 50 (2008): 262–85, especially 282–85.

though sometimes there were exceptions (*Digest of Justinian* 48.20.6; cf. Tacitus, *Hist.* 4.3).[563] Their principal task now complete, the soldiers "sat down there and kept watch over him" (**v. 36**).

Matthew reports that "Over his head they put the charge against him, which read, 'This is Jesus, the King of the Jews'" (**v. 37**). Matthew has added Jesus' name (cf. Mark 15:26). The epithet "king of the Jews" is Roman and was originally applied to Herod the Great (cf. Josephus, *Ant.* 15.409, "the king of the Jews, Herod"). As mentioned already, this epithet did not originate in Christian circles, for Christians referred to Jesus with different titles. The significance of the *titulus* is that it confirms the messianic self-understanding of Jesus. Jesus had encouraged his disciples to regard him as Israel's anointed king, or, in the language of Rome, the "king of the Jews."[564]

MATTHEW 27:38–44 – THE MOCKING OF JESUS

27:38: Then two bandits were crucified with him, one on his right and one on his left.

27:39: Those who passed by derided him, shaking their heads

27:40: and saying, "You who would destroy the temple and build it in three days, save yourself! If you are the Son of God, come down from the cross."

27:41: In the same way the chief priests also, along with the scribes and elders, were mocking him, saying,

27:42: "He saved others; he cannot save himself. He is the King of Israel; let him come down from the cross now, and we will believe in him.

27:43: He trusts in God; let God deliver him now, if he wants to; for he said, 'I am God's Son.'"

27:44: The bandits who were crucified with him also taunted him in the same way.

*M*atthew's account of the mockery of Jesus on the cross is derived from Mark 15:27–32. There are two important additions in Matthew's version of the story. In v. 40, the mocking priests invite Jesus, "If you are the Son of God...." We hear this again in v. 44, where the priests, scribes, and elders remind Jesus and others standing by that Jesus had said, "I am God's Son." This addition shifts the focus to a principal element of christology: Jesus' divine sonship (cf. Matt 3:17; 17:5).[565] The

---

[563] The allusion to Ps 22:18 (which in John 19:24 becomes explicit) obviously derives from Christians who passed on the story, phrasing it to take on scriptural overtones.

[564] On the role of the mockers in Matthew and the vindication of Jesus, see T. L. Donaldson, "The Mockers and the Son of God (Matthew 27:37–44)," *JSNT* 41 (1991): 3–18.

[565] A. Sand, *Das Evangelium nach Matthäus* (1986), 562; J. Nolland, *The Gospel of Matthew* (2005), 1199; R. T. France, *The Gospel of Matthew* (2007), 1071–72.

whole of v. 43 is the second important addition: "He trusts in God; let God deliver him now, if he wants to...." The words allude to Ps 22:8 ("Commit your cause to the Lord; let him deliver – let him rescue the one in whom he delights!") and prepare us for Jesus' quotation of Ps 22:1 in Matt 27:46.

In Matt 26:67–68 and 27:27–31, Jesus was taunted first by the ruling priests and then by Pilate's soldiers. Now Jesus is taunted by passersby (**vv. 39–40**), by the ruling priests once again (**vv. 41–42**), and even by the bandits who had been crucified with him (**vv. 38, 44**). He is supposed to be a powerful Savior, sent by God to save his people (cf. Matt 1:21). Now he hangs on a Roman cross, unable to save himself (v. 42).

Matthew's additions in v. 40 ("If you are the Son of God") and v. 43 ("He trusts in God ... 'I am God's Son'") underscore Jesus' identity. One thinks of the wicked, who say, "if the righteous man is God's son, he will help him and rescue him from the hand of his enemies" (Wisd of Sol 2:18). Jesus' claim, "I am God's Son," is evidently false, for God has not delivered this "King of Israel."

If Matthew's Gospel was published after the year 70 A.D., the year Jerusalem was captured and the temple was destroyed, then readers would have realized how off-target the mockery proved to be. The derision, "You who would destroy the temple and build it in three days" (v. 40), would no longer provoke laughter. Likewise, the mocking words, "he cannot save himself ... let God deliver him," became hollow in the light of the Resurrection. But none of this is yet known to the friends and opponents of Jesus.

MATTHEW 27:45–50 – THE DEATH OF JESUS

27:45: From noon on, darkness came over the whole land until three in the afternoon.

27:46: And about three o'clock Jesus cried with a loud voice, "Eli, Eli, lema sabachthani?" that is, "My God, my God, why have you forsaken me?"

27:47: When some of the bystanders heard it, they said, "This man is calling for Elijah."

27:48: At once one of them ran and got a sponge, filled it with sour wine, put it on a stick, and gave it to him to drink.

27:49: But the others said, "Wait, let us see whether Elijah will come to save him."

27:50: Then Jesus cried again with a loud voice and breathed his last.

Matthew's account of Jesus' death and the accompanying preternatural signs follows Mark 15:33–37, though not without a few interesting supplements.

Matthew reports, "From noon on, darkness came over the whole land until three in the afternoon" (**v. 45**). The darkness is the first of three preternatural events (the second is the tearing of the temple veil in v. 51, and the third is the earthquake in vv. 51, 54). In late antiquity, in Jewish (*b. Mo'ed Qatan* 25b) as well as in Roman traditions, strange events and omens were often thought to attend the death of a great figure (see Diogenes Laertius, 4.64, at the death of Carneades "the moon is said to have been eclipsed"; Plutarch, *Life of Caesar* 69.3–5; Virgil, *Georgics* 1.463–468, where the sun hid its face in response to the death of Caesar). The darkness may also allude ominously to such biblical stories as Exod 10:22, implying that divine judgment is being visited upon the earth (cf. Jer 15:9; Amos 8:9; Joel 2:10).

Jesus calls out from the cross, "Eli, Eli, lema sabachthani?" (**v. 46**). Unlike Mark's Aramaic "Eloi, Eloi" (Mark 15:34), Matthew transliterates Jesus' words into Hebrew, perhaps to match the Hebrew text of Ps 22:1 but perhaps also to show more clearly why bystanders (**v. 47**) thought Jesus was calling out to Elijah (i.e., the sound of *eli* ["my God"] is closer to *elia* ["Elijah"], a shortened form of the prophet's name). The darkness of the land signifies judgment; that Jesus cries out the way he does suggests that divine judgment has in part fallen on him.[566] This is consistent with his earlier allusion to Zech 13:7 in Matt 26:31. After they reject his son (see the parable of the vineyard tenants in Matt 21:33–46), God strikes his own people, beginning with Israel's shepherd. Darkness covers the land as God looks away from the obscenity that has taken place.[567]

Jesus has quoted Ps 22:1, a psalm whose details have been echoed in various places in the Passion narrative. Some wonder if Jesus has the whole psalm in mind, especially the concluding part that expresses the hope of vindication and restoration:

I will tell of your name to my brothers ... in the midst of the congregation I will praise you.... For he did not despise or abhor the affliction of the afflicted; he did not hide his face from me, but heard when I cried to him.... Posterity will serve him; future generations will be told about the Lord, and proclaim his deliverance to a people yet unborn, saying that he has done it. (Ps 22:22, 24, 30–31)

---

[566] See A. LaCocque, "Le grand cri de Jésus dans Matthieu 27,50," *ETR* 75 (2000): 161–87. LaCocque suggests that Jesus' loud cry is part of the apocalyptic symbolism described in the death, a symbolism that includes darkness, the tearing of the temple veil, and the earthquake. For more on this theme, see J. T. Carroll and J. B. Green, "'His Blood on Us and on Our Children': The Death of Jesus in the Gospel According to Matthew," in J. T. Carrol and J. B. Green, with R. E. Van Voorst, J. Marcus, and D. Senior, *The Death of Jesus in Early Christianity* (Peabody, MA: Hendrickson, 1995), 39–59, especially 48–49.

[567] For more on the symbolism of darkness, see G. Forbes, "Darkness over All the Land: Theological Imagery in the Crucifixion Scene," *Reformed Theological Review* 66 (2007): 83–96.

Perhaps Jesus did have the whole psalm in mind, including the optimistic conclusion.[568]

Matthew then says of the crowd that "One of them ran and got a sponge, filled it with sour wine ..." (**v. 48**). Readers will assume that this person "ran" because it was sensed that Jesus was about to die. The hope was to prolong Jesus' life to see if Elijah would indeed come to his aid (as the context, vv. 47, 49, seems to suggest). The "sour wine" would act as a stimulant and perhaps keep the failing Jesus breathing a bit longer. This was no act of kindness.

Someone in the crowd then says, "Let us see whether Elijah will come to save him" (**v. 49**). It was believed that Elijah, who will come and restore all things (cf. Matt 17:11; Sir 48:10), on occasion rescued the righteous (cf. *b. 'Aboda Zara* 17b; *b. Ta'anit* 21a; *Gen. Rab.* 33.3 [on Gen 8:1]). Given the exceptional nature of Jesus' public ministry, in which he rendered service to so many, perhaps Elijah will come to his aid.

But the life of Jesus comes to a sudden end: "Then Jesus cried again with a loud voice and breathed his last" (**v. 50**). Mark simply says that Jesus "breathed his last" (literally "expired"; Mark 15:37). Matthew says Jesus "dismissed [his] spirit."[569] The NRSV translation obscures the distinction between Mark and Matthew. Whereas in Mark Jesus merely "expired," in Matthew Jesus "dismissed" or permitted his spirit, his life, to depart. Matthew is implying that, even in death, Jesus remains a figure of authority.

MATTHEW 27:51–54 – SIGNS AND CONFESSION

27:51: **At that moment the curtain of the temple was torn in two, from top to bottom. The earth shook, and the rocks were split.**

27:52: **The tombs also were opened, and many bodies of the saints who had fallen asleep were raised.**

27:53: **After his resurrection they came out of the tombs and entered the holy city and appeared to many.**

27:54: **Now when the centurion and those with him, who were keeping watch over Jesus, saw the earthquake and what took place, they were terrified and said, "Truly this man was God's Son!"**

*T*he present passage is an expansion of Mark 15:38–39 (the tearing of the temple curtain and the centurion's confession). The expansion in Matthew primarily

---

[568]   For more on this topic, see R. E. O. White, "That 'Cry of Dereliction' ... ?" *ExpT* 113 (2002): 188–89.

[569]   See 2 *Enoch* 70:16, which describes the death of Methuselah, "as he was praying to him, his spirit went out." The word "spirit" (*pneuma*), used by Matthew, is a cognate of "expired" (*ekpneuein*), the verb Mark used.

consists of vv. 51b ("The earth shook …") to 53 ("… appeared to many"). This expansion brings the preternatural signs surrounding the death of Jesus to a dramatic climax: at the moment of Jesus' death, the temple curtain is torn and the righteous dead are raised, implying that it is through Jesus (and not the temple) that life and salvation are to be had. But is the expansion original? This difficult question will be addressed shortly.

The power of Jesus is displayed in his death audibly, in the loud shout of v. 46, but it is displayed even more impressively and more tangibly in the tearing of the "curtain of the temple": "At that moment the curtain of the temple was torn in two, from top to bottom. The earth shook, and the rocks were split" (**v. 51**). That the tearing of the curtain is the result of Jesus' sudden expiration, and not merely a coincidental omen, is probable. This death shout and the tearing of the temple curtain constitute a single action that counters all of the previous mocking. Jesus, mocked as a pseudo-prophet (Matt 26:67–68) and pseudo-king (Matt 27:42), who in his despair actually thinks Elijah might come to his aid (Matt 27:47–49), surprises the onlookers with an unexpectedly powerful shout, whose force actually tears the temple curtain. He who had spoken of the temple's destruction (cf. Matt 24:2; 26:61) has now on the cross struck it with his dying breath, tearing the curtain "from top to bottom" (*ap' anothen heos kato*); that is, tearing it completely. The torn curtain is but a token of the complete destruction that will someday befall the temple, when "not one stone will be left here upon another" (Matt 24:2). It is also the first step in the promised judgment that will overtake Jesus' priestly judges (Matt 26:64).[570]

The curtain (*to katapetasma*) should probably be understood as the curtain (or veil) that enshrouds the holy of holies. It is the word used in the Septuagint (e.g., LXX Exod 26:31–37). However, the outer veil, which covered the entrance to the holy place (Exod 27:16) and was easier to see (Josephus, *J. W.* 5.214, "a panorama of the entire heavens"), may be what is in mind in the Markan story. Against identification with the outer curtain is the fact that it is usually called *to kalumma* (as in Exod 27:16 and elsewhere), though there are some exceptions. Commentators are divided on the question of which curtain is meant, with some favoring the inner and others the outer. The evidence does not allow us to determine which veil is meant.[571]

Mark, Matthew's source, says nothing about an earthquake, one powerful enough to split rocks and open tombs. We may have an echo of Zech 14:4: "On that day … the Mount of Olives … shall be split.…" The splitting of rocks may recall the wilderness tradition of Moses splitting rocks to provide water (e.g., Exod 17:6; Isa 48:21; Ps 78:1), but that is probably not in view here. Matthew is fond of earthquakes (cf. Matt 8:24; 21:10; 24:7; 27:51, 54; 28:2, 4).

---

[570] For discussion of the temple curtain, see J. Nolland, *The Gospel of Matthew* (2005), 1211–13; D. M. Gurtner, *The Torn Veil: Matthew's Exposition of the Death of Jesus* (SNTSMS 139; Cambridge: Cambridge University Press, 2007), 97–137.

[571] For background, see D. M. Gurtner, *The Torn Veil* (2007), 29–96.

Matthew reports that "The tombs also were opened and many bodies of the saints who had fallen asleep were raised. After his resurrection they came out of the tombs and entered the holy city and appeared to many" (v. **52–53**). On the opening of tombs, see Ezek 37:12, "I am going to open your graves, and bring you up from your graves, O my people …";[572] Dan 12:2, "Many of those who sleep in the dust of the earth shall awake, some to everlasting life …"; and Zech 14:5b, "the Lord my God will come, and all the holy ones with him" (see also John 5:24–29). Early interpreters have tried to identify the "saints" who were raised and entered Jerusalem. Adam, Job, Moses, righteous Simeon (of Luke 2), and the Old Testament prophets have been suggested. All of this is mere speculation.

The story of the opening of the tombs and the emergence of dead saints may represent an early scribal supplement, probably inspired by Matt 28:2 and perhaps also by the aforementioned Ezek 37:7–14, Dan 12:2, and Zech 14:4–5 (cf. *Did.* 16:7), as well as the Christian belief that the resurrection of Jesus was but the "first fruits" of those who "sleep" (cf. 1 Cor 15:20).[573] Indeed, it has been suggested that vv. 52–53 constitute a fulfillment of sorts of Jesus' promise in Matt 16:18 in that he will build his church and "the gates of Hades will not prevail against it." That is, by raising the saints at the moment of death, the gates of Hades have been breached.[574]

The peculiar vv. 52–53 are not cited and evidently not alluded to in the writings of the church fathers prior to the Council of Nicaea in 325 A.D. The quotation in the longer form of one of the letters of Ignatius is almost certainly a later interpolation. Moreover, the suggestion that the Akhmîm Gospel fragment (assumed by most to be the *Gospel of Peter*) alludes to Matt 27:52 (cf. *Gos. Peter* 41: "Have preached to them that sleep?") is not convincing. *Peter* alludes to Christ's preaching to the saints when he descended into hell. Indeed, the story of the raised saints in Matthew, perhaps inspired by the tradition of Christ's harrowing of hell (cf. *Acts of Pilate* 20–26), is probably no earlier than late second century.

That this story is probably a post-Matthean gloss is also suggested by the chronological awkwardness created by vv. 52–53.[575] According to the story, it is at the

---

572   It has been plausibly suggested that Matt 27:52–53 was inspired by a vision based on Ezekiel 37. See W. Schenk, *Die Sprache des Matthäus* (Göttingen: Vandenhoeck & Ruprecht, 1987), 76–78.

573   For a different take on this theme, see S. Wüthrich, "Naître de mourir: la mort de Jésus dans l'Évangile de Matthieu (Mt 27.51–56)," *NTS* 56 (2010): 313–25. Wüthrich argues that the story of the raised saints depicts Jesus as the "first-born from the dead" (Col 1:18; Rev 1:5). On the connection between Matt 27:52–53 and the Pauline concept of the "first fruits" of the general resurrection, see J. Nolland, *The Gospel of Matthew* (2005), 1216.

574   For more on this interesting line of interpretation, see T. McLay, "Death, Descent and Deliverance in Matthew 27:51b–53," in R. G. Wooden et al. (eds.), *You Will Be My Witnesses* (A. A. Trites Festschrift; Macon, GA: Mercer University Press, 2003), 81–93.

575   For this reason, I find it unlikely that the evangelist Matthew found this story in tradition that he received, linked to Jesus' resurrection and the earthquake that took place when the stone was rolled aside (Matt 28:2), and then moved it forward to the time of Jesus' death, thus creating himself the chronological problem under consideration. This option is explored in J. P. Meier, *Matthew* (NTM 3; Wilmington: Glazier, 1980), 352.

moment of Jesus' death that the tombs open and the saints are raised. They are therefore raised *before Jesus is raised.* May Jesus still be regarded as the "first fruits" of the resurrection? It is probably for this reason that the scribe who added this story tells us that the raised saints remained in their tombs until *after* Jesus himself was resurrected the following Sunday.[576] Thus, we are to imagine these resurrected saints loitering in their tombs the remainder of Friday, all of Saturday, and the early hours of Sunday.[577]

There are other unanswered questions, too. Who were these saints supposed to be? If they were the patriarchs and prophets of old, then how would anyone have recognized them as such? (Remember, there were no photographs or painted portraits for identification!) And further, what happened to them? Did they return to their tombs a few days later?[578]

If vv. 52–53 are original, then the probable meaning of this strange story was to show that the death of Jesus brings life and that his life-giving death takes the place of the temple, which by the time of the publication of the Gospel of Matthew has ceased to be.[579] Those who wish to be numbered among the righteous raised up in the day of judgment must embrace Messiah Jesus, God's Son.[580]

---

[576]   D. C. Allison, Jr. and W. D. Davies, *A Critical and Exegetical Commentary on the Gospel According to Saint Matthew* (1988–1997), 3:634–35, think the words "after his resurrection" (v. 53a) were added to clear up the chronological problem of having the saints raised up before Jesus was. Allison and Davies are probably correct; see also P. Gaechter, *Das Matthäus Evangelium: Ein Kommentar* (Innsbruck: Tyrolia-Verlag, 1963), 933. But even this gloss does not solve the problem. The saints may have loitered in their respective tombs until Sunday morning, as "after his resurrection" implies, but they were still raised before Jesus was. The clumsy gloss of vv. 52b–53 led to the qualifying gloss of v. 52a. Admittedly, we possess no textual evidence or witness that suggests vv. 52–53 are a gloss. But one will recall that it was not until older manuscripts were discovered that glosses were recognized at Luke 22:43–44 (where Jesus perspires drops of blood and an angel appears) and John 5:3b–4 (where we hear of the angel who agitates the pool), not to mention larger passages, such as Mark 16:9–20 (and the ending of Mark, in which the risen Jesus is described) and John 7:53–8:11 (the story of the adulteress brought before Jesus).

[577]   The chronological difficulties are addressed in J. W. Wenham, "When Were the Saints Raised: A Note on the Punctuation of Matthew xxvii.51–3," *JTS* 32 (1981): 150–52. Wenham does not come to the conclusion made in the present commentary.

[578]   Early church fathers puzzled over these questions, speculating that Moses and Elijah, and perhaps other Old Testament prophets and the like, were among these "holy ones." Some Medieval interpreters thought that these resurrected ones lived on for centuries.

[579]   See D. P. Senior, "The Death of Jesus and the Resurrection of the Holy Ones (Mt 27:51–53)," *CBQ* 38 (1976): 312–29; D. P. Senior, "Revisiting Matthew's Special Material in the Passion Narrative: A Dialogue with Raymond Brown," *ETL* 70 (1994): 417–24. Linking vv. 51–53 to Matt 1:21, Senior argues that the raising of the saints reveals the evangelist's understanding of Jesus as Savior. See also D. M. Gurtner, "The Veil of the Temple in History and Legend," *JETS* 49 (2006): 97–114; D. M. Gurtner, *The Torn Veil* (2007), 147–52. Gurtner emphasizes the significance of Jesus' death for the temple.

[580]   See R. Schwindt, "Kein Heil ohne Gericht: Die Antwort Gottes auf Jesu Tod nach Mt 27,51–54," *Biblische Notizen* 132 (2007): 87–104. Schwindt suggests that the raising of the saints portends Jesus' return as eschatological judge. See also R. D. Witherup, "The Death

Matthew reports that a centurion who has witnessed the earthquake and other events exclaims, "Truly this man was God's Son!" (v. **54**). Matthew follows Mark 15:39 but adds a summary of the events that had just taken place. In Mark, the centurion sees how Jesus expired, but in Matthew the centurion sees "the earthquake and what took place." Moreover, in Matthew it is not only the centurion who sees all of this but also "those with him." Impressed by the manner of Jesus' death and the signs that attend it, the Roman centurion and those with him confess of Jesus what they should only confess of the Roman emperor: Caesar is not the "son of God"; Jesus the crucified Messiah is. The mockery is now over. In calling Jesus the Son of God, these men have switched their allegiance from Caesar, the official "son of God," to Jesus, the real Son of God.[581]

MATTHEW 27:55–56 – WOMEN WITNESSES OF JESUS' DEATH

27:55: Many women were also there, looking on from a distance; they had followed Jesus from Galilee and had provided for him.

27:56: Among them were Mary Magdalene, and Mary the mother of James and Joseph, and the mother of the sons of Zebedee.

*M*atthew has followed and slightly revised Mark 15:40–41. To be sure, the momentous events described in Matt 27:45–54 enhance the drama of Jesus' death. But now we learn that these events, including the death of Jesus and the startling confession of the centurion and those with him, were witnessed by some of Jesus' following.

"Many women were also there, looking on from a distance; they had followed Jesus from Galilee and had provided for him" (v. **55**). The surprising confession of the centurion and those with him, brought on by the stunning and awesome shout of Jesus and the ensuing earthquake, brings the death scene to a close. But Matthew must prepare for the discovery of the empty tomb in Matt 28:1–8, so he includes

---

of Jesus and the Raising of the Saints: Matthew 27:51–54 in Context," *SBLSP* 26 (1987): 574–85; R. D. Witherup, "The Death of Jesus and the Raising of the Saints: Matthew 27:51–54," in J. P. Galvin (ed.), *Faith and the Future: Studies in Christian Eschatology* (New York: Paulist, 1994), 574–85. Witherup sees in the story the promise of the vindication of the righteous. For a different view, see R. L. Troxel, "Matt 27.51–54 Reconsidered: Its Role in the Passion Narrative, Meaning and Origin," *NTS* 48 (2002): 30–47. Troxel thinks the evangelist has drawn upon *1 Enoch* 93:6, where visions of holy ones accompany the giving of the Law to Moses. It is not clear to me what the death of Jesus and the rising of the righteous ones have to do with the giving of the Law.

[581] This confession does not mean that the soldiers, who only hours earlier treated Jesus with brutality, are now Christians, but it does demonstrate a dramatic change in their opinion of Jesus, a point that I think has been underestimated in D. C. Sim, "The 'Confession' of the Soldiers in Matthew 27:54," *HeyJ* 34 (1995): 401–24.

Mark's notice of the women who observe all that happened. They will be witnesses to the empty tomb, yet one more dramatic omen that attends the death of Jesus, and they will be witnesses to the amazing events that took place when Jesus was crucified. (Noting that the women were present when Jesus was buried, in Matt 27:61, serves the same purpose.)[582]

Matthew says of the women who witnessed these events that "Among them were Mary Magdalene, and Mary the mother of James and Joseph, and the mother of the sons of Zebedee" (v. 56). To the list of female witnesses Matthew adds "the mother of the sons of Zebedee" (i.e., James and John; cf. Matt 4:21; 10:2, 20; 26:37). He had introduced her earlier in Matt 20:20, where she makes a request on their behalf. Mary Magdalene is probably the most famous of all the women who followed Jesus.[583] This is her first appearance in Matthew. She will reappear in Matt 27:61 and 28:1. (In the Gospel of Luke, she makes a much earlier appearance in the narrative; cf. Luke 8:2.) More will be said of the importance of the women as eyewitnesses. Knowing where Jesus has been buried will enable the women to return to the tomb Sunday morning (cf. Matt 28:1).

MATTHEW 27:57–61 – THE BURIAL OF JESUS

27:57: When it was evening, there came a rich man from Arimathea, named Joseph, who was also a disciple of Jesus.

27:58: He went to Pilate and asked for the body of Jesus; then Pilate ordered it to be given to him.

27:59: So Joseph took the body and wrapped it in a clean linen cloth

27:60: and laid it in his own new tomb, which he had hewn in the rock. He then rolled a great stone to the door of the tomb and went away.

27:61: Mary Magdalene and the other Mary were there, sitting opposite the tomb.

*M*atthew condenses Mark's version of the burial of Jesus (Mark 15:42–47) but adds a few finishing touches. Some scholars have suggested that the story is a fiction, perhaps motivated by apologetical interests, namely that Jesus was buried properly and that at least a few of his followers (i.e., the women mentioned in v. 61)

---

[582] On the women as witnesses at the cross and tomb, see B. Gerhardsson, "Mark and the Female Witnesses," in H. Behrens et al. (eds.), *Studies in Honor of Åke W. Sjöberg* (Philadelphia: The Samuel Noah Kramer Fund, 1989), 217–26; S. Byrskog, *Story as History – History as Story* (WUNT 123; Tübingen: Mohr Siebeck, 2000), 73–82, 190–97.

[583] See M. Hengel, "Maria Magdalena und die Frauen als Zeugen," in O. Betz et al. (eds.), *Abraham unser Vater: Juden und Christen im Gespräch über die Bibel* (Leiden: Brill, 1963), 243–56; and, more recently, G. O'Collins, "Mary Magdalene as Major Witness to Jesus' Resurrection," *TS* 48 (1987): 631–46; R. Bieringer, "Mary Magdalene in the Four Gospels," *Louvain Studies* 32 (2007): 186–254.

were present and so would have known where he was buried, thus preparing for the visit Sunday morning (as in Matt 28:1–8). It is more probable, these skeptics contend, that the family and followers of Jesus would have had no idea where Jesus had been buried, if anywhere. Indeed, they argue that it is likely his corpse was left on the cross. This skepticism, however, is unwarranted and reflects ignorance of Jewish burial customs and law.

First-century Jews buried their dead the day of death (Luke 7:12). Preparation for burial, which included washing, perfuming, and wrapping the corpse (cf. John 19:39–40; Acts 9:37; Josephus, *Ant.* 15.61; 17.196–99), and the burial process itself were accompanied by public lamentation, prayers, and hymns (cf. Matt 9:23; Josephus, *Ant.* 8.272). Fasting and graveside mourning perdured for seven days (Gen 50:10; 1 Sam 31:13; Josephus, *Ant.* 17.200; Josephus, *Against Apion* 2.205; *Semahot* 12.1). The ledge (or *loculus*) on which the corpse was laid was marked for purposes of identification (often with charcoal, as seen in excavations of tombs). One year later, family members gathered the bones (a practice called ossilegium) and placed them in a bone pit or in an ossuary (*b. Qiddushin* 31b; *Semahot* 3.2; 12.9). About one-fourth of all ossuaries bear inscriptions of the names of the deceased.[584]

For executed criminals, however, the rules were different. Criminals were to be buried properly (Josephus, *Ant.* 4.265, "we bury all whom the law condemns to die"), but not in places of honor, such as the family tomb. This is clearly taught in the earliest writings of the Rabbis (*m. Sanhedrin* 6:5; *Semahot* 13.7). Not only was the body of a criminal not to be buried in a place of honor, but also no public mourning for executed criminals was permitted: "they used not to make [open] lamentation … for mourning has place in the heart alone" (*m. Sanhedrin* 6:6). Burial before sunset is commanded in Scripture, even in the case of executed criminals (cf. Deut 21:22–23, "his corpse must not remain all night upon the tree; you shall bury him that same day"; 11QTemple 64:7–13a, "you are to hang him, also, upon a tree until dead. But you must not let their bodies remain on the tree overnight"). It fell to the Jewish council, or Sanhedrin, to bury those it had condemned to death (*m. Sanhedrin* 6:5–6; *Semahot* 2.13; 13.7; Josephus, *J.W.* 4.317; Josephus, *Against Apion* 2.205, 211). After one year, when the flesh had wasted away, the bones could be gathered and transferred to a place of honor, which normally was the family tomb (*m. Sanhedrin* 6:6; *Semahot* 13.7). In Jewish settings, these and other Jewish customs were respected by the Romans (*Digesta* 48.24.1, 3, "bodies of persons who have been punished should be given to whoever requests them for the purpose of burial"; Josephus, *J.W.* 4.317, "the Jews used to take so much care of the burial of men, that they took down those that were condemned and crucified, and buried them before

---

[584] For a lengthy and important sample of published ossuaries, see L. Y. Rahmani, *A Catalogue of Jewish Ossuaries in the Collections of the State of Israel* (Jerusalem: The Israel Antiquities Authority, 1994). On the relevance of this material for the study of Jesus, see C. A. Evans, *Jesus and the Ossuaries* (Waco, TX: Baylor University Press, 2003).

the going down of the sun"; *Against Apion* 2.73; Philo, *Flaccus* 83, "men who had been crucified ... being taken down and given up to their relations, in order to receive the honours of sepulture").[585] There is therefore no reason to dismiss the accounts of all four New Testament Gospels, namely that Jesus was buried before nightfall on the day of his death and that his burial was undertaken by a member of the Jewish council.[586]

Matthew reports that the body of Jesus was taken by "... a rich man from Arimathea, named Joseph, who was also a disciple of Jesus" (v. 57). Mark only says that Joseph was "a respected member of the council" (Mark 15:43). Matthew may have assumed that Joseph was rich because of his membership on the council and perhaps because of his willingness and ability to make available a new tomb. Once the body of Jesus is placed in this tomb, the tomb will be regarded as a burial place of no honor, for it has been occupied by the corpse of an executed criminal. Even after the body has been removed for reburial in the family tomb, Joseph's tomb can never be used for honorable burial. It is also possible that Matthew wanted to make explicit Joseph's affluence in order to remind his readers of the Suffering Servant Song, in which the Servant's burial is linked to a rich man (cf. Isa 53:9: "They made his grave with the wicked and his tomb with the rich").

The town of Arimathea has been identified with Ramathaim-zophim (1 Sam 1:1), Rathamin (1 Macc 11:34), and Ramathain (1 Macc 11:34; Josephus, *Ant.* 13.127), all of which are considered variants of the same place. If this city has been rightly recognized, it is about twenty miles northwest of Jerusalem.

The most interesting feature is that in Matthew's Gospel Joseph of Arimathea is said to be Jesus' *disciple* and not simply one who is "waiting expectantly for the kingdom of God," as it says in Mark 15:43. Again, Matthew's elaboration is probably based on an assumption, in this case the assumption that if one awaits the kingdom of God (which was at the center of Jesus' proclamation), then in some sense one is a disciple of Jesus.

Matthew says of Jesus' body that "Pilate ordered it to be given to him" (v. 58). Pilate's willingness to give the body to Joseph is in step with the practice of the time, as seen in texts such as *Digesta* 48.24.1, 3; Philo, *Flaccus* 83; and Josephus, *J.W.* 4.317. Matthew omits Mark's reference to Pilate's surprise at Jesus' early death and the verification from the centurion (Mark 15:44–45a).

---

[585] Archaeological evidence for this is seen in the 1968 discovery in Jerusalem (at Giv'at ha-Mivtar) of the remains of one Yehohanan, crucified during Pilate's administration. In the right heel bone was embedded an iron spike, which evidently those who buried the man had been unable to extract. Yehohanan was executed and then properly buried, with his bones later gathered and placed in an ossuary, which in turn was placed in the family tomb. For a discussion of this ossuary, see C. A. Evans, *Jesus and the Ossuaries* (2003), 98–103.

[586] For a further discusson, see C. A. Evans, "Jewish Burial Traditions and the Resurrection of Jesus," *JSHJ* 3 (2005): 233–48.

Matthew continues, "Joseph took the body and wrapped it in a clean linen cloth and laid it in his own new tomb" (**vv. 59–60a**). Matthew adds important details, noting that the linen cloth was "clean" and that the tomb was Joseph's (i.e., "his own") and was "new." These details mitigate the shame of a dishonorable burial. The newness of the tomb probably means that the tomb had not been used before, which is exactly how the evangelist Luke understands it (cf. Luke 23:53, "where no one had ever been laid"). If the tomb had not been used, then no criminals had been buried in it. Thus the tomb was not yet a "place of dishonor". But because no righteous person had been buried in it, it was not yet a "place of honor," in which an executed person like Jesus could not be buried. The tomb of Joseph was, in a sense, a neutral place – neither dishonorable nor honorable.

Matthew reports that "He then rolled a great stone to the door of the tomb and went away" (**v. 60b**). Most doors or entrance covers of tombs were square blocks, sometimes with recessed borders. About 10 percent of these doors were round. Matthew's "rolled" implies a round stone door. The Garden Tomb in Jerusalem offers a fine example of what Joseph's tomb may have looked like (though this is not the actual tomb).

Matthew then mentions others attending the burial: "Mary Magdalene and the other Mary were there, sitting opposite the tomb" (**v. 61**). That is, the women had a good view, enabling them to see precisely where Jesus had been interred.[587] Observing where the body of Jesus was placed will make it possible for them to visit the tomb on Sunday. On Mary Magdalene, see the commentary on v. 56.

MATTHEW 27:62–66 – GUARDING THE TOMB

27:62: The next day, that is, after the day of Preparation, the chief priests and the Pharisees gathered before Pilate

27:63: and said, "Sir, we remember what that impostor said while he was still alive, 'After three days I will rise again.'

27:64: Therefore command the tomb to be made secure until the third day; otherwise his disciples may go and steal him away, and tell the people, 'He has been raised from the dead,' and the last deception would be worse than the first."

27:65: Pilate said to them, "You have a guard of soldiers; go, make it as secure as you can."

27:66: So they went with the guard and made the tomb secure by sealing the stone.

---

[587]   On these women as eyewitnesses of the burial of Jesus, see S. Byrskog, *Story as History – History as Story* (2000), 73–82; R. Bauckham, *Gospel Women: Studies of the Named Women in the Gospels* (Grand Rapids, MI: Eerdmans, 2002), 257–310.

Only Matthew relates the story of the guard at the grave. (An expanded and embellished version is found in the second-century *Gospel of Peter*.) The purpose of this passage is found in Matt 28:11–15, where Matthew counters claims that Jesus had not been resurrected at all but that his disciples had removed his body. Not so, says Matthew, for the tomb had been sealed and a guard posted, making theft quite improbable.

Protecting tombs was a serious matter in late antiquity, among Gentiles as well as Jews. There were stiff laws against tampering with tombs, including vandalism, unauthorized entry, theft, and removing or adding corpses without authorization. An inscription of uncertain provenance, perhaps originally erected in Galilee and probably dating to the early first century A.D., records Caesar's edict against grave robbery (*SEG* 8.13):

Ordinance of Caesar: It is my pleasure that graves and tombs – whoever has made them as a pious service for ancestors or children or members of their house – that these remain unmolested in perpetuity. But if any person lay information that another either has destroyed them, or has in any other way cast out the bodies which have been buried there, or with malicious deception has transferred them to other places, to the dishonor of those buried there, or has removed the headstones or other stones, in such a case I command that a trial be instituted, just as if they were concerned with the gods for the pious services of mortals. For beyond all else it shall be obligatory to honor those who have been buried. Let no one remove them for any reason. If not, however [i.e., if anyone does so], capital punishment on the charge of tomb robbery I will to take place.[588]

In all probability, Matthew's readers would have understood the story of the posting of the guard and the sealing of the stone that covered the entrance in light of the laws and values expressed in this inscription, whatever its precise date and provenance. Caesar's edict forbids the removal or transfer of bodies. If one violates the edict, the emperor wills "capital punishment on the charge of tomb robbery."

Of course, Jewish readers would also be mindful of their own laws and customs that forbade full funeral rites for condemned criminals. These rules made it unlawful to remove the corpse from the dishonorable place of burial to a family crypt (cf. 1 Kings 13:21–22; Jer 22:19; Josephus, *Ant.* 5.44, "he was given the dishonorable burial

---

[588] See B. M. Metzger, "The Nazareth Inscription Again," in E. E. Ellis and E. Grässer (eds.), *Jesus und Paulus: Festschrift für Werner Georg Kümmel zum 70. Geburtstag* (Göttingen: Vandenhoeck & Ruprecht, 1975), 221–38. The inscribed stone came to light in modern times in Nazareth, but it is believed that it originated elsewhere. For further discussion, see A. D. Nock, "Tomb Violations and Pontifical Law," in *Essays on Religion and the Ancient World*, vol. 2 (ed. Z. Stewart; Oxford: Clarendon Press; Cambridge, MA: Harvard University Press, 1972), 527–33; P. W. van der Horst, *Ancient Jewish Epitaphs: An Introductory Survey of a Millennium of Jewish Funerary Epigraphy (300 bce – 700 ce)* (Kampen: Kok Pharos, 1991), 159–60; C. A. Evans, *Jesus and the Ossuaries* (2003), 35–37.

proper to the condemned"; *m. Sanh.* 6:5, "And they did not bury [the executed criminal] in the burial grounds of his fathers, but two burial places were kept in readiness for the use of the court"). Mourning was not allowed (cf. Jer 22:18, "They shall not lament for him"; *m. Sanh.* 6:6, "they did not go into mourning; but they observe a private grief, for grief is only in the heart"; *Semahot* 2.7, but mourning is allowed if the condemned person had been judged only by the Roman government; cf. *Semahot* 2.11). Sanctions against mourning and reburial (i.e., in an ossuary) were lifted after one year, or when the flesh had decomposed (cf. *m. Sanh.* 6:6, "when the flesh had wasted away they gathered together the bones and buried them in their own place"; *Semahot* 2.13, where there is also reference to execution by crucifixion). Only then would Jesus' followers and family be permitted to rebury his bones in an ossuary (or bone box) and inter it in the family tomb (see also the commentary on Matt 27:57–61).

Matthew states that "The next day, that is, after the day of Preparation, the chief priests and the Pharisees gathered before Pilate" (**v. 62**). The reference "after the day of Preparation" alludes to Mark 15:42, which Matthew did not mention earlier at Matt 27:57. The appearance of the Pharisees is surprising, for their absence in the Passion story is otherwise conspicuous. The "next day" is the Sabbath. The chief priests and Pharisees assemble before the Roman governor to make a request.

They address Pilate: "Sir, we remember what that impostor said while he was still alive, 'After three days I will rise again.' Therefore command the tomb to be made secure until the third day …'" (**vv. 63–64**). By asking for a guard and for the sealing of the tomb, the chief priests have in effect doubled the laws (and the penalties). To enter the tomb, whether to mourn, or – more seriously – to remove the body, was now forbidden by two jurisdictions: the Roman authority that condemned Jesus to the cross and the Jewish authority that had presented him to the governor and had laid charges. Matthew has made it clear that theft of Jesus' body was improbable if not impossible.

Pilate replies, "You have a guard of soldiers; go, make it as secure as you can" (**v. 65**). Although Pilate's reply is somewhat ambiguous, it probably means that he has granted the request. This is because of what is said in Matt 28:14 ("If this comes to the governor's ears, we will satisfy him and keep you out of trouble"), which makes sense in reference to Roman guards, not Jewish ones.[589] When the governor says "make it as secure as you can," he has acknowledged that the chief priests are

[589]   J. Schmid, *Das Evangelium nach Matthäus* (1959), 378; D. C. Allison, Jr. and W. D. Davies, *A Critical and Exegetical Commentary on the Gospel According to Saint Matthew* (1988–1997), 3:655, "must be Roman"; D. A. Hagner, *Matthew* (1993–1995), 2:863; U. Luz, *Matthew* (2001–2007), 3:588; J. Nolland, *The Gospel of Matthew* (2005), 1238–39. Some think Jewish temple police are envisioned; see D. A. Carson, "Matthew," in F. E. Gaebelien (ed.), *The Expositor's Bible Commentary*, vol. 8 (1984), 586; R. T. France, *The Gospel of Matthew* (2007), 1094–95. If that was the case, then why would the guards fear word reaching the governor's ears (Matt 28:14)?

more familiar with the rules pertaining to the burial of Jewish criminals – as to who can mourn quietly at tombside or perhaps even enter the tomb (as the women in Matt 28:1 intend to do; cf. Mark 16:1–3), and when the remains of the deceased can be removed and taken to the family tomb or place of honor. Pilate places a contingent of soldiers at the disposal of the ruling priests. How long they are expected to serve in this capacity is not made clear. As it turns out, their vigil is scarcely twenty-four hours.

Matthew reports, "So they went with the guard and made the tomb secure by sealing the stone" (**v. 66**). Nothing is said in Mark or the other Gospels about a guard or the stone being sealed. We do not know if in antiquity the tombs in which executed criminals were buried were normally guarded or "sealed." In Mark's account, the women expect to enter the tomb to anoint the body of Jesus and to mourn quietly within the tomb itself, as Jewish law allowed. Matthew seems to suggest that, because of the fear of theft, the tomb has been sealed (evidently by a Roman seal), and therefore the women will not be allowed to enter (unless escorted by one of the guards?).[590] Whatever the case, in the accounts of all four Gospels, the women discover the stone rolled aside, seal or no seal.

MATTHEW 28:1–7 – DISCOVERY OF THE EMPTY TOMB

28:1: After the sabbath, as the first day of the week was dawning, Mary Magdalene and the other Mary went to see the tomb.

28:2: And suddenly there was a great earthquake; for an angel of the Lord, descending from heaven, came and rolled back the stone and sat on it.

28:3: His appearance was like lightning, and his clothing white as snow.

28:4: For fear of him the guards shook and became like dead men.

28:5: But the angel said to the women, "Do not be afraid; I know that you are looking for Jesus who was crucified.

28:6: He is not here; for he has been raised, as he said. Come, see the place where he lay.

28:7: Then go quickly and tell his disciples, 'He has been raised from the dead, and indeed he is going ahead of you to Galilee; there you will see him.' This is my message for you."

*M*atthew follows Mark's account (Mark 16:1–8), though he omits a few details and adds a few others. The principal difference is that Matthew has emphasized the role of the angelic figure.

---

[590] This does not mean that the tomb is "sealed" in the sense that no one can enter. It means a seal has been affixed to the stone that prohibits entry (much like yellow police tape).

Matthew's account begins, "Mary Magdalene and the other Mary went to see the tomb" (**v. 1**). Mark mentions "Mary Magdalene, and Mary the mother of James, and Salome" (Mark 16:1). Matthew simply says the women "went to see the tomb." In Mark's account, the women visit the tomb in order to perfume Jesus' body and then mourn for him (Mark 16:1–3). It was the Jewish custom to mourn at graveside (including within the tomb itself) for seven days. The passage of time and the close proximity made it necessary to perfume the decomposing corpse. But Matthew has no interest in the women's plan to anoint the body or in their concern about who would be on hand to assist in rolling aside the stone. His concern is to call attention to the dramatic appearance of the angel.[591]

Matthew continues, "And suddenly there was a great earthquake" (**v. 2**). This earthquake may have inspired the scribal gloss in Matt 27:52–53, in which an earthquake occurs (v. 51) and tombs are opened (see the commentary there). As the text of Matthew stands, we have an earthquake Friday afternoon, when Jesus died, then another one early Sunday morning, when Jesus rose from the dead. The first earthquake opened the tombs of some saints, but they did not venture forth until the second earthquake and the resurrection of Jesus himself.

The cause of this earthquake was the action of the "angel of the Lord" who "rolled back the stone and sat on it." Whereas in Mark we are only told that the women saw "a young man, dressed in a white robe, sitting on the right side" (Mark 16:5), Matthew speaks explicitly of an angel whose "appearance was like lightning, and his clothing white as snow." One may wonder if this angel is none other than Michael, who in Dan 12:1–2 is associated with the resurrection of the dead. In this passage, we are told that the righteous will "shine like the brightness of the sky" and be "like the stars forever" (Dan 12:3). But reference to "clothing white as snow" may also allude to Dan 7:9, where it is said of God (i.e., the "Ancient One") that "his clothing was white as snow" and the "hair of his head like pure wool" (Dan 7:9). There will be additional allusions to Daniel 7 in the conclusion of Matthew, where the risen Jesus commissions his disciples.

Reference to the "angel of the Lord" explains how it is that the women found the stone rolled away (cf. Mark 16:4). The epithet angel of the Lord is commonplace in the Old Testament, occurring dozens of times. Matthew's description of the angel ("young man" in Mark 16:5) in this manner links the resurrection of Jesus with major events of Israel's sacred history. To say that this angel had descended from

---

591   For a related discussion, see W. Carter, "'To See the Tomb': Matthew's Women at the Tomb," *ExpT* 107 (1996): 201–5. On the temporal meaning of "after the sabbath," see J. M. Winger, "When Did the Women Visit the Tomb? Sources for Some Temporal Clauses in the Synoptic Gospels," *NTS* 40 (1994): 284–88; D. Boyarin, "'After the Sabbath' (Matt. 28:1) – Once More into the Crux," *JTS* 52 (2001): 678–88; K. L. Waters, "Matthew 28:1–6 as Temporally Conflated Text: Temporal-Spatial Collapse in the Gospel of Matthew," *ExpT* 116 (2005): 295–301.

heaven also clarifies Jesus' resurrection: just as the angel of the Lord descended from heaven to roll back the stone, so will the risen Jesus ascend to heaven.

Mark says nothing about guards at the tomb, but Matthew does (see Matt 27:62–66 and comments on this passage): "For fear of him the guards shook and became like dead men" (**v. 4**). On being fearful and dead-like from seeing an apparition, see the inscription of Onassanius, dedicated to his nephew M. Lucceius: "It happened, as I lamented my nephew, taken from me by premature death ... I saw a figure gliding down from heaven, radiant with light like that of the stars.... I straightened myself up, for terror had penetrated my being, so that my limbs were as rigid as ice...." (*CIL* XXI.521). The radiant figure described by Onassanius is none other than his nephew Lucceius, who at death was taken up to heaven.

Matthew then recounts the appearance of the angel to the women: "But the angel said to the women, 'Do not be afraid ...'" (**v. 5**). The tradition of the women as the first to learn of the resurrection of Jesus serves an important apologetic purpose, though perhaps not from the perspective of late antiquity. Surely in no invented tradition would women play such an important role. Whether the early church liked it or not, women came to the tomb first. In the first century, both in Jewish and (especially) in Greco-Roman society, women were not viewed highly as witnesses or spokespersons. Josephus offers a pretty clear example of this bias in his elaboration of the law of witnesses in Deut 19:15 ("on the evidence of two or three witnesses"). He says: "From women let no evidence be accepted, because of the levity and temerity of their sex" (*Ant.* 4.219). For examples of rabbinic texts that take a dim view of women as witnesses, see *m. Shebuot* 4:1 ("'an oath of testimony' applies to men but not to women"); *m. Rosh haShanah* 1:8 ("evidence a woman is not eligible to bring"); *b. Baba Qamma* 88a ("a woman ... is disqualified from giving evidence"); *Sipre Deut.* §235 (on Deut 22:13) ("A woman may not speak in a man's stead"); *y. Sota* 3.19a ("Better to burn the Torah than to teach it to a woman!"). For a pagan perspective, see Plutarch, *Moralia* 142CD, "Advice to Bride and Groom" 32, who opines that a "woman ought to do her talking either to her husband or through her husband, and she should not feel aggrieved if, like the flute-player, she makes a more impressive sound through a tongue not her own." For additional negative opinions regarding women as witnesses or speakers, see Aeschylus, *Seven against Thebes* 230–32; Democritus, frags. 110–11, 274; Euripides, *Heracles* 474–77; Euripides, *Phoenician Maidens* 198–201; Euripides, *Daughters of Troy* 651–56; Sophocles, *Ajax* 292–93. In light of both Jewish and pagan views of women as witnesses and public speakers, why would early Christians invent an Easter narrative in which women are witnesses and, as seen in v. 7, conveyors of the resurrection message to the male disciples?[592]

---

[592] For more on this important point, see C. Osiek, "The Women at the Tomb: What Are They Doing There?" *HTS Teologiese Studies/Theological Studies* 53 (1997): 103–18. Although in many Jewish and pagan texts negative opinions are expressed about women as witnesses

The angel explains Jesus' absence from the tomb: "He is not here; for he has been raised, as he said" (**vv. 6–7**). The tomb, naturally, is where the women expected to find Jesus. He is not in the tomb because "he has been raised"; that is, his corpse has not been removed and placed somewhere else (as the women may have imagined). The angel adds, "as he said," to remind the women that Jesus himself had foretold his resurrection "on the third day" (cf. Matt 16:21; 17:22–23; 20:17–19). The women are invited to look inside the dimly lit tomb to see for themselves that the body of Jesus is in fact no longer present. The women are then commissioned to take the good news of the Resurrection to the disciples of Jesus, assuring them that they will see him in Galilee.

MATTHEW 28:8–10 – ENCOUNTERING THE RISEN JESUS

28:8: So they left the tomb quickly with fear and great joy, and ran to tell his disciples.

28:9: Suddenly Jesus met them and said, "Greetings!" And they came to him, took hold of his feet, and worshiped him.

28:10: Then Jesus said to them, "Do not be afraid; go and tell my brothers to go to Galilee; there they will see me."

*M*atthew has rewritten Mark 16:8 ("So they went out and fled from the tomb, for terror and amazement had seized them; and they said nothing to anyone, for they were afraid"), with which our earliest copies of the Gospel of Mark conclude. (Later copies of Mark include either the Short Ending or the Long Ending – including vv. 9–20 – though usually with markings indicating textual doubt. It may well be that Mark's Gospel originally went beyond v. 8.) The most important elements in this brief passage are found in vv. 9 and 10.

Matthew's account of the women's response to the words of the angel reads: "So they left the tomb quickly with fear and great joy, and ran to tell his disciples" (**v. 8**). Compare this with Mark 16:8, where we are told that the women were afraid and spoke to no one. As mentioned, Mark's narrative probably continued beyond Mark 16:8, reporting that the women recovered and obeyed the angel's directive. In any case, Matthew has made it clear that they did so.

and spokespersons, it would be wrong to conclude that women were universally regarded as incompetent witnesses, as rightly noted in G. Luedemann, *The Resurrection of Jesus: History, Experience, Theology* (London: SCM Press, 1994), 158. The point is simply that in all probability men, not women, would be assigned the role of principal witnesses in a fictional story. An example of this is seen in the embellished narrative of the *Gospel of Peter*, in which a number of men – all hostile toward Jesus – witness his resurrection. On the importance of women in the Resurrection story, see G. O'Collins and D. Kendall, "Mary Magdalene as Major Witness to Jesus' Resurrection," *TS* 48 (1987): 631–46.

When the women see Jesus, Matthew reports: "And they came to him, took hold of his feet, and worshiped him" (v. 9). This is related in some way to John 20:17, where Jesus tells Mary, "Do not hold on to me," though we are not told specifically that Mary held Jesus' feet. A number of suggestions have been made as to the significance of the women's taking hold of the feet of Jesus. Perhaps it was out of joy, an act of obeisance or worship, or perhaps a demonstration of submission. Early Patristic interpreters, as well as a number of later commentators, believe the purpose is to show that the risen Jesus was truly physical and that he was not a ghost.[593] This is the position taken here. We see this concern in Luke 24:36–43, where the risen Jesus eats food in the presence of his disciples and invites his disciples to handle him. The same point is seen in John 20:24–29, where the risen Jesus invites skeptical Thomas to examine his hands and side. Matthew has defended the proclamation of the resurrection of Jesus by showing that the body of Jesus was not stolen by his disciples (Matt 27:62–66; 28:11–15) and that the post-Easter Jesus that the women and disciples encountered actually possessed a body.

Jesus instructs the women, "Do not be afraid; go and tell my brothers to go to Galilee; there they will see me" (v. 10). In Mark 16:6–7, followed but edited in Matt 28:5–7, the young man/angel of the Lord instructs the women to go and report to the disciples. Here in Matt 28:10, the risen Jesus himself repeats these instructions. As we shall see in Matthew 28:16–20, the report has reached the disciples and they do as they are instructed.

MATTHEW 28:11–15 – THE STOLEN BODY RUMOR

28:11: While they were going, some of the guard went into the city and told the chief priests everything that had happened.

28:12: After the priests had assembled with the elders, they devised a plan to give a large sum of money to the soldiers,

28:13: telling them, "You must say, 'His disciples came by night and stole him away while we were asleep.'

28:14: If this comes to the governor's ears, we will satisfy him and keep you out of trouble."

28:15: So they took the money and did as they were directed. And this story is still told among the Jews to this day.

*T*his passage completes the story begun in Matt 27:62–66, where the tomb is sealed and guarded. Apologetic interests are at work here, as Matthew tries to

---

[593] This interpretation has been recently and persuasively argued in D. C. Allison, Jr., *Studies in Matthew* (2005), 107–16.

counter claims that the tomb was found empty because Jesus' disciples had removed the corpse. It is not hard to see how skeptics could make such an accusation. They would assume that the disciples desired to remove the corpse of their beloved teacher from a place of dishonor. Moreover, had they heard that the corpse had actually been buried in a private tomb (the tomb of Joseph of Arimathea), instead of one of the tombs set aside for the burial of executed criminals, they may well have assumed the lack of proper custodial supervision, designed to prevent public lamentation and, more importantly, removal of the body for purposes of interment in the family tomb. The irregularity of Jesus' burial in the tomb belonging to Joseph (Matt 27:57–61) would have encouraged suspicion along these lines.

An imaginative retelling of this story appears in the apocryphal work known as the *Acts of Pilate*. It says that

there came some of the guard that the Jews had asked from Pilate to guard the tomb of Jesus, lest his disciples should come and steal him. And they told the rulers of the synagogue and the priests and the Levites what had happened, how there was a great earthquake. 'And we saw an angel descend from heaven, and he rolled away the stone from the mouth of the cave, and sat upon it, and he shone like snow and like lightning. And we were in great fear, and lay like dead men' [cf. Matt 28:2–4].... And the Jews took counsel, and offered much money and gave it to the soldiers of the guard, saying, 'Say that when you were sleeping his disciples came by night and stole him. And if this is heard by the governor, we will persuade him and keep you out of trouble.' (13:1, 3)

Matthew's account continues, "Some of the guard went into the city and told the chief priests everything that had happened" (**v. 11**). Reporting back to the chief priests supports the view that Pilate had placed the soldiers (whether regular Roman troops or auxiliaries) at the disposal of the priests (cf. Matt 27:65).

Matthew then says of the priests that "They devised a plan to give a large sum of money to the soldiers" (**v. 12**). Josephus relates incidents of bribery among the ruling priests: "Now the high priest Ananias [son of the high priest Annas of Luke 3:2; John 18:13, 24; Acts 4:6] daily advanced greatly in reputation and was splendidly rewarded by the goodwill and esteem of the citizens; for he was able to supply them with money" (i.e., he was able to pay them bribes; *Ant.* 20.205).

The priests instruct the soldiers, "You must say, 'His disciples came by night and stole him away while we were asleep'" (**v. 13**). Theft of Jesus' body for the purpose of perpetrating a hoax is most implausible. Graves were plundered for their valuables, not the theft of a corpse (e.g., Arrian, *Anabasis of Alexander* 6.29.4; Plutarch, *Moralia* 173B). However, from the perspective of Jesus' enemies, there was the very real possibility of illegally removing Jesus' body to a more secure location (perhaps in Galilee), where he may be buried in honor and where his tomb could become the focal point of a renewed restoration movement and antiestablishment activities. On guarding against (honorable) burial, see Sophocles, *Antigonus* 217; and

Plutarch, *Agis and Cleomenes* 39. On punishment for sleeping during one's watch, see Euripides, *Rhesus* 812–19, 825–27; and Tacitus, *Histories* 5.22, where only the incompetence of the commanding officer spared sleeping guards the punishment they deserved.

The priests try to reassure the soldiers that "If this comes to the governor's ears, we will satisfy him and keep you out of trouble" (**v. 14**). Indeed, the guards would be in very serious trouble (cf. Petronius, *Satires* 112, where a guard commits suicide after discovering the theft of a body from a cross). The chiefs were in a position to offer this assurance only because the guards had been acting under the authority of the priests themselves, not the governor.

Matthew concludes the exchange, saying: "So they took the money and did as they were directed. And this story is still told among the Jews to this day" (**v. 15**). The evangelist is now speaking from his own experience. His uncharacteristic reference to "the Jews" seems to suggest Gentiles are among his anticipated readership. The statement "this story is still told" brings to an end Matthew's defense of the Resurrection account. He has argued that the tomb was well guarded and that the disciples could not in fact have succeeded in illegally removing the body of Jesus. He has further implied that the Jesus the women met in Matt 28:9–10 (and the disciples will meet in Matt 28:16–20) was in fact bodily risen and not a spirit or phantom.

A Closer Look: The Stolen Corpse Lives On

The rumor that the disciples, or another party, removed the body of Jesus circulated among the Jewish people long after the publication of the Gospel of Matthew. According to Justin Martyr (ca. 160 A.D.): "... after you learned that he rose from the dead ... you have sent chosen and ordained men throughout all the world to proclaim that a godless and lawless heresy had sprung from one Jesus, a Galilean deceiver, whom we crucified, but his disciples stole him by night from the tomb, where he was laid when unfastened from the cross, and now deceive men by asserting that he has risen from the dead and ascended to heaven" (*Dialogue with Trypho the Jew* 108).

According to Tertullian: "This is he whom you purchased from Judas! This is he whom you struck with reed and fist, whom you contemptuously spat upon, to whom you gave gall and vinegar to drink! This is he whom his disciples secretly stole away, that it might be said he had risen again, or the gardener abstracted, that his lettuces might come to no harm from the crowds of visitors" (*De Spectaculis* 30).

Quotations from A. Roberts and J. Donaldson, *The Ante-Nicene Fathers* (10 vols., Grand Rapids, MI: Eerdmans, 1989), 1:253 and 3:91.

MATTHEW 28:16–20 – THE GREAT COMMISSION

28:16: Now the eleven disciples went to Galilee, to the mountain to which Jesus had directed them.

28:17: When they saw him, they worshiped him; but some doubted.

28:18: And Jesus came and said to them, "All authority in heaven and on earth has been given to me.

28:19: Go therefore and make disciples of all nations, baptizing them in the name of the Father and of the Son and of the Holy Spirit,

28:20: and teaching them to obey everything that I have commanded you. And remember, I am with you always, to the end of the age."

*M*atthew's Gospel ends on a majestic note with the risen Jesus charging his disciples with the Great Commission, whereby they proclaim the message of their Lord throughout the world. The guards at the tomb have been bribed to say that the disciples stole the body of Jesus (Matt 27:11–15), but Matthew tells his readers what really happened: Jesus has been raised up and has commanded his disciples to continue his mission. This final passage sums up the goal of the Gospel of Matthew – that of the missionary task of the church.[594]

Because Judas has died (Matt 27:5), there are no longer *twelve* disciples, so "the eleven disciples went to Galilee" (**v. 16**). Judas will be replaced by a disciple named Matthias (cf. Acts 1:15–26). The disciples have gone to Galilee, in obedience to the angel's word in Matt 28:7 (cf. 26:32) and to the word of Jesus in Matt 28:10. The disciples go "to the mountain to which Jesus had directed them." The Greek perhaps should be understood as "to the mountain where Jesus gave his commands." In the Gospel of Matthew, Jesus is often seen on mountaintops (cf. Matt 4:8; 5:1; 8:1; 14:23; 15:29; 17:1, 9).[595] One final appearance on a mountain brings the Gospel story to its conclusion.

Matthew says of the disciples' reunion with Jesus: "When they saw him, they worshiped him; but some doubted" (**v. 17**). According to an Aramaic fragment from Qumran, "all the nations" will worship the Son of God and the people of God, whom he will deliver (cf. 4Q246 2:4–7), although in the very presence of the risen Jesus there was doubt. The NRSV translates the phrase as "some doubted," but the Greek suggests that the eleven as a group both "worshiped" and "doubted."[596] What

---

594   See E. Krentz, "Missionary Matthew: Matthew 28:16–20 as Summary of the Gospel," *Currents in Theology and Mission* 31 (2004): 24–31.

595   T. L. Donaldson, *Jesus on the Mountain* (1985), 170–90.

596   On this point, see K. H. Reeves, "They Worshipped Him, and They Doubted: Matthew 28.17," *BT* 49 (1998): 344–49; J.-P. Stemberger, "Le doute selon Mt 28,17," *ETR* 81 (2006): 429–34.

was it that they doubted? They may have doubted that it was really Jesus or that he really was alive (as in the famous example of "doubting Thomas" in John 20:24–28). However, it is more likely that they had doubts as to what purpose the mission of Jesus now had, and what purpose they as disciples now had. Jesus may have been raised, but what of the promised kingdom of God? In what way would Jesus now "save his people" (recall Matt 1:21, "he will save his people from their sins")? In what sense have the messianic and restoration prophecies of Scripture been fulfilled?[597] What are the disciples to do now? To this doubt and confusion, the risen Jesus responds with assurance, commands, and instruction.

Jesus states, "All authority in heaven and on earth has been given to me" (**v. 18**). Reference to being given authority in heaven and on earth recalls the Son of Man in Dan 7:13–14, who in heaven was given "authority," an authority later claimed "on earth" (cf. Matt 9:6, "the Son of Man has authority on earth"; Matt 21:23, "By what authority are you doing these things, and who gave you this authority?"; Matt 7:29, "he taught them as one having authority"). The heavenly authority of Jesus is such that he even commands angels (cf. Matt 16:27, "the Son of Man is to come with his angels in the glory of his Father"; 24:31; 25:31, "the Son of Man comes in his glory, and all the angels with him").

The "authority" here in Matt 28:18 probably alludes to the authority granted to the "Son of Man" in Dan 7:14: "And royal authority was given to him … his authority is an everlasting authority" (NETS). The risen Jesus can speak of his authority "in heaven" because that is where the authority was granted – in heaven and in the very presence of God. The claim to have authority "on earth" recalls Jesus' earlier demonstration that he indeed does possess this authority, which he announced on the occasion of healing the paralyzed man (cf. Matt 9:6, "the Son of Man has authority on earth").[598]

Possessed with all the authority in heaven and on earth, the risen Jesus now commands his disciples, "Go therefore" (**v. 19a**). Literally, the Greek reads "having gone." In other words, the going precedes the making of disciples. Jesus' commissioning of his disciples appears to follow a commissioning pattern that we find in the Old Testament (e.g., Exod 7:2, "You shall speak all that I command you"; Josh 1:7, "being careful to act in accordance with all the law that my servant Moses commanded you"; 1 Chron 22:13, "if you are careful to observe the statutes and the ordinances

---

[597]   For a discussion of the reasons for the eleven disciples' doubt, see B. J. Walsh and S. C. Keesmaat, "Reflections on the Ascension," *Theology* 95 (1992): 193–200. Walsh and Keesmaat suspect, given the allusion to Daniel 7 in v. 18, that the disciples could not see how Jesus could live up to the prophecy and vision of the son of man figure who received from God authority and kingdom.

[598]   For discussion of Dan 7:14 and Matt 28:18, see J. Schaberg, *The Father, the Son, and the Holy Spirit: The Triadic Phrase in Matthew 28:19b* (SBLDS 61; Chico, CA: Scholars Press, 1982), 111–317; B. T. Viviano, "The Trinity in the Old Testament: From Daniel 7:13–14 to Matt 28:19," *TZ* 54 (1998): 193–209.

that the Lord commanded Moses"; Jer 1:7, "you shall go to all to whom I send you, and you shall speak whatever I command you.").[599]

Just as Jesus formally began his teaching ministry on a Mosaic note, by delivering his great sermon on the mountain (Matthew 5–7), now he concludes his earthly ministry on a similar note. In a sense, Jesus has sent out his disciples to conquer the nations, not with the sword but with a message of redemption.[600]

Jesus now instructs his disciples to "make disciples of all nations" (**v. 19b**). The imperative "make disciples" is the main verb in the commission of vv. 19–20. What is translated as "Go" is in fact a participle that simply assumes that the disciples will go forth – throughout Israel itself and eventually throughout the whole world. The commission is not so much fulfilled in the *going* but in the *disciple-making*.[601] Given Matthew's pronounced Jewish orientation, the commission to make disciples "of all nations" is at first blush somewhat surprising (recall Matt 10:5–6: "Go nowhere among the Gentiles"). However, Israel's place of priority has not been set aside (which would very much stand in tension with Matthew's theology); far from it.[602] Under the authority of its Messiah, Jesus, Israel's jurisdiction over the nations can now be fulfilled (and here again we may have an allusion to Dan 7:14, "that all peoples, nations, and languages should serve him"). All will be brought to an obedience and understanding of the faith of the patriarchs and the prophets. All will be taught a righteousness that must exceed the righteousness of the scribes and Pharisees (Matt 5:20). Israel will conquer the nations, not with the sword (Matt 26:52) but with the gospel, the good news of the reign of God.[603]

---

[599]   For the proposal that Matt 28:16–20 is modeled after Old Testament call narratives, see B. J. Hubbard, *The Matthean Redaction of a Primitive Apostolic Commissioning: An Exegesis of Matthew 28:16–20* (SBLDS 19; Missoula, MT: Society of Biblical Literature, 1974).

[600]   K. L. Sparks, "Gospel as Conquest: Mosaic Typology in Matthew 28:16–20," *CBQ* 68 (2006): 651–63.

[601]   D. A. Carson, "Matthew," in F. E. Gaebelien (ed.), *The Expositor's Bible Commentary*, vol. 8 (1984), 595–96; B. Witherington III, *Matthew* (2006), 534.

[602]   Some argue that "all nations" excludes Israel. For this view, see D. R. A. Hare and D. J. Harrington, "'Make Disciples of All Gentiles' (Mt 28:19)," *CBQ* 37 (1975): 359–69. The words allude to the promise made to Abraham long ago (cf. Gen 12:3), rightly noted by D. A. Carson, "Matthew," in F. E. Gaebelien (ed.), *The Expositor's Bible Commentary*, vol. 8 (1984), 596. The point is that the nations, as well as Israel, are to be evangelized. For a rebuttal of the study by Hare and Harrington, see J. P. Meier, "Nations or Gentiles in Matthew 28:19?" *CBQ* 39 (1977): 94–102. For support of the position taken here, see D. A. Hagner, *Matthew* (1993–1995), 2:887; J. Nolland, *The Gospel of Matthew* (2005), 1265–66; R. T. France, *The Gospel of Matthew* (2007), 1114–15. See also H. Kvalbein, "Hat Matthäus die Juden aufgegeben? Bemerkungen zu Ulrich Luz' Matthäus-Deutung," *TBei* 29 (1998): 301–14. Kvalbein emphatically denies that the evangelist Matthew has abandoned the Jewish people.

[603]   For further discussion of the idea that the Great Commission envisions the restoration of Israel, see A. von Dobbeler, "Die Restitution Israels und die Bekehrung der Heiden. Das

The making of disciples entails two principal elements: "baptizing them in the name of the Father and of the Son and of the Holy Spirit, and teaching them to obey everything that I have commanded you" (**vv. 19c–20a**). Jesus' command that his disciples baptize converts recalls the teaching of John the Baptist (or Baptizer): "I baptize you with water for repentance, but one who is more powerful than I is coming after me; I am not worthy to carry his sandals. He will baptize you with the Holy Spirit and fire" (Matt 3:11). John's baptism was for repentance, in anticipation of the coming of the mightier one. Now that the mightier one has come, has been exalted in his resurrection, and has been invested with "all authority in heaven and on earth" (v. 18), he commands his followers to baptize "in the name of the Father and of the Son and of the Holy Spirit." The qualifying phrase "in the name of" is interesting and takes different forms in the New Testament (e.g., Acts 2:38, "in the name of Jesus Christ"; 8:16, "in the name of the Lord Jesus"; 19:5, "in the name of the Lord Jesus") and in related literature (cf. *Did.* 9:5, "in the name of the Lord").

To act or speak "in the name of" God (or the Lord) is commonplace in the Old Testament (e.g., Deut 18:5, "to stand and minister in the name of the Lord"; Deut 18:22, "If a prophet speaks in the name of the Lord"; Deut 21:5, "the Lord your God has chosen them to minister to him and to pronounce blessings in the name of the Lord"; 1 Sam 17:45, "I come to you in the name of the Lord of hosts"; 2 Sam 6:18, "David … blessed the people in the name of the Lord of hosts"; Ezra 5:1; Pss 20:5; 118:10, 11–12, 26; Isa 50:10; Mic 4:5; Zeph 3:12). The most interesting parallel is found in Ps 118:10–12, where three times the Psalmist complains of being surrounded by the "nations" but predicts that "in the name of the Lord" he will be able to "cut them off" (i.e., destroy them). In contrast to this imprecation stands Jesus' charge to his disciples: "Go and make disciples of the nations."

The risen Jesus commands his disciples to baptize "in the name of the Father and of the Son and of the Holy Spirit." The three personages, Father, Son, and Holy Spirit, have already been mentioned in the Gospel of Matthew. God as "Father" occurs many times (Matt 5:16, 45, 48; 6:1; passim). There are a number of references to Jesus as the "Son" (Matt 11:27; 24:36) or "Son of God" (Matt 4:3, 6; 8:29; 14:33; 16:16), and Matthew makes reference to the "Spirit" or "Holy Spirit" (Matt 1:18, 20; 3:11, 16; 12:32; cf. 10:20, "Spirit of your Father"). Are there antecedents to this trinitarian or triadic language? Although Daniel 7 is probably echoed in Matt 28:18–19,

Verhältnis von Mt 10,5b.6 und Mt 28,18–20 unter dem Aspekt der Komplementarität: Erwägungen zum Standort des Matthäusevangeliums," *ZNW* 91 (2000): 18–44; M. Konradt, "Die Sendung zu Israel und zu den Völkern im Matthäusevangelium im Lichte seiner narrativen Christologie," *ZTK* 101 (2004): 397–425; A. J. Levine, "'To All the Gentiles': A Jewish Perspective on the Great Commission," *RevExp* 103 (2006): 139–58; D. W. Ulrich, "The Missional Audience of the Gospel of Matthew," *CBQ* 69 (2007): 64–83. These studies rightly call attention to themes in the Missionary Discourse (Matt 10, especially vv. 5–6) that parallel the Great Commission.

the triadic phrase itself probably does not derive from this passage. Binitarian descriptions of God are found in traditions prior to Jesus and his movement,[604] and triadic language is found in Paul.[605] The trinitarian understanding of the Godhead, as opposed to a binitarian understanding, may well have its roots in the pre-Easter teaching of Jesus. It was also part of the church's earliest preaching. The risen Jesus speaks of his Father (Acts 1:4, 7) and commands his disciples to await the promise of the Father (Acts 1:4), which is the giving of the Holy Spirit (Acts 2:33). The Holy Spirit figures prominently in the Book of Acts (Acts 1:2, 5, 8, 16; 2:4, 33, 38, etc.). Jesus is the Lord (Acts 1:21, 24; 2:36), Christ/Messiah (Acts 2:31, 36, 38; 3:6, 18, 20; 4:10; etc.), and Son (Acts 9:20; 13:33; 20:28). What is distinctive about Matt 28:18–20 is not its trinitarian understanding of the Godhead but its succinct formulation, probably reflective of early Christian baptism.[606]

Jesus also commands his disciples to teach the baptized converts "everything" that he had "commanded" them (**v. 20a**). That is, the disciples are to make disciples. These words echo Exod 7:2, especially as found in the Septuagint: "You shall speak all that I command you." Recall that Matthew used a phrase from the Pentateuch to conclude each of the five major discourses (see the commentary on Matt 7:28–29). Thus Jesus' language once again sounds a Mosaic ring. The new disciples are to learn what Jesus had taught the original disciples. They, too, are to learn the way of righteousness.

The Great Commission ends with a word of assurance: "And remember, I am with you always, to the end of the age" (**v. 20b**). Jesus' words may allude to Dan 12:13: "But you, go your way, and rest; you shall rise for your reward at the end of the days."[607] Readers of the Gospel of Matthew will also be reminded of the prophecy cited at the beginning of the narrative: "'Look, the virgin shall conceive and bear a son, and they shall name him Emmanuel,' which means, 'God is with us'" (Matt 1:23).[608] God became present with his people in a special way in the

---

[604] See L. W. Hurtado, *Lord Jesus Christ: Devotion to Jesus in Earliest Christianity* (Grand Rapids, MI: Eerdmans, 2003), 32–48. Prominent among Jewish texts is Philo's remarkable discussion of the "Word" (*logos*) as the "second God" (*deuteros theos*); cf. Philo, *Quaest. Gen.* 2.62.

[605] The relevant texts are discussed in G. D. Fee, "Paul and the Trinity," in S. T. Davis, D. Kendall, and G. O'Collins (eds.), *The Trinity: An Interdisciplinary Symposium on the Trinity* (Oxford: Oxford University Press, 1999), 49–72.

[606] See L. Hartman, *'Into the Name of the Lord Jesus': Baptism in the Early Church* (Edinburgh: T. & T. Clark, 1997), 147–53.

[607] The phrase "end of the age" occurs a number of times in the Old Testament and related literature (e.g., Dan 12:7; 2 Esd 2:34; 6:7). See also O. L. Cope, "'To the Close of the Age': The Role of Apocalyptic Thought in the Gospel of Matthew," in J. Marcus and M. Soards (eds.), *Apocalyptic in the New Testament: Essays in Honor of J. Louis Martyn* (JSNTSup 24; Sheffield: JSOT Press, 1989), 113–24.

[608] T. Zahn, *Das Evangelium des Matthäus* (1910), 724, aptly remarks: "Where Jesus is, God is there also." See also R. H. Gundry, *Matthew* (1982), 597; A. Sand, *Das Evangelium nach*

birth of his Son Jesus and remains with his people even after his earthly ministry is concluded. The missionary task of Jesus did not end with his death; it resumed with his resurrection and is carried on by his faithful disciples, with whom he is present.[609]

Matthäus (1986), 597; D. J. Harrington, *The Gospel of Matthew* (1991), 414; D. A. Hagner, *Matthew* (1993–1995), 2:888; J. Nolland, *The Gospel of Matthew* (2005), 1271; R. T. France, *The Gospel of Matthew* (2007), 1119.

[609]   The nonappearance of a reference to the ascension of Jesus may have left Matthew's readers with a stronger sense of the abiding presence of Jesus ("I am with you always"), as suggested by D. C. Allison, Jr. and W. D. Davies, *A Critical and Exegetical Commentary on the Gospel According to Saint Matthew* (1988–1997), 3:687. Recall also the words of assurance "where two or three are gathered in my name, I am there among them" (Matt 18:20).

Author Index

Note: Names with particles are alphabetized according to the family name.

Scripture and Apocrypha Index

Index of Extrabiblical Jewish and Christian Sources

Subject Index

Made in the
USA
Middletown, DE